Readings on Second Language Acquisition

Readings on Second Language Acquisition

H. Douglas Brown

San Francisco State University

Susan T. Gonzo

University of Illinois
at Urbana-Champaign

Prentice Hall Regents
Upper Saddle River, NJ 07458

Library of Congress Cataloging-in-Publication Data

Readings on second language acquisition / [edited by] H. Douglas
   Brown, Susan Gonzo.
         p. cm.
      Includes bibliographical references and index.
      ISBN 0-13-102260-1
      1. Second language acquisition.   2. Language and languages—Study
   and teaching.   I. Brown, H. Douglas, 1941–.   II. Gonzo, Susan.
   P118.2.R4   1994
   418—dc20   93-42222
                                                              CIP

Publisher: Tina Carver
Assistant Editor: Lizette Reyes Richards
Project Management: J. Carey Publishing Service
Interior Design: J. Carey Publishing Service
Cover Design: YES Graphics
Cover Photo: © SUPERSTOCK
Buyer: Raymond Keating

© 1995 by Prentice Hall Regents
Prentice-Hall, Inc.
Simon & Schuster/A Viacom Company
Upper Saddle River, NJ 07458

Printed in the United States of America
10 9 8 7 6 5 4

ISBN 0-13-102260-1

Prentice-Hall International (UK) Limited, *London*
Prentice-Hall of Australia Pty. Limited, *Sydney*
Prentice-Hall Canada Inc., *Toronto*
Prentice-Hall Hispanoamericana, S.A., *Mexico*
Prentice-Hall of India Private Limited, *New Delhi*
Prentice-Hall of Japan, Inc., *Tokyo*
Prentice-Hall of Southeast Asia Pte. Ltd., *Singapore*
Editora Prentice-Hall do Brasil, Ltda., *Rio de Janeiro*

Contents

Preface

An indispensable component of language teacher education programs world-wide is a survey of research in second language acquisition (SLA), which leads teacher-trainees to establish a firm set of principles on which to build practical classroom techniques. Such background information may be offered in the form of (a) research references embedded in methodology courses and text-books; (b) a course and/or textbook exclusively focusing on theories, models, and issues in the field of SLA; or (c) a collection of articles and chapters that capsulize prominent issues. Frequently, all three components are included in a teacher education program.

Readings on Second Language Acquisition (RSLA) is a collection of original articles designed to supply the third component above. It is a book for teachers and teacher-trainees who want to learn more about second language acquisition and who have virtually no background in conducting or reading research. We have put together this anthology to fulfill two major needs in teacher education programs: (a) to provide a set of original readings—not sum-maries or abstracts—with clear implications for classroom language teaching; and (b) by supplementing each article with guidelines for study and reflection, to develop the reader's ability to understand and evaluate research.

We have found in our own teaching of courses in SLA that original arti-cles and chapters form an important element of the course. Although overviews and summaries of research, as found in such textbooks as *Principles of Language Learning and Teaching,* Third Edition *(PLLT)* (Prentice-Hall Regents, 1994), may be enlightening, readers often have difficulty understand-ing what scholarship looks like if they have never read the primary material as it appears in major journals in our field. All of the readings included here have been previously published. They have been selected not only for the topics they cover but also because they serve as examples of different approaches to research and scholarship in second and foreign language acquisition. Further, to help readers become more familiar with some of the major journals in the field, we have selected articles from eight different journals as well as chapters from three books.

The second need—that of guidelines for study and for developing evalua-tive capacities—is often difficult to meet with current anthologies, many of which are unfortunately not designed to be used by teachers new to SLA research. Such books may be too narrow—focused on a single subtopic in SLA—or too broad and unfocused, with papers on a variety of topics, unified only by the fact that they were presented at the same conference. Without the assistance of the instructor, articles in these collections can be difficult to understand, evaluate, and place in the appropriate context in the field of SLA. After the introductory SLA course is over, students may be ill-equipped to continue to read about research on SLA, evaluate it, determine its applications to classroom language learning, and understand how new developments in the field relate to what has gone before.

RSLA can be used in conjunction with *PLLT*. But it is also designed to serve effectively as a companion to other textbooks that survey issues in the field. For example, the nine topics treated here are sequenced to correspond to the outline of *PLLT*, but they also represent nine major issues or areas in the field of SLA that would hardly be overlooked in any comprehensive summary of the field. With the exception of the introduction and Unit I, which should be read first, all of the other units could be reordered to suit an instructor's purpose. And, although a number of the study guidelines refer to the various chapters of *PLLT*, such references may be found in other, similar surveys of issues in language learning and teaching.

We gratefully acknowledge the contributions of a number of people who have been instrumental in bringing this project to fruition. We are primarily indebted to all of our students, who over the years have offered questions and insights that eventually made their way into our process of selection and of offering guidelines for study. We also appreciate our faculty colleagues, whose stimulation prods us to engage in these projects and whose support sustains us as we take time to put them all together.

H. D. B.
S. T. G.

Acknowledgments

Grateful acknowledgment is made to the following publishers for permission to reprint copyrighted material:

Academic Press, Inc., for material from:

Johnson, Jacqueline S., and Newport, Elissa L. 1989. Critical period effects in second language learning: The influence of maturational state on the acquisition of English as a second language. *Cognitive Psychology, 21,* 60–99.

Edward Arnold, for material from:

Chapelle, Carol, and Abraham, Roberta. 1990. Cloze method: What difference does it make? *Language Testing, 7,* 121–146.

J. Benjamins Company, for material from:

White, Lydia. 1992. Universal grammar: Is it just a new name for old problems? In Gass and Selinker (Eds.), *Language Transfer in Language Learning,* pp. 217–232.

Cambridge University Press, for material from:

Ellis, R. 1992. Learning to communicate in the classroom. *Studies in Second Language Acquisition, 14,* 1–23.

Gardner, R., and McIntyre, P. 1991. An instrumental motivation in language study: Who says it isn't effective? *Studies in Second Language Acquisition, 13,* 57–72.

Kachru, Braj. 1992. World Englishes: Approaches, issues, and resources. *Language Teaching, 25,* 1–14.

Lightbown, P., and Spada, N. 1990. Focus-on-form and corrective feedback in communicative language teaching. *Studies in Second Language Acquisition, 12,* 429–447.

xii   **Acknowledgments**

Heinle and Heinle, Publishers, for material from:

Bailey, Kathleen. 1983. Competitiveness and anxiety in adult second language learning: Looking *at* and *through* the diary studies. In Seliger and Long (Eds.), *Classroom Oriented Research in Second Language Acquisition,* pp. 67–102.

Scovel, Thomas. 1988. Genes and teens—sociobiological explanations for the presence of accents after puberty. In Scovel, *A Time to Speak,* pp. 103–123.

Language Learning—A Journal of Applied Linguistics, for material from:

Schumann, J. 1976. Second language acquisition: The pidginization hypothesis. *Language Learning, 26,* 391–408.

Tarone, E., and Parrish, B. 1988. Task related variation in interlanguage: The case of articles. *Language Learning, 38,* 21–44.

The Modern Language Journal, for material from:

Jamieson, J. 1992. The cognitive styles of reflection/impulsivity and field independence/dependence and ESL success. *Modern Language Journal, 76,* 491–501.

Oxford University Press, for material from:

Holmes, J. 1989. Sex differences and apologies: One aspect of communicative competence. *Applied Linguistics, 10,* 194–213.

O'Malley, J. M., Chamot, A. U., and Küpper, L. 1989. Listening comprehension strategies in second language acquisition. *Applied Linguistics, 10,* 418–437.

Teachers of English to Speakers of Other Languages, for material from:

Bachman, Lyle. 1991. What does language testing have to offer? *TESOL Quarterly, 25,* 671–704.

Brown, J. D. 1991. Statistics as a foreign language—Part I: What to look for in reading statistical language studies. *TESOL Quarterly, 25,* 569–586.

Long, Michael H. 1990. The least a second language acquisition theory needs to explain. *TESOL Quarterly, 24,* 649–666.

Watson-Gegeo, Karen Ann. 1988. Ethnography in ESL: Defining the essentials. *TESOL Quarterly, 22,* 575–592.

Readings on
Second Language
Acquisition

INTRODUCTION

Mention the word *research,* and many people envision a laboratory, with animals in cages and researchers busily writing voluminous notes on how many trials it takes for rats to find their way out of a maze. Teachers, in particular, have been suspicious of research because too often it seems to have little or nothing to say to them. Since the 1970s, when research in the field of second language acquisition (SLA) began to blossom, research has focused on two areas: the nature of the language acquisition process, and the identification and description of the factors that affect language learners (Larsen-Freeman, 1991). This focus seems arguably to be at the core of what teachers should know about second and foreign language acquisition. How, then, is it possible for much of the work on SLA that has been done over the past 20 years to seem so alien to those very people who have a stake in knowing as much as possible about how this process works—language teachers themselves?

If it is true that researchers and teachers have the same goal in mind—learning more about how second language learning works—we might expect that there would be some shared understanding of how to go about finding answers to this question. Suppose you, as a teacher, want to study language acquisition. What would you do? On the one hand, you might decide to test a particular question you had about language acquisition—for example, "Will my students learn more if I use this new method of teaching?" Before testing whether this new method was better, you would have to decide exactly how and what you would measure—before and after—in order to decide if the students had "learned more." You would have to carefully design your experiment so that you could compare one group of students with whom you used the new method with another group with whom you didn't use the method. And you would have to be sure that the two groups were identical, with the only difference between them being the method of instruction. If you wanted to try to demonstrate that the results of your experiment would also apply to other groups of learners, you would have to use inferential statistics in your data analysis.

On the other hand, you might decide to observe a language class, or even an individual learning a language. This observation could take place over a relatively short period of time, or it could go on for days, weeks, or even years. In the course of making your observations, you might make audio and/or video recordings, or you might only take notes on what you saw. You might stay completely out of the way of the learners, or you might decide to get some additional information about what was going on at a particular point in time by asking the learner(s) or the teacher to describe what they thought was happening. When you were finished collecting the data, or even while you were collecting it, you might formulate some hypotheses about particular aspects of language learning, based on your data. After the data collection was finished, you might use counting and categorizing in your data analysis, or you might write an interpretation of what you had concluded from your observations.

These two hypothetical examples represent two ends of a continuum of approaches to research on language acquisition. We can call the first approach experimental and the second nonexperimental. It is probably the case that when you think of research you think of studies that fit in the category demonstrated by our first example. For many of us, experimental research is synonymous with quantitative, number-crunching analyses that make use of statistical terms and procedures that we often don't understand. But we need to emphasize here that not all research is experimental and, further, that statistics need not remain a foreign language. Research also includes scholarship produced through other methods of inquiry—case studies, descriptions, surveys, formal linguistic research, and analyses and syntheses of previous research. (For examples of the latter, see the articles by Bachman, Kachru, and Long in this volume.)

For our purposes, we will look at research in terms of an experimental–nonexperimental continuum. Broadly speaking, experimental research seeks to predict and explain a phenomenon such as second language acquisition and uses quantitative techniques to do so. This approach currently dominates SLA research, which may explain why so many researchers use statistics. Nonexperimental research has a different, although equally valid, aim—namely, to describe and interpret SLA. This type of research is frequently ethnographic and tends to use qualitative techniques to investigate SLA. However, we should not make the mistake of equating nonexperimental research solely with ethnography, since there are a number of nonexperimental, qualitative approaches to research that could not strictly be categorized as "ethnographic." Further, this also ignores the fact that the work on Universal Grammar in linguistics, though nonexperimental, uses a distinctive research methodology that does not owe anything to ethnography. (See the article by White in this volume.)

On another level, we will look at research in terms of whether the data are quantitative or qualitative and whether the analysis is interpretive or statistical. We should be careful not to make overly rigid distinctions between quantitative and qualitative research, for a number of reasons, not the least of which is the fact that researchers often use both quantitative and qualitative techniques in the same study. (For example, see the study by Lightbown and Spada in this volume.) Nonetheless, there are some basic differences in quantitative and qualitative research methodologies that readers need to understand. Let us now look at what these differences might entail.

Quantitative and Qualitative Approaches to Doing Research

Most of us have an idea of what is meant by the terms *qualitative* and *quantitative* when used to describe research. In this context, *quantitative* suggests number-crunching and statistical analyses, whereas *qualitative* suggests just the opposite. If we played a game such as "Tell me what words come to mind when I say _____," for quantitative, we might hear words such as *deductive, objective, controlled, obtrusive, interventionist, reductionist, product-oriented,* and *generalizable.* For qualitative we might expect to hear *inductive, subjective, uncontrolled, naturalistic, unobtrusive, descriptive, process-oriented, ungeneralizable.* The two might be further distinguished by associating quantitative research with *hypothesis testing* and *obtaining proof,* whereas qualitative research is associated with *hypothesis generating* and *developing an understanding.* But are these associations accurate? What do we mean when we use these terms and expressions to describe quantitative and qualitative research? Are qualitative and quantitative research as clearly separable as these polarities would make it appear?

First, let's look more closely at the terms that we have identified as being commonly associated with either quantitative or qualitative research in order to get a better understanding of what the terms mean in this particular context. The contrast between deductive and inductive rests on which comes first, the theory or the data. Quantitative research is deductive, in that it starts with a theory or a hypothesis and then uses data to test it, whereas qualitative research is inductive, in that it collects data through observation and then comes up with a theory to account for the data. The *theory first* approach seeks to obtain data that provide proof and test hypotheses; the *data first* approach looks for hypotheses that can explain the data collected or the facts observed. In quantitative research, the researcher is obtrusive, intervening to control the variables under study. This stands in contrast to the qualitative researcher, who does not try to exert control, as an experimenter would, but instead observes naturally occurring behavior. Quantitative research is often described as *reductionist* because the researcher preselects the variables to be examined in the study, whereas in contrast, the qualitative researcher does not decide in advance what variables will be important but instead attempts to describe as fully as possible what is being observed. In this sense, quantitative research is interested in the end product—for example, whether a particular program seems to be more effective than another—whereas the interest of qualitative research is in the process itself—in other words, in what actually goes on in the classroom. Finally, although the results of quantitative research are assumed to be generalizable to the larger population, many researchers claim for a variety of reasons, that the results of qualitative research cannot (and often need not) be generalized.

Although there are obviously some clear distinctions between quantitative and qualitative research, some researchers suggest that it is an oversimplification to try to polarize them in this way. Chaudron (1988) argues that the two categories actually overlap. For example, quantitative methods are sometimes used to test hypotheses that were derived from a qualitative approach to defining a problem, and qualitative research is often supplemented by counting instances of the occurrences of some behavior. Grotjahn (1987; cited in Nunan, 1992) suggests that instead of identifying research in terms of the overly simplistic quantitative/qualitative distinction, we should look at the data—whether they are quantitative or qualitative; the data collection procedures—whether they are experimental or not; and the data analysis—whether it is statistical or interpretive. In his view, at one extreme we could find research that has a nonexperimental design, qualitative data, and an interpretive analysis of these data; at the other extreme we could find research that has an experimental design, quantitative data, and a statistical analysis of these data. In between we could find a range of research paradigms, differing from one another in terms of the categories outlined above—the data, the data collection procedures, and the data analysis.

Some researchers, such as Nunan (1992), however, believe that the there is a clear distinction between quantitative and qualitative research, in that the two are based on very different ways of understanding the world and very different views of whether or not there is an external truth out there waiting to be "discovered." These two polar views are represented on a methodological continuum by true or quasi-experiments on one end, and ethnography on the other. Along the continuum, we find a wide range of research methods—formal experiments, interviews and questionnaires, schemes for observing classes and individuals, introspective methods such as diaries, discourse analysis, case studies, and ethnographies. We will explore these differences further in the discussion that follows.

Quantitative Research

Experimental Research.   Researchers have investigated a wide variety of issues in classroom second language acquisition through experimentation. True experiments are designed to help researchers predict and explain human behavior. Ultimately, the researcher hopes to be able to establish a causal relationship between a particular *treatment* and a result or consequence. Larsen-Freeman and Long (1991) establish two minimal criteria for an experiment: at least two groups must be included in the study (a control group and an experimental group); and the subjects must be randomly assigned to one of the groups. The rationale for having a control group is quite clear—if one group is treated one way and the other group is treated a different way, *and* if there is a difference in the behaviors (e.g., test scores) of the two groups after the treatment, then the difference must be attributable to the different treatments (assuming that the researcher took care to ensure that no other difference between the groups existed that could account for the difference in behavior). The establishment of cause–effect relationships is one of the goals of experimental research. Another is to be able to extend the explanations/predictions of the results of the study to the broader population. In order to do this, researchers use *inferential statistics.* (For an explanation of inferential and descriptive statistics, see the article by J. D. Brown in this volume.)

Of all the articles in this volume, perhaps the one that comes closest to a true experiment is Gardner and MacIntyre's study of motivation. The authors began with a specific research question and then designed a study to test the hypotheses. Subjects were randomly divided into two groups. All subjects were given a test to determine how they scored on eight different attitudinal/motivational characteristics. Then they were tested in a laboratory-like setting in which they were given six trials to learn 26 English/French word pairs. Subjects in the experimental group were told that they would be paid $10 if they successfully learned the word pairs. Subjects in the control group were told to do their best. Inferential statistics were used in the analysis of the results, which the authors believe are generalizable to other language learners.

But language learning is very complex, and this complexity creates serious problems for the researcher trying to design a pure experiment. Because of these problems, most so-called *experimental* research in SLA is actually quasi-experimental. Another problem with experimental research is that the behavior it examines often takes place, of necessity, outside its natural context. Van Lier (1990) points out that as a result, when we think we are studying classroom language acquisition, in many instances we may be only approximating the classroom. Thus, an important problem for quasi-experimental research is how valid it is in a real-world context.

Elicitation of Experimental Data. There are a number of different methods of data elicitation that can be used in experimental research. These include setting up a particular task for the learners and then collecting language data elicited by that task; structured exercises designed to produce the particular structures of interest to the researcher; grammaticality judgment tasks; elicited imitation; oral interviews; guided compositions; and communicative games. The article by Tarone and Parrish in this volume reports on research that used several of these data elicitation techniques, including grammaticality judgments, oral interviews, and an oral narration task. In their research on the critical period, Johnson and Newport also used grammaticality judgments to measure the language proficiency of their subjects (the behavior being studied).

Other Data Sources.   Other sources of data include surveys and various test instruments, including standardized tests. The studies by Jamieson and by Chapelle and Abraham make use of a number of standardized tests or test types—TOEFL, various cloze tests, the Matching Familiar Figures Test, and the Group Embedded Figures Test, for example. These experimental studies are examples of correlation studies that attempt to demonstrate relationships among various tests. (See J. D. Brown's article for a discussion of correlation studies.)

Quantitative Data Analysis.   The aspect of experimental research that is most intimidating to the uninitiated is its quantitative approach to data analysis. The mere sight of a table of numbers induces some readers to skip immediately to the conclusions section of the article. It is important to keep in mind that quantification of data can be found in studies that are not at all experimental—for example, in survey research. Studies that appear to be based on relatively qualitative data—for example, transcriptions of classroom discourse—can use a data analysis procedure that may include coding, counting, and categorizing of the data. Or we might find a study in which the researcher looks at sentences produced by a learner and computes the average length of the sentence. This kind of quantification is an example of the use of *descriptive statistics,* which are actually quite easy to understand once we know what is represented on the tables and what words such as *mean* and *median* mean. More difficult to understand are the quantitative analyses known as inferential statistics. This kind of statistical analysis typifies psychometric research (experimental research that uses inferential statistics to analyze the data). Inferential statistics are used so that the researcher can make generalizations about the larger population from which the sample used in the study was drawn. To help you to better understand how to read statistical studies, we have included J. D. Brown's article, "Statistics as a Foreign Language," in this volume.

Qualitative Research

Ethnographic Research.   Ethnographic research comes to language acquisition from the fields of anthropology, sociology, and education. Although it has played an important role in naturalistic first language acquisition, its potential for use in second language acquisition research has only recently attracted attention. To provide a better understanding of what ethnography is and what it can contribute to research on second language acquisition and teacher training, we have included Watson-Gegeo's article, "Ethnography in ESL: Defining the Essentials," in this volume. Very briefly, however, whereas experimental research seeks to predict and explain behavior out of context, ethnographic research seeks to provide a contextually rich interpretation of behavior that leads to a grounded understanding of the phenomena that are being studied. Furthermore, generally speaking, in ethnographic research there is less concern with generalizing results obtained in one situation to other contexts. This is because each context is viewed as culturally unique, so that no single "truth" can be deduced from a particular set of circumstances and generalized to a general population of language learners.

More specifically, when you think about the fields in which ethnography originated, it is easy to understand why one of its fundamental principles is that it must look at behavior within its naturally occurring context rather than in an artificial or experimental setting. Anthropology, after all, is fundamentally concerned with the study of culture. Furthermore, as we noted above, ethnography assumes that reality is subjective—that the researcher cannot understand the behavior of the individuals or the group being studied without incorporating into the research the beliefs and perceptions of the subjects themselves. This is what is known as adopting a *participant's perspective* as opposed to an *analyst's perspective*—the perspective that characterizes experimental research. Because context is so important, ethnographic researchers attempt to minimize disruptions caused by their intrusion into the subjects' world. In other words, the researcher does not try to control or manipulate the phenomena under investigation. Thus, ethnographic research constructs theory by allowing hypotheses to emerge from the data. Although this doesn't mean that researchers begin with a blank slate, the ethnographer does not begin with a preconceived notion of what the research questions are (as in experimental research); rather, the questions emerge in the course of data collection. Ethnographic research is also described as *neutral,* in that the researcher attempts to avoid bias by studying interaction in context—that is, from the perspective of those being studied.

It is important to keep in mind that ethnography is both a set of procedures and a philosophy. In examples of *pure* ethnographic research based on ethnographic philosophies and using ethnographic procedures, researchers often spend years living in the culture being studied, functioning as *participant-observers.* In such cases, volumes of data are collected, often through recordings and field notes, with further notes as part of the ongoing analysis of the data. In the end, what we see published is only a small fraction of the data and the data analysis. (For examples of the researcher as *participant-observer,* see the studies by Ellis and Bailey in this volume.)

Diaries.   Diaries are first-person accounts of language learning or teaching. Although some researchers categorize them as ethnographic, they can also be viewed as examples of *introspective* research in which learners, with the aid of the researcher, try to examine their own behavior for insight into how they acquire a second/foreign language. Diaries are a particularly interesting form of qualitative data collection in second/foreign language acquisition research, since the researcher functions as a participant (the individual being studied) and as an observer (the researcher). In diary studies, the method is to keep a journal, to reread the entries soon after they are done to be sure that nothing has been omitted, and then to reread the entire journal after the learning experience being observed is over, in order to look for recurring patterns and possible explanations for these patterns. Kathleen Bailey's article in this volume provides an example of this kind of qualitative/ethnographic approach to studying language acquisition. Her study is more complex than most diary studies because she starts at what we might call "Stage II"; that is, she had already noticed a recurring theme—competition and anxiety—in her diary, so in this article she looks at diaries of other language learners to see if she can find the same themes in their diaries.

Case Studies.   The study of a single individual—a case study—looks like a kind of ethnography in terms of its methods and its concern for studying the phenomena in context; however, in a case study, the qualitative methods of ethnography can be supplemented by quantitative data and statistical analyses. The case study approach has been widely used to study first language development. The method of data collection is normally naturalistic and longitudinal—that is, the data consist of samples of spontaneous speech collected over a long period of time. John Schumann's study of a Spanish-speaking adult learning English naturalistically (in this volume) provides an example of a case study of a second language learner. In Schumann's study, what emerged in the course of the study was a hypothesis that second language development is governed by the learner's social and psychological distance from the target language group. Like the diary studies, what we see in the published reports of the research is only a small part of the data collected—only the portions that pertain to the particular theory generated by the data.

Discourse Analysis.   In its most general sense, *discourse analysis* focuses on the analysis of whole texts (oral or written) rather than discrete sentences. The language data can be naturally occurring, elicited, or invented. The procedures used in the analysis of language include both qualitative measures and quantitative measures such as coding and counting. Discourse analysts typically make audiotapes and/or videotapes of interactions (inside or outside the classroom) which they later transcribe and then analyze for recurring patterns. The articles by Holmes and Ellis in this volume exemplify a discourse analytic approach to studying SLA. Methodologically speaking, the essays embody an interesting mix of philosophies and methods. The data collection procedures they use are naturalistic, but their analyses are motivated by a research question drawn from the theoretical literature, not from the data, as would be the case in ethnography. The analysis of the data is primarily descriptive, and includes some descriptive statistics.

The article by Lightbown and Spada also provides an interesting mix of qualitative and quantitative approaches. The researchers collected a large corpus of naturalistic classroom data (qualitative) that was coded at the time it was observed. This was supplemented by an analysis of the audiotapes and/or transcriptions of the audiotapes. The Communicative Orientation of Language Teaching (COLT) scheme is arguably the most highly developed observation scheme for coding classroom behavior and is particularly noteworthy for combining the product-orientation typical of quantitative research with the process-orientation typical of qualitative research.

Qualitative versus Quantitative: Is One Better?

As we have seen, qualitative and quantitative research are not necessarily mutually exclusive. Some researchers make use of both approaches in a single study. Nevertheless, they probably do represent very different ways of looking at the world and very different conceptions of the nature of truth. Those who believe that there is a body of "truth" out there, independent of the researcher and waiting to be discovered, tend to favor what is called *psychometric* research, with its experimental design and inferential statistical analysis of the data. These researchers also believe that it is extremely important to be able to make generalizations about the results that can be applied to the larger population. For them, qualitative research is not normally generalizable or replicable, so it cannot be used to make meaningful inferences that are applicable to other cases. Most psychometric researchers argue that the only way to proceed in SLA research is to formulate and test hypotheses in a scientific way. They suggest that ethnographic research is useful largely as a tool to identify relevant concepts that will lead to the formation of testable hypotheses. Further, they argue that most researchers adopting qualitative or ethnographic techniques need to continue their analysis with some quantification. As Chaudron puts it, "the ultimate need for generality and for comparisons across classroom contexts inevitably requires such quantification of events" (Chaudron, 1988, p. 49).

From the perspective of the qualitative researcher, however, the price of scientific control—neglect of the social context—is too high. With regard to the question of generalizability, they argue, first, that some qualitative studies are generalizable, and second, that holistic, ungeneralizable studies are justifiable. For our part, we agree with Nunan, who says that "ethnography is a valid tradition in its own right, and should not be considered simply as a hypothesis-generating device for experimental research" (Nunan, 1992, p. 57). Or, as van Lier suggests, "it is in the interest of our profession to pursue both options"— that "ethnography serves as preparatory ground-clearing for causal research" and that "it is also theory building and theory testing" (van Lier, 1990, pp. 48–49). Ultimately, the type of approach each of us finds most convincing is probably a matter of personal taste, and it is up to you to decide which type of research you find most congenial and persuasive.

Understanding and Evaluating Research

✳ As we said earlier, one of the goals of this book is to help teachers and teacher-trainees learn to read, understand, and evaluate research in second and foreign language acquisition. For all of the articles, you should be able to answer the following questions:

1. What is the purpose of this study?
2. How does this study relate to other research that has been done in this area, as described in the literature review?
3. What data were collected and how were they collected?
4. What are the conclusions? Are generalizations about the results appropriate?
5. How does the study contribute to the field?
6. What are the implications of the study for language learning and teaching?

Although these questions are general enough to apply to the various examples of research in this volume, they should be supplemented with additional questions, depending on the approach to research that the article represents. As part of your analysis of each study, you need to ask the following questions (cf. Grotjahn, 1987): (1) Are the data quantitative or qualitative? (2) Are the data collection procedures experimental or not? (3) Is the data analysis statistical or interpretive? For some of the studies in this volume, the answers will not be simple because, for example, both quantitative and qualitative data may have been used or because some of the data may have been analyzed statistically and some interpretively. In reality, as you will see, it is not always easy to label a particular study as purely qualitative or quantitative.

Once you have identified the particular research approach that seems to best characterize the work in question, you will need to answer some additional questions. For research that is primarily quantitative and experimental, expand the questions on the list given earlier to include the following:

1. What are the research questions and hypotheses?
2. Who were the subjects in the study? How were they selected? What are their characteristics?
3. What variables does the researcher want to manipulate? Which ones are to be held constant?
4. What data were collected and how were they collected?
5. How were the data analyzed? (What statistical procedures were used?)
6. Are the results of the study generalizable to the broader population?

7. Has the researcher provided enough information so that someone else could replicate the study?

✳For research that is primarily qualitative research, particularly ethnographic research, you should be able to answer these additional questions:

1. What is the research problem or the goal of the study? (Notice that there are not specific "research questions" or hypotheses to be tested.)

2. Who were the participants in the study?

3. What was the role of the researcher in the study? (Observer? Participant/observer?)

4. What data were collected and how were they collected? Over what period of time were they collected?

5. In the course of collecting and analyzing the data, what questions emerged (or what hypotheses were generated)?

6. To what extent are the results generalizable or applicable to other contexts or groups?

As part of the process of evaluating the articles in this volume, you should think carefully about answers to some of the issues we touched on earlier in relation to the qualitative/quantitative distinction. What is the relationship between quantitative and qualitative research? Is one approach to research "better" than another, or is it simply the case that the research problem itself should determine whether one approach is more appropriate than another? For each of the works in this volume, does the approach taken seem to provide the best insight into the problem under investigation?

Using This Book

As we said in the preface, this book was designed to accomplish two separate goals. The first was to put together a collection of articles focusing on some of the major topics of interest to both teachers and SLA researchers that could supplement one of the standard introductory texts on second/foreign language acquisition and teaching. Topics covered include comparing and contrasting first and second language acquisition, cognitive styles and strategies, affective factors in language acquisition, sociocultural factors in language acquisition, interlanguage, communicative competence, language testing, and theories of second language acquisition.

The second goal was to help teachers and teacher-trainees learn to read, understand, and evaluate research published in the major journals in our field. For each work, we have provided sections called "Previewing the Article," "Understanding the Article," "Reflecting on Wider Issues," and "Going Beyond the Article." The "Previewing" section is designed to put the work in context and to give you some questions to guide your reading as you begin the article. Before reading each article, look ahead and scan the questions in the "Understanding" section that follows, and then work through the answers to the questions as you read. After reading the work, you should answer the questions in the "Reflecting" section, either alone or with a group of other students, either in or out of class. Finally, the "Going Beyond" section gives you a few suggestions for articles or books that cover related research by the same author or by other authors, with a brief commentary designed to put these suggested additional readings in context. We know that you won't have time to follow up on all the additional readings suggested for every article, but we hope that your interest in some of the topics will pique your curiosity enough to send you off in search of some of the materials we have suggested. The Appendix provides a list of some of the major journals that you should turn to in order to keep up with developments in the field of second and foreign language acquisition, and a list of books designed to help you as both a consumer and a producer of SLA research. Armed with a new understanding of SLA research, we hope that you will not only feel better equipped to understand the process of language learning in your own classroom but will also feel motivated to view yourself as a teacher-researcher—that is, as someone who not only teaches language but is also able to solve a broad range of practical language learning and teaching problems in a principled fashion.

References

Brumfit, C., & Mitchell, R. (Eds.). (1990). *Research in the language classroom.* London: Modern English Publications.

Chaudron, C. (1988). *Second language classrooms.* Cambridge: Cambridge University Press.

Grotjahn, R. (1987). On the methodological basis of introspective methods. In C. Faerch and G. Kasper (Eds.), *Introspection in second language research.* Clevedon, England: Multilingual Matters.

Johnson, D. (1992). *Approaches to research in second language acquisition.* New York: Longman.

Larsen-Freeman, D. (1991). Second language acquisition research: Staking out the territory. *TESOL Quarterly, 25,* 315–345.

Larsen-Freeman, D., & Long, M. (1991). *An introduction to second language acquisition research.* London: Longman.

Nunan, D. (1992). *Research methods in language learning.* Cambridge: Cambridge University Press.

van Lier, L. (1990). Ethnography: Bandaid, bandwagon, or contraband? In C. Brumfit & R. Mitchell (Eds.), *Research in the language classroom.* London: Modern English Publications.

UNIT I

UNDERSTANDING SECOND LANGUAGE ACQUISITION RESEARCH

1

STATISTICS AS A FOREIGN LANGUAGE— PART 1: WHAT TO LOOK FOR IN READING STATISTICAL LANGUAGE STUDIES

James Dean Brown
University of Hawaii at Manoa

Previewing the Article

A good deal of research in second language acquisition ultimately involves quantification of factors and variables under investigation. It is not uncommon for potential readers of the reports of such research to be overwhelmed by what appears to be a barrage of statistics and mathematical jargon, even to the point of avoiding such studies. Yet one can hardly enjoy the mystery and challenge of second language acquisition research without squarely facing those statistics. In fact, in this volume, many of the 18 articles involve some form of quantification.

James Dean Brown addresses this study to those who are bewildered by the statistics of our professional literature. Concepts and terms are explained simply and clearly, so that you can read and understand research reports. Before you read the article, scan it to find answers to the following questions:

Reprinted from *TESOL Quarterly, 25*:569–586, 1991.

1. What is the author's principal purpose?
2. How does the author organize the article (look at headings and subheadings) to accomplish that purpose?
3. What specific statistical terms or concepts are covered?

NOTE: To illustrate the concepts he wishes to discuss in this article, J. D. Brown refers to another article in the same issue of *TESOL Quarterly.* Immediately following this article, we have added an Editors' Appendix (pages 31–34) that includes the abstract and all of the tables in the example article to which Brown refers.

This article is addressed to those practicing EFL/ESL teachers who currently avoid statistical studies. In particular, it is designed to provide teachers with strategies that can help them gain access to statistical studies on language learning and teaching so that they can use the information found in such articles to better serve their students. To that end, five attack strategies are advocated and discussed: (a) use the abstract to decide if the study has value for you; (b) let the conventional organization of the article help you; (c) examine the statistical reasoning involved in the study; (d) evaluate what you have read in relation to your professional experience; and (e) learn more about statistics and research design. Each of these strategies is discussed, and examples are drawn from the article following this one in this issue of the *TESOL Quarterly*.

The *TESOL Quarterly* is currently the research journal of the organization, Teachers of English to Speakers of Other Languages. Ironically, many of the statistical studies on language learning and teaching that are found in the *Quarterly* may be incomprehensible to the very EFL/ESL teachers who make up the intended audience. Rather than bemoaning this situation (either by berating teachers for not knowing more about statistics or by criticizing researchers for producing articles that are frequently not accessible to teachers), this article will begin by accepting statistical language studies for what they are: legitimate investigations into phenomena in human language learning/teaching which include the use and systematic manipulation of numbers as part of their argument.

Notice that I purposely avoid terms such as *empirical* and *experimental* in referring to these statistical language studies. I am doing so for several reasons. First, there are other, nonstatistical studies that could be called empirical (e.g., ethnographies, case studies, etc.) since, by definition, empirical studies are those based on data (but not necessarily quantitative data). Second, there are statistical studies that are not exactly experimental in the technical sense of that word (e.g., quasi-experimental studies, posttest-only designs, etc.). Third, there are statistical studies that have little or nothing to do with experimentation (e.g., demonstrations, survey research, etc.).

Regardless of what studies are called, when confronted with statistics, many readers will either skip an article entirely, or take a rather cursory route through the paper. Such a route might include skimming the abstract and the introduction section, then skipping over the method and results sections (with their tables, figures, and statistics) to the conclusions (and/or discussion) section where they look to find out what the study was all about. If this strategy sounds similar to one that you use, you may be missing an opportunity. Statistical reasoning is just a form of argumentation; by skipping the method and results sections, readers not only miss the heart of the study, but also buy the authors' argument without critical evaluation. Most of us would not surrender so easily if the form of argument were expressed in words rather than numbers. We would read a prose article carefully and critically. We should not have to surrender professional skepticism just because the form of argument may be a bit alien, that is, numerical.

The purpose of this article is to provide some attack strategies for teachers to use in gaining access to statistical studies and in understanding them better. In the process, examples will be drawn from another study, the abstract and tabular results of which are included as an appendix to this article (see page 31).[1]

Attack Strategies for Statistical Studies

With the following strategies in hand, you may not understand every word of a statistical study, but you will be able to gain access to such studies and will have a purposeful way of grappling with the content.

Use the Abstract to Decide if the Study has Value for You

Let us begin with the familiar and work toward the less familiar. The portion of a statistical report that is probably most often read is the abstract. An abstract typically contains about 150 words in the *TESOL Quarterly*. Other journals may have somewhat longer or shorter abstracts. Regardless of their length, these handy summaries should contain enough information for the reader to know what the study was about, how it was conducted, and the general trend of the results. In other words, an abstract should tell the reader in a nutshell what is presented in the study and allow you to determine if an article is pertinent enough to your professional life and teaching situation to be interesting and worthy of your time.

Indeed, there is an overwhelming and increasing amount of information competing for our professional attention. Along with the *TESOL Journal* and

---

[1] Editor's note: See the appendix to this article for a description (abstract) of the second article and the seven tables from that article.

the *TESOL Quarterly,* EFL/ESL teachers choose among other journals, such as the *ELT Journal,* the *ESP Journal, Language, Language Learning, Language Testing, Modern Language Journal, Studies in Second Language Acquisition,* and *TESL Canada Journal/Revue TESL du Canada,* to name just a few in the United Kingdom and North America, as well as *Cross Currents* and the *JALT Journal* (Japan), *Prospect* (Australia), *RELC Journal* (Singapore), *System* (Sweden), and many others.

Because of this plethora of journals, it is essential to use the abstracts to advantage. Consider the abstract associated with the example article that follows this one. Is there sufficient information in that abstract for you to decide whether the article is of interest to you?

Let the Conventional Organization of the Paper Help You

The *TESOL Quarterly* and many other journals in our field generally follow the format and organization described in the *Publication Manual of the American Psychological Association* (APA) (American Psychological Association, 1983). That manual advocates using the following general sections and subsections in reporting a statistical study:

Introduction
    Introduction to the problem
    Background
    Statement of purpose
Method
    Subjects
    Materials (or Apparatus)
    Procedures
Results
Discussion (and/or Conclusions)
References

Typically in our journals, there are no headings for the introduction or its subparts. However, beginning with the method section (including any subjects, materials or apparatus, and procedure subsections) through the results, discussion, conclusion, and references sections, you will generally find clear headings and subheadings. Since the general purpose of the headings and subheadings is "to help readers find specific information" (American Psychological Association, 1983, pp. 25–26), you should use them to help you find and organize the information that you need in order to understand the study. There is not space here to provide details about what each of these sections should contain. Indeed, such details are not necessary here because existing sources give ample information on this topic (e.g., Brown, 1988, pp. 43–62; Hatch & Farhady, 1982, pp. 33–38; Hatch & Lazaraton, 1991, pp. 107–126).

Nevertheless, there are a number of questions that you might want to ask yourself as you read through a statistical study. These questions should help focus the information contained in these key sections and help readers critically evaluate a study. Notice that section and subsection headings are listed in parentheses after each of the questions below. These are meant to suggest where you would typically find the information that would answer each question.

1. What literature is reviewed? Is the review current and complete? Where does the study fit into the field? (Introduction section)

2. What is the purpose of the study? (Introduction section, especially the Statement of Purpose subsection)

3. Who was studied and how were they selected? Were there enough people in the study to make the results meaningful? (Subjects subsection)

4. What tests, questionnaires, rating scales, etc., were used? What do they look like? And, are they reliable and valid for the purposes of the study? (Materials subsection)

5. What actually happened to the subjects during the data gathering process? (Procedures subsection)

6. How were the data organized and analyzed? (Results section)

7. Is there enough information provided to replicate the study? (throughout the Method section including the Subjects, Materials, and Procedure subsections)

8. What were the descriptive results? What other statistical results came out of this study? (Results section)

9. What were the answers to the research questions and what do the answers indicate? (Discussion section)

10. What are the implications of the results, and how do they relate to the field as a whole? (Discussion or Conclusions section)

11. Which conclusions follow directly from the results and which ones are more speculative? (Discussion or Conclusions section)

12. What questions arose in the course of doing the study that might be useful for future research? (Discussion or Conclusions section)

Since answers to these questions are important in understanding any study, you can use the conventional organization of statistical studies as represented by the sections discussed here to find your way around published research articles.

However, be warned that, even though the APA format and organization are well known, some authors do not use exactly the sections and headings listed above. Sometimes there are good reasons for such deviations. For instance, in the example article, there is a separate procedures subsection as advocated in the APA manual. However, in other studies, the same author has chosen to use a combined materials and procedures subsection because the two issues were inextricably intertwined to the degree that they made little sense if explained separately. Regardless of the specific sections and headings used in a particular study, you should find sufficient information somewhere in any statistical study to answer the twelve sets of questions listed above.

Examine the Statistical Reasoning Involved in the Study

In order to understand the results of a statistical study, it is necessary to understand the statistical reasoning that underlies all such studies. There are several key concepts that are necessary parts of much statistical reasoning: (a) descriptive statistics, (b) statistical differences, (c) probability levels, (d) statistical tests, and (e) significance versus meaningfulness. These five concepts will be discussed in turn.

Descriptive statistics.   Part of the content of any statistical paper describes what happened in the study. As mentioned above, such description is partially accomplished within the various parts of the method section. However, description also occurs in the results section, which describes what happened statistically. Descriptive statistics (a phrase used in contrast to inferential statistics) describe or summarize a data set but, by themselves, cannot tell us the extent to which they represent a larger population or other, similar sets. The descriptive statistics that are most often used are indicators of the central tendency and dispersion. The central tendency (which can be viewed as a typical value for a set of numbers) is commonly reported in terms of a statistic called the *mean.* (A statistic is any number that can be computed based on the observed data.) The mean is usually exactly the same as the arithmetic average that we use in daily life. Dispersion (which can be viewed as the variation of the numerical values away from the central tendency) is usually reported in terms of a statistic called the *standard deviation.* The standard deviation summarizes how much the numbers vary away from the mean, or how much they are spread out around the mean. Ordinarily, we would expect most scores (about 68% for a normal distribution) to fall within one standard deviation of the mean. For a normal distribution, 95% of the data fall within 2 standard deviations. For instance, if the data being described are a set of test scores, their standard deviation can be defined as "a sort of average of the differences of all scores from the mean" (Brown, 1988, p. 69).

You now have enough basic information about descriptive statistics to consider the central tendency and dispersion in a real study. Such descriptive statistics most often take the form of a table. Table 2 in the example study is typical. Notice that it describes the results in terms of the various groupings involved in the study, that is, for each group and/or subgroup in the study. The first column labels groups that were created by considering the raters in two faculties (English and ESL) separately as well as combined. Across the top of the table, you will also find labels for the groups that were created by considering the different types of students separately (English and ESL composition students) and combined. The most important thing to note is that the data being grouped and described are the ratings for two types of students (English and ESL) as rated by two types of instructors (from English and ESL faculties).

Notice that for each possible combination of Student Type, and Rater Faculty, the table provides three statistics: the number of students involved in the group (n), the mean (m), and the standard deviation (SD). For instance, the descriptive statistics for the English students' compositions as rated by the English faculty indicate that there were 112 compositions involved, that the mean was 2.46 (on a 0-to-5-point scale), and that the standard deviation was 1.11. This information is interesting in itself because it indicates that the test is fairly well centered (i.e., the mean is almost exactly halfway between the lowest possible score of zero and the highest possible score of five), and the scores are spread out to a reasonable degree (i.e., there is room for 2 standard deviations above and below the mean within the range of possible scores from 0 to 5).

However, the information is also useful for comparing groups to each other. Consider the fact that the means for all of the groupings are very similar in this table. That may indicate that there were no major differences among the groups of compositions as produced by the two types of students and rated by the two types of teachers. However, note that the standard deviations for the compositions written by the English students are generally higher than those for the essays written by the ESL students. This indicates that the scores for the English composition students were more spread out than those for ESL students, that is, there was greater dispersion in the writing scores of the English course students.

Statistical differences.   As useful and informative as descriptive statistics can be, they are often not enough. There is a type of statistical reasoning that takes over at this stage in most studies: *Inferential statistics* investigate the extent to which descriptive statistics represent a larger population or other, similar data sets. This mode of reasoning hinges on the concept of *significant differences.* The significant differences most often of interest in statistical studies are the differences observed in comparing means, comparing frequencies, or comparing correlation coefficients to zero.

In *comparing means* (i.e., arithmetic average), it is possible that any observed differences are purely accidental. After all, if you give a test to a group of students on several occasions, you would expect the means to be slightly different because human beings simply do not perform exactly the same on every occasion (e.g., some students' scores might have been affected by the fact that they were sick, tired, depressed, etc., on one of the occasions). Indeed, it would be very surprising if the test results turned out to be exactly the same on successive occasions. The issue that researchers must grapple with is whether the differences that they observe between means are just such chance variations or are due to some other more systematic factor. The question being posed by the researcher and answered through statistical tests is whether or not there is a significant difference between means.

For example, consider a hypothetical study in which the average number of correctly defined words on a vocabulary test is compared for two groups: one group that received lessons using language teaching Method X for 6 weeks, and the control group that received 6 weeks of instruction based on Method Y. The problem is that the two means will naturally vary to some degree by chance alone. The question that the researchers must resolve is whether there is a significant difference between the means (i.e., whether the observed difference between the means is systematic or occurred by chance alone).

If there is a significant difference, the researcher can say with a certain amount of confidence that the observed difference between the two means was not just accidental. This is an important issue because, if the group learning vocabulary under Method X has a higher mean than the other group, the higher number of vocabulary words learned can probably be attributed to the effects of Method X (provided the experiment was conducted properly). This would constitute an argument in favor of Method X, which might be interesting to other language educators responsible for teaching vocabulary. As described here, it is an argument based entirely on comparing the mean performances of the groups involved.

In *comparing frequencies,* it is also possible that any observed differences are due to chance variations. After all, if we tally the numbers of Taiwanese and Korean students in an ESL class on successive days, we would expect the resulting frequencies (also known as tallies) to be slightly different on different days. It might turn out that there are 7 Taiwanese and 11 Koreans on the first day, 6 Taiwanese and 12 Koreans on the second day, 7 Taiwanese and 9 Koreans on the third day, etc. Indeed, it would be surprising if the frequencies turned out to be exactly the same every day. Similarly, by chance alone, one would expect the numbers of Taiwanese and Koreans to vary from group to group because of chance variations in the proportions of different nationalities. The issue that researchers must come to grips with is whether any difference that is observed between frequencies is a chance variation or is instead due to some other more systematic factor. In short, the question being posed by a researcher who is comparing frequencies is whether or not there is a significant difference between the observed frequencies and the frequencies that would be expected by chance alone.

An example of this type of study might occur in performing a needs analysis for a language course. Perhaps the researcher is interested in the frequency, or tally, of people who are interested in studying pronunciation as compared to those interested in studying grammar. The question that a researcher might pose is whether there is a significant difference between the existing frequencies and the fifty-fifty split that would be expected by chance. If the researcher can state that there is a significant difference, it will indicate that the observed difference is due to factors other than the chance fluctuations that would occur naturally.

Similar reasoning may be used in *comparing correlation coefficients to zero.* Correlation coefficients are indexes that represent the degree of relationship between two sets of numbers. Correlation coefficients can range from 0.00 (if there is no relationship) to 1.00 (if there is a very strong relationship). Consider the following data set:

Students	EFL Test A	EFL Test B	Last EFL Study (years since)	Age
Maria	100	97	0.0	26
Jaime	98	97	0.5	28
Carla	87	84	2.0	26
Jose	82	85	1.5	28
Juanita	77	74	4.0	27
Jimmy	55	52	3.5	27

EFL Tests A and B appear to be highly related in the sense that as one set of numbers goes up so does the other. The resulting correlation coefficient turned out to be a very high .99. If two sets of numbers are not related at all, the expected correlation coefficient is 0.00. This is the case for Age and Test B in the above example data where the correlation coefficient turned out to be very close to zero at 0.01.

It is important to note that correlation coefficients can also take on negative values anywhere between 0.00 (if there is no relationship) and -1.00 (if there is a strong but opposite relationship). In such cases, the two sets of numbers are related but in opposite directions. For example, Test B and Last EFL Study in the above example are fairly strongly related but in opposite directions. In other words, as one set of numbers goes up, the other set goes down. The result in this case is a high but negative correlation coefficient of -.86. In short, correlation coefficients can range from -1.00 (for strong, but opposite relationships) to 0.00 (for no relationship) to +1.00 (for strong relationships in the same direction).

One problem with correlation coefficients is that even for two sets of random numbers some degree of correlation may be found by chance alone. For instance, on successive sets of randomly selected numbers, correlation coefficients of .12, .07, -.17, -.01, etc., might be found by chance alone. Indeed, it would be surprising if a correlation coefficient of exactly 0.00 were found every time. The issue that researchers must deal with is whether the correlation coefficients that occur in a study are just such random (or chance) variations around zero, or rather are due to some more systematic relationship between the sets of numbers. The question being posed by the researcher is whether there is a significant relationship, i.e., a significant difference between the correlation coefficient that was observed in a study and a zero (or chance) correlation. If the researcher can state that there is a significant difference, the correlation coefficient observed in the study probably varied from zero for other than chance reasons. In simpler terms, it indicates that the relationship between the sets of numbers is probably systematic—not just a chance relationship.

Probabilities.   Since there is always at least some possibility that differences are due to chance, researchers use statistical tests to compute a particular significant difference in terms of the probability that observed differences would occur by chance alone. In other words, when a researcher states that there is a significant difference (between the two means, between observed and expected frequencies, or between a correlation coefficient and zero), these results will always be stated in terms of the probability that the observed difference was due to chance fluctuations.

These probabilities are usually expressed as p values in statistical studies. They will normally be written as $p < .01$, or $p < .05$, or as exact figures, e.g., $p = .9681$. The p stands for probability. In straightforward terms, p is the likelihood that the researcher will be wrong in stating that there is a statistical difference (whether between means, between observed and expected frequencies, or between a correlation coefficient and zero) if, in fact, there is no difference. Thus, if $p < .01$, the probability (assuming chance alone) is less than 1% that the observed difference would be so large, giving strong evidence against pure chance. Similarly, if $p < .05$, the probability is less than 5% that an observed difference this large could have occurred by chance alone.

The probability levels of .05 and .01 (also referred to as alpha levels) are used by convention in most social science research to define the threshold of statistical significance. The choice between the .01 and.05 values is governed by how strict the researcher wants to be with regard to the conclusions that are drawn from a study. When a study is about an important medicine, we want to be very sure that it will not hurt patients. Thus a conservative .01 value might be selected so that there is a 99% probability of nonchance results. If the study is about a new way of teaching reduced forms, the decision is perhaps not quite so crucial, and therefore, we can accept the .05 value, which indicates that we are willing to accept a less restrictive 95% probability of nonchance results.

The determination of significant differences and their associated probabilities takes many forms, but the most commonly reported types are the three that have to do with means, frequencies, and correlation coefficients. It is important to note that a study seldom compares only two means, or contrasts only two frequencies, or examines one correlation coefficient to see if it varies from zero. More commonly, there are a number of means involved, or a number of frequencies, or a number of correlation coefficients to complicate the picture. Nevertheless, the underlying processes of checking significant differences and determining probabilities are the same.

Statistical tests.   The process of determining statistical significance as described in the Statistical Differences and Probabilities subsections above is referred to as performing a statistical test. The three most commonly reported types of statistical tests are used in the example study: mean comparisons, comparisons of frequencies, and comparing correlation coefficients to zero.

Example mean comparisons are discussed in the example study:

> In short, the small differences among the means shown in Table 2 can only be interpreted as chance fluctuations, which are not attributable to systematic differences based on the variables used in this study.

In the above quote, the statistical reasoning for comparing pairs of means is explained. In this case, there were three comparisons of interest: (a) the difference between the mean scores for the two types of students, English composition or ESL composition students; (b) the difference between the mean scores assigned by the English faculty and ESL faculty raters; and (c) the difference between the mean scores that resulted from the two different orders in which compositions were rated (first or second). In all three comparisons, it turned out that there were no significant differences between the two types of students, the two types of raters, and the two types of orders.

The statistical test being used is the F test, the results of which are based on the F statistic reported in the second column from the right in Table 3 on the example study. The essential information is found in the column on the far right where the probabilities are given in the column labeled p. Notice that each of these p values has an asterisk next to it and that the asterisks refer to the statement at the bottom of the table indicating that $p > .05$. This is read as "the probability is greater than .05" and indicates that random chance alone could produce results like these more than 5% of the time; this is not convincing evidence against chance. Thus, the researcher would be wrong in stating that there was a significant difference. (In fact, the p values reported in the table are much higher than .05, so they indicate that the observed results are quite consistent with random chance.) The first, second, and fourth p values are associated with one F ratio each for the main factors in Table 3: Student Type, Rater Faculty, and Order. The quote cited above discusses what these three statistical tests indicate.

Example frequency comparisons are shown in Tables 4 through 7 of the example study. The statistical test being used is known as the chi-square test, or simply χ^2. You will notice the asterisks in each table refer to the statement at the bottom of the table that $p < .05$. In this case, the statement would be read as "the p value is less than .05" and indicates that the researcher was justified (in those cases marked with an asterisk) in stating that there was a significant difference between the relative frequencies of English faculty and ESL raters who chose a particular feature, that is, the observed differences are unlikely to have occurred due to chance alone. Hence, we conclude that there are systematic differences between English faculty and ESL raters.

Notice that there are two steps involved in interpreting Table 4. First, there is the overall χ^2 value to consider. This value, located in the bottom row, is found to be significant at $p < .05$ (as indicated in the line just below the table). This result simply suggests that one or more of the frequencies in the table differed from what would be expected, and more detailed analyses are justified. In order to investigate which of the specific pairs (English faculty and ESL raters) of relative frequencies might be contributing to the overall significant difference, the χ^2 values for pairs were also calculated. These χ^2 values are reported in the column furthest to the right. They indicate that there was a significant difference (at $p < .05$) for the English faculty raters and ESL raters on Cohesion, Organization, and Syntax (i.e., the frequencies observed for the English and ESL raters on Cohesion, Organization, and Syntax were significantly different). In contrast, the frequencies of response for English and ESL faculty were not significantly different from expectations for the rating categories on Content, Mechanics, and Vocabulary. Similar two-step interpretations can be drawn from each of the other frequency tables (Tables 5–7).

Example comparisons of correlation coefficients to zero are shown in Table 1. The statistical test results are based on the Pearson product-moment correlation coefficient, or simply r. The asterisks in the table once again refer to the statement at the bottom of the table that $p < .05$. The statement would be read as "the p value is less than .05," which, in this case, indicates that the researcher was justified in each case in stating that the correlation coefficient was significantly different from zero. More specifically, random chance produces such strong correlations less than 5% of the time. Based on this evidence against pure chance, the researcher was justified in stating that there was a significant difference between each correlation coefficient and zero. For instance, the results in Table 1 show that, even though it is relatively low in magnitude, the correlation coefficient of .37 between Groups A and B of the English faculty raters differs from zero for reasons other than chance. The same is true for all of the other correlation coefficients in this table. Such is not always the case. Other studies may well find correlation coefficients that are not significant, indicating just chance differences from zero with no systematic association between the sets of numbers involved.

Significance versus meaningfulness. It is important to recognize that a statistically significant difference is just that, and no more. Significant differences, whether working with means, frequencies, or correlation coefficients, simply indicate that we have concluded that the observed differences are due to other than chance factors. In other words, the differences are systematic in some way. It does not indicate that the differences are necessarily interesting or meaningful. In fact, a difference can be statistically significant, yet be so small that it is not at all meaningful or interesting.

For instance, the correlation coefficient of .37 was found to be statistically significant at .05 (i.e., the correlation coefficient is probably different from 0.00 for other than chance reasons), but the meaningfulness of the relationship between the two sets of numbers is a separate issue. In this case, the numbers are scores assigned by two raters and the low correlation coefficient indicates that there was some association between the two sets of scores but there are other important factors that are still not accounted for. The weakness of agreement found here is worrisome because it indicates that the scores may not be very reliable. Thus, this is an example of a correlation coefficient that is statistically significant, but not very meaningful in magnitude.

Similarly, if two means are statistically different at $p < .05$, yet only differ by two points out of 100, then the result might not be at all meaningful. Likewise, if a set of observed frequencies differs from expected frequencies at $p < .01$, yet differs to an uninteresting degree, the results may not be meaningful. Thus, it is always important to examine the descriptive statistics in any study and think about any statistical tests in terms of descriptive statistics so that you can determine whether any significant differences are also meaningful.

The important thing to remember, then, is that meaningfulness is a separate issue from statistical significance and that meaningfulness will depend on all of the factors involved in the situation in which the study was conducted. When reading a statistical study, you might want to check to make sure that the researcher has kept separate these two issues of significance (i.e., can we rule out chance?) and meaningfulness (i.e., is the difference large enough to be interesting?) and interpreted them clearly.

It is important to remember that statistical studies are no more likely to be infallible than any other form of argumentation. Authors make errors, and computers make errors. However, if a study is properly carried out and the results are adequately described and systematically explained, such studies can help us to view the important issues in our field in new and useful ways.

Evaluate What You Have Read in Relation to Your Professional Experience

There are six types of questions that may prove useful in thinking about an article after having read it. These questions will enable you to know, comprehend, analyze, apply, synthesize, and evaluate what you have read. (These six categories are taken from Bloom's [1956] taxonomy. Note that they are presented here in a slightly different order from the original.) In short, after reading an article, try to recall basic information about the article by asking yourself Questions 1–3 below; then try to relate the article to your professional life by asking yourself Questions 4–6:

1. *Know:* Who wrote the article? When? In what journal? (Useful for identifying the study when referring to it)

2. *Comprehend:* In a sentence, what was the article about? (Useful for briefly summarizing the study)

3. *Analyze:* What sections was the article divided into? (Useful for recalling the overall structure of the study)

4. *Apply:* How can you apply what you learned in the article to your professional EFL/ESL teaching situation? (Useful for determining whether the article is applicable to your teaching experience)

5. *Synthesize:* How does the article relate to other professional books or papers that you have read? (Useful for seeing how the study fits into the professional literature)

6. *Evaluate:* How good was the quality of the article internally (in terms of style, organization, reasoning, etc.)? How good was it externally (i.e., in terms of everything else you know about the profession)? (Useful for evaluating the overall quality of the article)

Going through these questions (or similar ones) will help you to remember which article you read, comprehend its essential message, analyze the constituent parts of the article, apply what was learned in the article to your professional situation, synthesize what you found in the article with other points of view in the profession, and evaluate the quality of the article (both internally and externally).

Learn More about Statistics and Research Design

Having gone this far in the process of understanding statistical studies, you may now be intrigued by the prospect of learning more. For instance, you may have heard about ANOVAs, regression analyses, factor analyses, and other analyses not directly covered in this article. It is only by learning more that you will be able to understand some of these more complex analyses. In fact, it is only by learning more that you will be able to decide whether the author of a given study chose the correct statistical tests at all, or whether the assumptions that are required for any statistical tests were met.

There are a number of ways to learn more about statistics and research design. In addition to Part 2 of this discussion, there are books specifically designed to help language teachers do statistical research: Butler (1985), Hatch and Farhady (1982), Hatch and Lazaraton (1991), Seliger and Shohamy (1989), Woods and Fletcher (1986), etc. Another book, Brown (1988), is designed to help readers who are only interested in reading (rather than doing) statistical research. If the topics that interest you are more closely related to the statistics and research in the area of language testing, it may be more appropriate to read references such as Bachman (1990) and Henning (1987). If you have no idea which book to choose, it might be useful to read Hamp-Lyons' (1989, 1990) book reviews which describe a number of the volumes listed above.

I am not advocating that every EFL/ESL teacher read and internalize all of the knowledge in these books. However, I am suggesting that a number of strategies are available to teachers: (a) for some teachers, a thorough reading of one or two of the books listed above may be just what is needed; (b) for other teachers, it may prove useful to use several of the books listed above as references to explore topics in more depth as need arises in reading statistical studies; (c) still other teachers may be more comfortable with the structure provided by taking an organized course in basic research design and statistics at a local college or university.

Regardless of the strategy that is used, learning more about statistical research can help not only in understanding the statistical studies in the professional literature but also in grappling with the research that is reported in the lay media, much of which is done in the same statistical research paradigm that is used in our field. (For an excellent and easy to read treatment of how numbers, figures, and tables are used to fool the general public, you may want to read a book appropriately titled *How to Lie with Statistics,* Huff & Geis, 1954. Yes, it is still in print.) Armed with such knowledge, teachers can then defend themselves against numbers, and understand the reasoning that surrounds their use.

Conclusion

This article set out to provide attack strategies for EFL/ESL teachers to use in gaining access to statistical studies. These strategies include using the abstract and conventional organization of statistical papers to guide reading, examining the statistical reasoning, critically evaluating what the results signify to each reader, and learning more about statistical studies. There are a number of reasons why I hope that some readers will find these suggestions useful. First, if the studies that appear in the *TESOL Quarterly* have a larger informed readership, such studies will have greater impact on the field. All of us must use all important information about language learning and teaching to improve the ways that we serve our EFL and ESL students. Second, it is only by having an informed readership that the quality of the statistical studies in the *TESOL Quarterly* can be assured. Though the review process for selection of articles is thorough and fair, there are no guarantees that the articles that appear in print are 100% correct or uncontroversial. It is therefore our responsibility to read any articles that interest us as carefully and critically as we can so that the interface between teaching and research can be strengthened.

Acknowledgments

I would like to thank Kathleen Bailey, Graham Crookes, Thom Hudson, Andrew F. Seigel, and Ann Wennerstrom for their insightful comments and suggestions on an earlier version of this paper.

References

American Psychological Association. (1983). *Publication manual of the American Psychological Association.* Washington, DC: Author.

Bachman, L. F. (1990). *Fundamental consideration in language testing.* Oxford: Oxford University Press.

Bloom, B. (Ed.). (1956). *Taxonomy of educational objectives: Handbook 1. Cognitive domain.* London: Longman.

Brown, J. D. (1988). *Understanding research in second language learning: A teacher's guide to statistics and research design.* Cambridge: Cambridge University Press.

Butler, C. (1985). *Statistics in linguistics.* Oxford: Blackwell.

Hamp-Lyons, L. (1989). Recent publications on statistics, language testing, and quantitative research methods: I. *TESOL Quarterly, 23,* 127–132.

Hamp-Lyons, L. (1990). Recent publications on statistics, language testing, and quantitative research methods: II. *TESOL Quarterly, 24,* 293–300.

Hatch, E., & Farhady, H. (1982). *Research design and statistics for applied linguistics.* Rowley, Mass.: Newbury House.

Hatch, E., & Lazaraton, A. (1991). *The research manual: Design and statistics for applied linguistics.* Rowley, Mass.: Newbury House.

Henning, G. (1987). *A guide to language testing.* Rowley, Mass.: Newbury House.

Huff, D., & Geis, I. (1954). *How to lie with statistics.* New York: Norton.

Seligor, H. W., & Shohamy, E. (1989). *Second language research methods.* Oxford: Oxford University Press.

Woods, A., Fletcher, P., & Hughes, A. (1986). *Statistics in language studies.* Cambridge: Cambridge University Press.

Editor's Appendix

The study from which the following seven tables are taken investigates the degree to which differences exist in the writing scores of native speakers and international students at the end of their respective first-year composition courses (ESL 100 and ENG 100, in this case). Eight members each from the ESL and English faculties at the University of Hawaii at Manoa rated 112 randomly assigned compositions without knowing which type of students had written each. A holistic 6-point (0–5) rating scale initially devised by the English faculty was used by all raters. Raters were also asked to choose the best and worst features (from among cohesion, content, mechanics, organization, syntax, or vocabulary) of each composition as they rated it. The results indicated that there were no statistically significant mean differences between native-speaker and ESL compositions or between the ratings given by the English and ESL faculties. However, the features analysis showed that the ESL and English faculties may have arrived at their scores from somewhat different perspectives.

TABLE 1.   Correlation Matrix for Rater Groups

	Interrater Correlations			
	ENG/A	ENG/B	ESL/A	ESL/B
ENG/A	1.00	.37°	.58°	.36°
ENG/B	.37	1.00	.45°	.37°
ESL/A	.58	.45	1.00	.47°
ESL/B	.36	.37	.47	1.00
	Combined Reliabilities			
ENG A&B	.54			
ESL A&B	.64			
All raters (ENG & ESL)	.76			

° $p < .05$, $n = 112$.

[1]These significance results along with those reported in Tables 4–7 and the F_{max} test based on the statistics in Table 2 should be interpreted cautiously: The 448 reported essay scores are based on multiple readings of 112 essays.

TABLE 2.   Descriptive Statistics for Student Type and Rater Faculty

| | Student Type | | | | | | | | |
| | ENG 100 Essay Scores | | | ESL 100 Essay Scores | | | Essay Scores Combined | | |
RATER FACULTY	n	m	SD	n	m	SD	n	m	SD
ENG	112	2.46	1.11	112	2.30	.77	224	2.38	.96
ESL	112	2.37	1.16	112	2.31	.96	224	2.34	1.06
Faculties combined	224	2.42	1.14	224	2.30	.87	448	2.36	1.01

TABLE 3.   Three-Way ANOVA with Repeated Measures

Source	SS	df	MS	F	P°
Between subjects effects					
Student type	2.315	1	2.315	1.003	0.319
Within groups	253.915	110	2.308		
Within subjects effects					
Rater faculty	0.487	1	0.487	0.819	0.367
Student X Rater	0.362	1	0.362	0.609	0.437
Within groups	65.386	110	0.594		
Order	0.799	1	0.799	1.150	0.286
Student X Order	0.049	1	0.049	0.070	0.792
Within groups	76.396	110	0.695		
Rater X Order	0.276	1	0.276	0.544	0.462
Student X Rater X Order	0.116	1	0.116	0.228	0.634
Within groups	55.864	110	0.508		

°$p > .05$

TABLE 4. Overall Best Features Identified by Each Faculty

	Raters						
	ENG		ESL		Total		
BEST FEATURE	NO.	%	NO.	%	NO.	%	χ^2
Cohesion	55	24.6	26	11.6	81	18.1	10.38°
Content	71	31.7	86	38.4	157	35.0	1.43
Mechanics	21	9.4	24	10.7	45	10.0	.20
Organization	32	14.3	65	29.0	97	21.7	11.23°
Syntax	29	12.9	6	2.7	35	7.8	15.11°
Vocabulary	16	7.1	17	7.6	33	7.4	.03
Total	224	100	224	100	448	100	38.39(df=5)°

Note: Due to rounding, column percentages may not total 100.
° $p < .05$ ($df = 1$).

TABLE 5. Overall Worst Features Identified by Each Faculty

	Raters						
	ENG		ESL		Total		
WORST FEATURE	NO.	%	NO.	%	NO.	%	χ^2
Cohesion	14	6.3	21	9.4	35	7.8	1.40
Content	59	26.3	88	39.3	147	32.8	5.72°
Mechanics	28	12.5	10	4.5	38	8.5	8.53°
Organization	21	9.4	30	13.4	51	11.4	1.59
Syntax	80	35.7	60	26.8	140	31.3	2.86
Vocabulary	22	9.8	15	6.7	37	8.3	1.33
Total	224	100	224	100	448	100	21.42(df=5)°

Note: Due to rounding, column percentages may not total 100.
° $p < .05$ ($df = 1$).

TABLE 6. Best Features for Each Score

BEST FEATURE	English Faculty Scores						English χ²	ESL Faculty Scores						ESL χ²
	Low NO.	Low %	Middle NO.	Middle %	High NO.	High %	χ²	Low NO.	Low %	Middle NO.	Middle %	High NO.	High %	χ²
Cohesion	17	42.5	32	20.0	6	25.0	6.60°	11	21.6	14	9.9	1	3.1	6.69°
Content	4	10.0	56	35.0	11	45.8	8.00°	12	23.5	50	35.5	24	75.0	14.42°
Mechanics	7	17.5	14	8.8	0	0.0	5.13	9	17.6	15	10.6	0	0.0	5.72
Organization	4	10.0	23	14.4	5	20.8	1.24	12	23.5	48	34.0	5	15.6	3.73
Syntax	5	12.5	22	13.8	2	8.3	0.48	2	3.9	4	2.8	0	0.0	1.16
Vocabulary	3	7.5	13	8.1	0	0.0	1.94	5	9.8	10	7.1	2	6.3	0.45
Total	40	100	160	100	24	100		51	100	141	100	32	100	

Note: Due to rounding, column percentages may not total 100.
° $p < .05$ ($df = 2$).

TABLE 7. Worst Features for Each Score

WORST FEATURE	English Faculty Scores						English χ²	ESL Faculty Scores						ESL χ²
	Low NO.	Low %	Middle NO.	Middle %	High NO.	High %	χ²	Low NO.	Low %	Middle NO.	Middle %	High NO.	High %	χ²
Cohesion	2	5.0	9	5.6	3	12.5	1.70	1	2.0	16	11.3	4	12.5	3.91
Content	19	47.5	35	21.9	5	20.8	8.29°	31	60.8	55	39.0	2	6.3	14.89°
Mechanics	4	10.0	21	13.1	3	12.5	0.25	3	5.9	1	0.7	6	18.8	19.31°
Organization	3	7.5	15	9.4	3	12.5	0.40	6	11.8	21	14.9	3	9.4	0.72
Syntax	8	20.0	64	40.0	8	33.3	3.63	10	19.6	38	27.0	12	37.5	2.35
Vocabulary	4	10.0	16	10.0	2	8.3	0.06	0	0.0	10	7.1	5	15.6	7.26°
Total	40	100	160	100	24	100		51	100	141	100	32	100	

Note: Due to rounding, column percentages may not total 100.
° $p < .05$ ($df = 2$).

Understanding the Article

1. How does Brown differentiate among the terms *statistical, empirical,* and *experimental?*

2. What kinds of statistics might you find in nonexperimental studies?

3. In your own words, explain the difference between *descriptive statistics* and *inferential statistics.*

4. Explain the following concepts: *mean, frequency, correlation coefficient.*

5. What is the difference between *significance* and *meaningfulness?*

Reflecting on Wider Issues

1. To what extent do other works on SLA follow the "conventional organization" described in Brown's article? To help answer this question, look ahead in this book at some of the nonstatistical studies.

2. What kinds of research do not make use of statistics at all?

3. To what extent do you think including statistical analyses of the data makes a study more credible? Why or why not?

Going Beyond the Article

In order to gain a better understanding of statistical studies, you should read the second of J. D. Brown's articles, "Statistics as a foreign language—Part 2: More things to consider in reading statistical language studies" (*TESOL Quarterly, 26,* 629–664). You might also want to examine the two review articles by Hamp-Lyons (1989, 1990)—"Recent publications on statistics, language testing, and quantitative research methods: I" (*TESOL Quarterly, 23,* 127–132) and "Recent publications on statistics, language testing, and quantitative research methods: II" (*TESOL Quarterly, 24,* 293–300).

2

ETHNOGRAPHY IN ESL: DEFINING THE ESSENTIALS

Karen Ann Watson-Gegeo
University of California, Davis

Previewing the Article

Not all research, by any means, uses statistics and principles of experimental design in order to draw significant conclusions. In fact, in a field such as second language acquisition, where (a) human behavioral factors are difficult to quantify, and (b) variables are equally difficult to control empirically, we must turn to other, more qualitative, research paradigms.

Karen Watson-Gegeo offers a description of a form of qualitative research: ethnography. Ethnographic studies have been used in the fields of anthropology and education for many years, but have only somewhat recently become popular in second language acquisition. Before you start reading the article, scan it for answers to the following:

1. What does *ethnography* mean?
2. What is the author's purpose? (See the end of the first section.)
3. Make some predictions on how ethnographic research differs from the statistically-based research discussed by J. D. Brown in the previous article.

Reprinted from *TESOL Quarterly, 22*:575–592, 1988.

Ethnography has recently become fashionable in ESL, second language classroom, and educational research. But many studies bearing the name ethnographic are impressionistic and superficial rather than careful and detailed. This article addresses two questions: What is ethnography? And what can it do for us in ESL? Ethnography is defined, and some principles of quality ethnographic work are discussed, including the focus on behavior in groups, holism, emic-etic perspectives, comparison, grounded theory, and techniques of data collection and treatment. The promise of ethnography for research and for improving teaching and teacher training is then addressed.

Classroom research in ESL, second language acquisition, and bilingual education has drawn on a variety of research methodologies over the past decade (for reviews, see Allwright, 1983; Chaudron, 1986, 1987; Gaies, 1983; Long, 1980; Mitchell, 1985). Recently, ethnographic methods have become fashionable in both educational and ESL research. Ethnography has been greeted with enthusiasm because of its promise for investigating issues difficult to address through experimental research, such as sociocultural processes in language learning, how institutional and societal pressures are played out in moment-to-moment classroom interaction, and how to gain a more holistic perspective on teacher–student interactions to aid teacher training and improve practice.

Yet an understanding of what constitutes high-quality, scientific ethnographic work has not kept pace with ethnography's increasing popularity in ESL. For some, *ethnography* has become a synonym for qualitative research, so that any qualitative approach may be called ethnographic in whole or part, as long as it involves observation in nonlaboratory settings. Some qualitative or "naturalistic" studies are structured by coding schemes based on predetermined categories. Others involve impressionistic accounts and very short periods of observation (e.g., Lightfoot, 1983). The superficial nature of many studies, which caricature rather than characterize teaching–learning settings, has led Rist (1980) to call them "blitzkrieg ethnography": The researcher "dive-bombs" into a setting, makes a few fixed-category or entirely impressionistic observations, then takes off again to write up the results.

If impressionistic accounts are not ethnography—and they are not—what *is* ethnography? What constitutes a methodological framework for ethnographic study? Why should we study second language learning and teaching ethnographically?

The purpose of this article is to address these questions through an overview of some essential characteristics of ethnography. It is not my intent to critique existing studies or to conduct a comprehensive review of the ethnographic literature. Instead, ethnography as a research perspective and method is outlined, and ways in which ethnography can serve second language learning and teaching are suggested.

Definition of Ethnography

Originally developed in anthropology to describe the "ways of living" of a social group (Heath, 1982), ethnography is the study of people's behavior in naturally occurring, ongoing settings, with a focus on the cultural interpretation of behavior (see also Firth, 1961; Hyes, 1982). The ethnographer's goal is to provide a description and an interpretive–explanatory account of what people do in a setting (such as a classroom, neighborhood, or community), the outcome of their interactions, and the way they understand what they are doing (the meaning interactions have for them). This characterization of ethnography, although general enough to include most forms of ethnographic work, also stays true to an anthropological perspective. (For discussions of varying kinds of ethnographic work and suggested classification schemes, see Hymes, 1982, and Werner & Schoepfle, 1987.)

The terms *ethnographic, qualitative,* and *naturalistic* are often used interchangeably in the educational literature, but they differ in essential ways. In its primary meaning, qualitative research is concerned with identifying the presence or absence of something and with determining its nature or distinguishing features (in contrast to quantitative research, which is concerned with measurement). *Qualitative research* is an umbrella term for many kinds of research approaches and techniques, including ethnography, case studies, analytic induction, content analysis, semiotics, hermeneutics, life histories, and certain types of computer and statistical approaches (Kirk & Miller, 1986). *Naturalistic research* is a descriptive term that implies that the researcher conducts observations in the "natural, ongoing environment where [people] live and work" (Schatzman & Strauss, 1973, p. 5). By these definitions, ethnography is qualitative and, like many other forms of qualitative research, also naturalistic. Ethnography differs from other forms of qualitative research in its concern with holism and in the way it treats culture as integral to the analysis (not just as one of many factors to take into consideration).

To accomplish the goal of providing a descriptive and interpretive-explanatory account of people's behavior in a given setting, the ethnographer carries out systematic, intensive, detailed observation of that behavior—examining how behavior and interaction are socially organized—and the social rules, interactional expectations, and cultural values underlying behavior.

Some Principles of Ethnographic Research

Several principles of ethnographic research are entailed by the above discussion. First, ethnography focuses on people's behavior in groups and on cultural patterns in that behavior. Ethnographers are of course interested in individuals, for it is individuals who are observed and interviewed and with whom the ethnographer develops personal relationships. Individual differences are also important for establishing variation in behavior. However, most ethnographic studies are concerned with group rather than individual characteristics because cultural behavior is by definition shared behavior. For example, an ethnographer in an ESL classroom is more likely to focus on the role of classroom organization in student access to types of language input or practice than to focus on individual language-learning problems. When ethnographic reports focus on an individual's behavior, the individual is usually treated as representative of a group. An example is Carrasco's (1981) article on social organization in a bilingual classroom, in which he illustrates how ethnographer—teacher collaboration can expand teacher awareness of unrecognized abilities in individual children whom the teacher may have "written off" as "not making it."

Second, ethnography is holistic; that is, any aspect of a culture or a behavior has to be described and explained in relation to the whole system of which it is a part (Diesing, 1971; Firth, 1961). An instance of teacher-student interaction occurring in a lesson on English conversation, for example, can be seen as embedded in a series of concentric rings of increasingly larger (more "macro") contexts. If we move from the microcontext of the interaction outward, these rings might include other interactions during the lesson, the lesson taken as a whole, the classroom with its characteristics and constraints, the school, the district (or other regional administrative level), and the society.

To fully account for an instance of teacher-student interaction may require tracing its meaning or implications across all the theoretically salient or descriptively relevant micro- and macrocontexts in which it is embedded. For example, in an ethnographic study of process writing in two sixth-grade, multiethnic, urban classrooms (Cazden, Michaels, & Watson-Gegeo, 1987), classroom writing lessons were examined in the context of whole classroom activities, the training and background of teachers, family and neighborhood cultures, the school's social organization and leadership, the district's implementation of process writing, and the state writing examination. Ulichny and Watson-Gegeo (in press) went on to demonstrate the importance of institutional and societal levels of analysis for explaining the discourse of teacher-student writing conferences.

Third, ethnographic data collection begins with a theoretical framework directing the researcher's attention to certain aspects of situations and certain kinds of research questions. The role of theory in guiding observation and interpretation in ethnography seems to be poorly understood outside anthropology. Ethnographers do not claim that they come to a situation like a "blank slate," with no preconceptions or guides for observation. Theory is important for helping ethnographers decide what kinds of evidence are likely to be significant in answering research questions posed at the beginning of the study and developed while in the field (Narroll & Cohen, 1970, 1973; Pelto & Pelto, 1970). If observation is not guided by an explicit theoretical framework, it will be guided only by the observer's "implicit ontology," that is, his or her values, attitudes, and assumptions about "what sorts of things make up the world [or universe of study], how they are related, and how they act" (Diesing, 1971, p. 124).

In classroom ethnography, the research literature now includes many studies detailing the characteristics of classroom organization and interaction; identifying and analyzing patterns, typologies, or models of interaction (e.g., Mehan's [1979] three-part instructional sequence; see also Mehan, 1982); and/or relating these to institutional, social, and cultural factors (e.g., Boggs, 1985; McDermott & Hood, 1982; Ulichny & Watson-Gegeo, in press). Although each classroom is a unique setting and situation, these studies have developed a conceptual vocabulary for examining patterns of social organization and interaction (e.g., speech activities [Levinson, 1979], participation structures [Philips, 1972], routines [Watson, 1975]) that directs the ethnographer's attention to ways in which behavior is typically organized or structured in classrooms and why. These studies provide theoretical grounding for comparison among settings and for the ethnographer's initial decisions on what to observe.

Though guided by received (especially ethnographically based) theory, ethnographic observation and interpretation are not determined by it. For one thing, each situation investigated by an ethnographer must be understood on its own terms. With regard to the research process, this means that the ethnographer shifts the focus of observation to include phenomena and interactions outside the scope suggested by prior theory, both to correct for what may be missing from or misleading in prior theory and to search for interactions, patterns of behavior, and other phenomena significant to and perhaps unique in the situation under study. Understanding a situation in its own terms is closely related to the generation of grounded theory (discussed below).

Moreover, each situation investigated by an ethnographer must be understood from the perspective of the participants in that situation. This latter characteristic of ethnographic research is often expressed as the *emic-etic* principle of analysis, to which we now turn.

Emic-Etic Analysis and Comparison

We owe the emic-etic distinction to Pike (1964), who extended the pho-n*etic*/phon*emic* distinction in linguistic meaning to cultural meaning. Pike pointed out that the emic or culturally specific framework used by the members of a society/culture for interpreting and assigning meaning to experiences differs in various ways from the researcher's ontological or interpretive framework (an etic framework) (see also Hymes, 1982).

Etic analyses and interpretations are based on the use of frameworks, concepts, and categories from the analytic language of the social sciences and are potentially used for comparative research across languages, settings, and cultures. To be useful in that way, however, etic terms must be very carefully defined and operationalized. Thus, for example, phonetic "distinctive difference" categories are relatively stable and therefore useful for cross-linguistic analyses. Perhaps the classic case of etic terminology is anthropological kin labels, which refer to biological relationships (e.g., mother's brother) rather than to social relationships (e.g., uncle). The English term *uncle* carries with it assumptions about obligations and behavior specific to American or British culture but not shared by other cultures.

However, etic terminology is rarely culturally neutral because its source is typically either the culture to which the researcher belongs or what we might call the "culture of research" itself (referring here to the traditions and ways of speaking that have evolved in particular research disciplines). For example, categories used in nonethnographic classroom-interaction coding schemes (e.g., the Flanders system and its descendants) are often problematic in this way. *Attitude, correction, praise, higher level question, initiates interaction, accepts feeling,* and similar terms or phrases have frequently been used in ESL and second language classroom research. Aside from the problem of inconsistency in defining and operationalizing such categories (Chaudron, 1986) and the problem that checklists obscure the contingent nature of interaction (Mehan, 1981), such terms, along with their operational definitions, may or may not have validity for the teachers and students whose behavior is being rated or evaluated.

Concern with the understanding participants themselves have of the situations in which they are observed has led ethnographers to emphasize emic analysis. As indicated above, *emic* refers to culturally based perspectives, interpretations, and categories used by members of the group under study to conceptualize and encode knowledge and to guide their own behavior. Emic terms, concepts, and categories are therefore functionally relevant to the behavior of the people studied by the ethnographer. An analysis built on emic concepts incorporates the participants' perspectives and interpretations of behavior, events, and situations and does so in the descriptive language they themselves use (see also Spradley, 1979).

It is important to recognize that an emic analysis does not merely substitute the terms used in one language or setting for the researcher's own. For example, an analysis is not emic simply if, in referring to a person whose occupation is to instruct others, it substitutes *profesora* for *teacher* because the setting studied is a classroom in Puerto Rico. To the contrary, what is important about the *teacher-profesora* distinction is that the two terms are part of *differing frameworks* involving what role the instructor takes in relation to her students, what she expects of them and they of her in terms of mutual obligations and behavior, largely societal expectations of instructors' responsibilities, and so on. These differences must become part of the analysis.

Ethnographic analysis is not exclusively emic. Rather, a carefully done emic analysis precedes and forms the basis for etic extensions that allow for cross-cultural or cross-setting comparisons. The fourth principle or characteristic of ethnographic research is that it is comparative (Firth, 1961). The ethnographer first seeks to build a theory of the setting under study, then to extrapolate or generalize from that setting or situation to others studied in a similar way. The comparison must be built on careful emic work, and it must be recognized that direct comparison of the details of two or more settings is usually not possible. Comparison is possible at a more abstract level, however.

For instance, I am particularly interested in developing culturally appropriate classroom strategies as a "bridge" for bilingual, minority, and Third World students whose cultural and/or linguistic background differs from that of the school. One successful example has been the Kamehameha Early Education Program (KEEP), where, in experimental classrooms, first-grade Hawaiian children's reading scores on nationally normed tests improved dramatically after the introduction of reading lessons based on "talk-story" speech events in the Hawaiian community. A key characteristic of talk story is conarration, the point presentation of personal experiences, information, and interpretations of events by two or more storytellers. KEEP researchers structured reading lessons around talk-story formats to create what Boggs (1985) called "talking story with a book" (p. 139), and they made culturally based changes in classroom organization (Au & Jordan, 1981; Boggs, 1985; see also Watson, 1975; Watson-Gegeo & Boggs, 1977).

The KEEP experience inspired my current work with rural communities in the Solomon Islands, where children enter English immersion classrooms beginning in kindergarten and where their failure rates are very high (Watson-Gegeo & Gegeo, 1988). As an ethnographer, my expectation had not been that I would find an exact equivalent to talk story (part of a Hawaiian emic framework) in the Solomons, but rather that I might discover a corresponding speech event that, like talk story, could be adapted for classroom use.

It now appears that a Solomon Islands speech event called "shaping the mind" may be the right candidate. As a speech event, shaping the mind involves the intensive teaching of language, proper behavior, forms of reasoning, and cultural knowledge in special sessions characterized by a serious tone, a formal register of speech, and tightly argued discussion. Because an important focus of shaping-the-mind activities is the direct teaching of linguistic skills (especially vocabulary and metalinguistic awareness [Watson-Gegeo, 1987]), it could prove highly valuable if adapted for use in English immersion classrooms. Shaping the mind is based on an emic teaching framework different from both Hawaiian talk story and from American/Western models of education (Watson-Gegeo, 1986; Watson-Gegeo & Gegeo, 1988).

As contrasting speech events based on differing cultural assumptions, Hawaiian talk story and Solomon Islands shaping the mind are emic concepts, not etic or directly comparable. However, at a more abstract level, we can talk about culturally appropriate strategies for teaching and can compare from one ethnographic study to another what such strategies are, how they relate to other aspects of the cultures in which they are found (e.g., values, local theories of learning, social structure, institutions), how they may be adapted to classroom pedagogy, and to what extent they are effective in terms of learners' improved performance.

The examples I have used to illustrate the principles of ethnographic research all assume a model of language learning through interaction. The ethnographic perspective on language learning is one of language socialization rather than one of language acquisition (Cook-Gumperz, Corsaro, & Streeck, 1986; Schieffelin & Ochs, 1986; Watson-Gegeo, in press). The substitution of *socialization* for *acquisition* places language learning within the more comprehensive domain of socialization, the lifelong process through which individuals are initiated into cultural meanings and learn to perform the skills, tasks, roles, and identities expected by whatever society or societies they may live in (Wuthnow, Hunter, Bergesen, & Kurzweil, 1984, p. 40).

The language socialization perspective implies that language is learned through social interaction. It also implies that language is a primary vehicle of socialization: When we learn a second language, we are learning more than a structure for communication; we are also learning (for example) social and cultural norms, procedures for interpretation, and forms of reasoning. The ethnographic study of language socialization therefore focuses the researcher's attention not only on the teaching and learning or acquiring of language skills, but also on the context of that learning and on what else (values, attitudes, frameworks for interpretation) is learned and taught at the same time as language structure.

Product and Process in Ethnography

As *product*, ethnography is a detailed description and analysis of a social setting and the interaction that goes on within it. A social setting might be a classroom, institution, neighborhood, or community, and settings may be defined at various levels of social inclusion. A completed ethnography offers a grounded theory (Glaser & Strauss, 1967) of the setting and its culture. By *grounded*, we mean theory based in and derived from data and arrived at through a systematic process of induction. Grounded theory may be either substantive (focused on an empirical topic, such as teacher–student interaction in second language classrooms) or formal (focused on a conceptual topic, such as a model for second language acquisition) (Diesing, 1971, p. 31; Glaser & Strauss, 1967, p. 32).

As *method*, ethnography includes the techniques of observation, participant-observation (observing while interacting with those under study), informal and formal interviewing of the participants observed in situations, audio- or videotaping of interactions for close analysis, collection of relevant or available documents and other materials from the setting, and other techniques as required to answer research questions posed by a given study. Historically, ethnographers have been methodologically very eclectic, using both quantitative and qualitative research methods where appropriate (Pelto & Pelto, 1970). Over the past 15 years, discourse analysis (of various types) has become a central approach to data analysis in ethnographic work (e.g., Boggs, 1985; Cazden, Johns, & Hymes, 1972; Heath, 1983; Mehan, 1979; Trueba, Guthrie, & Au, 1981).

One of the hallmarks of ethnographic method is intensive, detailed observation of a setting over a long period of time. Ideally, an ethnographer observing a university-level ESL class, for example, would observe all class meetings for the entire semester, conduct interviews with a sample of the students and the teacher, and observe the students in other settings, if possible. If the ethnographer is studying second language acquisition in community settings, he or she will systematically sample locations, participants, events, times, and types of interactions in the setting, conducting observations and interviews over the course of several months or years. Choices of settings, situations, and sample size for observation and interviewing depend on the research questions being asked and the aims of the study.

Ethnographers do not use quantified, fixed-category checklist observational schemes in their observations because such schemes cannot capture the complexity of classroom interaction and cannot address the relationship between verbal and nonverbal behavior or between behavior and context (Mehan, 1981, p. 39). Furthermore, most existing coding schemes involve short, recurrent periods of observation—for example, a coding sheet is marked once every 3 seconds for 2 minutes at intervals of 10 minutes over an hour of observation time in a classroom. Such arbitrary units of observational time fail to capture whole interactions, which may be played out over several minutes or even longer, and therefore further obscure the functional use of language and the complexity of interaction (Gleason, in press).

A long-term ethnographic project of a year or more usually involves three stages of work: comprehensive, topic oriented, and hypothesis oriented (to borrow Hymes's [1982] terms). In the comprehensive stage, the ethnographer studies all theoretically salient aspects of a setting, conducting a broad spectrum of observations, with mapping of the site, census taking, and interviewing. For example, in a bilingual classroom setting, the ethnographer observes classroom activities throughout the school day and also conducts observations in various microcontexts at the school, such as in the teachers' room, on the playground, and during lunch in the cafeteria (e.g., see Guthrie, 1985). All such locations may provide insights into children's bilingual skills, their attitudes toward and use of their linguistic repertoire; and other information on students, teachers, and parent involvement at the school. Triangulation—the putting together of information from different data sources and/or data collected through different research methods, such as participant-observation, interviewing, network mapping, and surveys (Fielding & Fielding, 1986)—is an important strategy for arriving at valid (or "dependable") findings in ethnographic work (Diesing, 1971).

During the topic-oriented stage, the ethnographer concentrates on clarifying and usually narrowing the study's main topic of interest through focused observations, interviewing, and analysis of the data already collected. The ethnographer concentrates on carefully describing interactions and events as they occur in context, with the aim of generating focused research questions and/or hypotheses. Data collected so far in the form of observation-based field notes are coded into categories salient to interaction in the setting and relevant to the evolving research questions. Tape recordings or videotapes are transcribed and annotated with the aid of observational notes, and where interaction is the focus of study, preliminary discourse analyses will be carried out on the transcripts.

The hypothesis-oriented stage involves the testing of hypotheses and answering of research questions through further focused observations, in-depth (often structured) interviews, continued discourse analysis, and other forms of systematic analysis (see Werner & Schoepfle, 1987). Some of the hypotheses considered during this stage may be generated from the literature, others from observation, interviews, or analysis. This stage may very well involve quantification in the form of frequency counts, tests of significance, or multivariate analyses of patterns and themes (such as in discourse data; see also Jacob, 1982).

Among Mehan's (1979) proposed set of methodological guidelines for ethnographic research is a crucial one often omitted in studies called ethnographic in ESL and education: *comprehensive data treatment.* By this, Mehan means that the analysis must be carried out on all the materials or data collected. One of the greatest weaknesses in many published studies is their reliance on a few anecdotes used to support the researcher's theoretical point of view or conclusions, but chosen by criteria usually not clarified for the reader (e.g., Preston, 1981, seems to equate anecdotal evidence with ethnography). When illustrative examples are presented in an ethnographic report, they should be the result of a systematic selection of *representative* examples, in which both variation and central tendency or typicality in the data are reflected. Anything less caricatures rather than characterizes what the ethnographer has observed and recorded. (See also Werner & Schoepfle's [1987] discussion of 28 minimum standards for ethnographic research design and analysis.)

Uses of Ethnography in ESL

So why should we study second language learning and teaching ethnographically? Ethnography is an important alternative to other forms of educational research because it allows us to address very basic questions of theory and practice.

One such basic question has to do with what is going on from moment to moment in settings where second languages are taught and learned. Second language *teaching* occurs in a wide spectrum of institutional contexts, including EFL classrooms in Japan, bilingual classrooms in New Mexico, and ESL pullout programs for Southeast Asian refugees in the Midwest. Second language *learning* occurs in an even wider spectrum of contexts, including family and community settings. Yet so far we have few careful studies characterizing these contexts and the teaching-learning interactions taking place within them (Breen, 1985).

Ethnographic methods offer us an approach for systematically documenting teaching-learning interactions in rich, contextualized detail with the aim of developing grounded theory (i.e., theory generated from data). This is an alternative to "top-down" research approaches based on preexisting models that may obscure important characteristics of previously unstudied settings (Glaser & Strauss, 1967). The long-term nature of ethnographic research allows for an examination of how teaching and other interactional patterns develop and change over time in a given setting. This dynamic perspective is an important corrective to the static nature of research involving single-time observations or testing.

Ethnographic research reminds us of the important role of culture in second language teaching and learning and gives us a way of addressing this issue. With regard to culture and teaching, for example, we can use ethnography to study the role of the classroom teacher in relation to how that role is defined and enacted in various societies. In Japan, teaching is a prestigious and respected role, the teacher–student relationship is one of polite distance, and the burden of responsibility for learning is placed on the student rather than on the teacher (White, 1987). In the United States, teachers do not enjoy such prestige or respect, and they are increasingly expected to meet more and more of their students' needs. Americans expect teachers to fill in as surrogate parents, and teachers are nearly always at the forefront of blame for their students' low achievement

Such differences in societal expectations should alert us to the fact that appropriate behavior between teachers and students varies substantially from one cultural setting to another. The advice we give to ESL student teachers— such as to be friendly, caring, and sharing to their students—may be very inappropriate in some cultural settings if it is given an American definition (for example, the teacher sharing his or her personal life with students would be inappropriate in many Asian societies). Ethnographic research can document and analyze what it takes to establish good relationships between teachers and students in the context of particular cultural or school settings, so that this information is available for teacher training.

Second, with regard to culture and learning, psycholinguistic research has explored the importance of schema theory for learning. Ethnography alerts us to the fact that many schemata are culturally based and capable of study through ethnographic means (e.g., see Quinn & Holland, 1986).

Another important contribution ethnography can make to ESL and educational research has been alluded to earlier: analysis of the institutional context of schooling, together with societal pressures on teachers and students (e.g., Ogbu, 1974, 1978). Only a few studies have focused on how societal and institutional pressures affect life in second language or second dialect classrooms. Guthrie's (1985) study of bilingual education in an American Chinese community illustrated well the complex role that the school district, federal policy and support for types of bilingual programs, and factions in the local community play in the debate between maintenance and transitional bilingual programs. Cleghorn and Genesee (1984) clearly illustrated the links between educational and societal factors affecting program objectives and outcomes in their analysis of Cleghorn's ethnographic study of a French immersion program in Montreal.

Similarly, ethnographic methods can be used to study institutional and societal pressures that affect educational innovations in ways unanticipated by those who have developed them. Two examples are the pedagogical use of computers in classrooms and the process for teaching writing. Cazden et al.'s (1987) study, mentioned earlier, showed that in two sixth-grade classrooms studied over a 2-year period, the teachers, instead of using microcomputers to change the way writing was taught, fitted the microcomputers into the existing classroom organization. The result was that the microcomputers were used as electronic typewriters to type up final copies, rather than for editing and revising drafts.

The classroom and institutional constraints that created this situation also affected the introduction of the process approach to writing in these classrooms. Because teachers were under institutional pressures to have their students (who were perceived as low achievers) pass the year-end writing test, they concentrated on students' mechanical errors in written drafts. Writing conferences (which were meant to help children focus on ideas and develop an awareness of standards for good writing; see Calkins, 1979) became correction-oriented interactions (Ulichny & Watson-Gegeo, in press; see also Zamel, 1985).

The holistic approach of ethnographic research allows us to integrate research on reading with research on writing and to address both as the acquisition of literacy. Heath's (1983) extensive ethnography on uses of reading and writing in black and white working-class children's homes and communities in the Carolinas has shown the importance of understanding the learner's prior experiences with language and literacy. Such an understanding is critical to effective teaching of standard English in the classroom (see also Spolsky, 1982). Her work has important implications not only for teaching nonstandard speakers, but also for teaching English to immigrants and refugees. Ethnographic studies in other societies could greatly assist ESL teachers working abroad to anticipate their students' needs in relation to their prior literacy experiences and ways of thinking and to develop appropriate learning materials for them. Ethnographic studies can also help teachers to understand the expectations that their students bring with them for what classroom life entails and for appropriate styles of interaction.

Ethnography can directly serve practice in two major ways, in addition to the application of research results to practice. First, ethnographic techniques of observation and interviewing can be applied to teacher supervision and feedback, whether in initial teacher training or in staff development. Because ethnographic observations take a holistic perspective on behavior in settings and because the ethnographer seeks to achieve an insider's understanding of interactions, ethnographic techniques can be used to provide helpful feedback to teachers about what is going on in the classroom, including interactions that are outside teacher notice or teacher behaviors outside the teacher's conscious awareness. Hymes (1981) refers to this kind of feedback to teachers as "ethnographic monitoring" of the classroom. Carrasco (1981), mentioned above, used his findings in just this way, with important outcomes for both the students and teacher involved. Other classroom ethnographers have emphasized the value of collaborative teacher–researcher relations for direct, positive changes in the quality of classroom teaching and learning (e.g., Florio & Walsh, 1981; Grimmett & Granger, 1983).

Second, ethnography can help teachers make a difference in their own classrooms. Teachers can learn ethnographic research methods either formally, by taking a course on ethnography, or informally, through a collaborative, apprenticelike relationship with an experienced ethnographer. By increasing their observational skills, teachers can gain new awareness of classroom organization, teaching and learning strategies, and interactional patterns in their own classrooms. These observations then become a basis for teachers to reflect on their own practice and to experiment with alternative teaching and classroom management techniques. The combination of intensive ethnographic research in classrooms and of teachers' ethnographic observations of their own practice can potentially produce the multilevel understanding of good teaching called for by Richards (1987).

Moreover, teachers can involve their students in doing ethnographic work in their own communities and then use the materials the students develop through observations and interviews as a basis for learning writing skills (Heath, 1983).

Conclusion

My aim in this article has been to show that true ethnographic work is systematic, detailed, and rigorous, rather than anecdotal or impressionistic. The promise of ethnography for ESL research, teacher training, and classroom practices lies in its emphasis on holistic, richly detailed descriptions and analyses of teacher–learner interactions and the multilevel contexts in which these interactions occur. It is important that research called ethnography actually be ethnographic—which means that it be conducted with the same standards of systematicity and rigor expected of quality ethnographic research in ESL's sister social science disciplines.

Acknowledgments

Research on Solomon Islands children's language learning referred to in this article has been supported by the National Science Foundation and the Spencer Foundation. The Microcomputers and Literacy Project work on computers and children's writing was supported by a grant from the National Institute of Education. I wish to thank Mike Long and Polly Ulichny for their helpful comments on an earlier draft of this article.

References

Allwright, D. (1983). Classroom-oriented research on language teaching and learning: A brief historical overview. *TESOL Quarterly, 17,* 191–204.

Au, K.H.-P., & Jordan, C. (1981). Teaching reading to Hawaiian children: Finding a culturally appropriate solution. In H. T. Trueba, G.P. Guthrie, & K.H.-P. Au (Eds.), *Culture and the bilingual classroom: Studies in classroom ethnography* (pp. 139–152). Rowley, MA: Newbury House.

Boggs, S.T. (with the assistance of K.A. Watson-Gegeo & G. McMillan) (1985). *Speaking, relating and learning: A study of Hawaiian children at home and at school.* Norwood, NJ: Ablex.

Breen, M.P. (1985). The social context for language learning—A neglected situation? *Studies in Second Language Acquisition, 7,* 135–158.

Calkins, L.M. (1979). Andrew learns to make writing hard. *Language Arts, 56,* 569–576.

Carrasco, R.L. (1981). Expanded awareness of student performance: A case in applied ethnographic monitoring in a bilingual classroom. In H.T. Trueba, G.P. Guthrie, & K.H.-P. Au (Eds.), *Culture and the bilingual classroom: Studies in classroom ethnography* (pp. 153–177). Rowley, MA: Newbury House.

Cazden, C.B., John, V.P., & Hymes, D. (Eds.) (1972). *Functions of language in the class-room.* New York: Columbia University, Teachers College Press.

Cazden, C.B., Michaels, S., & Watson-Gegeo, K.A. (1987). *Final report: Microcomputers and literacy project* (Grant No. G-83-0051). Washington, DC: National Institute of Education.

Chaudron, C. (1986). The interaction of quantitative and qualitative approaches to research: A view of the second language classroom. *TESOL Quarterly, 20,* 709–717.

Chaudron, C. (1987). *Second language classrooms: Research on teaching and learning.* Cambridge: Cambridge University Press.

Cleghorn, A., & Genesee, F. (1984). Languages in contact: An ethnographic study of interaction in an immersion school. *TESOL Quarterly, 18,* 595–625.

Cook-Gumperz, J., Corsaro, W., & Streeck, J. (Eds.) (1986). *Children's worlds and chil-dren's language.* The Hague: Mouton.

Diesing, P. (1971). *Patterns of discovery in the social sciences.* Chicago: Aldine.

Fielding, N.G., & Fielding, J.L. (1986). *Linking data.* Beverly Hills, CA: Sage.

Firth, R. (1961). *Elements of social organization.* Boston: Beacon.

Florio, S., & Walsh, M. (1981). The teacher as colleague in classroom research. In H.T. Trueba, G.P. Guthrie, & K.H.-P Au (Eds.), *Culture and the bilingual classroom: Studies in classroom ethnography* (pp. 87–104). Rowley, MA: Newbury House.

Gaies, S.J. (1983). The investigation of language classroom processes. *TESOL Quar-terly, 17,* 205–217.

Glaser, B., & Strauss, A. (1967). *The discovery of grounded theory.* Chicago: Aldine.

Gleason, J.J. (in press). *Special education in context: An ethnographic study of persons with developmental disabilities.* New York: Cambridge University Press.

Grimmett, S.A., & Granger, C. (1983). Resolution in context: A teacher-researcher part-nership. *Educational Horizons, 61,* 94–97.

Guthrie, G.P. (1985). *A school divided: An ethnography of bilingual education in a Chi-nese community.* Hillsdale, NJ: Lawrence Erlbaum.

Heath, S.B. (1982). Ethnography in education: Defining the essentials. In P. Gilmore & A.A. Glatthorn (Eds.), *Children in and out of schools: Ethnography and educa-tion* (pp. 33–58). Washington, DC: Center for Applied Linguistics.

Heath, S.B. (1983). *Ways and words: Language, life, and work in communities and classrooms.* Cambridge: Cambridge University Press.

Hymes, D. (1981). Ethnographic monitoring. In H.T. Trueba, G.O. Guthrie, & K. H.-P. Au (Eds.), *Culture and the bilingual classroom: Studies in classroom ethnogra-phy* (pp. 56–68). Rowley, MA: Newbury House.

Hymes, D. (1982). What is ethnography? In P. Gilmore & A.A. Glatthorn (Eds.), *Chil-dren in and out of school: Ethnography and education* (pp. 21–32). Washington, DC: Center for Applied Linguistics.

Jacob, E. (1982). Combining ethnographic and quantitative approaches: Suggestions and examples from a study on Puerto Rico. In P. Gilmore & A.A. Glatthorn (Eds.),

Children in and out of schools: Ethnography and education (pp. 124–147). Washington, DC: Center for Applied Linguistics.

Kirk, J., & Miller, M.L. (1986). *Reliability and validity in qualitative research.* Beverly Hills, CA: Sage.

Levinson, S. (1979). Activity types and language. *Linguistics, 17,* 363–369.

Lightfoot, S.L. (1983). *The good high school: Portraits of character and culture.* New York: Basic Books.

Long, M. (1980). Inside the 'black box': Methodological issues in classroom research on language learning. *Language Learning, 30,* 1–42.

McDermott, R.P., & Hood, L. (1982). Institutionalized psychology and the ethnography of schooling. In P. Gilmore & A.A. Glatthorn (Eds.), *Children in and out of school: Ethnography and education* (pp. 232–249). Washington, DC: Center for Applied Linguistics.

Mehan, H. (1979). *Learning lessons: Social organization in the classroom.* Cambridge, MA: Harvard University Press.

Mehan, H. (1981). Ethnography of bilingual education. In H.T. Trueba, G.P. Guthrie, & K.H.-P. Au (Eds.), *Culture and the bilingual classroom: Studies in classroom ethnography* (pp. 36–55). Rowley, MA: Newbury House.

Mehan, H. (1982). The structure of classroom events and their consequences for student performance. In P. Gilmore & A.A. Glatthorn (Eds.), *Children in and out of school: Ethnography and education* (pp. 59–87). Washington, DC: Center for Applied Linguistics.

Mitchell, R. (1985). Process research in second-language classrooms. *Language Teaching, 18,* 330–362.

Narroll, R., & Cohen, R. (1970). *A handbook of method in cultural anthropology.* New York: Natural History Press.

Narroll, R., & Cohen, R. (1973). *Main currents in ethnological theory.* New York: Appleton-Century-Crofts.

Ogbu, J.U. (1974). *The next generation: An ethnography of education in an urban neighborhood.* New York: Academic Press.

Ogbu, J.U. (1978). *Minority education and caste: The American system in cross-cultural perspective.* New York: Academic Press.

Pelto, P., & Pelto, G. (1970). *Anthropological research: The structure of inquiry.* New York: Harper & Row.

Philips, S.U. (1972). Participant structures and communicative competence: Warm Springs children in community and classroom. In C.B. Cazden, V.P. John, & D. Hymes (Eds.), *Functions of language in the classroom* (pp. 370–394). New York: Columbia University, Teachers College Press.

Pike, K.L. (1964). *Language in relation to a unified theory of structures of human behavior.* The Hague: Mouton.

Preston, D.R. (1981). The ethnography of TESOL. *TESOL Quarterly, 15,* 105–116.

Quinn, N., & Holland, D. (Eds.). (1986). *Cultural models in language and thought.* Cambridge: Cambridge University Press.

Richards, J.C. (1987). The dilemma of teacher education in TESOL. *TESOL Quarterly, 21,* 209–226.

Rist, R. (1980). Blitzkrieg ethnography: On the transformation of a method into a movement. *Educational Researcher, 9*(2), 8–10.

Schatzman, L., & Strauss, A.L. (1973). *Field research: Strategies for a natural sociology.* Englewood Cliffs, NJ: Prentice-Hall.

Schieffelin, B.B., & Ochs, E. (1986). Language socialization. *Annual Review of Anthropology, 15,* 161–191.

Spolsky, B. (1982). Sociolinguistics of literacy, bilingual education, and TESOL. *TESOL Quarterly, 16,* 141–151.

Spradley, J.P. (1979). *The ethnographic interview.* New York: John Wiley.

Trueba, H.T., Guthrie, G.P., & Au, K.H.-P. (Eds.). (1981). *Culture and the bilingual classroom: Studies in classroom ethnography.* Rowley, MA: Newbury House.

Ulichny, P., & Watson-Gegeo, K.A. (in press). Interactions and authority: The dominant interpretive framework in writing conferences. *Discourse Processes.*

Watson, K.A. (1975). Transferable communicative routines: Strategies and group identity in two speech events. *Language in Society, 4,* 53–70.

Watson-Gegeo, K.A. (1986). *Communicative routines in Kwara'ae children's language socialization: Final report to the National Science Foundation* (Grant Nos. BNS-83-16342 and BNS-86-41968). Washington, DC: National Science Foundation.

Watson-Gegeo, K.A. (1987) *"Heavy words and important silences": The social transfer of cognitive skills in Kwara'ae.* Paper presented at the Third International Conference on Thinking, Honolulu, January.

Watson-Gegeo, K.A. (in press). *The ethnographic study of language socialization.* Boston: University Working Papers in Linguistics and Education.

Watson-Gegeo, K.A., & Boggs, S.T. (1977). From verbal play to talk story: The role of routines in speech events among Hawaiian children. In S. Ervin-Tripp & C. Mitchell-Kernan (Eds.), *Child discourse* (pp. 67–90). New York: Academic Press.

Watson-Gegeo, K.A., & Gegeo, D.W. (1988). Schooling, knowledge and power: Social transformation in the Solomon Islands. *University of Hawaii Working Papers in ESL, 7*(1), 119–140.

Werner, O., & Schoepfle, G.M. (1987). *Systematic fieldwork: Vol. 1. Foundations of ethnography and interviewing; Vol. 2. Ethnographic analysis and data management.* Newbury Park, CA: Sage.

White, M. (1987). *The Japanese educational challenge: A commitment to children.* New York: Free Press.

Wuthnow, R., Hunter, J.D., Bergesen, A., & Kurzweil, E. (1984). *Cultural analysis.* Boston: Routledge & Kegan Paul.

Zamel, V. (1985). Responding to student writing. *TESOL Quarterly, 19,* 79–101.

Understanding the Article

1. How does Watson-Gegeo distinguish between *ethnography* and *qualitative research?*

2. Watson-Gegeo describes ethnographic research as *holistic*. What does she mean by this?

3. Briefly describe the principles of ethnographic research outlined in the article.

4. You should be familiar with terms such as *phonetic* and *phonemic* from an introductory course in linguistics or phonology. How does the distinction between *-etic* and *-emic* apply to ethnography?

5. Explain the distinction between ethnography as a *product* and as a *process.*

Reflecting on Wider Issues

1. To what extent do you think the increased interest in classroom research should bring with it an increased interest in ethnographic methods?

2. What research problems in second language learning or teaching could profitably be explored using an ethnographic approach? Keep this question in mind as you read the articles that follow.

Going Beyond the Article

For a clear and insightful description of the use of ethnography in classroom research, read Chapter 3 of van Lier (1988), *The Classroom and the Language Learner* (New York: Longman). For a shorter summary of the issues, read van Lier (1990), "Ethnography: Bandaid, bandwagon, or contraband?" in C. Brumfit and R. Mitchell (eds.), *Research in the Language Classroom* (London: Modern English Publications); and "Toward an ethnomethodological respecification of second language acquisition studies" by Markee, in A. Cohen, S. Gass, and E. Tarone (eds.), *Methodology and Second Language Acquisition* (Hillsdale, N.J.: Lawrence Erlbaum, in press). You might also be interested in reading Breen (1985), "The social context for language-learning—a neglected situation?" (*Studies in Second Language Acquisition, 7,* 135–158), in which he suggests a need to look at language learning ethnographically in family and community settings.

UNIT II

COMPARING AND CONTRASTING FIRST AND SECOND LANGUAGE ACQUISITION

3

GENES AND TEENS— SOCIOBIOLOGICAL EXPLANATIONS FOR THE PRESENCE OF ACCENTS AFTER PUBERTY

Thomas Scovel
San Francisco State University

Previewing the Chapter

Theories about critical—or "sensitive"—periods for language acquisition have fascinated researchers and teachers for decades. If there is a biologically determined critical period for first language acquisition, how powerful a predictor is it of the eventual success of a second language learner? What aspects of language acquisition are actually affected? And, as Thomas Scovel asks, might there be an evolutionary leftover in our genetic structure that once served a utilitarian purpose?

Before you read this chapter (from Scovel's book, *A Time to Speak* [New York: Newbury House, 1988]), review your understanding of what is meant by "critical period" (*PLLT,* Chapter 3). Set your mind to read a chapter that will have quite a few highly technical terms (e.g., "empidonax flycatchers" and "phenotypes") and constructs from other disciplines (biology, anthropology) that you don't need to define explicitly in

Reprinted from Scovel, *A Time to Speak: A Psycholinguistic Inquiry into a Critical Period for Human Speech.* New York: Newbury House, pp. 68–83, 1988.

order to understand the author's purpose and argument. Then, scan the chapter and answer the following questions:

1. What is meant by the term *sociobiological?*
2. What is Scovel's purpose? (Look at the title and the last two paragraphs.)
3. What do the subheadings tell you about what the author's line of argument is going to be?

Many years ago, an American wife and husband team of anthropologists embarked on an intriguing experiment concerning the impact of environment on behavior (Hayes, 1950). They devoted several years to raising a baby chimp as if she were their newborn human child, and because it was during the heyday of behaviorism in the social sciences, perhaps we can forgive their zealous expectation that a Pygmalion transformation might have ensued. Vicki (aka *Pan troglodytes*) certainly learned a great deal more about American households than the average chimpanzee, but she did not become particularly human. But Vicki never did learn to form even the most rudimentary form of speech, an achievement all human children acquire, albeit over the span of a few years. Apparently, she was able to pick up one or two words (e.g., *cup, momma*), but that was about the extent of her linguistic prowess.

The Genes of Chimps—Constraints on Speech

Ironically, it was the limited achievement of this privileged primate which set the stage for a wide variety of creative experiments on other chimps by subsequent researchers. Largely through Vicki's failures, people interested in attempting to teach language to chimps have realized the anatomical limitations for human speech production in this species and have designed quite elaborate communicative systems using sign language (Gardner & Gardner, 1971), plastic symbols (Premack & Premack, 1972), and computer-operated electronic consoles (Rumbaugh & Gill, 1976). These studies have led some to suggest that although the production of human speech is not possible, as the Hayeses inadvertently demonstrated with Vicki, symbolic language, previously thought to be only the domain of humans, can be acquired by chimps (Linden, 1976). Personally, I would side with the many linguists (e.g., Katz, 1976) and psychologists (Terrance, 1979) who claim that these elaborate experiments provide no convincing proof that chimps or gorillas have come close to learning human language. Getting back to Vicki, I begin this chapter with her restricted linguistic performance because her behavior so neatly contrasts with that of her human counterparts. As anyone would expect, the behaviors of two infants, chimp and human, if they were raised together in the same house, would invariably differ because we are dealing with two disparate gene pools. Put tersely, it is hard to conceal the DNA molecules of a *Pan troglodytes,* even in a *Homo sapiens* household. (Although some human parents might sometimes suspect genes of the former are scattered among those of their own overactive offspring!) So the genetic script is exceedingly important, and we must learn something of its composition if we are to understand the critical period for language and to appreciate its role in determining foreign accents.

The Sociobiological Perspective

It is necessary to consider the research of Edward Wilson in our deliberations about a sociobiological explanation for a critical period for language in humans, especially as detailed in his magnus opus, *Sociobiology: The New Synthesis* (Wilson, 1975). Wilson and his fellow sociobiologists are sometimes viewed controversially as scientists who have tried to rationalize or justify the ancient and universal oppression of women by men, for example. Because this misperception creates antipathy toward both the topic and its proponents, sociobiology has frequently become the whipping boy of academic conclaves for political but not scientific reasons (Gaulin, 1978). Part of this misunderstanding can be eliminated if we recognize, right off the bat, that sociobiology is not an academic field or discipline (like psycholinguistics or neurolinguistics) but a viewpoint or perspective (like rationalism or behaviorism). Thus, Wilson's tone is not an introductory textbook, but an encyclopedia of research on various phenomena in animals ranging from ants to zebras, all carefully scrutinized within "the systematic study of biological basis of all social behavior" (Wilson, 1975, p. 4).

Once we accept this prefatory qualification, it is useful to realize that the Nobel laureates and Lenneberg were sociobiologists even before this brand-new term gained currency, and several years before the publication of Wilson's treatise, Lenneberg was clearly advocating a sociobiological stance in the ninth chapter of his major work, titled, "Toward a biological theory of language development":

> The role of language is so important for social integration that such abnormality (language deficits) reduces the opportunity for finding a partner, and if the deviation is marked enough, the individual will become virtually incommunicado with great probability of exclusion from the gene-pool. Furthermore, genetically based alterations of a given trait are likely to be accompanied by other deviations, and thus there is a greater proportion of multiply abnormal individuals among the group of people with latent structure alterations than among a random sample of the population. This is corroborated by the fact that children seen in clinics with complaints of

severely defective language abilities have a greater incidence of associated abnormalities than children admitted with infectious diseases. Such confluence of abnormalities in the latent structure deficient group raises barriers to mixing in the general gene-pool and reduces the chances for perpetration of the trait. (Lenneberg, 1967, p. 384)

Given the transparent sociobiological tone of this statement from Lenneberg, is there any difference between the traditional Darwinian view of natural selection that has been the basis of our discussions of evolution, ethology, and imprinting and this "new synthesis" which Wilson propounds? Yes, Wilson and others of like mind are eager to point out. Biologists and ethologists of the Darwinian tradition assume that natural selection is for the group or the species, whereas proponents of sociobiology argue that natural selection is confined to the single gene:

Natural selection is the process whereby certain genes gain representation in the following generations superior to that of other genes located at the same chromosome positions. . . . Samuel Butler's famous aphorism, that the chicken is only an egg's way of making another egg, has been modernized: the organism is only DNA's way of making more DNA. (Wilson, 1975, p. 3)

Like any approach, sociobiology carries with it the baggage of new terms or of new meanings for familiar terminology, and we witness both lexical types in a couple of ideas that are fundamental to the understanding of what the process of genetic natural selection portends for human language acquisition. Wilson distinguishes between "proximate" causes, those that are found internal or external to the organism within its lifetime, and "ultimate" causes, which are the collective conditions in the environmental history of the genetic evolution of the organism which have ultimately caused certain kinds of adaptive behaviors in that organism. If I understand Wilson correctly, when we focus on the presence or absence of a sign stimulus (e.g., a moving red object for a male stickleback fish in heat), we are talking about proximate causation, but if we look at the propensity for the male stickleback to attack moving red objects (and the failure of other species, like the greylag geese, to act in this manner), then we are talking about ultimate causation. Somewhere in the chromosomal memory of each male stickleback fish is a gene that reflects this "ultimate" sociobiological behavior.

Wilson and other sociobiologists also use traditional terms in new ways, and perhaps this is one reason why they are occasionally misunderstood by the public. The words *altruism, selfness,* and *spite* are examples of this terminological revisionism, and they are best defined in Figure 1, taken from Wilson but based on the earlier work of Hamilton (1972).

Another pair of characteristics that Wilson uses divides animals into two groups, based on the rate of population density plotted against the rate of population growth. "r strategists" are the fugitives of the animal kingdom, recolo-

The basic conditions required for the evolution of altruism, selfishness, and spite by means of kin selection. The family has been reduced to an individual and a brother, the fraction of genes in the brother shared by common descent ($r = 1/2$) is indicated by the shaded half of the body. A requisite of the environment (food, shelter, access to mate, and so on) is indicated by a vessel, and harmful behavior to another by an axe. *Altruism:* The altruist diminishes his/her own genetic fitness but raises the brother's fitness to the extent that the shared genes are actually increased in the next generation. *Selfishness:* The selfish individual reduces the brother's fitness but enlarges his/her own to an extent that more than compensates. *Spite:* The spiteful individual lowers the fitness of an unrelated competitor (the unshaded figure) while reducing that of his/her own or at least not improving it, however, the act increases the fitness of the brother to a degree that more than compensates.

FIGURE 1. Altruism, Selfishness, and Spite in Genetic Evolution (*Source:* From Wilson, 1975, p. 119.)

nizing rapidly in a new location when wiped out from a previous haunt. These animals are asocial, mature rapidly, have a short life-span, and exhibit little intra- or interspecies competition. The bane of the household pet, the common flea, is a typical "r strategist." By contrast, the "K strategist" is highly social, matures slowly, lives long, and displays keen intra- and interspecies competitiveness (Wilson, 1975, p. 101). Among the animals on earth, none is a better exemplar of the mark of "K" than our species. The consequences of our being a "K strategist" in terms of the way we populate the earth and the way we aggressively compete with ourselves and with other species will be considered later in this chapter, because there are implications here for why a human gene might want to carry with it information about a critical period for human language acquisition.

The Genes of a Sparrow—A Genius for Song

We have delved adequately into sociobiology, but you should be forewarned, if you need any words of caution whatsoever, that at this point I am taking the liberty of applying this oversimplified glimpse of sociobiology as a fruitful perspective for looking at how natural evolution in hominid and human groups has selectively reinforced both the emergence and the recognition of foreign accents in human beings by puberty. In short, I want to claim that the critical period for language acquisition is part of our biological endowment because it is the result of ultimate causation and enhances our status as a K strategist.

An excellent way in which to introduce this sociobiological perspective for human language learning is to look at the fine research that has been performed on the singing of another, though less complicated, K strategist, the white-crowned sparrow. Gould and Marler (1987) review the extensive research done on the acquisition of species-specific songs in these common birds (much of the work undertaken by Marler himself), and they prove that there is an innate releasing mechanism (the bird's inherent ability to sing in its own "accent"), the necessary presence of a sign stimulus (the presence of the songs of mature white-crowned sparrows), and the meeting of both within a critical or sensitive period of time (before 50 days after hatching). Obviously, the transmission of all this information genetically has been important to the maintenance of the white-crowned gene pool, and it is evident from Figure 2 that the genes have orchestrated natural, nurtural, and time-related components into one harmonious blend to compose the songs of this species.

Before we examine possible analogies between birdsongs and human speech from a sociobiological perspective, I want to distinguish between those *songs,* which are generally used only by males during mating season, and bird *calls,* which, like other animal calls, tend to be used by all members of the species at any time for signaling danger or distress, maintaining contact, and similar purposes. Because calls are rudimentary forms of communication, they are not subject to the complex imprinting pattern depicted in Figure 2, and they are almost entirely innately specified; they are nearly identical to the knee-jerk reflex in humans. But the melodic bursts of singing by white-crowned sparrows and many other species of birds are positively operatic compared with the cacophony of the common calls, and the very complexity of the score demands the interplay of the several and often competing factors shown in the figure. If white-crowned sparrows and a vast number of other species can communicate about food and fancy, fight and flight so effectively with simple calls, why have their genes carried with them the cumbersome and complicated legacy of singing? Surely it is not solely a gift from nature to soothe the troubled heart of man. Wilson goes into some depth in answering this sociobiological question:

> Why are bird songs so complex? It has been recognized that the vocalizations of males are important premating isolating mechanisms. This means that they collaborate with other kinds of genetically based differences to prevent species from interbreeding. In fact, as W. H. Thorpe has said, "it is virtually impossible to think of two closely related species of birds which,

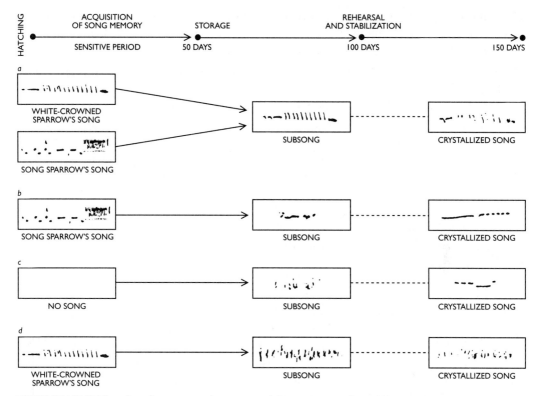

SONG LEARNING in the white-crowned sparrow exhibits great specificity: Young male birds can instinctively identify and preferentially learn the song of their own species. If a young male white-crown is played tape recordings of adult white-crown song and adult song-sparrow song (a), it first begins a period of experimentation, known as a subsong, and then produces a crystallized song very similar to the white-crown song it has heard. If it is played only a tape recording of song-sparrow song (b), it will not learn the song: it still goes through subsong, but its final, crystallized song does not resemble either the song-sparrow song or the white-crown song. A bird that is played no song (c) also learns nothing. If the young bird hears a white-crown song but is deafened before subsong begins (d), it is unable to learn how to produce the song it heard; it produces an amorphous song with no melodic structure.

FIGURE 2.   White-Crowned Sparrow Song Learning (*Source:* From Gould & Marler, 1987, p. 80.)

possessing full song, are not thereby specifically distinguishable." Bird watchers know that many complexes of similar species, such as the Empidonax flycatchers of North America, are best identified in the field by their songs, the same cues the birds themselves use during the breeding season. According to current speciation theory, most or all bird species begin the multiplication process when a single, ancestral species is broken into two or more geographically isolate populations.... As these daughter populations subsequently evolve, they inevitably diverge from one another in many genetically determined traits, representing multiple differences in the environment they inhabit.... The theoretically expected result, which can take place in as little as ten generations, is character displacement, in this case the reinforcement of premating isolating mechanisms. (Wilson, 1975, p. 237)

The identification of birdsong is consequently crucial for mating identification and for the ultimate survival of the genes.

Another way of looking at this evolution of species-identifying song is to recognize that this process is a compromise between constantly competing pressures, and that selection moves from a situation of imbalance (or what Wilson calls "dynamic selection") among social and environmental forces to a balanced or "stabilizing" situation. The further a species moves to the right of the graphs in Figure 3, the more "advanced" it becomes phylogenetically, and I would surmise that the possession of speech and language is a trait that would account for a great deal of "stabilization" in our species, and since a critical period for acquisition seems to be a significant component of this human trait, it too contributes to the "stabilizing selection" of the gene pool of *Homo sapiens.*

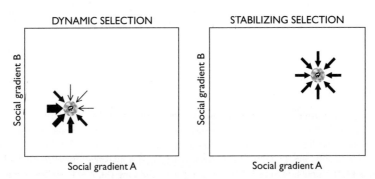

Evolution in two social traits is viewed here as the movement of an entire population of organisms on a plane of phenotypes. The rate and direction of movement is determined by the force field of opposing selection pressures (left figure). The stable states of social traits are reached when the selection pressures balance, the condition called stabilizing selection (right figure).

FIGURE 3.   Dynamic and Stabilizing Selection (*Source:* From Wilson, 1975, p. 131.)

The Primacy of Sound in Human Social Interaction

We need one more piece of the puzzle before we can see the possible role of genetics in the existence of a critical period for human speech. We need evidence that even more than birds, who rely so heavily on calls and songs, humans are a highly auditory animal and rely more heavily on the oral/aural channel than on any other sense for social organization. When we generalize about the five senses that most animals possess, it is impossible to specify in a quantifiable or empirical manner how much a certain species relies on a specific sense relative to any other species, but Wilson, an entomologist by training and experience, and a comparative biologist of high repute, when comparing the use of the major senses for social organization among all the animals, ranks *Homo sapiens* as just about the most "acoustical" species in the entire animal kingdom (Figure 4).

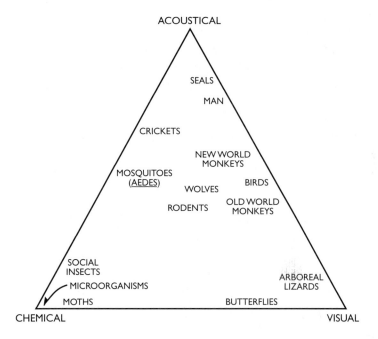

The relative importance of sensory channels in selected groups of organisms. The nearness of the group to each apex indicates, by wholly subjective and intuitive criteria, the proportionate usage of the channel in the species signal repertory. Tactile, surface-wave, and electrical channels are not included.

FIGURE 4.   Comparative Use of Senses among the Animals (*Source:* From Wilson, 1975, p. 240.)

Wilson is not alone, of course, in emphasizing the role of sound and voice in the evolution of human social organization. In the famous conference on the origins and evolution of language and speech, convened by the New York Academy of Sciences (Harnad, Stecklis, & Lancaster, 1976), many presenters and discussants argued for the "oralist" interpretation of the emergence of language in man, and though it is neither prudent nor necessary to fully discount the import of a "gesturalist" interpretation for language origins, it is clear from the sum total of all the 93 formal presentations made that speech and language evolved much more definitely from hearing the sounds of the human voice than from seeing the gestures made by the face and body. At this conclave, Andrew (1976), speculated that one of the many advantages of vocalic communication is for affectionate group cohesion, especially in the open vegetation where hominids foraged. Sladen (1981) goes so far as to suggest that dyslexia, the inability to learn how to read, is a contemporary social consequence of our sociobiologically programmed propensity to communicate most efficiently via the auditory rather than the visual channel.

Strong evidence for the primacy of sound in the evolution of human social organization is found in the existence of feature detectors, groups of neurons in the brain that are organized for the perception of a very narrowly defined type of sensory activity. For example, Lettvin, Maturana, McCullock, and Pitts (1959) showed that a frog's brain has feature detectors for specific types of visual movement—for example, one for horizontal left-to-right motion and another for vertical top-to-bottom movement. Although research on the human brain is naturally more restricted and complicated, some, but certainly not all, speech researchers speculate that the identification of the segmental and suprasegmental phonemes of human speech are ultimately dependent on the presence of auditory feature detectors in the human temporal lobe (Abbs & Sussman, 1971; Stevens, 1975; Tartter & Eimas, 1975).

Tartter (1986) presents a useful analysis of how the human ear and brain are wired to perceive exquisitely minute changes in auditory information, and how the existence of feature detectors for speech plays a role in this processing, in the chapter of her text called "Speech perception and production." Studies of neonates, only a couple of months old, give us further corroboration of the presence of genetically specified feature detectors in humans which can develop to play a crucial role in the identification of human voices and language. In studies showing correlations to exposures to voiced/voicing contrasts, human infants have demonstrated a change in sucking rhythm (Morse, 1972), a change in heartbeat (Morse, 1974), and changing brain wave patterns on the left side of the skull measured by an electroencephalograph (Molfese et al., 1975). A detailed review of these and other studies is presented by Reich (1986) in the first chapter of his superb book on language development in children. These neonatal studies all imply that because little babies attend to very discrete kinds of vocalic information, such as changes in voice onset timing that are less than 35 milliseconds (that is, about a third of a hundredth of a second!), it is almost certain that the human brain is evolutionarily programmed with feature detectors (or some other perceptual system that specializes in acoustic processing) that are tuned to the kinds of acoustic information that are relevant to the processing of human speech and to the recognition of the human voice. Strange and Jenkins (1978) summarize the import of all of these findings on the relationship of innate natural abilities and early nurturing:

> Infant studies suggest that prior to any extended linguistic experience, several "natural" phonetic boundaries are observed. Such boundaries have been found in linguistic environments where such distinctions are not utilized by adult speakers. Yet, adult studies across languages show marked insensitivity to acoustic dimensions that do not have phonetic significance in the adult's language. Thus, it appears that appreciable modification of

> innate sensitivities takes place over the formative years while one acquires
> his native language. (Strange & Jenkins, 1978, p. 161)

What adaptive or selective advantage would there be for having acoustic feature detectors programmed into human DNA chains? First and foremost, they allow for the rapid acquisition of the richly detailed and complicated phonetic and phonological information that underlies all mother tongues. Human speech would not exist if nature compelled us to learn everything about it after birth, and did not provide us with a genetic head start. This is true for every level of human language, not just at the level of phonology, and Chomsky (1976) has been most vocal in arguing for the existence of prepackaged, innate abilities for a universal grammar. But my contention is that there is at least one other reason why the infant *Homo sapiens* comes already assembled with linguistic feature detectors, and this is because they are instrumental in vocal identification. I am not talking about the amazing ability of all people to recognize hundreds and hundreds of individuals simply on the basis of a phrase or two, although this skill is surely based on this same network of acoustic detection. Nor am I considering the equally astounding ability to recognize a stranger's sex (Coleman, 1971), age (Ptacek & Sander, 1966), or whether or not someone is smiling when speaking (Tartter, 1980), though these skills again are based in part not on environmental learning but on inborn propensities. Marvelous and beneficial as these acoustic abilities are for social interaction, it is the talent to identify groups and not individuals that should be our focus here, and so the question naturally arises, what adaptive advantage is there for human beings to possess the innately programmed ability to distinguish *groups* of human voices from each other?

The Costs and Benefits of a Critical Period for Speech

A sociobiologist looks at a question like this in the same way an accountant examines a new acquisition—what are the costs and benefits of such a trait? That is, a genetically encoded behavior can be seen as an *adaptation,* a trait determined by ultimate causation to have survival value for the gene. Human language behavior, at least the part of it that is biologically specified, is an example of adaptation, though my specific point is that the emergence and recognition of foreign accents in man is also adaptive. In contrast, a trait can also be viewed as a *susceptibility.* Here, the characteristic is viewed as a negative consequence of evolution—part of the cost inherent in a greater benefit. Looking at a critical period for foreign accents in this light, we could consider them a susceptibility, part of the price we must pay for being an articulate ape. Notice that, either way, we would accept a critical period for phonological acquisition as an inherent trait of our species, but its presence in our genes could be either a benefit or a liability.

Gaulin (personal communication, July 23, 1980) explains the situation like this. When we look at the evolution of the hemoglobin molecule in animal circulatory systems, its ability to carry oxygen is distinctly an adaptive trait; however, a consequence of this is that hemoglobin is also "susceptible" to carrying carbon monoxide, since the latter has the same molecular appearance as oxygen. The possibility of CO poisoning has no real selective advantage for any species, and thus it is the kind of susceptibility that must be paid to nature as tribute for the adaptive value of efficient oxygen intake into the bloodstream. Too little is known about the evolution of human speech and language to determine whether the emergence of accents is an adaptation or a susceptibility, but let me try to make a case for its possible evolutionary benefits.

Wilson devotes an entire chapter of his major work to animal aggression, a behavior that is all too apparent in the human animal, though he differs with writers like Robert Ardrey and says that man is not necessarily the most aggressive creature on this planet (Wilson, 1975, p. 247). Regardless of our fame or infamy as a belligerent species, if we fit the biological mold described by Wilson for all other living beings, it is the presence of a stranger that incites the greatest amount of belligerence within us:

> The strongest evoker of aggressive response in animals is the sight of a stranger, especially a territorial intruder. This xenophobic principle has been documented in virtually every group of animals displaying higher forms of social organization. Male lions, normally the more lethargic adults of the prides, are jerked to attention and commence savage rounds of roaring when strange males come into view. Nothing in the day-to-day social life of an ant colony, no matter how stressful, activates the group like the introduction of a few alien workers. The principle extends to the primates. (Wilson, 1975, p. 249)

Recall that K strategist animals, of which we humans are the paragon, are marked by their competitiveness, both within and outside the species, and then consider the statements just made by Wilson. Now reflect, if you will, on the evolution of the hominids and their predecessors, the Hominoids. How were these competing groups of roving and foraging prehumans able to tell each other apart? They did not possess the distinctive scents of insect pheromones, the remarkable plumage of birds, or the melodies of white-crowned sparrows, but they did have their voices, already evolved as a sensitive system of communication. Is it not logical to assume, then, that their voices also served as a means of identification? Through them, individuals could recognize their own groups and distinguish themselves from others; with them, they could identify strangers, even at a great distance. And so, if competitiveness and aggression are part and parcel of biological behavior, the sound of a voice was sufficient to keep friend and foe apart. Remember that among the hominids, racial differences between contiguous groups were minimal, if present at all. Remember too that poor visibility at night limited visual recognition, and once small bands grew into larger groups, it was necessary to cue in on broad, phonemic features of speech for social recognition and not just on the paralinguistic features that identify individual voices. The recognition of strangers and intimates by voice alone seems to me to be the very kind of trait that is adaptive, and this argument appears to fit the "new synthesis" of Wilson, as summarized here, as well as the overall sociobiological perspective apparently presented by Lenneberg in the quote that was cited early in this chapter.

And even if you are unwilling to accept my premise that accent emergence and recognition is an adaptive feature of hominid evolution, you could still accept its presence as a susceptible trait, a costly consequence of our biological endowment for language. In other words, an accent emerging after puberty is the price we have to pay for our preordained ability to be articulate apes: Accents are the carbon monoxide that get picked up in the natural flow of communication. Biologists like Williams (1966) have cautioned that adaptation should not be used as an explanatory factor unless absolutely necessary, so to view the emergence of accents in human language learning as a chance susceptibility is a conservative interpretation of the data. But even this non-adaptive explanation remains firmly grounded in sociobiology.

Adaptive Values of Accents for Teens in the Genes

The evolutionary question to answer is why has nature left us with a time constraint of about a dozen years for accentless language acquisition? It seems plausible to assume that both the emergence and the recognition of accents should develop around puberty because, as with all other animal learning, typified by the white-crowned sparrows discussed earlier in this chapter, the imprinting takes place only after an early period of social exposure. But as with all other imprinting behaviors we know of, there is a cutoff time limit for this learning, and for language acquisition in hominid evolution, imprinting wanes at puberty. Why? This is the time that hominids—and humans too, of course—are sexually prepared to contribute to the gene pool, and so it is imperative that by this point the individual is capable of distinguishing mates who might enhance the chances of future genetic success from those who might inhibit those chances.

A speculation very similar to this comes from a rather surprising source. A year after the publication of my 1969 article rearguing the Penfield and

Lenneberg claims about a biologically based critical period for language, Jane Hill, an anthropologist and linguist wrote a rejoinder to my paper in the same journal (Hill, 1970). In sum, although she expressed interest in many of the ideas I had propounded, she questioned the validity of my version of the critical period hypothesis from the perspective of anthropological linguists. I found it rather surprising, then, that a few yeas later, she came out with a fascinating article in *American Anthropologist* entitled "On the evolutionary foundations of language" (Hill, 1972), for in this second publication, she makes an articulate and convincing case for an evolutionary explanation for the very phenomenon that was introduced in the 1969 article:

> Scovel (1969) has noted a particularly interesting aspect of this development: the presence in adult language learners (but generally not in children after the early stages) of "foreign accents." Scovel suggests, based on experimental and general observational grounds, that all normal adults beyond early adolescence can recognize a foreign accent in their native language, and are incapable of learning any new language without a foreign accent with which they can, in turn, be recognized. Scovel relates these properties to the completion of cerebral lateralization. I have suggested elsewhere (Hill 1970) that the data are not all in on this proposed universal, but let us suppose for the moment that it is genuine (and the evidence for it is very strong). What could be the adaptive significance of such a trait? The foreign accent seems, if anything, maladaptive in the present world context. However, this feature may have had considerable importance in ancient times. (Hill, 1972, pp. 312–313)

In the quotation above, Hill apparently recants her original objections to the ideas I had originally advocated about the critical period, but much more importantly, Hill herself considers the existence of foreign accents from a sociobiological perspective and sets the stage for her explanation of the emergence of accents at puberty:

> Neel (1970, p. 816) has emphasized that a population structure involving small, relatively endogamous, highly competitive demes between which only occasional cross-breeding takes place is a structure which favors extremely rapid evolution, giving great adaptive flexibility to populations displaying this type of organization. The inability of humans to ever blend imperceptibly into new social groups after puberty would surely foster such a population structure, and make populations in which an upper limit on language acquisition was established perhaps better off evolutionarily than one where language and dialect variation was easily overcome. I do not wish to suggest that gene flow across dialect lines is at all unusual, but we may assume in discussing long-term evolutionary trends that very minor variations in population structure might be of great significance. This

hypothesis about the adaptive relevance of the foreign accent phenomenon links it, and cerebral lateralization in general, at the age at which breeding becomes possible; in evolutionary terms, this is a much more significant correlation than simply the two terms of foreign accent and cerebral dominance. (Hill, 1972, p. 313)

A completely independent source of information that tends to substantiate Hill's idea about the linking of foreign accents, cerebral dominance, and evolutionary success comes from very recent research done on the way hormonal changes in the body appear to affect the destiny of brain maturation. Although the experimental work on this topic is so far mainly confined to laboratory animals, the findings are suggestive. Nordeen and Yahr (1982) surgically placed pellets of estrogen on either the left or the right sides of the lower part of the brains of newborn female rats and discovered that the degree of "feminized" behavior of the rats, when they grew to maturity, appeared to be affected by whether estrogen was placed on the left or on the right side of the brain. The authors were thus able to demonstrate a link between postpubescent behavior, the presence of a sex hormone, and laterality differences in the brain. Though differing greatly in focus and content from this experiment on rats, more recent studies of humans suggest that there is a natural link between certain changes in the brain (e.g., the loss of plasticity), hormonal transformations during puberty, and the presence (or absence) of certain language abilities in adults (Geshwind & Behan, 1982; Sundet, 1986).

However tentative they might be, I find these various ideas from different scholars and different fields all sympathetic to a sociobiological explanation for the presence of a critical period for language in our species. Further, they also appear supportive of the reason why our genes are programmed to complete the acquisition of accentless speech by the time we are in our teens. Whether this phenomenon came about because it was adaptive, as Hill, for example, seems to argue, or whether it arose as a consequence of susceptibility, either way, from the sociobiological way of looking at human history, they are part of our genetic heritage, and thus, to paraphrase both Samuel Butler and Edward Wilson, accents are nature's way of keeping the language of the genes separate!

Because we have dealt with evolution and prehistoric time in this chapter, our evidence has been indirect and our logic has been necessarily inferential. I hope this excursion back to our genetic roots has not been without insight, and having laid a strong foundation in the natural reasons why time has constrained our ability to learn language, I believe we are now prepared to look at the effects of nurture. And by looking at the possible effects the environment might play on our ability to acquire a new tongue, we will be able to approach these factors much more empirically, but, I trust, with just as much relevance and fascination.

References

Abbs, J., & Sussman, H. (1971). Neurophysiological feature detectors and speech perception: A discussion of theoretical implications. *Journal of Speech and Hearing Research, 14*, 23–36.

Chomsky, N. (1976). *Reflections on language.* New York: Pantheon Books.

Coleman, R. (1971). Male and female voice quality and its relationship to vowel formant frequencies. *Journal of Speech and Hearing Research, 14*, 565–577.

Gardner, R., & Gardner, B. (1971). Two-way communication with an infant chimpanzee. In A. Schrier & F. Stollnitz (Eds.), *Behavior of nonhuman primates* (pp. 117–184). New York: Academic Press.

Gaulin, S. (1978). Sociobiology and Hubbard's 19th century pseudoscience (Letter to the editor). *Pitt News,* December, 6.

Geschwind, N., & Behan, P. (1982). Left-handedness: Association with immune disease, migraine, and developmental learning disorder. *Proceedings of the National Academy of Sciences, USA, 79*, 5097–5100.

Gould, J., & Marler, P. (1987). Learning by instinct. *Scientific American,* January, 74–85.

Harnad, S., Stecklis, H., & Lancaster, J. (Eds.). (1976). *Origins and evolution of language and speech.* New York: New York Academy of Sciences.

Hayes, J. (1950). Vocalization and speech in chimpanzees. *American Psychologist, 5*, 275–276.

Hill, J. (1970). Foreign accents, language acquisition, and cerebral dominance revisited. *Language Learning, 20*, 237–248.

Hill, J. (1972). On the evolutionary foundations of language. *American Anthropologist, 74*, 308–317.

Katz, J. (1976). A hypothesis about the uniqueness of natural language. In S. Harnad, H. Steklis, & J. Lancaster (Eds.), *Origins and evolution of language and speech* (pp. 33–41). New York: New York Academy of Sciences.

Lenneberg, E. (1967). *Biological foundations of language.* New York: Wiley.

Lettvin, J., Maturana, H., McCullock, W., & Pitts, W. (1959). What the frog's eye tells the frog's brain. *Proceedings of the IRE, 47*, 1940–1951.

Linden, E. (1976). *Apes, men, and language.* New York: Penguin Books.

Molfese, D., Freeman, R., & Palermo, D. (1975). The ontogeny of brain lateralization for speech and nonspeech. *Brain and Language, 2*, 356–358.

Morse, P. (1972). The discrimination of speech and nonspeech stimuli in early infancy. *Journal of Experimental Child Psychology, 14*, 477–492.

Morse, P. (1974). Infant speech perception: A preliminary model and review of the literature. In R. Schiefelbusch & L. Lloyd (Eds.), *Language perspectives: Acquisition, retardation, and intervention.* Baltimore: University Park Press.

Nordeen, E., & Yahr, P. (1982). Hemispheric asymmetries in the behavioral and hormonal effects of sexually differentiating mammalian brain. *Science, 218*, 391–394.

Premack, A., & Premack, D. (1972). Teaching language to an ape. *Scientific American,* October, 92–99.

Ptacek, P., & Sander, E. (1966). Age recognition from voice. *Journal of Speech and Hearing Research, 9,* 273–277.

Reich, P. (1986). *Language development.* Englewood Cliffs, NJ: Prentice-Hall.

Rumbaugh, D., & Gill, T. (1976). The mastery of language-type skills by the chimpanzee (Pan). In S. Harnad, H. Steklis, & J. Lancaster (Eds.), *Origins and evolution of language and speech* (pp. 562–578). New York: New York Academy of Sciences.

Scovel, T. (1969). Foreign accents, language acquisition, and cerebral dominance. *Language Learning, 19,* 245–253.

Stevens, K. (1975). The potential role of property detectors in the perception of consonants. In G. Fant & M. Tatham (Eds.), *Auditory analysis and perception of speech* (pp. 303–330). New York: Academic Press.

Strange, W., & Jenkins, J. (1978). The role of linguistic experience in the perception of speech. In R. Walk & H. Rick (Eds.), *Perception and Experience* (pp. 125–169). New York: Plenum.

Tartter, V. (1980). Happy talk: The perceptual and acoustic effects of smiling on speech. *Perception and Psychophysics, 27,* 24–27.

Tartter, V. (1986). *Language Processes.* New York: Holt, Rinehart & Winston.

Tartter, V., & Eimas, P. (1975). The role of auditory feature detectors in the perception of speech. *Perception and Psychophysics, 18,* 293–298.

Terrance, H. (1979). *Nim: A chimpanzee who learned sign language.* New York: Washington Square Press.

Wilson, E. (1975). *Sociobiology: The new synthesis.* Cambridge, MA: Harvard University Press.

Understanding the Chapter

1. How does Scovel use the distinction between *r strategists* and *K strategists* to help explain why a critical period for human language acquisition might be genetically programmed?

2. Explain how human beings rely on sound for social organization. In what ways does Scovel claim this is similar to or different from birds?

3. What are the *costs* and *benefits* of a critical period for speech in humans?

4. According to Scovel, what is the *adaptive value* of accents for teens?

Reflecting on Wider Issues

1. How does Scovel's sociobiological explanation for a critical period relate to the notion that there is a neurologically-based critical period?

2. Explanations for the existence of a critical period for language learning fall into two categories—those attributable to nature, and those attributable to nurture. If biological and neurological factors fall into the category of *nature,* what factors attributable to *nurture* might be used to explain the existence of a critical period for language learning?

Going Beyond the Chapter

If you are interested in pursuing the comparison of language acquisition in humans and in animals, read the article by Neapolitan et al. (1988) on "Second language acquisition: Possible insights from studies on how birds acquire song" (*Studies in Second Language Acquisition, 10,* 1–11.) Some researchers argue that there are different "sensitive periods" for acquiring different aspects of the linguistic system, with the earliest of these applying to the phonological system. For a discussion of age and accent, you might read Flege (1987), "A critical period for learning to pronounce foreign languages?" (*Applied Linguistics, 8,* 162–177), and Patkowski's response to Flege, "Age and accent in a second language: A reply to James Emil Flege" (*Applied Linguistics, 11,* 73–89, 1990).

4

CRITICAL PERIOD EFFECTS IN SECOND LANGUAGE LEARNING: THE INFLUENCE OF MATURATIONAL STATE ON THE ACQUISITION OF ENGLISH AS A SECOND LANGUAGE

Jacqueline S. Johnson
University of Virginia

Elissa L. Newport
University of Rochester

Previewing the Article

In the previous chapter, Scovel fashioned a *sociobiological* argument for a critical period and appealed to zoological, neurological, and anthropological evidence to state his case. A good deal of research on the critical period hypothesis involves quantitative, experimental research. In this article by Johnson and Newport, just such an approach is taken specifically to study critical period effects in *second* language learning.

Before you dig in to this somewhat lengthy article, make sure, if you haven't already done so, that you understand the general issues in the critical period hypothesis (see *PLLT,* Chapter 3). Then, answer the following:

Reprinted from *Cognitive Psychology, 21*:60–99, 1989.

1. What is the purpose of the study? That is, what is the single most important question that the researchers want to answer?

2. What are the research questions?

3. What kinds of data are gathered to answer those questions, and what kinds of statistical tests are used?

Lenneberg (1967) hypothesized that language could be acquired only within a critical period, extending from early infancy until puberty. In its basic form, the critical period hypothesis need only have consequences for first language acquisition. Nevertheless, it is essential to our understanding of the nature of the hypothesized critical period to determine whether or not it extends as well to second language acquisition. If so, it should be the case that young children are better second language learners than adults and should consequently reach higher levels of final proficiency in the second language. This prediction was tested by comparing the English proficiency attained by 46 native Korean or Chinese speakers who had arrived in the United States between the ages of 3 and 39, and who had lived in the United States between 3 and 26 years by the time of testing. These subjects were tested on a wide variety of structures of English grammar, using a grammaticality judgment task. Both correlational and *t*-test analyses demonstrated a clear and strong advantage for earlier arrivals over the later arrivals. Test performance was linearly related to age of arrival up to puberty; after puberty, performance was low but highly variable and unrelated to age of arrival. This age effect was shown not to be an inadvertent result of differences in amount of experience with English, motivation, self-consciousness, or American identification. The effect also appeared on every grammatical structure tested, although the structures varied markedly in the degree to which they were well mastered by later learners. The results support the conclusion that a critical period for language acquisition extends its effects to second language acquisition.

In most behavioral domains, competence is expected to increase over development, whether gradually or in stages. However, in some domains, it has been suggested that competence does not monotonically increase with development, but rather reaches its peak during a "critical period,"[1] which

---

[1] In this article we use the term *critical period* broadly, for the general phenomenon of changes over maturation in the ability to learn (in the case under consideration in this paper, to learn language). We therefore include within this term maturational phenomena which other investigators have called sensitive, rather than critical, periods. By using the term in this broad fashion, we mean to avoid prejudging what the degree or quality of such maturational change may be (e.g., is it a sharp qualitative change vs. a gradual quantitative one?) and what the nature of the underlying maturational mechanism may be (e.g., is it a change in a special language faculty vs. a more general change in cognitive abilities?). These further questions will be addressed in part by the nature of our findings, and in part by future research.

may be relatively early in life, and then declines when this period is over. For example, in the development of early visual abilities, the development of attachment, or—in the case considered here—the acquisition of language, it has been suggested that learners are best able to achieve the skill in question during a maturationally limited period, early in life. Elsewhere we have presented evidence that first language learning is indeed limited in this way (Newport & Supalla, 1987). The present article focuses on the acquisition of a *second* language, asking whether this type of learning, undertaken only after a native language is already acquired, is nevertheless still maturationally constrained.

We will begin by reviewing prior evidence on this hypothesis, for both first and second language learning, and will then present a new empirical study which we believe shows evidence for a maturational function in second language learning. Such evidence leaves open, however, whether the underlying maturational change occurs in a specific language faculty, or rather in more general cognitive abilities involved in language learning. We will conclude by considering the types of mechanisms which are consistent with our findings.

Evidence for a Critical Period Effect in First Language Acquisition

The critical period hypothesis, as advanced by Lenneberg (1967), holds that language acquisition must occur before the onset of puberty in order for language to develop fully. As will be detailed in the subsequent section, Lenneberg's hypothesis concerned only first language acquisition; he left open the question of whether this critical period extended to second language acquisition, which would occur after a first language was already in place.

Lenneberg's argument contained two parts. First, he reviewed available behavioral evidence suggesting that normal language learning occurred primarily or exclusively within childhood. At the time his book was written, no direct evidence for the hypothesis (from normal individuals who had been deprived of exposure to a first language for varying lengths of time in early life) was available. His review therefore included various types of indirect evidence, for example, differences in recovery from aphasia for children vs. adults, and differences in progress in language acquisition, before vs. after puberty, in the mentally retarded.

Second, he proposed a mechanism which might be responsible for a maturational change in learning abilities. The proposed mechanism was fundamentally neurological in nature. He suggested that the brain, having reached its adult values by puberty, has lost the plasticity and reorganizational capacities necessary for acquiring language. Subsequent research has questioned whether all of the neurological events he cited occur at an appropriate time for them to serve as the basis for a critical period (Krashen, 1975). Nevertheless, the hypothesis that there *is* such a critical period for language learning has remained viable.

Since Lenneberg's writing, behavioral studies approximating a direct test of the critical period hypothesis for first language acquisition have become available. One such study is a well-known case of Genie, a girl who was deprived of language and social interaction until her discovery at the age of thirteen (Curtiss, 1977). Her lack of linguistic competence, particularly in syntax, after seven years of rehabilitation supports the critical period hypothesis. However, the abnormal conditions under which Genie was reared, including nutritional, cognitive, and social deprivation, have led some investigators to question whether her language difficulties have resulted only from lack of linguistic exposure during early life.

More recently, Newport and Supalla (Newport, 1984; Newport & Supalla, 1987) have studied language acquisition in the congenitally deaf, a population in which exposure to a first language may occur at varying ages while other aspects of social and cognitive development remain normal. Their data come from congenitally deaf subjects for whom American Sign Language (ASL) is the first language. However, since 90% of the congenitally deaf have hearing (speaking) parents, only a few deaf individuals are exposed to this language at birth. The majority of deaf people are exposed to ASL only when they enter residential school for the deaf and first associate with other deaf individuals; this can be as early as age four or as late as early adulthood.

Newport and Supalla separated subjects by their age of exposure into three groups: *native learners,* who were exposed to ASL from birth by their deaf parents; *early learners,* who were first exposed to ASL between the ages of 4 and 6; and *late learners,* who were first exposed to ASL at age 12 or later. Wishing to test asymptotic performance (i.e., ultimate command of the language), they chose subjects who had at least 40 years of experience with the language as their primary, everyday communication system. The subjects were tested on their production and comprehension of ASL verb morphology. The results show a linear decline in performance with increasing age of exposure, on virtually every morpheme tested. That is, native learners scored better than early learners, who scored better than late learners, on both production and comprehension.

This study thus provides direct evidence that there is a decline over age in the ability to acquire a first language. It also tells us, however, that Lenneberg's portrayal is at least partially incorrect in two regards. First, the results show a continuous linear decline in ability, instead of a sudden drop-off at puberty as his hypothesis implies. (This study does not tell us whether the linear function asymptotes or continues to decline after puberty, since separate groups of later learners, before vs. after puberty, were not tested.) Second, it should be noted that, while the postpubescent learners did not reach as high a level of proficiency as the native or early learners, language had not become totally unlearnable for them. This rules out any extreme interpretation of the critical period hypothesis.

In sum, current evidence supports the notion of a maturationally delimited critical period for first language acquisition, with some modifications from Lenneberg's original formulation. However, this evidence is compatible with a number of quite different accounts of the nature of the underlying maturational change. Evidence concerning age effects on *second* language learning can contribute to a further delineation of critical period accounts.

Second Language Acquisition

What it can and cannot tell us about the critical period.   Given the early difficulties of performing a direct test of the critical period hypothesis on first language acquisition, many researchers undertook studies of second language acquisition over age as a test of the hypothesis. Some investigators have suggested that a critical period theory must predict that children are better than adults at learning second languages, as well as first languages. Consequently, they have viewed any evidence to the contrary as evidence against the critical period hypothesis (cf. Snow, 1983, for discussion).

In our opinion, data on this issue do have an important consequence for a critical period theory of language acquisition. However, it is not that the critical period hypothesis could be rejected on such evidence, but rather that it can be refined or clarified by such evidence. A critical period theory for language acquisition would have quite a different character depending upon whether second language acquisition were included in its effects.

To capture this distinction there are two different ways we can state the critical period hypothesis, one which does not include second language acquisition in its effects and one that does:

Version One: The exercise hypothesis.   Early in life, humans have a superior capacity for acquiring languages. If the capacity is not exercised during this time, it will disappear or decline with maturation. If the capacity is exercised, however, further language learning abilities will remain intact throughout life.

Version Two: The maturational state hypothesis.   Early in life, humans have a superior capacity for acquiring languages. This capacity disappears or declines with maturation.

Notice that, although very different in character, the two versions make the same predictions with regard to first language acquisition. They differ, however, in their predictions for second language acquisition.

The exercise hypothesis predicts that children will be superior to adults in acquiring a first language. By this account, if learners are not exposed to a first language during childhood, they will be unable to acquire any language fully at a later date. However, as long as they have acquired a first language during childhood, the ability to acquire language will remain intact and can be utilized at any age. On such a hypothesis, second language learning should be equivalent in children and adults, or perhaps even superior in adults due to their greater skills in their first language as well as in many related domains.

This hypothesis is not unlike the conception of the visual critical period described for cats (Hubel & Wiesel, 1963), where early visual experience is required to maintain and refine the structure of the visual cortex, or the conception of the critical period described for attachment in dogs (Scott, 1980), where early attachment to one dog is required for subsequently normal socialization and permits unlimited later attachments to other members of the same species. Indeed, as will be discussed below, some of the current evidence on second language learning could be interpreted to support an exercise hypothesis.

In contrast, the maturational state hypothesis claims that there is something special about the maturational state of the child's brain which makes children particularly adept at acquiring *any* language, first as well as second. This hypothesis predicts that language learning abilities decline with maturation, regardless of early linguistic experience: acquiring a first language early in life will not guarantee the ability to acquire a second language later in life. In this version, then, children will be better in second language learning as well as first.

With certain qualifications, the critical period hypothesis that Lenneberg put forth can be subsumed under either version. In fact, it is not absolutely clear which version he would have favored. Some comments he made suggest that he thinks the young learner has a superior capacity for acquiring second languages, and therefore that he would favor the maturational state hypothesis:

> . . . the incidence of "language learning blocks" rapidly increases after puberty. Also automatic acquisition from mere exposure to a given language seems to disappear after this age and foreign languages have to be taught and learned through a conscious and labored effort. Foreign accents cannot be overcome easily after puberty. (Lenneberg, 1967, p. 176)

However, other comments within the same paragraph sound as if he would have favored the exercise hypothesis:

> . . . our ability to learn foreign languages tends to confuse the picture. Most individuals of average intelligence are able to learn a second language after the beginning of their second decade . . . a person can learn to communicate in a foreign language at the age of forty. This does not trouble our basic hypothesis on age limitation because we may assume that the cerebral organization for language learning as such has taken place during childhood, and since natural languages tend to resemble one another in many fundamental aspects the matrix for language skills is present. (Lenneberg, 1967, p. 176)

Since Lenneberg's was one of the first proposals in this area, it is not surprising that he did not take a definitive stand on this issue, particularly since there were at that time few data to support either view. Nevertheless, it is a crucial distinction that should be made in any subsequent account of a critical period.

Research on Age Effects on Second Language Acquisition

Is there an age-related limitation on the learning of a second language? A number of studies have investigated this question since the time of Lenneberg's book, focusing particularly on the acquisition of phonology and grammar. Superficially, these studies appear to contradict one another; some have been said to demonstrate an adult advantage, some a child advantage.

This apparent contradiction is resolved when one separates performance in the early stages of learning from eventual attainment in the language. (For a review of these studies, with a conclusion similar to the one presented here, see Krashen, Long, & Scarcella, 1982.) Most of the studies of second language learning have examined just the early stages of learning; these studies tend to show an adult advantage in both phonology (Asher & Price, 1967; Olson & Samuels, 1973; Snow & Hoefnagel-Hohle, 1977) and syntax (Snow & Hoefnagel-Hohle, 1978). Adults thus seem to begin moving toward second language proficiency more quickly. However, this advantage appears to be short-lived.

In contrast, studies of eventual attainment in the language show a superiority for subjects who began learning in childhood, both in phonology (Asher & Garcia, 1969; Oyama, 1976; Seliger, Krashen, & Ladefoged, 1975) and in syntax (Oyama, 1978; Patkowski, 1980). However, most of the studies of child-adult differences in ultimate attainment have focused on pronunciation. With anecdotal evidence that late learners do carry an accent and experimental findings that support it, most investigators will concede a child advantage for acquiring phonology (though not necessarily a maturational one; see, for example, Olson & Samuels, 1973; Snow & Hoefnagel-Hohle, 1977).

There is much less available evidence on child-adult differences in the ultimate attainment of grammar. To our knowledge, only two studies have been done. In both, the subjects were U.S. immigrants who were exposed to English upon moving to the United States and who had lived in the United States for at least five years at time of the test.

In one study, subjects' syntactic ability was assessed by trained judges who assigned syntactic ratings to written transcripts of the subjects' speech from tape recorded interviews (Patkowski, 1980). For purposes of analysis, subjects' scores were divided along two variables: age of arrival in the United States (before vs. after age fifteen), and years in the United States (under vs. over 18 years). Additionally, measures of the subjects' exposure to English in both natural and classroom settings were taken. Using either the results from the analysis of variance test or correlations, age of arrival was the only significant predictor of syntactic proficiency, with the prepubescent learners outperforming the postpubescent learners. The correlation of age of arrival with score was -.74, which indicates a linear trend; however, the exact shape of the relationship cannot be determined from the reported results.

In the second study mentioned, subjects were measured on their ability to repeat spoken English sentences which had been masked with white noise (Oyama, 1978). This task was meant to tap the ability to integrate different sources of linguistic knowledge including phonology, syntax, intonation, and redundancy patterns. Admittedly this is not a pure measure of syntactic ability; however, it presumably involves syntactic knowledge (along with other factors). This study found the same pattern of results just reported: age of arrival was the only significant predictor of test performance.

In addition, the Oyama study addressed important claims regarding whether children's superiority over adults in final attainment is due to factors other than maturation, which happens to be correlated with age. For example, it has been argued that the adult is less *motivated* than the child to learn the language fully, is more *self-conscious* about speaking (i.e., practicing and making errors), does not have the cultural *identification* with the host country necessary to become fluent, and in general is less able to achieve the open attitudinal and affective state required for language acquisition to take place (for reviews of this view, see Krashen, 1982; Schumann, 1975). To test these claims, Oyama measured each of these variables, plus other candidate predictors, using interview and questionnaire material. Simple correlations showed a good association between these variables and test score; however, partial correlations removing the effects of age of arrival become essentially zero. In contrast, when the reverse procedure was performed, removing each of these variables from the relationship between age of arrival and test score, the partial correlation remained large and significant. In short, age of arrival, rather than the attitudinal variables, predicted language performance.

These are important findings, for they support the view that age effects are not simply an artifact of child-adult differences in affective conditions of learning. However, a more rigorous test of this question could be performed. Nonmaturational hypotheses do not typically propose that one attitudinal variable, for example, self-consciousness, will alone predict performance; rather, they propose that the combination of all of these variables favor children over adults. Thus a more stringent test would involve partialling out all of the attitudinal variables together from age of arrival, and then determining whether there is any predictive power left.

The study we present in the present paper is an attempt to supplement the findings of these earlier studies. It is similar to the two studies discussed above, in that the focus is on ultimate command of the grammar of the second language as a function of age of exposure to that language. It differs from previous studies, however, in the way subjects' proficiency in the language is assessed and in the types of analyses performed. First, a detailed evaluation of subjects' knowledge of numerous aspects of English morphology and syntax is performed. This allows us to examine the relationship between age of exposure and an overall measure of English proficiency, as well as the possible differential effects of age of exposure on various aspects of grammatical structure. Second, a wide range of ages of exposure is examined, so that the precise shape of the function relating age to proficiency can be determined. Third, multivariate analyses are used to evaluate the relative contributions to proficiency of age as well as a number of affective, sociological, and environmental conditions of learning.

In detail, the primary questions that we address are as follows:

1. Is there an age-related effect on learning the grammar of a second language?

2. If so, what is the nature of this relationship? What is the shape of the function relating age to learning and ultimate performance, and where (if anywhere) does the relationship plateau or decline?

3. Can experiential or attitudinal variables, separately or together, explain the effects obtained for age of learning?

4. What areas of the grammar are the most and least problematic for learners of different age groups?

In answering these questions we hope to gain a better understanding of the nature of the critical period and, most particularly, to be able to decide between the two versions of the critical period outlined above.

Method

Subjects

Subjects were 46 native Chinese or Korean speakers who learned English as a second language. Chinese and Korean were chosen as the native languages because of their typological dissimilarity to English. (For consideration of the effects of the first language on the second, see Discussion.) No differences were found in the results for the two language groups, so they will be presented together throughout the paper.

The primary criterion for selecting subjects was that they vary in the age at which they moved to the United States and thereby first became immersed in English. All subjects were exposed to English by native speakers in the United States. In addition, to be sure that subjects had sufficient experience with English to be considered at their ultimate attainment in the language, every attempt was made to obtain subjects who had lived in the United States for many years. Minimum criteria were as follows: all subjects had to have at least five years of exposure to English and had to have lived in the United

States for an unbroken stay of at least three years prior to the time of test. Finally, to ensure ample exposure to English and to ensure some homogeneity of social background, all subjects were selected from the student and faculty population at an American university (University of Illinois). Subjects were recruited through posted sign-up sheets, letters, and by word of mouth.

The resulting 46 subjects varied in age of arrival in the United States from ages 3 to 39; throughout that range there was a fairly even distribution of ages of arrival. Age of arrival was considered the age of first exposure to English. Three additional subjects were tested but eliminated from data analysis when our posttest interview revealed that they did not meet the above criteria: One did not have an unbroken stay in the United States for three years prior to test; the second did not arrive in the United States until adulthood but was immersed in English through attending an all-English-speaking school in a foreign country. For both of these subjects, then, age of immersion could not be determined unambiguously. The third subject was eliminated because her early exposure to English was from her Chinese parents, who had no prior experience with English but nevertheless decided to speak only English in the home upon their arrival in the United States. Most of her early exposure to English was therefore not to standard English.

Additional experiential characteristics of the subjects varied for subjects arriving in the United States early vs. late in life, and will be discussed separately for these two groups. In all cases, these experiential characteristics, as well as age of arrival, will be evaluated for their relationship to performance in English.

Early arrivals.   There were 23 subjects, 12 males and 11 females, who had arrived in the United States before age 15. These early arrivals were, at the time of test, for the most part freshman or sophomore undergraduates who received money or class credit for their participation. All of these subjects, from the time of arrival until college, lived in an environment where their native language was spoken in the home and English spoken outside of the home. Once they entered college, all lived predominantly in an English-speaking environment.

Late arrivals.   The remaining 23 subjects were 17 males and 6 females who had arrived in the United States after age 17. Prior to coming to the United States, all of these subjects had had between 2 and 12 years of mandatory formal English instruction in their native country. This raised two possible concerns: One, the classroom experience might reduce the effect of age of arrival on learning, since age of first exposure to English for these subjects is earlier than age of arrival. Two, "age of learning" may turn out to be better defined by age of starting classes rather than age of arrival, which would result in a narrower range of ages than desired. Whether point 2 is true is an interesting question itself and will be examined empirically in the results section.

At the time of test, these subjects were primarily professors, research associates, and graduate students. All subjects, in both the early and late arrival groups, had at least some years of schooling while in the United States. Within the late arrivals, the smallest number of years of school in the United States was 3 years, the largest 10, with an average of 6 years for the group.

For some of the subjects, the language environment was analogous to that of the early arrivals, in which the native language was spoken in the home and English spoken at school and work; for others, particularly those that were unmarried, the language environment was almost all English. Thus in terms of exposure on a day to day basis, it does not appear that the early arrivals have any advantage over the late arrivals.

In terms of years of exposure in the United States the late and early arrivals also are fairly even. See Table 1. The average number of years in the United States for early and late arrivals is 9.8 and 9.9, respectively. The main difference between the two groups is that the late arrivals have a larger range of years in the United States.

TABLE I. The Distribution of Early and Late Arrivals in Terms of the Number of Years They Lived in the U.S.

	Age of Arrival	
YEARS IN THE U.S.	3–15	17–39
3–6	4	7
7–10	10	11
11–15	9	3
23–26	0	2

To provide a baseline performance on tests of English, 23 native speakers of English were run. Two additional native subjects participated but were not included in the analysis, one because the posttest interview revealed that he acquired English outside of the United States, and one because she spoke a nonstandard dialect of English.

Procedure

The subjects were tested on their knowledge of English syntax and morphology by being asked to judge the grammaticality of spoken English sentences of varying types (see Materials). While such a task, of course, in principle requires metalinguistic skills in addition to knowledge of the language, virtually perfect performance is shown on the same task by 6- and 7-year old native speakers in subsequent studies (Johnson, Newport, & Strauss, in press). This suggests that the metalinguistic skills necessary for our task can only be minimally demanding for an adult and that any variation obtained in performance on the task among adults must be due to variation in knowledge of the language.

The test sentences were recorded on tape by a native American female voice (E.N.). Each sentence was read twice, with a 1–2 second pause separating the repetitions. They were said clearly, with normal intonation at a slow to moderate speed. The ungrammatical sentences were spoken with the intonation pattern of the grammatical counterpart. There was a 3–4 second delay between the different sentences.

Subjects were tested individually in the laboratory. They were instructed to make a grammaticality judgment for each sentence, guessing if they were not sure. It was made clear to the subject that if the sentence was incomplete or otherwise wrong for any reason, they should regard it as ungrammatical. The subject recorded yes/no responses on an answer sheet by circling Y or N. To avoid giving cues to the subject, the experimenter did not face the subject during the testing session while the tape was going. Subjects were given a break halfway through the test, but were told prior to starting that they should tell the experimenter to stop the tape at any time if they needed to break sooner, either if the tape was too fast for them or if they were simply getting tired.

Following the grammaticality judgment test, subjects were interviewed for approximately half an hour about their language background. Information was gathered about the type and amount of exposure to English they had, from when they were first learning the language until the time of test. Motivational and attitudinal measures were also taken, by having the subjects rate themselves on a scale of 1 to 5 with regard to those measures.

None of the subjects were blind as to the nature of the experiment. They were told prior to participating that we were interested in determining whether children or adults are better at learning second languages; they were not told, however, what type of results were expected.

Materials

The judgments of grammaticality test was modeled loosely after one used by Linebarger, Schwartz, and Saffran (1983) in a study unrelated to the present one. Our test, however, has a different set of English constructions and corresponding test sentences than those of Linebarger et al., which the exception of two rule types which are noted.[2]

Our test was composed of 276 sentences.[3] Of these, 140 were ungrammat-

---

[2] We thank Marcia Linebarger for making these and other tests available to us.

[3] An additional six sentences, three ungrammatical and three the grammatical counterparts of these, were included in the test but were eliminated from scoring because native speakers of English made large numbers of errors in judging their grammaticality, due to either auditory problems or dialect variations.

ical. The other 136 formed the grammatical counterparts of these sentences.[4] The pairs that were formed, between the ungrammatical and grammatical counterparts, were sentences that were exactly the same except for one rule violation contained in the ungrammatical sentence. The pairs of sentences were constructed to test 12 types of rules of English, listed in Table 2. The test contained between 6 and 16 pairs of sentences testing each rule type. The members of a pair were, however, not adjacent to each other, but rather were placed in opposite halves of the test. Within each half, sentences were presented in random order (see Design for further details.)

TABLE 2.   12 Rule Types Tested in Grammaticality Judgment Task

1. Past tense	7. Particle movement
2. Plural	8. Subcategorization
3. Third person singular	9. Auxiliaries
4. Present progressive	10. Yes/no questions
5. Determiners	11. Wh-questions
6. Pronominalization	12. Word order

To ensure as much as possible that the sentences tested the rules under study and not extraneous factors, sentences were constructed to contain only relatively high frequency words, most of which were only one or two syllables in length. The location of the grammatical error (at the beginning, middle, or end of the sentence), the basic phrase structure of the sentence, and the sentence length (ranging from 5 to 11 words per sentence) were balanced across pairs of sentences testing each rule type, so that each rule type was tested by a set of sentences comparable in all of these regards.

The 12 rule types we tested were chosen to represent a wide variety of the most basic aspects of English sentence structure. (Indeed, according to our expectations, native speakers of English found the test very easy, with ungrammatical sentences producing strong feelings of ungrammaticality.) Within the 12 rules types, there were four rule types which dealt specifically with English morphology: past tense, plural, third person singular, and present progressive. They will be discussed together since many of the violations were constructed along similar lines. The other eight types involved various rules of English syntax. Within each rule type, the violations were formed on the basis of a few basic formats, with several pairs of sentences (typically 4) using each format. These are discussed in more detail, with examples of the structure of the pairs, below.

---

[4] The numbers of ungrammatical and grammatical sentences are unequal because some rule types have more than one grammatical sentence, or more than one ungrammatical sentence, within each set of counterparts (see, for example, the section on particle movement). For the most part, however, the grammatical and ungrammatical sentences form pairs, and for ease of presentation they will be referred to as "pairs" throughout the paper.

Morphology: Past tense, plural, third person singular, and present progressive. For morphology, the grammatical sentence always contained the target morpheme in a required context, while the grammatical violation was created using one of four formats:

1. by omitting the required morpheme;
2. by replacing the required morpheme with an inappropriate morpheme from a different class;
3. by making an irregular item regular;
4. by attaching a regular marking to an already irregularly marked item.

The first format was used to make ungrammatical sentences for all four types of morphology. The sentence pairs were constructed so that the grammatical context required the target morpheme, making it a grammatical violation when the morpheme was omitted in one of the sentences of the pair. For example, in sentences (1a) and (1b), a plural marker is required on the noun "pig," and is present in (1a) but is omitted in (1b). In sentences (2a) and (2b), the present progressive ending is required on the verb "speak"; it is present in (2a) but omitted in (2b).

1a.   The farmer bought two pigs at the market.
*1b.   The farmer bought two pig at the market.
2a.   The little boy is speaking to a policeman.
*2b.   The little boy is speak to a policeman.

Sentences were structured similarly for the other classes of morphemes.

The second format applied only to the verb morphology. One sentence of the pair was correct; the other had an inappropriate tense marking for the context. Consider, for example, sentences (3a) and (3b).

3a.   Yesterday the hunter shot a deer.
*3b.   Yesterday the hunter shoots a deer.

In (3a), the verb is in the past tense form as required, while in (3b) the verb "shoot" occurs in present tense form in a past tense context.

The last two formats for creating the ill-formed sentences could be used only for past tense and plural forms. An ill-formed sentence created by making an irregular item regular is exemplified in sentence (4b), with its grammatical counterpart in (4a). Similarly, the ungrammatical sentence (5b) has a regular marking added on an already marked irregular.

4a.   A shoe salesman sees many feet throughout the day.
*4b.   A shoe salesman sees many foots throughout the day.
5a.   A bat flew into our attic last night.

*5b.   A bat flewed into our attic last night.

The test was constructed so that there was an equal number of sentence pairs (4) in each format used for each type of morphology. However, due to the nature of the morphemes, it was impossible for all of the formats to be applied to all of the four rule types. Therefore the past tense and plural are tested by more sentence pairs than are the third person or the present progressive.

Determiners.   To test subjects' knowledge of determiners, the grammatical member of the sentence pairs was constructed so that a determiner in a particular position was either necessary or not allowed. The ungrammatical counterparts were then formed by one of three methods: (1) by omitting them in required contexts, as in sentence (6b); (2) by substituting the indefinite for the definite, as in (7b); and (3) by inserting them where neither article is allowed, see (8b). These examples can be contrasted with their grammatical counterparts (6a), (7a), and (8a), respectively:

6a.   Tom is reading a book in the bathtub.

*6b.   Tom is reading book in the bathtub.

7a.   The boys are going to the zoo this Saturday.

*7b.   A boys are going to the zoo this Saturday.

8a.   Larry went home after the party.

*8b.   Larry went the home after the party.

In many cases, there are other ways of construing the errors; for example, (6b) may be construed as a plural error, instead of a determiner error, for not having the plural marking on the noun "book." In cases like these, where the error classification was ambiguous, the semantic contexts were created to try to bias the listener into the preferred reading. For example, in (6) the reason Tom is in the bathtub is to sway the subject into expecting that he is reading only one book rather than many.

Pronominalization.   The sentence pairs for this rule type contain some type of pronominal. The ungrammatical sentences were formed to include one of the following violations: (1) the wrong case marking on the pronoun; (2) an error in gender or number agreement for the pronoun; or (3) an erroneous form of the possessive adjective.

The violations of case involved using nominative pronouns in objective positions (see (9a) and (9b)), and objective pronouns in nominative positions:

9a.   Susan is making some cookies for us.

*9b.   Susan is making some cookies for we.

Gender and number were tested by capitalizing on the fact that reflexive pronouns have to agree with the noun they are coindexed with. Sentence (10a) is an example of correct gender agreement, while (10b) shows a gender agreement violation:

10a.   The girl cut herself on a piece of glass.

*10b.   The girl cut himself on a piece of glass.

For possessive adjectives, the error is in the form the word takes. So, for example, some ungrammatical items have a possessive adjective with the possessive marker added, as in (11b). Compare this to the correct form in (11a):

11a.   Carol is cooking dinner for her family.

*11b.   Carol is cooking dinner for hers family.

Particle movement.   With some minor changes, all of the items in this rule type are from Linebarger et al. (1983). Here the sentences take advantage of the differences between particles and prepositions. The ill-formed sentences were created by treating prepositions as particles, that is, by moving the preposition to the right of the object NP as in (12b), as compared to the correct form in (12a). These were contrasted with grammatical sentences with particles in their moved and unmoved positions, as in (13a) and (13b). Additionally, other sentences were ill-formed by moving the particle outside its own clause as in (13c). Notice that, for this rule type, the sets of counterpart sentences are not pairs but triples:

12a.   The man climbed up the ladder carefully.

*12b.   The man climbed the ladder up carefully.

13a.   Kevin called up Nancy for a date.

13b.   Kevin called Nancy up for a date.

*13c.   Kevin called Nancy for a date up.

Subcategorization.   The items in this rule type are also from Linebarger et al. (1983). These items test subjects' knowledge of the subcategorization frames of various verbs. In English, individual verbs determine the type of syntactic frames that may follow them. For example, some verbs require a direct object, while others require prepositional phrases. Because the details of these frames are lexically determined, ill-formed sentences could be created by changing the structure of the required frame for a particular verb while keeping the meaning intact. Thus, the change in these sentences involved using the subcategorization frame of a semantically similar verb. See, for example, the contrasts below.

14a.   The man allows his son to watch T.V.

*14b.   The man allows his son watch T.V.

15a.   The man lets his son watch T.V.

*15b.   The man lets his son to watch T.V.

The ungrammatical sentences were formed by exchanging the different subcategorization frames of the two semantically similar verbs "allow" and "let."

Auxiliaries. In this rule type, the affix requirements for different auxiliary verbs were tested. In particular, the ungrammatical sentences were formed by violating three rules of auxiliaries. Each rule, with an example of the correct and incorrect forms, is given below:

"Have" requires a past participle.

16a. The baby bird has fallen from the oak tree.

*16b. The baby bird has fall from the oak tree.

Following any form of "be," the main verb must take the progressive.

17a. Fred will be getting a raise next month.

*17b. Fred will be get a raise next month.

Only the first element of Aux is tensed.

18a. Leonard should have written a letter to his mother.

*18b. Leonard should has written a letter to his mother.

Yes/no questions. For this rule type, the ungrammatical sentences contain primarily errors in subject-aux inversion. The errors are of three types. In one, two auxiliaries are moved in front of the subject, as in (19b). In another, both the auxiliary and the verb are fronted (20b); and in the third, the verb is fronted in a sentence where do-insertion would normally occur, as in (21b). The grammatical counterparts are (19a), (20a), and (21a), respectively.

19a. Has the king been served his dinner?

*19b. Has been the king served his dinner?

20a. Can the little girl ride a bicycle?

*20b. Can ride the little girl a bicycle?

21a. Did Bill dance at the party last night?

*21b. Danced Bill at the party last night?

Additionally, there were some ungrammatical sentences formed by copying, instead of moving, the auxiliary verb, the difference being shown in (22a) and (22b):

22a. Can the boy drive a tractor?

*22b. Can the boy can drive a tractor?

Wh-questions. The ungrammatical wh-questions have three forms, two of them also dealing with aux. In one form, no subject-aux inversion occurs, as in (23b) as compared with (23a); in the other, do-insertion is omitted, as in (24b) compared to (24a):

23a. When will Sam fix his car?

*23b. When Sam will fix his car?

24a.   What do they sell at the corner store?

*24b.   What they sell at the corner store?

The third form of the ungrammatical wh-questions was lexical. A question was ill-formed by substituting an incorrect wh-word for a correct one. In sentence (25b), for example, "why" cannot be used unless the subcategorization frame of the verb "put" is satisfied by supplying a locative. Sentence (25a) satisfies this restriction by replacing the locative with a locative wh-word.

25a.   Where did she put the book?

*25b.   Why did she put the book?

Word Order.   In this last rule type, basic word order rules are tested. Sentences of three types were used: intransitive (NP-V), transitive (NP-V-NP), and dative (NP-V-NP-NP). Within each type, the ungrammatical sentences were formed by systematically rearranging the verbs and noun phrases so that all of the possible orders of constituents occurred. Thus the simplest ill-formed sentence involves the reversal of an NP and intransitive verb, as in (26a) versus (26b); the most complex involves the rearrangement of NPs and V in double-object structures, as in (27a) versus (27b).

26a.   The woman paints.

*26b.   Paints the woman.

27a.   Martha asked the policeman a question.

*27b.   Martha a question asked the policeman.

Design

The test was divided into two halves. An equal number of exemplars of each rule type and subrule type were represented in each half. The grammatical and ungrammatical members of a pair were in opposite halves of the test. Within each half, sentences were randomized in such a way that no rule type was concentrated in one section of the test, and no run of grammatical or ungrammatical sentences was longer than four.

Results

Age of Acquisition

Age of acquisition and ultimate performance.   The primary question of this study involved examining the relationship between age of learning English as a second language and performance on the test of English grammar. The results show a clear and strong relationship between age of arrival in the United States and performance. Subjects who began acquiring English in the

United States at an earlier age obtained higher scores on the test than those that began later, $r = -.77$, $p < .01$.

A more detailed understanding of this relationship can be gained from Table 3 and Fig. 1. Subjects were grouped by age of arrival into categories similar to those used in past research (e.g., Snow & Hoefnagel-Hohle, 1978). Table 3 presents the mean score, standard deviation, and the ranges of the number of correct responses and the number of errors for each group and for the native English comparison group. The means are also presented graphically in Fig. 1. The adjacent age groups were compared, two at a time, by a set of two-sample t tests using separate variance estimates.[5]

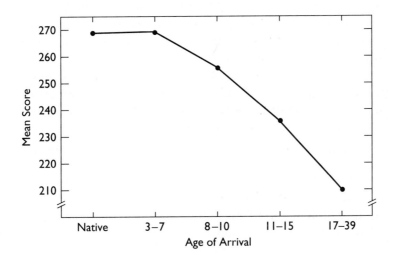

FIGURE 1. The Relationship between Age of Arrival in the United States and Total Score Correct on the Test of English Grammar

TABLE 3.   Mean Scores of Nonnative and Native Speakers of English

		Age of Arrival			
	NATIVES ($n = 23$)	3–7 ($n = 7$)	8–10 ($n = 8$)	11–15 ($n = 8$)	17–39 ($n = 23$)
Means	268.8	269.3	256.0	235.9	210.3
SD	2.9	2.8	6.0	13.6	22.8
Range	275–265	272–264	263–247	251–212	254–163
(Errors)	(1–11)	(4–12)	(13–29)	(25–64)	(22–113)

Note. Maximum score = 276.

---

[5] Using a two-sample t statistic where the variance of each group is estimated separately is appropriate whenever the population variances are not assumed to be equal, as is the case here.

The first comparison involved determining whether there was any difference between the age 3-7 group and the native group in their performance in English. The two groups were not significantly different from each other, $t(10.4) = 1.28$, $p > .05$; indeed, the two groups were entirely overlapping in performance. In contrast, all of the other age groups performed significantly below the natives (for natives vs. the next closest group (8-10), $t(8.1) = 6.67$, $p < .01$). This suggests that, if one is immersed in a second language before the age of 7, one is able to achieve native fluency in the language;[6] however, immersion even soon after that age results in a decrement in ultimate performance.

Given that the 3-7 group is the only group that reached native performance, it is perhaps not surprising that the difference between the means of the 3-7 and 8-10 age groups is significant, $t(10) = 5.59$, $p > .01$. As can be seen in Table 3, while the absolute difference between the means of these two groups is small, both groups have very small SDs, and the range of scores for the 3-7 group is entirely nonoverlapping with the 8-10 group. All of the later adjacent age groups are also significantly different from each other. The age 8-10 group obtained higher scores than the 11-15 group, $t(9.7) = 3.83$, $p < .01$, with almost nonoverlapping distributions between the two groups, and the age 11-15 group obtained higher scores than the 19-39 (adult) group, $t(21) = 3.78$, $p < .01$.

In sum, there appears to be a strong linear relationship between age of exposure to the language and ultimate performance in that language, up to adulthood. In the next section we examine the shape of this function in more detail.

The effects of age of acquisition before vs. after puberty.   An important question to answer is whether, throughout adulthood, performance continues to decline as a function of age of exposure or whether it plateaus at some point (H. Gleitman, personal communication). If the explanation for late learners' poorer performance relates to maturation, performance should not continue to decline over age, for presumably there are not many important maturational differences between, for example, the brain of a 17-year old and the brain of a 27-year old. Instead, there should be a consistent decline in performance over age for those exposed to the language before puberty, but no systematic relationship to age of exposure, and a leveling off of ultimate performance, among those exposed to the language after puberty. This is precisely what was found.

Subjects were divided into two groups in terms of age of exposure, from age 3-15 versus 17-39, with an equal number of subjects ($N = 23$) in each group. The correlations between age of exposure and performance for these two groups were strikingly different. For the group first exposed to English between the ages of 3 and 15, the correlation was -.87, $p < .01$. Note that this

---

[6] It is always possible, however, that the equivalence in performance between natives and the 3-7 group is due to a ceiling effect on our test, and that tests of more complex aspects of English syntax would show differences even between these groups.

correlation is even more substantial than that for the subjects as a whole. In contrast, for the group first exposed to English between the ages of 17 and 39, there is no significant correlation, $r = -.16$, $p > .05$. Scatterplots demonstrating this effect are presented in Figs. 2a and b.

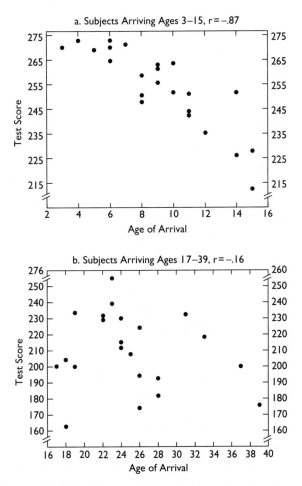

FIGURE 2. Scatterplots of Test Score in Relation to Age of Arrival for Subjects Arriving in United States Before vs. After Puberty

Age of acquisition and variance in ultimate performance. Another age-related result, which is obvious from inspecting the scatterplots of Fig. 2 and the SDs in Table 3, is the heterogeneous variance. For groups who acquired English at early ages, the variance is very small; with increasing age of exposure, variance gets larger, creating a megaphone shape, so that for subjects exposed to English after 15 the variance is very large. Note that it would have been quite possible to find that the means of these groups increased but the variance stayed constant over the age groups. The heterogeneity of variance obtained, and the relation between age of acquisition and variance, is an independent result.

This heterogeneity of variance underscores two simple but important points:

1. Before age 15, and most particularly before age 10, there are very few individual differences in ultimate ability to learn language within any particular age group; success in learning is almost entirely predicted by the age at which it begins.

2. For adults, later age of acquisition determines that one will not become native or near-native in a language; however, there are large individual variations in ultimate ability in the language, within the lowered range of performance.

Age of exposure to formal instruction.   It has been assumed thus far that age of arrival in the United States is the best measure of age of exposure to the language. For early arrivals it is the only measure available, since these subjects had no prior experience with English at all. However, for the late arrivals there are two measures possible: age of arrival in the United States, or age of beginning English instruction in school within the native country. There is already a high correlation between age of arrival and test score for the subjects as a whole, $r = 2.77$; if age of classes is a better measure of first exposure for the late arrivals, then the correlation should be even higher when using that as a measure of time of exposure. This is not what was found. The correlation for the subjects as a whole between age of exposure, defined as classes or immersion (whichever came first), and test score is -.67. These correlations, however, are not statistically different from each other, $t(43) = 1.26$, $p > .05$. This is not surprising since, due to the early arrivals, half of the measurements are exactly the same; moreover, most of the late arrivals are defined as later learners (pubescent or postpubescent) either way they are measured. Because of this overlap in measurement, the best way to evaluate the effect of age of classes is to do so using only the subjects who had classroom instruction. For these subjects alone ($N = 23$), the correlation between age of classes and test score is -.33, which is not significant, $p > .05$.

This result has two implications. First, it means that we are using the right measure for "age of exposure"; age of arrival in the United States, with its resulting immersion in English, is more strongly related to ultimate performance in English than is age of beginning formal English instruction. More profoundly, it means that the learning which occurs in the formal language classroom may be unlike the learning which occurs during immersion, such that early instruction does not necessarily have the advantage for ultimate performance that is held by early immersion. It should be noted, however, that the last conclusion may be limited by the relatively narrow age range for formal instruction found in our subjects: our subjects all began their English classes between the ages of 7 and 16, with most subjects beginning at ages 12–15. This conclusion may also be restricted to the type of formal instruction received in Chinese and Korean schools (and, of course, any other schools in which the instruction is similarly formal), and should be less true the more formal instruction approximates immersion in the United States. In any event, age of arrival in the United States appears to be the better measure of age of acquisition for the population we studied.

Experiential and Attitudinal Variables

Experiential variables.   Years of exposure in the United States was also a variable of interest in this study. First, careful attention was paid to balance the years of exposure between early and late learners. This was done in order to avoid the possibility that obtained age effects would be due to differences in years of exposure, rather than to true differences in age of exposure. That we were successful in controlling for years of exposure between the early and late learners is apparent from the lack of correlation between age of arrival and years in the U.S., $r = -.09$, $p > .05$.

Beyond controlling for this potential confound, it is also important to ask what effect years of exposure has on learning, independent of the age effects. It is known that number of years has some effect on subjects' competence during the initial stages of learning a second language (see, for example, Snow & Hoefnagel-Hohle, 1978). At an extreme, people who have been in a host country for 1½ years must perform better than those who have only been there half a year. The question here is, however, do people continue to improve over time through continued exposure to the language, or do they reach an asymptote after a certain number of years? To answer this question, a correlation coefficient was computed between years of exposure in the United States and test performance. The resulting correlation, $r = .16$, is not significant, $p > .05$ (see also Table 4). This is in agreement with other studies, (Oyama, 1978; Patkowski, 1980), also showing no significant effect of the number of years of exposure on language performance for learners beyond the first few years of exposure.

In addition to years of exposure, Table 4 also presents other variables which we considered possible experiential correlates with ultimate performance, such as amount of initial exposure to English, classroom experience, and attitude. Most of these variables were computed from information provided by the subjects; amount of initial exposure (measured as the percentage of time English was used during the first year or two in the United States) and motivation to learn in English classes (rated 1 to 5) were estimates provided by the subjects. None of the correlations are significant.

**TABLE 4.   Correlation Coefficients of Experiential Variables
with Score**

Interview Variable	Correlation w/Score
Length of exposure (years in the U.S.)	.16
Amount of initial exposure (first year or two in U.S.)	.03
Age of English classes[a]	−.33
Years of English classes[a]	.25
Motivation to learn in classes[a]	.05

[a] Correlations for late learners only; measure not applicable to other subjects.

Regarding amount of initial exposure, the mean percentage for the group is 51.4%, with a standard deviation of 20.2%. Unless subjects' estimates are inaccurate, it appears that ultimate performance is not sensitive to fairly large differences in amount of initial exposure to the language, at least not after the subjects have been immersed in the language for a number of years.

The classroom variables include the age at which the subjects began English classes in their native country (already discussed in the previous section), the number of years they took English classes, and their ratings of how motivated they were to learn English in the classroom. Again, none of these variables correlate significantly with performance. It may be of interest for future research, however, that age of starting English classes is the highest of the (nonsignificant) experiential correlations. This may suggest some benefit of early classroom exposure, if classroom exposure occurred earlier than in the population we studied, and particularly if the classroom were more like immersion.

Attitudinal variables.   Some investigators (see Krashen, 1982, and Schumann, 1975, for reviews) have suggested that age effects are secondary by-products of changes in people's level of self-consciousness, in their cultural identification, and in their motivation to learn a second language well, rather than maturational changes in learning. To address this claim, correlation and regression analyses were performed. Table 5 presents correlations of such attitudinal variables with test score as well as with age of arrival. These variables were measured by asking subjects to rate themselves according to the questions presented at the bottom of Table 5.

The correlations show a strong relationship between these attitudinal variables and both test score and age of arrival. Higher ratings of American identification and increased measures of motivation were associated with better performance in English and with younger age of arrival, while higher ratings of self-consciousness were associated with poorer performance and with later age of arrival. Both of these sets of results would be predicted by a theory which attempted to explain age differences in language learning as a function

TABLE 5. Correlation Coefficients of Attitudinal Variables with Test Score and Age of Arrival

Attitudinal Variables	Test Score	Age of Arrival
Identification	.63**	−.55**
Self-consciousness	−.36*	.19
Motivation	.39**	−.48**

* p < .05.
** p < .01.
Questions:
1. How strongly would you say you identify with the American culture? (subjects reply) If 5 means you strongly identify with the American culture, that is, you feel like a complete American, and 1 means not at all, how would you rate your identification?
2. Did you feel self-conscious while learning English in the United States? (Most often an explanation was needed here.) How would you rate that on a scale from 1 to 5, where 5 is very self-conscious and 1 is not at all?
3. Motivation is a composite of two questions: (a) Is it important to you to be able to speak English well? (subject's reply) On a scale of 1 to 5, where 5 means very important and 1 means not at all, how would you rate it? (b) Do you plan on staying in the United States? The composite was formed by adding one point to their importance rating if they planned on staying in the United States, and by subtracting one point if they did not.

of maturation. The other possibility is, of course, the reverse; the attitudinal variables may have obtained their correlations with test score as a result of the correlation with age of arrival. Thus it becomes a question as to which is the better measure: age of arrival or attitudinal variables?

It is clear that age of arrival is the better measure over any of the attitudinal variables considered alone. The correlation between age of arrival and test score (r = −.77) surpasses the correlation between any of the attitudinal variables and test score. Furthermore, the attitudinal variables are more adversely affected when age of arrival is parcelled out than is age of arrival when each of the attitudinal variables is partialled out, as shown in Table 6. This is in complete agreement with Oyama's (1978) results.

TABLE 6. Partial Correlations of Age of Arrival and Attitudinal Variables with Test Score

	Attitudinal Variables w/Age of Arrival Removed	Age of Arrival w/Attitudinal Variables Removed
Identification	.39*	−.65**
Self-consciousness	−.34*	−.76**
Motivation	−.04	−.72**

* p < .05.
** p < .01.

As stated earlier, however, the most powerful evidence against this alternative hypothesis is to show that age of arrival can account for variance not accounted for by the attitudinal variables combined. To test this, a regression analysis was performed using the three attitudinal variables together, which resulted in a regression coefficient of .47. This was compared to the .69 regression coefficient obtained with the three attitudinal variables plus age of arrival. The contribution made by age of arrival is statistically significant $F(1,41) = 28.1$, $p < .01$. This shows that, independent of any possible attitudinal effects, age of arrival has an effect on learning a second language.

Of independent interest is whether the attitudinal variables can account for any of the variance not accounted for by age of arrival. Even though it is clear that age of exposure to a language is an important variable for predicting ultimate performance, other variables may contribute to this as well. Unlike previous studies (e.g., Oyama, 1978), we did find added predictive value with two attitudinal variables: self-consciousness and American identification. Each of the two makes a significant contribution to a regression model including only age of arrival ($F(1,43) = 5.6$, $p < .05$., for self-consciousness, and $F(1,43) = 7.5$, $p < .05$., for identification), as well as a significant contribution to a regression model including age of arrival and the other attitudinal variable ($F(1,42) = 5.0$, $p < .05$, for the addition of self-consciousness to age plus identification, and $F(1,42) = 6.9$, $p < .05$., for the addition of identification to age plus self-consciousness). Motivation, whether analyzed separately or in conjunction with the other two variables, failed to add significantly to the regression coefficient. Thus it appears at first glance that a model of second language learning would have to include both age effects and the effects of self-consciousness and identification, though not the effects of motivation. Such a model might argue, for example, that while age of arrival affects language learning, so does the self-consciousness and the cultural identification of the learner.

At this time one might, however, be cautious about inferring a direct causal link between self-consciousness and cultural identification to language learning, until this result is corroborated in future studies. Not only are the effects of self-consciousness and cultural identification not supported in other studies, but also possible mediating variables have not been ruled out. For example, language performance may be correlated with subjects' evaluation of their performance, which may in turn affect how self-conscious they are and how much they identify with the host country. Thus poorer learners may, as a result of their performance problems, become more self-conscious and identify less with the United States. In this account, greater self-consciousness and less identification would be the result rather than the cause of the performance problems. In any case, apart from whether attitudinal variables do or do not play a role, there is a clear independent effect of age of arrival on ultimate performance.

Age of Acquisition and Rule Type

The results show a striking effect of age of acquisition on performance in our test of English syntax and morphology. It is of interest to know what particular areas of the grammar create the most and least problems for second language learners. Are the errors random, with an even dispersal across rule type, or do late learners err more frequently on a particular type of rule? To answer this question, an analysis was performed on age of learning in relation to the differing types of rules evaluated on the test. This analysis used only the ungrammatical items, since it is only the ungrammatical items which can be said to be testing any particular rule type. That is, when a subject marks a grammatical sentence as ungrammatical, it is unclear what part of the sentence, or grammar, (s)he is having problems with. In contrast, when a subject marks an ungrammatical sentence as grammatical, (s)he must have failed to represent just that structure under test as a native speaker would. For purposes of this analysis, the age groups were the same as those used previously, except that the late learner group was further divided into two groups, (17-24) and (25-39), with an approximately equal number of subjects in each. This was done to reach a more nearly equal number of subjects in each of the age of learning groups. A two-way analysis of variance was performed, using the 12 rule types (outlined in the methods section above) and six ages of acquisition.

The results of the anova showed a significant effect of rule type $F(11,693) = 53.2$, $p < .01$, a significant effect of age of acquisition, $F(5,63) = 32.3$, $p < .01$, and an interaction between rule type and age of acquisition, $F(55,693) = 8.3$, $p < .01$. The age effect here is simply a reproduction of the finding that early learners perform better than the late learners; apparently there is no reduction of this effect when scoring only the ungrammatical test items. The effect of rule type shows that subjects made more errors on certain rule types than on others. Finally, the interaction appears mainly to be the result of late learners making proportionately more errors on some rules types, and proportionately fewer on others. Thus, many of the late learners' errors do not appear to be random; rather, there are particular parts of the grammar that seem more difficult.

The pattern of errors for each age group across the 12 rule types can be seen in Fig. 3. In Fig. 3, rule types are ordered along the x-axis in decreasing order of difficulty for late learners.[7] As can be seen, determiners and plural morphology appear to be the most difficult for the two latest groups of learners, with scores significantly worse than chance for determiners ($t = 3.35$, $p < .01$), and no different from chance for plurals ($t = .16$, $p > .05$). While all of the remaining rule types receive scores significantly better than chance (t ranges from 3.46 to 26.1, $p < .01$), they vary widely in level of performance. Most

---

[7] This ranking of rule type difficulty remains the same when using other criteria, for example, ordering rule type according to the number of subjects who score almost perfectly on that rule (that is, 0 or 1 item wrong, out of 6 to 16 possible, depending on the rule type).

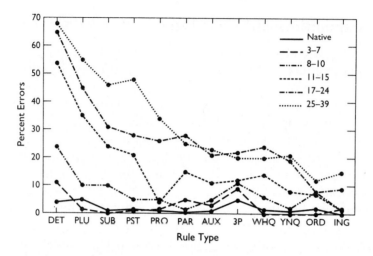

FIGURE 3.   Mean Percentage of Errors on 12 Types of English Rules

notably, basic word order rules and the present progressive are giving very few problems, with most subjects getting virtually all of the items of these types correct.[8]

Why are subjects performing better on some rule types and worse on others? One uninteresting possibility is that the items testing some rule types are inherently easier than those testing other rule types, since in some cases different rules are tested by quite different sentential variations. On the other hand, it is clear that this is not the whole account of our effects. Rule types tested in very similar ways on our test (e.g., the various rule types involving morphology) did not show similar degrees of difficulty for late learners, suggesting that these rule type effects are not due to the difficulty of the format by which we tested the rules.

A second possibility is that the subjects suffered from phonological difficulties which made the items for that rule type difficult to process. Again, although we cannot definitely eliminate this possibility, we do not believe it is the whole account of the rule type effects. Rule types with exactly the same phonological form (e.g., plural and third person singular, both -s) did not show similar degrees of difficulty for late learners. Also, rule types testing forms which were phonologically more substantial and therefore easier to hear (e.g., rule types with whole words reversed or eliminated) were not necessarily easier for late learners than those that involved smaller phonological units.

---

[8] Some other rule type scores also benefited from subjects' apparent ease with basic word order rules. For example, those items testing yes/no question formation by presenting questions in a V-N-N order (e.g., "Learns Jane math from Mr. Thompson?") were particularly easy for subjects. This pattern fit in with a general tendency for V-first items to be easily judged ungrammatical.

A third possibility is that subjects suffered from interference from the nature of their first language (Chinese or Korean), and so should show special difficulty with rule types most different from the first language. Once again this did not appear to be the full account of our effects. Rule types equally absent from Chinese and Korean (e.g., past tense and present progressive) did not show similar degrees of difficulty for late learners.

Most important, our rule type ordering corresponds in certain striking ways to the order of difficulty obtained in studies of second language learners from other first language backgrounds, as well as in studies of the isolated girl Genie. In particular, the relative ease of word order and the present progressive show up in all of these studies. We believe, then, that the rule type effects we obtained are at least in part reflections of what is generally difficult or easy for a late learner. We will return to this issue in the Discussion section below.

One final question involved the relationship between age of arrival and each of the individual rule types. Given that late learners' competence varies over rule types, it is of interest to know whether age of arrival predicts performance on only certain selected rules of the second language. The data show, however, that this is not the case. Table 7 presents the correlations between age of arrival and the scores on each of the 12 rule types. Despite late learners' proficiency on some rule types, all of the rule types showed significant correlations with age of arrival. This result shows that age of exposure to the language

TABLE 7. Correlation Coefficients between Age of Arrival and Rule Type[a]

Rule Type	Correlations
Determiners	.64**
Plural	.75**
Subcategorization	.53**
Past tense	.79**
Pronouns	.73**
Particles	.44**
Auxiliaries	.45**
Third person singular	.29*
Wh-questions	.39**
Yes/no questions	.50**
Word order	.48**
Present progressive	.32*

[a] These correlations, unlike others with age of arrival, are positive correlations, since they relate age of arrival to number of errors.

 * $p < .05$.

 ** $p < .01$.

affects all of the structures we examined, despite variations across rule types in the absolute level of performance late learners achieved.

Discussion

This study was designed to answer certain empirical questions about critical period effects in second language learning, and thereby to clarify and refine theoretical proposals regarding a critical period for language acquisition more generally. We will begin our discussion by reviewing the empirical findings, and then turn to the general theoretical issues.

The Basic Empirical Findings

Age of acquisition and ultimate performance.   The first question we asked was whether there was a relation between age of acquisition and ultimate performance in the grammar of a second language. The results of this study clearly show such a relation, and therefore support the notion that children have an advantage over adults in acquiring a second language. The overall correlation between age of arrival in the United States and performance on our test of English grammar was -.77; and, for those subjects arriving in the United States before puberty, this correlation was -.87. Indeed, there was a significant correlation between age of arrival and performance on every type of syntactic and morphological rule we tested.

These findings are in accord with the results of the previous studies which have tested asymptotic performance, despite the fact that these studies used very different measures of English proficiency. (Oyama, 1978, measured number of words detected through white noise; Patkowski, 1980, measured syntactic ratings of production). The present study enhances the previous studies' findings by providing a much more detailed examination of English syntax and morphology. The three studies, however, complement each other well, for each emphasizes a different aspect of language use. Oyama's study, for example, taps some aspect of on-line processing in comprehension, Patkowski's measures free production, and in our study we presume to be measuring underlying grammatical competence via sentence judgments. Because these studies complement each other, the compatibility of the results is all the more impressive. Together they provide a strong case for the conclusion that children are indeed better than adults in their ultimate attainment in a second language.

The effects of age of acquisition before vs. after puberty.   The second question we asked concerned the shape of the relationship between age of acquisition and ultimate performance. Due to the large range of ages in the learners we tested, and our division of the early learners into small age groups, we are able to make a fairly good generalization about the shape of this relationship. Subjects who arrived in the United States before the age of seven reached native performance on the test. For arrivals after that age, there was a linear decline in performance up through puberty. Subjects who arrived in the United States after puberty performed on the average much more poorly than those who arrived earlier. After puberty, however, performance did not continue to decline with increasing age. Instead, the late arrival group, while performing on the whole more poorly than the younger arrivals, distinguished itself by having marked individual differences in performance, something which was not found in the earlier arrivals.

The pattern of this relationship supports a maturational account of the age effects found. It does this by the fact that the age effect is present during a time of ongoing biological and cognitive maturation and absent after maturation is complete (i.e., at puberty). Thus it appears as if language learning ability slowly declines as the human matures and plateaus at a low level after puberty. The precise level of this plateau differs between individuals.

Again, these findings are in line with previous studies, although no previous study has asked this question in detail. Both Oyama (1978) and Patkowski (1980) reported only overall correlation and grouped means, with groupings which were larger and slightly different from our own and with a more limited range of ages of acquisition than our own. Both studies found the general linear decline of performance with age of acquisition that we found, but the groupings of their subjects make it difficult to tell whether the precise ages at which we found changes in the function are supported by their results as well. In addition, in a study of age of acquisition in relation to first (rather than second) language acquisition, Newport and Supalla (1987; Newport, 1984) found a linear decline in ultimate performance over three age groups: subjects exposed to American Sign Language from birth vs. at age 4–6 vs. after age 12.[9] In short, the surrounding literature on both first and second language acquisition appears to be generally consistent with the more detailed results obtained in the present study.

Experiential and attitudinal variables.   The third question we asked was whether the effects of age of acquisition could be due to experiential or attitudinal variables coincidentally related to age, rather than to maturational changes in language learning. Our results suggest that entirely nonmaturational explanations for the age effects would be difficult to support. Certainly the attitudinal variables (motivation, American identification, and self-consciousness) were unable to explain away the age effects, in accord with

---

[9] One discrepancy between the Newport and Supalla results for first language acquisition and the present results for second language acquisition is in the level of performance attained by subjects who began learning the language between the ages of 3 and 7. In the Newport and Supalla data, the 4-6 age group performed consistently, although not always significantly, below natives. In the present study, the 3-7 age group was entirely within native performance. This difference will be discussed below, in the section entitled "The age at which a decline in performance is first detected."

Oyama's (1978) study. This held true in the present data even when all three variables together were pitted against age.

It is also doubtful that the age effects are the result of differences in the amount of English exposure between the younger and older arrivals. This is true for several reasons. First, the younger arrivals did not differ significantly, if at all, from the adult arrivals in the amount of English they were exposed to during learning (see the Method section for description of the subjects' experiential characteristics). Second, the nonsignificant correlation between amount of initial exposure and performance suggests that second language learning is not particularly sensitive to differences in the amount of exposure, at least when that exposure has occurred over a number of years and is fairly high in the first place.

Some researchers have claimed that there are differences in the quality of the exposure that adults and children receive, rather than in the mere quantity, and that this difference may account for the age differences found in language learning success. According to this view, children receive the ideal type of input for successful language learning, while adults do not. Many have said, for example, that children receive "simple," reduced input which refers to concrete objects, existing in the here and now. Adults, on the other hand, are exposed to syntactically more complex input which most often refers to abstract concepts and events that are displaced in space and time. The simple concrete input of the child is thought to be helpful for language acquisition, while the complex input of the adult is thought to interfere with language acquisition (Dulay, Burt, & Krashen, 1982).

Both the empirical and theoretical assumptions underlying this approach have been disputed. First, the assumption that language is easier to learn from limited simple input has been questioned (Gleitman, Newport, & Gleitman, 1984; Wexler & Culicover, 1980). Second, the empirical evidence for this claim has also been brought into question. Freed (1980) performed a study which compared the type of input given to adult and child language learners and found that adults and children actually receive comparable input in terms of syntactic complexity (as measured by the number of clause boundaries). Interestingly, however, the adult-directed input contained a more limited range of constructions than the child-directed input. Adults received input which tended to maintain the canonical shape of a sentence, while children received sentences with more deformations. Thus in terms of transformational complexity, adults received the simpler input. From this it would be just as reasonable to argue that adults learn less well because their input is not as complex and varied as the child's. In any case, the role of input in second language learning needs to be better formulated before we can decide whether children have any advantage in learning a language due to the type of input they receive.

Age of acquisition and rule type.   The fourth question we asked concerned the nature of the effects of age on the attained grammar of the second language. Our results suggested that, although there was an effect of age of acquisition on every rule type we examined, some rules of English grammar were more profoundly affected by age of acquisition than others. In particular, knowledge of the basic word order of the language was acquired by all of our subjects, regardless of their age of learning. Similarly, knowledge of the present progressive (-ing) was acquired by all of our subjects. These areas of competence likewise appear in other studies of second language learning (see Krashen, 1982, for a review of the order of morpheme difficulty in second language learning). Perhaps even more striking, they are the only two aspects of English which were successfully acquired by Genie, who was exposed to English as a first language only after puberty (Curtiss, 1977; Goldin-Meadow, 1978). In contrast, other aspects of English syntax and morphology gave late learners much more difficulty.

We believe that these rule type results are at least in part reflections of universal factors in learnability, and not merely the result of item difficulty or transfer from the first language. Newport, Gleitman, and Gleitman (1977; Gleitman, Newport, & Gleitman, 1984) and Goldin-Meadow (1978) have suggested that basic word order is a highly resilient property of languages, appearing in the acquisition of a first language under widely varying conditions of both input and age of exposure. The present results on the acquisition of a second language under varying conditions of age of exposure are in accord with these claims. However, accounting for why word order and -ing are partially easy for learners remains for future research.

Before turning to a more general discussion of critical period hypotheses in language learning, we must consider whether the set of results we have obtained will be replicable on other second language learning groups or whether they are confined in any way to the particular second language learners (Chinese and Koreans) we have studied.

Possible effects of the first language on second language learning. We have thus far presented our results as though the findings were generalizable to second language learning, regardless of the nature of the first language or the relationship between the grammar of the first language and that of the second language. Indeed we believe this is the case, although we also recognize that certain aspects of the structure of one's first language are likely to have some effects on the learning of the second language (see, for example, Hakuta & Cancino, 1977, and Zehler, 1982, for a review of transfer effects in second language learning). Here we wish to raise two points of relevance to the question of whether our results are limited in any way to the Chinese and Korean speakers we studied.

First, we do not believe that the relationship found here between age of exposure and ultimate performance in the second language is unique to the circumstances where Chinese or Korean is the first language and English is the second. We did purposely choose to concentrate on first and second languages where the grammars were sufficiently different that a significant second language learning problem would arise. Chinese and Korean are relatively more isolating languages than English and have syntaxes which are different in many ways from that of English. However, studies currently underway, as well as certain details of our present results, suggest that the basic findings do not depend on these particular language combinations.

Several studies in progress (Johnson & Newport, in press) examine performance on our test by subjects with a wide variety of first languages. It is too early to say from these data whether there is any effect of the nature of the first language (we expect that there might be); however, it is already clear that the strong correlation between age of arrival and test performance replicates with subjects from these other first-language backgrounds.

In addition, the detailed results of the present study suggest that the nature of the first language cannot fully explain the difficulties of the second language learner. The examination of performance on the 12 rule types reveals relationships to age of arrival on every structure we examined, regardless of how similar or different these structures were to ones in the first language. For example, determiners and plural inflection, which gave late learners their most serious difficulties on our test, are notably lacking in Chinese and Korean; but so are inflections for the present progressive, on which late learners performed exceptionally well. A more detailed understanding of which of our effects, if any, may arise from first language characteristics should emerge from our studies in progress.

Second, we do not believe that our results derive in any important way from the input or cultural circumstances which characterize Chinese and Korean speakers. The Chinese and Korean speakers we tested were perhaps unusual, compared with many second language learners of English, in that they often continued close associations with other speakers of their first language. One might wonder, therefore, whether their exposure to English or their maintenance of their first language somehow influenced their second language. Again, this is an empirical question which is best resolved by the results of our studies in progress, which include many speakers isolated from their first language group as well as speakers of first languages with large communities. Within the present study, all of our subjects (both early and late learners) continued speaking their first language with their families and others into adulthood, and all were exposed to English from native English speakers. In addition, all had a significant amount of exposure to English, since they were all active members of an English-speaking community (that is, American schools and universities). These factors therefore could not be responsible for the differences we found between early and late learners of English. Whether these factors have an additional effect on learning, beyond the effect of age of exposure, was not the focus of our study, although some of our results do bear on this question.

In sum, we believe that in other language groups the strong effects of age of acquisition may be accompanied by effects of input, first language typology, or other variables that do not appear in our data on Chinese and Korean learners. Most importantly, however, we have reason to expect, on the basis of our data, that these effects of age of acquisition will persist.

Theoretical Conclusions for a Critical Period Hypothesis in Language Acquisition

The present study was performed primarily for the purpose of understanding the nature of the critical period for language acquisition. In particular, we wanted first to discover whether the critical period occurs at all in second language acquisition or whether it is exclusively a first-language phenomenon. To delineate this distinction we began by presenting two possible versions of a critical period hypothesis. They are repeated here for convenience.

Version One: The exercise hypothesis.   Early in life, humans have a superior capacity for acquiring languages. If the capacity is not exercised during this time, it will disappear or decline with maturation. If the capacity is exercised, however, further language learning abilities will remain intact throughout life.

Version Two: The maturational state hypothesis.   Early in life, humans have a superior capacity for acquiring languages. This capacity disappears or declines with maturation.

To reiterate the differences between these two versions, the exercise hypothesis only requires that a first language be acquired during childhood; as long as this occurs, the capacity for successful language learning will remain intact. Thus it predicts no differences between child and adult learners, due to maturation itself, in the ability to acquire a second language to native proficiency. In contrast, the maturational state hypothesis says that any language, be it first or second, must be acquired during childhood in order for that language to develop fully. Our results support the maturational state hypothesis, and not the exercise hypothesis. Human beings appear to have a special capacity for acquiring language in childhood, regardless of whether the language is their first or second.

The maturational state hypothesis is, however, not itself an explanation of critical period phenomena in language; rather, it merely outlines a class of explanations which would be compatible with our results (namely, those which posit maturational changes in general language learning abilities). In order to approach a more precise theoretical account of the phenomena, our study has also provided additional information which should aid in understanding the nature of the critical period: namely, information about the shape of the function relating age of acquisition and ultimate performance. Our results provide three sets of facts which any theory regarding critical period would have to account for: the gradual decline of performance, the age at which a decline in performance is first detected, and the nature of adult performance.

The gradual decline of performance.   Lenneberg's original proposal of a critical period in language acquisition seemed to predict a rectangular function in the relationship between age of acquisition and ultimate performance. That is, Lenneberg hypothesized that "normal" language learning was possible during the period from infancy to puberty, with a loss of abilities after puberty. However, the data on second language learning in the present study did not have this shape. We did not find a flat relationship between performance and age of learning throughout childhood, with a sudden drop in performance marking the end of the critical period; instead, performance gradually declined from about age seven on, until adulthood. Insofar as such data are available from other studies of first and second language acquisition, the same linear trend seems to appear (Newport, 1984; Newport & Supalla, 1987; Oyama, 1978; Patkowski, 1980).

Although this gradual decline is not in accord with Lenneberg's implied function, it is in accord with results from other behavioral domains in which critical periods have been hypothesized. As research accumulates on critical period, whether it be on imprinting in ducks (Hess, 1973), socialization in dogs (Scott, 1978), or song learning in birds (Kroodsma, 1981), it is becoming apparent that most, if not all, critical periods conform to the more gradual function. This point has recently been noted by several investigators (Immelman & Suomi, 1981; Tanner, 1970).

> . . . usually these periods consist of . . . beginning and end parts . . . [during] which the organism is slightly sensitive to the specific influence, with a period of maximum sensitivity in the middle. It is not as a rule an all-or-none phenomenon. (Tanner, 1970, p. 131).

Whatever mechanisms underlie a critical period effect in language learning, then, must be compatible with this gradual decline of performance over age.

The age at which a decline in performance is first detected.   Lenneberg's proposal also seemed to imply that a decline in performance should first appear at puberty. Instead of puberty, we found a small but significant decline in performance in subjects who had arrived in the United States as early as age 8 to 10. Indeed, the only discrepancy we know of between our results and other data is that, in first language acquisition, this decline may occur even earlier (Newport, 1984; Newport & Supalla, 1987); in the Newport and Supalla data, a 4–6 age group scored consistently, although not always significantly, below native performance. It is possible that a similarly early decline may occur in second language acquisition as well on a test that included more complex aspects of syntax than our own; on our present test, the age 3–7 group scored at ceiling.

Further research is therefore necessary to determine with certainty the exact point at which a decline in learning begins for second language acquisition. It is clear from the present data, however, that this decline begins well before puberty. It also appears that this early decline is small, and that another more major change occurs around puberty. Proposed mechanisms underlying a critical period effect in language learning must therefore account for the details of timing of these changes and, particularly, for the fact that the decline in learning ability begins earlier than initially thought by most researchers.

The nature of adult performance. There are two aspects of adult performance with which any theoretical account of the critical period must be compatible. The first is that language does not become totally unlearnable during adulthood. This has held true in all of the studies which have tested age differences in asymptotic performance, including both first and second language learning. In the present study, late learners scored significantly above chance on all of the rule types tested except for determiners and plurals. It appears to be the case, then, that quite a few aspects of language are learnable to a fair degree at any age, even though deficiencies in this learning occur.

The second aspect of adult performance with which any theory must be compatible is the great variability found among individuals. For adult learners, age does not continue to be a predictor of performance; thus any proposed mechanisms accounting for adult performance likewise cannot be correlated with age. Moreover, while early learners are uniformly successful in acquiring their language to a high degree of proficiency, later learners show much greater individual variation (see also Patkowski, 1980, for related comments). A theoretical account of critical period effects in language learning must therefore consider whether the skills underlying children's uniformly superior performance are similar to those used by adult learners, or rather whether adult language learning skill is controlled by a different set of variables.

Final remarks on a critical period theory of language acquisition. In sum, we now have a number of findings which should be accounted for in any explanation of a critical period. There is the nature of the relationship between age of arrival and performance: a linear decline in performance up through puberty and a subsequent lack of linearity and great variability after puberty. There is also the pattern of errors found for the wide range of aspects of syntax and morphology of English studied: age effects were found for every rule type, and low levels of performance on every rule type except word order and present progressive. The primary and most general finding to accommodate for any critical period theory, of course, is that the critical period is not just a first language phenomenon, but extends to a second language as well.

These findings rule out certain types of accounts of a critical period for language acquisition and make other types of accounts more plausible. We have suggested that our results are more naturally accommodated by some type of maturational account, in which there is a gradual decline in language learning skills over the period of ongoing maturational growth and a stabilization of language learning skills at a low but variable level of performance at the final mature state. This leaves open, however, the precise explanation of such a phenomenon. The traditional view of critical period effects in language learning has been that there is maturational change in a specific language acquisition device (Chomsky, 1981; Lenneberg, 1967). Such a view, with some modifications to incorporate the detailed points of maturational change, is consistent with our results. Also consistent with our results are views which hypothesize more general cognitive changes over maturation (see, for example, Newport, 1984). From this view, an increase in certain cognitive abilities may, paradoxically, make language learning more difficult. We are hopeful that future research will provide more detailed results which may differentiate these views from one another. In any event, the present study makes clear that some type of critical period account for language acquisition is necessary and that the proper account of a critical period will include both first and second language in its effects.

Acknowledgment

This research was supported in part by NIH Grant NS16878 to E. Newport and T. Supalla, and by NIH Training Grant HD07205 to the University of Illinois. We are grateful to Geoff Coulter, Henry Gleitman, and all of the members of our research group for discussion of the issues raised here, to Lloyd Humphreys for advice on statistical matters, to Marcia Linebarger for the loan of test materials, and to Carol Dweck, John Flavell, Dedre Gentner, Doug Medin, and two anonymous reviewers for helpful comments on earlier drafts of this paper.

References

Asher, J., & Garcia, R. (1969). The optimal age to learn a foreign language. *Modern Language Journal, 53,* 334–341.

Asher, J., & Price, B. (1967). The learning strategy of total physical response: Some age differences. *Child Development, 38,* 1219–1227.

Chomsky, N. (1981). *Lectures on government and binding.* Dordrecht, Netherlands: Foris.

Curtiss, S. (1977). *Genie: A psycholinguistic study of a modern day "wild child."* New York: Academic Press.

Dulay, H., Burt, M., & Krashen, S. (1982). *Language two.* New York: Oxford University Press.

Freed, B. (1980). Talking to foreigners versus talking to children: Similarities and differences. In R. Scarcella and S. Krashen (Eds.), *Research in second language acquisition*. Rowley, MA: Newbury House.

Gleitman, L. R., Newport, E. L., & Gleitman, H. (1984). The current status of the motherese hypothesis. *Journal of Child Language, 11,* 43–79.

Goldin-Meadow, S. (1978). A study in human capacities. *Science, 200,* 649–651.

Hakuta, K., & Cancino, H. (1977). Trends in second language acquisition research. *Harvard Educational Review, 47,* 294–316.

Hess, E. H. (1973). *Imprinting.* New York: Van Nostrand.

Hubel, D., & Weisel, T. (1963). Receptive fields of cells in striate cortex of very young, visually inexperienced kittens. *Journal of Neurophysiology, 26,* 994–1002.

Immelmann, K., & Suomi, S. J. (1981). Sensitive phases in development. In K. Immelmann, G. W. Barlow, L. Petrinovich, & M. Main (Eds.), *Behavioral development: The Bielefeld interdisciplinary project.* Cambridge: Cambridge University Press.

Krashen, S. (1975). The development of cerebral dominance and language learning: More new evidence. In D. Dato (Ed.), *Developmental psycholinguistics: Theory and applications: Georgetown round table on language and linguistics.* Washington, DC: Georgetown University.

Krashen, S. (1982). Accounting for child-adult differences in second language rate and attainment. In S. Krashen, R. Scarcella, & M. Long (Eds.), *Child-adult differences in second language acquisition.* Rowley, MA: Newbury House.

Krashen, S., Long, M., & Scarcella, R. (1982). Age, rate, and eventual attainment in second language acquisition. In S. Krashen, R. Scarcella, & M. Long (Eds.), *Child-adult differences in second language acquisition.* Rowley, MA: Newbury House.

Kroodsma, D. E. (1981). Ontogeny of bird song. In K. Immelmann, G. W. Barlow, L. Petrinovich, & M. Main (Eds.), *Behavioral development: The Bielefeld interdisciplinary project.* Cambridge: Cambridge University Press.

Lenneberg, E. (1967). *Biological foundations of language.* New York: Wiley.

Linebarger, M. C., Schwartz, M. F., & Saffran, E. M. (1983). Sensitivity to grammatical structure in so-called a grammatic asphasics. *Cognition, 13,* 361–392.

Newport, E. L. (1984). Constraints on learning: Studies in the acquisition of American Sign Language. *Papers and Reports on Child Language Development, 23,* 1–22.

Newport, E. L., Gleitman, H., & Gleitman, L. R. (1977). Mother, I'd rather do it myself: Some effects and noneffects of maternal speech style. In C. E. Snow & C. A. Ferguson (Eds.), *Talking to children: Language input and acquisition.* Cambridge: Cambridge University Press.

Newport, E. L., & Supalla, T. (1987) *A critical period effect in the acquisition of a primary language.* University of Illinois, manuscript under review.

Olson, L., & Samuels, S. (1973). The relationship between age and accuracy of foreign language pronunciation. *Journal of Educational Research, 66,* 263–267.

Oyama, S. (1976). A sensitive period for the acquisition of a nonnative phonological system. *Journal of Psycholinguistic Research, 5,* 261–285.

Oyama, S. (1978). The sensitive period and comprehension of speech. *Working Papers on Bilingualism, 16,* 1–17.

Patkowski, M. (1980). The sensitive period for the acquisition of syntax in a second language. *Language Learning, 30,* 449–472.

Schumann, J. (1975). Affective factors and the problem of age in second language acquisition. *Language Learning, 2,* 209–235.

Scott, J. P. (1978). Critical periods for the development of social behavior in dogs. In J. P. Scott (Ed.), *Critical periods.* Stroudsburg, PA: Dowden, Hutchinson, & Ross.

Scott, J. P. (1980). The domestic dog: A case of multiple identities. In M. A. Roy (Ed.), *Species identity and attachment: A phylogentic evaluation.* New York: Garland STPM Press.

Seliger, H., Krashen, S., & Ladefoged, P. (1975). Maturational constraints in the acquisition of a nativelike accent in second language learning. *Language Sciences, 36,* 20–22.

Snow, C. (1983). Age differences in second language acquisition: Research findings and folk psychology. In K. Bailey, M. Long, and S. Peck (Eds.), *Second language acquisition studies.* Rowley MA: Newbury House.

Snow, C., & Hoefnagel-Hohle, M. (1977). Age differences in pronunciation of foreign sounds. *Language and Speech, 20,* 357–365.

Snow, C., & Hoefnagel-Hohle, M. (1978). The critical period for language acquisition: Evidence from second language learning. *Child Development, 49,* 1114–1128.

Tanner, J. M. (1970). Physical growth. In P. H. Mussen (Ed.), *Carmichael's manual of child psychology.* New York: Wiley.

Wexler, K., & Culicover, P. (1980). *Formal principles of language acquisition.* Cambridge, MA: The MIT Press.

Zehler, A. M. (1982). *The reflection of first language-derived experience in second language acquisition.* Unpublished doctoral dissertation. University of Illinois.

Understanding the Article

1. In the literature review, what evidence do the authors cite that supports the notion that there is a critical period for first language acquisition?

2. In your own words, explain the two different ways of defining the term *critical period.* What is the difference between them? Which version of the critical period hypothesis does this study support?

3. Describe the study: Who were the subjects? What data were used in the study? How were these data collected?

4. Years of exposure to English is one of the variables of interest to the researchers. List the other variables they wanted to consider.

5. Reading the tables and figures:

   a. Figure 1 provides a graphic view of the relationship between age of arrival and mean (average) score on the test of English grammar. What information from Table 3 is not included in Figure 1? In your own words, what does Figure 1 show?

   b. What does dividing the subjects into two rather than four groups (Figure 2) reveal?

   c. Tables 4, 5, and 6 depict the correlations (relationships) between experiential variables, attitudinal variables, age of arrival, and test scores. In your own words, explain what each of these tables tells us.

   d. In your own words, from looking at Table 7, what can we conclude about the relationship between the age of acquisition and subjects' scores on the various rule types tested?

6. Look back at the research questions stated at the end of the introductory section. Briefly, what were the answers to these questions?

Reflecting on Wider Issues

1. How do the researchers explain the apparent contradiction between studies that seem to show that adults have the advantage in SLA and others that appear to demonstrate that children have the advantage?

2. Some researchers argue that instead of a *critical period* for SLA we should talk about a *sensitive period.* To what extent does this study lend support to one or the other of these two concepts?

Going Beyond the Article

For an excellent article summarizing and critiquing the research on critical/sensitive periods for language acquisition, read Long (1990), "Maturational constraints on language development" (*Studies in Second Language Acquisition, 12*, 251–285). You might also want to look at Johnson's 1992 article "Critical period effects in second language acquisition: The effect of written versus auditory materials on the assessment of grammatical competence" (*Language Learning, 42*, 217–248).

UNIT III

COGNITIVE STYLES AND STRATEGIES

5

THE COGNITIVE STYLES OF REFLECTION/IMPULSIVITY AND FIELD INDEPENDENCE/DEPENDENCE AND ESL SUCCESS

Joan Jamieson
Northern Arizona University

Previewing the Article

The cognitive styles of second language learners clearly affect the pathways that learners will take in successfully or unsuccessfully reaching their goals. Field independence has been of interest in the profession for quite some time, as Joan Jamieson notes in her article. Reflection/impulsivity has been less studied, however, and so the author is breaking some new ground here in this study.

Before you start a careful reading of the article, make sure you understand what cognitive styles are (*PLLT*, Chapter 5) and especially what their limitations may be. Then, scan the article to find the answers to the following questions:

1. How are reflection/impulsivity and field independence/dependence defined?

Reprinted from *Modern Language Journal,* 76:491–501, 1992.

> 2. What is the purpose of the study?
>
> 3. What are the research questions identified in the procedures section?
>
> 4. What kind of statistical analysis will be used to draw conclusions?

"Reflection/Impulsivity" may sound unfamiliar, but both teachers and theorists have had experience with this construct. Teachers know that some students are slow and accurate workers, while others work too fast, making many mistakes. Second language acquisition (SLA) theory proposes that good guessers are good learners (Rubin, 1975; Stern, 1974), but essentially this proposal is an intuitive hypothesis, lacking empirical investigation. This article attempts to help rectify that lack.

Characteristics of the learner are considered to play a role in SLA variation (Duda & Riley, 1990; Gardner, 1985). Work in this area has been grouped as the "good language learner studies." These studies ask the question: Since intelligence is not the factor that determines successful language learning, what other factor (or, more precisely, what group of factors) explains individuals' language learning abilities?

This question has led some researchers to concentrate on the characteristics of successful or unsuccessful language learners. Characteristics of the learner that are unchangeable (age, sex, native language) or predispositions (motivation, attitude, anxiety, tolerance of ambiguity, and cognitive style) have all been examined in varying degrees. The focus of this study is narrowed to one characteristic—cognitive style—and finally, narrowed even further to only two cognitive styles, Reflection/Impulsivity and Field Independence/Dependence. Field Independence/Dependence has received greater attention in language learning research than has Reflection/Impulsivity.

What is the role of the cognitive style of Reflection/Impulsivity when adults are learning English as a second language? I believe that Reflection/Impulsivity will provide a method for classifying successful and unsuccessful language learners within a construct that is easy to understand and easy to work with in instructional settings. This is theoretically and empirically important because it will provide construct-related evidence validating a model of SLA that includes cognitive style as a source of individual variation. Pragmatically, understanding the predisposition of language learners in terms of cognitive style could provide a basis for materials development both for the classroom and computer lab—training in strategies to adapt performances, altering natural tendencies (Brown, 1989; Oxford, 1990; Rubin & Thompson, 1982).

Reflection/Impulsivity and Field Independence/Dependence

The study of the cognitive styles of interest began in the 1940's in an effort to understand individual difference in terms other than intelligence. Initial work on Reflection/Impulsivity (R/I) and Field Independence/Dependence (FI/D) was carried out simultaneously (Sperry, 1972). Ehrman and Oxford traced the dimensions of FI/D and R/I to the tradition of ego psychology and efforts to learn about autonomous ego functions and cognitive controls; they suggest that these two cognitive styles may be different measures of one construct.

R/I describes the disposition to reflect on the solution to a problem where several alternatives are possible and there is high uncertainty over which is correct (see Kagan, Rossman, Day, Albert, and Phillips (1964) for the initial development of R/I). As Kagan (1966) explained, the "impulsives" reach decisions and report them very quickly with little concern for accuracy. Others, of equal intelligence, are more concerned with accuracy and consequently take more time to reach a decision. These are "reflectives."

The construct of R/I has been operationalized in terms of response time and errors on a visual recall task—the Matching Familiar Figures Test (MFFT). A double median split for time and errors results in a 2x2 matrix. The four cells are slow-accurate (reflective), fast-inaccurate (impulsive), slow-inaccurate (inefficient), and fast-accurate (efficient). It is this last category, the fast-accurate, that seems to depict the "good guesser." However, because two-thirds of the subjects usually fall in the reflective/impulsive cells, the subjects in the fast-accurate and slow-inaccurate cells have been less frequently studied (Abraham, 1983; Block, Block, & Harrington, 1974; Doron, 1973; Jamieson & Chapelle, 1987; Joffe, 1987; Meredith, 1978; Messer, 1976; Paulson & Arizmendi, 1982; Salkind & Wright, 1977). I believe that the fast-accurate students will be better language learners than both reflectives and impulsives, who are lacking speed and accuracy, respectively. Although this sounds like common sense, there is no empirical evidence to support this claim.

The cognitive style Field Independence/Dependence (FI/D) has been defined as ". . . the extent to which a person perceives part of a field as discrete from the surrounding field as a whole, rather than embedded. . . . Or, to put it into everyday terms, the extent to which a person perceives analytically" (Witkin, Moore, Goodenough, & Cox, 1977, p. 7). Throughout its development, FI/D has been operationalized by a number of measures; today the Embedded Figures Test (EFT) is widely used. A Field Independent (FI) person may be described as relying on an internal orientation, whereas a Field Dependent (FD) person relies on an external orientation.

Witkin, Moore, Goodenough, and Cox investigated the differences between FI/D subjects and reported several correlates to this style. Specifically,

FD subjects learn material with social content better than FI subjects. FDs are more positively influenced by their teachers. FDs perform better on structured tasks than unstructured tasks. FDs are distracted by nonsalient cues. On the other hand, FIs impose structure on unstructured material. FIs do better without teacher interference. FIs learn better with intrinsic motivation, depending upon themselves rather than someone else. Finally, FIs approach problem solving situations analytically.

In recent years, the cognitive style of FI has been theorized as being related to L2 acquisition. The two extremes of this cognitive style can be expected to do well in different types of situations. The FD person, for example, is considered to have an interpersonal orientation (Hansen & Stansfield, 1981). Moreover, FD individuals are thought to be socially oriented and would be apt to converse and communicate (Brown, 1987). Thus, the FD person might do well in L2 acquisition when acquiring the language by interfacing with native speakers (Krashen, 1977). The other cognitive style, FI, is thought to be independent and attendant to details. Hansen and Stansfield depict FIs as those who rely on internal frames of reference, as self-reliant types. Thus, the analytical FI person might be good at language learning activities such as finding patterns, organizing data to make generalizations, and learning rules (Krashen, 1977).

Several studies have examined the relationship between FI and L2 acquisition. Tucker, Hamayan, and Genesee attempted to define the constellation of factors associated with success in French as a second language in Canada. The subjects were English speaking high school students studying French. They reported that FI, along with French class anxiety and ethnocentrism, predicted success on a French achievement test. Seliger (1977) examined L2 acquisition in terms of the extreme ends of the FI continuum and reported a high correlation between success on a sentence disambiguation task and FI. Bialystok and Frohlich (1978) studied high school students learning French in Toronto. They found a significant, positive correlation between FI and reading, writing, and grammar tests; however, when FI was combined with other experimental factors, it was not a significant predictor of success. Naiman, Frohlich, Stern, and Todesco (1978) reported that FI predicted success on an imitation test. In another study, Hansen and Stansfield (1981) found FI to be related to three factors of L2 competence and thus related to better performance in a Spanish course. Abraham (1981) reported FI to be a significant predictor for performance on a fill-in-the-blank grammar test as well as composition for adult ESL students. Another study of adult ESL students by Chapelle and Roberts (1986) examined the relationships among a set of cognitive and affective variables and reported that FI was a significant predictor of success on the TOEFL, a multiple choice structure test, a dictation test, and on an oral communication test (for a more thorough discussion, see Chapelle, 1988). Carter (1988) directly addressed the hypothesis that FIs will perform better in linguistic achievement and FDs will perform better in functional communicative proficiency (in college level Spanish); her results indicate that FIs performed better than FDs in both areas.

In sum, evidence seems to indicate a positive relationship between FI and selected linguistic tasks. This is in sharp contrast to Ellis' (1986, p. 116) statement that FI/D "does not appear to be an important factor in SLA." Note that these tasks include discrete point tests such as sentence disambiguation and grammar, but also more integrative tests such as dictation, reading, writing, oral communication, and functional proficiency. In addition, many of the tasks are described as "achievement" tests—testing what has been taught in the language classroom. It must be noted that no such evidence exists for FD as a positive attribute for L2 success.

In terms of the relationship between FI/D and R/I, Kagan et al. (p. 35) concluded that "the data summarized indicate no strong relationship between field independence and reflection impulsivity." Messer (1976, pp. 1003–1034) reported a "consistent, moderate association may be due to the similarity of tests; however, both contribute independently to problem solving." Field Dependence/Independence and Reflection/Impulsivity are considered two distinct cognitive styles.

Procedure

The research design of this study was ex post facto. As a correlational study, it investigated the extent to which variation in one factor related to variation in another factor based on correlation coefficients and multiple regression (Isaac & Michael, 1982). All of the variables were continuous.

Sample.   The hypothetical population of this study was adult second language learners who were immersed in the target culture. The target population included those learners who were in an academically oriented intensive English program in the United States. An intact sample of forty-six students attending the University of Illinois from January to May 1985 was studied. The subjects represented sixteen countries: Chile, Colombia, Indonesia, Iran, Japan, Jordan, Jordan/Brazil, Korea, Lebanon, Mexico, Republic of China (Taiwan), Saudi Arabia, Syria, Thailand, Turkey, and Yemen. Threats to generalizability are due to the fact that eighteen of the subjects were males from Lebanon and that an intact sample was used.

Variables.   Reflection/Impulsivity was chosen as the major variable of interest because common sense seems to indicate its importance, but we lack empirical support. Field Independence/Dependence was included because it was the cognitive style most often reported to predict L2 success in other studies. It was of interest to determine the relation between R/I and FI/D as well as their respective relationships with ESL success.

Instrumentation and Scoring.   The adolescent/adult version of the Matching Familiar Figures Test (MFFT) first used by Yando and Kagan (1968)

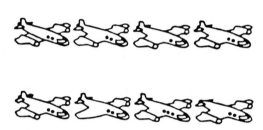

FIGURE 1.   Item from the Matching Familiar Figures Test (MFFT)

was chosen as the measure of R/I. The test was designed so that the subject saw two pages simultaneously. On one page was the standard; on the other page were eight variants, only one of which was exactly the same as the standard. An item from the MFFT is illustrated in Figure 1. The student's task was to match the single picture on one page with the only one on the other page that was exactly the same. The researcher told the student to point to the picture that was exactly the same as the standard. The researcher recorded the time it took for the student to make his/her first response and the total number of tries. There were twelve items.

Salkind and Wright's method of scoring was used to calculate two continuous variables. Impulsivity and Efficiency (I and E), both having positive negative values, as illustrated in Figure 2.[1]

The Group Embedded Figures Test (GEFT), developed by Witkin, Oltman, Raskin, and Karp (1971) was chosen as the measure of FI/D. This was a three section, pencil and paper test. The first section was for practice and was two minutes long. The second and third sections consisted of nine items each and were both five minutes long. The task was to outline a geometric figure which was embedded in a larger, more complex design. The score was the number of

---

[1] Salkind and Wright's (pp. 381–82) method of scoring was calculated. Impulsivity and efficiency scores (I and E, respectively) were generated from raw latency and error scores by the following formulas: $I = z_{ei} - z_{li}$, and $E = z_{ei} + z_{li}$ where I_i = impulsivity for the ith individual; E_i = efficiency for the ith individual; z_{ei} = a standard score for the ith individual's total errors; and z_{li} = a standard score for the ith individual's mean latency. Large positive I scores are indicative of impulsivity, and large negative I scores indicate reflectivity. High positive E scores indicate inefficiency and high negative E scores indicate efficiency.

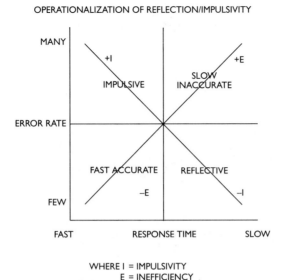

OPERATIONALIZATION OF REFLECTION/IMPULSIVITY

WHERE I = IMPULSIVITY
E = INEFFICIENCY

FIGURE 2.   Relationship between Impulsivity and Efficiency
Adapted from Salkind and Wright

correct answers, ranging from zero to eighteen. A high score indicated FI, a low score, FD.

The Test of English as a Foreign Language (TOEFL) was chosen as the measure of English proficiency. The TOEFL consists of three parts, all of which are multiple choice: a listening test, a grammar test, and a reading test. According to the TOEFL manual (ETS, 1983, pp. 7–8), the listening comprehension section measures the "ability to understand English as it is spoken in the United States." There are three subparts: choosing one statement that is closest in meaning to a statement heard; choosing an answer to a spoken question based on a dialogue between two speakers; and answering questions based on short talks, conversations, or presentations. The grammar section (structure and written expression) measures "mastery of important structural and grammatical points in standard written English." Its two subparts include selecting a word or phrase to complete a sentence, and identifying an unacceptable word or phrase. The reading comprehension and vocabulary section "tests the ability to understand the meanings and uses of words in written English as well as the ability to understand a variety of reading materials." Its two subparts include selecting a synonym of an underlined word in a sentence, and answering several questions that follow reading passages dealing mostly with main and supporting ideas.

The stated purpose of the TOEFL (ETS, 1983, p. 6) is to evaluate English proficiency of students whose native language is not English and who want to study at colleges and universities in the United States. Criterion-related evidence for validity of the TOEFL is provided in the test manual, where TOEFL scores were relatively highly correlated with essay tests, university English ratings, interviews, and GRE scores. Construct-related evidence is presented by the results that indicate the TOEFL is relatively easy for native speakers and that "the points tested represent basic features of English . . . indispensable for effective academic work at the undergraduate level" (p. 31).

Scoring was done by the Educational Testing Service in Princeton, New Jersey. Total and part scores were examined. Since the study was concerned with success in terms of improvement as well as proficiency, both beginning and end of semester TOEFL scores were collected (Linn & Slinde, 1977).

Administration.   The forty-six subjects were grouped into three classes at the University of Illinois during the Spring semester, 1985. They were required to take the TOEFL, which was administered to the entire group at the end of the second week of instruction. Cognitive style measures were administered two to three weeks later. First, the subjects took the Field Independence/Dependence test (GEFT) in one of their regularly scheduled English classes; absent students were later tested in the researcher's office. For the Reflection/Impulsivity test (MFFT), the subjects arranged to meet with the researcher for individual half-hour appointments. The TOEFL was administered again at the end of the semester.

Research Questions.   There were three research questions: (1) Were the I (impulsive) and E (inefficient) dimensions of Reflection/Impulsivity related to L2 success? (2) Are R/I and FI/D related to the degree that they can be considered two measures of the same construct? and (3) Were these two cognitive styles independently related to ESL success?

Analysis.   The analysis used the SPSS statistical software package (Nie, Hull, Jenkins, Steinbrenner, & Gent, 1975). First, descriptive statistics were computed. Next, reliability as a measure of internal consistency was computed for Reflection/Inpulsivity and Field Independence/Dependence. For R/I, there were forty-six subjects. Time to respond (mean response time) had a Spearman Brown reliability coefficient of .93. Number of errors had a Spearman Brown reliability coefficient of .51. These findings are in line with previous studies. Messer reports typical reliabilities for time to respond at .89 and numbers of errors at .52. This low reliability of errors will lead one to question an individual's consistency in performing the task from item to item. There were forty-three subjects for FI/D. The Spearman Brown reliability coefficient was .88. Witkin et al. (1971) reports Spearman Brown coefficients for the Embedded Figures Test ranging between .61 and .92. In a study using a sample similar to this study's, Roberts reported a Spearman Brown coefficient of .92. The next part of the analysis used Pearson-product moment correlations to examine the relationships between R/I, FI/D, and English proficiency. Finally, stepwise multiple regression analysis was done to determine whether R/I and FI/D were independent predictors of English proficiency and/or improvement.

Results

Descriptive Statistics.   This section presents and describes the data collected for each area in turn. Means and standard deviations of the variables which measured each construct will be followed by correlations of variables.

The dimension of Impulsivity was represented by I; a high I score signified an impulsive subject whereas a low score signified a reflective one. E represented Inefficiency; a high E score indicated an inefficient subject and a low E score indicated an efficient subject. Because of the standardization of the data, the means of I and E were 0 and the standard deviation of E was near one, while that of I was 1.7, as shown in Table 1.

TABLE 1.   Descriptive Statistics for the Whole Group on Cognitive Styles and TOEFL

| | | Statistic | |
MEASURE	*M*	*SD*	*N*
I	−.00	1.73	46
E	−.00	1.01	46
FI/D	12.47	4.74	43
TL1	43.89	6.15	45
TL2	46.56	4.69	45
TS1	41.22	8.25	45
TS2	44.76	8.87	45
TR1	40.58	8.26	45
TR2	43.11	7.17	45
TT1	419.49	69.91	45
TT2	448.02	62.02	45

Key
I = Impulsivity on Reflection/Impulsivity measure; standardized score
E = Inefficiency on Reflection/Impulsivity measure; standardized score
FI/D = Field Independence/Dependence raw score
TL1 = TOEFL Listening pretest score; TL2 = TOEFL Listening posttest score
TS1 = TOEFL Structure pretest score; TS2 = TOEFL Structure posttest score
TR1 = TOEFL Reading pretest score; TR2 = TOEFL Reading posttest score
TT1 = TOEFL Total pretest score; TT2 = TOEFL Total posttest score
N = 46. Three students did not take the FI/D measure; one student did not take the TOEFL pretest; one other did not take the posttest.

Field Independence (FI) was measured by the Group Embedded Figures Test (GEFT). A range of scores from zero to eighteen was possible. The students' scores ranged from two to eighteen. The number of subjects, means, and standard deviations are also in Table 1. The FI group mean of 12.47 and the standard deviation of 4.74 were similar to those of American male college students, 12.0 and 4.1 respectively, in Witkin et al. (1971).

The descriptive statistics for the TOEFL test are also in Table 1. The test had two scores, one given at the beginning of the semester and the other given at the end. Since scores were converted by the Educational Testing Service based upon item difficulty, it is difficult to state the limits of the scores. Basically the scales ranged from 200 to 800 for the total and twenty to eighty for the sections, although scores do not exceed sixty-eight for the sections nor 677 for the total (ETS, 1983). The scores were typical of an intensive English program in which students were preparing for study in an American college.

Correlations.   To answer questions concerning relationships between the variables tested, three sets of Pearson-product moment correlations were calculated: (1) correlations among cognitive styles; (2) correlations among language measures; and (3) correlations among cognitive styles and language measures. All correlations were significant at <.05, unless otherwise indicated.

The intercorrelations among the variables constituting R/I and FI/D are presented in Table 2. I and E are not related. The E dimension of R/I and FI correlate moderately significantly at -.36, which indicates that FI subjects are negatively related to inefficients and positively related to efficients.

TABLE 2.   Pearson-product Moment Correlations among Cognitive Style Variables

SCALE	I	E	FI
I	1.00	.00	−.14
E		1.00	−.36*
FI			1.00

Key
N = 43
I = Impulsivity on Reflection/Impulsivity
E = Inefficiency on Reflection/Impulsivity
FI = Field Independence on Field Independence/Dependence
*p < .05, one-tailed

The intercorrelations among the part and total TOEFL scores for the group are displayed in Table 3. All of the measures were strongly positively correlated.

Table 4 displays the correlations among the cognitive styles of Reflection/Impulsivity and Field Independence/Dependence, and TOEFL. Overall, only the inefficiency dimension (E) of Reflection/Implusivity was related to the TOEFL scores. I scores were totally unrelated to TOEFL scores, with most

TABLE 3.   Pearson-product Moment Correlations among Language Measures

SCALE	TLI	TSI	TRI	TTI	TL2	TS2	TR2	TT2
TLI	1.00	.76	.77	.90	.78	.64	.61	.74
TSI		1.00	.80	.93	.75	.85	.69	.86
TRI			1.00	.94	.69	.73	.71	.80
TTI				1.00	.80	.80	.73	.86
TL2					1.00	.65	.64	.81
TS2						1.00	.76	.93
TR2							1.00	.91
TT2								1.00

Key
TLI = TOEFL Listening pretest   TL2 = TOEFL Listening posttest
TSI = TOEFL Structure pretest   TS2 = TOEFL Structure posttest
TRI = TOEFL Reading pretest   TR2 = TOEFL Reading posttest
TTI = TOEFL Total pretest   TT2 = TOEFL Total posttest
N = 45. One student did not take the TOEFL pretest; one other did not take the posttest. All correlations significant <.05, one-tailed

TABLE 4.   Pearson-product Moment Correlations among Language Measures and Cognitive Styles

SCALE	I	E	FI
TLI	−.02	−.30*	.42*
TSI	.08	−.37*	.37*
TRI	.04	−.21	.39*
TTI	.04	−.32*	.42*
TL2	−.02	−.16	.39*
TS2	−.10	−.33*	.39*
TR2	.01	−.16	.44*
TT2	−.05	−.26*	.45*

Key
I = Impulsivity on Reflection/Impulsivity measure
E = Inefficiency on Reflection/Impulsivity measure
FI = Field Independence on Field Independence/Dependence
Dependence
TLI = TOEFL Listening pretest   TL2 = TOEFL Listening posttest
TSI = TOEFL Structure pretest   TS2 = TOEFL Structure posttest
TRI = TOEFL Reading pretest   TR2 = TOEFL Reading posttest
TTI = TOEFL Total pretest   TT2 = TOEFL Total posttest
N = 45 for I and E correlations; 43 for FI correlations
*p < .05

correlations close to 0; thus, Impulsives and Reflectives did not differ in their TOEFL scores. On the other hand, E scores were significantly moderately negatively related to most of the TOEFL part scores and to both of the totals. The negative correlations mean that those with low E scores (in other words, fast-accurate or efficient subjects) had high TOEFL scores. High TOEFL scores were also related to Field Independence (high GEFT scores) on all of the language measures.

Multiple Regression Analyses. The investigation of the relationship among R/I, FI/D, and ESL proficiency and/or improvement was at the heart of this study. When two or more variables showed significant correlation (such as both E and FI with TOEFL scores), the question naturally arose as to which was more important, or whether they were equally important. In order to clarify the relative contribution of these variables, a multiple regression analysis was done. Cognitive styles were regressed on language measures first to determine relationships with proficiency. Then, cognitive styles and pretest language measures were regressed on posttest language measures to determine relationships with improvement.

Table 5 illustrates the pattern evident in all analyses that investigated the relationship with proficiency. E (the inefficiency dimension of R/I) was a significant predictor of variance on the TOEFL listening pretest only when it was entered into the equation on the first step. For the TOEFL scores that were correlated with both E and FI, when FI was entered first, it accounted for all of the shared variance, and rendered E insignificant. The significance of FI in both structure tests was less strong, though still significant. In general, the r^2 change for FI was between .15 to .20 on the TOEFL scores. In terms of predicting high

TABLE 5.   Example of Cognitive Styles Regressed on Language Measures

Language Measure	Step	Variable Entered	r^2	r^2 Change	B	t
TLI	1	E	.10	.10*	−.19	−1.26
	2	FI	.21	.11*	36	2.36*
	1	FI	.18	.18*	.36	2.36*
	2	E	.21	.03	−.19	−1.2

Key

N = 42

TLI = TOEFL Listening Pretest

E = Inefficiency on Reflection/Impulsivity

FI = Field Independence on Field Independence/Dependence

B = slope

t = Student's t

*p < .05

scores on the TOEFL then, Field Independence was the more important cognitive style; Reflection/Impulsivity contributed almost no information not already contained in FI.

Finally, the two cognitive styles and pretest TOEFL scores were regressed on posttest TOEFL scores in order to determine which was more important for improvement, Field Independence or Reflection/Impulsivity. Neither FI nor R/I were significant predictors of improvement based on any of the four language measures.

Discussion

To summarize the salient features of the analysis at this point, several findings are of interest. In terms of the relationships among cognitive styles and language measures, the results were what was expected. Field Independence was moderately related to a high score for all of the language measures. In terms of Reflection/Impulsivity, an Efficient worker (a fast-accurate subject—the hypothesized "good guesser") was moderately related to a good performer on the language measures. Also, there was a moderate negative correlation between FI and E. Even though Field Independence and E were interrelated, as well as both being related to the language measures, a regression analysis showed that FI was the more important contributor to proficiency.

The first research question asked whether there were differences between the dimensions of Reflection/Impulsivity and ESL success. This question can be answered "yes" since a fast-accurate (good guesser) was positively related to TOEFL proficiency. Interestingly, Reflection and Impulsivity were neither positively nor negatively related to language proficiency. Some might propose that these two dimensions cancel each other out on a timed test where reflectives answer fewer questions but get more of them right, and impulsives answer many more questions but make more errors; however, the TOEFL is scored by the number of questions answered correctly in each part, which should favor reflectives. These findings support the claim, reported above, that fast-accurates are better language learners than both reflectives and impulsives.

Whether Field Independence and Reflection/Impulsivity were simply two measures of the same construct was asked in the second research question. Although there is some degree of overlap in the two cognitive styles, in general it is reasonable to conclude that Field Independence and Reflection/Impulsivity are independent cognitive styles. First, no significant correlation was uncovered between FI and I. In other words, no relationship was found between either fast-inaccurate performance on the MFFT (Impulsivity) or slow-accurate performance (Reflection) and Field Independence. Therefore, the prior finding that Reflectives are significantly more Field Independent than Impulsives (Messer, 1976) is not supported in this study; although the correlation was negative, it was neither strong nor significant. Secondly, there was only a moderate correlation between E and FI (-.36), which accounts for eighteen percent of the shared variance. This negative relationship indicates that Field Independence is negatively related to slow-inaccurate performance and conversely, positively related to fast-accurate performance. This relationship, while significant, is moderate in strength and in line with previous studies (Messer, 1976).

Were these two cognitive styles independent contributors to L2 success? This was the third and final research question of this study. L2 success can be defined in two ways: proficiency or improvement over a semester. It was operationalized as the subparts of the TOEFL test (listening, structure, and reading) and the total score on pre- and posttest administrations. Although Field Independence was positively related to proficiency in English as a second language, it was not predictive of improvement over the course of a semester.

In terms of proficiency, no relation was found between any of the language measures and I (reflectives and impulsives). In terms of the other dimension, E, the slow-inaccurates (inefficients) are at the positive end of the continuum and the fast-accurates (efficients) are at the negative end. All of the correlations between E and the language measures were negative, indicating that the fast-accurates did well on the two administrations of the TOEFL. Field Independence was significantly positively related to all of the language measures. It must be noted that when Field Independence was entered into the regression equations before E, E was rendered insignificant. In other words, Field Independence accounted for everything that Reflection/Impulsivity did, and more, on all of the individual language tasks.

Finally, neither R/I nor Field Independence were predictive of L2 improvement over the course of a semester. This might be due to the effects of multicollinearity in which two independent variables, FI and the pretests, were correlated (FI had positive correlations of .42, .37, .39, and .42 with TL1, TS1, TR1, and TT1, respectively) so that the inclusion of the pretest first in the equation accounted for all of FI's contribution. Another explanation might be found in the TOEFL scores themselves. In general, the r^2 value for the pretest on the posttest ranged from .50 to .74, not leaving much variance to be accounted for, requiring at least a .6 correlation coefficient for significance.

Implications

Overall, this study provides continuing evidence for the positive relationship between Field Independence and English as a second language proficiency. Contrary to what had been expected, Field Independence/Dependence provided more information about ESL proficiency than did Reflection/Impulsivity.

What, then, is the role of Reflection/Impulsivity in learning ESL? This study has indicated that it might not be a fruitful line of continued inquiry; however, I intend to investigate this cognitive style further, seeking to confirm or refute my findings presented here. Work can be done in two areas, testing and teaching. The psychometric quality of the reliability of the MFFT can be improved by lengthening it to twenty items (Cairns & Cammock, 1989). A way to increase its practicality in terms of administration time would be to computerize the MFFT; this would have the added advantage of immediate scoring and results.

Reflection/Impulsivity has a common sense explanation that is intuitively appealing and provides practitioners with a means to diagnose and test slow or careless students (in terms of speed and accuracy). Studies have shown that Reflection/Impulsivity is a trait that carries beyond the test into the activities of school children in the classroom (Kagan, 1971) and while students interact with computerized lessons (Jamieson & Chapelle, 1987). Teachers can observe these traits in their classrooms and make students aware of their own behavior while encouraging them to delay or guess—both tangible tasks for students to work on.

Future studies should be alerted to a limitation of this study: the TOEFL was used as the only measure of English proficiency. It could be argued that better performance by Field Independent and Efficient students might be an artifact of test method, rather than evidence of association with language skill. Perhaps FI/D, the ability to perceive analytically, is associated with understanding language as a system, which is being tested by the test content and the test method of TOEFL. As measured by the TOEFL, the notion of English proficiency is by design limited in two ways: its setting is restricted to an academic environment, and it tests receptive rather than productive skills. The TOEFL is often criticized as a discrete point test reflecting a dated view of language proficiency, and indeed, reviews of the TOEFL from communicative competence perspectives have pointed out shortcomings particularly in context (both reduced and non-authentic) and sociolinguistic competence (Duran, Canale, Penfield, Stansfield, & Liskin-Gasparo, 1985; Stansfield, 1986). However, these same reviewers remind us that for its purpose in admission decisions at universities, the TOEFL performs well. Based on their conclusions, it seems reasonable to generalize the findings of this study beyond the TOEFL to the academic domains of reading and listening, and to infer that FI students are better in these areas of English proficiency than their FD counterparts.

In order to get a clear perspective on the interaction between cognitive styles and second language learning, a variety of language tasks should be analyzed in relation to both Reflection/Impulsivity and Field Independence/Dependence. For example, tests of pragmatic competence focusing on illocutionary or sociolinguistic skills (Bachman, 1990) might reveal a very different pattern of relationships since they might best elicit the social strengths of the Field Dependent and impulsive students. In addition, Reflection/Impulsivity might be more associated with strategies—the learning activities—than with the product of language proficiency.

References

Abraham, R. (1981). The relationship of cognitive style to the use of grammatical rules by Spanish-speaking ESL students in editing written English. Doctoral dissertation, University of Illinois.

Abraham, R. (1983). Relationships between use of the strategy of monitoring and cognitive style. *Studies in Second Language Acquisitions, 6,* 17–32.

Bachman, L. (1990). *Fundamental considerations in language testing.* Oxford: Oxford Univ. Press.

Bialystok, E. & Frohlich, M. (1978). Variables of classroom achievement in second language learning. *Modern Language Journal, 32,* 327–336.

Block, J., Block, J., & Harrington, D. (1974). Some misgivings about the matching familiar figures test as a measure of reflection-impulsivity. *Developmental Psychology, 10,* 611–632.

Brown, H. D. (1987). *Principles of language learning and teaching.* Englewood Cliffs, NJ: Prentice-Hall.

Brown, H. D. (1989). *A practical guide to language learning.* New York: McGraw-Hill.

Cairns, E. & Cammock, T. (1989). The 20-item matching familiar figures test: Technical data. Unpublished manuscript, University of Ulster.

Carter, E. (1988). The relationship of field dependent/independent cognitive style to spanish language achievement and proficiency." *Modern Language Journal, 72,* 21–30.

Chapelle, C. (1988). Field independence: A source of language test bias? *Language Testing, 5,* 62–82.

Chapelle, C. & Roberts, C. (1986). Field independence and ambiguity tolerance as predictors of proficiency in English as a second language. *Language Learning, 36,* 27–45.

Doron, S. (1973). Reflection-impulsivity and their influence on reading for inference for adult students of ESL. Unpublished manuscript, University of Michigan.

Duda, R. & Riley, P. (Eds). (1990). *Learning styles.* France: Presses Universitaires de Nancy.

Duran, R., Canale, M., Penfield, J., Stansfield, C., & Liskin-Gasparro, J. (1985). *TOEFL from a communicative viewpoint on language proficiency: A working paper.* TOEFL Research Report 17. Princeton, NJ: ETS.

Educational Testing Service (1983). *TOEFL Test and Score Manual.* Princeton, NJ: ETS.

Ehrman, M., & Oxford, R. (1990). Adult language learning styles and strategies in an intensive training setting. *Modern Language Journal, 74,* 311–327.

Ellis, R. (1986). *Understanding second language acquisition.* Oxford: Oxford University Press.

Gardner, R. C. (1985). *Social psychology and second language Learning—The roles of attitudes and motivation.* London: Arnold.

Hansen, J., & Stansfield, C. (1981). The relationship of field dependent-independent cognitive styles to foreign language achievement. *Language Learning, 31,* 349–367.

Isaac, S., & Michael, W. (1982). *Handbook in research and evaluation.* San Diego.

Jamieson, J., & Chapelle, C. (1987). Working styles on computers as evidence for second language learning strategies. *Language Learning, 37,* 523–544.

Joffe, R. (1987). Reflection-impulsivity and field dependence-independence as factors in the reading achievement of children with reading difficulties. Doctoral dissertation, Temple University.

Kagan, J. (1966). Reflection-impulsivity: The generality and dynamics of conceptual tempo. *Journal of Abnormal Psychology, 71,* 359–365.

Kagan, J. (1971). *Change and continuity of infancy.* New York: Wiley.

Kagan, J., Rossman, B., Day, D., Albert, J., & Phillips, W. (1964). Information processing in the child: Significance of analytic and reflective attitudes. *Psychological Monographs, 78,* 1–37.

Krashen, S. (1977). The monitor model for adult second language performance. In M. Burt, H. Dulay, & M. Finocchiaro (Eds.), *Viewpoints on English as a second language* (pp. 152–161). New York: Regents.

Linn, R., & Slinde, J. (1977). The determination of the significance of change between pre- and posttesting periods. *Review of Educational Research, 47,* 121–150.

Meredith, R. A. (1978). Improved oral test scores through delayed response. *Modern Language Journal, 62,* 321–327.

Messer, S. (1976). Reflection-impulsivity: A review. *Pyschological Bulletin, 86,* 1026–1052.

Naiman, N., Frohlich, M., Stern, H. H., & Todesco, A. (1978). *The Good Language Learner.* Research in Education Series 7. Toronto: Ontario Institute for Studies in Education.

Nie, N., Hadlai Hull, C., Jenkins, J., Steinbrenner, K., & Bent, D. (1975). *SPSS statistical package for the social sciences.* New York: McGraw-Hill.

Oxford, R. (1990). *Language learning strategies—What every teacher should know.* New York: Newbury House.

Paulson, K., & Arizmendi, T. (1982). Matching familiar figures test norms based on IQ. *Perceptual and Motor Skills, 55,* 1022.

Roberts, C. (1983). Field independence as a predictor of second language learning for adult ESL learners in the U.S. Doctoral dissertation, University of Illinois.

Rubin, J. (1975). What the 'good language learner' can teach us. *TESOL Quarterly, 9,* 41–51.

Rubin, J. & Thompson, I. (1982). *How to be a more successful language learner.* Boston: Heinle.

Salkind, N., & Wright, J. (1977). The development of reflection-impulsivity and cognitive efficiency. *Human Development, 20,* 377–387.

Seliger, H. (1977). Does practice make perfect?: A study of interaction patterns and L2 competence. *Language Learning, 27,* 263–278.

Sperry, L. (1972). *Learning performances and individual differences.* Glenview, IL: Scott, Foresman.

Stansfield, C. (Ed.). (1986). *Toward communicative competence testing: proceedings of the Second TOEFL Invitational Conference,* TOEFL Research Report 21.

Stern, H. H. (1974). What can we learn from the good language learner? *Canadian Modern Language Review, 30,* 304–318.

Tucker, G. R., Hamayan, E., & Genesee, F. (1976). Affective, cognitive and social factors in second language acquisition. *Canadian Modern Language Review, 32,* 214–226.

Witkin, H., Moore, C. A., Goodenough, D., & Cox, P. W. (1977). Field-dependent and field-independent styles and their educational implication. *Review of Educational Research, 47,* 1–64.

Witkin, H., Oltman, P., Raskin, E., & Karp, S. (1971). *A manual for the embedded figures tests.* Palo Alto, CA: Consulting Psychologists.

Yando, R., & Kagan, J. (1968). The effect of teacher tempo on the child. *Child Development, 39,* 27–34.

Understanding the Article

1. What is the hypothesized relationship between the cognitive styles of Reflection/Impulsivity and Field Dependence/Independence and second language acquisition?

2. In the Procedures section, the author describes the subjects, the variables studied, and the tests used and how they were scored.

    a. Who were the subjects? Do we know how they were selected?

    b. Describe the test instrument used to measure Reflection/Impulsivity.

    c. Describe the test instrument used to measure Field Dependence/Independence.

    d. What was the purpose of administering the TOEFL to the subjects?

3. The Results section contains both the descriptive statistics (means and standard deviations) and the inferential statistics (correlations or relationships among the variables).

    a. What descriptive statistics are used and in which table(s) are they displayed? What inferential statistics are used? In your own words, explain the correlations or relationships that are shown in the tables.

   b. Which cognitive style was more important in predicting **beginning** TOEFL score? Which, if any, was more important in predicting **improvement** in TOEFL score?

4. Look back at the research questions identified in the Procedures section of the study. Are there specific answers to these questions in the Discussion section? If so, what are they?

5. What are the implications of the results for future research?

Reflecting on Wider Issues

1. Do the results of this study support the notion that an optimal cognitive style for a "good language learner" is not too extreme in either direction?

2. Explain why you would agree or disagree with the researcher's concern about the possible limitations of this study due to its reliance on the TOEFL as the only measure of language proficiency.

Going Beyond the Article

Research on Field Dependence/Independence is not without controversy. To get an idea of the different perspectives on whether on not FI/D is relevant to second language learning, you should read the following: Griffiths and Sheen (1992), "Disembedded figures in the landscape: A reappraisal of L2 research on field dependence/independence" (*Applied Linguistics, 13,* 133–48); Chapelle (1992), "Disembedding 'disembedded figures in the landscape': An appraisal of Griffiths and Sheen's 'Reappraisal of L2 research on field dependence/independence,'" (*Applied Linguistics, 13,* 376–384); and Sheen (1993), "A rebuttal to Chapelle's response to Griffiths and Sheen" (*Applied Linguistics, 14,* 98–100).

6

LISTENING COMPREHENSION STRATEGIES IN SECOND LANGUAGE ACQUISITION

J. Michael O'Malley, Anna Uhl Chamot,
Georgetown University
InterAmerica Research Associates

Lisa Küpper
Interstate Research Associates

Previewing the Article

One recent trend in language pedagogy that is rapidly gaining momentum is the incorporation of learner strategy training into classroom teaching methodology. Researchers have compiled considerable data on strategies that have enabled learners to be more successful in their second language learning process. This article by O'Malley, Chamot, and Küpper focuses specifically on strategies for successful acquisition of listening comprehension skills.

Before reading the article, do a little background review of "good language learner" research and of strategies employed by successful second language learners (see *PLLT,* Chapter 5). Also, if possible, think of the kinds of cognitive skills that good listeners employ. Then, scan the article to answer the following:

Reprinted from *Applied Linguistics, 10*:418–437, 1989.

1.   What is the purpose of the study?
2.   What are the research questions that the authors address?
3.   What kinds of data are gathered and how are they interpreted?

Listening comprehension is viewed theoretically as an active process in which individuals focus on selected aspects of aural input, construct meaning from passages, and relate what they hear to existing knowledge. This theoretical view has not been sufficiently supported by direct research which clarifies what listeners actually do while engaged in listening tasks. This study focused on the mental processes second language learners use in listening comprehension, the strategies they use in different phases of comprehension, and the differences in strategy use between students designated by their teachers as effective and ineffective listeners. The students in this study were all from Hispanic backgrounds, intermediate in English proficiency, and were enrolled in ESL classes at the secondary level. Data were collected using think-aloud procedures in which students were interrupted during a listening comprehension activity and asked to indicate what they were thinking. Findings indicated that mental processes students use in listening comprehension paralleled three theoretically-derived phases of the comprehension process: perceptual processing, parsing, and utilization. Each phase was characterized by active processing and by the use of learning strategies. Three predominant strategies which differentiated effective from ineffective listeners were self-monitoring, elaboration, and inferencing. The findings were related to implications for instructional practice.

Introduction

Listening comprehension has become the keystone of many theories of second language acquisition and instruction which focus on the beginning levels of second language proficiency (for example, Asher 1969; James, 1984; Krashen, Terrell, Ehrman, & Herzog, 1984; Winitz, 1978; Wipf, 1984). The principal assumption underlying these theories is that language acquisition is an implicit process in which linguistic rules are internalized by extensive exposure to authentic texts (Postovsky, 1974; Winitz, 1978) and particularly to comprehensible input that provides a modest challenge to the listener (Krashen, 1980). When applied to instructional settings, the assertion in these theories is that modified teacher input will enhance comprehension, and enhanced comprehension will in turn promote acquisition (Long, 1985). The focus in these discussions is exclusively on adaptations of teacher input to enhance comprehension rather than on the ways in which learners process the input. The learner's conscious processing is said to be de-emphasized during instruction because language acquisition is an implicit process (Brown, 1984). This exclusive focus on teacher behaviors is constrained by a failure to understand deliberate learner strategies for comprehending language texts, for processing new information, and for learning and retaining concepts related to academic language and content.

There has been little direct research that would clarify what listeners actually do while listening to oral texts in academic settings (Richards, 1983). This article will identify theoretically-derived components of listening comprehension that parallel conscious and strategic mental processes used by second language learners, and will illustrate the characteristics and variation in these components and strategies with the support of empirical data. The components of listening comprehension will be identified initially through an inspection of cognitive and second language acquisition theory, and further examined through interviews in which students of English as a second language (ESL) 'think aloud' or describe their thoughts while in the process of responding to a listening comprehension task. The language samples to which students listened were selected to represent the kind of academic language task that ESL students might typically encounter in content area classrooms. Student verbal reports while thinking aloud were examined to determine the types of and differences in processing strategies between students who had been designated by their teachers as effective or ineffective second language listeners. The article concludes with implications for theory, research, and practice.

Background

Components of Listening Comprehension

As a complement to the focus on what teachers can do to aid listening comprehension in instructional settings, there has been a parallel but apparently independent emphasis on what listeners do while comprehending. Listening to spoken language has been acknowledged in second language theory to consist of active and complex processes that determine the content and level of what is comprehended (Byrnes, 1984; Call, 1985; Howard, 1983; Richards, 1983). These processes use utterances as the basis for constructing meaning-based propositional representations that are identified initially in short-term memory and stored in long-term memory. Anderson (1983, 1985) differentiates comprehension into three interrelated and recursive processes: perceptual processing, parsing, and utilization. During a single listening event, the processes may flow one into the other, recycle, and may be modified based on what occurred in prior or subsequent processes. These three processes overlap with and are consistent with listening comprehension processes identified elsewhere (for example, Call, 1985; Clark & Clark, 1977; Howard, 1983).

In perceptual processing, attention is focused on the oral text and the sounds are retained in echoic memory (Loftus & Loftus, 1976; Neisser, 1967).

The essential characteristics of echoic memory are that capacity limitations prevent specific word sequences from being retained longer than a few seconds, and that new information to which the listener attends replaces the former information almost immediately. While the oral text is still in echoic memory, some initial analysis of the language code may begin (Howard, 1983), and encoding processes may convert some of the text to meaningful representations (Anderson, 1985). It seems likely that the same factors in perceptual processing that focus attention on oral text to the exclusion of other competing stimuli in the environment also focus attention selectively on certain key words or phrases that are important in the context, on pauses and acoustic emphases that may provide clues to segmentation and to meaning, or on contextual elements that may coincide with or support the interpretation of meaning such as the listener's goals, expectations about the speaker's intent, and the type of speech interaction involved (for example, a conversation or a lecture).

In the second listening comprehension process, parsing, words and messages are used to construct meaningful mental representations. The basic unit of listening comprehension is a *proposition*, which consists of a *relation* followed by an ordered list of *arguments* (Anderson, 1985; Kintsch, 1974). For example, in the statement:

I will give each student a blue test booklet.

the relations correspond to the verbs (give) and adjectives (blue), while the arguments correspond to the nouns (I, student, booklet), and the timing (will). While the proposition suggested here is relatively simple, propositional analysis recognizes that complex propositions may be differentiated into simpler propositions that can be recombined by the listener to generate new sentences whose essential meaning does not change. Thus, through parsing, a meaning-based representation of the original sequence of words can be retained in short-term memory; this representation is an abstraction of the original word sequences but can be used to recreate the original sequences or at least their intended meaning.

The size of the unit or segment (or 'chunk') of information processed will depend on the learner's knowledge of the language, general knowledge of the topic, and how the information is presented (Richards, 1983). The principal clue for segmentation in listening comprehension is meaning, which may be represented syntactically, semantically, phonologically, or by any combination of these (Anderson, 1983, 1985). Thus, an interplay between various kinds of knowledge about language is involved in segmentation, although semantic information in the text is more effective at reducing sentence response time than syntactic information (Byrnes, 1984). Second language listeners may have difficulty in understanding language spoken at typical conversational rates by native speakers if they are unfamiliar with the rules for segmentation, even though they may understand individual words when heard separately.

Findings from research with second language learners indicate that memory span for target language input is shorter than for native language input (Call, 1985). Complex texts may be especially difficult to understand in a second language because they require concatenation or combining of parsed segments during comprehension, thereby placing an additional burden on short-term memory which already may be loaded with unencoded elements of the new language.

The third process, utilization, consists of relating a mental representation of the text meaning to existing knowledge. Existing knowledge is stored in long-term memory in propositions of the type discussed above and in *schemata*, or interconnected networks of concepts. Connections between the new text meaning and existing knowledge occur through *spreading activation* in which knowledge in long-term memory is activated to the degree that it is related to the new meanings in short-term memory. As Faerch and Kasper (1986, p. 264) note, "Comprehension takes place when input and knowledge are matched against each other."

Listeners make use of two kinds of information to identify the meaning of propositions: real world knowledge, and linguistic knowledge (Richards, 1983). Real world knowledge is stored either in propositions or schemata. Listeners may augment existing propositions or schemata with new information instead of being required to build entirely new knowledge structures. The listener *elaborates* on the new information by using what is known or in some cases by connecting interrelated portions of the new text. The more additional processing one does that results in "related, or redundant propositions, the better will be memory for the material processed" (Reder, 1980, p. 7). In some cases existing knowledge is stored in terms of *scripts,* which are special schemata consisting of situation-specific knowledge about the goals, participants, and procedures in real-life situations, and in *story grammars,* which are special schemata representing the discourse organization of fables, stories, narratives, and so on. The advantages of these schemata are that they enable the listener to anticipate what will occur next, to predict conclusions, and to infer meaning where a portion of the text was incompletely understood. Listeners who make effective use of schematic knowledge can be said to use "top-down" processing because they are drawing upon information in memory or upon analysis of text meaning for comprehension.

Listeners who make use of linguistic knowledge are also using propositions and schemata in long-term memory but the information used consists of grammatical or syntactic rules. Listeners who interpret meaning based on the linguistic characteristics of the text are using "bottom-up" processing and are forced to determine the meaning of individual words and then aggregate upwards to larger units of meaning. This approach is problematic in that the sounds, segmentations, and linguistic markers are subject to interference from the first language (Byrnes, 1984). It should not be surprising, as was noted earlier, that sentence-level response time for syntactic processing is greater than for meaning-based processing.

Bialystok and Ryan (1985) proposed two orthogonal dimensions of cognitive skill which underlie linguistic knowledge: analyzed knowledge and cognitive control. The knowledge dimension extends from low to high analyzed knowledge on features such as units of speech, the relationships between forms and meanings, and awareness of syntax (Bialystok, 1986). The control dimension also varies along a continuum and involves the selection and coordination of information to solve a linguistic task. Control mechanisms select knowledge about form or meaning depending on the difficulty of the linguistic task (for example, conversation vs. reading a difficult text) and the time available to complete the task. With difficult tasks, the control function may require more highly analyzed linguistic knowledge for an adequate solution. However, individuals who are proficient at a linguistic task may perform these actions automatically and without awareness (Anderson, 1983, 1985). Bialystok's analysis of knowledge and control features has a stronger resemblance to bottom-up processing than to top-down processing.

Strategic Processing

As has been discussed, listeners engage in a variety of mental processes in an effort to comprehend information from oral texts. Yet there is rarely a perfect match between input and knowledge; gaps in comprehension occur and special efforts to deduce meaning or to facilitate new learning may be required, especially with second language learners (Færch & Kasper, 1986). Mental processes that are activated in order to understand new information that is ambiguous or to learn or retain new information are referred to as *learning strategies*. The defining features of learning strategies are that they are conscious and they are intended to enhance comprehension, learning, or retention (Rabinowitz & Chi, 1987; Weinstein and Mayer, 1986). The importance of analyses of strategic processing lies in three research-based conclusions: (1) the frequency and type of strategies used differentiates effective from ineffective learners, (2) strategic modes of processing can be trained, and (3) use of strategic processing can be shown to enhance learning (Derry & Murphy, 1986; O'Malley, Chamot, Stewner-Manzanares, Küpper, & Russo, 1985a; O'Malley, Chamot, Stewner-Manzanares, Russo, & Küpper, 1985b; Weinstein & Mayer, 1986). One additional finding of significance in the context of this discussion is that strategies for second language acquisition do not appear to differ from general strategies used with other skills such as reading and problem solving, although the specific applications may differ (O'Malley et al., 1985a).

Two types of learning strategies that second language learners regularly report using are metacognitive strategies and cognitive strategies (O'Malley et al., 1985a; Wenden & Rubin, 1987). Metacognitive strategies involved knowing about learning and controlling learning through planning, monitoring, and evaluating the learning activity. Monitoring has been described as a key process that distinguishes good learners from poor learners (Nisbet & Shucksmith, 1986). In listening comprehension, monitoring consists of maintaining awareness of the task demands and information content. Two metacognitive strategies that support monitoring are selective attention, or focusing on specific information anticipated in the message, and directed attention, or focusing more generally on the task demands and content. Metacognitive strategies are generally considered to be applicable across a variety of tasks, whereas cognitive strategies may be more tailored to specific learning activities. Cognitive strategies involve active manipulation of the learning task and include the following:

— rehearsal, repeating the names of objects or items that have been heard, or practicing a longer language sequence

— organization, or grouping information to be retained in ways that will enhance comprehension and retention

— elaboration, or relating new information to information that has previously been stored in memory, or interconnecting portions of the new text.

Elaboration is a particularly significant strategy because of the benefits for comprehension and retention that have been demonstrated with its use (for example, Reder, 1980; Weinstein & Mayer, 1986). Furthermore, elaborative strategies may be considered a superordinate category for other strategies such as inferencing, transfer, deduction, imagery, and summarization (O'Malley, Chamot, & Walker, 1987).

A third strategy category, social/affective strategies, is less often reported by second language learners (Chamot & O'Malley, 1987). These strategies entail cooperative learning, questioning for clarification, and affective control over learning experiences.

The distinctions among learning, communication, and production strategies are important in second language acquisition (Færch & Kasper, 1983; Tarone, 1981). Learning strategies are concerned with language acquisition, while production and communication strategies refer to language use. Production strategies are used to accomplish communication goals, and communication strategies are an adaptation resulting from the failure to realize a language production plan. Communication strategies therefore may be important in negotiating meaning between individuals (Tarone, 1981). These distinctions are dependent upon the intentions of an individual for learning in the target language or for language use.

Research Questions

While the conceptual view of listening comprehension presented earlier provides a reasonably well-formulated analysis of the listening process, questions remain concerning the ways in which second language listeners process information, and the specific learning strategies they use while listening to academic texts. The differentiation of listening comprehension into three phases, while consistent with other theoretical formulations, has not been analyzed empirically. The importance of conscious processing in second language acquisition has been questioned and should be analyzed to determine the precise nature of the processing which occurs, the degree to which the processing is automatic, and the extent to which the processing is related to the learning process (for example, McLaughlin, Rossman, & McLeod, 1983). The use of learning strategies with academic texts is particularly important in ESL because of the difficulties limited English proficient students encounter in mainstream academic areas such as science, math, and social studies. While general descriptions of mental processing during second language acquisition have been presented (for example, O'Malley et al., 1985a; Wenden & Rubin, 1987), these analyses have usually been based on retrospective analysis rather than concurrent analysis of an ongoing task.

The "think aloud" data collection technique to be used in this study has a number of strengths and some limitations. One of the strengths of concurrent analysis of an ongoing task, or thinking aloud, is that the mental processing in short-term memory, which is lost in retrospection, can be described and reported (Ericsson & Simon, 1980; Garner, 1984). Other advantages of this data collection technique are in providing information about the individual's approach to the task, their levels of decision making, and the factors which govern their decisions (Færch & Kasper, 1987). One limitation with respect to collecting data on learning strategies is that individuals may report only a limited range of strategies of which they are consciously aware at the moment for any particular task. A second is that the process of interrupting informants to report on their thoughts may change the nature of the thinking and precipitate strategic processing which otherwise might not occur. A third concern is whether or not the strategic processes involved in learning can be identified or if these simply reflect strategies underlying language use (Seliger, 1983). That is, in a study focusing on listening comprehension, are strategies for learning necessarily unconscious and, if they are unconscious, are they accessible? The view we prefer on this issue is expressed by Dechert, who noted that a cognitive theory based on memory organization, schemata, and spreading activation avoids an imposed dichotomy on conscious and unconscious mental processing and "enables us to better understand the processing of language in lexical search as revealed through concurrent think-aloud data" (1987, p.109).

The specific research questions this study addressed concern the comprehension processing of ESL students while listening to academic texts. The questions were as follows:

1. Can the listening comprehension processes of students be differentiated into phases such as perceptual processing, parsing, and utilization?

2. Can the learning strategies used in each phase of listening comprehension be clearly identified?

3. Are there differences in listening comprehension strategies between students designated as effective and ineffective listeners?

Methodology

Subjects

The participants in this study were 11 high school age students enrolled in ESL classes in two suburban public high schools in the northeastern United States. All students were classified by the school district at the intermediate level of English proficiency, which the district defined as limited proficiency in understanding and speaking English, and little or no skill in reading and writing English. All participants were from Spanish speaking countries in Central or South America.

Students were nominated for participation in the study by their ESL teachers, who also designated students as effective or ineffective listeners. Criteria for being an effective listener were determined in advance collectively by the teachers with assistance from the researchers and consisted of attentiveness in class, ability to follow directions without asking for clarification, ability and willingness to comprehend the general meaning of a difficult listening passage, ability to respond appropriately in a conversation, and ability and willingness to guess at the meaning of unfamiliar words and phrases. Application of these criteria resulted in the selection of eight effective and three ineffective listeners, although data are reported here only on the five effective listeners who attended successive sessions and the three ineffective listeners. The grade equivalent scores on a standardized reading test of functional vocabulary for the designated effective listeners were significantly greater than those for the ineffective listeners (Mann-Whitney U, $p < .05$). Analysis of the reading scores on a locally developed reading comprehension test were in the expected direction but yielded a value of U which only approached significance ($p < .08$).

Procedures

Students were pretrained on thinking aloud in an hour-long session consisting of three stages conducted entirely in Spanish and one stage using English materials. In each stage, small groups of two to four students were asked to describe what they were thinking as they worked on an activity. The activities for the three stages conducted in Spanish consisted of word associations, associations during writing, and associations during a board game in which students thought aloud as they responded to a multiple choice question in a subject area. In the game, points were given for the completeness of the student's think aloud as well as for the correct answer. In the English language activity, students were asked to listen to a taped passage in English which contained eight pauses. After each pause, students were asked to think aloud about how they had made sense of what they had heard: whether there were unfamiliar words, what they had not understood, how they had figured it out, and whether memories or images had occurred to them while they listened. Students had the option of thinking aloud in Spanish or in English. They were told that this phase of training was similar to what they would do in later sessions.

The data collection sessions were conducted individually and were tape recorded for later coding and analysis. Neither interviewers nor data coders were informed which students had been designated effective or ineffective listeners. The data collection sessions each lasted about one hour and were conducted at roughly two-week intervals.

Each data collection session consisted of three phases: a warm-up, transition, and verbal report. In the *warm-up* the interviewer asked general questions about the student's country of origin, length of residence in the United States, level of education in the native language, or other general questions appropriate for introductions in each session. In the *transition,* the interviewer presented a math or a logic problem to the student, asked the student to think aloud while working on the solution, and then asked the student to evaluate how completely what they had reported captured their actual thinking processes. In the *verbal report stage,* students were presented three listening activities per session selected from among the following types of activities: a history lecture, a science experiment, a science lecture, a short story, and taking dictation. Each listening passage typically contained several pauses during which the interviewer stopped the tape and asked the students to relate as much as they could about their thoughts while listening. Students were permitted to think aloud either in Spanish or in English; most students chose to think aloud in Spanish and make occasional remarks in English. The interviewer usually asked questions in Spanish. Probe questions were used when a student seemed uncertain how to proceed, such as "What are you thinking?," and "What didn't you understand?" At the completion of the think-aloud, the interviewer asked comprehension questions about the main idea of the passage or the meaning of specific terms.

Tape-recorded data were collected for three activities in each of three sessions for the effective listeners and in the first session for the ineffective listeners. After a preliminary screening of the tapes, interviews were transcribed for all tasks from session one, two tasks from session two, and two tasks from session three. The listening passages used in data analyses, which averaged about 150–175 words each, were on the following topics (numerals indicate the session and sequence):

1a. History lecture—the story of the American Indian Massasoit, his responsibility as Chief of the Wampanoag Tribe, the assistance he gave the English Pilgrims, and the peace treaty he signed with them.

1b. Dictation—a brief (84 word) narrative about life span expectations in 1900 and in current times.

1c. Business lecture—a lecture about bad decisions made by two businesses; a toothpaste manufacturer's attempt to sell their product in an area of the world where chewing betel nuts was considered prestigious; and the decision by American and British car manufacturers not to take over the Volkswagen factory as part of a deal for reparations from World War II.

2b. Science lecture—a story about a volcanic eruption in 1816 and the unusual climatic variations which resulted around the globe.

2c. Short story—"The baboon and the tortoise," a story of an attempted friendship and the misunderstanding which occurred.

3a. History lecture—the explorations of James Cook in the eighteenth century to the South Pacific and to Australia and Antarctica.

3c. Science lecture—a narrative about the inventor Edmund Halley as an astronomer, physicist, engineer, and underwater adventurer and particularly his invention of the diving bell and diving suit.

The verbatim transcripts were coded for the appearance and incidence of learning strategies. Two members of the research team who had worked on prior learning strategies studies coded two test transcripts and compared the results. With each test transcript the question marks and disagreements were resolved through discussion. For both test transcripts combined, the agreement rate was 47 out of 55 strategies identified (85 per cent). The remaining transcripts were then coded by one of the test transcript coders who was checked by the other coder on 12 of the 34 remaining transcripts, resulting in agreements on 478 out of 499 strategies coded (96 per cent), excluding uncertainties (7 per cent of the total in the 34 transcripts), which were coded through discussion. Once the coding had been completed, the frequency of different strategies was determined and representative examples of specific strategies were identified.

Results

The focus of analyses presented in this report is on qualitative examples of the strategies in order to provide evidence related to the research questions which have been identified. Student comments during think-aloud sessions were examined to determine the distinctions between different phases of listening comprehension, the types of strategies used in each phase, and the differences between strategy use for effective versus ineffective listeners. Prior to beginning the qualitative analyses, however, an initial statistical analysis was performed to determine whether effective and ineffective listeners differed significantly on any of the strategies. Analyses using a Mann-Whitney U test indicated that significant differences ($p < .05$) were found between effective and ineffective listeners on self-monitoring, or checking one's comprehension or production while it is taking place; elaboration, or relating new information to prior knowledge or to other ideas in the new information; and inferencing, or using information in a text to guess at meaning or to complete missing ideas. In the discussion of qualitative findings which follows, these strategies also emerge as playing an important role in assisting listening comprehension.

In the following sections, original remarks by students in Spanish have been translated (all translations were verified independently by a second person who was also fluent in Spanish). The presentation of results is differentiated into three sections related to the comprehension phases: perceptual processing, parsing, and utilization. The description of each phase contains information pertaining to the strategies used in that phase and the differences between effective and ineffective listeners.

Perceptual Processing

The three-stage theory of listening indicates that attentional factors during perceptual processing are fundamental for comprehension. Because attention is limited, however, individuals attending to an unfamiliar language can be expected to have difficulty in identifying and retaining important portions of the oral text. One factor that caused students to stop attending in the present study was the length of the listening task. Some students reported that they started thinking about or translating the first part of a passage, and then did not attend to the next part. However, effective listeners seemed to be aware when they stopped attending and to make an effort to redirect their attention to the task, as in these examples:

— (Student describes what she was thinking about when the maintenance man came into the room, how the noise prevented her from concentrating, and then that she heard something on the tape that redirected her attention.) "Then when she (the voice on the tape) said that, it was like I took more interest in understanding it. That's what I was thinking. I was telling myself just now that I should pay more attention."
— (Student puzzles over the meaning of an item.) "I kept thinking about what she (voice on the tape) had said before, and while she was ahead, I was behind. Then I said (to myself), forget it, and I went on ahead."

Thus, effective listeners became aware of their inattentiveness and consciously redirected their attention back to the task. In contrast, ineffective listeners reported that when they encountered an unknown word or phrase in a listening text, they usually just stopped listening and failed to be aware of their inattention or to try to redirect their attention to the oral text.

In some cases elaborations interfered with rather than assisted comprehension. If the text reminded students of something they knew well, they sometimes got so involved in recalling prior knowledge that their attention wandered from the listening task. Thus, elaborations could have a negative effect if the students did not carefully monitor their attention, as in this example:

> — "I was thinking about what I've studied before in social studies." (Student then elaborated on what she remembered of the topic.) "I didn't pay much attention because of thinking of all that." (But the student went on to say) "And then I started to pay attention and I concentrated on it" (the listening task).

Student attention was also affected by fatigue. The students had spent a full day in school, and many of the students had evening jobs which prevented them from going to bed early. Effective listeners nevertheless seemed to be able to monitor their attention lapses and redirect their attention to the text, especially if they were interested in the material.

Parsing

Listeners segment and parse portions of the oral text based on cues to meaning or on structural characteristics. The basis for chunking and the size of the segments can be expected to vary depending on the student's level of proficiency and whether they are effective or ineffective listeners. The following examples illustrate ways in which effective and ineffective listeners chunked units of meaning.

Effective Listeners

— Listening for intonation and pauses:

"I listened for whole sentences." (How big?) "One line long." (How do you know?) "Because when you are talking there is some punctuation that you have to stop a little bit and then keep going."

— Listening for phrases or sentences:

(Are you listening for exact words or phrases?) "No, for phrases. I put them together and then I figure it out more or less."

Ineffective Listeners

— Listening for each word:

"Well, first I listened to each word that she (the tape) was saying. I grasped it—but not really all of them."

(Do you listen for words, phrases, or the meaning?)

"Words."

— Listening for words and sentences:

"I concentrate on the most difficult words and also on the sentences."

In general, the effective listeners seemed to be listening for larger chunks, shifting their attention to individual words only when there was a breakdown in comprehension. With the second effective listener, there was evidence of concatenating segments to produce overall meaning. Ineffective listeners seemed to approach listening as a task primarily requiring comprehension on a word-by-word basis. Thus, the general approach of the more effective learners was to use top-down processing and to rely upon bottom-up processing only as needed. In contrast, the approach of less effective listeners was consistently a bottom-up strategy.

Students who were effective listeners inferred the meanings of new words that were important for comprehension of the oral text by using the context of the sentence or paragraph in which the unfamiliar word appeared. The following example shows an effective listener using semantic information to infer the meaning of the word "belly."

> — Text listened to: "Of course, the tortoise could not sit for a long time. Whenever he reached for the food, he fell flat on his belly and all the baboons laughed. They ate the delicious food and the tortoise got very little."

> — Student response: "That one ... (there's) a word there that I think that ... I imagine that it must mean 'carapace' (shell) or something like that of the tortoise. When she (voice on tape) said that he would fall on his carapace that he wanted to reach the fruit (sic) and would fall on his ... what was it?"

This student's ability to use inferencing as a strategy resulted in his parsing the sentence meaningfully, although not with the exact equivalent of the unfamiliar English word "belly." Another example of meaningful parsing occurred with his substitution of the word "fruit" for "food," which was not an unfamiliar word. It may be that the phrase "reached for the food" had the connotation of reaching up, as for fruit from a tree. This student, in common with other effective listeners, showed that he is adept at constructing meaningful sentences from the input he receives, even though the meaning may be slightly different from the actual text.

There were also instances in which direct parsing in English failed to be effective due to the difficulty of the text. In these instances, students invoked multiple strategies, as identified in parentheses for the first student below. The second student illustrates the use of inferencing with one or more unencoded words in short-term memory which may be defined later from additional contextual information. The third student illustrates the use of translation and the awareness of the complexities of using this as a strategy. And the fourth student illustrates the use of self-monitoring while attempting to use existing knowledge to parse the meaning of a phrase.

— (Regarding dictations) "But if the story is too difficult . . . I go on writing what I understand and the words that I don't know, I write them in Spanish (transfer). From there I go back again in the story to where the words are (contextualization). I underline them so I don't make a mistake, I look up their meanings if a dictionary is available (resourcing), and I write them on another piece of clean paper (note-taking). In order to do well . . . I revise it . . . to know if everything makes sense (self-evaluation) . . . because if it doesn't, they're going to laugh at me" (affective component).

— "I let it (what isn't understood) pass and I think about the rest, and if I can remember back, that is, I try to record (mentally) the word, but I go on with the lecture. Then I understand the rest afterwards, if I remember, I go back to the word. To see if I understand."

— "There are times that I hardly know what they (the words) mean but to translate them into Spanish then seems a bit difficult for me. When I understand them only in English, I stay like that."

— (The student had just listened to the segment of Massasoit which said, "The war lasted two years, and many Indians and English colonists were killed.") "I was thinking when, the first thing that she (the voice on the tape) read was about the war. It had lasted up to two years, but I wasn't sure what she said because she said, 'the war lasts?'. Since 'lasts' is the last thing, right? Then I got confused, and I was trying to think if it was 'to finish' or 'to endure.'"

Thus, in parsing the text they heard, students used a variety of strategies. Elaboration, self-monitoring, and inferencing appeared to be most useful in aiding comprehension. Translation was reported as a tool that was often problematic.

Utilization

In utilization, information attended to and parsed stimulates related concepts or prior information in long-term memory through spreading activation. Effective listeners either have more prior information available than ineffective listeners, have the information better organized, access the prior information more efficiently, or use the prior information more strategically to comprehend and recall new information (Rabinowitz & Chi, 1987). Listeners in this study appeared to make use of prior knowledge at two points; to assist comprehension and to assist recall.

When listeners call upon prior knowledge to assist comprehension, the way in which they use elaborations may depend on whether they are an effective or an ineffective listener. Analyses of listening comprehension transcripts indicated that effective listeners made use of elaborations in three major ways:

World knowledge   using world knowledge acquired either in an academic or a non-academic context:

—Academic elaboration:

(After listening to the introduction to a lecture about Halley's underwater inventions, the interviewer asks the student what she thought when she heard "Halley's Comet") "I imagined the comet." (Have you read something about the comet?) "That comet, no. Only when I was in school they taught us definitions of comets and about space."

(After listening to a lecture about Captain Cook's expeditions, the student had difficulty with the idea that the south could be cold.) "I was really confused, but then I remembered that in south—no, north pole and the south pole there is cold. And I said 'How is it going to be cold in the south pole?' But I remember that it can be."

—Non-academic elaboration:

(After listening to the description of Halley's underwater diving suit): It's like when they go to space and when they, the people, went to the moon and they are out in the moon, they put those things to get air . . .

Personal knowledge   relating the new information to something meaningful on a personal level, such as making a judgment about the information or relating it to a personal experience.

(Responding to the statement that the average life expectancy in North America has increased from 47 to 72 years): "I'm thinking that that's true because my grandmother is 83. (There are) many people that are older than 47. And it's true that today many people live (longer)."

Self-questioning   asking oneself questions about the material listened to, or anticipating possible extensions of the information.

(After hearing about the pipe on Halley's diving suit which carried air to the diver.) "How can you say, hum, 'pipes'"? For example, you can use the pipe to irrigate the flowers in the garden. What's the other word you say? (Interviewer: Hose)

Effective students tended to relate new information to prior knowledge in all three types of elaborations. They frequently related the new information to

their three types of elaborations. They frequently related the new information to their personal experiences and made critical judgments about the value of the information. In contrast, the ineffective listeners not only had fewer elaborations but also did not make connections between the new information and their own lives.

The familiarity of the information students listened to also had an effect on their ability to use prior knowledge. All students had difficulty comprehending a section of one lecture which mentioned World War II since few of them had prior knowledge about this period of history. The following example from an effective listener illustrates this difficulty:

> —Text listened to: "... At that time, Germany owed a lot of money as a result of the Second World War. The British and American (car) experts thought they might take over the Volkswagen factory. By taking over the manufacture of Volkswagens, they thought Germany could pay back some of the money she owed."

> —Student response: "On that bit I really did get lost ... like Germany is going to pay the United States. That the United States is ... and England owes it. Like ... ah! Now I understand. It was because of the Volkswagen. Since they are going to sell it over here, they make more money, and then with that money Volkswagen is going to pay back all that money they lost."

This student knows that the Volkswagen is a popular car that sells well and interprets the text as indicating that by exporting Volkswagens to the States, Germany will be able to get back all the money she lost. The concept of Germany's war debt or the fact that the British and American plan was to take over the Volkswagen factory escaped her altogether. However, rather than abandoning the text as ineffective listeners often did, this student used elaborations related to her own knowledge to create something that was personally meaningful if inaccurate.

Given the apparent influence of elaborations on initial comprehension, the elaborations would be expected to form the basis for schemata that would be useful later in recall. The data were examined to determine if elaborations formed while listening reemerged later during the interview on a recall task. The success students experience in doing this is mixed, as can be seen in the following two sets of examples. In the first set, the student is elaborating on the meaning of "salvage"; the second set of examples relate to how air was kept inside Halley's diving bell.

> —Initial elaboration: (After listening to lecture on Halley's inventions in which the word "salvage" is explained.) "It was about salvage, that people go into the water. You know, when a ship fight? And it goes down into the sea ... the people go and they can find whatever valuable things."

—Recall elaboration: (Student was asked what "salvage" meant, and to give an example of a salvage effort in the present time.) "I think salvage means to when the people drown? You know, they put the kids in a pool ... if somebody is drowning, that guy can go and help it. You know, like that airplane that splash into the ... that is ... that bridge that's here." (Referring to an airplane disaster in Washington, DC).

In the recall elaboration, this student apparently forgot that he had previously defined "salvage" correctly. The explanation in the second passage appears to be based on the Spanish cognate "salvar" (to save). Thus, having forgotten the text of the comprehension task, the student nevertheless used a different kind of elaboration to fill in other information from prior knowledge.

A second example contrasting an initial with a recall elaboration also shows the contribution of prior knowledge:

—Initial elaboration: (After listening to a description of Halley's diving bell) "His problem was how to keep the air inside the bell. He used ... uh ... he took some ... I don't know what they could be called ... some tubes full of air that prevented ... uh ... that he, each time that they went deeper, he opened the air valve ... so that the water would stay outside with the air inside."

—Recall elaboration: (One of the comprehension questions asked how Halley kept the diving bell full of air and free of water.) "Each time that he was going down, he would open the valve (so) that the water wouldn't come in and the air wouldn't go out."

The listening text on Halley did not mention a valve, but the student's stepfather was a diver, and she had a great deal of prior knowledge about diving, which she apparently superimposed on the listening task. Unlike the student in the first example, however, this student retained the elaboration she generated at the time of initial listening. This and other examples indicated that students either made assumptions about the text and did not verify them or supplied missing narrative by using personal knowledge at a later time. Whether or not initial elaborations are retained and are available to aid recall may depend upon the strength and richness of the schemata activated at the time of listening.

Elaborations were also used to support inferencing about the meaning of unfamiliar words or phrases. In some cases, students inferred meaning based on an analogy with prior knowledge, as in the following examples:

—"I was thinking about what 'chewing betel nut' means. And as each time that she (voice on the tape) repeated it, I tried to see what it was that she was saying, (and) how it was pronounced. I don't think it could be chewing gum ... perhaps some kind of plant. Something like that. Like here some people chew tobacco."

—(When asked if she heard the word "tip" in the Captain Cook lecture, as used in the phrase "the tip of South America") "I heard it but I don't know it. I know it means tip (as in a gratuity left in a restaurant). But I know there's another meaning because I was playing softball and every time that I didn't hit the ball, they said 'tip.' And I said, 'Why are you saying that to me?'"

In the first example, the student is using nonspecialized prior knowledge to infer that betel nut is some kind of plant that is chewed in much the same way as tobacco. In the second example, the student is trying to infer meaning by using a personal experience where the word in question appeared. This use of prior knowledge to infer meaning was a characteristic of effective listeners but rarely of ineffective listeners.

Summary and Conclusions

The picture of listening comprehension of ESL students that emerged in this study was consistent with the depiction of general comprehension processes in the cognitive literature (for example, Anderson, 1983, 1985; Howard, 1983; Pearson, 1985). Listening comprehension is an active and conscious process in which the listener constructs meaning by using cues from contextual information and from existing knowledge, while relying upon multiple strategic resources to fulfill the task requirements. The task requirements varied depending on the phase in listening comprehension and included perceptual processing, or maintaining attention to the aural text; parsing, or encoding the information to develop a meaningful representation that is stored in short-term memory; and utilization, or drawing upon existing knowledge both to enhance the meaning of the information and to store the information for later retrieval.

The principal strategic resources students deployed to aid in comprehension—self-monitoring, elaboration, and inferencing—differentiated effective from ineffective listeners and were applied in a variety of ways depending on the phase of comprehension. In general, however, the effective listeners made use of both top-down and bottom-up processing strategies, while ineffective listeners became embedded in determining the meanings of individual words. In few instances was there clear evidence of using specific linguistic cues for meaning; rather, students seemed to rely upon contextual inferencing and elaborative strategies to aid in both comprehension and retention.

What these findings imply is that instructional approaches which rely exclusively upon teacher input or other teaching techniques for their effectiveness are failing to draw upon what the students can contribute to the learning process. There is ample evidence (for example, Derry & Murphy, 1985; O'Malley et al., 1985b; Weinstein & Mayer, (1986) that less effective students can learn to use learning strategies and apply them. To fail to draw upon the students as a resource in instruction is to diminish the chances of students' success and exclude them from opportunities to gain independent control over the learning process.

Acknowledgment

This study was based on a report prepared with support from the US Army Research Institute for the Behavioral and Social Sciences under Contract No. MDA 903-85-C-0200. The views and opinions contained in this paper are those of the authors and should not be construed to represent official Department of the Army position or policy.

References

Anderson, J. R. (1983). *The architecture of cognition.* Cambridge, Mass.: Harvard University Press.

Anderson, J. R. (1985). *Cognitive psychology and its implications.* (2nd ed.) New York: W. H. Freeman.

Asher, J. J. (1969). The total physical response approach to second language learning. *The Modern Language Journal, 53,* 3–17.

Bialystok, E. (1986). Factors in the growth of linguistic awareness. *Child Development, 57,* 498–510.

Bialystok, E., & Ryan, E. B. (1985). Toward a definition of metalinguistic skill. *Merrill-Palmer Quarterly, 31,* 229–251.

Brown, H. D. (1984). The consensus: Another view. *Foreign Language Annals, 17,* 277–280.

Byrnes, H. (1984). The role of listening comprehension: A theoretical base. *Foreign Language Annals, 17,* 317–329.

Call, M. E. (1985). Auditory short-term memory, listening comprehension, and the input hypothesis. *TESOL Quarterly, 19,* 765–781.

Chamot, A. U., & O'Malley, J. M. (1987). The cognitive academic language learning approach: A bridge to the mainstream. *TESOL Quarterly, 12,* 227–249.

Clark, H. H., & Clark, E. V. (1977). *Psychology and language.* New York: Harcourt Brace Jovanovich.

Dechert, H. W. (1987). Analyzing language processing through verbal protocols. In C. Færch and G. Kasper (Eds.), *Introspection in second language research.* Philadelphia, Pa: Multilingual Matters.

Derry, S. J., & Murphy, D. A. (1986). Designing systems that train learning ability: From theory to practice. *Review of Educational Research, 56.* 1–39.

Ericsson, K. A., & Simon, H.A. (1980). Verbal reports as data. *Psychological Review, 87,* 215–251.

Færch, C., & Kasper, G. (1986). The role of comprehension in second-language learning. *Applied Linguistics, 7,* 257–274.

Færch, C., & Kasper, G. (Eds.). (1987). *Introspection in second language research.* Clevedon, Avon: Multilingual Matters.

Garner, R. (1984). Verbal-report data on cognitive and metacognitive strategies. Paper presented at the Learning and Study Strategies Conference, College Station, Texas.

Howard, D. V. (1983). *Cognitive psychology: Memory, language, and thought.* New York: Macmillan.

James, C. J. (1984). Are you listening? The practical components of listening comprehension. *Foreign Language Annals, 17,* 129–133.

Kintsch, W. (1974). *The representation of meaning in memory.* Hillsdale, NJ: Erlbaum.

Krashen, S. D. (1980). The input hypothesis. In J. E. Alatis (Ed.),*Current Issues in Bilingual Education.* Washington, DC: Georgetown University Press.

Krashen, S. D., Terrell, T. D., Ehrman, M. E., & Herzog, M. (1984). A theoretical base for teaching receptive skills. *Foreign Language Annals, 17,* 261–275.

Loftus, G. R., & Loftus, E. F. (1976). *Human memory: The processing of information.* Hillsdale, NJ: Earlbaum.

Long, M. H. (1985). Input and second language acquisition theory. In S. Gass and C. Madden (Eds.), *Input and second language acquisition.* Rowley, Mass.: Newbury House.

McLaughlin, B., Rossman, T., & McLeod, B. (1983). Second language learning: An information processing perspective. *Language Learning, 33,* 135–158.

Neisser, U. (1967). *Cognitive psychology.* New York: Appleton-Century-Crofts.

Nisbet, J., & Schucksmith, J. (1986). *Learning strategies.* Boston, Mass.: Routledge and Kegan Paul.

O'Malley, J. M., Chamot, A. U., Stewner-Manzanares, G., Küpper, L., & Russo, R. P. (1985a). Learning strategies used by beginning and intermediate ESL students. *Language Learning, 35,* 21–46.

O'Malley, J. M., Chamot, A. U., Stewner-Manzanares, G., Küpper, L., & Russo, R. P. (1985b). Learning strategy applications with students of English as a second language. *TESOL Quarterly, 19,* 557–546,

O'Malley, J. M., Chamot, A. U., & Walker, C. (1987). Some applications of cognitive theory to second language acquisition. *Studies in Second Language Acquisition, 9,* 287–306.

Pearson, P. D. (1985). Changing the face of reading comprehension instruction. *The Reading Teacher, 38,* 724–738.

Postovsky, V. A. (1974). Effects of delay on oral practice at the beginning of second language learning. *The Modern Language Journal, 58,* 229–239.

Rabinowitz, M., & Chi, M. T. (1987). An interactive model of strategic processing. In S. J. Ceci (Ed.), *Handbook of cognitive, social and neuropsychological aspects of learning disabilities.* Hillsdale, NJ: Erlbaum.

Reder, L. M. (1980). The role of elaboration in the comprehension and retention of prose: A critical review. *Review of Educational Research, 50,* 5–53.

Richards, J. C. (1983). Listening comprehension: Approach, design, procedure. *TESOL Quarterly, 17,* 219–239.

Seliger, H. W. 1983. The language learner as linguist: Of metaphors and realities. *Applied Linguistics, 4,* 179–191.

Ratone, E. (1981). Some thoughts on the notion of communication strategy. *TESOL Quarterly, 15,* 285–295.

Weinstein, C. E., & Mayer, R. E. (1986). The teaching of learning strategies. In M. C. Wittrock (Ed.), *Handbook of research on teaching.* (3rd ed.) New York: Macmillan.

Wenden, A., & Rubin, J. (Eds.) (1987). *Learner strategies in language learning.* Englewood Cliffs, NJ: Prentice-Hall.

Winitz, H. (1978). Comprehension and language learning. In C. H. Blatchford & J. Schachter (Eds.), *On TESOL '78 EFL policies, programs, practices.* Washington, DC: TESOL.

Wipf, J. A. (1984). Strategies for teaching second language listening comprehension. *Foreign Language Annals, 17,* 345–348.

Understanding the Article

1. How do the processes of perceptual processing, parsing, and utilization function in listening comprehension?

2. What role do learning strategies play in listening comprehension?

3. Describe the study. Who were the subjects and how were they selected? What data were collected and what was the data collection procedure? How were the data analyzed? What inferential statistics were used?

4. What were the answers to the research questions?

5. How can effective listeners be distinguished from ineffective listeners in terms of the learning strategies they used?

Reflecting on Wider Issues

1. Look back at the description of how the subjects were selected. Do you think that the method of classifying the subjects as effective or ineffective listeners is valid? What are the advantages and disadvantages of other ways of identifying effective and ineffective listeners?

2. The study relies exclusively on self-reports by the subjects in order to identify the learning strategies being used. What sorts of problems might be inherent in self-reports? In an earlier study (O'Malley et al., 1985), two other methods of identifying learning strategies were also used: teachers' observations and observations by the researcher. Which method(s) of data collection do you predict would be most successful?

Going Beyond the Article

For an excellent review of research on language learning strategies, read Oxford and Crookall (1989), "Research on language learning strategies: Methods, findings, and instructional issues" (*Modern Language Journal, 73,* 404–419). O'Malley and Chamot (1990), *Learning Strategies in Second Language Acquisition* (New York: Oxford University Press) provides an in-depth treatment of issues and relevant research on learning strategies.

UNIT IV

AFFECTIVE FACTORS

7

COMPETITIVENESS AND ANXIETY IN ADULT SECOND LANGUAGE LEARNING: LOOKING *AT* AND *THROUGH* THE DIARY STUDIES

Kathleen M. Bailey
Monterey Institute of International Studies

Previewing the Chapter

Personality variables often emerge as key factors in second language learners' eventual success. However, research on such factors is mitigated by the difficulty of empirical measurement of such constructs as anxiety and competitiveness; elusive affective factors are, in fact, sometimes impossible to quantify meaningfully. In this chapter, Kathleen Bailey argues for a markedly different approach to the study of affective variables.

Before you begin to read this somewhat lengthy chapter, make sure you are familiar with what anxiety is (*PLLT*, Chapter 6), and predict how competitiveness might relate to anxiety. Then ask yourself some questions:

1. What is the purpose of the study?
2. How does Bailey's study differ from statistically quantifiable studies?

Reprinted from Selinger and Long (Eds.), *Classroom-Oriented Research in Second Language Acquisition*. Rowley, Mass.: Newbury House, pp. 67–102, 1983.

3. Glance at the last section of the chapter ("Describing and defining affective factors"). What are the seven characteristics of competitiveness? Try to use those seven characteristics to organize your reading of the study.

Problems in Research on Affect: Anxiety in Second Language Learning

Affective factors are generally assumed to influence second language acquisition (SLA). Yet there are many difficulties associated with research on such variables. The tasks of defining, manipulating, and quantifying affective factors pose serious problems for researchers. A case in point is anxiety. In reviewing the research on anxiety and second language learning, Scovel borrows from work in psychology by Hilgard, Atkinson, and Atkinson (1971) and defines anxiety as an emotional state of "apprehension, a vague fear that is only indirectly associated with an object" (Scovel, 1978, p. 34).

Empirical research on affect in language learning usually takes the form of correlation studies. An example which is relevant to the present study is a paper by Gardner, Smythe, Clement, and Glicksman (1976), who conducted research "concerned with delineating components of the integrative motive" (p. 199). One of those components in a formal instructional setting is what Gardner et al. have termed French Classroom Anxiety, or "feelings of anxiety in the French classroom situation" (ibid., 200). In that study data from a self-report survey of approximately one thousand high school students in seven communities across Canada were correlated with four measures of French achievement (aural comprehension, speech skills, final course grade, and opportunity to use French).

A negative correlation was found to exist between reported French Classroom Anxiety and scores on an oral production test of speech skills. Gardner et al. report, "The negative correlation of French Classroom Anxiety indicates that the more anxious students are less proficient in Speech Skills" (ibid., 202). This finding is not surprising, but it is restricted by a limitation of all correlational studies: one cannot identify the causal variable. Does anxiety impair students' oral fluency, or do they become anxious in oral production tasks because their speech skills are low? Whatever the relationship of French Classroom Anxiety to oral production, the trend varied among the grade levels of the students surveyed:

> Whereas French Classroom Anxiety plays a minimal role in Grade Seven, it becomes more dominant in the later grades. In fact, by Grade Eleven, French

> Classroom Anxiety is among the best three predictors of all four variables. It would seem therefore, that anxiety possibly plays a more important role as students begin to achieve a better grasp of the language, (ibid., 203)

An alternative interpretation of these findings is that older language learners are generally more anxious. (See Schumann, 1975, for a discussion of age and affective factors in SLA.)

Because affective factors, such as anxiety, are so complex, many studies have produced conflicting findings and varied terminology. In a paper which reviews the research on the role of anxiety in SLA, Scovel (1978) discusses several attempts to define affective factors. He summarizes by saying,

> ... Most of the constructs and behaviors which have been misclassified as affective factors in the literature can be subsumed under the category "learner variables," either intrinsic or extrinsic to the learner, but affect, if we adhere to its traditional definition in psychology, is itself only one variable within intrinsic learner variables, and, therefore, if we are to proceed with an examination of the relationship of anxiety to foreign language learning, we must first of all realize that we are talking about only one affective variable among many intrinsic learner variables. (p. 130)

Scovel turns to Buddhist philosophy and borrows the concept of *vedana* (feelings) in developing a broad definition:

> ... Affective factors are those that deal with the emotional reactions and motivations of the learner, they signal the arousal of the limbic system and its direct intervention in the task of learning. (ibid., 131)

After discussing various studies of anxiety in SLA (many of which produced conflicting findings), Scovel suggests that "anxiety can be viewed, not as a simple unitary construct, but as a cluster of affective states, influenced by factors which are intrinsic and extrinsic to the foreign language learner" (ibid., 134). He then considers research on anxiety in the fields of athletics and applied psychology. Typically anxiety is measured by behavioral tests, self-report, or physiological tests, but Scovel cites Beeman, Martin, and Meyers (1972, p. 427) as saying that there is generally "a low correlation between clinically rated anxiety, self-rated anxiety, and psychometric anxiety" (Scovel, 1978, p. 136).

Scovel points out that the research in applied psychology has contributed a number of ideas which are relevant to SLA research on anxiety. For instance, research by Verma and Nijhavan (1976) revealed an interaction between IQ and anxiety level: "higher states of anxiety facilitate learning at upper levels of intelligence, whereas they are associated with poorer performance at lower IQ levels" (Scovel, 1978, p. 136). In addition, Beeman et al. (1972) found that "increased anxiety is likely to improve performance at later stages in a learning activity, but conversely hinders academic performance at earlier stages of the same activity" (Scovel, 1978, p. 136). Scovel feels that other conflicting findings can be accounted for by Spielberger, Gorusch, and Lushene's (1970) distinction between *state anxiety*, which is (relatively) momentary, and *trait anxiety*, a "more permanent predisposition to be anxious" (Scovel, 1978, p. 137).

Finally, Scovel notes that the issue of *facilitating* versus *debilitating* anxiety (Alpert & Haber, 1960) may be central to research on anxiety in SLA. These concepts are related to work by Chastain (1975), who investigated the correlation between language test scores and anxiety. His conflicting results led him to conclude that mild anxiety could be beneficial while too much anxiety could be harmful (Scovel, 1978, p. 132). This concept was tested in a study by Kleinmann (1977) in which subjects with high facilitating anxiety attempted to use syntactic structures unlike those of their native language, while subjects with high debilitating anxiety avoided such structures. Scovel explains facilitating and debilitating anxiety as products of the limbic system, "the source of all affective arousal" (1978, p. 139):

> Facilitating anxiety motivates the learner to "fight" the new learning task; it gears the learner emotionally for approach behavior. Debilitating anxiety, in contrast, motivates the learner to "flee" the new learning task; it stimulates the individual emotionally to adopt avoidance behavior. (ibid.)

Findings from psychological research on performance are related to the issue of facilitating and debilitating anxiety. In discussing the effect of an audience or the presence of coactors on task performance, Davis states that

> the performance which was *facilitated* involved tasks requiring well-learned behavior; social *inhibition* occurred where the *acquisition of new information* was required by the task. (1969, p. 16)

There is an important distinction here: "Learning is the acquisition of new responses, and performance is the emission of old (that is, well-learned) ones" (ibid.). To restate, then, inhibition occurs when learners must publicly produce new responses which are not yet well-learned. However, in language classes it is not unusual for students to be called upon to *perform* during the early stages of *learning*. Such demands for public performance could be premature and may lead to anxiety on the part of the learner.

Scovel ends his review on a note of cautious optimism. He feels that it is possible to isolate affective variables in SLA research and that anxiety is, in fact, a subject worthy of investigation. However, he also points out that the more we study language learning, the "more complex the identification of particular variables becomes" (1978, p. 140):

> . . . Before we begin to measure anxiety, we must become more cognizant of the intricate hierarchy of learner variables that intervene: the intrinsic/extrinsic factors, the affective/cognitive variables, and then the various measures of anxiety and their relationship to these other factors. (ibid.)

Thus Scovel's paper addresses the problems of identifying and defining affective variables, with anxiety being the case in point. In a paper which focuses on methodological issues, Oller discusses the various difficulties involved in language learning research on the affective domain in general. The first problem is that the measurement of affective variables is "necessarily inferential and indirect" (1979, p. 9):

> While many sorts of behavior can be directly observed . . . attitudes can only be inferred from behaviors or statements of the person in question. The difficulty of validating such inferences is increased by the need to establish some more or less stable set of values against which attitudes can be referenced. This need is complicated by the fact that attitudes are typically unstable sorts of things. (ibid., 10)

Because affective variables are usually not directly observable, data are often based on "inferences made by an observer concerning how the person really feels or thinks or would behave under certain circumstances" (ibid., 11).

One way of minimizing the problems of inference[1] in research on affective variables is to query the subjects directly, either in questionnaires or interviews. In these cases the subjects themselves provide the data on their attitudes and feelings. Since such feelings are often hidden, especially in adults, "the necessary reliance on self-reports would seem to be an entirely unavoidable weakness" of research on affective variables (ibid.).

Unfortunately, self-reports are often problematic because the subjects "tend to give answers that are associated with the respondents' perceptions of the predispositions of the researcher" (ibid., 17). That is, the subject may say what he or she thinks the researcher wants to hear. A related problem has been termed "self-flattery" by Oller and Perkins (1978), who showed that self-evaluations on given traits correlate with the subjects' judgments of the desirability of those traits. Oller states, "On the whole, it was possible to show that as much as 25% of the variance in self-ratings may be attributed to the self-flattery factor" (1979, p. 18).

In discussing the problems of inference and self-reports, Oller points to yet another serious issue in research on affective variables. He hypothesizes that questionnaires designed to assess affective variables may in fact be measuring language proficiency or intelligence instead (ibid., 16). It is beyond the scope of this paper to do more than mention this important and complicated issue. At this juncture it is sufficient to state that research into affective variables in language learning poses numerous challenging problems at all levels—definition, description, measurement, and interpretation.

Yet, for many people involved in language teaching and learning, the hypothesis that the affective domain is significant in second language learning

---

[1]See Long (1979) for a discussion of the degree of inference involved in various observational instruments used in language classroom research.

is intuitively sound. It is a widely held belief that what the learner experiences in a language lesson is as important as the teaching method, the sequence of presentation, or the instructional materials. In responding to Oller's criticism of the research on affective factors, Tucker has said,

> Although we would all presumably agree with the proposition that affective variables (somehow defined) are important in some way during the course of foreign or second language learning or teaching, their precise description and measurement remains a problematic issue. (1979, p. 3)

Given the complexities of research on affective variables, finding out exactly what the learner experiences is a complicated venture. How can a researcher in a language classroom minimize the problems of observational inference and/or obtain valid self-report data from subjects? Given the variety of learners' needs, motivation, and learning styles, how can a classroom researcher discover what individual students really do and think and feel during the language lesson?

One recent response to this dilemma has been the use of intensive journals to provide the data base for studying personal and affective variables in language learning. The diary studies are first-person case studies: the researcher becomes the language learner in question.

The Use of Personal Diaries as Language Learning Research Tools

Early work using intensive journals as language learning research tools was conducted by Francine and John Schumann. While studying Arabic in Tunisia and Persian in Iran and California the Schumanns recorded "daily events and the thoughts and feelings related to them in a loglike fashion, paying particular attention to cross-cultural adjustments and efforts made and avoided in learning the target language, both in and out of class" (1977, p. 243). In keeping a language learning diary, the researcher/learner records anything and everything perceived to be important to his or her current learning experience. The diaries often include early impressions of the people and culture of the target language environment, the teacher and fellow students in a language class, comments about the learner's fears and frustrations, and the difficulties or successes experienced by the learner.

Several of the diarists have also documented their personal language learning histories in their reports. These accounts of the diarist's previous language learning experience are by definition retrospective. The language learning histories are included in hopes that they will contribute to an understanding of the personal factors involved in the current language learning experience.

In studying their own language learning, diarists assume the role of participant observers in ethnographic research. Methodologically speaking, the diary studies can be classified as belonging to the anthropological research tradition (Long, 1979). For both ethnographers and second language diarists, the research questions are not predefined, and open-ended note-taking is the typical data collection procedure:

> Ethnographers do not set out to test particular hypotheses in any formal sense. Instead, they try to describe all aspects of whatever they experience in the greatest possible detail. This they accomplish principally by making extensive witness notes, usually recording their observations as soon as possible *after* involvement in the day's activities in order to avoid compromising their own participant role. Note-taking is as systematic and thorough as the individual ethnographer cares to make it . . . (ibid., 26)

Most of the diarists have kept written logs, although others have preferred to use tape-recorded comments for storing journal entries (Kheredmand, personal communications). Some find writing cumbersome and slow while others feel inhibited by the presence of a microphone and find they are better able to express themselves in writing. Diary research is largely introspective since the learner reflects on his or her own experiences;[2] however, some diarists (e.g., Bailey, 1978) in formal classrooms include commentary on other learners as well (Long, 1979).

In introspective research on personal variables, it is important for the diarist to record his or her feelings honestly and openly during the initial data-collection phase of a diary study. Otherwise, if the original journal is prematurely edited, significant information could be automatically censored if it were painful or embarrassing for the diarist.[3] The Schumanns point out that since the diaries

> must be as candid as possible and entries are uncensored, they are essentially private documents. Therefore, for the study, this raw data was rewritten by each subject, keeping all relevant detail but eliminating highly personal entries. (1977, p. 243)

In practice it seems that very little is edited in the public versions of the diaries. The names of the participants are changed and comments damaging to others are usually deleted. However, one finds that writing about a painful or embarrassing incident often renders it harmless. In rewriting the journal, the diarist can take a clinical view of the entries. Time, introspection, and the catharsis of writing usually divest the diarist of any painful personal involvement in the episodes reported.

Once the journal has been "revised" for public consumption, the

---

[2]See Boring (1953) for an overview of the history of introspection as a tool of scientific psychological inquiry.

[3]Throughout this article I use the terms diary and journal interchangeably. In addition, the terms diarist, language learner, and researcher typically refer to one person since that individual is functioning in all three roles.

researcher rereads the entries, looking for significant trends. An issue is usually deemed important if it arises frequently or with great salience (J. Schumann, personal communication). Papers reporting on the findings may or may not include the journal excerpts. Thus, simply stated, the process of doing a diary study entails five major steps:

1. The diarist provides an account of his or her personal language learning history.

2. The diarist/learner/researcher systematically records events, details and feelings about the current language-learning experience in a confidential and candid diary.

3. The journal entries are revised for public perusal. Names are changed and information damaging to others or extremely embarrassing to the learner is deleted.

4. The researcher studies the journal entries as data, looking for "significant" trends.

5. The factors identified as important to the language-learning experience are discussed, either with or without illustrative data.

Although diarists may try to relate their findings to theories of learning or language acquisition, the introspective diary studies that have been conducted to date have been largely heuristic. It is normally in the fourth step, the sifting of the data, that specific research questions are defined. In a broad sense, the diary studies are guided by one main question: "What factors are important in *my* language learning experience?" As personal variables emerge, the diarist continues to reread the data, seeking insights and further examples of the phenomena in question.

This article is an example of a language classroom diary study, or at least a part of one. It is based on a journal I kept while studying French as a foreign language in a low-level college class.

Competitiveness and Anxiety in an Adult Learning French

As a doctoral student in Applied Linguistics I was faced with the requirement of passing translation exams in two languages. I enrolled in French 2R, a reading and grammar course designed primarily for people who want to pass language exams rather than learn to speak French. The class met three hours a week on Mondays, Wednesdays, and Fridays, for ten weeks. There was no required lab session. I felt that such a course would provide me with the review I needed to prepare for the linguistics translation exam. Three years before enrolling in French 2R I had completed two quarters of introductory French. Those courses had been taught with the direct method. During the interim I had made no effort to study French.

The French 2R teacher was a female native speaker of French. During the previous quarter French 1R, the prerequisite course, had been taught by a more experienced teacher and four of the French 2R students had taken that class together. Thus they were familiar with one another, the textbooks, and a particular teaching style.

In conducting this research I kept a journal of experiences related to my language learning. Typical entries include comments about French class meetings, tests and homework, my classmates, conversations, commercials and television programs in French, class parties, etc. An initial analysis of the diary revealed three prevalent factors or themes which are discussed elsewhere (Bailey, 1979). These themes were (1) my response to the language learning environment, (2) my preference for a democratic teaching style, and (3) my need for success and positive reinforcement.

In rereading the diary I kept during the French 2R course, I noticed that I often compared myself to the other students in the class. A closer examination revealed a great deal of competitiveness on my part, although I would not have characterized myself as a competitive learner. This realization surprised me and led to two questions, both of which could be answered by the diary. First, I wanted to determine what specific evidence the diary provides of competition in the French classroom, or of competitiveness in my approach to learning French. Second, I wondered what effect such competitiveness may have had on my efforts to learn French. Excerpts from the journal are examined in order to answer these questions.

It appears that during the first two weeks of the ten-week course I was highly anxious about learning French because I felt I could not compete with the other students. After that period I became more confident but was still competitive with regard to tests and grades. Although the nature of my competitiveness changed during the quarter, it appears to have been important in my language-learning experience, at least in this formal instructional setting.

After just the first hour of the class, when much of the journal entry is devoted to my first impressions of the teacher and my entry-level French proficiency, I seemed to be "sizing up" the other students. The diary says,

> I have just come from the first class meeting. The teacher's name is Marie. She seems nice—young, enthusiastic, and willing to slow down for the students. She encourages us to tell her when we don't understand something. She also stops lecturing in French to give us grammatical explanations, and she often writes on the board when she sees we don't understand what she has said. . . . I am interested in the problems of one man in the class who has taken the ETS French exam and failed. He is desperate and somewhat discouraged. I hope I can encourage him. He is really trying. He talked to the teacher after class but he's using a lot of energy fighting with his own frustrations. There are only ten or twelve students in the class. The girl who had been in France seemed to try to align herself with the teacher, but Marie

made an effort to distribute turns evenly and not play favorites. I think this will be a good class for me and I'll try to write in my journal after each meeting. (1979, pp. 38–39)

It may be that in referring specifically to the woman who had been in France and the man who had failed the ETS test, I was identifying the sources of the greatest and least threat to me as a learner in that class. In the journal entries for the second meeting it is clear that I was experiencing what Gardner et al. (1976) called "French Classroom Anxiety":

> ... Today I was panicked in the oral exercise where we had to fill in the blanks with either the past definite or the imperfect. Now I know what ESL students go through with the present perfect and the simple past. How frustrating it is to be looking for adverbial clues in the sentence when I don't even know what the words and phrases mean. I realized that the teacher was going around the room taking the sentences in order, so I tried to stay one jump ahead of her by working ahead and using her feedback to the class to obtain confirmation or denial of my hypotheses. Today I felt a little scared. I'm so rusty! (ibid., 40)

This fear of public failure seems to have been caused or at least aggravated by comparing myself with the other students (or with an idealized self-image), rather than by any fear of rebuke from the teacher. In fact, the journal entry for that same day shows that I actually ranked my French fluency against that of the other students:

> ... I hope Marie will eventually like me and think that I am a good language learner, even though I am probably the second lowest in the class right now (next to the man who must pass the ETS test). The girl who has been in France seems to think that she's too good for the rest of us, but she didn't do all that well today. I want to have the exercises worked out perfectly before the next class. Today I was just scared enough to be stimulated to prepare for next time. If I were any scareder I'd be a nervous wreck. I feel different from many of the students in the class because they have been together for a quarter with the other teacher. They also don't seem very interested in learning French. Today Marie was explaining something and some of the students looked really bored (ibid., 41)

I was apparently very uncomfortable throughout the third class meeting as well. My feelings of inadequacy in comparing myself to the other students led me to seek out allies and react negatively to some students. On Friday of the first week, the third day of instruction, I wrote,

> Today I decided to speak to the man who is so uptight about this ETS test. I was sad that he didn't come to class. I hope he doesn't drop the course. I said hello to another student in the hall (Robert is his name) but he just nodded. I would have liked to have someone to commiserate with. ... I am

absolutely worn out. I floundered through the class, making at least four stupid mistakes out loud. I felt so lost! . . . Today my palms were sweating and I was chewing my lip through the entire class. My emotional state wasn't helped by the blond girl who sat next to me. She had already taken French 3 and was just looking for a three-unit course. She made several comments about how slow the class is and then decided this isn't the right course for her. I offered to buy her grammar book and I'm relieved she agreed to sell it to me; that means she won't be back. . . . I'm not having any trouble understanding Marie's grammar explanations. My grammar background is probably stronger than most of the students'. I'm just having trouble in recognizing and producing the spoken language. I want to work on French a lot over the weekend (ibid., 42–43)

These journal entries from the first week of the French course reveal a learner who was very uncomfortable and extremely anxious about the class. After only three hours of instruction I had ranked myself as the second lowest in a group of ten or twelve students. Yet I was consoled by the thought that even though my spoken French was poor, my knowledge of grammar was probably better than the other students'. In other words, although I couldn't compete with the others orally, I thought I would have an edge in the grammar competition.

Since the student who had to take the ETS test didn't come to class on Friday, I had become the lowest person in the rankings of French fluency. Seeing myself as weaker than the other students motivated me to study French in order to avoid the embarrassment of making public errors. However, the feeling that I couldn't compete in class became so intense that I soon withdrew from this painful situation. On the fourth day of instruction I wrote,

Today I skipped my French class. Last Friday after class I spoke to Marie and apologized for slowing down the class. I asked her how far they had gone the previous quarter in the grammar book, so that I could try to catch up over the weekend. She was very encouraging and said that I hadn't slowed the class down. Over the weekend I had planned to do a total review of the French grammar book, but I didn't get to it because I had so much department business to do. Last night I began reading the assigned chapter but I got bogged down and discouraged and I quit. Coming to school today I vowed to leave my office an hour before class so I could prepare. Some things came up though and twenty minutes before the class was supposed to start, I decided to skip class and use the time to review instead. Then I discovered I had left my French books at home! I feel very anxious about this class. I know I am (or can be) a good language learner, but I hate being lost in class. I feel like I'm behind the others and slowing down the pace. Since I didn't have the French books, I decided to go to the library and study for my other class . . . I tried to read but I was so upset about the French class that I couldn't concentrate so I've just been writing in my journal. I *must* get caught up in French or I'll never be able to go back to the class. (ibid., 43–44)

This journal entry shows that in this case, French Classroom Anxiety definitely interfered with language learning (at least in the short-term perspective) when I temporarily withdrew from the instructional setting. My *perceived* inability to compete with the other students was so strong that I either didn't heed or didn't believe the teacher's encouraging comments.[4] Apparently I felt that the other students had a "head start" on me because they had been studying French together for a quarter. The sense of competition is clearly revealed in the foot-race imagery used in the diary: "I apologized for *slowing down* the class" and asked "*how far they had gone*" so I could "*try to catch up.*" This racing imagery is particularly apparent in the comment, "I feel like I'm *behind the others and slowing down the pace*. . . . I must get *caught up* in French. . . ." Thus, the language with which I expressed my frustrations in the diary reveals the development of competition as a prevalent theme in my perceptions of this classroom situation. (It is unlikely that an observer or a videotape camera could have captured these intense feelings of inadequacy. It is also doubtful that I would have revealed them on a questionnaire.)

> Today we had our first test. It consisted of two paragraphs in French, which we were to translate into English. These were followed by six sentences in French, also to be translated, and five multiple choice questions in which we were to choose the correct English interpretation of a word or phrase. I felt pretty good about this test. I finished and left while the others were still working. (ibid., 52–53)

This last sentence is curious. Apparently I felt I had caught up with the group in terms of my French proficiency, but I never felt accepted by them. "Beating them" by finishing the test early may have been a basic form of revenge. I was very surprised, however, when the teacher returned the exams. The journal entry says,

> Today we went over the exam we took last week. I got a "B+." The grade was all right with me but I was amazed to see that I had skipped one sentence within a paragraph and the entire middle section of the test. I just didn't notice those six sentences to be translated into English. No wonder I finished before the others! It is strange that I did finish early but I didn't go back over the test. I honestly thought I had done my best on the entire test. In retrospect, I am pleased to have gotten a "B+" after having jumped over so much of the exam. I wonder what grades the others got. (ibid., 53)

In fact, this entry reveals an error on my part: I *had noticed* those parts of the test; otherwise I wouldn't have been able to describe them in the entry cited

---

[4]In a related phenomenon, research on friendship groups in classrooms showed that a student's perception of holding low status—more than the fact of actually having such status—was related to incomplete use of intellectual abilities and to holding negative attitudes toward self and toward the school (Schmuck & Schmuck, 1971)

above. The diary shows that I had unwittingly skipped those sections even though I had been aware of them at some point during the test.

This pattern of rushing through tests persisted throughout the quarter. When the second test was returned I wrote,

> Much to my surprise I skipped part of the test again. I missed an entire section by not copying it onto the paper I handed in. I even had correct notes about the sentence on the ditto sheet, but I neglected to follow through on them. Why an I so careless as a test-taker in French? (ibid., 63)

At the time I didn't realize that my competitiveness in test-taking situations was causing me to do poorly. I attributed the gaps in my test-taking behavior to a lack of monitoring, insensitivity to context, or just plain carelessness. Yet none of these explanations was intuitively appealing. After the third classroom examination I wrote,

> I am disgusted with myself for skipping something once more. This time it was just a phrase in the passage that I could not translate, but the silly thing is that the term was included on the vocabulary list provided. Thus I missed a section on the translation because I misinterpreted a term that was actually defined for me! This is more evidence that I am not as good a test-taker in a foreign language as I am in my native language. (ibid., 83)

Although I couldn't identify the cause of this gapping, I tried to disrupt the pattern by concentrating on systematically completing the tasks on the fourth test, the final examination. This time I was more successful. At the beginning of the exam I seemed to be competing with the task, but when the first student left I was tempted to compete with her, which would have damaged my performance on the test. In this journal entry, as in the first two weeks of the course, competitiveness and anxiety again coincide. Here it is difficult to tell which is the cause and which the effect.

To summarize then, the diary contains numerous indications that, at least in the French 2R class, I was a competitive language learner. Sometimes this competitiveness hindered my language learning (as in the case of debilitating anxiety when I avoided contact with the language by skipping class) and at other times it motivated me to study harder (as in the case of facilitating anxiety when I completed an intensive review so I would feel more at ease during oral classroom work). Journal entries which reveal this competitiveness have involved the following characteristics:

1. Overt—though private—comparison of myself with other students (e.g., self-ranking, use of comparatives and superlatives, comparison in particular skill areas, etc.).

2. Emotive responses to such comparisons (anxiety when I didn't compare favorably with the others and elation when I did), including

emotional reactions to other students (e.g., the girl who'd been to France, the girl whose grammar book I bought, etc.): connotative uses of language (for instance, the foot-race imagery) in the diary entries sometimes reveal this emotion.

3. The desire to outdo the other students; here realized as the tendency to race through exams in order to finish first.

4. Emphasis on tests and grades, especially with reference to the other students.

5. The desire to gain the teacher's approval.

6. Anxiety experienced during the language class, often after making errors on material I felt I should have known (i.e., a discrepancy between an idealized self-image and a realistic assessment of myself as a language learner.

7. Withdrawal from the language-learning experience when the competition was overpowering.

In many cases, these manifestations of competitiveness coincided with comments about French Classroom Anxiety, but whether as a cause or as an effect—or in a cyclic relationship—is difficult to determine.

Competitiveness and Anxiety Among Other Language Learners

The excerpts from my French class journal are concerned with one perceived characteristic of one language learner. The question is often raised as to whether the findings of the diary studies are generalizable. That is, can the findings be attributed to a larger population of language learners? In order to answer this question, let us consider the work done by other diarists in language-learning situations.

Three caveats are in order here. The first is that in reading the diary studies one notices various degrees of introspection and observational acuity among the authors. The obvious conclusion is that some of the studies are more accurate and hence more reliable than others. Second, some of the papers reviewed here (Fields, Jones, Lynch, Scheding, & Walsleben) included the rewritten diaries, or substantial excerpts from them. Others (Bernbrock, Moore, Plummer, & F.E. Schumann) are discussions of trends in the diaries and do not include the actual journals. (Leichman's [1977] paper is a summary of her journal.) In these latter cases I may sometimes be drawing inferences from the diarists' comments, since I am not examining primary data. Finally, these ten papers were all written in English by adult native speakers of English. The "sample" is further restricted by the fact that, except for Moore and Fields, the diarists cited are all language teachers themselves. As readers of these studies we should probably assume that these diarists possess a certain degree of linguistic sophistication as well as the dual perspective of teachers-turned-learners. The purpose of considering these papers is to see what evidence, if any, the various diary studies provide of the relationship between competitiveness and anxiety in other language learners.

Francine Schumann (1978) identifies competition versus cooperation as a major trend in the diary she kept in Tunisia and Iran. She reports that she felt guilty when her husband was studying and she wasn't. She also says,

> This guilt was a result of my competitive feeling that if I didn't work as much as he did, he would get further ahead. . . . Instead of causing me to work harder, this competitiveness resulted in my feeling frustrated and led to a reduced effort. (pp. 5–6)

The Schumanns were able to resolve this problem by working together with materials that appealed to both of them. Francine Schumann further suggests that language-training programs that involve couples (e.g., Peace Corps training) should recognize the competition/cooperation phenomenon in order to "maximize cooperation and minimize competition" (ibid., 7). This last statement shows that, for Francine Schumann, cooperative language-learning situations are perceived as preferable to competitive situations.[5]

A British psychologist named Terence Moore studied his own behavior and reactions when he moved to Denmark to assume a post at the university of Aarhus. Unlike the researchers who have kept diaries to study language learning, Moore used his "personal experience of being partially deprived of the normal modes of communication" (1977, p. 107) to gain insights into "the problems of the immigrant, the deaf, the aphasic, the person confined to a 'restricted code,' and especially perhaps to the child in the class where work is too difficult for him" (ibid.). Moore discusses the problems he encountered in the areas of (a) decoding and comprehension, (b) encoding and expression, and (c) the effects of and his reactions to restricted communication (ibid., 108). It is in this last area that Moore makes comments which are pertinent to the present study. Quoting from notes he made when he joined a Danish class, he writes,

> This is a good reminder of how a child feels when a lesson goes over his head. One feels bewildered; ashamed and inferior when everyone else

---

[5]The issue of competition and cooperation in language learning has also been discussed by Stevick (1976) in describing the Silent Way. He points out that one positive feature of this method "is the absence of destructive competition: when students are depending on one another, the unique contributions of each are clearly recognized and valued by all, for even the slower students will, from time to time, remember something or figure something out that has escaped the others" (p. 142).

> appears to understand except oneself; sympathetic, a little victorious and anxious to help when it happens to someone else; humiliated when one has to admit ignorance openly, however kind the teacher is . . . (ibid., 109)

Although I don't have enough information to conclude that Moore is a competitive learner, it is clear that comparing himself to others in the oral language lesson was a source of some anxiety for him. Moore's conclusion is relevant to the issue of hidden affective variables which a diary study may reveal. Of his restricted communicative ability he writes,

> My experience has shown me how communication failure . . . can produce mystification, frustration, and many counterproductive emotional and behavioral responses. Because these are mostly silent, however, the magnitude of the problem has in my opinion been seriously underestimated. It calls for an imaginative and multifaceted approach by social and educational psychologists jointly with the teaching profession. (ibid., 110)

Cheryl M. Fields, writing in *The Chronicle of Higher Education,* has reported on her experiences as a participant observer in a language class. Her article is based on a diary she kept while taking an introductory Spanish course, the small group option offered by a Berlitz school. She enrolled ostensibly to learn enough Spanish to be able to conduct interviews in Mexico, but also to do a story on nonacademic language-training programs. Fields, who had studied French for two years in college, says of herself, "I'd never studied Spanish before and had no particular aptitude for foreign languages—an understatement if I ever had uttered one" (1978, 4). Yet for her, knowing a second language would have been desirable:

> I always felt ashamed when I went to Europe and found that people there seemed to routinely speak at least two or three languages. (ibid.)

Fields's early entries about the Spanish class (like mine in the French 2R journal) are filled with comments about her classmates. After the first session she wrote,

> My first Spanish lesson was both reassuring and a little troubling. The other person in the class is a young woman who has never studied a foreign language before, and despite the fact that her mother is Mexican, knows absolutely no Spanish. . . . As a result the instructor spent a lot of time helping my classmate pronounce every word and attach the proper article. That didn't bother me particularly, but I hoped my classmate would quickly catch on to the basics. . . . It was clear that Berlitz didn't or couldn't match people in their group lessons according to their language sophistication. I certainly didn't know much but my grounding in traditional language training had given me an obvious starting edge I hadn't imagined I had. (ibid., 4)

Fields's choice of words here when she refers to "an obvious starting edge" is an example of the connotative power of language revealing something about the diarist's attitude.

At the end of the second meeting Fields again overtly compares the students' performances:

> A third person joined the class during the second lesson. The new fellow had had two years of high school French and had taken Chinese in college, so he quickly caught on as the instructor reviewed the first lesson. The instructor . . . carefully divided her attention during class. But she introduced a number of new words and concepts as the fellow and I progressed, even though it was clear that the other woman wasn't catching on as quickly. (ibid.)

At this early stage of language learning the speed with which she learned a structure or grasped a concept seems to have been important to Fields. She has already used the phrase, "to catch on quickly" three times in discussing her Spanish class. After the above entry the reader senses that Fields saw herself as better than the female student and roughly equal to the male student. But at the fourth class meeting a new person joined the group. Fields wrote, apparently with some envy,

> A fourth person joined the class today. Although it was the fourth lesson he had no trouble catching up with the rest of us because he had spent several months in Spain and had studied Spanish briefly in Madrid. He spoke with what is known as "the Castillian lisp." . . . The other woman in our class was absent and the fellows and I made pretty good progress. The new student commented during the break that he hoped the other man and I weren't confused by his lisp. We weren't; we couldn't understand anything he said, so there was nothing to be confused about. (ibid.)

Again the image of the language class as a race emerges in the diary. After this entry Fields continued to be sensitive to the presence of other students in her Berlitz class. Three weeks after the first class she wrote, "There were only two of us in class last night and things went smoothly . . ." Two weeks after that she wrote, "The other woman in the original group hasn't been here for several lessons." (ibid., 5)

Like Francine Schumann, Fields seems to have been competing with her husband, who was not, in this case, a member of the class. There are two revealing comments about her husband which indicate that she envied his abilities as a Spanish speaker. Following the first Berlitz class Fields wrote,

> After much patient repetition, my husband—one of the few people I had ever known to emerge from two years of college language training able to speak the language and with a good accent—had taught me to "roll my r's." (ibid., 4)

A month later, after gaining some functional proficiency in Spanish, Fields wrote,

> I wish I could practice my Spanish more, but when I try to speak it to my husband, I find there are a lot of common verbs I still don't know. Also, since I can use only the present tense, my husband finds my conversational attempts disconcerting at times. He keeps trying to tell me the future or past tenses of the verbs I use, but that doesn't do me much good, since I don't know the rules for formalizing them. (ibid., 5)

Again it would be premature to say that Fields is a competitive language learner. It is safe to say, however, that she actively compared herself to other learners in the classroom, envied her husband's abilities and wished to be able to communicate better in a second language than she really could. She may have been competing with the other students, her husband, and/or an idealized vision of herself as a fluent foreign language speaker.

Brian Lynch (1979) kept a journal of his experiences in a college Spanish class. Although this study focuses primarily on his learning strategies, there are entries documenting overt comparison with his classmates. These entries frequently deal with his efforts to achieve correct pronunciation:

> Following the exam we went over some oral exercises in which individuals were called upon to deliver a series of substitutions out loud. One of the drills I was called upon for included "trabajo" and "hijas"—the difficult velar fricative which no one in the class seems to be able to produce. At first I did produce the fricative quite well, surprising myself, and I sensed a reaction from the students around me—just recognition, not good or bad—but I was immediately self-conscious and struggled between wanting to produce the correct form and not wanting to sound funny. The next few times I did not produce the fricative well at all. . . . Here the classroom is not an environment where your peers are producing, or I believe even trying to produce, the correct speech sounds. Most people in the class seem not to care about speaking fast. (Lynch, 1979, pp. 30–31)

Lynch attributed this difference between himself and his classmates to motivation: "Most of these students are taking Spanish as a requirement and therefore aren't motivated in any integrative way to learn to speak Spanish without an accent" (ibid., 31). Because he saw himself as both integratively and instrumentally motivated, Lynch continued to be concerned with achieving native-like pronunciation and fluency. In one entry he ranked himself as third among the students in pronunciation ability and made some observations on his two competitors:

> . . . I have the impression that I speak with a better accent, i.e., produce Spanish phonology better, than almost everyone else in the class. Only two exceptions come to mind—Senorita F., . . . who occasionally makes errors involving the use of French words instead of Spanish, and an Iranian stu-

dent who seems to have studied Spanish before and has a larger vocabulary than the rest of the class. He is the person who approached me . . . to ask if I thought the teacher was any good. . . . (His) complaint was that the class was moving too slow. My reaction was that if it was moving too slow, no one in the class would be making mistakes on the simple matters that even he was guilty of from time to time. (ibid., 38)

Later in Lynch's journal competition is specifically mentioned, although not as a major trend and only with regard to pronunciation:

. . . We took turns reading the lesson out loud by paragraphs. Only one person read very well and that was Senorita F. . . . She is the only person who speaks with something resembling an authentic Spanish accent—and at times I have been aware of competing with her. Today she read so well that I felt a sudden urge to compliment her. It was nice not to feel competitive about it, and for once I felt a positive motivation as a result of the classroom environment (even if it was only one person). When I was called upon to read I was inspired to try and speak as clearly as possible and with good pronunciation. . . . Overall I was pleased with the results. I didn't feel like I was competing with Senorita F., but I was definitely serious about sounding good. (ibid., 56)

This entry is noteworthy in that Lynch, like Francine Schumann, sees the absence of competitiveness as a positive change.

The public performance aspect of his Spanish class seems to have been a source of some anxiety for Lynch:

I was aware today of the difference in my speaking ability between being called on in class and speaking out loud while studying (or even reading or speaking to someone outside of class). In class, where you are performing and being judged by instructor and classmates, there is much more tenseness and I became very much afraid of making mistakes, and I am not as aware of how closely I am approximating correct Spanish pronunciation. Sometimes the horrible accents I hear others using in class . . . shock me. It almost seems like they don't even want to overcome the accent problem. Today made me aware that in the classroom drills I tend to focus on speaking with a correct accent because I am so preoccupied with the right form of the answer—and that I may be sounding as poor as most of the class. (ibid., 41)

Lynch's fear of public failure was apparently aggravated by the reactions of one vocal student. The following entry reveals the type of hostility I experienced in my French 2R class:

One of the tangents we got off onto today actually involved only one student and the teacher, as near as I could tell. At least there were a few people who I noticed were looking around bored, annoyed, or laughing at the somewhat ridiculous questions this person tends to come up with regularly. This same person has the annoying (not just to me I believe) habit of exclaiming out loud in a "whiny" tone, "No-oo-o" when someone in class gives the wrong answer—a tone which seems to say, "How *could* you say *that!*" Until today I thought I was the only one who reacted this way to her, but I noticed a comrade or two sharing my look of irritation and smiling at me in recognition. (ibid., 44)

Here the word *comrade* provides an example of the connotative power of the language used in the diary entries.

Lynch felt that his fear of public failure contributed to poor oral performance, especially in short responses to questions:

I noticed that I still continue to stutter quite a bit—a problem I don't seem to have in English. It's usually (perhaps always) when I'm called upon for a one-sentence response. I tend to get very nervous and it takes me a few seconds before I can even start to speak, even when it's a relatively simple task or phrase. I'm obviously very afraid to make a mistake in front of the class— and I always feel very embarrassed about stammering. When I read a long passage or get involved in more of an on-going conversation, this seems to be less of a problem. (ibid., 53)

Earlier in the semester Lynch had observed that he had more difficulty in pronouncing the first few responses. After a warm-up period he found that he loosened up and felt more fluent (ibid., 29). One can hypothesize that in reading a longer passage or being involved in a prolonged conversation, Lynch has time to calm himself, relax and control his anxiety, which in turn improves his oral performance.

Another example of overt comparison with other students arose in Lynch's communicative use of Spanish during a classroom lesson. When called upon to form a question, Lynch asked the teacher in Spanish what he had read the day before. Although the question contained an accent error, it

got the teacher onto the subject of V. Nabokov—and as it turned out, I was the only person in the class who had heard of him. I was asked to say who he was, in Spanish—a good test of my communicative abilities. . . . I was fairly happy with my answer. It was slowly constructed with many "uh's" and a questioning to the teacher on two of the words . . . but I did manage to deliver a whole sentence and use the preterite. . . . After class the professor initiated a conversation with me, in English, about my plans for next year. I was flattered by his interest. We talked about ESL (which he taught at night for twelve years) and about opportunities for travel that the field affords me. (ibid., 50–51)

In this instance the teacher rewarded Lynch's performance by (a) prolonging his turn by setting a new task,[6] and (b) engaging him in social conversation, in which they discovered their common interest in ESL. Here it is apparently

---

[6]See Allwright (forthcoming) for a discussion of the relationship between turns, topics and tasks in the language classroom.

Lynch's difference from the other students (i.e., his unique knowledge of Nabokov) which led to these rewards.

Lynch's journal includes numerous remarks on tests and graded assignments, but never with reference to the other students. For him a key issue seems to have been whether a grade was inaccurately high. The following comments reveal Lynch's desire for true grades (i.e., an accurate assessment of his progress):

> Today in class we had our exams (lesson 3) returned. Mine was scored as "O/A" even though I forgot three accent marks. (ibid., 26)

> Today I handed in the rough draft of my Spanish essay, and, to my surprise, was greeted with a tentative "A+ excelente" reaction from the professor. I think he was pleased with my content mostly as he had made twenty or so corrections on my grammar and word choice—which despite the "A+ excellent" marking upset me very much . . . (ibid., 42)

> After getting my test back I noticed that he had scored mine as "−1, A", which I was sure was a mistake since I had remembered making so many (errors) . . . (ibid., 49)

Thus, Lynch's diary portrays a relatively secure language learner who is not highly prone to competitiveness. Only in instances of oral classroom performance (i.e., cases of potentially high anxiety and fear of public failure) do overt comparisons with other students emerge.

In a review of diary studies by six language learners, Snell (1978) identifies the attitude of the language learner toward other students as a source of competition for a number of the subjects. It appears that a language learner may face competition from other sources too. As well as competing with other students, the learner may compete with the teacher's expectations or with an idealized self-image. Evidence of these possibilities appeared in my French class diary when I wrote, "I hope Marie will like me and think that I am a good language learner. . . ." (Bailey, 1978, p. 41) and later, "I know I am (or can be) a good language learner, but I hate being lost in class" (ibid., 43).

Competition with other students and with one's idealized self-image can often be intertwined with the desire to gain the teacher's approval. For example, in keeping a diary of her experience while studying Indonesian as a foreign language, Hindy Leichman (1977) reports a fear of public failure and a need for success:

> When in class I still had the fear of being called on. I was afraid that I would fumble on the material I had worked so hard to learn. Each time I did fumble, I became a little less confident. On the other hand, each time I understood what was being said, I felt better. . . . In almost every class hour I would fluctuate between feelings of success or failure. (p. 2)

Apparently part of her sense of failure is based on her past history as a language learner—a history which is not documented in this particular paper. But part is attributable to the diarist's comparison of herself with the other students, rather than to a purely linguistic assessment of her fluency. In discussing the Indonesian classroom Leichman writes,

> From the beginning I believed that the other students were not struggling as much as me. Very often they would process the question and start to answer before I had a chance. This scared me because I did not know what I was doing wrong not to be able to think as quickly as them. So many of my hangups about language learning were my own perceptions of what I do and what others do. Unfortunately, I did not know which were distortions of the truth; maybe others were struggling as much, maybe I was speaking as fluently or at least not any worse than everyone else. So much depended on how I viewed myself and others. Very often I would try to stop concerning myself with how I thought they were doing and try concentrating on me. (1977, p. 3)

The paper does not include a language-learning history, but Leichman says she was not successful in her earlier attempts to learn a foreign language. Thus she had to overcome her own negative expectations.[7] She wrote, "Throughout the course there was a struggle within myself between my old feelings (of failure) and my desire for success" (ibid., 6). The impact of the word *struggle* here provides further evidence of her emotional state.

Leichman also identifies tests and grades as a source of apprehension for her. In discussing an exam she took in the Indonesian course she said,

> I had not done nearly as well as I had hoped, and was ashamed to let anyone see my grade. . . . During the review I volunteered to put something on the blackboard because I wanted the teacher to consider my class participation more than my test grade. (ibid., 4)

Here the learner seems to be competing for the teacher's approval as well as performing well in comparison to the other students. Leichman wrote that her performance on this exam "caused a temporary backslide" (ibid.) in her study of Indonesian. That evening she tried to study but couldn't concentrate:

> I just kept thinking that there was no point in learning the vocabulary since I would only fail again. I felt resentment at having to spend so much time studying when it did not pay off. Why should I study if I only do badly on a test? Eventually my feelings won over my better judgment and I gave up. (ibid., 4–5)

---

[7]Schmuck and Schmuck, in discussing group processes in the classroom, cite a definition of expectations from Finn (1972, p. 320):

Expectations are evaluations—whether conscious or unconscious—that one person forms of another (or of himself) which lead the evaluator to treat the person evaluated as though the assessment were valid. The person doing the expecting typically anticipates that the other person will act in a manner consistent with the assessment. (Schmuck & Schmuck, 1971, pp. 42–43)

Leichman's journal entry for the next class period reveals the power of grades:

> The next day I did not want to go to class. I still was upset about the test and was unprepared emotionally to be confronted by other students as to my grade. Since it was a Tuesday, we were getting back our logs about the week before. I was scared that I would not do well on it and that would only compound my existing feelings. When I saw a good grade I was not only relieved, I was encouraged. Maybe I could not do well on tests, but I could succeed in other requirements of the course. I volunteered a lot during the review and left my paper open so anyone (and everyone) could see I had done well. (ibid., 5)

That day Leichman was successful in the Indonesian class and wrote that she didn't mind doing her homework that night because she had been successful in class.

Several of the other classroom diary studies also make reference to grades and tests. In a paper based on a diary which he kept while learning to read Thai in an individualized course, Chris Bernbrock (1977) recalls that he "could only manage to obtain mediocre grades" while studying French and Latin in high school, and that he saw "language studies as something to be avoided because he could not excel in them" (p. 1). Bernbrock also reports that a test grade led him to withdraw from a Russian course in college:

> After having failed to perform in a distinguishing manner on the midterm examination, the learner withdrew and resigned himself to reading Dostoyevsky in English translation. (ibid., 1–2)

Yet in an immersion situation in Thailand, the student "learned Thai quite well and was proud of his ability to use the language" (ibid., 2). Later Bernbrock was able to pursue the individualized programmed course in reading Thai syllables. In this course he worked alone with a professor who had studied Thai. They agreed on a reasonable syllabus—in effect, a learning contract. Bernbrock was also tutored by his wife, a native speaker of Thai. Of this experience he wrote,

> In this particular course I did not have to worry about my performance compared to other students or what the teacher expected of me. . . . I experienced none of the anxiety or fear of making mistakes that was so detrimental to my attempts to learn languages in the past. (ibid., 9)

Here Bernbrock explicitly identifies competition with other students and with the teacher's expectations as problems in his former efforts to learn a foreign language. In reflecting on his experiences Bernbrock suggests that a language course syllabus should "encourage learners to measure up against the goals of the course rather than measure up against the other learners" (ibid., 5). (The assessment method Bernbrock suggests is basically a type of criterion-referenced testing, as opposed to norm-referenced testing of achievement.) Like

Francine Schumann and Brian Lynch, Bernbrock sees competition as undesirable in a language-learning situation.

It is difficult to determine the origins of a learner's responses to perceived competition. In reading journal studies that include a retrospective discussion of the diarist's language-learning history, one is often tempted to indulge in a little armchair psychology. The influence of the family seems to play a role in some learners' attitudes about performing in a language classroom. For example, as Snell points out (1978), Marjorie Walsleben's efforts to learn Persian seem to involve a long-standing rivalry with her younger sister. In comparing her own background as a language learner with that of her sister, Walsleben says,

> I was very envious of her apparent ability to be at ease when attempting to speak French or Spanish. . . . With a thinly disguised competitive reaction, I began a self-study of German. (1976, pp. 6–7)

Walsleben's sensitivity to competition is apparent in the discussion of a beginning Persian class she took as a graduate student. Like me in the French 2R class, she rated herself as being one of the less fluent members of the group:

> Two of the students had lived and worked in Iran and could speak Farsi to some extent; ten of the students were already familiar with the language through association with Persian friends; seven of the students were actual "beginners." I classed myself with the group of seven. (ibid., 13)

This last characterization of herself is curious since Walsleben had several Persian friends and some exposure to the language at the time she recorded this entry.

Walsleben saw her inability to compete with her more proficient classmates as causing her a great deal of anxiety. This anxiety is directly attributable to the stressful competitive nature of oral public performance in the Persian class. Walsleben reports that the class became polarized into the group that "knew" Farsi and the group that did not:

> Three of the more voluble students delighted in "racing" each other to see who could repeat the choral drills first and loudest. My anxiety level increased daily and I developed a feeling of frustration and incompetence which was only intensified by my wanting so very much to speak the language. (ibid., 15)

Whether or not this anxiety affected her language learning is open to debate. It is clear that she felt it did. As is often the case in the journal studies, what the diarist perceives as real may be more important to that person's language-learning experience than any external reality. At any rate, Walsleben's introspection led her to conclude, "I never feel that I do my best work or make my best efforts when I am anxious, insecure or feel threatened in any way" (ibid., 18).

The remarks above are excerpted from Walsleben's detailed language-learning history. In keeping a personal journal of a subsequent Persian class she often commented on her conflicting desire to gain the teacher's approval and her frustration with the way he taught and the tests he assigned:

> As class was dismissed (the teacher) assigned a vocabulary test for the following Wednesday to be derived from the thousand-word glossary that accompanied the first-year Persian text. I said that I felt such a test was unreasonable. . . . I knew that I did not have twenty-five hours to spend studying for such a vocabulary test, yet I was frustrated because I wanted to perform well on the test. I felt torn between wanting to somehow show him that I could do well, yet feeling that such a test at that point would not truly reflect anyone's basic productive capabilities. (ibid., 23–24)

Later she wrote, "I knew I would not do well on the test, and it bothered me though I continued to feel it was a meaningless exercise" (ibid., 25). Throughout the remaining journal entries Walsleben comments on the frequent vocabulary tests, but these quizzes do not become objects of competition between her and the other students in this particular class. In fact, Walsleben's diary reveals a very empathic learner who was concerned with the feelings of the other students. Her own feelings of frustration were aimed at the teacher and his teaching methods, which she felt were wasting her time. Apparently she was not alone in this opinion. Toward the end of the journal Walsleben documents a classroom blow-up, triggered by yet another vocabulary test:[8]

> After the break (the teacher) announced that he would give the vocabulary test, "If that's okay." Shirley stated again her difficulty in studying uncontextualized words for a vocabulary test, and (the teacher) explained that he nonetheless felt that it was a justifiable way of building up our vocabularies. When he repeated that he was going to give the test and looked at me when he said, "If that's okay," I responded tersely, "You're the professor, but in my opinion it's a poor use of time." That was the proverbial last straw. For the next hour and a half the whole class was embroiled in a very emotional exchange of opinions dealing with what the class was and was not, what it could and should be, who would let whom do what.
>
> My seven weeks of pent-up anger and frustration made my voice quaver and my hands tremble so that I could not lift my coffee cup without spilling the coffee. (The teacher's) voice too was unsteady. I was terribly uncomfortable, feeling like the class "heavy" and feeling little or no support from the other members of the class at first. At one point, when I saw Davis's and Ramona's faces flush with what I interpreted as being discomfort, I tried to stop talking, but by then (the teacher) insisted that we continue.

---

[8]See Bailey (1979) for a description of a similar classroom incident which was also touched off by the students' reaction to a test.

> Gradually our voices became lower and more calm, and one by one, the students expressed their own opinions and suggestions. But when we finished talking, I was feeling an internal conflict between my belief that (the professor) had *heard* our criticisms and suggestions and my doubt that he would actually do anything in response to them. I felt exhausted and empty. (ibid., 34–35)

Besides Walsleben two other students in the class were experienced language teachers, and throughout the journal there is much discussion of how the course should be taught. In this case it seems that the diarist is not competing with her classmates, but is struggling with the instructor for control of her language-learning experience. This idea is supported by the argument about "who would let whom do what" and her comment, "You're the professor." During the eighth week of the ten-week quarter she wrote,

> By Thursday I knew I would not go to class again—at least for the remainder of the quarter. . . . All quarter long I had spent hours and hours studying Farsi because I wanted to and was determined to keep progressing. Whenever I had several assignments to do I always did my Farsi first because to me it was not work at all, but fun. Reading and translating was like working a puzzle. I had reread all the texts and marked all the relative clauses to see if I could grasp the pattern that was being used; it did not always appear to fit the rules (the teacher) had given us, so I wanted to ask questions about them whenever he reached the point where he intended to explicate grammatical points in the texts. I had also noted other grammatical questions in the text margins. But suddenly—it did not seem to matter. (ibid., 36)

Walsleben had not enrolled in this course for credit: she was there just to learn Persian. But she could not accept the teacher's methodology because of her own training as an ESL teacher. The over-emphasis on tests in the course seemed unproductive to her and in spite of her high integrative motivation, Walsleben left the Persian class.[9]

---

[9]Francine Schumann also discusses withdrawal from learning due to nonacceptance of the teaching method:

> I hated the method. My anger bred frustration, a frustration which I acutely felt as my goal was to be a star performer in class, and I found it impossible to be so under these circumstances.
>
> Instead of resorting to a solution which would allow me to cope with this learning environment and learn in spite of the method, my reaction was to reject it and withdraw from learning. This withdrawal was gradual and displayed itself in a variety of ways. Some days I would assume such a low profile in class, making no attempts to participate, that only my physical presence allowed that I was indeed a member of the group. Other days this withdrawal took the form of my cutting-up during the lesson. Eventually the withdrawal led to my leaving class early, walking out on exams, and on some days not showing up at all. (Schumann & Schumann, 1977, p. 244)

Another unhappy experience is reported by Rebecca Jones, who studied Indonesian in an eleven-week intensive program while she was immersed in the target culture. The journal of her experiences reveals a sharp contrast between the positive environment in the home of her Indonesian host family and the discomfort and frustration she felt within the formal classroom situation. The competitiveness she experienced in the Indonesian course is evident throughout the journal.

Much of Jones's unhappiness with the program started in an early encounter with the director. A diary entry made at the beginning of the course says,

> I can't believe Dr. Fox. He has just informed me that I am lucky that I am one of the ten participants in this program as I was a borderline case and on Indonesian tests I took to get admitted to the program I wasn't that good. Then he said it was because I hadn't used his books, *that* was the main problem. I can barely write this down. One of my friends warned me. If he likes you, you will do fine; if he doesn't, WATCH OUT. So I have to swallow my pride and hide my feelings and try to make him like me and avoid him or ignore what he says. I feel like telling exactly what I think of him, but that would do nothing but alienate me from the program and antagonize him more. (1977, p. 27)

Thus from the beginning of the course, Jones had to compete with the negative expectations communicated to her by the director. To salvage her pride she had to do better than he expected her to do—better than her test scores predicted she would do. Later in the week she wrote,

> ... We have been divided into two groups, "good" and "not so good." I'm in the "not so good" group with Peter, Cindy and Laura. Those in the upper group are those who used Fox's book in the United States, who are his students, or who previously had been in Indonesia longer than three months. (ibid., 31)

Her status as a member of the less advanced group was apparently upsetting to Jones, who had been to Indonesia twice before—once as an exchange student for three months.

In Jones's case the program director seems to have promoted the competition by overtly comparing the students in the class. Apparently hurt by this action, Jones wrote,

> Dr. Fox stated in front of the entire group that he was pleased with Peter's memorization of the dialogue; Laura's was OK; and he was not pleased with mine *at all.* In other words, he said, "A for Peter, B for Laura and C for Becky." That had the effect of turning me off entirely from the rest of the lectures for the rest of the day. I am writing in my journal and not listening at all. ... (ibid., 36)

Peter and Laura, the two learners with whom Jones is compared, were both in the "not so good" group of students. According to the diarist, this public humiliation caused her to mentally withdraw from instruction for at least the remainder of the day. The director's comment was apparently very damaging to Jones's attitude about the program as a whole. At the end of this episode she wrote,

> I am building up a lot of resentment and negative feelings. If I learn Indonesian, it is in spite of Dr. Fox and this program. The program has the tendency of stripping away all support and exposing all my inadequacies in Indonesian. It crushes my ego, *especially when I wanted to be top in the class.* (ibid., 36) (emphasis mine)

This last comment is an example of an overtly stated desire to outdo the other students (like my predicting I would be the best student in the French 2R class). However, Jones was facing some severe obstacles: it seems she was competing with an idealized self-image as well as with her classmates and the director's negative expectations.

The competitiveness that developed in Jones's Indonesian classes spilled over into her free-time activities as well. During the second week of the program she wrote,

> I went downtown tonight with Sony and Laura. My Indonesian was good and I felt confident. I spoke in Indonesian all night and felt secure in my use of it. This is probably because I compared myself to Laura, whose language is terrible. She has difficulty understanding anything. I felt more confident because I know she is not going to correct my Indonesian. (ibid., 34)

Like me in the French 2R class, Jones seems to capitalize (emotionally and—indirectly—linguistically) on the presence of another learner with whom she can compare herself favorably.

Jones's first edge in the classroom competition appeared when the group began to study Jawi, Indonesian in Arabic script. Of this experience she wrote,

> Jawi began today. I did better than the others, except Glenn, because of my previous study of Jawi in Hawaii. I feel good because of that. (ibid., 46)

There is no further reference to Jawi in the edited diary, so the reader doesn't know if the Jawi writing practice continued to be a source of success for Jones. However, like me in the French 2R class, Jones found some satisfaction in ranking herself differentially (against the other students) in the various language skills. Nearly two months after the beginning of the course, Jones wrote,

> In comparison with the other members of the group, I would say that my pronunciation is the best, but my vocabulary is by far the most limited because I've stopped doing the readings. (ibid., 57)

In discussing the trends in her journal, Jones, like Francine Schumann, identifies her competitiveness with the other participants as one of the major personal factors influencing her language learning experience:

> Prompted by Dr. Fox's and the Indonesian staff's behavior toward me in the
> classroom situation, I began to feel more and more in competition with the
> other participants. A curious form of sibling rivalry developed among us.
> Dr. Fox . . . functioned in the role of the parent with all of the learners acting
> as children, competing in order to achieve recognition and attention. . . . I
> disliked this competitiveness in the classroom as I was not the top student
> and could not achieve my need for positive reinforcement and reassurance.
> So I essentially stopped working altogether on my language learning in the
> classroom situation. In order to gain favor with the parent figure of Dr. Fox, I
> turned my energies to organizing parties and trips for the group and totally
> abandoned anything more than a polite attempt in keeping up with the
> lessons. (ibid., 77–78)

Thus, Jones saw the competitive climate in her Indonesian program as detri-
mental (or at least not conducive) to language learning. Although her Indonesian fluency improved (as measured by pre- and posttesting, as well as by her
own estimation), she attributed this gain to her life with the Indonesian host
family and to being immersed in the target language environment, rather than
to the classroom instruction. Because she could not compete with many of the
other students in the formal instructional setting, she channeled her energies
into other ways of pleasing the director/parent figure.

In a paper based on a diary she kept while studying Indonesian as a foreign language, Deborah Plummer (1976) also discusses the teacher as a parent
figure. In reviewing her journal entries, Plummer identified three phases in her
classroom language-learning experience. These stages were determined more
by affective factors than by linguistic ability. Plummer's journal reveals that in
the first phase of classroom language learning she adopted a childlike persona,
which (she felt) enabled her to learn more easily:

> The best way I can describe my psychological state in the class is childlike.
> At the beginning I felt free from adult responsibility. I was expected to bring
> to the class no previous knowledge of the language. All of the students
> began at the same level. I felt like I could play. I knew I was not expected to
> make no errors in my L2 speech so I took advantage of my freedom. This
> does not mean that I made errors on purpose. It simply means that I was
> able to experiment and learn in the way I find easiest, that is, learning by
> doing. . . . (Plummer, 1976, p. 5)

Plummer's attitude toward the Indonesian teacher in this first phase seems to
have promoted this childlike state. In discussing the professor she wrote,

> She became very much of a parental figure to me, in whom I could place my
> trust. I knew that she understood the changes I went through each day from
> 9:00 to 9:50 A.M. Before and after that time I was an adult who could
> express herself on an intellectual linguistic level, but during class I was an
> adult who struggled to talk about elementary concrete objects in the most
> simple, childlike speech. Instead of being frustrated by such a dichotomy, I

found it much easier to adopt a childlike identity in the new language. I consider this a major factor in promoting the learning of the target language. Because of the threats a second or foreign language class often poses, this new identity helped preserve my adult ego and self-confidence. (ibid., 5–6)

Plummer's description of herself in the first phase of her language-learning experience is remarkably similar to Walsleben's discussion of the highly vocal students who annoyed her so much in her Persian class:

My childlike behavior in class was manifest in a variety of ways, what I was most conscious of was shouting out words. I particularly liked playing with the new sounds of the target language.[10] I liked repeating words and phrases after the professor and I did so in a loud voice. I liked trying to be the first to get it out. . . . I found myself just wanting to talk and make noise and play with the language until it became a part of me. . . . I realize that in such a language class there needed to be order. The professor, very much like a parent, let those of us play who needed to, but there was an understood limit and discipline. (ibid., 6)

During the first phase Plummer also reports that she had a "language-learning buddy" (i.e., a cooperative coactor):

We usually sat together and laughed about the sounds of the new words as we shouted them out. . . . We incorporated Indonesian words into English phrases and took the liberty to invent some words. It was very much like child-play with language. . . . Our goal was to use Indonesian communicatively. (ibid., 6–7)

Plummer and her language-learning buddy were apparently aggressive and fun-loving in their approach to learning Indonesian. Yet Plummer too was extremely sensitive to competition in the language classroom. At one point she saw herself as being out of favor with the instructor, for reasons she cannot (or does not) explain. This period she identifies as the second phase of her language learning:

Outside of class I had felt very distant from the professor—an abrupt change from the in-class parental figure. In and out of class she was a person I highly respected and from whom I sought recognition and approval—as if she were a parent. . . . I felt that I had lost her recognition, approval and favor. I lost my self-confidence and most of all I lost my childlike feeling. I was an adult. As an adult I was responsible for my actions and my L2 errors became ego deflating and wounding. In my mind errors were no longer to be laughed at. (ibid., 8–9)

During this second phase Plummer also reports a change in the relationship with her friend:

---

[10]See Peck (1977, pp. 86–90) for a discussion of adults and language play.

> He began sitting away from me and his attention was on another friend. I knew him better than anyone in the class so as a result I felt very much alone and isolated. I did not have much desire to communicate so my new language was useless. (ibid., 9–10)

Plummer reports that she continued to be sensitive to the attention other students received and was bothered by one person in particular. In her journal she wrote, "more than anything, I was jealous." This entry provides an example of the kind of hidden emotions sometimes experienced by learners in language classrooms.

Eventually Plummer discussed these feelings with her professor in an oral exam situation. The teacher apparently responded appropriately because Plummer saw this discussion as another turning point in her language-learning experience:

> Phase III began after this session. I began to feel a little more self-worth and acceptance from my parental figure. She was more sensitive to my needs in class and her subtle attention, unnoticed by others, was very encouraging. I began enjoying the class again. She tried not to let any students dominate the class, which was difficult to do with the few very verbose students. I found those students very intimidating because I could not compete with them for the professor's attention. (ibid., 10–11)

Although Plummer was unable to completely recapture the childlike attitude she had perceived as so beneficial to her early language learning, she saw herself as progressing in Indonesian. Because she had discussed her unhappiness with the teacher, she was able to regain a certain equilibrium in the class, although the competition from the highly vocal students continued to bother her.

In contrast, a diary study conducted by Susan Scheding (1978) in an introductory German class seems to portray an unanxious language learner. Scheding's description of herself leads one to think that Walsleben, Leichman, Bernbrock, Plummer, and I might not be comfortable in a language class with her. On the first day of her college German class she wrote,

> The teacher handed out the syllabus and discussed quizzes, grades, etc. I could feel the anxiety among my fellow students during this discussion, but it doesn't affect me. Many of these students are probably taking German to fulfill some sort of university requirement. I'm hoping to have a good time. . . . (1978, p. 4)

Scheding's approach to classroom language instruction is to seek out as much input and correction as possible. On the fourth day of the class she wrote,

> Somehow I have the feeling that not everybody is participating in the oral drills. I can't really see, as I sit in the front and the chairs are in the traditional rows behind me. But there are thirty students in here and I seem to be

> awfully loud. . . . Why would anyone want to sit in the back of a language class anyway? I always sit close to the instructor in the beginning in order to make sure I'm hearing correctly. Besides, sitting in the front means the teacher is likely to correct me if I mispronounce a word, even in choral drill. This is something the students in the back can't benefit from. (ibid., 5)

Like me in the French 2R class, Scheding compares herself to the other students, but since she is a confident language learner, the results are quite different. Scheding often comments on the lack of challenge in her German class. The following entries are representative:

> We spent most of the hour on grammar explanations. Even though they were in German, I found myself getting impatient with this. Why explain the obvious? I just have to tell myself that for some students it must not be so obvious. . . . (ibid., 6)

> We reviewed for the quiz on Monday. This was very boring. The teacher seemed to avoid calling on me in class; he was looking for those students he is unsure of. But if no one else answered, he usually looked at me. . . . (ibid., 7)

> The quiz was returned. I did very well, as I had expected. The teacher reassured those students who did poorly. I sympathize with those who are struggling. . . . Foreign language learners may not have to deal with culture shock, but most must face other anxieties, and one of them is grade anxiety. (ibid., 8)

Other entries reveal Scheding's annoyance when her classmates would ask picky questions or break into English during the German class.

Before enrolling in this particular course, Scheding had studied Spanish, Latin, French, Mandarin Chinese, Ameslan (American Sign Language), Indonesian, and Quecha. Her self-image was one of a successful language learner. Yet even a confident learner can experience anxiety in a situation where he or she feels incompetent (i.e., unable to compete). Scheding's journal provides a nice illustration of this idea. She reports that she had arranged to miss one class period and the regular teacher had told her he doubted she'd have any trouble with the new material when she returned. However, on returning to the German class, Scheding was surprised:

> Today for the first time all quarter, I experienced the kind of anxiety I once used to experience in language classes when I wasn't prepared and had to go anyway. I had been away skiing with (the teacher's) blessings. During this time they had begun a new chapter. I had made arrangements with (the teacher) to make up the work, but (he) wasn't there today. We had a substitute and *he* didn't know I'd been away. He called on everyone several times during the hour and I really didn't know what was going on. I felt very anxious from the beginning, wishing he wouldn't call on me and keeping my

head down, as though absorbed in the book. (It's the old ostrich syndrome: if I can't see him, he can't see me.) This hour passed very slowly and I was glad when it was over. (ibid., 11–12)

Thus, with her confidence temporarily damaged by not knowing as much as her classmates (or as much as she normally knew), Scheding, like the other diarists, felt inadequate and anxious. This diary entry supports the distinction between state and trait anxiety, made by Spielberger, Gorusch, and Lushene (1970). Although not prone to state anxiety, Scheding's temporary incompetence generated state anxiety.

Except in this one instance, the diary portrays Scheding as a highly confident language learner who compares herself favorably with her classmates because of her past experiences in learning languages (like Fields in the Berlitz class but with much broader exposure to language learning). Scheding may not have experienced much competitiveness because there was no need for her to compete. She was already at the top of her class, in her own opinion as well as the teacher's. And except for the one occasion when she was unprepared and vulnerable, there was no discrepancy between her real self and her ideal self.

Describing and Defining Affective Factors in Second Language Learning

The purpose of this review has been to see what evidence of the relationship between competitiveness and anxiety these ten diary studies provide. In discussing my own journal I listed seven characteristics of the entries involving competitiveness. Those characteristics, with some additions, have appeared in the journals of the other diarists as follows:

1. *Overt self-comparison of the language learner*
   (a) with classmates (Bailey, Bernbrock, Fields, Jones, Leichman, Lynch, Moore, Plummer, Scheding, Schumann, Walsleben); (b) with other language learners not in the classroom (Fields, Walsleben); and (c) with personal expectations (Bailey, Bernbrock, Fields, Walsleben).

2. *Emotive responses to the comparisons* in (1) above (Bailey, Bernbrock, Fields, Jones, Leichman, Lynch, Moore, Plummer, Scheding, Schumann, Walsleben), including (a) hostile reactions toward other students (Bailey, Lynch, Plummer); and (b) connotative uses of language in the diary (Bailey, Fields Leichman, Lynch) which reveal the diarist's emotional state.

3. *A desire to out-do other language learners* (Bailey, Jones), including (a) racing through examinations (Bailey); and (b) students shouting out answers in class (Plummer, and reported on by Walsleben).

4. *Emphasis on or concern with tests and grades*[11] (Bailey, Bernbrock, Leichman, Lynch, Walsleben) (a) especially with reference to other students (Bailey, Leichman); or (b) with a discussion of how tests interfere with language learning (Leichman, Walsleben); although (c) one "unanxious" student (Scheding) documents a notable lack of concern with tests and grades.

5. *A desire to gain the teacher's approval* (Bailey, Jones, Leichman, Plummer, Walsleben), including (a) perception of the teacher as a parent figure (Jones, Plummer); and (b) the need to meet or overcome a teacher's expectations (Bernbrock, Jones).

6. *Anxiety experienced during the language lesson* (Bailey, Bernbrock, Jones, Leichman, Lynch, Moore, Plummer, Scheding, Walsleben).

7. *Withdrawal from the language-learning experience* (Bailey, Bernbrock, Jones, Schumann, Walsleben), which can be either (a) mental (Jones) or physical (Bailey, Bernbrock, Walsleben); and (b) temporary (Bailey) or permanent (Bernbrock, Jones, Walsleben); (c) one diarist (Leichman) wanted to withdraw temporarily but continued to attend the language class.

The components of this description could be used in a correlation study to design a questionnaire or scale for measuring competitiveness and anxiety. In addition, some of the manifestations of competitiveness listed above may be directly observable by classroom researchers. For example, teachers may overhear discussions of grades, or notice students rushing through tests. Observers could identify students who shout out answers in classroom drills, or who withdraw from the learning environment following public humiliation or failure. But attributing such behaviors to the learners' competitiveness is still an inferential step, and the other items on the list may be examples of the hidden classroom responses Moore has called "a melee of emotions, rational and irrational" (1977, p. 108). Thus the diary studies, if they are candid and thorough,

---

[11]Davis discusses the research on feedback as it relates to the quality of group performance:

If the task permits individual contributions to be recovered or graded in the final group product, then individual members may be selectively rewarded accordingly. Alternatively, the group may be paid off as a whole. The result ... is that cooperative behavior is usually evident in the latter kind of group, while a competitive interaction style typically characterizes the former sort of group. (1969, p. 81)

In a language classroom, achievement or improvement is normally measured on an individual basis by examination. Therefore, the language classroom is more closely related to the former type of group, in which members are rewarded selectively (i.e., by grades) than to the latter, in which the group members receive group "payoff."

can provide access to the language learner's hidden classroom responses, especially in the affective domain.[12]

It is not my purpose to argue in favor of introspective diary studies over empirical research on second language learning. In fact, these two approaches to knowing can provide us with very different types of information, and each methodology can inform the other, as I have tried to show.[13] In discussing what he calls the "anthropological approach" and the "interaction analysis approach" to investigating language classroom processes, Long calls for "future research on classroom language learning which uses a combined approach, thereby avoiding some of the limitations of each and taking advantage of the strengths of both" (1979, p. 40). Ochsner has also argued forcefully for the use of both traditions—nomothetic (empirical) science and hermeneutic (here, introspective) investigation—in SLA research. He describes a poetics of SLA which would allow us to "develop a perceptual bilingualism; that is, the ability to study SLA from at least two points of view" (1979, p. 71).

As research on classroom language learning progresses, we must question first the form and then the content of the diary studies. The medium, the methodology, is introspective and descriptive—not necessarily predictive. Cause and effect are determined by the diarist's perceptions rather than by controlling and manipulating variables. This being the case, what is the value of the diarists' conclusions? Can they be generalized, and what can they teach us about language learning?

Based on this review we may conclude that the findings of the diary studies can be *compared,* whether or not they can be *generalized.* In fact, it may not even be desirable to try to generalize from the results of such language learning journals. Their main purpose is to discover what factors influence the individual diarist's language learning. As Long has pointed out, the diary studies

> are concerned with individuals in unique learning environments, so generalization of their findings to other learners and environments is precluded on the basis of the studies themselves. They may be relevant to many or even all learners, in other words, or idiosyncratic. (1979, p. 36)

Of course, in the complex, real-life world of the language classroom, given enough details of history, motivation, aptitude, etc., every student can be

---

[12]In discussing the research on group processes, Davis states:

It is possible to distinguish two basic methods for obtaining data concerning interpersonal behavior: (a) the observation of interpersonal behavior by trained observers, and (b) the self-report of the individual member concerning his own reaction to others and his perceptions of the reactions of fellow group members to each other. (1969, p. 7)

To the extent that each individual diarist can be considered a "trained observer," the diary studies can tap both of these sources of information.

[13]See Bellack (1978) for a comparison of these two traditions, which he calls "mainstream scientific ideology" and "interpretive ideology," in research on teaching.

viewed as functioning in a unique learning environment. For this reason, the question of generalizability, as the term is used in the empirical research tradition, is inappropriate here.[14] Thus, it is primarily in the area of *personal variables* (Schumann & Schumann, 1977) or *learner variables* (Scovel, 1978) that the diary studies can contribute to our knowledge of second language learning (Long, 1979; Schumann & Schumann, 1977).

But questions of content, here the personal affective factors under consideration, must also be raised. What good does it do us to investigate competitiveness in language classrooms when competition surrounds us and permeates our lives? Caillois (1961) describes competition as both "a law of nature" (p. 46) and "a law of modern life" (p. 50). (Indeed the entire free enterprise system is based on economic competition.) He sees competition as a product of *agon,* the desire to win, which is one of four primary attitudes toward play among humans.[15] In a treatise on the play element in culture, Huizinga (1950) describes the agonistic impulse as innate and practically universal:

> From the life of childhood right up to the highest achievements of civilization, one of the strongest incentives to perfection, both individual and social, is the desire to be praised for one's excellence. . . . Doing something well means doing it better than others. In order to excel, one must prove one's excellence; in order to merit recognition, merit must be made manifest. Competition serves to give proof of superiority. (p. 63)

Such competition is well known, indeed integral, to prevalent trends in education. Reporting on ethnographic field work in elementary school classrooms, Roberts and Akinsanya (1976) characterize competition as one of "the most prominent emotions" of children:

> . . . It is difficult to see how, in the present state of our culture, competitiveness can be overlooked. It would seem, perhaps, that the important outcome to avoid is that the competitiveness should become destructive of peers, while reinforcing dependence on the teacher. (p. 181)

Huizinga too discusses competition in knowledge as a universal theme:

> The urge to be first has as many forms of expression as society offers opportunities for it. The ways in which men compete are as various as the prizes at stake. . . . The astonishing similarity that characterizes agonistic customs in all cultures is perhaps nowhere more striking than in the domain of the human mind itself, that is to say, in knowledge and wisdom (1950, p. 105).

If competition is practically all-pervasive, how can studying competitiveness contribute to our understanding of second language acquisition?

---

[14]Long (1979, pp. 35–36) summarizes the arguments regarding generalizability in social science research.

[15]In classifying games Caillois proposed "a division into four main rubrics, depending on whether, in the games under consideration, the role of competition, chance, simulation, or vertigo is dominant. (He calls) these agon, alea, mimicry and ilinx, respectively" (1961, p. 12).

The answer lies in the complex relationship of competitiveness and anxiety, and then of anxiety to language learning. For several of the diarists cited above, entries which may be interpreted as revealing competitiveness or a perceived inability to compete often reveal anxiety as well. This trend leads us to the already obvious conclusion that Gardner et al.'s term "French Classroom Anxiety" (1976) should be broadened to the more general term "Language Classroom Anxiety."

At this point we should recall Tucker's comment regarding the present "state of the art" in research on affective variables:

> Although we would all presumably agree with the proposition that affective variables (somehow defined) are important in some way during the course of foreign or second language learning or teaching, their precise description and measurement remains a problematic issue (Tucker, 1979, p. 3).

Using the description above we can distill a definition of competitiveness as it occurs in the language classroom. Competitiveness is the desire to excel in comparison to others. The *others* are typically the learner's classmates, but as these diaries have shown, a learner may compete with an idealized self-image or with other learners not directly involved in the language classroom (a spouse, a friend, a sibling, etc.). Competitiveness arises when the comparison is emotive rather than objective. If the comparison is invidious (i.e., if the learner perceives himself as lacking), such competitiveness can lead to anxiety. It may also lead to active *competition,* either through increased personal efforts to master the language or through striving to out-do other students (e.g., racing through tests, shouting out answers, over-emphasizing grades, etc.).

As Long notes, ethnographic field work—to which the diary studies are closely related—"is primarily a hypothesis-generating, not hypothesis-testing, undertaking" (1980, p. 27). This paper suggests the hypothesis that Language Classroom Anxiety can be caused and/or aggravated by the learner's competitiveness when he sees himself as less proficient than the object of comparison. Anxiety can also lead to competitiveness in the form of increased efforts to learn the language. (Such competitiveness, in Scovel's terms, is an intrinsic learner variable, which is influenced by extrinsic factors, including the behavior of the teacher[16] and other learners.) A corollary to this hypothesis is that as the learner

---

[16]The exact role of the teacher in promoting competitiveness and/or Language Classroom Anxiety is as yet unclear. In discussing group processes in (content) classrooms, Schmuck and Schmuck suggest that the actions of authoritarian teachers "encourage high dependency, high competition among students, feelings of some powerlessness, and at times, feelings of being alienated from the subject matter" (1971, p. 75). They also say that, "the teacher who encourages high amounts of dependency or competition through influence behaviors often is reaping debilitating outcomes for students" (ibid.). In pursuing the issue one step further, Schmuck and Schmuck point out that teachers too are susceptible to what Scovel calls "the effect of affect" (1978, p. 129):

If teachers have feelings of comfort and rapport in relationships with colleagues, they are supported in their feelings of self-worth and are better able to relate positively to students. Feelings of hostility, competition or alienation lead to anxiety and low levels of tolerance with students. (Schmuck & Schmuck, 1971, p. 196)

becomes, or perceives himself as becoming, more competent (that is, better able to compete), his anxiety will decrease. Several of the diary entries cited above suggest that as anxiety decreases, the quality and quantity of performance increases, and vice versa. Thus I am suggesting a cyclic relationship between anxiety and negative competitiveness (i.e., invidious comparisons with other learners in which the learner perceives himself as lacking and attaches emotional significance to that perception). In formal instructional settings, if such anxiety motivates the learner to study the target language, it is *facilitating.* On the other hand, if it is severe enough to cause the learner to withdraw from the language classroom (either mentally or physically, temporarily or permanently), such anxiety is *debilitating* (Alpert & Haber, 1966: Kleinmann, 1977; Scovel, 1978). An over-simplified schematic representation of this complex relationship is presented in Figure 1.

At this point we should recall Tucker's comment regarding the present "state of the art" in research on affective variables:

> Although we would all presumably agree with the proposition that affective variables (somehow defined) are important in some way during the course of foreign or second language learning or teaching, their precise description and measurement remains a problematic issue. (1979, p. 3)

Thus, one value of the first-person diary studies is that the researcher/learner/diarist begins to study an affective factor by acknowledging its presence and psychological reality in the journal entries. He or she can then use the rich details of these entries to describe and define the variable under consideration. This approach to knowing is quite different from that of traditional empirical research, in which an investigator must operationally define his terms before beginning an experiment.

A second advantage is that, like other longitudinal case studies, the diary studies can provide developmental data. But since the diaries are first-person accounts, such data can yield information on the instability of attitudes discussed by Oller (1979, p. 10). Because the journals are systematic chronological records of personal responses to language learning situations, attitudinal changes can be traced through the sequential entries. An example is Susan Scheding's sudden state anxiety on the one day she was not prepared to participate in her German class. The gradual decrease in the comparison of myself with other students in the French 2R class is another.

A third advantage is linked to the complaint that the diary studies are not generalizable. Because they provide an in-depth portrait of the individual diarist, his or her unique history and idiosyncracies, the diary studies can give teachers and researchers insights on the incredible diversity of students to be found even within a homogeneous language classroom.

Finally, the journal studies enable the researcher/learner to document, and perhaps overcome, avoid, or counteract factors that are apparently detri-

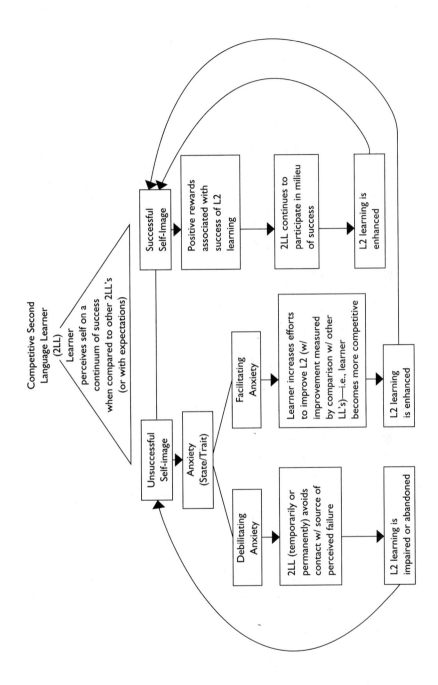

FIGURE 1.   Competitiveness and the Second Language Learner

mental to his or her language learning. There is some evidence that even the act of writing in the diary, whether or not the learner ever systematically reviews the entries, can be therapeutic for the learner. Ultimately, if we can use the diaries to identify the events and emotions leading up to changes in affect, we may be able to control or induce such changes. For instance, if we can determine the perceived causes of Language Classroom Anxiety, we might then be able to reduce this reaction or eliminate it entirely. Following the research of Gardner et al. cited above (1976), we can hypothesize that reduced Language Classroom Anxiety would lead to improved oral production on a measure of speech skills. Of course, we can also hypothesize that improved oral production would lead to a reduction in Language Classroom Anxiety. Either way, the diary studies allow us to see the classroom experience as a dynamic and complex process through the eyes of the language learner.

A portion of this article was presented at a workshop for teachers at the American Language Institute, San Diego State University, on October 13, 1979. The title is based in part on work by Robert Ochsner (1979), who argues that we must "look at SLA; however, we must also learn to see through it" (p. 71). I am indebted to Robert Ochsner, Diane E. Larsen-Freeman, and Michael H. Long, who gave me references, constructive criticism, and moral support. I also appreciate the guidance of my teachers, José L. Galvan and John H. Schumann.

References

Allwright, R. A. (1980). Turns, topics and tasks: Patterns of participation in language learning and teaching. In D. Larsen-Freeman (Ed.), *Discourse analysis in second language acquisition.* Rowley, Mass.: Newbury House, 1981.

Alpert, R., & Haber, R. (1960). Anxiety in academic achievement situations. *Journal of Abnormal and Social Psychology, 61,* 207–215.

Bailey, K. M. (1978). Mon journal de la classe de Français: An introspective analysis of an individual's language learning experience. Unpublished manuscript, University of California, Los Angeles, English Department (ESL Section).

Bailey, K. M. (1979). An introspective analysis of an individual's language learning experience. In S. Krashen & R. Scarcella (Eds.), *Research in second language acquisition: Selected papers of the Los Angeles second language research forum.* Rowley, Mass.: Newbury House.

Beeman, P., Martin, R., & Meyers, J. (1972). Interventions in relation to anxiety in school. In C. Spielberger (Ed.), *Anxiety: Current trends in theory and research.* New York: Academic Press.

Bellack, A. (1978). Competing ideologies in research on teaching. In Ahlstrom, Berglund, Dahllof, & Wallin (Eds.), *Uppsala reports on education, 1.* Department of Education, Uppsala University.

Bernbrock, C. (1977). An introspective study of second language learning. Unpublished manuscript, English Department (ESL Section). University of California, Los Angeles.

Boring, E. G. 1953. A history of introspection. *Psychological Bulletin, 50,* 3, 169–189.

Caillois, R. (1961). *Man, play and games.* Translated from the French by M. Barash. New York: The Free Press.

Chastain, K. (1975). Affective and ability factors in second language acquisition. *Language Learning, 25,* 153–161.

Davis, J. H. (1969). *Group performance.* Reading, Mass.: Addison-Wesley.

Fields, C. M. (1978). How Berlitz taught me Spanish rapidamente. *The Chronicle of Higher Education,* (July 17, pp. 4–6, and July 24, p. 7).

Gardner, R. C., Smythe, P. C., Clement, R., & Glicksman, L. (1976). Second language learning: A social-psychological perspective. *Canadian Modern Language Review, 32,* 198–213.

Huizinga, J. (1950). *Homo ludens: A study of the play-element in culture.* Boston: Beacon Press.

Jones, R. A. (1977). Psychological, social and personal factors in second language acquisition. Unpublished MA thesis, English Department (ESL Section), University of California, Los Angeles.

Kleinmann, H. (1977). Avoidance behavior in adult second language acquisition. *Language Learning, 27,* 93–107.

Leichman, H. (1977). A diary of one person's acquisition of Indonesian. Unpublished manuscript, English Department (ESL Section), University of California, Los Angeles.

Long, M. (1979). Inside the "black box": Methodological issues in research on teaching. Paper presented at the 1979 TESOL Convention, Boston, Mass.

Lynch, B. (1979). The adult second language learner: An introspective analysis of an individual learning Spanish as a second language. Unpublished manuscript, California State University, San Jose.

Moore, T. (1977). An experimental language handicap (personal account). *Bulletin of British Psychological Society, 30,* 107–110.

Ochsner, R. (1979). A poetics of second language acquisition. *Language Learning, 29,* 53–80.

Oller, J. (1979). Research on the measurement of affective variables: Some remaining questions. Paper presented at the Colloquium on Second Language Acquisition and Use Under Different Circumstances, 1979 TESOL Convention, Boston, Mass.

Oller, J., & Perkins, K. (1978). Intelligence and language proficiency as sources of variance in self-reported affective variables. *Language Learning, 28,* 85–97.

Peck, S. (1977). Play in child second language acquisition. Unpublished master's thesis, English Department (ESL Section), University of California, Los Angeles.

Plummer, D. (1978). A summary of a foreign language learning diary. Unpublished manuscript, English Department (ESL Section), University of California, Los Angeles.

Schmuck, R. A., & Schmuck, P. A. (1971). *Group processes in the classroom.* Dubuque, Iowa: William C. Brown.

Schumann, F. E. (1978, October). Diary of a language learner: A further analysis. Paper presented at the Los Angeles Second Language Research Forum, University of Southern California, Los Angeles.

Schumann, F. E., & Schumann, J. H. (1977). Diary of a language learner: An introspective study of second language learning. In H. D. Brown, R. H. Crymes, & C. A. Yorio (Eds.), *Teaching and learning: Trends in research and practice.* Washington, D.C.: TESOL.

Schumann, J. H. (1975). Affective factors and the problem of age in second language acquisition. *Language Learning, 25,* 209–235.

Scovel, T. (1978). The effect of affect on foreign language learning: A review of the anxiety research. *Language Learning, 28,* 129–142.

Snell, R. (1978). A review of six diary studies. Unpublished manuscript, English Department (ESL Section), University of California, Los Angeles.

Spielberger, C., Gorusch, & Lushene (1970). *State-trait anxiety inventory.* Palo Alto, Calif.: Consulting Psychologist Press.

Stevick, E. (1976). *Memory, meaning and method.* Rowley, Mass.: Newbury House.

Tucker, G. R. (1979). Comments on J. W. Oller, Research on the measurement of affective variables: Some remaining questions. Paper presented at the Colloquium on Second Language Acquisition and Use under Different Circumstances, 1979 TESOL Convention, Boston, Mass.

Verman, P., & Nijhawan, H. (1976). The effect of anxiety, reinforcement, and intelligence on the learning of a difficult task. *Journal of Experimental Child Psychology, 22,* 302–308.

Walsleben, M. (1976). Cognitive and affective factors influencing a learner of Persian (Farsi) including a journal of second language acquisition. Unpublished manuscript, English Department (ESL Section), University of California, Los Angeles.

Understanding the Chapter

1. How does this kind of research compare with experimental research in terms of (a) the data collection procedures, (b) the role of the researcher, and (c) the way in which the research questions are defined?

2. What are the recurring themes or patterns Bailey identified in the analysis of her own language learning diary?

3. How does Bailey use information from the ten diary studies by other language learners that she cites?

4. Restate the research question(s) and briefly summarize the answer(s).

5. What are the implications of the results? To what extent are the results generalizable to other language learners?

Reflecting on Wider Issues

1. There is general agreement that affective variables are hard to measure. What different ways might researchers try to measure anxiety? Do you think that some of the methods are more or less problematic than others? Why?

2. Like ethnographic studies, diary studies are often described as "hypothesis-generating," not "hypothesis-teaching." What are the advantages and disadvantages of this approach to looking at second language acquisition?

Going Beyond the Chapter

As we have noted, diary studies are often criticized for being too subjective. In a case study of a native speaker of English learning Portuguese, Schmidt and Frota respond to attacks on this kind of research by combining evidence from recordings of the learner conversing in Portuguese with data from the learner's diary. See Schmidt and Frota, "Developing basic conversational ability in a second language: A case study of an adult learner of Portuguese," in R. D. Day (ed.), *Talking to Learn* (Rowley, Mass.: Newbury House, 1986).

If you want to read more about the effect of anxiety on language learning, you might want to look at *Language Anxiety: From Theory and Research to Classroom Implications,* a collection of original contributions edited by Horwitz and Young (Englewood Cliffs, NJ: Prentice Hall, 1991).

If you would like to see how researchers attempt to study affective variables such as anxiety experimentally, read MacIntyre and Gardner (1991), "Investigating language class anxiety using the focused essay technique" (*Modern Language Journal, 75,* 296–304); and "Language anxiety: Its relationship to other anxieties and to processing in native and second languages" (*Language Learning, 41,* 513–534).

8

AN INSTRUMENTAL MOTIVATION IN LANGUAGE STUDY
Who Says It Isn't Effective?

Robert C. Gardner and Peter D. MacIntyre
University of Western Ontario

Previewing the Article

One of the most widely known affectively-based constructs in second language acquisition research is instrumental/integrative motivation, as first studied by Robert Gardner and Wallace Lambert in the late 1960s. In the early findings, they found substantial support for the effectiveness of an integrative orientation for successful language acquisition; soon, however, studies were published that demonstrated the superiority of an instrumental orientation. Here, in a relatively recent study, Gardner and his colleague, Peter MacIntyre, find new evidence for the desirability—but not necessarily superiority—of instrumental motivation.

Before you read the article, review definitions of instrumental and integrative motivation (see *PLLT*, Chapter 6) and arguments for their respective desirability. Then, scan the article to find answers to the following:

1. What is the purpose of the study?
2. What kinds of data are collected in this study?
3. What kinds of statistical tests are used to support the conclusions?

Reprinted from *Studies in Second Language Acquisition,* 13:57–72, 1991.

The major purpose of this study was to investigate the effects of integrative motivation and instrumental motivation on the learning of French/English vocabulary. Integrative motivation was defined in terms of a median split on scores obtained on subtests from the Attitude/Motivation Test Battery, while instrumental motivation was situationally determined in terms of monetary reward for doing well. The results demonstrated that both integrative motivation and instrumental motivation facilitated learning. Other results indicated that instrumentally motivated students studied longer than noninstrumentally motivated students when there was an opportunity to profit from learning, but this distinction disappeared when the incentive was removed. Both integratively and instrumentally motivated students spent more time thinking about the correct answer than those not so motivated, suggesting that both elements have an energizing effect. A secondary purpose of this study was to assess the consequences of computer administration of the Attitude/Motivation Test Battery. In this respect the results were most encouraging. Computer administration appeared not to detract from the internal consistency reliability of the subscales used, and moreover there was an indication that an index of reaction time to individual items might provide a way of identifying social desirability responding.

Considerable research has demonstrated that attitudes and motivation play a role in the learning of a second language. Gardner (1985) summarized much of the literature dealing with this topic and discussed various conceptual, analytic, and theoretical issues associated with this area. A major feature of his socioeducational model of second language learning (see also Gardner & Smythe, 1975) is the proposition that attitudes play a role in language learning through their influence on motivation.

In the socioeducational model, the integrative motive is viewed as a constellation of attitudes and motivation involving various aspects of second language learning, with the prime determinant of achievement being the motivational component. Gardner (1985) stated that "motivation to learn a second language is influenced by group related and context related attitudes, integrativeness and attitudes toward the learning situation, respectively" (p. 168). He argued that many other variables might also be implicated in second language learning, including an instrumental orientation. "To the extent that it (an instrumental orientation) is a powerful motivator, it too will influence achievement, but the major aspect in it is not the instrumentality *per se* but the motivation" (p. 168). There is, therefore, a major distinction between orientations and motivation. Orientations refer to reasons for studying a second language, while motivation refers to the directed, reinforcing effort to learn the language.

The distinction between integrative and instrumental orientations is a common one in this field of research. An integrative orientation reflects an interest in learning another language because of "a sincere and personal interest in the people and culture represented by the other language group" (Lambert, 1974, p. 98), while an instrumental orientation emphasizes "the practical value and advantages of learning a new language" (p. 98). Although some studies have used orientation items as their major affective measures (see, for example, Chihara & Oller, 1978; Lukmani, 1972; Oller, Baca, & Vigil, 1977; Oller, Hudson, & Liu, 1977), this approach places too much emphasis on orientation. In the research that has demonstrated the importance of affective factors (see, for example, Gardner, 1985; Gardner & Lambert, 1972), it has been shown repeatedly that it is not so much the orientation that promotes achievement but rather the motivation. If an integrative or instrumental orientation is not linked with heightened motivation to learn the second language, it is difficult to see how either could promote proficiency.

Research that focuses only on orientations is faced with at least two conceptual difficulties. First, as might be expected, the integrative and instrumental orientations have been shown to be positively correlated with one another and indeed often contribute to the same dimension in factor analytic studies (Gardner, Smythe, & Lalonde, 1984). This seems reasonable since someone who is oriented to learn a language for integrative reasons might well recognize the instrumental value of learning the language and vice versa. Spolsky (1989) made a similar observation when he pointed out that there are many possible bases for motivation. He stated: "A language may be learned for any one or any collection of practical reasons. The importance of these reasons to the learner will determine what degree of effort he or she will make, what cost he or she will pay for the learning" (p. 160). Second, as demonstrated by Clément and Kruidenier (1983), there are many possible orientations depending on the linguistic/cultural context, and even the definition of integrative and instrumental orientations differs in different settings. Thus, even if one finds that one orientation correlates higher with achievement than another (cf. Lukmani, 1972), there is little theoretical significance in the result.

A basic tenet of the socioeducational models is that the integrative motive facilitates second language acquisition because it reflects an active involvement in language study. This active component has been demonstrated in studies that show that, in addition to being more successful in learning a second language, integratively motivated students are more active in language class, are more likely to participate in excursions to the other cultural community when given the opportunity and to interact with members of that community when there, and less likely to drop out of language study in subsequent years (Gardner, 1983). This does not imply that an instrumental motivation would not also be effective. However, to date, there has been relatively little research conducted on an instrumental motive (as distinct from an instrumental orientation).

In order to study instrumental motivation in language study, it is necessary to establish a situation in which such motivation will be salient. One possible paradigm suitable for laboratory research was used by Dunkel (1948), though he did not use the term *instrumental motivation.* Dunkel was concerned with investigating the effects of motivation (among other factors) on learning Modern Persian. He offered rewards of up to $4 for superior performance in the learning of grammar. Although this strategy tended to be associated with higher mean performance on the grammar test, the results were not significant, possibly because the study lacked sufficient power. Dunkel concluded: "One could then suggest that the observed differences might be educationally significant even if not statistically significant" (p. 103). Regardless of the results, that study does provide a useful methodology for studying the role of an obvious form of instrumental motivation on second language learning.

An analogue task has already been used to study the effects of attitudinal/motivational characteristics on second language learning. Gardner, Lalonde, and Moorcroft (1985) used an English/French paired associates learning paradigm and found that the rate of learning French nouns was faster for students with favorable attitudes and motivation as compared with those with less favorable ones (as defined by a median split on the Attitude/Motivation Index [AMI]). In addition, subjects above the median in language aptitude also learned faster than those below the median. Such results demonstrate that an analogue situation can be used to study the effects of various factors on second language learning.

The major purpose of the present study was to investigate the role of both instrumental and integrative motivations in language study by determining how they influenced the learning of 26 English/French word pairs. The instrumental motivation was situationally defined in terms of a $10 reward offered randomly to one-half of the subjects if they achieved a superior level of success on the final trial of the learning task. The offer of an incentive can be viewed as a form of environmentally defined instrumental motivation. To the extent that this was a subject's sole reason for learning the material, it might also be considered as reflecting an instrumental orientation for that person, but to the extent that subjects were not asked this question, this cannot be determined. The point is then that this reflects an environmentally defined form of instrumental motivation. Results obtained in this study support the generalization that it was, in fact, motivating for the participants.

Following Gardner (1985), an individual difference measure of integrative motivation was defined by aggregating scores on six attitude and motivation tests involving elements of integrativeness (Integrative Orientation, Attitudes toward French Canadians, and Interest in Foreign Languages), attitudes toward the learning situation, and motivation (Attitudes toward Learning French, Desire to Learn French). It was hypothesized that both instrumental and integrative motivations would influence the learning of second language material. It was also felt that the two different motivational states may have differing but unspecified effects on how subjects approached the task of learning the word pairs. Two measures of effort expended during the learning task were also investigated (Viewing Time and Study Time). Carroll (1962) argued that time devoted to learning was an index of motivation; thus, both measures seem ideally suited as indices of motivation in this context.

A secondary purpose of this study was to assess the feasibility of administering elements of the Attitude/Motivation Test Battery (Gardner, 1985) by computer since research has demonstrated that this approach may provide a means of identifying social desirability responding. A recent article by Hsu, Santelli, and Hsu (1989) reviewed much of this literature and concluded that deliberate faking tends to be associated with shorter latencies in responding to individual items. Their own results supported this conclusion. In the present investigation, rather than focus on faking, we were interested in determining how response latencies related to scores on the attitude/motivation measures, and whether the different instructions with respect to the learning task influenced either attitude/motivation scores or item response latencies.

Method
Subjects

Ninety-two introductory psychology students participated in this study in order to fulfill a course requirement. None of the subjects had studied French since their penultimate year of high school. The reason for using subjects who had not studied French for some time was not taken lightly. Given the materials to be learned, it was known on the basis of previous research (Gardner, Lalonde, & Moorcroft, 1985) that such individuals would not know any of the vocabulary items at the outset of the study, and that consequently the rate of learning would reflect factors operating in the learning task itself as opposed to transfer from previous knowledge. Since the major focus was on the effects that attitudes and motivation, on the one hand, and monetary rewards, on the other, had on the French vocabulary learning (and other relevant behaviors), such control seems mandatory. A possible criticism of this strategy is that since the individuals were not students of French, none could be said to be truly integratively motivated to learn French. This, however, would tend only to moderate any effects between those classified as integratively or not integratively motivated, thus making any significant effects for this factor all the more impressive.

Materials

There were two parts to this study. In the first part, subjects responded to items assessing eight different attitudinal/motivational characteristics adapted from Gardner, Lalonde, and Moorcroft (1985) as well as the trait of social desirability responding. These Likert items were presented in an individually determined random order on a Zenith microcomputer. The computer recorded both the individual's response and the time it took for the individual to make the response. The variables assessed, and their Cronbach alpha (α) reliability coefficients, were as follows:

1. Attitudes towards French Canadians (α = .88). Ten items, five positively worded and five negatively worded, were presented. A sample positively worded item is "If Canada should lose the French culture of Quebec, it would indeed be a great loss." A high score reflected a positive attitude.

2. Interest in Foreign Languages (α = .79). Five items expressing a positive interest and five a relative disinterest were administered. A sample item is "I enjoy meeting and listening to people who speak other languages." This test was scored such that high scores reflect a strong interest in foreign languages.

3. Desire to Learn French (α = .87). This is a 6-item scale with equal numbers of positively and negatively keyed items. A high score denoted a relatively strong desire to learn French. A sample item is "I wish I were fluent in French."

4. French Use Anxiety (α = .86). This 8-item scale had four positively and four negatively worded items. A high score indicated that subjects would feel anxious if called upon to use the French they knew. A sample item is, "When making a telephone call, I would get flustered if it were necessary to speak French."

5. Attitudes toward the Learning Situation (α = .72). This 8-item scale included four items referring to French teachers in general and four referring to French courses. Half of the items were positively keyed and half negatively keyed in each case. A sample item is "French courses offer an excellent opportunity for students to broaden their cultural and linguistic horizons."

6. Integrative Orientation (α = .71). Four items expressing the importance of learning French for integrative reasons were presented. A sample item is "Studying French can be important because it allows people to participate more freely in the activities of other cultural groups."

7. Instrumental Orientation (α = .68). Four items expressing the importance of learning French for instrumental reasons were presented. A sample item is "Studying French can be important because it is useful for one's career."

8. Attitudes toward Learning French (α = .85). This 6-item scale included three items expressing a positive attitude and three items expressing a negative attitude. A sample item is "I would really like to learn French."

9. Social Desirability (α = .23). Three positively worded and three negatively worded items were adapted from Jackson's (1974) social desirability subscale of the Personality Research Form. Although they were presented in a True/False format in the original, they were presented in a Likert format in this study; this change might account for the low index of reliability.

In the second part of the study, subjects were given six trials to learn 26 English/French word pairs using the anticipation method. Testing was done by computer, which registered the amount of time they viewed the English stimulus word (viewing time, VT), their actual French response (VOC), and the amount of time spent reviewing the English/French pair (study time, ST).

Procedure

Subjects were tested individually. On arriving at the laboratory they were informed that this study involved learning a series of English/French word pairs. Subjects were told that they were first going to be asked to respond to a series of items dealing with their opinions about a number of issues associated with learning French, such as their attitudes toward learning French, French use anxiety, etc. They were told that the items would be presented on the computer monitor, and that they were to give their immediate spontaneous reaction to each item by depressing the appropriate number key from 1 to 7 that indicated the extent to which they agreed or disagreed with each item.

Subjects were tested in one of two conditions. Those in the experimental condition were informed that they would be paid $10 if they were successful in their learning of the English/French word pairs. Success was defined as 24 out of 26 pairs absolutely correct in form and spelling on the sixth trial. This was determined by the computer to eliminate any debate, and the number correct was displayed on the monitor at the conclusion of that trial. Subjects in the control condition were simply instructed to do their best.

During the learning task, a trial involved the administration of all 26 paired associates in the following manner. An English noun was displayed at the top of the screen, and below this the prompt, "Translation?" Subjects were instructed that they could view this for up to 10 seconds, or if they preferred they could move on by depressing the return key. The time spent considering each item constitutes the measure of viewing time (VT). They then typed the French translation including both the definite article and the French noun. If they did not know the answer they simply pressed the return key. At this point, the complete pair (English noun, French article and noun) were presented, and subjects could view them for up to 10 seconds, or move on by depressing the return key. This provided the index of study time (ST) for each item. The order of presentation was randomized separately for each trial. The computer recorded the viewing time, the French response typed by the subject, and the study time for each item, and then stored them in a fixed standard order. At the end of the sixth trial, the computer indicated the number that the subject had gotten correct (i.e., correct article and correctly spelled French noun). Those subjects in the experimental condition who achieved a score of at least 24 out of 26 were given $10. Nine subjects achieved this criterion.

For the analyses involving number correct (VOC), a research assistant scored each item. Subjects were given 1 point for the correct article, plus 2 points for the correct noun (allowing for minor spelling variations) (cf. Gardner, Lalonde, & Moorcroft, 1985).

Results

The major results of this study concern the effects of situationally based motivation (Instrumental Motivation) and individual-based motivation (Integrative Motivation) on the learning of second language material. This was assessed by means of a 2 x 2 x 6 analysis of variance. One factor was Incentive Condition (Reward vs. No Reward). Fifty of the 92 subjects, based on random assignment, were told that they would receive $10 if they got at least all but two items correct on the last trial. This was considered to reflect an instrumental motivation to the extent that subjects were learning the vocabulary items simply for the monetary reward. The second between subjects factor was Integrative Motivation (High vs. Low) defined in terms of a median split within each Incentive group on the aggregate of the measures of Attitudes toward French Canadians + Interest in Foreign Languages + Integrative Orientation + Attitudes toward the Learning Situation + Desire to Learn French + Attitudes toward Learning French. Differences on this factor were considered to reflect differences in integrative motivation in that subjects in the high integrative motive condition had more favorable attitudes, etc., than subjects in the low integrative motive condition even though none of these students were studying French as part of their curriculum. The third factor was based on repeated measures, and it comprised the six trials of the learning task.

Three dependent measures were investigated. The major one was achievement on each trial (VOC). The second dependent variable of interest was the mean time spent on each trial studying the pairs when they were presented together (ST). The third dependent variable was the mean time spent viewing the English word before subjects attempted to type in the French equivalent (VT).

Vocabulary Acquisition

Significant main effects were obtained for Integrative Motivation, Incentive Condition, and Trials, with the general pattern of results being as expected. The effect for Integrative Motivation, $F(1, 88) = 4.48$, $p < .05$, resulted because subjects high in Integrative Motivation performed better overall ($M = 30.55$) than subjects who were low ($M = 25.61$), while that for Incentive Condition, $F(1, 88) = 10.56$, $p < .01$, occurred because those offered financial rewards performed better ($M = 31.77$) than those who weren't (M 23.69). There were also significant learning effects across trials, $F(5, 440) = 414.81, p < .001$.

These main effects were tempered, however, by two significant interactions. The interaction between Integrative Motivation and Trials, $F(5, 440) = 3.35 \ p < .01$, is presented in Figure 1, where it will be noted that the rate of learning is steeper for subjects with a high level of Integrative Motivation than those with a low level. Simple contrasts between the two groups at each trial reveal, furthermore, that the differences are significant at Trials 3, 4, 5, and 6. The significant interaction between Incentive Condition and Trials (see Figure 2) is very similar, $F(5, 440) = 8.35 \ p < .001$. Again, contrasts between the two groups differed significantly beginning at Trial 3.

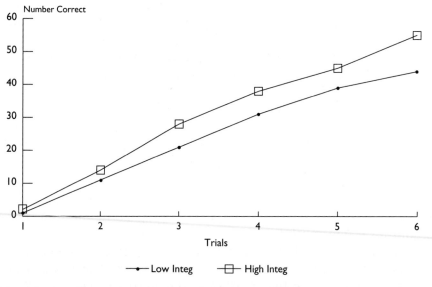

FIGURE 1.   Number Correct by Integrative Motivation and Trials

Study Time

Significant main effects were obtained for both Incentive Condition, $F(1, 88) = 22.84, p < .001$, and Trials, $F(5, 440) = 109.73, p < .001$. The effect for

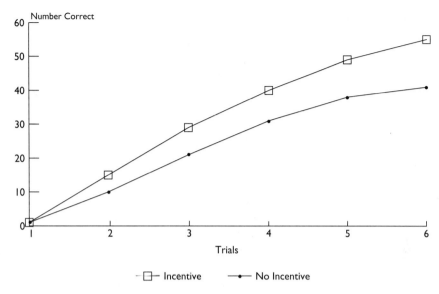

FIGURE 2.   Number Correct by Incentive Condition and Trials

Incentive Condition occurred because overall those promised money for superior performance spent more time studying each pair ($M = 5.17$ seconds) than those with no reward ($M = 3.24$ seconds). The effect for trials resulted because subjects tended to spend less time studying the pairs as learning progressed. The interpretation of these two main effects is tempered somewhat, however, by the significant interaction between Incentive Condition and Trials, $F(5, 440) = 6.34$, $p < .001$. This interaction is presented in Figure 3. As can be seen, both the incentive group and the no incentive group evidence less study time as trials progress. Tests of means comparing these two groups at each trial indicate, however, that the incentive group spent significantly ($p < .05$) more time studying the word pairs on every trial but the last one, on which the two groups did not differ significantly.

Viewing Time

Significant main effects were obtained for Integrative Motivation, $F(1, 88) = 8.20$, $p < .01$; Incentive Condition, $F(1, 88) = 11.59$, $p < .001$; and Trials, $F(5, 440) = 41.40$, $p < .001$. Integratively motivated subjects spent more time ($M = 2.57$) viewing the English stimulus than those who were not so motivated ($M = 2.07$). Subjects who were promised a reward spent more time ($M = 2.59$ seconds) viewing the English stimulus than subjects who were not ($M = 2.00$ seconds). Moreover, the mean viewing times for the six trials were 2.69, 2.95, 2.56, 2.14, 1.92, and 1.64. Viewing time increased slightly from Trial 1 to Trial

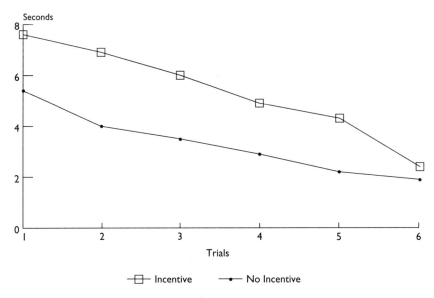

FIGURE 3.   Study Time by Incentive and Trials

2, but thereafter viewing time decreased as learning progressed. All but the difference between Trial 1 and Trial 3 were significant at the .05 level using post-hoc t tests.

In addition to these three analyses of variance, correlations were computed between each of the attitude/motivation and social desirability measures and the learning scores, viewing times, and study times for each of the six trials. Since there were two distinct groups, those in the Incentive Condition and those in the control group, the data were first standardized within groups before the correlations were computed to eliminate any effects attributable to groups. The resulting correlations are presented in Table 1.

As can be seen in Table 1, there were a substantial number of significant ($p < .05$) correlations involving vocabulary scores (VOC). Of the 54 correlations, 30 (56%) were significant. Moreover, the patterns are very consistent. Desire to Learn French and Attitudes toward Learning French (the two motivational components) were positively correlated with achievement for all six trials, while Attitudes toward French Canadians correlated significantly with Achievement on Trials 2 through 6. Moreover, Attitudes toward the Learning Situation resulted in significant correlations for Trials 3 to 6, French Use Anxiety correlated significantly (negatively) with vocabulary on Trials 1 to 3, and Integrative Orientation correlated significantly only with achievement on Trial 1. The patterns for the other variables (Interest in Foreign Languages and Instrumental Orientation) were not that meaningful, and the two significant correlations involving Social Desirability were not expected.

TABLE 1. Correlations of attitude/motivation subscales with behaviors on the learning task

	VOC1	VOC2	VOC3	VOC4	VOC5	VOC6	VT1	VT2	VT3	VT4	VT5	VT6	ST1	ST2	ST3	ST4	ST5	ST6
AFC	.13	.22*	.29**	.32**	.33***	.31**	.24*	.29**	.26*	.24*	.13	.09	.18	.16	.12	.07	.12	.09
IFL	.23*	.16	.22*	.15	.16	.15	.16	.17	.10	.11	.08	.05	.06	-.01	-.05	-.10	-.05	-.09
INT	.23*	.10	.17	.15	.19	.20	.06	.14	.22*	.29**	.22*	.20	.06	.02	.10	.05	.11	.03
D	.27**	.22*	.28**	.26*	.25*	.25*	.14	.14	.12	.07	.06	.01	.13	.08	.11	.07	.15	.09
ALF	.23*	.27**	.27**	.22*	.29**	.27**	.17	.25*	.22*	.19	.19	.12	.12	.08	.13	.08	.16	.07
ALS	.16	.17	.24*	.22*	.26*	.24*	.20	.18	.15	.20	.17	.13	.16	.16	.21*	.13	.14	-.04
FUA	-.44***	-.27**	-.21*	-.17	-.20	-.16	-.08	.04	-.01	-.07	-.04	-.09	.17	.12	.12	.15	.20	.19
INST	.19	.13	.21*	.15	.15	.14	.04	.15	.14	.12	.11	.15	.03	-.04	.03	.00	.10	.11
SD	.00	.19	.18	.21*	.25*	.18	-.15	-.12	-.02	-.06	-.10	-.09	-.03	-.03	.01	-.01	-.02	.05

AFC, Attitudes toward French Canadians; IFL, Interest in Foreign Languages; INT, Integrative Orientation; D, Desire to Learn French; ALF, Attitudes toward Learning French; ALS, Attitudes toward the Learning Situation; FUA, French Use Anxiety; INST, Instrumental Orientation; SD, Social Desirability; VOC1–VOC6, Vocabulary scores on Trials 1–6; VT1–VT6, Viewing time on trials 1–6; ST1–ST6, Study time on Trials 1–6. * $p < .05$; ** $p < .01$; *** $p < .001$.

There were far fewer significant correlations involving Study Time (1 of 54) and Viewing Time (9 of 54) as might be expected given the results of the analyses of variance. For Viewing Time, four of the correlations involved Attitudes toward French Canadians (Trials 1–4), three involved Integrative Orientation (Trials 3–5), and two involved Attitudes toward Learning French (Trials 2 and 3).

Analysis of Attitude/Motivation Test Behavior

A secondary purpose of this study was to determine the implications of administering the Attitude/Motivation Test Battery by computer. Three questions were relevant to this study. One concerns the reliability of the subtests administered in this format, but the comparability of the reliability coefficients obtained in this study with those from other studies suggests that computer administration does not materially influence the internal consistency reliability of the measures. In fact, the reliability coefficients for this study were higher for seven of the eight measures than those reported by Gardner, Lalonde, and Moorcroft (1985) for a comparable sample. The median reliability for this study is .82, while it was .71 in the earlier study. Since some items were changed, this improvement in reliability cannot necessarily be attributed to the computer administration; nonetheless, it is clear that reliability is not lowered as a result of computer administration of the items. A second question concerned whether or not offering an incentive to do well in the learning task would influence scores on the various attitude and motivation measures or mean item latencies. Tests of the differences between the means using t tests failed to obtain any significant effect, indicating that the differing instructions did not influence individuals' attitudes or motivation or the latency in responding to attitude and motivation items (all $ps < .05$).

The third question concerns the relation between speed of reaction to the attitude/motivation tests, including social desirability, and scores obtained on these measures. Correlations between speed of reaction to the items on a particular test and scores on that test yielded only two significant correlations. Subjects with high scores on the measure of French Use Anxiety had higher reaction times ($r(90) = .21$, $p < .05$), and subjects evidencing high social desirability had lower reaction times ($r(90) = -.32$, $p < .01$). Furthermore, the only measure to correlate significantly with Social Desirability was the French Use Anxiety scale ($r(90) = -.24$, $p < .02$).

Discussion

A major finding in this study was simply that both motivating conditions, the individual difference of integrative motivation and the environmentally

determined instrumental motivation established by means of financial induce-
ments, influenced the learning of French vocabulary pairs. Subjects with
higher levels of integrative motivation learned more words overall than did
subjects with low levels, and those who anticipated a possible financial
reward learned more than those who didn't. As indicated in Figures 1 and 2,
these differences became more pronounced as learning progressed. These
results support the generalization that motivation facilitates learning, and that
by and large any factors that motivate an individual to learn will result in successful acquisition (cf. Gardner, 1985, p. 168; Spolsky, 1989, p. 160). That is,
both instrumentally motivated and integratively motivated subjects learned
better than subjects not so motivated.

Other results from this study help to clarify the processes by which such
types of motivation facilitate learning. There was a significant difference in
favor of subjects in the incentive condition in the amount of study time, suggesting that a monetary reward can motivate individuals to study longer (and
also learn more). However, the interaction between Incentive Condition and
Trials (Figure 3) is even more instructive. It will be noted that, although the
subjects in the incentive condition studied significantly longer than subjects in
the control condition on the first five trials, this difference all but disappeared
on the sixth trial when the reward was no longer applicable, since subjects had
either satisfied the criterion or had not. Once any chance for receiving the
reward was eliminated, subjects in the incentive condition simply ceased
applying any more effort. This, if anything, is a major disadvantage of an
instrumental motivation.

Although integratively motivated subjects learned more than those not
integratively motivated, there was no significant difference between these two
groups on study time. This lack of a difference appears to question Gardner's
(1985) conclusion that integrative motivation is effective because it causes
individuals to work harder, though as reviewed by Gardner (1983) there is still
a wealth of evidence supporting that generalization. In the real life context,
integratively motivated students work harder, are more likely to participate in
excursion programs, and are less likely to drop out of language study. Each of
these findings support the active interpretation of integrative motivation. One
possible explanation for not finding such differences in effort expended in the
present study might be due to the fact that this is a laboratory study, and perhaps the setting is somewhat artificial. Moreover, other evidence in this study
does suggest that integratively motivated students are trying harder, as are
those motivated by reward. The analysis of viewing time—that time spent by
individuals considering the English stimulus before giving their response—
indicated that integratively motivated individuals spent more time thinking
about their response than subjects who weren't integratively motivated. Similarly, subjects who were in the incentive condition spent more time consider-

ing their responses. Both results support the "effort" interpretation of the results. Subjects who were motivated, either integratively or instrumentally, tried harder to think of the correct answer and apparently were more successful in finding it.

The results of the correlational analysis also help to clarify the nature of the roles of individual attitude and motivation attributes in second language learning. Individual differences in Desire to Learn French, Attitudes toward Learning French, and Attitudes toward French Canadians tend to correlate with French vocabulary acquisition at each trial (with the one exception). Furthermore, Attitudes toward the Learning Situation tends to relate to proficiency in the latter stages of learning (as if subjects were reminded of their earlier classroom experiences as the trials continued), while French Use Anxiety was significantly related (negatively) to achievement in the initial trials. Based on Tobias (1979) and MacIntyre and Gardner (1989), it seems reasonable to anticipate such correlations in the initial trials between anxiety and achievement. As trials progress, anxiety over the use of French would become less relevant. Finally, as expected from the arguments presented in the introduction, neither the integrative nor instrumental orientation scales were appreciable correlates in their own right. This is important because it demonstrates clearly that orientations may not relate to achievement while motivations do. It is not surprising, therefore, that studies that consider only the correlations between orientation and achievement often fail to find associations.

The few but nonetheless consistent correlations between some attitude measures and viewing time are also impressive. The major correlates of viewing time are Attitudes toward French Canadians, and Integrative Orientation—the only two measures that refer directly to the other language group. The absence of correlations with study time was not expected, but may be a function of the task at hand. It was our expectation (cf. Carroll, 1962) that study time would reflect motivation (as it certainty did in the distinction between the Incentive and Nonincentive Conditions), but it did not relate meaningfully to the individual difference measures. It seems possible, however, that the demands of the task itself played a much more dominant role than any individual differences.

These results demonstrate, therefore, that both integrative motivation and instrumental motivation can influence second language learning. Both the individual difference factor of integrative motivation and the situationally determined one of instrumental motivation had consistent and meaningful effects on learning, and on behavioral indices of effort. This, despite the fact that the study was conducted in a laboratory setting. None of the students were actually enrolled in French language classes, and the measure of integrative motivation involved differences in a series of attitude and motivation scales that may not be as applicable to them as they would be if the students were currently studying French. Even so, the results clearly confirm the role of attitudinal/motivational variables and incentives on second language learning. Generalizing these results to the language context seems fairly straightforward, and, if anything, one might expect that the effects would be even stronger in the classroom context. A major conclusion suggested from these results, therefore, is that both integrative and instrumental *motivation* can influence second language learning. This does not mean to imply, however, that integrative and instrumental *orientations* will necessarily influence learning. The important element is the motivation, not the orientation. Even in this study, the orientations were not particularly predictive of achievement, while the two forms of motivation were clearly so.

A question might be raised about the external validity of these results. That is, is it meaningful to generalize the results of this study to a real-life language learning context. Since the results of this study tend to agree with those of many studies that have investigated students in language classrooms, it seems meaningful to argue that they are generalizable. In this study as in others, individual differences in integrative motivation relate to achievement in the second language and to an index of effort expended in learning. The present study, however, introduces more control of the learning environment and prior characteristics of the students so that it is clear that the motivational factors influence actual learning as opposed to performance on an achievement test, for example, which could also reflect differences in prior knowledge, test-taking motivation, etc. Of course, it is possible that the effects of instrumental motivation may not generalize, though one would wonder why not. Presumably, because the time period is much longer and the task less circumscribed than that used in this study, any financial inducement might have to be larger, but it seems reasonable to expect that, to the extent that a monetary inducement was seen as instrumental by the students, comparable effects would be achieved. At least, this is the expectation that would derive from the socio-educational model of second language acquisition. Provided that a monetary reward has motivational properties, it would result in instrumental motivation, which would in turn effect high levels of achievement. Of course, to test the generalizability, actual research in a classroom environment would be required. Some context where language training leads to salary increments could provide a meaningful setting. If it were found that such students did perform well in such programs, but then failed to continue to make use of their skills once language training ended, this would provide further support for the notion that an instrumental motive will facilitate learning until the reward has been achieved, but then lose its potency.

The findings of this study also have implications for the socioeducational model of second language acquisition. First, they demonstrate once again that motivation—and in particular integrative motivation—facilitates second language acquisition. They show too that there is a big difference between orientations and motivation. They also help to point out a potential major distinction between integrative and instrumental motivation. Because integrative motivation has an attitudinal foundation in favorable attitudes toward the other ethnic community, other groups in general, and the language learning context, it is reasonable to expect it to have a continuing influence on language learning and use. To the extent that an instrumental motive is tied to a specific goal, however, its influence would tend to be maintained only until that goal is achieved. This then could well be a major difference between integrative and instrumental motives, and one that warrants further investigation. On the other hand, if the goal is continuous, it seems possible that an instrumental motivation would also continue to be effective. To a considerable extent this is the point made by Spolsky (1989) in his analysis of the role that economic factors could play in promoting second language acquisition in some contexts.

The findings with respect to computer administration of the Attitude/Motivation Test Battery provide some information attesting to the utility of this procedure. The internal consistency reliability of the subtests were comparable to, or better than, those obtained with paper and pencil administration. Instructions concerning the financial advantages of doing well in the learning phase of the study had no effects on either the attitude/motivation test scores or the latency of responding to the items. Finally, there was some evidence that reaction time to individual attitude/motivation test items might reflect social desirability responding. Only one measure, French Use Anxiety, correlated significantly with Social Desirability. The correlation indicated that those who expressed low levels of anxiety were also those who tended to respond in a socially desirable fashion. Thus, the measure of French Use Anxiety might be viewed as one influenced by social desirability responding. If this is the case, its correlation with reaction time might similarly be interpreted as suggesting that those who respond faster seek to reflect a nonanxious state when contemplating using French. That is, one component of variation in French Use Anxiety scores is due to social desirability. This interpretation is strengthened by the finding that there is also a significant negative correlation between Social Desirability and reaction time to that test only. Such results suggest that one way of identifying social desirability responding in the Attitude/Motivation Test Battery is by considering how quickly individuals respond to the items. Future research is obviously required, but this is an exciting first step.

Acknowledgments

This research was facilitated by grant number 410-88-0158 from the Social Sciences and Humanities Research Council of Canada for research on the topic "Social Factors in Second Language Learning and Ethnic Relations."

We would like to thank V. Galbraith and A. Young for their invaluable assistance.

References

Carroll, J. B. (1962). The prediction of success in intensive language training. In R. Glaser (Ed.), *Training research and education* (pp. 87–136). Pittsburgh, PA: University of Pittsburgh Press.

Chihara, T., & Oller, J. W. (1978). Attitudes and attained proficiency in EFL: A sociolinguistic study of adult Japanese speakers. *Language Learning, 28,* 55–68.

Clément, R., & Kruidenier, B. G. (1983). Orientations in second language acquisition: I. The effects of ethnicity, milieu and target language on their emergence. *Language Learning, 33,* 273–291.

Dunkel, H. B. (1948). *Second-language learning.* Boston: Ginn.

Gardner, R. C. (1983). Learning another language: A true social psychological experiment. *Journal of Language and Social Psychology, 2,* 219–239.

Gardner, R. C. (1985). *Social psychology and second language learning: The role of attitudes and motivation.* London: Edward Arnold.

Gardner, R. C., Lalonde, R. N., & Moorcroft, R. (1985). The role of attitudes and motivation in second language learning: Correlational and experimental considerations. *Language Learning, 35,* 207–227.

Gardner, R. C., & Lambert, W. E. (1972). *Attitudes and motivation in second language learning.* Rowley, Mass.: Newbury House.

Gardner, R. C., & Smythe, P. C. (1975). Motivation and second-language acquisition *The Canadian Modern Language Review, 31,* 218–230.

Gardner, R. C., Smythe, P. C., & Lalonde, R. N. (1984). *The nature and replicability of factors in second language acquisition* (Research Bulletin No. 605). Department of Psychology, University of Western Ontario, London, Canada.

Hsu, L. M., Santelli, J., & Hsu, J. R. (1989). Faking detection validity and incremental validity of response latencies to MMPI subtle and obvious items. *Journal of Personality Assessment, 53,* 278–295.

Jackson, D. N. (1974). *Personality research form manual.* Goshen, NY: Research Psychologists Press.

Lambert, W. E. (1974). Culture and language as factors in learning and education. In F. E. Aboud & R. D. Meade (Eds.), *Cultural factors in learning and education.* Proceedings of the Fifth Western Washington Symposium on Learning (pp. 91–122). Bellingham: Western Washington State College.

Lukmani, Y. M. (1972). Motivation to learn and learning proficiency. *Language Learning, 22,* 261–273.

MacIntyre, P. D., & Gardner, R. C. (1989). Anxiety and second language learning: Toward a theoretical clarification. *Language Learning, 39,* 251–275.

Oller, J. W., Baca, L., & Vigil, F. (1977). Attitudes and attained proficiency in ESL: A sociolinguistic study of Mexican-Americans in the Southwest. *TESOL Quarterly, 11,* 173–182.

Oller, J. W., Hudson, A., & Liu, P. (1977). Attitudes and attained proficiency in ESL: A sociolinguistic study of native speakers of Chinese in the United States. *Language Learning, 27,* 1–27.

Spolsky, B. (1989). *Conditions for second language learning.* Oxford: Oxford University Press.

Tobias, S. (1979). Anxiety research in educational psychology. *Journal of Educational Psychology, 71,* 573–582.

Understanding the Article

1. In the literature review, why do the authors stress the importance of distinguishing between *orientations* and *motivation*? How do they define *instrumental motivation*?

2. Who were the subjects and how were they selected? On what basis were the subjects divided into two groups for the purpose of the study?

3. How did the researchers determine the degree to which a subject was integratively motivated?

4. How were the subjects tested on vocabulary acquisition? In addition to the number of correct responses achieved by the subjects in each of six trials, what two other measures were investigated?

5. In your own words, describe the relationships depicted in Figures 1 and 2.

6. What is the purpose of looking at correlations among the attitude/motivation subscales and vocabulary scores, viewing times, and study times on the various trials, as depicted in Table 1? What did this analysis reveal about these relationships?

7. What are the answers to the research questions?

Reflecting on Wider Issues

1. Gardner and Lambert modified their original statement that integrative motivation was better than instrumental motivation in order to allow for special cases in which instrumental motivation could have a powerful effect on the learner. Can you think of instances in which instrumental motivation might be superior to integrative motivation?

2. How does the researchers' conception of motivation differ from what teachers and students usually think of when they use the term? Does Gardner and MacIntyre's concept of motivation apply to situations other than SLA?

Going Beyond the Article

As you have seen, instrumental orientation appears to function as an effective motive for language learning in some learning environments. For evidence of learning environments that might favor integrative motivation, see Gardner, Day, and MacIntyre (1992), "Integrative motivation, induced anxiety, and language learning in a controlled environment" (*Studies in Second Language Acquisition, 14*, 197–214).

Within the field of SLA, motivation has been linked to social-psychological variables such as attitudes toward self and toward the speakers of the target language. This concept of motivation does not reflect what teachers and students usually think of as motivation or the way the term is used in the related fields of psychology and education. For an excellent review of the standard SLA approach to motivation contrasted with the approach to the study of motivation in the field of education, you should read Crookes and Schmidt (1991), "Motivation: Reopening the research agenda" (*Language Learning, 41*, 469–512).

UNIT V

SOCIOCULTURAL FACTORS

9

WORLD ENGLISHES: APPROACHES, ISSUES, AND RESOURCES

Braj B. Kachru
University of Illinois

Previewing the Article

As English has rapidly spread to become an international language, a number of related sociopolitical issues have surfaced. We can no longer simply view English as a worldwide lingua franca; rather, as many nonnative varieties of English become standardized, the *nativization* of these varieties poses some interesting questions.

Braj Kachru is widely known for his many writings on the topic of the internationalization of what he coined *World Englishes.* In this article, issues and research are summarized. Before you read it, review some of the general cultural and sociopolitical research in second language acquisition (see *PLLT,* Chapter 7). Keep in mind the fact that one's language is the means through which one "transacts" oneself. Then, briefly answer the following questions:

1. What does the title of this study tell you about its purpose?

2. Scan the work before you read it, and take note of the various subheadings through which the purpose is achieved.

3. As you are reading, try to think of English speakers you know from both *outer* and *expanding* circles and apply Kachru's comments to their speech or writing.

Reprinted from *Language Teaching, 25:*1–14, 1992.

Introduction

The conceptualisation of World Englishes within a theoretical framework actually goes back to the early 1960s (Kachru, 1965). However, organized efforts in discussing the concept and its formal and functional implications were not initiated until 1978. I will, therefore, provide a brief historical context and a survey of resources, primarily since 1978. It was during that year, just three months apart, that the international and intranational functions of English became the focus of two independently organised international conferences. The first conference was organised by Larry E. Smith in April (1–15) at the East–West Culture Learning Institute (now the Institute for Culture and Communication) of the East–West Center, Honolulu, Hawaii, USA. The second was organised by me (30 June–2 July), in conjunction with the Linguistic Institute of the Linguistic Society of America, hosted by the University of Illinois at Urbana–Champaign, USA. These conferences had considerable conceptual similarities and shared several participants. The conferences resulted in two publications, Smith (1981) and Kachru (1982; 1992).

At the end of the Honolulu conference all the participants signed a statement and an agenda for the future which articulated their views. In that conference, as Kachru and Quirk (1981, p. xiii) observe:

> there were almost as many varieties of English—native and nonnative, Western and non-Western—as there were participants, including voices from Bangladesh, Singapore, Malaysia, Thailand, India, the Philippines, New Zealand, Britain, Germany, and the USA. Numerous cultural, linguistic, ideological and other differences could be found among the participants, but they all had this one thing in common: all of them used the English language to debate, discuss, and argue questions which concern both native and nonnative users of English as well as global uses of English in various sociolinguistic contexts in different parts of the world.

The Urbana conference (Kachru, 1982)

> ...broke the traditional pattern of such deliberations: no inconvenient question was swept under the rug. The professionals, both linguists and literary scholars, and native and nonnative users of English, had frank and stimulating discussions. The English-using community in various continents was for the first time viewed in its totality. A number of cross-cultural perspectives were brought to bear upon our understanding of English in a global context, of language variation, of language acquisition, and of the bilinguals'—or a multilingual's—use of English.

At these conferences the questions discussed included: the sociolinguistic and political contexts of the countries where English is used as a nonnative language; the factors which determine the retention of English after the end of the colonial period; the sociolinguistic and linguistic profile of each variety, particularly with reference to their *range* of functions and *depth* of societal penetration; and the linguistic and other processes of nativisation and acculturation.

The Honolulu conference resulted in the following statement on behalf of the participants (Kachru & Quirk, 1981, pp. xvii–xix):

1. As professionals, members of the Conference felt that the stimulus given to the question of English used as an international or auxiliary language has led to the emergence of sharp and important issues that are in urgent need of investigation and action.

2. These issues are seen as summarised in the distinction between the uses of English for international (i.e., external) and intranational (i.e., internal) purposes. This distinction recognises that, while the teaching of English should reflect in all cases the sociocultural contexts and the educational policies of the countries concerned, there is a need to distinguish between (a) those countries (e.g., Japan) whose requirements focus upon international comprehensibility and (b) those countries (e.g., India) which in addition must take account of English as it is used for their own intranational purposes.

3. So far as we know, no organisation exists that takes account of any language in the light of this fundamental distinction.

4. It is not for us to define or prescribe the policies to be adopted, but the papers and discussions at the Conference have identified a number of fundamental issues. These issues can be considered under four headings: (a) Basic research; (b) Applied research; (c) Documentation, dissemination and liaison; (d) Professional support activities.

The statement asks for more than a shift in emphasis; it seeks a new direction consistent with the identities and functions of World Englishes.

In the past decades special colloquia were organised as part of the annual International TESOL, and once with IATEFL in Belgium, and twice with the Georgetown University Round Table on Languages and Linguistics (1986 and 1987), see Lowenberg (1988). And in 1986 (6–13 August), yet another conference was organised: "Language and power: Cross-cultural dimensions of English in media and literature" at the East–West Center, Honolulu. This conference was more specific and its aim was (Kachru & Smith 1986, p. 117):

a. to explore the concept of the linguistic "power" of English with a cross-cultural perspective; and

b. to provide data for the study of such "power" from various English-using countries in the domains of literature and the media (film and journalism).

A variety of theoretical and applied research areas were identified and discussed, with special reference to the Outer Circle and the Expanding Circle (see section 1 below). These included:

a. preparation of in-depth empirical studies on the national uses of English;

b. identification of the main characteristics of English for international communication at various linguistic levels (e.g., syntactic, phonological, morphological, lexical, stylistic, and discoursal);

c. descriptions of registers of English (e.g., films, newspapers, and advertising);

d. development of extensive sociolinguistic profiles of English in various regions;

e. comparison of context and methods of language teaching in diverse cultural and educational settings;

f. promotion of and research in literatures in English around the world ("World Literatures in English" and "Literatures in English"), and the encouragement of their use in the study of literatures and literary criticism and in (i) the teaching of the English language (ii) cross-cultural communication (e.g., commerce, business, diplomacy, and journalism), and (iii) teacher preparation);

g. investigation into the possibility of implementing the recommendations of the Quirk Committee (Smith, 1981, pp. xvii–xix) to establish resource centers which will serve as archives for linguistic data and as clearing houses for various areas of English studies;

h. the study of local grammatical, linguistic, and literary traditions, and the applications of these traditions to the analysis and description of World Englishes; and

i. the initiation and coordination of research in lexicographical studies of English.

At the 1988 International TESOL convention in Chicago the Interim Committee which organised the 1986 conference in Honolulu met and formed the International Committee for the Study of World Englishes (ICWE). One charge of ICWE is to establish a network of interested scholars working on various aspects of World Englishes. In April (2–4), 1992, the ICWE met at the University of Illinois at Urbana, USA, as a cosponsor of a conference of "World Englishes Today."

The contexts, sociolinguistic and linguistic, within which English was discussed in these conferences were *inter*national and *intra*national. The term "World Englishes" and its sociolinguistic and pragmatic justification came later.

Why the use of "Englishes" (Kachru, 1985a; Kachru & Smith, 1988)? The term symbolises the functional and formal variations, divergent sociolinguistic contexts, ranges and varieties of English in creativity, and various types of acculturation in parts of the Western and non-Western world. This concept emphasizes "WE-ness," and not the dichotomy between *us* and *them* (the native and nonnative users). In this sense, then, English is a valuable linguistic tool used for various functions. The approaches to the study of World Englishes, therefore, have to be interdisciplinary and integrative, and different methodologies must be used (literary, linguistic and pedagogical) to capture distinct identities of different Englishes, and to examine critically the implications of such identities in cross-cultural communication.

There is also another wider implication. In the past four decades we see that almost the total spectrum of applied linguistic research, the strengths and limitations of theoretical frameworks and applications of such theories, have been demonstrated with reference to varieties of English. It is, therefore, not surprising that the past four decades in applied linguistics have been dominated by English; its use in such fields as first- and second-language acquisition, stylistics, bilingual and monolingual lexicography, theory of translation, and so on (Kachru, 1990a, p. 5).

This survey highlights the current approaches to the study of theoretical and applied issues and controversies related to English in the Outer and Expanding Circles (see 1, below). The survey is divided into the following sections:

1. The spread and stratification of English
2. Characteristics of the stratification
3. Interactional contexts of World Englishes
4. Implications of the spread
5. Descriptive and prescriptive concerns
6. The bilingual's creativity and the literary canon
7. Multicanons of English
8. The two faces of English: Nativisation and Englishisation
9. Fallacies concerning users and uses
10. The power and politics of English
11. Teaching World Englishes
12. Conclusion

The Spread and Stratification of English

The unparalleled spread of English demands a fresh conceptualisation in terms of its *range* of functions, and the *degree* of penetration in different non-Western societal contexts (Kachru, 1986f, pp. 129–131). The traditional dichotomy between native and nonnative is functionally uninsightful and linguistically questionable, particularly when discussing the functions of English in multilingual societies (Kachru, 1988a). The earlier distinction of English as a native (ENL), second (ESL), and foreign (EFL) language has come under attack for reasons other than sociolinguistic. Quirk now rejects this "terminological triad": he says that "...I doubt its validity and frequently fail to understand its meaning" (1988a, p. 236; see also Kachru, 1991, p. 5).

Kachru (1985a and later) represents the spread of English in terms of three concentric circles: the Inner Circle, the Outer Circle, and the Expanding Circle.

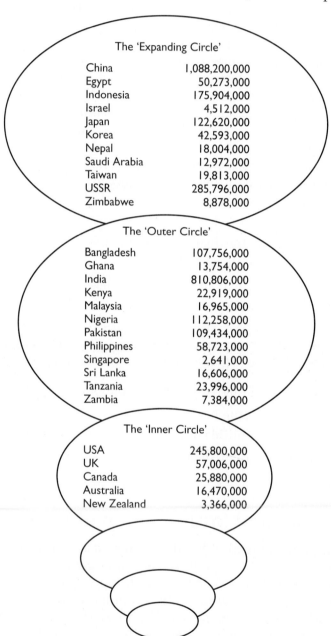

The 'Expanding Circle'	
China	1,088,200,000
Egypt	50,273,000
Indonesia	175,904,000
Israel	4,512,000
Japan	122,620,000
Korea	42,593,000
Nepal	18,004,000
Saudi Arabia	12,972,000
Taiwan	19,813,000
USSR	285,796,000
Zimbabwe	8,878,000

The 'Outer Circle'	
Bangladesh	107,756,000
Ghana	13,754,000
India	810,806,000
Kenya	22,919,000
Malaysia	16,965,000
Nigeria	112,258,000
Pakistan	109,434,000
Philippines	58,723,000
Singapore	2,641,000
Sri Lanka	16,606,000
Tanzania	23,996,000
Zambia	7,384,000

The 'Inner Circle'	
USA	245,800,000
UK	57,006,000
Canada	25,880,000
Australia	16,470,000
New Zealand	3,366,000

These circles are defined with reference to the historical, sociolinguistic, and literary contexts. The Inner Circle represents the traditional bases of English, dominated by the "mother tongue" varieties of the language. In the Outer Circle, English has been institutionalised as an additional language. The estimated population of the countries represented in this circle is over 1,303 million. Out of this population, if only ten per cent use English, it adds up to 130 million. And that is a very conservative estimate indeed. The Expanding Circle includes the rest of the world where English is used as the primary foreign language, and the uses of English are unpredictably increasing, as in, for example, what used to be the Soviet Union, in China, and in Eastern Europe. Note that countries such as South Africa (pop. 29,628,000) and Jamaica (pop. 2,407,000) are not placed within the above concentric circles, since their sociolinguistic situation is rather complex, particularly with reference to the English-using populations and the functions of English.

A major question here is: What is the number of users of English across the world? The answer to this question depends on what we mean by an "English-knowing" person. There is no one answer to this question; various educational and functional variables have been used. The estimates of the users of English range from a conservative figure of 700 to 800 million to a rather liberal figure of two billion people with some competence in English (see e.g., Fishman et al., 1977; Crystal, 1985).

Characteristics of the Stratification

The study of the spread and stratification of English in the non-Western world, within various theoretical frameworks, is essentially a post-1960 phenomenon. Such studies are the consequence of the theoretical and methodological insights gained by what are termed "socially realistic linguistic" approaches to language study, particularly those of the British linguist J. R. Firth (see Kachru, 1986b), and William Labov in the USA. Lyons (1978, p. xvi) is right in showing parallels "between Labov's approach to linguistics and that of the 'British' school, which draws its inspiration from J. R. Firth." The result of "socially realistic" paradigms and the activism of their proponents was that linguistic pluralism and diversity were considered a part of multiculturalism and societal interaction. What started originally as a ripple resulted in a challenge to various traditionally held linguistic assumptions.

The exponents of stratification in the Outer Circle have been interpreted in two ways: as a lectal range (e.g., Platt, 1977; Platt & Weber, 1979) and as a cline in English bilingualism (Kachru, 1983a and earlier; Pakir, 1991a, 1991b; Bamgbose, 1982). In terms of a lectal range, Platt and Weber describe Singapore English in terms of three reference points on a continuum: acrolect, mesolect, and basilect, following Bickerton's use of these terms in describing the creole continuum (Bickerton, 1975). This taxonomy of Singapore English is not accepted by all (Tay, 1986). The cline of bilingualism is related to the users and uses of English: one end of the cline represents what has been termed an educated variety (e.g., Indian English, Nigerian English), and at the other are the varieties termed, for example, Nigerian Pidgin (see for discussion and references, Bamiro, 1991), colloquial English in Malaysia and Singapore (see Pakir, 1991a; Lowenberg, 1991), bazaar English and butler English (see Kachru, 1983a; Hosali & Aitchison, 1986). These varieties are not restricted to the spoken mode, but are also used in new English literatures to characterise various types of interlocutors, social classes, and group identities, and to provide local colour (see Kachru, 1990a, pp. 10–13).

Interactional Contexts of World Englishes

Another result of the application of socially realistic linguistics has been the shift of the focus on to the functions of English in various types of interactional contexts, both in the Inner and Outer Circles. The approaches and methodologies suggested by, for example, Halliday (1970, 1973, 1974, 1978), Hymes (1974; see also Saville-Troike, 1981), and Labov (1972a, 1972b) have been particularly insightful. Approaches using Halliday's and Hymes's models have been used to describe the communicative and discoursal strategies in non-native varieties of English (e.g., Kachru, 1986a; Magura, 1984, 1985; Richards, 1979; Valentine, 1988, 1991).

A natural next step in this research was to extend these approaches to language pedagogy (e.g., Brumfit, 1988, for the British perspective; see review of Brumfit by Berns, 1991; for bibliographical references, specifically on communicative competence, see Ramaiah, 1985; Savignon & Berns, 1984).

The study and analysis of English in interactional contexts has resulted in studies such as the following:

    a. *Discourse strategies* (e.g., Kachru, 1982b; Smith, 1987).

    b. *Speech acts* (e.g., Kachru, 1983, pp. 128–144, for written texts; Kachru, 1992; Y. Kachru, 1991, includes a bibliography and illustrative studies by D'souza, Y. Kachru, Nelson, Tawake, and Valentine; Sridhar, 1989, pp. 99–116).

    c. *Code-mixing* (for references, see Kamwangamalu, 1989); see also for English in code-mixing across languages, Bhatia & Ritchie, 1989).

Implications of the Spread

The linguistic, cultural, canonical and literary implications of the spread of English in the Outer and Expanding Circles are discussed in, for example, Dissanayake (1985); Görlach (1991); Kachru (1987, 1988a, 1992); McCrum et al. (1986); Thumboo (1985, 1992).

Descriptive and Prescriptive Concerns

The theoretical, methodological, and ideological questions related to World Englishes have gone beyond the concerns of pedagogy, which was virtually the main concern before the 1960s. And now a number of the sacred cows of theoretical and applied linguistics are under attack as a consequence of two major developments: the impact of description, analysis, methodology, and relevance shown in sociolinguistic models, and the research initiatives and ideas provided by scholars from the Outer Circle. That the ideas and concerns of these scholars are generally not discussed by scholars in the Inner Circle is a different story, and thereby hangs a tale of linguistic attitudes, ethnocentrism, and economics (see section 10).

The sacred cows are of five types (Kachru, 1988a): acquisitional, sociolinguistic, pedagogical, theoretical, and ideological (what constitutes the sacredness of these sacred cows and how these attained that status are in themselves interesting topics that will not be discussed here).

The acquisitional questions relate to the relevance of concepts such as *interference, interlanguage, error,* and *fossilisation* (cf. Kachru, 1990a; Lowenberg, 1984, 1986a, 1986b; Sridhar & Sridhar, 1986). The sociolinguistic questions relate to, for example, the *pluricentricity* of English, its ideological connotations, the new ideologies represented by Englishes in the Outer Circle, and the expansion of literary and cultural canons (for discussion and references, see, e.g., Kachru, 1988a, pp. 210–211, 1990a, pp. 13–14; Mazrui, 1973; Nagugi, 1986, 1991; Phillipson & Skutnabb-Kangas, 1986). The pedagogical issues relate to models for teaching, methods of teaching, and curriculum design relevant for various methods (Berns, 1991; Phillipson, 1992). The theoretical issues surrounding World Englishes concern three vital concepts: the *speech community,* the *native speaker,* and the *ideal speaker–hearer* of English (Kachru, 1988a, pp. 213–218).

The definition of a speech community varies from Bloomfield's vague definition to the complex definitions of Le Page and Gumperz (Hudson, 1980, pp. 25–30). However, when we seek a definition for the English users in multilingual societies, the task becomes more complex. I believe that the sociolinguistic reality of the uses and users of English across cultures is captured by the term *speech fellowships* suggested by Firth (Kachru, 1988a, p. 224). And related to speech community is the concept *native speaker,* used as a lighthouse by both linguists and language teachers. Ferguson (1982, p. vii) warns us that:

> Linguists, perhaps especially American linguists, have long given a special place to the "native speaker" as the only truly valid and reliable source of language data, whether those data are the elicited texts of the descriptivist or the institutions the theorist works with . . . In fact, the whole mystique of native speaker and mother tongue should probably be quietly dropped from the linguists' set of professional myths about language.

In the same passage, Ferguson rightly says that the concept mother tongue is misleading, particularly in multilingual societies which form the largest components of the world, monolingualism not being a norm:

> Yet much of the world's verbal communication takes place by means of languages which are not the users' mother tongue, but their second, third, or nth language, acquired one way or another and used when appropriate.

These two statements by Ferguson and others have yet to be seriously applied to our understanding and description of World Englishes (Christopherson, 1988; Kachru, 1986a and earlier; Paikeday, 1985; Pride, 1981).

The concept ideal speaker–hearer (Chomsky, 1965) has been treated as a sacred cow in the literature. This concept is an abstract idealisation; however, the question remains: What, if any, is the relationship of this concept to *shared conventions,* linguistic and sociocultural? And, more pertinent to this survey, what are the shared conventions of users of World Englishes (Kachru, 1988a, pp. 213–218)?

The prescriptive concerns are directly related to the diversification of English. And diversification, like Hydra, is multiheaded and raises many issues of prescriptivism. It is argued that diversification is "symbolic of subtle sociolinguistic messages." The intended message may be to use diversity as an exponent of *distance,* as a marker of *creativity potential,* or as an expression of the "Caliban syndrome" (Kachru, 1988a, p. 218).

The most debated question in diversification is about the models, norms and standards for English in the Outer Circle. This question has been discussed in detail, with references, in Kachru (1982b, originally presented in 1979); see also Kachru (1983b, 1986a, 1992); Bédard and Maurais (1983); Tickoo (1991). During the past decade, the issues related to models have again been revived, and the two approaches to the controversy are presented in Quirk (1988, 1989) and Kachru (1988a, 1990a, 1991, 1992). For more extensive discussion, other viewpoints, and additional references see the papers in Tickoo (1991; including Honey, 1991). The main motivations for codification seem to be (a) attitudinal, based on markers of power and elitism and class and caste; (b) social standing and ethnicity; (c) social acceptance; and (d) integration, with a preference for the *melting pot* hypothesis.

In terms of diversification, there are now broadly three types of English using speech fellowships: norm-providing, norm-developing, and norm-dependent. The norm-providing varieties are used in the Inner Circle. Among these varieties, American and British Englishes (to use cover terms) are considered more appropriate than the varieties used in Australia and New Zealand. The situation, however, is dynamic. Until recently, the British variety (Received Pronunciation) was attitudinally a preferred pronunciation model, but the situation is now reversed in favour of the American model (Kachru, 1981a, pp. 21–43).

The norm-developing speech fellowships are institutionalised in the Outer Circle. The users of such varieties do not have identical attitudes about an endocentric (locally defined) norm—far from it. Among the users of these varieties, there is confusion between linguistic norm and linguistic performance, but generally the localised norm has a well-established linguistic and cultural identity (e.g., Singapore English, Nigerian English, Indian English; see Cheshire, 1991; Kachru, 1982).

The norm-dependent varieties are used in the Expanding Circle (e.g., Korea, Iran, Saudi Arabia). The norms are essentially external (American or British).

A string of questions concerning norms, codification and attitudes have been raised in recent studies (see Finegan, 1980; Greenbaum, 1985; see also related papers by Baxter, 1980; Kachru, 1976; Newbrook, 1986; Nihalani, 1991; Prator, 1968).

There are two other questions related to descriptive and prescriptive concerns about English in the Outer Circle: What determines the difference between an error (or a mistake) and an innovation? And, what are the variables of intelligibility for World Englishes across languages and cultures? The first question has been addressed in Kachru (1982) with relevant references (see also Y. Kachru, 1991). The second question has a long history of discussion mainly in pedagogical literature. The most insightful work on this topic has been done by Smith, who approaches this question within the framework of English as an international and intranational language (EIIL). An extensive partly annotated bibliography of over 163 items, divided into five sections, is in Smith and Nelson (1985). This bibliography covers general, sociolinguistic, and language-specific, syntactic, phonological, and reading studies. The question of intelligibility is viewed in a wide context, making a distinction between (a) *intelligibility:* word/utterance recognition, (b) *comprehensibility:* word/utterance meaning (locutionary force), (c) *interpretability:* meaning behind word/utterance (illocutionary force). Smith and Nelson also suggest "some of the issues" which should be on the agenda of researchers on this topic (pp. 335–336). These include: (1) How does the English proficiency of the speaker correlate with the intelligibility, comprehensibility and interpretability of his/her speech? (2) How does the English proficiency of the listener correlate with his/her ability to comprehend, interpret, and find intelligible what he/she hears? (3) How does topic difficulty for the speaker correlate with the intelligibility, comprehensibility and interpretability of his/her speech? (4) How does topic difficulty for the listener correlate with his/her ability to comprehend, interpret and find intelligible what he/she hears? (5) How does the communicative setting (quiet living room v. noisy bar, for example) affect intelligibility, comprehensibility and interpretability? (6) What are the effects of familiarity, either with the individual speaker or with the variety of the language spoken, on intelligibility, comprehensibility, and interpretability? They further suggest that (7) future research should investigate the correlation of speaker and listener effort to communicative success; (8) more research is needed on the effects of listener and speaker attitudes toward different varieties of spoken English on the intelligibility, comprehensibility and interpretability of those variables; (9) intelligibility, comprehensibility, and interpretability studies should be undertaken with nonnative speakers who come from different countries; (10) studies should be undertaken to determine how intelligible, comprehensible, and interpretable native speakers are to nonnative speakers as well as other native speakers of different national varieties of English.

The Bilingual's Creativity and the Literary Canon

The term 'bilingual's creativity' is used for "those creative linguistic processes which are the result of competence in two or more languages" (Kachru, 1986d, p. 20). This concept is not used for acquisitional inadequacies in a language, but refers to "... first, the designing of a text which uses linguistic resources from two or more—related or unrelated—languages; second, the use of verbal strategies in which subtle linguistic adjustments are made for subtle psychological, sociological, and attitudinal reasons" (ibid; for a detailed discussion and references, see Kachru, 1986c, 1986d). A paradigm example of the bilingual's creativity is the development of contact literatures in World Englishes (Kachru, 1986c; King, 1974, 1980).

The contact literatures in English are the result of the contact of English with other languages in multilingual and multicultural contexts in, for example, Africa and Asia. As time passes, the contact varieties acquire stable characteristics in their pronunciation, syntax, vocabulary and discoursal and style strategies. The long-term contact manifests itself in *nativisation* and *acculturation*. Nativisation refers to the processes which create a localised linguistic identity of a variety (e.g., *Indian* English, *Scottish* English; see Pandharipande, 1987). On the other hand, acculturation gives English distinct local cultural identities. It is in this sense that claims have been made that World Englishes have acquired multicultural identities and pluricentricity (Kachru, 1986a, 1991 and earlier; Steiner, 1975). One serious, and as yet not fully recognised, result of this contact is that the literary and cultural canons related to the English language are expanded (see section 7).

The contact literatures in English are thus both nativised and acculturated. A long tradition of such writing is found in South Asia, West Africa, the Philippines, and Southeast Asia. These literatures have by now gained national and international recognition, as is evident, for example, by the award of the Nobel Prize in literature to Nigerian English writer Wole Soyinka in 1986 and to Derek Alton Walcott of the West Indies in 1992, and the Neustadt award to Indian English writer Raja Rao in 1988.

In contact literatures in English there is convergence of two or more distinct linguistic and literary traditions. The three paradigms of research to study the bilingual's creativity in English relate to linguistic, literary and pedagogical studies (Kachru, 1986c, pp. 159–173).

In linguistic studies the shift is from an *interference-oriented* approach to models of contrastive discourse, the emphasis is on interactional context, contextualisation and contrastive stylistics. In literary studies the bilingual's creativity in English demands recognition of at least three facts: that the institutionalised nonnative varieties have an educated variety and a cline of subvarieties; that writers in contact literatures in English engage in *lectal mixing;* and that in such writing there are style-shifts which are related to the underlying sociolingustic and cultural context. The result of such style-shifts, appropriate to non-Western cultural contexts, is new discourse strategies, use of distinctly different speech acts, and development of new registers in English (for references, illustrations and discussion, see Kachru, 1982a, 1983a, 1987; Y. Kachru, 1991; Sridhar, 1989; see also relevant sections in Bailey & Gorlach, 1982; Kachru, 1985a; Platt et al., 1984).

In pedagogical studies the impact of bilingualism in the classroom is currently under study both in the UK and the USA, but very little empirical research has been done in the non-Western countries. (A useful annotated bibliography on this topic is Devaki et al., 1990, which lists 855 items; see also Strevens, 1988).

There is now awareness, though muted, of the fact that traditional (and some contemporary) approaches to the teaching of English developed in the Western contexts cannot be accepted without question for the non-Western contexts (see, e.g., Y. Kachru, 1985a; Tickoo, 1988). The main reasons for questioning these approaches are (see Kachru, 1986d, pp. 24–25):

a. the data for analysis are restricted to classroom assignments, etc., on the basis of which broad variety-specific generalisations are made;

b. the sociolinguistic context and its implications on creativity are not taken into consideration;

c. a majority of approaches ignore nativisation and acculturation in the institutionalised varieties (for further discussion see Y. Kachru, 1985a, 1987; Kachru, 1982b; Lowenberg, 1984; Pride, 1982; Sridhar, 1989).

With reference to literary creativity in English, Thumboo (1992) raises some interesting questions and argues:

> This challenge confronts every bi- or multilingual writer. His bilingualism is one of three broad types—proficient, powerful, or limited—his position in this cline is not static, because quite often one language gains dominance. A bilingual person has at least two language universes, and each language works with its own linguistic circuits. How the two associate depends on

whether the languages as neighbours inhabit the same space and time and can bend to serve creative purposes.

Why is it important to study bilinguals' creativity in English? It is not recognised that such creativity, both literary and of other types, has opened up research avenues with wide implications for language acquisition, language function and language identity. The following issues come to mind.

The first is the much-debated question of language *deficiency v. difference.* These two aspects were traditionally studied within the paradigm of error analysis (e.g., Richards, 1979). Only since the 1960s have analyses been provided which introduce the concepts of innovation and creativity in understanding the differences (Kachru, 1965, 1983a, and later). The second issue is the recognition of innovations used for stylistic effect as "foregrounding." I am particularly thinking of what are termed "new" English literatures (see, e.g., King, 1974, 1980). Referring to such writing, Carter and Nash (1990, p. 20) observe that there is continually a need to point out that there are

> ... many literatures in the world which are written in English but which are produced a long way from England. There is English literature written in the United States, Australia and South Africa; and less obviously, there is English literature written in countries in which English is an institution-alised second language, for example, India, Singapore, Nigeria, Kenya, or the Philippines, and where it is produced by writers for whom English is not a mother tongue ... (see also Steiner, 1975, p. 4).

The third issue is the recognition of various text types—code-mixed or noncode mixed—which are internationally meant for bilingual readers who share the writer's linguistic repertoire and cultural and literary canon. The writers of such texts do not seem to make concessions to the native speaker of the language. This is evidence in written media, literary genres, and localised culturally dependent registers (e.g. matrimonial advertisements, invitations, obituaries, etc.; see, e.g., Dubey, 1991; Kachru, 1982, chapter 20 and earlier; Nwoye, 1992). The fourth issue is recognising the functional appropriateness of localised sublanguages and registers. For example, it is argued that there is a need for a paradigm shift in the claims of ESP research and methodology (see, e.g., Kachru, 1988b (presented in 1985); Swales, 1985). The fifth issue is providing contrastive typologies of linguistic and cultural conventions. It is the differences in these conventions which result in the pragmatic failure or success of various language types (see Candlin, 1987; Kachru, 1986c; Sridhar, 1989; Y. Kachru, 1991 and earlier; Valentine, 1988, 1991). The sixth issue is describing the formal and functional characteristics of bilinguals' language mixing and switching (see case studies and references in Bhatia and Ritchie, 1989, particularly Kamwangamalu's bibliography).

Multicanons of English

Interlocutors in World Englishes have a variety of linguistic, cultural, and social backgrounds; the situation is that a speaker of a Bantu language may interact with a speaker of Japanese, a Taiwanese, an Indian, and so on. There are some historical analogues of this situation, though the degree of the spread and uses of English is unparalleled. The analogues that come to mind are Latin in medieval Europe (see Kahane & Kahane, 1979, 1986) and Sanskirit in traditional South Asia. The result of this extensive use of English over a long period has resulted in multicanons of English and a "shift of the canon" (Kachru, 1991).

This development of multicanons is particularly vital when English is being used as a tool to present distinct canons unrelated to the traditional canonical associations of English. This, of course, is not always done consciously. It is part of the acculturation of English in 'un-English' sociocultural and linguistic contexts. This has happened to the English language in the United States and Australia, too, but the situation is somewhat different in these two countries. They share with "mother English" a Judeo-Christian tradition, a literary past, and a general cultural heritage. This is not the case for English in Africa, in South Asia, in Southeast Asia, and in the Philippines (see Kachru, 1992; for an overview of such literatures, see King, 1974; see also Chishimba, 1984; Magura, 1984).

The Two Faces of English: Nativisation and Englishisation

The contact and convergence of English with other languages and cultures has resulted in two processes, *nativisation* and *Englishisation* (Kachru, 1989). These two processes have developed, as it were, two faces of English, one showing what the contact has formally done to various varieties of English, and the second showing what impact the English language and literature have had on other languages of the world. This process of "give and take" has, again, been unprecedented, and has contributed to the development of new English-mixed codes in various parts of the world (Kachru, 1983a, pp. 196–197). Englishisation is not restricted to phonology, grammar and lexis, but has had a deep impact on discourse, registers, styles and literary genres. One can see this process active in three major spheres associated with the spread of English: the traditional region of cultural and literary contact in which mostly cognate languages of English are used (e.g., in Western and parts of Eastern Europe); the English-using regions of the world in the Outer Circle of English which are noncontiguous with English geographically, and unrelated or not closely related in a genetic sense (e.g., parts of Africa and Asia); and the Expanding Circle which includes, in various degrees of use of English, the rest of the world, such as Japan, China, and Latin America.

The vocabularies of the languages of the world have been most receptive to borrowing from English. It is claimed, for example, that 81% of the borrowed vocabulary of Japanese are words of English origin. There are three ways in which such lexical borrowing manifests itself: in loan words, loan shifts (calques), and hybridisation, in which English and another language are combined (see, e.g., 1989; Bhatia & Ritchie, 1989; Viereck & Bald, 1986).

In grammar, Englishisation shows in several types of constructions, for example, the development of impersonal constructions in the Dravidian and Indo-Aryan languages, and the use of the passive constructions in a variety of ways (in the Indo-Aryan languages, passivisation with the agent NP, for example, *The plays were written by Shakespeare;* in Korean the *euihan* "by" expression, which has been traced to the contact with English; passivisation with extended semantic functions, as in, for example, Chinese, Japanese, Thai, and Swahili. In Thai, for example, passivisation has traditionally been used with an adversative connotation (the use of *thuuk*). However, this semantic constraint is now changing due to the influence of English).

Englishisation beyond the sentence level has resulted in Englished styles and registers (see Bhatia & Ritchie, 1989; Kachru, 1983a; for references, Kamwangamalu, 1989).

The literary impact of this influence is equally important. English provides a model for developing literary genres, has contributed thematic innovations, and has introduced new ideological paradigms, which in turn have resulted in new literary movements. The result is that classical stylistic traditions have changed, and innovations have become institutionalised (Kachru, 1990b).

Fallacies Concerning Users and Uses

It is evident in the literature that a variety of fallacies dominate the profession and professional societies involved in the teaching of English. Consider, for example, the following myth: that English is learnt essentially for its international currency. It is generally overlooked that actually English is also used as an important vehicle for intranational communication across diverse linguistic, ethnic, and religious groups. It is likewise often held that English is learnt exclusively or primarily to interact with a person from the Inner Circle who represents Judeo-Christian traditions. This is only partly true. English is also used as an important tool for imparting local cultural traditions and cultural values (Kachru, 1983a, 1990a, 1990b, 1992). It has also been claimed that the goal of learning and teaching English is to adopt a native model. Attitudinally this may be true of norm-dependent countries, but this assumption cannot be generalised. A number of scholars have held the view that a majority of Outer Circle English-using countries use interlanguages (e.g., Selinker, 1972). The validity of this hypothesis has been questioned in several studies (e.g., Sridhar & Sridhar, 1986). It is also believed that native speakers as teachers, consultants, advisers, and evaluators, have a serious input in the teaching of English, in policy formation and in organising the channels for the spread of

English. That actually is not true of the real ELT contexts in most of the world. Finally, it is argued that recognition of sociolinguistic and pragmatic realities of World Englishes reveals underlying philosophical and political positions. In the background of such positions, in Quirk's view, is "liberation theology" (1989). If recent history has given us a liberation theology, why not also a "liberation linguistics," Quirk asks. And then he adds:

> The trouble, as the Kingman Committee sees it [in reference to the report of the Committee presided over by Sir John Kingman], is that such an educational fashion went too far, grossly undervaluing the baby of standard English while overvaluing the undoubtedly important bathwater of regional social and ethnic varieties: giving the impression that any kind of English was as good as any other, and that in denying this, nothing less was at stake than 'personal liberty' itself (1989; for a detailed discussion of this fallacy, see Kachru, 1988a and 1991).

The Power and Politics of English

A number of recent studies address issues related to the ideological, cultural, and elitist power of English. And related to such power is the immense economic advantage of English to the countries in the Inner Circle, particularly Britain and the United States. An urge to derive maximum economic benefit has also resulted in competition between these two countries. The economic stakes are immense, as is obvious from the following statement: "The worldwide market for EFL training is worth a massive £6.5 billion a year according to a new report from the Economic Intelligence Unit" (*EFL Gazette,* March, 1989).

The very existence of their power thus provides the Inner Circle with incentives for devising ways to maintain attitudinal and formal control; it is both a psychological and sociopolitical process. And linguistic control is yet another such strategy, exercised in three ways: by the use of various channels of codification and by controlling these channels; by the attitude towards linguistic innovations (in the Outer Circle); and by suggesting dichotomies which are sociolinguistically and pragmatically unrealistic. These dichotomies divide the users of English into *us v. them* (see Kachru, 1986f, pp. 132–133; McArthur, 1978, 1986). In Kachru (1986f), "a blueprint for the study and conceptualization of selected issues related to the power and politics" of English is presented. The following studies discuss aspects of this question, either specifically with reference to English, or in relation to language in general: Knappert (1968); Kramarae et al. (1984); McArthur (1986); Ngũgĩ (1986, 1991); Mazrui (1967, 1973); O'Barr (1976); O'Barr et al. (1976); Phillipson & Skutnabb-Kangas (1986); Phillipson (1992); Ram (1983, 1991); Read (1974); Singh (1987); Tollefson (1991); Trömel-Plötz (1981). See also Kachru (1986f, pp. 133–134). For a discussion of the role of English in language "death" or "lingocide," see McDougal et al. (1976).

Teaching World Englishes

In planning a course on World English one is generally confronted with three questions: two relate to the conceptualisation of the topic, and one to resources for teaching such a course. The two content-related questions are: Why teach World Englishes? And, how does one motivate a paradigm-shift—attitudinally and methodologically—in the classroom? The third question concerns the resources available for teaching such a course. These will, of course, vary according to the linguistic, cultural and academic situations, and with respect to the experience of the instructor and goals of the students.

Why Teach World Englishes?

It is obvious that World Englishes provide a challenging opportunity to relate three academic areas—language, literature, and methodology.

The approach to World Englishes has to be cross-cultural and cross-linguistic. The sources involve diverse cultures, languages, and literatures in contact with English. One has to have interdisciplinary perspectives focusing on the linguistic face of World Englishes; one or more of the following aspects can form the basis for concentration. The references given below provide a framework and further references for understanding the shift in the paradigm, especially for English in the Outer Circle.

1. *Bilinguals' creativity* (Kachru, 1986c; Pride, 1981; McArthur, 1987)

2. *Contact and convergence* (for references see Kachru, 1989; Pandhari-pande, 1987; Viereck & Bald, 1986)

3. *Cross-cultural discourse* (Chishimba, 1984; D'souza, 1988; Garcia & Ortheguy, 1989; Y. Kachru, 1985b, 1985c, 1991; Magura, 1984; Nelson, 1985; Smith, 1981, 1987; Valentine, 1988, 1991)

4. *Textual competence and interpretation* (Nelson, 1982, 1984; Smith & Nelson, 1985)

5. *Language acquisition* (Sridhar & Sridhar, 1986; Williams, 1989)

6. *Language attitudes* (Finegan, 1980; Greenbaum, 1985; Smith, 1983)

7. *Language in society* (Bokamba, 1982; Cheshire, 1991; Kachru, 1976 and later)

8. *Lexicography* (Carter, 1987; Kachru, 1976, 1980; Kandiah, 1981; McArthur, 1978, 1986)

In lexicographical research on English, the observation of Carter (1987, p. 211) is very timely. He warns us that

> . . . it is important to bear in mind that English is an international language and there are several cultures which use English as a second language or as

an institutionalised variety. The kinds of associations described and the meanings defined in monolingual dictionaries for nonnative speakers reflect usage in British English (though variants in American English are plentiful in the OALD and especially the LDCE). Thus, in important respects British culture will be lexicalised. The consequences of this are partly ideological . . .

The literary face of World Englishes open up a mine of topics in textual, stylistic, and thematic terms (see, e.g., Brumfit & Carter, 1986; Kachru, 1986; see references in Bailey & Carter, 1986; Kachru, 1986e; see references in Bailey & Görlach, 1982).

The pedagogical issues have been addressed in Strevens (1980, 1988). Tickoo (1991) and Berns (1991); for the Western perspective on the history of English language teaching, see Howatt (1984), and for a critique of the Western approaches to English language teaching see Tollefson (1991) and Phillipson (1992).

What Motivates the Paradigm-Shift?

The issue concerning the need for paradigm shift raises the questions related to the sociolinguistic profiles in each English-using region: the underlying dynamic forces characteristic of the spread of English and its retention in the postcolonial period; the typologies of nativisation and Englishisation; the sociological and educational contexts in which English is taught and the implications of such contexts on methods of teaching and curriculum development; the types of personnel staffing and administering the EFL/ESL programmes; the attitudes of planners, teachers, and learners toward exonormative varieties and the localised educational varieties and subvarieties; the role writers and the media play in the Outer Circle in diffusion of local ideology through English; the role English plays in "modernisation" and "Westernisation" in non-Western regions; the role, if any, the Inner Circle plays in the ongoing spread of English and its codification; and the ways in which the nonnative literatures in English (e.g., Asian, African) can be used as a resource for cross-cultural awareness and for understanding linguistic creativity and innovations.

The aim is to make professionals and advanced students aware of the following aspects, among others:

1. *Sociolinguistic profile:* An overview of World Englishes in their world context, with in-depth focus on selected major varieties, their users and uses. It is useful to make a distinction between the use of English in a monolingual society as opposed to a complex multilingual society (e.g., Ferguson, 1966).

2. *Variety exposure:* A discussion of the repertoire within major native and nonnative varieties of English, varieties within a variety, their uses and users, specific texts related to different interactional con-

texts, mixing and switching and their implications, and shared and nonshared features at various linguistic levels.

3. *Attitudinal neutrality:* One might focus on one specific variety, and demonstrate the formal and functional reason for the distinctiveness of a variety. It is desirable to show why attitudinal neutrality is essential to capture, for example, the Africanness (Bokamba, 1982), and the Indianness (Kachru, 1965, 1983a) of the African and Indian varieties, respectively.

4. *Range of uses:* The functional and pragmatic appropriateness of the lectal range of English in private and public discourse and the reasons for the use of pidgins and basilectal (or colloquial) varieties in such contexts, and the importance of variety-shift for various types of identities. The range of uses may be related to the concept *cline* with reference to (a) the participants in a speech event, (b) intelligibility within the speech fellowship(s), and (c) roles in which English is used (see Kachru, 1983a, pp. 236–237).

5. *Contrastive pragmatics:* The rationale for the use of distinct discoursal and stylistic innovations, and their appropriateness to the local conventions of culture (e.g., linguistic strategies used for persuasion, phatic communion, apologies, condolences, obituaries).

6. *Multidimensionality of functions:* The linguistic implications of the functional ranges of English in the media, literary creativity, administration, government, and the legal system.

7. *Expansion of the canons:* The literary, linguistic, and cultural implications of multiple Western and non-Western canons of English.

8. *Cross-cultural intelligibility:* The implications of the diffusion and multilinguistic and literary identities of English on international and intranational intelligibility.

What are the Resources for Teaching?

In the 1970s, this question would have been difficult to answer. One would have had to depend primarily on papers from journals and selected notes. However, as Görlach (1991a, p. 11) rightly observes, "the books published in 1982-84 make up a particularly impressive list: It is no exaggeration to say that the following ten books more or less suffice to teach a full academic course on the topic." Görlach lists the following books: Bailey and Görlach (1982); Kachru (1982, 1983a [1990]); Platt et al. (1984); Pride (1981); Todd (1984); Trudgill and Hannah (1982; 2nd edition 1985); Trudgill (1986); Wells (3 vols., 1982). This is an impressive list indeed. I would add to this list Cheshire (1991), McCrum et al. (1986), and Smith (1981, 1987). McCrum et al. have also the advantage of an accompanying series of films which students of any level would find very instructive. Three other books useful for focusing on specific theoretical and pedagogical topics are: Lowenberg (1988); Quirk and Widdowson (1985); and Tickoo (1991). Out of the small number of books published before the 1980s, one stands out: Fishman et al. (1977).

Bibliographies: Viereck, Schneider, and Görlach (1984) provide a general bibliography, up to the early 1980s (reviewed in Kachru, 1986g). A supplement to the bibliography, published in 1992 (*English, World Wide, 13,* 1, 1–50), includes 794 entries and covers the period 1984–91. There are several bibliographies specifically for various regions, for example, Aggarwal (1982) for South Asia. See also references in Kandiah (1991); Kachru (1983a, 1986b), and Schmied (1990).

The following studies provide valuable bibliographical references for specific areas: Southeast Asia: Bloom (1986); Foley (1988); Noss (1983); Tay (1991); Ireland: Harris (1991); Canada: Chambers (1991); New Zealand: Bell and Holmes (1991); Australia: Guy (1991); East Africa: Abdulaziz (1991); Southern Africa: Chishimba (1991); West Africa: Bokamba (1991); the Caribbean: Winford (1991); the Pacific: Romaine (1991). Another bibliographical source for an overviewing and relevant references is Burchfield (forthcoming).

Issue-oriented studies: (a) Models: Kachru (1982, 1985, 1986a, 1992 ed.); Strevens (1982); Tickoo (1991). *(b) Intelligibility:* extensive and partly annotated bibliography in Smith (1981); Smith and Nelson (1985). *(c) Sociolinguistic issues:* Cheshire (1991); Kachru (1986a, 1988a, 1990a); K. Sridhar (1986); Tickoo (1991). *(d) Testing:* Lowenberg (1992).

Literatures in English: Kachru (1986a); King (1974, 1980); Taiwo (1976); Thumboo (1992). For South Asia, see Singh et al. (1981).

Reference: The Cambridge History of the English Language will provide a survey in seven volumes: Vol. I (The beginnings to 1066); Vol. II (1066 to 1476); Vol. III (1476 to 1776); Vol. IV (1776 to the present day); Vol. V (Present-day English: Origins and development) is planned in two parts (English in the British Isles, and English in the former colonies except North America); Vol. VI (American English); and Vol. VII (English as a second language). Part two of Vol. V, edited by Robert Burchfield, will be of special interest to students of World Englishes. *The Oxford Companion to the English Language,* edited by Tom McArthur (Oxford: Oxford University Press, 1992), includes extensive entries on English in the Outer and Expanding Circles.

Journals: There are four major journals that specifically focus on World Englishes: *English World-Wide: A Journal of Varieties of English* (1980–; John Benjamins; Amsterdam & Philadelphia); *World Englishes: Journal of English as an International and Intranational Language* (1985–; Blackwells, Oxford); *English Today* (1985–; Cambridge University Press, Cambridge); and *World Literature Written in English (WLWE)* (1961–; University of Guelph, Guelph, Ontario, Canada).

The International Corpus of English (ICE): The Survey of English Usage, at University College London was originally initiated by Sir Randolph Quirk.

In 1988, the new Director of the Survey, Sidney Greenbaum, proposed an International Corpus of English (ICE). The scope of the corpus has now been extended to the countries where English is an official second language. The proposal to extend the scope of the corpus received enthusiastic support and now scholars from the following countries are participating in the project: Australia, Belgium, Canada, Denmark, Germany, Hong Kong, India, Jamaica, Kenya, The Netherlands, New Zealand, Nigeria, Northern Ireland, The Philippines, Singapore, Sweden, Tanzania, UK, USA, Wales, Zaire, Zambia, and Zimbabwe. The extension of the corpus and participation of the countries from the Outer Circle "is a splendid example of international cooperation in research" (Greenbaum, 1991, p. 7; see also Greenbaum, 1990).

Conclusion

I believe that for proper conceptualisation and study of World Englishes, two types of shifts are needed. First, a paradigm shift in research, teaching, and application of sociolingiustic realities to the functions of English. Second, a shift from frameworks and theories which are essentially appropriate only to monolingual countries. It is indeed essential to recognise that World Englishes represent certain linguistic, cultural and pragmatic realities and pluralism, and that pluralism is now an integral part of World Englishes and literatures written in Englishes. The pluralism of English must be reflected in the approaches, both theoretical and applied, we adopt for understanding this unprecedented linguistic phenomenon.

References

Abdulaziz, M. M. H. (1991). East Africa (Tanzania and Kenya). In J. Cheshire (Ed.), *English around the world: Sociolinguistic perspectives* (pp. 391–401). Cambridge: Cambridge University Press.

Aggarwal, N. K. (1982). *English in South Asia: A bibliographical survey of resources.* Gurgaon and Delhi: Indian Documentation Service.

Bailey, R. W. & Gorlach, M. (Eds.) (1982). *English as a world language.* Ann Arbor, MI: University of Michigan Press.

Bamgboṣe, A. (1982). Standard Nigerian English: Issues of Identification. In B. B. Kachru (Ed.), *The other tongue: English across cultures* (pp. 99–111). Urbana, IL: University of Illinois Press.

Bamiro, E. O. (1991). Nigerian Englishes in Nigerian English literature. *World Englishes, 10,* 7–17.

Baxter, J. (1980). How should I speak English? American-ly, Japanese-ly, or internation-ally? *JALT Journal, 2,* 31–61.

Bell, A., & Holmes, J. (1991). New Zealand. In J. Cheshire (Ed.), *English around the world: Sociolinguistic perspectives* (pp. 153–68). Cambridge: Cambridge University Press.

Berns, M. (1990). *Contexts of competence: Social and cultural considerations in communicative language teaching.* New York: Plenum.

Berns, N. (1991). Review of *Communicative language teaching,* special issue of *Annual Review of Applied Linguistics,* Vol. 8. *World Englishes, 10,* 102–106.

Bhatia, T. K., & Ritchie, W. (Eds.) (1989). *Code-mixing: English across languages.* [Special issue]. *World Englishes, 8,*(3).

Bickerton, D. (1975). *Dynamics of a creole system.* Cambridge: Cambridge University Press.

Bloom, D. (1986). The English language and Singapore. In B. K. Kapur (Ed.), *Singapore studies: Critical surveys of the humanities and social sciences,* (pp. 337–458). Singapore: Singapore University Press.

Bokamba, E. G. (1982). The Africanisation of English. In B. B. Kachru (Ed.), *The other tongue: English across cultures* (pp. 77–98). Urbana, IL: University of Illinois Press.

Bokamba, E. G. (1991). West Africa. In J. Cheshire (Ed.), *English around the world: Sociolinguistic perspectives* (pp. 493–508). Cambridge: Cambridge University Press.

Bright, W. (Ed.) (1966). *Sociolinguistics.* The Hague: Mouton.

Brown, A. (Ed.) (1991). *Teaching English pronunciation.* London: Routledge.

Brumfit, C. J. (Ed.) (1988). *Communicative language teaching* [Special issue]. *Annual Review of Applied Linguistics, 8.*

Burchfield, R. (Ed.) (in press). *Cambridge history of the English language* (Vol. V). Cambridge: Cambridge University Press.

Candlin, C. (1982). English as an international language: Intelligibility vs. interpretability. In C. J. Brumfit (Ed.), *Notes on a theme: English for international communication,* (pp. 95–98). Oxford: Pergamon Press.

Candlin, C. (1987). Beyond description to explanation in cross-cultural discourse. In L. E. Smith (Ed.), *Discourse across cultures: Strategies in World Englishes* (pp. 22–35). London: Prentice-Hall.

Carter, R. (1987). *Vocabulary: Applied linguistic perspectives.* London: Allen & Unwin.

Carter, R. A., & Nash, W. (1990). *Seeing through language.* Oxford: Basil Blackwell.

Chambers, J. K. (1991). Canada. In J. Cheshire (Ed.), *English around the world: Sociolinguistic perspectives* (pp. 89–107). Cambridge: Cambridge University Press.

Cheshire, J. (1991). The UK and the USA. In J. Cheshire (Ed.), *English around the world: Sociolinguistic perspectives* (pp. 13–34). Cambridge: Cambridge University Press.

Cheshire, J. (Ed.) (1991). *English around the world: Sociolinguistic perspectives.* Cambridge: Cambridge University Press.

Chishimba, M. M. (1984). *African varieties of English: Text in context.* Unpublished doctoral dissertation, University of Illinois at Urbana-Champaign.

Chishimba, M. M. (1991). Southern Africa. In J. Cheshire (Ed.), *English around the world: Sociolinguistic perspectives* (pp. 435–445). Cambridge: Cambridge University Press.

Chomsky, N. (1965). *Aspects of the theory of syntax.* Cambridge, Mass.: MIT Press.

Christopherson, P. (1988). Native-speakers and world English. *English Today, 4*(3), 15–18.

Crystal, D. (1985). How many millions? The statistics of English today. *English Today, 1,* 7–9.

Devaki, L., Ramasamy, K., & Srivastava, A. K. (1990). *An annotated bibliography on bilingualism, bilingual education and medium of instruction.* Mysore: Central Institute of Indian Languages.

Dissanayake, W. (1985). Towards a decolonised English: South Asian creativity in fiction. *World Englishes, 4,* 233–242.

D'souza, J. (1988). Interactional strategies in South Asian languages: Their implications for teaching English internationally. *World Englishes, 7,* 159–171.

Dubey, V. D. (1991). The lexical style of Indian English newspapers. *World Englishes, 10,* 19–32.

Ferguson, C. A. (1966). National sociolinguistic profile formulas. In W. Bright (Ed.), Sociolinguistics (pp. 309–315). The Hague: Mouton.

Ferguson, C. L. A. (1982). Foreword. In B. B. Kachru (Ed.), *The other tongue: English across cultures* (pp. vii–xii). Urbana, IL: University of Illinois Press.

Ferguson, C. A. & Heath, S. B. (Eds.) (1991). *Language in the U.S.A.* New York: Cambridge University Press.

Finegan, E. (1980). *Attitudes toward English usage: The history of a war of words.* New York: Teachers College Press.

Fishman, J. A., Cooper, R. L., & Conrad, A. W. (1977). *The spread of English: The sociology of English as an additional language.* Rowley, Mass.: Newbury House.

Foley, J. (Ed.) (1988). *New Englishes: The case of Singapore.* Singapore: Singapore University Press.

Garcia, O., & Ortheguy, R. (Eds.) (1989). *English across cultures, cultures across English.* New York: Mouton de Gruyter.

Görlach, M. (1991). Lexicographical problems of new Englishes. In M. Gorlach, *Englishes: Studies in varieties of English 1984–1988* (pp. 36–68). Amsterdam/Philadelphia: John Benjamin.

Greenbaum, S. (1990). Standard English and the international corpus of English. *World Englishes, 9,* 79–83.

Greenbaum, S. (1991). ICE: the International Corpus of English. *English Today, 28*(7.4), 3–7.

Guy, G. R. (1991). Australia. In J. Cheshire (Ed.), *English around the world: Sociolinguistic perspectives* (pp. 213–226). Cambridge: Cambridge University Press.

Halliday, M. A. K. (1970). Language structure and language function. In J. Lyons (Ed.), *New horizons in linguistics,* 140–165. Harmondsworth: Penguin.

Halliday, M. A. K. (1973). *Explorations in functions of language.* London: Edward Arnold.

Halliday, M. A. K. (1974). *Learning how to mean: Explorations in the development of language.* London: Edward Arnold.

Halliday, M. A. K. (1978). *Language as a social semiotic: The social interpretation of language and meaning.* London: Edward Arnold.

Harris, J. (1991). Ireland. In J. Cheshire (Ed.), *English around the world: Sociolinguistic perspectives* (pp. 37–50). Cambridge: Cambridge University Press.

Honey, J. (1991). The concept 'standard English' in first- and second-language contexts. In M. L. Tickoo (Ed.), *Languages and standards: Issues, attitudes, case studies* (pp. 22–32). Singapore: SEAMO Regional Language Centre.

Hosali, P., & Aitchison, J. (1986) Butler English: A minimal pidgin? *Journal of Pidgin and Creole Linguistics, 1,* 51–79.

Howatt, A. P. R. (1984). *A history of English language teaching.* Oxford: Oxford University Press.

Hudson, R. (1980). *Sociolinguistics.* Cambridge: Cambridge University Press.

Hymes, D. (1974). *Foundations of sociolinguistics: An ethnographic approach.* Philadelphia: University of Pennsylvania Press.

Kachru, B. B. (1965). The *Indianness* in Indian English. *Word, 21,* 391–410.

Kachru, B. B. (1976). Models of English for the third world: White man's linguistic burden or language pragmatics? *TESOL Quarterly, 10,* 221–230.

Kachru, B. B. (1977). The new Englishes and old models. *English Language Forum, 15,* 29–35.

Kachru, B. B. (1980). The new Englishes and old dictionaries: Directions in lexicographical research on nonnative varieties of English. In L. Zgusta (Ed.), *Theory and method in lexicography: Western and non-Western perspectives* (pp. 71–104). Columbia, SC: Hornbeam Press.

Kachru, B. B. (1981a). American English and other Englishes. In C. A. Ferguson and S. B. Heath (Eds.), *Language in the U.S.A.* (pp. 21–43) New York: Cambridge University Press.

Kachru, B. B. (Ed.) (1982a). *The other tongue: English across cultures.* Urbana, IL: University of Illinois Press.

Kachru, B. B. (1982b). The bilingual's linguistic repertoire. In B. Hartford, A. Valdman, and C. Foster (Eds.), *Issues in bilingual education: The role of the vernacular.* New York: Plenum.

Kachru, B. B. (1982c). Meaning in deviation: Toward understanding nonnative English texts. In Kachru (Ed.), *The other tongue: English across cultures* (pp. 325–350). Urbana, IL: University of Illinois Press.

Kachru, B. B. (1983a). *The Indianisation of English: The English language in India.* New Delhi: Oxford University Press.

Kachru, B. B. (1983b). Norms régionales de l'anglais, In E. Bédard and J. Maurais (Eds.), *La norme linguistique* (pp. 707–730). Québec: Direction Générale des Publications Gouvernementales du Ministère des Communications.

Kachru, B. B. (1985a). Standards, codification and sociolinguistic realism: The English language in the Outer circle. In R. Quirk and H. G. Widdowson (Eds.), *English in the world: Teaching and learning the language and literatures* (pp. 11–30). Cambridge: Cambridge University Press.

Kachru, B. B. (1985b). Institutionalised second language varieties. In S. Greenbaum (Ed.), *The English language today* (pp. 19–32). Oxford: Pergamon Press.

Kachru, B. B. (1986a). *The alchemy of English: The spread, functions, and models of nonnative Englishes.* Oxford: Pergamon Press. Reprinted 1990, University of Illinois Press, Urbana, IL.

Kachru, B. B. (1986b). Socially-realistic linguistics: The Firthian tradition. *International Journal of the Sociology of Language, 31,* 65–89.

Kachru, B. B. (1986c). The bilingual's creativity and contact literatures. In B. B. Kachru, *The alchemy of English: The spread, functions, and models of nonnative Englishes* (pp. 159–173) Oxford: Pergamon Press.

Kachru, B. B. (1986d). The bilingual's creativity. *Annual Review of Applied Linguistics (1985), 6,* 20–33.

Kachru, B. B. (1986e). Nonnative literatures in English as a resource for language teaching. In C. J. Brumfit and R. A. Carter (Eds.), *Literature and language teaching* (pp. 140–149). Oxford: Oxford University Press.

Kachru, B. B. (1986f). The power and politics of English. *World Englishes, 5,* 121–140.

Kachru, B. B. (1986g). Review of *A bibliography of writings on varieties of English* by W. Viereck et al. *English World-Wide, 6,*(2), 132–5.

Kachru, B. B. (1987). The past and prejudice: Toward demythologising the English canon. In R. Steel and T. Threadgold (Eds.), *Linguistic topics: Papers in honor of M. A. K. Halliday,* (pp. 245–256). Philadelphia: J. Benjamin.

Kachru, B. B. (1988a). The spread of English and sacred linguistic cows. In P. H. Lowenberg (Ed.), *Language spread and language policy: Issues, implications, and case studies* (pp. 207–228). Washington, DC: Georgetown University Press.

Kachru, B. B. (1988b). ESP and nonnative varieties of English: Toward a shift in paradigm. In D. Chamberlain and R. J. Baumgardner (Eds.), *ESP in the classroom: Practice and evaluation,* (pp. 9–28). London: Macmillan.

Kachru, B. B. (1989). Englishisation and contact linguistics: Dimensions of linguistic hegemony of English. Unpublished manuscript.

Kachru, B. B. (1990a). World Englishes and applied linguistics. *World Englishes, 9,* 3–20.

Kachru, B. B. (1990b). Cultural contact and literary creativity in a multilingual society. In J. Toyama and N. Ochner (Eds.), *Literary relations east and west.* (pp. 194–203). Honolulu: University of Hawaii Press.

Kachru, B. B. (1991). Liberation linguistics and the Quirk concern. *English Today, 7.1,* 3–13.

Kachru, B. B. (1992). The second diaspora of English. In T. W. Machan and C. T. Scott (Eds.), *English in its social contexts: Essays in historical sociolinguistics.* New York: Oxford University Press.

Kachru, B. B. (Ed.) (1992). *The other tongue: English across cultures.* (2nd revised edition). Urbana, IL: University of Illinois Press.

Kachru, B. B. & Quirk, R. (1981). Introduction. In L. E. Smith (1981), *English for cross-cultural communication* (pp. xiii–xx) London: Macmillan.

Kachru, B. B. & Smith, L. E. (1988). World Englishes: An integrative and cross-cultural journal of We-ness. In R. Maxwell (Ed.), *Forty years' service to science, technology and education* (pp. 674–678). Oxford: Pergamon Press.

Kachru, B. B. & Smith, L. E. (Eds.) (1986). The power of English: Cross-cultural dimensions of literature and media. [Special issue] *World Englishes, 5*,(2/3).

Kachru, Y. (1983). Cross-cultural texts and interpretation. *Studies in the Linguistic Sciences, 13,* 57–72.

Kachru, Y. (1985a). Applied linguistics and foreign language teaching: A non-Western perspective. *ERIC Document ED* 256175.

Kachru, Y. (1985b). Discourse analysis, nonnative Englishes and second-language acquisition research. *World Englishes, 4,*(2), 223–232.

Kachru, Y. (1985c). Discourse strategies, pragmatics and ESL: Where are we going? *RELC Journal, 16,* (2), 1–30.

Kachru, Y. (1987). Cross-cultural texts, discourse strategies and discourse interpretation. In L. E. Smith (Ed.), *Discourse across cultures: Strategies in World Englishes* (pp. 87–100). London: Prentice-Hall.

Kachru, Y. (Ed.) (1991). Symposium on speech acts in world Englishes, *World Englishes, 10* (3).

Kahane, H. & Kahane, R. (1979). Decline and survival of Western prestige languages. *Language, 55,* 183–198.

Kahane, H. & Kahane, R. (1986). A typology of the prestige language. *Language, 62,* 495–508.

Kamwangamalu, N. (1989). A selected bibliography of studies on code-mixing and code-switching (1970-1988). *World Englishes, 8,* 433–440.

Kandiah, T. (1981). Lankan English schizoglossia. *English World-Wide: A Journal of Varieties of English, 2,* 63–81.

Kandiah, T. (1991). South Asia. In J. Cheshire (Ed.), *English around the world: Sociolinguistic perspectives* (pp. 271–287). Cambridge: Cambridge University Press.

King, B. (1980). *The new English literatures: Cultural nationalism in the changing world.* New York: St. Martin Press.

King, B. (Ed.) (1974). *Literatures of the world in English.* London: Routledge & Kegan Paul.

Knappert, J. (1968). Language in a political situation. *Linguistics, 39,* 59–67.

Kramarae, C., Schulz, M., & O'Barr, W. M. (Eds.) (1984). *Language and power.* Beverly Hills, CA: Sage.

Labov, W. (1972a). *Language in the inner city: Studies in the black English vernacular.* Philadelphia: University of Pennsylvania Press.

Labov, W. (1972b). *Sociolinguistic patterns.* Philadelphia: University of Pennsylvania Press.

Lowenberg, P. H. (1984). *English in the Malay Archipelago: Nativisation and its functions in a sociolingusitic area.* Unpublished doctoral dissertation, University of Illinois at Urbana-Champaign.

Lowenberg, P. H. (1986a). Sociolinguistic context and second-language acquisition: Acculturation and creativity in Malaysian English. *World Englishes, 5,* 71–83.

Lowenberg, P. H. (1985b). Nonnative varieties of English: Nativisation, norms, and implications. *Studies in Second-Language Acquisition, 8,* 1–18.

Lowenberg, P. H. (1991). Variations in Malaysian English: The pragmatics of languages in contact. In J. Cheshire (1991), *English around the world: Sociolinguistic perspectives* (pp. 364–375). Cambridge: Cambridge University Press.

Lowenberg, P. H. (1992). Testing English as a world language: Issues in assessing non-native proficiency. In B. B. Kachru (Ed.), *The other tongue: English across cultures* (2nd ed.). Urbana, IL: University of Illinois Press.

Lowenberg, P. H. (Ed.) (1988). *Language spread and language policy: Issues, implications and case studies.* (GURT 1987). Washington, DC: Georgetown University Press.

Lyons, J. (1978). Foreword. In W. Labov, *Sociolinguistic patterns* (British ed.) (pp. xi–xxiii). Oxford: Blackwell.

McArthur, T. (1978). The vocabulary control movement in the English language, 1844–1953. *Indian Journal of Applied Linguistics, 4,* 47–68.

McArthur, T. (1986). The power of words: Pressure, prejudice and politics in our vocabularies and dictionaries. *World Englishes, 5,* 209–219.

McArthur, T. (1987). The English languages? *English Today,* July/September, 9–11.

McCrum, R., Cran, W., & MacNeil, R. (1986). *The story of English.* New York: Viking.

McDougal, M. S., Lasswell, H. D., & Chen, L. C. (1976). Freedom from discrimination in a choice of language and international human rights. *Southern Illinois University Law Journal, 1,* 151–174.

Machan, T. W., & Scott, C. T. (Eds.) (1992). *English in its social contexts: Essays in historical sociolinguistics.* New York: Oxford University Press.

Magura, B. (1984). *Style and meaning in Southern African English.* Unpublished doctoral dissertation, University of Illinois at Urbana-Champaign.

Magura, B. (1985). Southern African Black English. *World Englishes, 4,* 251–256.

Mazrui, A. A. (1967). Language and politics in East Africa. *Africa Report, 12,* 59–56.

Mazrui, A. A. (1973). *The political sociology of the English language: An African perspective.* The Hague: Mouton.

Nelson, C. (1982). Intelligibility and nonnative varieties of English. In B. B. Kachru (Ed.), *The other tongue: English across cultures* (pp. 58–73). Urbana, IL: University of Illinois Press.

Nelson, C. (1984). *Intelligibility: The case of nonnative varieties of English.* Unpublished doctoral dissertation. University of Illinois at Urbana-Champaign.

Nelson, C. (1985). My language, your culture: whose communicative competence? *World Englishes, 4,* 43–50.

Newbrook, M. (1986). Received pronunciation in Singapore: a sacred cow? *Commentary, 7,* 20–27.

Ngũgĩ Wa Thiong'o (1986). *Decolonising the mind: The politics of language in African literature.* London: James Currey.

Ngũgĩ Wa Thiong'o (1991). English: A language for the world? *The Yale Journal of Criticism, 4,* 283–293.

Nihalani, P. (1991). Coarticulation and social acceptability: Pragmatic implications for World Englishes. *World Englishes, 10,* 15–29.

Noss, R. B. (Ed.) (1983). *Varieties of English in Southeast Asia.* Singapore: Regional Language Center.

Nwoye, O. G. (1992). Obituary announcements as communicative events in Nigerian English. *World Englishes, 11,* 15–28.

O'Barr, W. M. (1976). The study of language and politics. In W. M. O'Barr and J. F. O'Barr (Eds.), *Languages and politics* (pp. 1–27). The Hague: Mouton.

Paikeday, T. M. (1985). *The native speaker is dead!* Toronto: Paikeday Publishing.

Pakir, A. (1991a). The status of English and the question of "standard" in Singapore: a sociolinguistic perspective. In M. L. Tickoo (Ed.), *Languages and standards: Issues, attitudes, case studies* (pp. 109–30). Singapore: SEAMEO Regional Language Centre.

Pakir, A. (1991b). The range and depth of English-knowing bilinguals in Singapore. *World Englishes, 10,* 167–180.

Pandharipande, R. (1987). On nativisation of English. *World Englishes, 6,* 149–158.

Phillipson, R. (1992). *Linguistic imperialism.* London: Oxford University Press.

Phillipson, R., & Skutnabb-Kangas, T. (1986). *Linguisticism rules in education, 1.* Denmark: Roskilde University Center, Institute VI.

Platt, J. (1977). The subvarieties of Singapore English: Their sociolectal and functional status. In W. J. Crew (Ed.), *The English language in Singapore.* Singapore: Eastern University Press.

Platt, J., & Weber, H. K. (1979). *English in Singapore and Malaysia: Status, features, functions.* Kuala Lumpur: Oxford University Press.

Platt, J., Weber, H., & Lian, H. M. (1984). *The New Englishes.* London: Routledge.

Prator, C. (1968). The British heresy in TESL. In J. A. Fishman, R. L. Cooper, & A. W. Conrad, (Eds.), *Language problems in developing nations.* New York: Wiley & Sons.

Pride, J. B. (1981). Native competence and the bilingual/multilingual speaker. *English World-Wide, 2,* 141–153.

Pride, J. B. (Ed.) (1982). *New Englishes.* Rowley, Mass.: Newbury House.

Quirk, R. (1988). The question of standard in the international use of English. In P. H. Lowenberg (Ed.), *Language spread and language policy: Issues, implications and case studies* (pp. 229–241). Washington, D.C.: Georgetown University Press.

Quirk, R. (1989). Language varieties and standard language. *JALT Journal, 11,* 14–25.

Quirk, R. & Widdowson, H. G. (Eds.) (1985). *English in the world: teaching and learning the language and literatures.* Cambridge: Cambridge University Press.

Ram, T. (1983). *Trading in language: The story of English in India.* Delhi: G.D.K. Publication.

Ram, T. (1991). English in imperial expansion. In R. S. Gupta and K. Kapoor (Eds.), *English in India: Issues and problems,* (pp. 28–57). Delhi: Academic Foundation.

Ramaiah, L. S. (1985). *Communicative language teaching: A bibliographical survey of resources.* Gurgaon: Indian Documentation Service.

Read, A. W. (1974). What is "linguistic imperialism"? *Geolinguistics, 1,* 5–10.

Richards, J. (1979). Rhetorical and communicative styles in the new varieties of English. *Language Learning, 29,* 1–25.

Richards, J. (Ed.) (1979) *Error analysis: Perspectives on second language analysis.* London: Longman.

Romaine, S. (1991). The Pacific. In J. Cheshire (Ed.), *English around the world: Sociolinguistic perspectives* (pp. 619–636). Cambridge: Cambridge University Press.

Savignon, S. (1983). *Communicative competence: Theory and classroom practice.* Reading, Mass.: Addison-Wesley.

Saville-Troike, M. (1981). *Ethnography of communication: An introduction.* Oxford: Basil Blackwell.

Schmied, J. (Ed.). (1990). *Linguistics in the service of Africa, with particular reference to research on English and African languages.* Bayreuth: University of Bayreuth.

Selinker, L. (1972). Interlanguage. In B. W. Robinett and J. Schachter (Eds.), *Second-language learning, error analysis, and related aspects,* (pp. 173–196). Ann Arbor, MI: University of Michigan Press.

Singh, A., Verma, R., & Joshi, I. M. (Eds.) (1981). *Indian literature in English 1927-1979: A guide to information sources.* Detroit, MI: Gale Research Company.

Singh, F. B. (1987). Power and politics in the context of grammar books: The example of India. *World Englishes, 6,* 195–199.

Smith, L. E. (Ed.) (1981). *English for cross-cultural communication.* London: Macmillan.

Smith, L. E. (Ed.) (1983). *Readings in English as an international language.* London: Pergamon.

Smith, L. E. (Ed.) (1987). *Discourse across cultures: Strategies in World Englishes.* London: Prentice-Hall.

Smith, L. E., & Nelson, C. L. (1985). International intelligibility of English: Directions and resources. *World Englishes, 4,* 333–342.

Sridhar, K. (1986). Sociolinguistic theories and nonnative varieties of English. *Lingua, 68,* 85–104.

Sridhar, K. (1989). *English in Indian bilingualism.* New Delhi: Manohar.

Sridhar, K. K., & Sridhar, S. N. (1986). Bridging the paradigm gap: Second-language acquisition theory and indigenised varieties of English. *World Englishes, 5,* 3–14.

Steiner, G. (1975). *Why English?* London: The English Association.

Strevens, P. (1980). *Teaching English as an international language.* Oxford: Pergamon.

Strevens, P. (1982). World English and the world's Englishes: Or, whose language is it, anyway? *Journal of the Royal Society of Arts,* London, CXX, 5311, 418–431.

Strevens, P. (1988). Language learning and language teaching: Toward an integrated model. In D. Tannen (Ed.), *Linguistics in context: Connecting observation and understanding* (pp. 299–312). Norwood, NJ: Ablex.

Swales, J. (1985). ESP—the heart of the matter or the end of the affair. In R. Quirk and H. G. Widdowson (Eds.), *English in the World: Teaching and learning the language and literatures* (pp. 212–223). Cambridge: Cambridge University Press.

Taiwo, O. (1976). *Culture and the Nigerian novel.* New York: St. Martin's Press.

Tay, M. W. J. (1986). Lects and institutionalised varieties of English: The case of Singapore. *Issues and Developments in English and Applied Linguistics, 1,* 93–107.

Tay, M. W. J. (1991). Southeast Asia and Hong Kong. In J. Cheshire (Ed.), *English around the world: Sociolinguistic perspectives* (pp. 319–332). Cambridge: Cambridge University Press.

Thumboo, E. (1985). Twin perspectives and multiecosystems: Traditions for a commonwealth writer. *World Englishes, 4,* 213–222.

Thumboo, E. (1992). The literary dimensions of the spread of English. In B. B. Kachru (Ed.), *The other tongue: English across cultures.* Urbana, IL: University of Illinois Press.

Tickoo, M. L. (1988). In search of appropriateness in EF(S)L teaching materials. *RELC Journal, 19,* 39–50.

Tickoo, M. L. (Ed.) (1991). *Languages and standards: Issues, attitudes, case studies.* Singapore: SEAMEO Regional Language Centre.

Todd, L. (1984). *Modern Englishes: Pidgins and creoles.* Oxford: Blackwell.

Tollefson, J. W. (1991). *Planning language, planning inequality: Language policy in the community.* London: Longman.

Trömel-Plötz, S. (1981). Languages of oppression. *Journal of Pragmatics, 5,* 67–80.

Trudgill, P., (1986). *Dialects in contact.* Oxford: Blackwell.

Trudgill, P., & Hannah, J. (1982). *International English: A guide to varieties of Standard English.* London: Arnold.

Valentine, T. (1988). Developing discourse types in nonnative English: Strategies of gender in Hindi and Indian English. *World Englishes, 7,* 143–158.

Valentine, T. (1991). Getting the message across: Discourse markers in Indian English. *World Englishes, 10,* 325–334.

Vierbeck, W., Schneider, E. W., & Görlach, M. (1984). *A bibliography of writings on varieties of English, 1965–1983.* Amsterdam/Philadelphia: Benjamins.

Viereck, W., & Bald, W. (Eds.) (1986). *English in contact with other languages.* Budapest: Akademiai Kiado.

Wells, J. C. (1982). *Accents of English* (Vols. 1–3). Cambridge: Cambridge University Press.

Williams, J. (1989). Language acquisition, language contact and nativised varieties of English. *RELC Journal, 20,* 39–67.

Windord, D. (1991). The Caribbean. In J. Cheshire *English around the world: Sociolinguistic perspectives* (pp. 565–584). Cambridge: Cambridge University Press.

Understanding the Article

1. What reasons does Kachru give for abandoning the traditional dichotomy between *native* and *nonnative* varieties of English?

2. How does the acceptance of varieties of English other than the five listed in Kachru's "Inner Circle" affect our concept of linguistic norms for English?

3. What is the difference between the "Outer Circle" and the "Expanding Circle"?

4. What does Kachru suggest about the viability of concepts such as *ideal speaker-hearer* and *mother tongue*?

Reflecting on Wider Issues

1. How do the concepts of motivation (integrative and instrumental) and acculturation operate in the kinds of sociolinguistic contexts Kachru describes for the acquisition of English in the Outer Circle?

2. Does the model Kachru describes for World Englishes apply to other languages as well? Can you think of any examples?

3. Imagine the following three situations and describe what decisions you would have to make about linguistic norms, error correction, selection of literary texts, and even the goal of learning English:

   a. You are a native speaker of American English teaching high school English in Nigeria.

    b. You are a speaker of Indian English teaching high school in Zambia.

    c. You are a speaker of Singaporean English teaching high school English in Singapore.

4. Some scholars have suggested that International English should be considered an interlanguage. What support can you provide for or against this position?

Going Beyond the Article

How can we distinguish between the varieties that constitute English as an International Language and the interlanguages of nonnative speakers learning English? For an interesting discussion of this issue and related issues, read Davies (1989), "Is International English an interlanguage?" (*TESOL Quarterly, 23,* 447–467).

There is a growing body of literature on varieties of English. You might want to look at the articles in Kachru (1992), *The Other Tongue: Englishes Across Cultures, 2nd. ed.* (Urbana: University of Illinois Press), in particular the articles by Nelson ("My language, your culture; whose communicative competence?") and Lowenberg ("Testing English as a world language: Issues in assessing nonnative proficiency"). You might also look at Cheshire (1991), *English Around the World: Sociolinguistic Perspectives* (New York: Cambridge University Press) or issues of the journal *World Englishes.*

10

SECOND LANGUAGE ACQUISITION: THE PIDGINIZATION HYPOTHESIS

John H. Schumann
University of California at Los Angeles

Previewing the Article

As second language acquisition research gathered momentum in the 1970s, researchers began to make a rather interesting comparison between linguistic forms produced by adult second language learners and pidginized forms of language. John Schumann was the first researcher to draw the comparison between pidginization and SLA and to support this analogy in some detail with data from a second language learner. His argument was doubly interesting because he attributed the pidginized forms of his subjects to *social and psychological distance.*

Before you read this article of historical significance, review the research on social and psychological distance and its potential effect on language acquisition. If possible, try to acquaint yourself with the meaning of *pidgin* in its original definition. Then, answer these questions:

1. What is the purpose of this study?
2. How does the author go about demonstrating his hypothesis?
3. What kinds of data are reported and how are they analyzed?

Reprinted from *Language Learning, 26*:391–408, 1976.

This paper is a case study of the untutored acquisition of English by a 33-year-old Costa Rican named Alberto. His language learning was examined longitudinally for a ten month period. During that time he evidenced very little linguistic growth. Three causes for Alberto's lack of development are considered: ability, age, and social and psychological distance. Performance on a test of adaptive intelligence indicated that lack of ability is not adequate to explain his acquisition pattern. Also, due to the inadequacy of the arguments for a biological critical period in language acquisition, age is also rejected as a cause. However, Alberto's English speech showed evidence of pidginization. Pidginization is seen as the result of the learner's social and psychological distance from speakers of the target language. Hence, it is argued that Alberto's lack of development in English is the result of his social and psychological distance from native speakers of English.

In the fall of 1973 a research project (Cazden, Cancino, Rosansky, & Schumann, 1975) was undertaken to make a ten-month longitudinal study of the untutored acquisition of English by six native speakers of Spanish—two children, two adolescents, and two adults. Data collection involved the recording of both spontaneous and experimentally elicited speech. This report is a case study of one of the six subjects, a 33-year-old Costa Rican named Alberto, who evidenced very little linguistic development during the course of the project. It was felt that by attempting to account for his lack of learning, significant insight could be gained on what is involved in successful second language acquisition in general.

Developmental Patterns in the Negative, Interrogative, and Auxiliary

The research focused on the subjects' acquisition of negatives, wh- questions, and auxiliaries. The analysis revealed several clear patterns of development. In the negative all subjects began with *no + verb* (*no V*) constructions in which the negative particle, while internal to the sentence, was external to the verb: *I no can see, But no is mine . . . , I no use television.* Simultaneously or shortly afterwards the subjects started using *don't + verb* (*don't V*) constructions. Here *don't* did not consist of *do + not,* but was simply an allomorph of *no* which was also kept external to the verb: *I don't hear, He don't like it, I don't can explain.* In the third stage, *auxiliary + negative* (aux-neg), the subjects learned to place the negative particle after the auxiliary. In general, the first auxiliaries to be negated in this way were *is* (isn't) and *can* (can't). In the final stage (*analyzed don't*), the learners acquired the analyzed forms of *don't* (do not, doesn't, does not, didn't, did not): *It doesn't spin, Because you didn't bring, He doesn't laugh like us.* At this point *don't* was no longer negative chunk, but actually consisted of *do* plus the negative particle. The stages in this sequence were not discrete and there was a good deal of overlap among them. Each stage was defined by the negating strategy that was used predominantly at that time.

The analysis of the acquisition of wh- questions revealed a developmental pattern which consisted of two stages (undifferentiation and differentiation). The first stage involved three periods (uninverted, variable inversion, and generalization). This developmental sequence is summarized below:

Stage 1–Undifferentiation: Learner did not distinguish between simple and embedded *wh- questions.*

> a. uninverted: Both simple and embedded *wh- questions* were uninverted.
>
> simple: *What you study?;*
>
> embedded: *That's what I do with my pillow.*
>
> b. variable inversion: Simple *wh- questions* were sometimes inverted, sometimes not.
>
> inverted: *How can you say it?;*
>
> uninverted: *Where you get that?*
>
> c. generalization: increasing inversion in *wh- questions* with inversion being extended to embedded questions.
>
> simple: *How can I kiss her if I don't even know her name?;*
>
> embedded: *I know where are you going.*

Stage 2–Differentiation: Learner distinguished between simple and embedded *wh- questions.*

> simple: *Where do you live?;*
>
> embedded: *I don't know what he had.*
>
> (from Cazden, Cancino, Rosansky, & Schumann, 1975, p. 38).

In the analysis of the acquisition of auxiliaries we found that *is* (*cop*) was acquired first by all the subjects and that generally *do* and *can* followed shortly afterwards. The other auxiliaries appeared in a highly variable order.

Alberto's Development

As mentioned above, one of the adult subjects, Alberto, showed very little linguistic development during the course of the study. Whereas four stages were found in the acquisition of the English negative (*no V, don't V, aux-neg, analyzed don't*), throughout the study Alberto remained in the first period of the first stage. In addition, in yes/no-questions he inverted considerably less frequently than the other subjects. The four inflectional morphemes (possessive, past tense, plural, and progressive) which were studied showed little or no growth over time. In terms of auxiliary development, *am* (*cop*), *can* and *are* (*cop*) could be classified as appearing in his speech (i.e., they were supplied 80% of the time in three consecutive samples), but only *is* (*cop*) approaches the criterion for acquisition (correctly supplied in 90% of obligatory contexts for three successive samples). In general, then, Alberto can be characterized as using a reduced and simplified form of English:

a. in which the negative particle remains external to the verb and is not placed after the first auxiliary element as required in well-formed English;

b. in which inversion is virtually absent in questions;

c. in which no auxiliaries [except possibly *is* (*cop*)] can be said to be *acquired,* and using a less stringent criterion only four auxiliaries [*is* (*cop*), *am* (*cop*), *can* and *are* (*cop*)] can be said to have *appeared*;

d. in which the possessive tends to be unmarked;

e. in which the regular past tense ending (ed) is virtually absent;

f. in which positive transfer from Spanish can account for the plural inflection being supplied 85% of the time, for *is* (*cop*)'s being correctly supplied to a greater extent than other auxiliaries and for *am* (*cop*), *are* (*cop*), and *can* reaching criterion for appearance;

g. and in which the progressive morpheme (*-ing*) is supplied only about 60% of the time.

Reasons for Alberto's Development

Three explanations are considered in accounting for the lack of development in Alberto's speech: ability, age, and social and psychological distance from speakers of the target language.

Ability. Performance on a Piagetian test of adaptive intelligence (Feldman et al., 1974) indicated that Alberto had no gross cognitive deficits that would have prevented him from acquiring English more fully. Therefore, lack of ability does not seem adequate to explain his acquisition pattern.

Age. It was once thought that the completion of cortical lateralization at puberty was the cause of adult difficulties in acquiring second languages. However, Krashen (1973) has demonstrated that the lateralization process which gradually locates language functions in the left hemisphere of the brain may be completed by the age of five. Therefore, since we know that six-, seven-, and eight-year olds learn second languages without great difficulty, we are left with no substantially clear age-related biological or neurological explanation for Alberto's lack of development in English.

Pidginization.   Alberto's essentially reduced and simplified English contains several features that are characteristic of pidgin languages. A pidgin language is a simplified and reduced form of speech used for communication between people with different languages. The type of pidginization referred to here is secondary hybridization, not tertiary hybridization (see Whinnom, 1971); the position taken here is that secondary hybridization is legitimate pidginization. The grammatical structure of pidgins is characterized by a lack of inflectional morphology and a tendency to eliminate grammatical transformations. Alberto's English shared the following features with other pidgin languages:

a. He used the uniform negative "no" for most of his negative utterances as in American Indian Pidgin English (AIPE) (Leachman & Hall, 1955) and English Worker Pidgin (EWP) (Clyne, 1975).

b. He did not invert in questions as in Neo-Melanesian Pidgin (N-MP) (Smith, 1972) and EWP.

c. He lacked auxiliaries as in EWP.

d. He tended not to inflect for the possessive as in AIPE.

e. He used the unmarked form of the verb as in English-Japanese Pidgin (E-JP) (Goodman, 1967), AIPE and EWP.

f. He deleted subject pronouns as in EWP.

Since Alberto's English appears to be pidginized, we want to answer the question, "What causes pidginization?" The answer lies in the functions which a pidginized language serves. Smith (1972) sees language as having three general functions: communicative, integrative, and expressive. The communicative function operates in the transmission of referential, denotative information between persons. The integrative function is engaged when a speaker acquires language to the extent that it marks him as a member of a particular social group. That is, his speech contains those features (such as correct noun and verb inflections, inversion in questions, and correct placement of the negative particle) that are unnecessary for simple referential communication, but which are necessary in order to sound like a member of the group whose language contains these features. The expressive function goes beyond the integrative in that through it, the speaker becomes a valued member of a particular linguistic group. In other words, he displays linguistic virtuosity or skill such that he becomes an admired member of the community. Examples of such people are storytellers (especially in nonliterate societies), comedians, orators, poets, etc. Since many native speakers do not command the expressive functions of their language, in order to be considered a fluent speaker of a language, one need only master the communicative and integrative functions. According to Smith, pidgin languages are generally restricted to the first function—communication. That is, their purpose is merely to convey denotative, referential information. Since pidgins are always second languages, the integrative and expressive functions are maintained by the speakers' native languages. As a result of this functional restriction, pidginization produced an interlanguage which is simplified and reduced.

The next question to be answered, then, is "What causes restriction in function?" Martin Joos (1971, p. 187) suggests that "the skeletonizing/skeletonized pattern of pidgin-formation + emerges automatically from lack of actual/prospective *social* solidarity between speaker and addressee" (emphasis mine). To this I would also add the lack of actual or prospective psychological solidarity between the two parties. If we turn this formulation around, restriction in function can be seen as resulting from social and/or psychological distance between the speaker and addressee. Placing this notion within the framework of second language acquisition, we would argue that the speech of the second language learner will be restricted to the communicative function if the learner is socially and/or psychologically distant from the speakers of the target language. The extent and persistence of the pidginized forms in the second language learner's speech will result automatically then from the restriction in function.

Social distance pertains to the individual as a member of a social group which is in contact with another social group whose members speak a different language. Hence social distance involves such sociological factors as domination versus subordination, assimilation versus acculturation versus preservation, enclosure, size, congruence, and attitude. Psychological distance pertains to the individual as an individual, and involves such psychological factors as resolution of language shock, culture shock and culture stress, integrative versus instrumental motivation, and ego-permeability. In the following two sections each form of distance will be discussed.

Social distance.   The following notions about social distance (Schumann, 1976) evolve from the literature on bilingualism, second language acquisition, sociolinguistics, and ethnic relations. They represent societal factors that either promote or inhibit social solidarity between two groups and thus affect the way a second language learning group (2LL group) acquires the language of a particular target language group (TL group). The assumption is that the greater the social distance between the two groups the more difficult it is for the members of the 2LL group to acquire the language of the TL group. The following issues are involved in social distance: In relation to the TL group is the 2LL group politically, culturally, technically, or economically *dominant, nondominant, or subordinate?* Is the integration pattern of the 2LL group *assimilation, acculturation, or preservation?* What is the 2LL group's degree of *enclosure?* Is the 2LL group *cohesive?* What is the *size* of the 2LL group? Are the cultures of the two groups *congruent?* What are the attitudes of the two groups toward each other? What is the 2LL group's *intended length of residence* in the target language area? The above terms are defined as follows:

1. Dominant—2LL group is politically, culturally, technically, or economically *superior* to the TL group.

2. Nondominant—2LL group is politically, culturally, technically, and economically *equal* to the TL group.

3. Subordinate—2LL group is politically, culturally, technically, and economically *inferior* to the TL group.

4. Assimilation—2LL group gives up its own life style and values and adopts those of the TL group.

5. Acculturation—2LL group adapts to the life style and values of the TL group, but at the same time maintains its own cultural patterns for use in intragroup relations.

6. Preservation—2LL group rejects the life style and values of the TL group and attempts to maintain its own cultural pattern as much as possible.

7. Enclosure—The degree to which the two groups have separate schools, churches, clubs, recreational facilities, professions, crafts, trades, etc.

8. Cohesiveness—The degree to which members of the 2LL group live, work and socialize together.

9. Size—How large the 2LL group is.

10. Congruence—The degree to which the cultures of the two groups are similar.

11. Attitude—Ethnic stereotypes by which the two groups either positively or negatively value each other.

12. Intended length of residence—How long the 2LL group intends to remain in the TL area.

It is argued that social distance and hence a bad language learning situation (see rows A and B in Tables 1 and 2) will obtain where the 2LL group is either dominant or subordinate, where both groups desire preservation and high enclosure for the 2LL group, where the LL group is both cohesive and large, where the two cultures are not congruent, where the two groups hold negative attitudes toward each other and where the 2LL group intends to remain in the target language area only for a short time. It is also argued that social solidarity and hence a good language learning situation (see row C in tables) will obtain where the 2LL group is nondominant in relation to the TL group, where both groups desire assimilation for the 2LL group, where low enclosure is the goal of both groups, where the two cultures are congruent, where the 2LL group is small and noncohesive, where both groups have positive attitudes toward each other, and where the 2LL group intends to remain in the target language area for a long time.

    In comparing Alberto's social distance from Americans with that of the other subjects in Cazden, Cancino, Rosansky, and Schumann's (1975) study,

TABLE I. Analysis of Political, Economic, Technical, Cultural, and Structural Characteristics for Good and Bad Language Learning Situations and for Worker vs. Professional Immigrants from Latin America to the United States[1]

	Political, Economic, Technical, Cultural						Culture						Structure					
	TLgp Views 2LLgp			2LLgp Views Itself			TLgp Desires of 2LLgp			2LLgp Desires for Itself			TLgp Desires for 2LLgp			2LLgp Desires for Itself		
	dominant	– dominant	subordinate	dominant	– dominant	subordinate	assimilation	acculturation	preservation	assimilation	acculturation	preservation	high enclosure	moderate enclosure	low enclosure	high enclosure	moderate enclosure	low enclosure
A. Bad language learning Situation I	*					*			*			*	*			*		
B. Bad language learning Situation II	√					√			√			√	√			√		
C. Good language learning situation		X			X		X			X					X			X
D. Latin American workers	√					√			√			√		√			√	
E. Latin American professionals		X			X			X			X				X			X

[1] Corresponding √'s and X's indicate similarity of situations.

TABLE 2. Analysis of Second Language Group Characteristics, Attitudes, and Social Distance for Good and Bad Language Learning Situations and for Worker vs. Professional Immigrants from Latin America to the United States[1]

	2LLgp Characteristics								Attitudes				Social Distance	
	Cohesiveness		Size		Culture		Length of Stay		TLgp's Attitude Toward 2LLgp		2LLgp's Attitude Toward TLgp			
	+ cohesive	– cohesive	large	small	+ congruent with TLgp	– congruent with TLgp	short	long	positive	negative	positive	negative	great	little
A. Bad language learning Situation I	*		*			*	*			*		*	*	
B. Bad language learning Situation II	√		√			√	√			√		√	√	
C. Good language learning situation		X		X	X			X	X		X			X
D. Latin American workers	√		√		√→								√	
E. Latin American situation		X		X	X		X				X			X

[1] Corresponding √'s and X's indicate similarity of situations.

Alberto can be regarded as belonging to a social group designated as lower class Latin American worker immigrants, and the other four subjects can be classified as children of upper-middle class Latin American professional immigrants. There was insufficient background on the second adult subject to include her in this classification.

Latin American worker immigrants (see row D) are subordinate in relation to Americans since they represent an unskilled labor group whose modal socioeconomic status is lower than that of Americans in general. This view is probably shared by both the worker immigrants and the Americans. The worker immigrants probably fall somewhere between preservation and acculturation with regard to their desired integration into American society. American society in general expects them to assimilate as it does all immigrants, but it does not necessarily make the assimilation easy. In terms of enclosure the Latin American workers have access to American institutions, but generally live in immigrant neighborhoods where they share schools, churches, and associations with other immigrants having the same socioeconomic status and usually having the same language and culture. This enclosure by neighborhood fosters cohesiveness, particularly in Alberto's case where Costa Rican immigrants are a small minority within a Portuguese minority area. The culture of the Latin American worker immigrants is relatively congruent to that of the Americans (both being Western and Christian), but since the Latin American workers may represent the "culture of poverty" more than does the model American culture, there may also be an element of incongruence between the two cultures (indicated by the arrow, ↓, in Table 2). The attitudes of the two groups toward each other would have to be measured before accurate judgments could be made. It is also difficult to assess the intended length of stay in the United States by Latin American workers.

Upper-middle class Latin American professional immigrants (see row E in the tables) are probably viewed by Americans and also view themselves as nondominant in relation to the English-speaking TL group because their educational background and socioeconomic status more closely match that of Americans in general (particularly in the Boston/Cambridge area). The Latin American professionals are solidly acculturative in their integration pattern. They have to be able to demonstrate culturally appropriate behavior in their relationships with American colleagues and therefore must adapt to American life styles and values. But since their length of residence in the United States is often confined to a period of postgraduate education, they generally integrate into the university and professional communities and do not live in immigrant neighborhoods. Therefore, their enclosure is low and they are less cohesive than the worker immigrants. The size of the professional group is likely to be smaller than that of workers, and the congruity of the two cultures is relatively high. Once again attitudinal orientations would have to be empirically assessed in order to be correctly classified.

When both profiles are considered we find that the Latin American worker-immigrant group is at a considerably greater social distance from Americans than are the professionals. Thus, we would expect the workers' use of English to be functionally restricted and to pidginize. This is precisely what we find in Alberto.

Psychological distance.   As the classification of the 2LL group in either the good or bad language learning situations becomes less determinant (that is, if a group stands somewhere between the bad and good situations), then success in acquiring the target language becomes more a matter of the individual as an individual rather than of the individual as a member of a particular social group. In addition, in either a good or a bad language learning situation, an individual can violate the modal tendency of his group. Thus, an individual might learn the target language where he is expected not to, and not learn the language where successful acquisition is expected. In these cases it is *psychological distance* (Schumann, 1975b) or proximity between the learner and the TL group that accounts for successful versus unsuccessful second language acquisition. The factors which create psychological distance between the learner and speakers of the target language are affective in nature and involve such issues as the resolution of language shock and culture shock, motivation and ego permeability.

In experiencing language shock (Stengal, 1939), the learner is haunted by doubts as to whether his words accurately reflect his ideas. In addition, he is sometimes confronted with target language words and expressions which carry with them images and meanings which he interprets differently than do native speakers of the target language. Also, the narcissistic gratification to which the learner is accustomed in the use of his native language is lost when he attempts to speak the target language. Finally, when speaking the second language the learner has apprehensions about appearing comic, childlike, and dependent.

The learner experiences culture shock (Larsen & Smalley, 1972; Smalley, 1963) when he finds that his problem-solving and copying mechanisms do not work in the new culture. When they are used they do not get the accustomed results. Consequently, activities which were routine in his native country require great energy in the new culture. This situation causes disorientation, stress, fear, and anxiety. The resultant mental state can produce a whole syndrome of rejection which diverts attention and energy from second language learning. The learner, in attempting to find a cause for his disorientation, may reject himself, the people of the host country, the organization for which he is working, and even his own culture.

Motivation (Gardner & Lambert, 1972) relates to the goals of second language learning. In terms of psychological distance, the integratively motivated learner would seek maximum proximity in order to meet, talk with, and perhaps even become like the speakers of the target language. An instrumentally motivated learner would achieve a level of psychological solidarity that would only be commensurate with his instrumental goals. Consequently, if the learner's goal were mere survival, he might maintain a good deal of psychological distance between himself and the speakers of the target language.

Another source of psychological distance may be the relative rigidity of the learner's ego boundaries (Guiora, 1972). Some experimental evidence indicates that people who have ego permeability, that is, the ability to partially and temporarily give up their separateness of identity, are better second language learners. This essentially psychoanalytic concept is intuitively appealing and provides another perspective from which the concept of psychological distance can be understood.

In sum, then, factors causing psychological distance, like those causing social distance, put the learner in a situation where he is largely cut off from target language input and/or does not attend to it when it is available. The language which is acquired under these conditions will be used simply for denotative referential communication in situations where contact with speakers of the target language is either absolutely necessary or unavoidable. The learner's psychological distance will prevent him from identifying with the speakers of the target language such that he will not attempt to incorporate into his speech those linguistic features that would help to identify him as a member of the TL group. Hence, his use of the target language will be functionally restricted and, therefore, we would expect it to pidginize.

In order to get some assessment of Alberto's psychological distance from English speakers, at the end of the study, he was asked to fill out a short questionnaire which elicited information concerning his attitude and motivation. In terms of his questionnaire, he seemed to have a positive attitude and good motivation, and hence little psychological distance. However, there is some question as to whether he was entirely candid in his answers. Alberto tended not to like to displease and therefore his answers may reflect what he thought the experimenter wanted to hear.

There are several aspects of Alberto's life-style that appear to contradict the positive attitude and motivation expressed in the questionnaire. First of all, he made very little effort to get to know English-speaking people. In Cambridge he stuck quite close to a small group of Spanish-speaking friends. He did not own a television and expressed disinterest in it because he could not understand English. On the other hand, he purchased an expensive stereo set and tape deck on which he played mostly Spanish music. Also, he chose to work at night (as well as in the day) rather than attend English classes which were available in Cambridge.

The other subjects were not given the attitude and motivation questionnaire, but in general they seemed to be psychologically much closer to Americans. All the children attended American schools and had American friends. The second adult baby-sat for American children, studied English on her own, and tried to get to know and speak with Americans.

The effect of instruction.   From the point of view of the pidginization hypothesis we would argue that Alberto did not seek out instruction in English because his pidginized speech was adequate for his needs. Nevertheless, it might be argued that with instruction his simplified linguistic system might have reorganized and come to conform more closely with the target language. The opportunity to test this idea presented itself after the study was completed. At the end of the ten-month project, twenty, one-hour speech samples had been collected. As mentioned earlier, throughout this period Alberto had maintained essentially a *no V* negation system.

The experimenter then undertook to teach him how to negate in English to see if his intervention would cause him to alter his pidginized system of negation. Extensive instruction was provided during the collection of speech sample 21 and then intermittently in samples 22 through 32. This program covered a seven-month period. At the same time in samples 22–30 Alberto was given extensive sets of positive sentences which he was asked to negate. These elicited negatives were then compared with the negative utterances in his spontaneous speech. In elicited speech after instruction, Alberto's negatives were about 64% (216/335) correct. His spontaneous negatives, however, were only about 20% (56/278) correct. His *don't V* utterances were correct only by coincidence simply because *don't,* as an allomorph of *no,* was occasionally used in the appropriate linguistic environment. Therefore, we see that instruction influenced only Albert's production in a testlike, highly monitored situation; it did not affect his spontaneous speech which he used for normal communication. This result is even more striking when we compare it with spontaneous and elicited negatives prior to instruction. In samples 16–20, Alberto's spontaneous negatives were 22% (23/105) correct and his elicited negatives were 10% (7/71) correct. This indicates that instruction has radically improved his performance in an artificial, highly monitored elicitation task, but that it had virtually no effect on his spontaneous speech which he uses in normal communication with native speakers of English. Hence we can conclude that instruction is evidently not powerful enough to overcome the pidginization engendered by social and psychological distance.

Cognitive Processes in Pidginization

The social and psychological forces that cause the persistence of pidginization in a second language learner's speech have been discussed. The term "persistence" is used because, as predicted in Schumann (1974a, 1974b), pidginization appears to be characteristic of early second language acquisition in general. What has been described as pidginization in Alberto's speech corresponds to the early stages of the acquisition of English by all six learners. Alberto remained in stage one of negation (the *no V* stage) and in stage one, period *a* of interrogation (univernsion in both simple and embedded wh- questions). Since it is reasonable to assume that, as with Alberto, inflectional marking tended to be absent in the early speech of the other five subjects (this was not specifically examined in Cazden, Cancino, Rosansky, & Schumann, 1975), evidence exists that pidginization may characterize all early second language acquisition and that under conditions of social and psychological distance it persists. Since pidginization may be a universal first stage in second language acquisition, it is important to explore what cognitive processes either cause or allow the pidginization to occur.

Kay and Sankoff (1974) believe that contact vernaculars such as pidgins and other varieties of incomplete competence such as child language, second language acquisition, bilingualism, and aphasia are all potential areas for examining linguistic universals. Referring to contact vernaculars in particular they state that "since the communicative functions fulfilled by contact vernaculars are minimal, these languages may possibly reveal in a more direct way than do most natural languages the universal cognitive structure and process that underlie all human language ability and use" (Kay & Sankoff 1974, p. 62).

Smith (1973, p. 3) notes that the early speech of children is largely unmarked (hence the term telegraphic speech) and that in the process of socialization the child learns to mark his language with those features which characterize his speech community. The result of this development is that adult speech is naturally and normally marked. However, pidgin languages which are spoken by adults are characteristically unmarked. Smith attempts to account for the fact that pidginization produces a generally unmarked language by viewing unmarking and marking as part of the same process. The child at one point in his development has had the ability to unmark. Smith speculates that this ability is not lost and can be retrieved under certain social conditions. One of these conditions is the pidginogenic social context where the function of the language is restricted to communication of denotative referential information. Both the child in early native language acquisition and the pidgin speaker reduce and simplify the language to which they are exposed into a set of primitive categories which undoubtedly are innate (Smith, 1973, p. 11). These primitive categories emerge in speech as utterances relatively unmarked by inflections, permutations and functors. Within this framework unmarking is not seen as a deficiency, but as a positive cognitive strategy to which a language learner turns at certain development stages and under certain social conditions.

Corder (1975) maintains a similar position, but argues that "simple codes" spoken by children, neophyte second language learners, pidgin speakers, and adults using baby-talk or foreigner talk are not "implied," i.e., they are not reductions of a more complicated and expanded code. Instead they represent a basic language which, in the process of learning, is expanded and compli-cated. Following Kay and Sankoff (1972), Corder (1975, p. 4) suggests that sim-ple codes are "nearer," in some sense, to the underlying structure or "inner form" of all languages, i.e., more overtly reflect semantic categories and rela-tions. He goes on to speculate that this basic language, and all intermediate linguistic systems between basic and complex, once learned are never obliter-ated. These approximate systems remain "available both for special commu-nicative functions in the mother tongue [baby talk, foreign talk] and as an 'initial hypothesis' in the learning of second language" (p. 9).

Within this framework, pidginization in second language acquisition can be viewed as initially resulting from cognitive constraints and then persisting, due to social and psychological constraints. Hence, early second language acquisition would be characterized by the temporary use of a nonmarked, sim-ple code resembling a pidgin. This code would be the product of cognitive constraints engendered by lack of knowledge of the target language. The code may reflect a regression to a set of universal primitive linguistic categories that were realized in early first language acquisition. Then, under conditions of social and/or psychological distance, this pidginized form of speech would persist.

Conclusion

The pidginization hypothesis predicts that where social and psychologi-cal distance prevail we will find pidginization persisting in the speech of sev-eral language learners. There are several experimental and several clinical studies that could be undertaken to further explore this hypothesis. In order to experimentally test the social distance aspect of the hypothesis, one might choose a population of worker immigrants in the United States and compare its success in the acquisition of English to the success in the acquisition of English experienced by a group of professional immigrants. To experimentally test the psychological distance aspect of the hypothesis one could make an intensive examination (using questionnaires, interviews, etc.) of those worker immigrants who *do* successfully learn English and the professional immi-grants who fail to learn it.

To clinically examine social distance phenomena, a questionnaire might be developed which would be filled out by experimenters doing research in second language acquisition. In it they would attempt to classify the subjects with whom they were working (either groups or individuals) on social dis-tance dimensions. The questionnaire would be designed to permit the researcher to rate a particular 2LL group's dominance, cohesiveness, enclo-sure, etc., on a numerical scale, to compute a social distance score for the group and then to relate that score to the extent of pidginization found in his subject(s)' speech.

Psychological distance might receive clinical examination by studying a small group of subjects (six to ten) who will be living in a foreign language environment for a fairly long period of time. The subjects might be a group of Peace Corps Volunteers or foreign service personnel who have a good opportunity to become bilingual as a result of training in and exposure to the target language. At the beginning of the study the subjects would be assessed on as many relevant variables as possible, including: language learning aptitude, motivation, ego-permeability (assuming a valid measure is available), experiences in learning other second languages, and general social adjustment. The subjects would be asked to keep diaries in which they would describe daily exposure to the target language, efforts to learn the language, and feelings about language learning and the new culture. In addition, the subjects would be interviewed once every two weeks in order that the researchers could probe the same issues verbally. Finally the subjects' achievement in the second language would be tested monthly by means of an oral interview which could then be analyzed for aspects of pidginization. The object of this approach would be to develop several case studies in which an individual's pattern of second language acquisition could be related longitudinally to factors involving his psychological distance from speakers of the target language.

Such research strategies could shed light on the interaction between the phenomena of social and psychological distance; uncover new factors contributing to both phenomena and perhaps indicate ways in which social and psychological distance can be overcome and thus free those affected to become bilingual.

Finally, by studying the second language speech of learners affected by social and/or psychological distance in a variety of contact situations (for example, Chinese-English, English-Persian, Italian-French) a further contribution could be made to our knowledge of the linguistic aspects of pidginization and the processes of simplification and reduction in natural languages in general.

References

Cazden, C. B., Cancino, H., Rosansky, E. J., & Schumann, J. H. (1975). *Second language acquisition sequences in children, adolescents and adults.* Final Report, National Institute of Education (Grant No. NE–6–00–3–0014).

Clyne, M. G. (1975). *German and English working pidgins.* Paper presented at the International Congress on Pidgins and Creoles, Honolulu, Hawaii.

Corder, S. P. (1975). *'Simple codes' and the source of the second language learner's initial heuristic hypothesis.* Paper presented at the Colloque 'Theoretical Models in Applied Linguistics' IV, University de Neuchatel.

De Camp, D. & Hancock, I. F. (Eds.) (1974). *Pidgins and creoles: Current trends and prospects.* Washington, D.C.: Georgetown University Press.

Feldman, C., Lee, B., McLean, J. D., Pellemer, D., & Murray, J. (1974). *The development of adaptive intelligence.* Chicago: Jossey-Bass Publishers.

Gardner, R. C. & Lambert, W. E. (1972). *Attitudes and motivation in second-language learning.* Rowley, Mass.: Newbury House.

Goodman, J. S. (1967). The development of a dialect of English-Japanese pidgin. *Anthropological Linguistics, 9,* 43–55.

Guiora, A. Z. (1972). Construct validity and transpositional research: Toward an empirical study of psychoanalytic concepts. *Comprehensive Psychiatry, 13,* 139–150.

Hymes, D. H. (Ed.). (1971). *Pidginization and creolization of languages.* Cambridge: Cambridge University Press.

Joos, M. (1971). Hypotheses as to the origin and modification of pidgins. In D. H. Hymes (Ed.), *Pidginization and creolization of languages* (p. 187). Cambridge: Cambridge University Press.

Kay, P. & Sankoff, G. (1974). A language-universal approach to pidgins and creoles. In D. De Camp and I. F. Hancock (Eds.), *Pidgins and creoles: Current trends and prospects* (pp. 61–72). Washington, D.C.: Georgetown University Press.

Krashen, S. D. (1973). Lateralization, language learning, and the critical period: Some new evidence. *Language Learning, 23,* 63–74.

Larsen, D. A. and Smalley, W. A. (1972). *Becoming bilingual: A guide to language learning.* New Canann, Ct.: Practical Anthropology.

Leachman, D. & Hall, Jr., R. A. (1955). American Indian pidgin English: Attestations and grammatical peculiarities. *American Speech, 30,* 163–171.

Schumann, J. H. (1974). The implications of interlanguage, pidginization and creolization for the study of adult language acquisition. *TESOL Quarterly, 8,* 145–152.

Schumann, J. H. (1975a). The implications of pidginization and creolization for the study of adult second language acquisition. In Schumann & Stenson (Eds.), *New frontiers in second language learning* (pp. 137–152). Rowley, Mass: Newbury House.

Schumann, J. H. (1975b). *Second language acquisition: The pidginization hypothesis.* Unpublished doctoral dissertation, Harvard University.

Schumann, J. H. (1975c). Affective factors and the problem of age in second language acquisition. *Language Learning, 25,* 209–235.

Schumann, J. H. (1976). Social distance as a factor in second language acquisition. *Language Learning, 26,* 135–143.

Schumann, J. H. and Stenson, N. (Eds.) (1975). *New frontiers in second language learning.* Rowley, Mass.: Newbury House.

Smalley, W. A. (1963). Culture shock, language shock and the shock of self-discovery. *Practical Anthropology, 10,* 49–56.

Smith, D. M. (1972). Some implications for the social status of pidgin languages. In D. M. Smith & R. Shuy (Eds.), *Sociolinguistics in cross-cultural analyses* (pp. 47–56). Washington D.C.: Georgetown University Press.

Smith, D. M. (1973). *Pidginization and language socialization: The role of marking.* Unpublished paper, Georgetown University.

Smith, D. M., & Shuy, R. W. (Eds.) (1972). *Sociolinguistics in cross-cultural analyses.* Washington, D.C.: Georgetown University Press.

Stengel, E. (1939). On learning a new language. *International Journal of Psychoanalysis, 2,* 471–479.

Whinnom, K. (1971). Linguistic hybridization and the 'special case' of pidgins and creoles. In D. H. Hymes (Ed.), *Pidginization and creolization of languages,* (pp. 91–115). Cambridge: Cambridge University Press.

Understanding the Article

1. This article is described as "a case study of the untutored acquisition of English by a 33-year-old Costa Rican named Alberto." How does this kind of study differ from an experimental study?

2. Describe the larger study: What was the purpose? Who is/are the subject(s)? How were the data collected?

3. Describe the linguistic data which are the focus of the current study.

4. Look at the section called "Reasons for Alberto's Development." Here Schumann attempts to provide an explanation for Alberto's lack of development in English.

   a. What evidence does the author cite to reject ability as a possible explanation?

   b. What evidence does Schumann cite to reject age as a possible explanation?

   c. What evidence does the author cite in support of social and psychological distance as a possible explanation?

5. In your own words, what can you conclude from looking at Tables 1 and 2?

6. In the section entitled "The Effect of Instruction," Schumann describes the researcher's attempts to teach the subject how to negate in English. How does this phase of the study differ from the initial case study?

7. To what extent do the conclusions follow directly from the results of the study?

Reflecting on Wider Issues

1. There is general agreement that it is difficult to measure affective variables and social distance. To what extent does this cause problems for Schumann's theory?

2. Is this theory generalizable to all kinds of second language acquisition—for example, classroom SLA?

Going Beyond the Article

After this early study, John Schumann continued to develop and revise his theory of second language acquisition. His 1978 book, *The Pidginization Hypothesis: A Model for Second Language Acquisition,* contains the fullest description of his case study of Alberto and its implications for a theory of second language acquisition. You might also read his 1986 article, "Research on the acculturation model for second language acquisition" (*Journal of Multilingual and Multicultural Development, 7,* 379–392), in which he argues that the role of acculturation is to bring the learner into contact with TL speakers, thereby leading to communicative interaction and the negotiation of input. In more recent work, Schumann (1990) attempts to link affective factors with cognition ("Extending the scope of the acculturation/pidginization model to include cognition," *TESOL Quarterly, 24,* 667–684).

If you are interested in looking at a case study that appears to disprove Schumann's acculturation hypothesis, read Schmidt (1983), "Interaction, acculturation and the acquisition of communicative competence: A case study of an adult," in N. Woolfson and E. Judd (Eds.), *Sociolinguistics and language acquisition* (Rowley, MA: Newbury House).

UNIT VI

INTERLANGUAGE

11

TASK-RELATED VARIATION IN INTERLANGUAGE: THE CASE OF ARTICLES

Elaine Tarone
University of Minnesota

Betsy Parrish
Hamline University

Previewing the Article

When interlanguage theories first appeared in the early 1970s, the perspective adopted by most research was to look for systematicity in learner language. In fact, it was the discovery of such systematicity that propelled interlanguage research into prominence in the field of SLA. More recently, researchers have focused on the variation among and within learners in their interlanguage development, with the intent of determining sources of such variation.

In this study by Tarone and Parrish, we see an excellent example of an attempt to clearly identify causes of certain interlanguage variation. Before you read this article, make sure you understand what is meant by *interlanguage* and what interlanguage research has revealed about learners' stages of systematic development. Then, answer the following:

1. What is the importance of the previous (Tarone 1985) study with respect to the present one?

2. What is the purpose of the present study?

3. What were the three tasks that this study refers to?

Reprinted from *Language Learning, 38*:21–44, 1988.

There is no doubt that second-language learners vary in the accuracy of their production when asked to perform different tasks. For example, Tarone (1985) found that the accuracy with which English articles and other grammatical forms were used by nonnative speakers at a single point in time varied depending on the *tasks* which the learners were asked to perform. Quantitative measures showed that the shifts in accuracy of article use were highly significant. The *causes* of this variability, however, were unclear. Researchers such as Arditty & Perdue (1979) have suggested a variety of possible causes of task-related variability.

In this study, a more fine-grained quantitative and qualitative analysis of the Tarone (1985) data focuses on the *function* which articles played in the different tasks. It is found that different tasks elicited different types of noun phrases, which in turn demanded different uses of the article. In addition, it is found that there was some tendency of learner accuracy with articles occurring with one type of noun phrase to change across the tasks used. It is argued that this change in accuracy is due to the communicative demands and discourse characteristics of the tasks. Finally, it is argued that task-related variability in interlanguage must be due, not to a single variable called "attention to form," but to a complex of variables, at least one of which must be the differing communicative functions which forms may perform in different tasks, as, for example, when these tasks place different degrees of communicative pressure upon the speaker, or elicit discourse which varies in its cohesiveness.

In recent years, there has been increasing interest in the way in which the accuracy of learner language (or interlanguage: IL) varies depending upon task conditions. In particular, there has been interest in discovering, first, the way in which attention to language form is related to this *style-shifting,* and second, whether learners shift between essentially two styles—monitored and unmonitored—or whether a continuum of styles exists. The research which has been done in this area (described in detail in Tarone, 1988) has focused upon the distribution of surface forms across tasks. The function which these forms play in the various tasks has not been addressed; thus little can be said about possible *causes* of task-related variation.

An example of this problem occurs in Tarone (1985), in which a study was done to examine task-related IL variation in some detail. Twenty second-language learners (SLLs) studying English as a Second Language at the University of Minnesota were asked to participate in the study; ten were native speakers of Japanese and ten were native speakers of Arabic. The learners were asked to perform three tasks:

1. a written "grammaticality judgment" task containing five English sentences with missing articles. Subjects were asked to "star" any sentence which was grammatically incorrect, and to rewrite the erroneous portion correctly.

2. an oral interview with a native speaker of English, focusing on the subject's field of study, plans for academic work in the United States, and plans to apply that work in his or her own country.

3. an oral narration task which required subjects to look at a sequence of events depicted (nonverbally) on a video screen, and then to "tell the story" to a non-native listener clearly enough so that the listener could select the correct picture sequence. Japanese and Arabic speakers were paired for this task, and the order of speaking and listening counter-balanced between the two NL groups.

It was felt that most attention to language form would be required by the judgment task and the least by the narrative, with the interview requiring an intermediate degree of attention to form. Channel cues present in the tapes of the oral interview and the oral narrative seemed to validate the ordering of these two tasks relative to one another: the narratives contained fewer hesitations, were generally more fluent, and contained more laughter and joking comments—all these are channel cues which Labov (1969) uses to confirm a subject's use of the vernacular.

It was hypothesized that learners would supply articles and other grammatical forms most accurately on the grammar test (with most attention to form), and least accurately on the narrative (with least attention to form), with the interview producing intermediate levels of accuracy. It was also hypothesized that the three tasks would produce *three* distinct accuracy rates, not just a monitored and unmonitored style.

Result I

The learners' accuracy in article use on the three tasks is illustrated in Figure 1.

An analysis of variance for repeated measures was performed on the learners' scores on production of the article on the three tasks. A greenhouse Geisser *p* value of .0000 indicates that the subjects' scores on the three tests were indeed significantly different.

Discussion I

Three different levels of accuracy did seem to occur with the article. However, the hypothesis that the learners would achieve most grammatical accuracy on measures requiring most attention to language form was not upheld for all the grammatical forms studied. While the third-person singular verb marker -s did follow this pattern, the opposite pattern held true for articles: these were produced *least* accurately on the measure assumed to require attention to form, and *far more accurately* on measures assumed to require less attention to form.

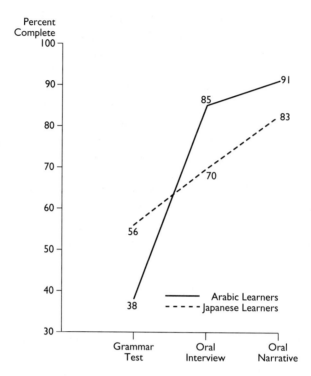

FIGURE 1.   Grammatical Accuracy of Articles under Three Task Conditions (from Tarone 1985)

Tarone (1985) concluded that the variable of "attention to language form" was simply not able to explain the pattern of style-shifting we see in Figure 1. Rather, it was suggested that other task factors might be more helpful in explaining these patterns.

The Present Analysis

This paper is an attempt to return to the data elicited in Tarone (1985), and to re-analyze article production from the point of view of function in discourse. It is hoped that this analysis will shed some light on the relationship between the form and function of the article in the discourse of these three tasks, and lead to some insight into the possible reasons for the variation in accuracy which occurred.

We are, therefore, adding to the quantitative analysis which has already been applied to the data—a statistical measure showing highly significant differences in article accuracy across tasks—a more fine-grained qualitative analysis in the tradition of Bickerton (1981), Huebner (1983), and Perdue (1984:3.1) which attempts to identify the *function* played by the language forms under study. Also, a more fine-grained quantitative measure was added:

the *t*-test (since the ANOVA is not able to tell us which tasks produced the most significant differences in accuracy, and also since there is some question as to the appropriateness of the ANOVA for data sets as small as those represented in this study). It is our belief that excessive reliance on either quantitative or qualitative methods of analysis *alone* will lead researchers to an unnecessarily incomplete view of interlanguage, and that the sort of interplay of quantitative and qualitative methodologies which we attempt here will lead to a richer insight into the workings of interlanguage.

Huebner (1983) and Parrish (1987) have used systems of analyzing articles which do not look at the presence or absence of articles in obligatory context, but rather at the functions of the articles used by learners of English. Huebner developed a system of analysis which accounts for article use in all pre-noun positions. His system describes three things: 1) the semantic function of each noun phrase used; 2) the articles used in conjunction with each semantic class of noun phrase; and 3) the way in which this article + NP function relationship changes over time.

Huebner analyzes the semantic function of NPs in terms of two binary features:

[+/− information assumed known to the hearer] ([+ HK])

[+/− specific referent] ([+ SR])

The four possible combinations of these two binary features define what Huebner calls semantic *Types.* The semantic wheel in Figure 2 (borrowed from Bickerton 1981) illustrates the four types. Each NP belongs to one of the four Type categories, permitting us to assign a semantic function to each. To determine with what accuracy articles are used in the interlanguage, one must first consider what is used in Standard English. Table 1 outlines the four Noun Phrase Type categories and their semantic functions.

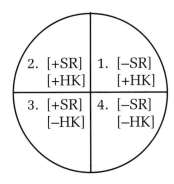

FIGURE 2.   Semantic Wheel of Noun Phrase Types (from Huebner 1983)

TABLE I.   Four NP Type Categories and their Semantic Functions in Standard English

1.   [– Specific Referent][+ Hearer Knowledge] ("Generics")

   Standard English: definite, indefinite, 0
   e.g., The lion is a beautiful animal.
   e.g., 0 Lions are beautiful animals.
   e.g., A lion is a beautiful animal.

2.   [+ Specific Referent][+ Hearer Knowledge]

   Standard English: definite article
   a. Unique referent or conventionally assumed unique referent;
      e.g., The Pope
   b. Referent physically present; e.g. Ask the guy over there.
   c. Referent previously mentioned in the discourse:
      e.g., A. So he married a woman from England.
      e.g., B. Yes, the woman's from London.
   d. Specific referents assumed known to the hearer:
      e.g., He went over to the book store.

3.   [+ Specific Referent][– Hearer Knowledge)

   Standard English: indefinite, 0.
   a. First mention in a discourse of [+ SR] NP which is assumed not
      known to the hearer;
      e.g., Dad gave me a car.
   b. First mention of [+ SR] NP following existential have and assumed
      not known to the hearer;
      e.g., Our house has a garage.

4.   [–Specific Referent][–Hearer Knowledge]
   Standard English: indefinite, 0.

   a. Equative noun phrases;
      e.g., He's a nice man.
   b. Noun phrases in the scope of negation;
      e.g., I don't see a pencil.
   c. Noun phrases in the scope of interrogative;
      e.g., Do you see a pencil?
   d. Noun phrases in irrealis scope;
      e.g., If I had a million dollars, I'd buy a big yacht.

Huebner classifies the noun phrases in his data according to whether they are of Types 1, 2, 3, or 4. In order not to distort his data, he omits all reformations and repetitions, proper nouns, idioms, and commonly-used expressions such as "in the morning," "go home," and "in the future" which he notes seem to be learned as formulae. In addition, he eliminates second and subsequent noun phrases in a series, as in *the men and the women.*" Noun phrases preceded by possessives are eliminated as well, because in these cases the [+ HK] [+ SR] distinction is neutralized. In Standard English we can say "my brother" without having mentioned him previously or without the hearer knowing whether the phrase "my brother" refers to a unique referent, i.e., my only brother, or one of many brothers. Parrish (1987) has adapted Huebner's system, accounting only for the use of *the, a,* and *0,* but also for the use of quantifiers and demonstratives since quantifiers can be used with Type 3 and Type 4 noun phrases and demonstratives can be used with Type 2 noun phrases, as in the following examples:

1. They don't have *any* children. (Type 4 NP)
2. I have *one* sister. (Type 3 NP)
3. Give me *that* book. (Type 2 NP)

Quantifiers and demonstratives are obviously not articles; however, if they occur in positions where articles are used, and if, in terms of the NP Type classification they can serve the same purpose, they should be included in a complete analysis of article usage. For this reason, we have included quantifiers and demonstratives in the figures provided in Appendix 1, and will discuss these in our analysis, although our quantitative analysis will be restricted to the learners' use of articles alone, for purposes of comparison with the original study.

For purposes of comparison with Tarone (1985), we will use the term "article" to refer to the use of *a/an, the, 0,* in the three tasks, and we will use the term "pre-modifier" to refer to the full set of articles, demonstratives and quantifiers.

In using this system to reanalyze the article usage in Tarone's (1985) study, we are interested in the distribution of noun phrase Types across tasks, to determine whether or not a given task favors the use of a particular Type of noun phrase. Stated in the form of a null hypothesis, we are testing the following:

1. There will be no difference in the proportion of NP Types produced by learners on the two oral tasks.

The second question we are interested in is the possible variation in learner accuracy related to NP Type. That is, since the rules for article use are different for each NP Type, it is possible that learners might; (a) learn some of these rules better than others, thus achieving higher accuracy rates within one NP

Type than another, or (b) adopt an interlanguage rule which might result in higher accuracy within one NP Type than another. (A hypothetical IL rule of this type might be, "Use the definite article with all NPs." Such an IL rule would favor higher accuracy with Type 2 NPs than with the others. Interestingly, the subject in Huebner's study went through a phase where he seemed to employ precisely this rule.) Stated in the form of a null hypothesis, we are testing the following:

2. There will be no overall difference in learners' accuracy rates in article production related to NP Type.

Finally, we must examine the interaction of the variables of task, NP Type, and accuracy. It is possible that certain tasks might encourage higher accuracy of article use within some NP Types than within others.

3. There will be no difference in accuracy rates in article production related to NP Type, when learners move from one oral task to another.

Using the system of analysis which we have described, we recounted and reanalyzed all NPs in all three tasks in terms of Type category. All repetitions of NPs, reformations, proper names and idioms were omitted, as in Huebner's methodology. We tabulated the learners' use of premodifiers[1] (that is, articles, quantifiers and demonstratives) with these NPs, and also their use of articles alone with these NPs).

Results II

A summary of the productions of all 20 subjects, analyzed in terms of the distribution of NP types on all three tasks, and the learners' accuracy in premodifier and article usage on each task, in relation to each NP Type, is provided in Appendix 1. In Appendix 2, we present article matrices (see Parrish, 1987 for a discussion of this means of data display) based on data obtained from 10 of the 20 subjects. These 10 included 5 randomly selected Japanese and 5 randomly selected Arabic speakers. In Appendix 3, we again present data on all 20 subjects, this time broken down in terms of native language group. In Appendix 4, we show the proportion of NP Types elicited from each subject on each oral task. In Appendix 5, we show the rate of accuracy for each subject on each NP Type on each oral task. Examining first the *distribution* of

---

[1]The score for quantifiers and demonstratives may be inflated, however; since quantifiers and demonstratives serve a similar function to articles in modifying an NP, it is difficult when a learner omits one of these forms in front of an NP to determine whether it is an article, or a quantifier/demonstrative which is missing. In other words, an omission is usually judged to be omission of an article rather than omission of a quantifier or demonstrative. This is a problem with "obligatory context" type scoring.

TABLE 2.   Proportion of NP Types Elicited by Two Oral Tasks[a]

	INTERVIEW (%)	NARRATIVE (%)	(DIFF) MEAN	t-VALUE	PROB.
Type 1	27.2	.15	27.05	7.85	.000
Type 2	36.6	69.4	−32.8	−8.04	.000
Type 3	27.6	26.5	1.1	.29	.77
Type 4	8.5	4.05	4.4	2.29	.03

[a]Scores were computed by establishing for each subject the total number of NPs on each task, and the percentage of that total which was Type 1, 2, 3, & 4. The sum of these individual scores was divided by the number of subjects, to obtain a group mean score for each Type on each task.

NP Types across tasks, we can make the following observations: Only Types 2 and 3 were elicited on the grammar test. Furthermore, the number of NPs elicited on the test was small, and these types were selected by the researcher and not by the learners. Therefore, no further quantitative analysis will be made here between the grammar test and the other two tasks—although we will discuss the implications of the information provided by the test in our Discussion.

We note that, across both oral tasks, some NP Types are more frequently produced than others. Type 2 is by far the most frequently produced NP Type.

A paired-samples 2-tailed t-test was used to assess the difference between the mean suppliance of each NP type on each oral task. Based on this analysis, the first hypothesis must be rejected. The two oral tasks did in fact elicit different proportions of NP Types. Table 2 illustrates these differences. While Type 3 was produced at the same rate on both tasks, the other Types clearly were not. In particular, Types 1 and 2 were produced at markedly different rates in the Interview and Narrative tasks, and Type 4 at somewhat different rates on the tasks. In the Interview, almost one-third of the NPs were Type 1, while Type 1 was almost never used on the Narrative. By contrast, almost 70% of the NPs in the Narrative were Type 2—a more than 30% increase over their frequency in the interview.

Examining the rate of accuracy of article and premodifier use within each NP Type in both tasks, we find the results summarized in Table 3.

We see first that the pattern of accuracy in moving from Type to Type seems to be the same for both articles and premodifiers, although premodifier accuracy with Type 3 seems higher than article accuracy with that Type. Accuracy in the use of articles with Type 3 NPs was significantly lower than article accuracy with either Type 1 or Type 2 NPs (prob. .007 and .003 respectively).

Finally, we examine the way in which accuracy rates varied across tasks, within each NP Type. Here we turn to Appendix 5, and Table 4. We can see by inspection of Table 3 that article and premodifier accuracy rates were not particularly different from one another.

TABLE 3.   Rate of Accuracy of Article and Premodifier Use Within Each NP Type in the Oral Tasks[a]

	ARTS (%)	PREMODS (%)	COMPARISON OF ART. MEANS	(DIFF) MEANS	*t* VAL	PROB.
Type 1	87	85	1 & 2	2.21	.41	.687
Type 2	85	85	2 & 3	12.05	3.01	.007
Type 3	73	80	1 & 3	12.63	3.47	.003
Type 4	80	83				

[a]Scores were computed by establishing the percent correct for each subject for each Type in both oral tasks combined. Cases where a subject provided no or only 1 obligatory context for any particular Type were omitted. The sum of these individual scores was divided by the number of remaining subjects to obtain a group mean score for each Type. A paired-samples 2-tailed *t*-test was used to measure the significance of difference between mean article accuracy scores for Type 1 vs. Type 2, Type 2 vs. Type 3, and Type 1 vs. Type 3. Not enough Type 4 contexts were generated for us to feel confident applying measures of significance.

Therefore, we limit our statistical analysis for Table 4 to accuracy in the use of articles alone. Here again we use a paired-samples 2-tailed *t*-test to assess the significance of differences between mean scores for each NP Type on each of the two oral tasks.

We see that Hypothesis 3 is upheld, but just barely. Inspection of Table 4 shows that the rate of accuracy of article use seemed to vary across tasks within some NP Types but not others. While the general pattern of accuracy with Type 4 NPs is similar to that found in Tarone (1985) (greater accuracy occurs on the narrative, and less accuracy is evidenced on the interview), not enough obligatory contexts were provided for Type 4 to permit us to make confident conclusions; in general, Type 4 NPs rarely occurred. Future studies might profitably look at this NP Type in more detail.

The most interesting change in accuracy rate is the greater accuracy of article use with Type 2 NPs on the narrative task. While this increase in accuracy does not turn out to be statistically significant at the .05 level (as

TABLE 4.   Rate of Accuracy of Article Use Within Each NP Type

	INTERVIEW (%)	NARRATIVE (%)	(DIFF) MEANS	PROB.
Type 1	87	—		n.a.
Type 2	82.6	90.6	8	.067
Type 3	71.7	71.7	0	1.0
Type 4	80	90.3	10.3	n.a.

(No statistical analysis was run on Type 4 NPs as the N was felt to be too small to permit accurate probability measurement.)

measured by the more conservative 2-tailed *t*-test,[2] the data do show a strong trend toward higher accuracy on the Narrative. An examination of individual scores in Appendix 5 shows interesting individual variation on this point. The group trend toward greater accuracy on the narrative is moderated by individual trends in the opposite direction. Thirteen individuals improved markedly in accuracy with Type 2 NPs as they moved from Interview to Narrative—four did not shift in accuracy at all—and article accuracy of three subjects (J4, 11A, and 14A) decreased markedly from the Interview to the Narrative. Another study, with a larger number of subjects, may be able to show statistical significance in the group trend we see in Table 4, and tease out the frequency and possible causes of opposing trends such as those exhibited by J4, 11A, and 14A.

Although the learners' scores on the grammar task were not included in the quantitative analysis, it is worth pointing out that article accuracy with NP Types 2 and 3 (shown in Figure 1) was *far lower* than on either of the oral tasks: 50% for Type 2 NPs and 46% for Type 3.

We felt it would be useful to examine the performance of native speakers of English on some of these tasks. Nine native speakers of English performed the same narrative task with one another in a study (Tarone and Yule, 1987) which looked at another aspect of IL. The transcript of these native speaker narrations were re-analyzed using Parrish's system. The results of this analysis are provided in Table 5.

We can observe that there is a slightly greater number of Type 4 NPs used on the narrative task by nonnative speakers than by these native speakers, 4% versus 1%. However, the distribution of NP Types for nonnative speakers is generally consistent with distribution of NP types for native speakers.[3]

Discussion II

What can we make of these results? First, it does seem that at least some of the variability in article usage found in Tarone (1985) is due to the learners' use of different types of noun phrase in the different oral tasks. In the *Interview*,

---

[2]A note about our choice of statistical measures is worth making here. We have chosen to use a more conservative measure of significance: a two-tailed rather than a one-tailed *t*-test. While a one-tailed *t*-test would be more likely to show significance or difference, we decided to use a 2-tailed test because of our inability to predict directionality of improvement in accuracy scores. As more data on this phenomenon accumulate, we may be able to use a more powerful one-tailed *t*-test.

[3]It is interesting to note that native speaker accuracy in article use was less than 100% in conjunction with Type 3 NPs. These were all cases where native speakers made first mention in the discourse of a referent using a definite, rather than an indefinite, article, but where the hearer could not reasonably be assumed to be able to identify the referent; e.g., "Then she put it on the student's desk" (not previously mentioned). Similar patterns are found in the speech of native-speaker adolescents in Anderson, Brown, and Yule (1982). Although learners also had somewhat lower accuracy scores in Type 3 contexts, their errors were of a different nature.

TABLE 5. Native Speaker Performance on Narrative Task

TYPE	TOTAL NPS WITH PRE-MODIFIERS	% OF TOTAL	% ACCURACY IN PRE-MODIFIERS
1	0		
2	181	68	100
3	81	31	95
4	2	1	100

TYPE	TOTAL NPS WITH ARTICLES	% OF TOTAL	% ACCURACY IN ARTICLES
1	0		
2	173	73	100
3	62	26	94
4	2	1	100

learners produced approximately equal proportions of NP Types 1, 2, & 3, with a smaller proportion of Type 4. In the *Narrative*, the learners *and native speakers* used mostly (about 70%) Type 2 NPs, with Type 3 NPs occurring less frequently. Type 1 and 4 NPs were rarely used in the narrative task. Since both learners and native speakers produced a similar pattern on this task we might hypothesize that there is something about this sort of narrative that encourages the use of certain types of NPs and not others. In particular, it seems likely that this narrative task required a set proportion of "first-mention" NPs (Type 3) and "subsequent-mention" NPs (Type 2) in the discourse.

The Interview seemed to require a different pattern of NP Types: NP Types 1, 2, and 3 were common, and were produced frequently, while Type 4 NPs were much rarer. The Interview task was more successful than the Narrative in eliciting both Type 1 and Type 4 NPs. Again, intuitively this makes sense, because in the Interview task the learners were being asked about their field of study; they typically used a large number of "generic" NPs (Type 1)—for example, "agronomy," "profit"—and Type 4's—for example, "I want to be a secretary." With regard to NP Type and article usage, it seems then that task influences the type of NP which is used by the learner, and as we have seen, different NP Types require different patterns of article usage. In particular, this fact should be important in designing formal tests which examine article and premodifier use. The test used in Tarone (1985), while possibly typical of classroom tests, was flawed by its omission of NP Types 1 and 4.[4]

---

[4]It might be worthwhile to examine other frequently-used research tools (e.g., the Bilingual Syntax Measure, the SCOPE test) to determine the Types of NP used to elicit articles.

Hypothesis Two must be rejected; learners' accuracy in article use was significantly lower in the context of Type 3 NPs than in the context of Types 1 and 2. We see this pattern on both oral tasks, which we should recall, did not differ in the proportion of Type 3 NPs elicited.

A third conclusion is that there is a tendency (nonsignificant or nonmeasurable in this study) for learner accuracy in article and premodifier use to vary with task and NP Type. Accuracy was by far the lowest on the grammar test, for the only two NP Types tested: 2 and 3. Statistical measures applied in Tarone (1985) indicate that this difference was highly significant.

On the oral tasks, article accuracy was higher on the narrative than on the interview for Type 2 NPs (a difference approaching but not reaching statistical significance). This is interesting since Type 2 NPs were also more frequently supplied on the narrative. That is, not only were Type 2 NPs *used* far more in the narrative task, the articles used with Type 2 NPs tended to be *more accurate* on the Narrative than on the Interview task. The modest increase in accuracy of the subjects with article use with Type 2 NPs, *combined with* the very great increase in *number* of Type 2 NPs on the Narrative task, may help us to understand the way in which the learners' overall accuracy with article use increased as they moved from the Interview to the Narrative task. The accuracy with which articles were used with Type 2 NPs was lowest on the test and highest on the narrative; this steady increase in accuracy with Type 2 NPs is quite marked, ranging from 50% on the test, to 82.6% on the Interview, to 90.6% on the Narrative.

Why should this be? If we recall that one use of Type 2 NPs is for referents previously mentioned in the discourse, it seems most likely that the demands of the Narrative task itself can explain not only the increased presence of such NPs but any increased accuracy of article use with them as well. Effective story-telling requires that the narrator keep track over time of persons and objects important to the story-line; frequently subsequent mention of such persons and objects must demand the use of Type 2 NPs, and the marking of such NPs as referring to "previous" rather than "new" mentions is crucial to the listener's understanding of the story. It is simply more important for the speaker to mark such NPs accurately in producing an effective narrative than it is to attend to the same forms in a sentence-level grammar test. Here, we define an *effective* narrative as one which is comprehensible to a listener who needs the information in the story for some purpose; recall that the speaker was telling the story face to face with a listener who needed the information in the story in order to perform a task. It is suggested here that the importance of marking "subsequent-mention" NPs in such an extended narrative task is greater than in performing a sentence-level written exam. Its importance also seems to be greater than in describing one's field of study to an interviewer who has no obvious need for the information being conveyed; while the discourse in the Interview and Narrative tasks was, in both cases, extended discourse, we believe the pressure for clarity was greater in the case of the Narrative than in the case of the Interview.

This explanation does not at first seem to account for the lack of a similar increase in accuracy of articles with Type 3 NPs on the narrative. Recall that one use of Type 3 NPs is to mark first-mention referents clearly. However, article accuracy with Type 3 NPs, which was significantly low on both oral tasks, did not improve on the narrative. Although we do not have more fine-grained data on the performance of all 20 subjects, as to where their general difficulties lay in the use of Type 3 NPs in the oral tasks, we do have such data for ten of the subjects (see matrices in Appendix 2). For those subjects, it seems that most of the incorrect uses of articles with Type 3 NPs consisted of the incorrect use of 0 article in place of the indefinite. Such an error would not, we submit, lead to substantial confusion on the part of a hearer trying to follow a narrative; in such a case, there is not as much communicative pressure brought to bear upon the speaker to be accurate, as there is in the case of accurate marking of Type 2 NPs in the narrative. In fact, communicative pressure for accuracy with Type 3 NPs must be low on both oral tasks for this same reason, and may be a cause of the lower accuracy which actually occurred with Type 3 NPs.

Thus, we would like to argue that the increased accuracy of articles in the Narrative task as opposed to the Interview task (and certainly as opposed to the grammar test) is due to the general influence of communicative pressure. The task itself demands that, if the speaker is to communicate effectively, she or he must accurately mark certain types of NP in such a way that a hearer can keep track of referents as the narrative progresses. A second factor, mentioned in Tarone (1985), which favors increased accuracy on both the oral tasks as opposed to the grammar test, is likely to be the cohesiveness of the discourse elicited by the task; sentence-level discourse is likely to be less favorable to accuracy of article use with Type 2 and 3 NPs than more extended discourse. At the same time, as Tarone (1985) hypothesizes, grammatical forms such as the third person singular –s would seem to become more and more redundant as the discourse becomes more cohesive. This factor would seem to be able to account satisfactorily for the fact that such grammatical forms in the Tarone (1985) study became less accurate as discourse became more cohesive, while the article became more accurate under the same conditions.

Littlewood (1981) listed the importance of the communicative function of a feature as a primary factor likely to influence variability in interlanguage. He speculated that, if a feature was semantically redundant in a particular communicative context, it would be more likely to be omitted, but if that same feature became important to communication in another communicative context, it would be much less likely to be omitted. Littlewood suggested that three factors are likely to influence variability in interlanguage: (1) the communicative function of a feature, (2) the linguistic environment of that feature, and (3) social/situational factors (which include formality of situation and ability of the speaker to attend to adjustment of his or her speech toward the norm). It now seems that recent theoretical formulations modeling variation in interlanguage (e.g., Ellis (1985), Krashen (1981), and Tarone (1983)) have tended to focus too much upon factors (2) and (3), and particularly upon "attention to speech" as a causal factor in IL variability; the results of our analysis in this paper suggest that we would do well to return to Littlewood's earlier framework and broaden our considerations to include communicative function as a factor which directly influences the pattern of variability which we observe in interlanguage.

Conclusion

This paper has examined, in more detail, the form and function of articles in the production of second-language learners on two oral tasks. It was found that different tasks elicited different types of noun phrases to different degrees. Learner accuracy with article usage in the context of Type 3 NPs was significantly lower than accuracy in the context of Type 1 and Type 2 NPs. This difference in accuracy did not correlate in this study with oral task differences, since the two oral tasks both happened to elicit the same proportion of Type 3 NPs; however, one could imagine a task which did demand a large proportion of Type 3 NPs, or first-mention referents, (for example, an oral task asking learners to describe entities in a picture) and which might result in lower article accuracy related to task. In addition, it was found that learner accuracy in the articles used with Type 2 NPs did increase across the three tasks used, the greatest difference being between the grammar task and the two oral tasks, and the difference in accuracy on the two oral tasks approaching but not reaching statistical significance. It was argued that the change in accuracy which occurred was due to the differing communicative demands of the tasks. Finally, it is argued that task-related variation in interlanguage must be due, not to a single variable called "attention to language form," but to a complex of factors, at least one of which must be the communicative function of particular forms in the language. The function of these forms may vary with the communicative demands of the task, and the cohesiveness of the discourse produced in response to the task. The learner responds differently to different task demands, and at least some of this differential response will result in different accuracy scores for different grammatical forms.

It was concluded that this analysis provides support for Littlewood's (1981) proposal that three factors influence variation in interlanguage: the communicative function of a feature, the linguistic environment of that feature, and social/situational factors such as formality of situation and ability to attend to form.

It is clear that we need more data of the sort presented in this paper in order to learn more about the dynamics of style-shifting across tasks, and in order to be able to make stronger conclusions about this phenomenon. In particular, in order to show that the trend to increase accuracy of article usage with Type 2 NPs in narrative tasks of the sort used in this study is statistically significant, and to ascertain the extent of individual deviation from that trend, we need well-designed studies with larger numbers of subjects. (It would also be useful to test the suggestion made in this paper that tasks eliciting a large number of Type 3, or first-mention, NPs, might produce a lower article accuracy rate than tasks of the sort used in this study.) But we feel that the analysis we have represented here is important in that it shows patterns in learner performance related to tasks which have not heretofore been reported empirically, and which violate assumptions previously made by many in the field—ourselves included.

References

Anderson, A., Brown, G., & Yule, G. (1982). Hearers make better speakers: Hearer-effects on speaker performance in oral communication tasks. *Work in Progress 14*, Department of Linguistics, Edinburgh University.

Arditty, J. & Purdue, C. (1979). Variabilité et connaissances en langue étrangère. In C. Perdue & R. Porquier (Eds.) *Linguistique appliquée*. Special issue of *Encrages*. Paris: Presses Universitaires de Vincennes.

Bickerton, D. (1981). *Roots of language*. Ann Arbor: Karoma.

Ellis, R. (1985). *Understanding second language acquisition*. London: Oxford University Press.

Huebner, T. (1983). *A longitudinal analysis of the acquisition of English*. Ann Arbor: Karoma Publishers.

Krashen, S. (1981). *Second language acquisition and learning*. Oxford: Pergamon.

Labov, W. (1969). The study of language in its social context. *Studium Generale, 23*, 30–87.

Littlewood, W. (1981). Language variation and second language acquisition theory. *Applied Linguistics 2*, 150–158.

Parrish, B. (1987). A new look at methodologies in the study of article acquisition for learners of ESL. *Language Learning 37*, 361–383.

Perdue, C. (1984). *Second language acquisition by immigrants: A field manual*. Rowley, Massachusetts: Newbury House.

Tarone, E. (1983). On the variability of interlanguage systems. *Applied Linguistics 4*, 143–163.

Tarone, E. (1985). Variability in interlanguage use: a study of style-shifting in morphology and syntax. *Language Learning, 35*, 373–404.

Tarone, E. (1988). *Variation in Interlanguage*. London: Edward Arnold Publishers.

Tarone, E., & Yule, G. (1987). Communication strategies in East-West interactions. In L. Smith (Ed.). *Discourse Across Cultures*, Englewood Cliffs, New Jersey: Prentice-Hall.

Appendix 1

TABLE A1.   Distribution of NP Type and Accuracy of Article Usage Within Types, Produced by Twenty Subjects on Three Tasks

TASK ONE: GRAMMAR TEST

	TOTAL NPS REQUIRING ARTICLES	% OF TOTAL NPS	% OF ACCURACY ARTICLES
Type 1	0	0	—
Type 2	40	40	50
Type 3	60	60	46
Type 4	0	0	—

TASK 2: INTERVIEW

	TOTAL NPS WITH PRE-MODIFIERS	% OF TOTAL	% OF ACCURACY IN PRE-MODIFIER USE
Type 1	358	26	86
Type 2	526	38	85
Type 3	404	29	79
Type 4	101	7	80
	TOTAL NPS WITH ARTICLES	% OF TOTAL NPS WITH ARTICLES	% OF ACCURACY IN ARTICLE USE
Type 1	353	30	87
Type 2	439	37.5	86
Type 3	301	24.5	77
Type 4	91	8	78

TASK 3: NARRATIVE

	TOTAL NPS WITH PRE-MODIFIERS	% OF TOTAL	% OF ACCURACY IN PRE-MODIFIER USE
Type 1	1	0	—
Type 2	422	67	92
Type 3	186	29	79
Type 4	24	4	96
	TOTAL NPS WITH ARTICLES	% OF TOTAL NPS WITH ARTICLES	% OF ACCURACY IN ARTICLE USE
Type 1	1	—	—
Type 2	405	71	92
Type 3	142	25	71
Type 4	21	4	91

Appendix 2

TABLE A2. Average Distribution of Types Produced by Ten Japanese and Arabic Subjects for Each Task

	Nonnative Interview			
	TYPE 1 [−SR] [+HK]	TYPE 2 [+SR] [+HK]	TYPE 3 [+SR] [−HK]	TYPE 4 [−SR] [−HK]
Definite Article				
Correct	16	201	0	0
Incorrect	20	0	6	2
Indefinite Article				
Correct	7	0	71	30
Incorrect	4	2	2	0
Ø				
Correct	174	0	43	9
Incorrect	7	38	25	9
Quantifiers				
Correct	0	0	59	7
Incorrect	2	1	1	1
Demonstratives				
Correct	0	47	0	0
Incorrect	0	0	0	0
TOTALS				
Correct	197	248	173	46
Total	230	289	207	58
Percent Correct	85.7	85.8	83.6	79.3
	Nonnative Interview			
Definite Article				
Correct	0	186	0	0
Incorrect	0	0	3	0
Indefinite Article				
Correct	0	0	45	7
Incorrect	0	0	1	0
Ø				
Correct	0	0	10	3
Incorrect	0	7	11	2
Quantifiers				
Correct	0	0	27	3
Incorrect	0	0	0	0
Demonstratives				
Correct	0	10	0	0
Incorrect	0	0	0	0

TOTALS				
Total Correct		196	82	15
Total	0	203	97	15
Total Percent Correct		96.6	84.5	86.7

Appendix 3

TABLE A3.   Distribution of NP Type and Accuracy of Article Usage within Types, for Twenty Subjects on Three Tasks: Analysis in Terms of Native Language of Subjects

Interview Task
NPs With Pre-Modifiers

	Japanese Only			Arabic Only		
TYPE	TOTAL NPS WITH PRE-MODS.	% OF TOTAL	% OF ACCURACY	TOTAL NPS WITH PRE-MODS.	% OF TOTAL	% OF ACCURACY
I	109	22	77	249	28	91
II	176	35	79	350	39	92
III	158	32	73	246	28	85
IV	56	11	79	45	5	80

NPs with Articles Only

	Japanese Only			Arabic Only		
TYPE	TOTAL NPS WITH ARTS	% OF TOTAL	% OF ACCURACY	TOTAL NPS WITH ARTS	% OF TOTAL	% OF ACCURACY
I	106	25.5	84	247	32	89
II	140	34	76	299	39	91
III	122	29	71	179	23	82
IV	48	11.5	75	43	6	81

Narrative Task
NPs With Pre-Modifiers

	Japanese Only			Arabic Only		
TYPE	TOTAL NPS WITH PRE-MODS.	% OF TOTAL	% OF ACCURACY	TOTAL NPS WITH PRE-MODS.	% OF TOTAL	% OF ACCURACY
I	0	—	—	1	.3	100
II	191	65.5	87	231	67.7	95
III	83	28.5	81	103	30	77
IV	18	6	89	6	2	100

NPs With Articles Only

	Japanese Only			Arabic Only		
TYPE	TOTAL NPS WITH ARTS	% OF TOTAL	% OF ACCURACY	TOTAL NPS WITH ARTS	% OF TOTAL	% OF ACCURACY
I	0	—	—	I	.3	100
II	183	70.5	86	222	71.85	96
III	59	23	66	83	26.85	74
IV	17	6.5	88	3	1	100

Appendix 4

TABLE A4.   Proportion of NP Types elicited from each Subject on the Interview and Narrative Tasks

	Interview					Narrative			
TYPES: SUBJECTS	1	2	3	4		1	2	3	4
J1	18	55	25	3		0	75	15	10
J5	49	26	16	9		0	61	29	10
J4	18	9	36	36		0	68	30	4
J8	33	14	38	14		0	81	19	0
J9	20	32	34	14		0	80	19	3
J12	9	36	39	16		0	29	57	14
J13	33	47	19	0		0	76	15	9
J16	11	47	36	6		0	58	37	5
J17	3	55	38	3		0	85	8	8
J20	42	16	26	16		0	59	33	7
2A	46	26	18	11		0	42	50	8
3A	30	47	18	4		0	92	8	0
6A	44	31	18	7		0	50	50	0
7A	35	33	26	6		0	84	16	0
10A	56	25	12	8		0	72	24	3
11A	36	36	26	2		0	73	27	0
14A	13	50	31	6		0	59	41	0
15A	22	54	24	0		0	93	7	0
18A	17	43	37	3		3	66	31	0
19A	9	50	36	5		0	85	15	0

(In this table, the proportion with which each subject supplied each NP Type, out of the total NP's she or he produced on the task, is given. The proportion is based upon a total of 100. Proportion scores are necessary here in order for us to be able to compare all the subjects, because some subjects produced far more total discourse than others.)

Appendix 5

TABLE A5.   Individuals' Rate of Accuracy of Article Use by NP Type on Two Tasks

TYPES SUBJECTS	Interview				Narrative			
	1	2	3	4	1	2	3	4
J1	7/7	13/22	8/10	1/1	0/0	11/15	2/3	2/2
J4	4/6	2/3	7/12	10/12	0/0	4/18	6/8	11/13
J5	32/36	15/19	7/12	4/7	0/0	17/19	8/9	2/3
J8	7/7	3/3	7/8	1/3	0/0	21/21	5/5	0/0
J9	10/13	19/21	17/22	7/9	0/0	26/28	5/6	1/1
J12	4/4	11/16	16/17	7/7	0/0	2/2	2/4	1/1
J13	11/12	10/17	3/7	0/0	0/0	31/31	5/6	1/4
J16	1/4	16/17	8/13	2/2	0/0	11/11	5/7	1/1
J17	1/1	15/16	6/11	1/1	0/0	22/22	1/2	2/2
J20	11/16	2/6	3/10	3/6	0/0	10/16	6/9	2/2
2A	24/26	11/15	9/10	6/6	0/0	9/10	8/12	2/2
3A	28/34	46/53	16/20	5/5	0/0	23/23	1/2	0/0
6A	46/48	30/33	15/19	7/8	0/0	17/17	17/17	0/0
7A	23/25	23/24	15/19	3/4	0/0	39/41	8/8	0/0
10A	45/59	24/26	9/13	4/8	0/0	21/21	3/7	1/1
11A	20/21	21/21	11/15	1/1	0/0	21/22	6/8	0/0
14A	7/8	30/31	16/19	4/4	0/0	14/16	7/11	0/0
15A	10/10	22/25	8/11	0/0	0/0	13/14	1/1	0/0
18A	5/5	12/13	10/11	0/1	1/1	21/23	7/11	0/0
19A	11/11	54/58	30/42	6/6	0/0	35/35	4/6	0/0

(In the fractions provided in this table, the nominator indicates the number correct and the denominator, the number of obligatory contexts provided by each subject for articles in the context of that NP Type.)

Understanding the Article

1. Summarize the purpose, results, and conclusions of the 1985 study by Tarone. How did the results of this study lead the authors to conduct the present study?

2. For the present study, the authors have added a *qualitative* analysis of the data used in the 1985 study. Describe their method of analyzing the functions of articles and explain why this kind of analysis is called *qualitative*.

3. Appendix 1 summarizes the results of the analysis. In order to understand Table A1, you need to review the following: the three tasks; the four noun phrase (NP) types; examples of NPs requiring articles and NPs with pre-modifiers. In what ways do the results elicited on the grammar test differ from the results elicited on the oral tasks?

4. In your own words, describe the differences in the proportion of NP types produced by the two oral tasks (as depicted in Table A2).

5. What do the results indicate about the relationship between the two oral tasks and the rate of accuracy of use of articles and pre-modifiers (as depicted in Table A3)?

6. What were the answers to the research questions (i.e., were the three null hypotheses upheld or rejected)?

7. How do the authors explain their findings—for example, the change in accuracy across tasks? Do these findings support or contradict previous research in this area?

Reflecting on Wider Issues

1. Tarone's research on interlanguage variation emphasizes variability due to context. How does this paper by Tarone and Parrish provide support for her position?

2. What other explanations might there be for variability in the interlanguages of learners? What evidence would you look for to support those other positions?

Going Beyond the Article

In addition to context as a source of variation in interlanguage, researchers have shown that the task and the time allotted for its completion can also have an effect. Read Crookes (1989), "Planning and interlanguage variation" (*Studies in Second Language Acquisition, 11,* 367–384) for the results of a study of the effect of the learner's planning on variation in learner interlanguage.

On the basis of her earlier research, Tarone went on to develop a theory of interlanguage variability, outlined in her 1988 book, *Variation in Interlanguage* (London: Edward Arnold). After reading this book, you might want to look at an argument against Tarone's theory—Gregg's "The variable competence model of second language acquisition and why it isn't" (*Applied Linguistics, 11,* 364–383, 1990). Then read Tarone's response ("On variation in interlanguage: a response to Gregg," *Applied Linguistics, 11,* 392–400, 1990).

12

FOCUS-ON-FORM AND CORRECTIVE FEEDBACK IN COMMUNICATIVE LANGUAGE TEACHING
Effects on Second Language Learning

Patsy M. Lightbown
Concordia University

Nina Spada
McGill University

Previewing the Article

One of the more intriguing issues prevailing throughout the last few decades of second language acquisition research is the question of how much focus should be placed in the classroom on the grammatical forms of language, as opposed to its communicative functions. There are mixed findings on the effectiveness of form-focused instruction, leading to a wide range of classroom implications.

Lightbown and Spada's study adds some further support to those who advocate specific focus on formal aspects of language. Before you read the work, review some of the issues on error correction in the classroom (see *PLLT*, Chapter 8, end-of-chapter vignette), and contemplate

Reprinted from *Studies in Second Language Acquisition*, 12:429–447, 1990.

some of the arguments one might advance for and against form-focused instruction. Then, find answers to the following questions:

1. What is the overall purpose of the study? Where is it stated?
2. What are the specific research questions?
3. What kinds of data are gathered and how are they analyzed?

The developing oral English of approximately 100 second language learners (four intact classes) was examined in this study. The learners were native speakers of French (aged 10–12 years) who had received a 5-month intensive ESL course in either grade 5 or grade 6 in elementary schools in Quebec. A large corpus of classroom observation data was also analyzed.

Substantial between-class differences were found in the accuracy with which students used such English structures as progressive -*ing* and adjective–noun order in noun phrases. There was some evidence that these differences (which were not correlated with performance on listening comprehension tests) were due to differences in teachers' form-focused instruction. These findings are discussed in terms of current competing views of the role of form-focused instruction in second language learning.

The study reported in this article was an investigation of the effects of form-focused instruction and corrective feedback provided in the context of teaching programs that were based on principles of communicative language teaching (CLT). The research was carried out in recently implemented, intensive ESL programs for francophone children in elementary schools near Montreal, in the majority French-speaking province of Quebec in Canada. These programs provide students in grade 5 or grade 6 (aged 10–12 years) with 5 hours of daily ESL instruction for 5 months of the school year. In the remaining 5 months of the year, the children complete the rest of their academic program (primarily French language arts and mathematics).[1]

The purpose of the research presented in this article is to examine relationships between classroom instruction and interaction and the learners' developing second language (L2) ability (specifically in terms of some aspects of grammatical accuracy in this case). The context of the investigation is a

---

[1]The intensive programs differ considerably from the regular ESL programs for primary schools in Quebec, which provide less than 2 hours a week of ESL instruction in grades 4, 5, and 6. These programs also differ from Canadian French immersion programs in that no subject matter is taught in the target language (English). In Quebec it is illegal for French-language schools to teach subject matter in a language other than French. As a result, students in the intensive programs do not receive instruction in mathematics, social studies, etc. The "content" of these courses is organized around interest areas such as food, housing, music, or careers.

controversial issue in L2 learning and teaching research: To what extent is form-focused instruction beneficial to classroom learners of a second language?

The first section of the article is a review of the literature, addressing both empirical and theoretical aspects of the role of formal instruction in L2 learning. This is followed by some background information on the ongoing research within which the present study was carried out and a statement of the specific research questions. The third section describes the methodology and procedures for the collection of data on classroom interaction and learner language. The results for the various analyses are presented following each of these descriptive sections. Finally, conclusions are presented and suggestions are made for further research.

Previous Research

Over the past 20 years there have been many changes in L2 instruction. The major change is the shift from an explicit focus on language itself (i.e., grammar, phonology, and vocabulary) to an emphasis on the expression and comprehension of meaning through language. This change has led to a greater tolerance for error in learners' speech and an emphasis on creating opportunities for learners to use language in more authentic and spontaneous ways. The theory behind these pedagogical shifts is that learners can develop greater L2 communicative abilities through instruction that more closely resembles the characteristics of a "natural" environment. It has also been argued, by Krashen (1982, 1985) and others, that such approaches can lead eventually to mastery of the target language in much the same way that a child's first language (L1) gradually comes to match that of the environment, provided that the learner manages to get enough exposure to the language.

There is some evidence that CLT does lead to higher levels of fluency and "communicative confidence" in the L2 than approaches that are exclusively or primarily form-focused and "metalinguistic" in orientation. There is also some concern that high levels of accuracy or nativelike language use cannot be achieved by adolescent or adult learners whose experience in the second language is limited to such "natural contexts" (Higgs & Clifford, 1982).

Research providing evidence that CLT does not necessarily lead to grammatical accuracy comes from Canadian French immersion programs. These programs are referred to by Krashen (1984) as "communicative programs *par excellence*" since the focus is almost exclusively on meaning through subject-matter instruction rather than on the form of the language itself. It has been demonstrated that, while children learn to speak French fluently and confidently, their accuracy in French syntax and morphology is still far below what one might expect of learners who have spent several years immersed in the second language (Harley & Swain, 1984; Swain, 1985, 1989). Indeed, some observers have concluded that French immersion is the best demonstration of the inadequacy of CLT (Hammerly, 1987).

In addition to studies of the L2 development of learners in programs in which there is very little structural grading or explicit reaction to grammar (such as the immersion context), there have been studies investigating the relative contributions of form-focused instruction and communication-focused instruction on the L2 learning of students who get both types. Savignon (1972) compared the grammatical and communicative skills of three groups of college students, all of whom were enrolled in regular audiolingual (thus, form-focused) French language classes for 4 hours a week. One experimental group which had an additional hour devoted to communicative tasks outperformed the other two groups on the "communicative" measures and did not perform differently on the "linguistic" measures. This was one of the earliest studies providing empirical support for the development of L2 teaching programs that included at least some opportunities for spontaneous communicative interaction.

More recent studies investigating the effects of combined CLT and form-focused instruction on L2 development have also been interpreted as supporting the inclusion of natural communicative interaction in L2 language classes. In an evaluation of an experimental ESL course for adults, Montgomery and Eisenstein (1985) compared the L2 performance of learners enrolled in an experimental communicative program in addition to their required grammar-based ESL course with learners who were taking only the required grammar course. The results of learners' pre- and posttest performance on a revised version of the Foreign Service Institute Oral Interview indicated that the subjects receiving the communicative instruction made greater gains on accent, grammar, vocabulary, and comprehension than the subjects who received only the required grammar course. Somewhat unexpectedly, the area of greatest improvement for the group getting communicative practice as compared with the group getting only the grammar-based instruction was in grammatical accuracy. The authors interpret this finding as support for the argument that a "combination of form-oriented and meaning-oriented language teaching was more beneficial than form-oriented teaching alone" (p. 329). Similar conclusions have been reached in studies of (nonimmersion) French L2 programs for children (Allen, Swain, Harley, & Cummins, 1990). (See Long, 1988, and Schachter, 1982, for research overviews and a theoretical discussion of this issue.)

These studies were based in large part on learners who received communicative experience in contexts where the emphasis was on grammar. Few studies have compared learners receiving primarily grammatical instruction. One such study was reported by Beretta and Davies (1985) in their evaluation of an experimental, task-based program of ESL instruction in schools in Bangalore, India. (For a full description of this program, see Prabhu, 1987.) This evaluation revealed that learners in the communicative (task-based) programs performed better on a communicative test than learners in the regular grammar-based program, and that learners in the regular grammar-based program performed better on a discrete-point grammar test. A more interesting finding is that two groups of learners in the communicative program significantly outperformed learners in the grammar-based program on contextualized grammar and dictation tests. This provided partial support for the researchers' hypothesis that "the acquisition of nonsyllabus based structure is best achieved without focus on form" (Beretta & Davis, 1985, p. 126).

In other research the effects of form-focused instruction within a primarily communicative program have been investigated. The findings of one study suggest that classrooms that provide a focus-on-form within contexts of meaningful communication work better than either those that avoid form-focused instruction altogether or those that emphasize form-focused instruction to the virtual exclusion of communicative activities. Spada (1987) investigated the L2 development of adults in ESL programs that were essentially communicative but varied in terms of the proportion of time spent on explicit grammatical instruction. In this study, learners who received more form-focused instruction performed as well or better on grammatical measures and just as well on communicative measures as learners who received less form-focused instruction.

Thus, while there is some evidence from post hoc observations to support the claim that fluency without accuracy is the outcome of CLT that excludes form-focused instruction altogether, there is, at present, little comparative research evidence to support the claim that early emphasis on grammar and accuracy is essential if early fossilization is to be prevented (see VanPatten, 1988, for a discussion of this). The exact role of form-focused instruction in CLT will become clear only when experimental research succeeds in isolating and examining this type of instruction. Some recent experimental research within the context of French immersion programs has focused on the provision of explicit language instruction in an attempt to improve particular aspects of the linguistic performance of learners in these programs (Harley, 1989). Results of this experiment showed some short-term improvements which disappeared in a later follow-up testing.[2]

---

[2]There are many possible explanations for these findings. For example, the structures chosen for teaching (French past tense forms) may not have been amenable to the kind of form-focused activities used in the experiment, too little time may have been devoted to the form-focus, students may not have been developmentally ready for the structures that were presented, and—as is so often the case in educational research—it is not completely clear that the control groups received no comparable form-focused instruction on the same structures during the period of the experiment. If we are eventually to isolate the specific contributions of form-focused and meaning-focused interaction in second language learning, this line of experimental research will have to be refined and extended.

A somewhat different perspective on the role of form-focused instruction has been taken by Pienemann and his colleagues, who have hypothesized that while certain developmental sequences are fixed and essentially inalterable by instruction, other aspects of the target language (called "variational features") are subject to the influence of a number of factors, including instruction (Meisel, Clahsen, & Pienemann, 1981; Pienemann, 1985, 1987; Pienemann, Johnston, & Brindley, 1988). Pienemann's experimental work has emphasized learners' progression from one developmental stage to another. This progression has been defined in terms of the "emergence" (the appearance in learners' spontaneous language production) of even a small number of tokens of the structural types of the relevant stage. He has been less interested in the development of the accuracy with which certain structures are used within stages. Nevertheless, it seems to be consistent with Pienemann's theory that, while instruction cannot guarantee the achievement of high accuracy in learners who are not motivated to achieve high-level skills, motivated learners may be able to improve their accuracy within their developmental stage. That is, instruction cannot cause learners to skip a natural stage of development, but once a given stage is reached, instruction may be effective in increasing the likelihood that the stage-appropriate rules will be applied. For example, while one cannot provide instruction that will prevent learners from passing through a natural stage of using declarative word order for questions in English, once learners reach the stage where they begin spontaneously to produce some questions with subject-auxiliary inversion, instruction may have some influence on the frequency with which learners actually produce the structure correctly.

The question of *when* attention to form may be most useful to learners was explored in two articles by Tomasello and Herron (1988, 1989). In an essentially structure-based program for teaching French as a foreign language to American college students, the experimenters manipulated the focus-on-form in such a way that some learners were alerted in advance to a potential problem (in this case, exceptions to some general rules or some unexpected restrictions on the transferability of an L1 rule), while others were led to make the error (the "garden path" treatment) and were then corrected only when they had actually made the error. On both immediate and delayed posttests, the "garden path" learners performed better on the structures used in the experiment. Because the Tomasello and Herron studies were carried out in classes where the focus seems to have been on language form most of the time, they cannot be interpreted as being directly relevant to classes where the focus is on communication. Nevertheless, the findings suggest that the timing of the focus-on-form is of an importance equal to that of the techniques used in teaching or correcting grammatical points.

Timing may thus be important both in terms of determining whether learners are at an appropriate stage in their language learning to benefit from correction (the position that would be congruent with Pienemann's proposals) and in terms of the more immediate matter of choosing the most propitious moment for drawing the point to the learner's attention.

As this review of research has shown, most classroom-based research on the extent to which form-based instruction is beneficial to L2 learners has been undertaken in contexts where the instruction is either exclusively or primarily form-focused. There has been far less research on the effects of form-focused instruction in programs that are primarily communicative. This research was carried out in such a program.

Background

The research to be reported here was carried out within a project that has been underway for several years. Learner language data have been collected from more than 1,000 students in nearly 40 intensive ESL classes and from over 200 students in regular ESL programs. Approximately 320 hours of classroom observation data from 20 of these classes have also been collected. The children's listening and reading comprehension skills as well as their ability to speak English have been analyzed. In addition, the amount of contact learners have with English outside the classroom, and their attitudes toward the target language, and the type of instruction they receive have been examined.

Overall, the results have been very positive. The children in the intensive programs develop significantly higher levels of comprehension ability than learners in the regular programs. They also achieve greater fluency in their oral production, and, although they still have much to learn, they achieve considerably higher levels of fluency and communicative confidence in using the second language than has ever been achieved in the regular programs at the primary level. The students who have had the intensive ESL experience usually perform as well as—and often better than—older ESL students who have accumulated the same total number of hours of ESL instructional time, spread out over 5 to 7 years rather than condensed into 5 months (Lightbown, in press; Lightbown & Spada, 1987; Paris, 1987; Spada & Lightbown, 1989).

Our observations have confirmed that the children in the experimental intensive programs receive instruction that is "communicative" in nature, instruction that focuses on meaning-based activities, opportunities for the negotiation of meaning in group work, and the provision of rich and varied, comprehensible input. Errors are viewed as a necessary part of the developmental process, and the classroom observation data show that error correction by the teachers is relatively rare. This type of instruction meets the requirements of the Ministry of Education of Quebec, which designed and implemented a communicative syllabus and related methodology for ESL approximately 8 years ago.

The new "communicative" program is more effective than the previous audiolingual program in creating opportunities for learners to use language meaningfully and communicatively in the limited time they have for instruction in English. Such a program may also be more effective in keeping learners motivated over the period of 8 years of ESL instruction at school. However, we believe that in the intensive program, where students have considerably more time to learn the L2 and to develop greater levels of communicative competence and confidence, the inclusion of more form-focused instruction within a communicative framework may be useful.

One example of the impact that form-focused teaching may have on specific aspects of L2 development emerged from our analysis of learner language in one of the intensive ESL classes. In examining the transcripts of francophone learners' performance on an oral picture description task, we saw time and again over the years that a substantial majority of learners used the verb *have* rather than *be* in their introducer or "presentational" forms. For example, when describing a picture of a classroom with three children in it, most of the learners would start by saying, "We have a classroom" or "It have three children" instead of the form overwhelmingly preferred by native speakers of the same age, "There's a classroom and there's three kids in it" or "It's a classroom with three kids in it" (Lightbown, 1984). However, we were surprised to find that the learners in one class did not use the *have* form in their introducers. Most of them used a correct *be* form (either *there is* or *it's*). The frequency with which *be* and *have* were used in four classes is shown in Table 1.[3]

Clearly class 1 is different from the other classes, even though all had had the same amount of English instruction under essentially similar circumstances. Naturally, we were curious to know why the children in this class behaved so differently from the others in their use of this particular form. When we asked the teacher whether she had specifically focused on the *have/be* distinction in presentational forms, she said emphatically that she had, so much so, in fact, that it had become a kind of joke in the classroom. When someone introduced a descriptive statement by saying "You have a . . . ," she (or another student) would look at her empty hands or look around behind herself and say, "I do? I have a . . . ? Where?" (See Lightbown, in press, for further details of this study.)

An examination of the classroom observation data indicated that this class was the one in which the greatest amount of time overall was spent on form-related instruction, that is, instruction that explicitly dealt with grammar, vocabulary, phonology, or syntax. It must be emphasized right away, however, that although the teacher in this class spent more time on form-focused activi-

---

[3]Comparisons are based on the analysis of variance (ANOVA) procedure, which sought to establish whether there were any significant differences between classes. When significant differences were found, the Tukey post hoc comparison procedure was used to specify which classes were significantly different from which others.

TABLE 1.   Percentage of Introducer Forms with Be

	CLASS 1 (GRADE 5)	CLASS 2 (GRADE 5)	CLASS 3 (GRADE 6)	CLASS 4 (GRADE 6)
N	19	25	26	24
Mean (%)	93.95	35.84	43.00	31.08
SD	18.60	27.93	35.27	34.23

Note: $F(3, 90) = 18.54$, $p < .001$. Mean scores joined by a solid line differ significantly from one another according to the Tukey multiple comparison procedure, $p < .05$.

ties than the other intensive program teachers we observed, the overall focus of the class (more than 70% of class time) was on communicative activities or classroom management.

Based on this finding, we undertook a more detailed examination of the amount and type of form-focused instruction provided in this class and in three others that we had observed in other schools during the same school term. The specific question we asked in examining the classroom observation and learner language data was:

> Are there other differences in learner language outcomes that may be related to differences in instruction?

Investigating this question led to further post hoc analysis of the type of form-focused behavior that occurred in these four classes (two at the grade 5 level and two at grade 6) and an analysis of the oral performance data of all the students in these classes (N = approximately 100) in terms of (a) their use of *have* and *be* as presentational forms; (b) their use of two grammatical morphemes (plural -*s* and progressive -*ing*); (c) adjective placement in noun phrases; and (d) the use of appropriate gender in possessive determiners. These features were chosen for analysis principally because they were known to cause difficulty for fracophone ESL learners in the classroom research we had previously carried out (Lightbown, 1981, 1983, 1984; Lightbown & Spada, 1978; Martens, 1988; Paris, 1987).

Classroom Observation

A modified version of the Communicative Orientation of Language Teaching (COLT) scheme was used to collect the observation data. This scheme was designed to measure the communicative orientation of instruction at the level of activity type (Part A) and verbal interaction between teachers and students (Part B; Allen, Fröhlich, & Spada, 1984; Fröhlich, Spada, & Allen, 1985; Spada,

1990). For this study, a modified version of Part A was used to analyze all the observation data from the four classes (approximately 20 hours per class). This analysis is referred to as the macrolevel analysis. A revised and expanded section of Part B (specifically "code reaction") was used with a 2-hour segment of the observation data for each class. This analysis is referred to as the microlevel analysis.

The macrolevel analysis involved a real-time coding procedure that described classroom behaviors at the level of activity type, participant organization (student-centered/teacher-centered), modality practice (listening/speaking/reading/writing), and content of the activities (focus-on-form/focus-on-meaning). This analysis also permitted a description of the type for form-based and meaning-based focus within activities. For example, if an activity was described as form-focused, the aspect of language that was targeted (vocabulary/pronunciation/grammar/discourse) was specified.

The microlevel analysis was a post hoc analysis of the audiotapes and/or transcriptions of the audiotapes. This analysis included an assessment of the extent to which the teachers' form-focused behaviors were "instruction" (where the teacher presented a language point and led students to practice it) or "reactive" (where the teacher reacted to an error or apparent difficulty that a student exhibited during a communicative activity). Thus, when a form-focused activity had been observed in the macrolevel analysis, the microlevel analysis was used to investigate how form was dealt with (i.e., the nature of the teaching methods). Further, when a form-focused activity with a focus on grammar was observed, the microlevel analysis was used to determine the specific grammatical point that the teacher had addressed (e.g., verb forms or adjective placement).

Results

The macrolevel analysis indicated that all four classes were primarily communicative in their approach, and classroom interaction focused on meaning, not form, most of the time. However, the four teachers differed from each other in terms of the total amount of time they gave to form-focused activities. For example, the teacher in class 1 devoted the most time to form-focus (almost 29% of the total observed class time), whereas the teachers in classes 2 and 4 spent 13%, and the teacher in class 3 spent 11% of her instructional time on form (see Table 2). The teachers also differed with regard to the aspects of form on which they focused. For example, the teacher in class 1 tended to focus on grammatical errors, whereas the teacher in class 4 focused most often on vocabulary problems.

The microlevel analysis showed that the teachers almost never taught "grammar lessons" and rarely presented rules about the target language. Instead, their form-focused behaviors were almost always reactions to learners'

TABLE 2.   Percentage of Instructional Time with a Focus on Code (Grammar, Vocabulary, and Phonology)

CLASS 1 (GRADE 5)	CLASS 2 (GRADE 5)	CLASS 3 (GRADE 6)	CLASS 4 (GRADE 6)
28.77%	13.49%	10.73%	13.42%

errors or to student requests for assistance with some aspect of language use. This analysis showed further that, even within a grammar focus, teachers differed in the aspect of grammar to which they reacted. For example, the teacher in class 1, as noted earlier, had a particular concern about the students' use of the presentational forms *there is/there are*. (See Spada, in press, for further details of the microlevel analyses.)

On the basis of these findings, we hypothesized that the learner language in each class might show signs of the influence of specific items on which an individual teacher had chosen to focus.

Learner Language

It is important to emphasize, before presenting the results of the analysis of learner language, that the learners in these four classes began their intensive ESL instruction with very little knowledge of English apart from what they had learned in 2 hours a week (or less) of ESL instruction in grade 4 (for the students in grade 5) or grades 4 and 5 (for students in grade 6).[4] These students had practically no contact with speakers of English outside the classroom. At the end of the intensive program, they were given a test of listening and reading comprehension developed by the provincial Ministry of Education for secondary school learners. The class results for this test are presented in Table 3. With the exception of class 2, all groups performed substantially better than the provincial average for students finishing Secondary 3 (grade 9). The performance of class 2 was right at the grade 9 mean (see Spada & Lightbown, 1989, for a fuller discussion of test results).

For our analyses, the learner language data were collected using an oral communication task referred to as the "picture card game" (PCG). In this task a learner describes a picture until the interviewer can guess which of a set of four similar (but not identical) pictures is being described. (For more detailed descriptions of the PCG and procedures, see Lightbown, 1983; Lightbown &

---

[4]A pretest was administered to all classes in this study at the beginning of the 5-month intensive program. On this test (a listening comprehension test), class 1 had a significantly higher score than class 2. There were no other significant differences (see Spada & Lightbown, 1989, for details.)

TABLE 3.   MEQ Posttest Results

	CLASS 1 (GRADE 5)	CLASS 2 (GRADE 5)	CLASS 3 (GRADE 6)	CLASS 4 (GRADE 6)
N	20	25	28	25
Mean (%)	65.45	53.48	72.64	67.96
SD	12.04	9.09	15.00	17.18

Note: $F(3, 94) = 8.88$, $p < .001$. Mean scores joined by a solid line differ significantly from one another according to the Tukey comparison procedure, $p < .05$.

Spada, 1978, 1987). Audiotaped recordings were made as learners played the PCG, and these were transcribed (in standard orthography). All analyses reported in this article were based on these transcriptions.

Global analyses of the transcripts confirmed that virtually all students spoke and understood English with confidence and enthusiasm. No student had difficulty completing the task and, although there were differences in the speech styles and speech rates, most of the students would be described as "fluent" within the limitations of their "low intermediate" command of the language. When they lacked specific vocabulary, they readily used circumlocution or asked the interlocutor for a word. The Appendix provides excerpts from transcripts from three learners representing a range of communicative ability among these students.

Results

Accuracy on plural -s and progressive -ing.   The first analysis of the learner language data was an examination of their spontaneous use of two inflectional morphemes, the -s plural and the progressive -ing, in obligatory contexts. Table 4 presents the results of the -s plural. The lowest results were

TABLE 4.   Accuracy on Plural -s

	CLASS 1 (GRADE 5)	CLASS 2 (GRADE 5)	CLASS 3 (GRADE 6)	CLASS 4 (GRADE 6)
N	20	25	27	25
Mean (%)	50.20	59.04	58.63	37.36
SD	25.00	18.51	27.93	20.98

Note: $F(3, 93) = 4.76$, $p < .01$. Mean scores joined by a solid line differ significantly from one another according to the Tukey multiple comparison procedure, $p < .05$.

obtained by class 4 (plural -s was supplied in only 37% of obligatory contexts). Accuracy in class 1 was 50%; in classes 2 and 3, accuracy was approximately 59%. Analysis of variance (ANOVA) revealed that there were group differences. The Tukey test showed that the significant difference was between class 4 on the one hand and classes 2 and 3 on the other.

The results on plural accuracy need to be interpreted in the context of the fact that even highly proficient francophone speakers of English often omit the plural in spoken English. Lightbown (1983) found, in a study of plural accuracy among francophone learners whose instruction had included extensive presentation and practice of the plural in audiolingual classes, that accuracy rates for advanced secondary school students were often below 60%. A partial explanation for this may lie in the fact that, although written French also marks the plural noun with -s, the -s is not pronounced in oral French. It may be that learners in all four classes analyzed for this study have reached a level of accuracy in oral English beyond which they will not progress without some specific concerted effort. This may not be true of the -ing, which has emerged in the speech of a smaller number of learners but which may be likely to continue to develop to higher levels of accuracy because it will not be influenced by a partial overlap with an aspect of the learners' native language (see Lightbown, in press; White, 1987).

Table 5 shows the accuracy in learners' use of the progressive -ing. Class 4 had the lowest accuracy, followed by classes 2 and 3. The learners in class 1 had the highest accuracy, and the difference between class 1 and class 4 is significant. When we examined individual learners' performance in the four classes, we found that 7 of 24 students in class 1 had a 0% level of accuracy. That is, 29% of those whose spontaneous speech included obligatory contexts for the -ing failed to use the -ing at least once. It can be seen in Table 6 that in the other classes, the frequency of 0% accuracy was considerably higher, and was the highest in class 4 where 76% of the students (19 of 25), whose speech created obligatory contexts for the -ing, never supplied the morpheme.

TABLE 5.   Accuracy on Progressive -ing

	CLASS 1 (GRADE 5)	CLASS 2 (GRADE 5)	CLASS 3 (GRADE 6)	CLASS 4 (GRADE 6)
N	19	25	25	25
Mean (%)	28.21	13.16	14.80	5.44
SD	28.04	19.30	23.02	11.60

Note: $F(3, 90) = 4.36$, $p < .01$. Mean scores joined by a solid line differ significantly from one another according to the Tukey multiple comparison procedure, $p < .05$.

TABLE 6. Number of Students with Zero Accuracy on -ing

CLASS 1 (GRADE 5)	CLASS 2 (GRADE 5)	CLASS 3 (GRADE 6)	CLASS 4 (GRADE 6)
7/24	14/25	14/28	19/25

A possible explanation for the higher accuracy of -ing in class 1 is that this class is the one in which the teacher reported spending time on the progressive -ing verb form in her instruction, although always in a communicative context. The class differences in the accuracy rates on the plural are more difficult to interpret, since we do not have an indication that any of the classes had a substantial amount of focused instruction on the plural.

Adjective placement in noun phrases.   The next feature examined was the learners' use of adjectives in noun phrases. It has been argued that English has typologically "disharmonic" word order as regards nouns and adjectives. Most languages with a dominant SVO order tend toward postnominal placement of the adjective. Gass and Ard (1984) reported that Spanish speakers rarely use the (incorrect) noun—adjective order in English—even though both their native language and universal tendencies in word order would point in that direction. Gass and Ard noted, however, that English speakers learning Spanish do have difficulty with postnominal placement of the adjective, even though, according to typological tendencies, noun–adjective word order accords best with the basic SVO order of Spanish. It has been our experience, both in this study and in our previous research with francophone learners of English, that the prenominal placement of adjectives can be a problem. French, like Spanish, has predominantly postnominal adjective placement, but many high-frequency adjectives usually occur before the noun.

The results of the analysis of the intensive program learners' placement of adjectives in noun phrases are shown in Table 7. Learners in class 2 were sig-

TABLE 7. Accuracy on Adjective/Noun Placement

	CLASS 1 (GRADE 5)	CLASS 2 (GRADE 5)	CLASS 3 (GRADE 6)	CLASS 4 (GRADE 6)
N	19	23	28	25
Mean (%)	74.63	88.74	74.71	58.96
SD	33.33	16.93	26.96	37.46

Note: $F(3, 91) = 4.07$, $p < .01$. Mean scores joined by a solid line differ significantly from one another according to the Tukey multiple comparison procedure, $p < .05$.

nificantly more accurate on this feature than students in class 4, who had the lowest accuracy. Students in classes 1 and 3 fell between the two, but were not significantly different from either.

On the surface, the classroom observation data do not suggest that the strong performance by class 2 was influenced by focus-on-form or error correction, since the teacher was observed to do little form-focused teaching in general, and there were no examples of her correcting postnominal adjective placement in the 2 hours analyzed for the microlevel analysis. Other observations of this class suggest, however, that the teacher was sensitive to a number of error types that were typical of most students in the class, and, even though she virtually never "taught grammar," when students produced one of these error types, she slipped in a quick correction—often in the form of a funny face or dramatically raised eyebrows, or sometimes with a chanted, laughing repetition of the correct form.

Possessive determiners.   Another aspect of English known to be difficult for francophones is the pronoun system, particularly the choice of gender in possessive determiners. In French, the gender of the determiner agrees with the grammatical gender of the object possessed rather than with the gender of the possessor:

Elle (f) lit son (m) livre (m).

She (f) reads her (f) book (m).

Zobol (1985) observed an apparently developmental progression in the acquisition of the possessive determiners by francophone students:[5]

Stage 1: the use of definite articles rather than possessive determiners, for example,

She reads the book.

Stage 2: the use of a generalized possessive determiner for all persons, genders, and numbers, for example,

She reads your book.

Stage 3: the use of a third person determiner where third person is required, but an overgeneralization of only one form (usually the masculine) of the determiner, for example,

She reads his book.

---

[5]Note that this presentation of Zobl's research is based on a somewhat simplified summary of that author's findings. It should not be understood that one stage ends before another begins or that all learners exhibit all stages equally. Nevertheless, the summary does describe the main findings and implications of Zobl's study.

Stage 4: differentiated use of possessive determiners with some possessed nouns, although learners continue to have difficulty when the object possessed has "natural" gender, for example,

She reads her book to his brother.

Stage 5: the correctly differentiated use of possessive determiners with all types of nouns, including those with natural gender, for example,

She reads her book to her brother.

The use of possessive determiners in the spontaneous speech of the learners in these four classes was analyzed in two ways: (a) group accuracy for use of *his* or *her* in appropriate contexts, and (b) the number of students in each class who used both *his* and *her* at least once correctly. These results are shown in Tables 8 and 9.

Table 8 shows that the overall accuracy of class 1 was greater than that of the other classes, but it is striking that only in classes 1 and 3 did the majority of students use enough examples (at least three) to make the analysis possible. Only six students in class 4 used at least three possessive determiners, and among these students, the mean accuracy was only 42%. As table 9 shows, no student in class 4 used at least one correct example of *his* and one of *her*.[6] In these analyses, the use of sentences such as "There is a boy sitting at the desk" or "The hair is brown and the shirt is red" were not counted as errors in possessive determiners. Counting such errors would have further reduced the

TABLE 8.   Accuracy in Use of Possessive Determiners by Students Who Used at Least Three Determiners

	CLASS 1 (GRADE 5)	CLASS 2 (GRADE 5)	CLASS 3 (GRADE 6)	CLASS 4 (GRADE 6)
N	17	11	19	6
Mean (%)	74.00	62.90	56.00	42.00

TABLE 9.   Number of Students Who Used Both *His* and *Her* Correctly at Least Once

CLASS 1 (GRADE 5)	CLASS 2 (GRADE 5)	CLASS 3 (GRADE 6)	CLASS 4 (GRADE 6)
8/23	4/25	9/28	0/25

[6]Because the numbers were so small, no statistical analysis was considered appropriate for these data.

accuracy of students in class 4, but would have had little effect on the results for class 1. This suggests that students in class 4 were not only less accurate than those in the other classes, but may also have been at a different level of development from the others. Martens (1988) carried out a study involving a different group of students who had the same teacher for intensive ESL, finding that they were very poor at finding ungrammatical uses of the possessive determiner in a grammaticality judgment task, and that, in their spontaneous language, there was an overwhelming tendency to use the masculine determiner (*his*) for all cases, although a few female students overgeneralized the feminine. There is no evidence that the teacher in question ever intentionally taught the possessive determiners, and one may question, in fact, whether she was sensitive to the error when it was committed.

Conclusions

It is important to repeat that since this study is a post hoc description of some specific classroom events and outcomes, it can only be taken as suggestive of directions for future research. Furthermore, the classroom observation data are limited, and there can be no claim that only the instructional variables differ between the classes. The observed differences between classes lead us to further research on the question of the specific effects of form-focused instruction and error correction in communicative language teaching.

The profiles of the learner language in these four classes are quite different, even though the students had very similar exposure to English both in their intensive ESL program and in their limited contacts with English outside school. In some cases, it appears that the differences are related to the type of instruction provided. For example, in class 1, where the most form-focused instruction was provided, the learners were more accurate in their use of the progressive -*ing,* were more likely to use the presentational forms preferred by native speakers (*there is* rather than *you have*), and were at a more advanced stage in their use of possessive determiners.

Students in class 4 had the lowest accuracy on all the features examined in the analysis of spontaneous language samples. The teacher in this class was the only one who virtually never focused—however briefly—on grammar. When language was in focus, it was generally because the teacher was reacting to vocabulary difficulties that students were experiencing. Note, however, that students in class 4 showed no disadvantage in their overall performance. Their comprehension skills were very good. Indeed, as shown in Table 3, they performed better than both the grade 5 classes (classes 1 and 2) and not significantly differently from the other grade 6 class (class 3).

Having acknowledged the limitations of the classroom observation data, we can nevertheless confirm that certain teachers seemed to have a particular set of structural features on which they placed more emphasis and for which they had greater expectations for correct use. Such focus seems to have been effective in some cases, and less so in others. Teachers in these programs rarely presented a grammar lesson, but tended instead to react to errors or difficulties as they occurred. Such a pedagogical technique is in accord with the notion that learners can benefit from "consciousness raising" (Rutherford, 1987, 1988; Rutherford & Sharwood Smith, 1988). It is also consistent with research on developmental sequences in language acquisition (e.g., Pienemann, 1985) and research on the effectiveness of form-focus at different points in teacher-student contact (Tomasello & Herron, 1988, 1989).

In interpreting the results of this study, we do not mean to imply that instructional intervention in the form of either grammatical presentation or reaction works with all aspects of language form. Nor do we wish to suggest that all structural features of the language will require instructional intervention. Clearly, students in the intensive ESL programs have acquired a great deal of English through communicative interaction in the classroom. What we are suggesting is that some components of the language may not only be amenable to instructional intervention, but may, as Bley-Vroman (1986), White (1987, 1990), and others argue, depend on it for further development and improvement. Unfortunately, not enough is known about the L2 acquisition process to be able to specify a large range of features that are more or less affected by form-focused instruction. Some of this research is currently underway in the work of Pienemann and his colleagues (Pienemann, 1987), and we are currently carrying out some experimental studies (White, 1989; White, Spada, Lightbown, & Ranta, 1990).

The results presented in this article provide further support for the hypothesis that form-based instruction within a communicative context contributes to higher levels of linguistic knowledge and performance. The findings of the study suggest that accuracy, fluency, and overall communicative skills are probably best developed through instruction that is primarily meaning-based but in which guidance is provided through timely form-focus activities and correction in context. The crucial question is what particular aspects of linguistic knowledge and performance are more or less affected by such instruction. We intend to continue pursuing this line of investigation in a series of experimental studies within the intensive program classes, where the learners' main source of input for English language learning is the classroom itself.

Acknowledgments

This research was funded by grants from the Quebec Ministry of Education's research granting agency (Fonds pour la formation de chercheurs et l'aide à la recherche) and the Social Science and Humanities Research Council of Canada, and by supplementary grants from several of the school boards in which the intensive programs have been developed. We wish to acknowledge the exceptional cooperation we have always enjoyed in dealing with students and teachers in the programs. We are grateful to our fine research assistants who have helped us at every stage of the research. We particularly acknowledge the help of Randall Halter, Leila Ranta, Catherine Poulsen, and Mary Jo Martens.

An earlier version of this article was presented at the Second Language Research Forum in Los Angeles in February 1989. We are grateful to Paul Meara and an anonymous SSLA reviewer whose critical reading of the manuscript made this a better article.

References

Allen, P., Fröhlich, M., & Spada, N. (1984). The communicative orientation of second language teaching: An observation scheme. In J. Handscombe, R. Orem, & B. Taylor (Eds.), *On TESOL '83* (pp. 231–252). Washington, DC: TESOL.

Allen, P., Swain, M., Harley, B., & Cummins, J. (1990). Aspects of classroom treatment: Toward a more comprehensive view of second language education. In B. Harley, P. Allen, J. Cummins, & M. Swain (Eds.), *The development of second language proficiency* (pp. 57–81). Cambridge: Cambridge University Press.

Beretta, A., & Davies, A. (1985). Evaluation of the Bangalore project. *ELT Journal, 39,* 121–127.

Bley-Vroman, R. (1986). Hypothesis testing in second-language acquisition theory. *Language Learning, 36,* 353–376.

Fröhlich, M., Spada, N., & Allen, P. (1985). Differences in the communicative orientation of L2 classrooms. *TESOL Quarterly, 19,* 27–57.

Gass, S., & Ard. J. (1984). The ontology of language universals. In W. Rutherford (Ed.), *Language universals and second language acquisition* (pp. 33–68). Amsterdam: John Benjamins.

Hammerly, H. (1987). The immersion approach: Litmus test of second-language acquisition through classroom communication. *Modern Language Journal, 71,* 395–401.

Harley, B. (1989). Functional grammar in French immersion: A classroom experiment. *Applied Linguistics, 10,* 331–359.

Harley, B., & Swain, M. (1984). The interlanguage of immersion students and its implications for second language teaching. In A. Davies, C. Criper, & A. P. R. Howatt (Eds.), *Interlanguage* (pp. 291–311). Edinburgh: Edinburgh University Press.

Higgs, T., & Clifford, R. (1982). The push toward communication. In T. Higgs (Ed.), *Curriculum, competence and the foreign language teacher* (pp. 57–79). Skokie, IL: National Textbook Co.

Krashen, S. (1982). *Principles and practice in second language acquisition.* New York: Pergamon.

Krashen, S. (1984). Immersion: Why it works and what it has taught us. *Language and Society, 12,* 61–64.

Krashen, S. (1985). *The input hypothesis: Issues and implications.* New York: Longman.

Lightbown, P. M. (1983). Acquiring English L2 in Quebec classrooms. In S. Felix & H. Wode (Eds.), *Language development at the crossroads* (pp. 101–120). Tübingen: Gunter Narr.

Lightbown, P. M. (1983). Exploring relationships between developmental and instructional sequences in L2 acquisition. In H. Seliger & M. Long (Eds.), *Classroom-oriented research in second language acquisition* (pp. 217–243). Rowley, Mass.: Newbury House.

Lightbown, P. M. (1984). Input and acquisition in second language classrooms. *TESL Canada Journal, 1,* 55–67.

Lightbown, P. M. (in press). What have we here? Some observations on the influence of instruction on L2 learning. In R. Phillipson, E. Kellerman, L. Selinker, M. Sharwood Smith, & M. Swain (Eds.), *Foreign language pedagogy research: A commemorative volume for Claus Faerch.* Clevedon: Multilingual Matters.

Lightbown, P. M., & Spada, N. (1978). Performance on an oral communication task by francophone ESL learners, *SPEAQ Journal, 2,* 35–54.

Lightbown, P. M., & Spada, N. (1987). *Learning English in intensive programs in Quebec schools (1986–87): Report on the first year of research.* Montreal: Concordia University.

Long, M. (1988). Instructed interlanguage development. In L. Beebe (Ed.) *Issues in second language acquisition: Multiple perspectives* (pp. 115–141). New York: Newbury House.

Martens, M. J. (1988). *Recognition and production of pronouns by francophone learners of English as a second language.* Unpublished master's thesis, Concordia University, Montreal.

Meisel, J., Clahsen, H., & Pienemann, M. (1981). On determining developmental stages in natural second language acquisition. *Studies in Second Language Acquisition, 3,* 109–135.

Montgomery, C., & Eisenstein, M. (1985). Reality revisited: An experimental communicative course in ESL. *TESOL Quarterly, 19,* 317–334.

Paris, L. (1987). *Some aspects of the second language development of children in intensive programs.* Unpublished master's thesis, Concordia University, Montreal.

Pienemann, M. (1985). Learnability and syllabus construction. In K. Hyltenstam & M. Pienemann (Eds.), *Modelling and assessing second language acquisition* (pp. 23–75). Clevedon: Multilingual Matters.

Pienemann, M. (1987). *Determining the influence of instruction on L2 speech processing.* Paper presented at the colloquium of the Scientific Commission on Second Language Acquisition at the Eighth AILA Congress, Sydney, Australia.

Pienemann, J., Johnston, M., & Brindley, G. (1988). Constructing an acquisition-based procedure for second language assessment. *Studies in Second Language Acquisition, 10,* 217–243.

Prabhu, N. S. (1987). *Second language pedagogy.* Oxford: Oxford University Press.

Rutherford, W. (1987). *Second language grammar: Learning and teaching.* London: Longman.

Rutherford, W. (1988). The meaning of grammatical consciousness-raising. *World Englishes, 6,* 209–216.

Rutherford, W., & Sharwood Smith, M. (Eds.). (1988). *Grammar and second language teaching.* New York: Newbury House.

Savignon, S. (1972). *Communicative competence: An experiment in foreign-language teaching.* Philadelphia: Center for Curriculum Development.

Schachter, J. (1982). Nutritional needs of language learners. In M. Clarke & J. Handscombe (Eds.), *On TESOL '82: Pacific perspectives on language learning and teaching* (pp. 175–189). Washington, DC: TESOL.

Spada, N. (1987). Relationships between instructional differences and learning outcomes: A process-product study of communicative language teaching. *Applied Linguistics, 8,* 137–161.

Spada, N. (1990). Observing classroom behaviours and learning outcomes in different second language programs. In J. Richards & D. Nunan (Eds.), *Second language teacher education: Content and process.* Cambridge: Cambridge University Press.

Spada, N. (in press). A look at the research process in classroom observation: A case study. In C. Brumfit & R. Mitchell (Eds.), *ELT Documents: Special issue on classroom centered research.* London: Macmillan.

Spada, N., & Lightbown, P. M. (1989). Intensive ESL programs in Quebec primary schools. *TESL Canada Journal, 7,* 11–32.

Swain, M. (1985). Communicative competence: Some roles of comprehensible input and comprehensible output and its development. In S. Gass & C. Madden (Eds.), *Input in second language acquisition* (pp. 235–253). Rowley, Mass.: Newbury House.

Swain, M. (1889). Manipulating and complementing content teaching to maximize second language learning. *TESL Canada Journal, 6,* 68–83.

Tomasello, M., & Herron, C. (1988). Down the garden path: Inducing and correcting overgeneralization errors in the foreign language classroom. *Applied Psycholinguistics, 9,* 237–246.

Tomasello, M., & Herron, C. (1989). Feedback for language transfer errors: The garden path technique. *Studies in Second Language Acquisition, 11,* 385–395.

VanPatten, B. (1988). How juries get hung: Problems with the evidence for a focus on form in teaching. *Language Learning, 38,* 243–260.

White, L. (1987). Against comprehensible input: The input hypothesis and the development of second language competence. *Applied Linguistics, 8,* 95–110.

White, L., (1989, August). *Adverb placement in SLA: Some effects of consciousness raising.* Paper presented at the Language Acquisition Research Symposium, Utrecht, Holland.

White, L. (1990). Implications of learnability theories for second language learning and teaching. In M. A. K. Halliday, J. Gibbons, & H. Nicholas (Eds.), *Learning, keeping and using language.* Amsterdam: John Benjamins.

White, L., Spada, N., Lightbown, P. M., & Ranta, L. (1990, March). *Consciousness raising and syntactic accuracy in L2 acquisition.* Paper presented at the Tenth Second Language Research Forum, University of Oregon, Eugene, Ore.

Zobl, H. (1985). Grammars in search of input and intake. In S. Gass & C. Madden (Eds.), *Input in second language acquisition* (pp. 329–344). Rowley, Mass.: Newbury House.

Appendix

Learner #1: Relatively Proficient Speaker

They have five students. And—,[1] the—, the teacher is outside of the classroom. The have uh, a boy with uh—, drawing the picture of the teacher. The boy have uh—, a—, red top and jeans. They are blue. They have a girl who is watching outside the *in the of the *[2] classroom to see if the teacher is coming. She have a purple uh top and a—, brown uh shirt. On the desk of the teacher they have a—, a book with writing "English." Uh, they have a girl who uh—, do an airplane for pitch uh on the classroom. There's a girl have blond hair and a blue dress. And uh they have another boy who is said to the to uh this girl uh—, shut up, close your mouth. Uh this boy have the finger uhn on his mouth. He have un* a grey a green* top and uh blue jeans. And on the desk of the girl they have uh a book open. It's writing something, but I don't know what it is. They have another boy *who said uh who show* to the classroom uh what uh the boy uh is uh drawing the board. This boy have uh—, a sweater uh green and a white top.

(Is that the same as yours?)[3]

—Yes.

(Is everything the same? Look closely at the books on the students' desks. Are they the same?)

—Oh, no, is just one.

(Tell me about yours. What's different about yours?)

—Uh they have uh—, in front of the book *of one of the* student who is showing to the classroom *the draw the drawing* uh the book is open uh it's closed, excuse me.

(And on mine it was open. So it's this one.)

—Yes.

(Excellent! That's it.)

Learner #2: Average Speaker

—He have five person. He have one in the boar[4] the board. Is uh draw her teacher. Uh he have one is look on the door. He have one is point. Uh he has *three book two book* *on the desk on the table* and one book on the desk. The teacher put the—, the uh glasses on the board. On the board he have the teacher he put the glasses. Is a funny picture.
(Hmm. Can you tell me anything else about your picture?)
—Uh—, he has two girl, three boy. *The one* boy* is he said* uh chut don't uh don't talk.
(Let me guess which one. Uh—, is that the same as yours?)
—Uh—, Mais, I don't know is is uh the same parce que the hair is/uninterpretable/is not the same color. Look, the mine is uh—,
(Mhm.)
—Mine is your is is it the same?
(Well, more or less the same. I think there's something else that's different though.)
—Yes, it is not the same.
(Okay, tell me about yours. What's different?)
—Me, the boy is to this is uh have uh—, the little comme for me là the little/uninterpretable/.
(Like a vest?)
—Yes, green and your is black.
(Aha! Is that the one you have?)
—Yes
(Mhm. Yes. Okay.)

Learner #3. Relatively Nonproficient Speaker

—Mm, the people go to the board and uh—, uh write the the teacher on the board. And the—, the—, /uninterpretable/ dessiner how do you say dessiner, dessiner?
(Uh, draw.)
—Draw the, the—, the teacher, mais is uh—, bein oui uh—, hm uh—, is very uh—, is not very good, the the the teacher. And un—, the people in the class is uh—, in uh—, in is uh—, because the, the te^ teachers is not on the class, and uh the people is uh—, uh, batailler, how do you say batailler? Uh—, the people is uh—
(Misbehaving?)
—Yes, And uh—, and the girl uh—, and the girl uh—, have uh—, uh in the blue. And the purple. Uh write the teacher in the red and in the—, in the blue. That's finish.
(Okay, Let's see. Is this the same as yours?)
—Yes.

(Exactly?)

—No! No.

(No. What's different?)

—Because uh—, *the girl the the boy* i^ have uh—, a jacket—, black and his is uh—, the green.

(Ah. Okay, green. Mmm—how about this one?)

—Yes. Ah! Yes.

Appendix Notes

1. —, indicates a pause.

2. Speech bounded by a pair of asterisks (* . . . *) indicates self-correction.

3. The interviewer's speech is in parentheses.

4. A carat indicates an incomplete word.

Understanding the Article

1. The section titled *Previous Research* provides the literature review. What questions has previous research addressed? According to the authors, what issues need further research? In what important way does the research reported in this study differ from the previous research cited?

2. The background section describes the ongoing research project of which this study was a part. Who are the subjects of the larger study? What were the general findings of the larger study that led the authors to undertake the present study?

3. What specific research questions do the authors want to address in the present study? Who are the subjects of this study?

4. The data used in the present study were collected as part of the larger study but reanalyzed for this study. These data were of two different types: data from classroom observation and data from an analysis of learner language. How were the classroom data collected and analyzed? (What is the COLT scheme? Is this a quantitative or a qualitative approach to the data?)

5. What were the results of the data analysis?

6. As described in the Background section, for the analysis of learner language the researchers selected four grammatical

features that were known to cause difficulty for speakers of French learning English. What were these four grammatical features? How were the learner language data collected? What were the results of the data analysis for each of the features?

7. Look back at the specific research question(s) identified in the *Background* section of the study. Are there specific answers to these questions in the Conclusions section? If so, what are they?

Reflecting on Wider Issues

1. What is the difference between *focus on form* and *focus on forms?*

2. Some researchers and methodologists (such as Stephen Krashen) claim that formal instruction in second language acquisition is of little use, whereas others (such as Michael Long) claim that instruction may be essential in order for the language learner to acquire some of the grammatical structures of the target language. To what extent do you think this debate is clouded by different conceptions of what is meant by *formal instruction?* How do you think the concept should be defined?

Going Beyond the Article

For a review of research on the effects of instruction (covering research through 1987), read Long (1988), "Instructed interlanguage development" in *Issues in Second Language Acquisition,* L. Beebe, (Ed.), (New York: Newbury House). In a more recent article, Lightbown and Spada (1993) investigate the role of instruction in the development of interrogatives ("Instruction and the development of questions in L2 classrooms," *Studies in Second Language Acquisition, 15,* 205–224). You might also be interested in recent research on the effect of focus-on-form on English speakers' acquisition of Spanish. Read, for example, VanPatten (1990), "Attending to form and content in the input: An experiment in consciousness" (*Studies in Second Language Acquisition, 12,* 287–301); or VanPatten and Cadierno (1993), "Explicit instruction and input processing" (*Studies in Second Language Acquisition, 15,* 225–243).

UNIT VII

COMMUNICATIVE COMPETENCE

13

LEARNING TO COMMUNICATE IN THE CLASSROOM
A Study of Two Language Learners' Requests

Rod Ellis
Temple University Japan

Previewing the Article

Research on the acquisition of communicative functions, although sometimes difficult to carry out, has contributed considerably to our understanding of the development of communicative competence. In this study, Rod Ellis carries out an ethnographic study of two child second language learners in their acquisition of requesting functions.

Before you read the article, remind yourself of what language *functions* are, and how the potentially hundreds of functions are a part of what is commonly called communicative competence. Then, answer the following questions:

1. What is the purpose of the study?
2. What are the research questions?
3. What kinds of data are reported and how does the author analyze them?

Reprinted from *Studies in Second Language Acquisition, 14*:1–23, 1992.

It is now generally accepted that second language (L2) acquisition can take place as a result of learning how to communicate in the L2. It is less clear, however, whether the kind of communication that occurs in a classroom is sufficient to ensure development of full target language competence. This essay examines the extent to which the opportunities for communication in an English as a Second Language (ESL) classroom result in the acquisition of one particular illocutionary act—requests. A total of 410 requests produced by two child learners over 15–21 months were examined. The results suggest that although considerable development took place over this period, both learners failed to develop either the full range of request types or a broad linguistic repertoire for performing those types that they did acquire. The learners also failed to develop the sociolinguistic competence needed to vary their choice of request to take account of different addressees. One explanation for these results is that although the classroom context fostered interpersonal and expressive needs in the two learners, it did not provide the conditions for real sociolinguistic needs.

This article will investigate the relationship between the opportunities for production that arise in a classroom setting and the development of one specific illocutionary act—requests—in the speech of two second language (L2) learners. In so doing it seeks to contribute to our growing understanding of how and to what extent interaction in the classroom shapes the process of L2 acquisition.

Classroom Communication and L2 Acquisition

The view that communication serves as one of the primary ways in which learners obtain data with which to construct their interlanguages is now well established (cf. Hatch, 1978; Van Lier, 1988). In addition, Allwright (1984) has argued that interaction is "the fundamental fact of pedagogy" and that "successful pedagogy" involves the successful management of classroom interaction" (p. 156). Much of the work to date, however, has focused on the extent to which the classroom provides opportunities for negotiating comprehensible input (Long, 1983; Pica, 1987). The focus in this article is on the opportunities for *production* that occur in an L2 classroom.

Swain (1985) has argued that successful language learning needs more than comprehensible input. She suggested that the acquisition of higher levels of grammatical competence is dependent on opportunities for "pushed output" (i.e., production that is characterized by precision, coherence, and appropriateness). Classroom data collected from Canadian immersion classrooms (which, in comparison to other types of language classrooms, might be expected to provide ample opportunities for pushed output) indicate that little extended learner talk occurs (cf. Allen, Swain, Harley, & Cummins, 1990). In addition, as often noted, the prevalence of three-phase (initiate-respond-feedback) exchanges in classroom discourse (Sinclair & Coulthard, 1975) restricts learners to the performance of a relatively narrow range of speech acts associated with the responding role assigned to them. This, in turn, may limit the development of a full sociolinguistic competence and the extended linguistic repertoire that this requires.

The nature of the output that learners produce in the classroom may be influenced by a number of factors, one of which is the interactional goal. Ellis (1984) distinguished three types of interactional goals—core goals (i.e., goals concerning explicit pedagogic aims), framework goals (i.e., goals relating to the organization of classroom activity), and social goals (i.e., goals linked to the use of language for purposes of socializing). He illustrated the typical kinds of interaction that arose in communication centered around each type of goal in a beginner ESL classroom and speculated how these may have contributed to the learners' interlanguage development. He argued that interactions centering around framework goals may be especially effective in promoting acquisition in the early stages of L2 acquisition—providing, of course, that English serves not only as the *target* of instruction but also as the *means* for managing lessons. Framework goals afford learners opportunities for the production of a range of illocutionary acts that they might not need to perform in interactions centering on core goals. Mitchell (1988) found that even in foreign language classrooms (where all the learners shared the same first language), extensive use of the L2 for classroom management by the teacher proved feasible, although special efforts were needed to ensure that pupils also used the L2 for this purpose. Although Mitchell did not provide any evidence to suggest that the use of the L2 for management purposes contributed to acquisition, it is clearly seen as a significant feature of communicative language teaching, which, in turn, is seen as a means of promoting effective language learning.

Another factor influencing output is the classroom setting. Cathcart (1986) investigated the language used in different classroom settings (recess, free play, seatwork, interview and storytelling, playhouse, and ESL introduction) by eight Spanish-speaking children in an English-Spanish bilingual class. She found that both the quantity and the type of illocutionary acts performed by the children varied according to setting. The playhouse elicited by far the most acts, including some (e.g., describe, label object, label action, and express intent) not observed in any other setting. However, some illocutionary acts that occurred in other settings (e.g., refusing and giving information) did not occur in the playhouse. Overall, Cathcart found that four situational variables affected language behavior—conversational control, the interlocutors, the task stage, and the task type.

It should be noted, however, that there have been few attempts to establish a direct relationship between classroom communication and the acquisition of new linguistic features. The studies referred to above classify, describe, and illustrate types of classroom interaction and then, on the basis of a theoretic view of language acquisition or language pedagogy, speculate how communication in the classroom contributes to interlanguage development. Recent studies that have attempted to establish a direct relationship have not been very successful. Day (1984) found no relationship between learner participation in the classroom and gains in learner proficiency. Slimani (1987) also failed to find any relationship between learner production and learner uptake (i.e., items that learners reported having learned after a lesson was over).

One approach that may prove profitable for exploring how classroom communication affects acquisition is the detailed study of specific illocutionary acts that learners perform in different kinds of interaction. McNamara (1973) has proposed that the primary motivation for learning an L2 derives from the desire that learners have to participate in acts of communication and from the success that they experience. The aim of this approach, then, is to demonstrate to what extent the classroom affords opportunities for learners to perform a given illocutionary act and whether these opportunities motivate the acquisition of the full range of linguistic exponents associated with the performance of this act in native speaker speech.

Illocutionary Acts and L2 Acquisition Research

A speech act has an illocutionary force, which can be glossed as an attempt to use words in order to perform an interpersonal function. Taxonomies of illocutionary acts (e.g., Searle, 1976) have been based on a classification of the various communicative functions that occur in speech (and, to a lesser extent, in writing). As Levinson (1981) and Flowerdew (1990) have pointed out, there are a number of problems with speech act theory (such as the question of how many illocutions there are in any single language and how the illocutionary force of a speech act comes to be communicated). Research into the use and acquisition of L2 English has focused on a fairly narrow set of illocutions (e.g., compliments, apologies, requests, refusals, complaints, and thanking), which are "relatively well defined" (De Beaugrande & Dressler, 1981, p. 117) in the sense that they are associated with a set of specifiable linguistic exponents. Wolfson (1983), for instance, reports that 80% of the American English compliments that she collected were realized by three easily identifiable sentence patterns.

Much of the research into the performance of L2 illocutionary acts has been cross-sectional in nature and has made use of elicited rather than naturally occurring data. The Cross-Cultural Speech Act Realization Project (CCSARP; Blum-Kulka, House, & Kasper, 1989a) is a good example of such research. This project entailed the collection of data from both native and nonnative speakers of a variety of languages by means of a discourse completion test. This consisted of descriptions of different situations calling for two illocutionary acts, carefully selected to reflect different factors (such as the social distance between the interactants and the degree of imposition on the addressee) that were considered likely to affect linguistic choice. The subjects were given an incomplete dialogue which they were asked to complete in writing. In other studies oral data have been collected by means of role-play activities (cf. Kasper & Dahl, 1991, for a review of such studies). These elicited data have provided a number of insights relating to cross-linguistic differences in the performance of illocutionary acts and also to the nature of their realization in learners' interlanguages. However, there is some uncertainty as to whether elicited data reflect natural language use (cf. Wolfson, Marmor, & Jones, 1989). Moreover, with only a few exceptions (e.g., Blum-Kulka & Olshtain, 1986), the studies to date have not examined how L2 speech act performance changes over time with the result that, although information is available about the use of speech acts in an L2, little is known about their acquisition.

Research Questions

The study reported below seeks to investigate how one illocutionary act—requests—was performed by two L2 learners in a classroom context over a period of 2 years. It addresses the following general questions:

1. What opportunities for performing requests did the classroom afford the two learners?

2. What range of linguistic devices did the learners use to perform the requests and how did these change over time?

3. To what extent did the learners succeed in learning to perform different request realization strategies and their linguistic exponents?

It is hoped that answering these questions will contribute to our understanding of the relationship between classroom communication and L2 acquisition.

Requests and the L2 Learner

Searle (1976) distinguished five general classes of speech acts, one of which is *directives.* This consists of all those specific acts whose function is to get the hearer to do something, including requests for information, goods and services, and permission. The focus of this study is on one specific illocutionary act—requests (i.e., attempts on the part of the speaker to get the hearer to perform some kind of action or cessation of action). This definition is intended to exclude requests for information and permission.

Requests, so defined, have a number of general characteristics:

1. They often serve an initiating function in discourse. In this, they differ from many of the other illocutionary acts that learners may be required to perform in the responding role they are often assigned in the classroom.

2. They can be performed in a single turn, for example:

> TEACHER: Read your book, Asiz.

or over more than one turn, in which case there may be a preparatory act or prerequest:

> TEACHER: Have you finished your work?
>
> PUPIL: Yes.
>
> TEACHER: Read your book then.

3. They can be realized linguistically in a variety of ways. Blum-Kulka, House, and Kasper (1989b) identified three dimensions of request modification:

    a.   directness level,

    b.   internal modification of the request act, and

    c.   external modification of the request act.

Examples of these different kinds of modification are given later. A request act can also be realized by means of a declarative, interrogative, or imperative sentence.

4. They can be encoded from the speaker's perspective, the hearer's perspective, or an impersonal perspective.

5. A request act may also be supported by some additional speech act designed to prepare for the request itself, give a reason or justification for the request, minimize the degree of imposition, and so forth.

6. The choice of linguistic realization depends on a variety of social factors to do with the relationship between the speaker and the addressee and the perceived degree of imposition that a particular request makes on the hearer (cf. Brown & Levinson, 1978; Ervin-Tripp, 1976). Speakers can elect to go baldly on record (i.e, perform the request with a high risk of loss of face), use a positive politeness strategy (i.e., emphasize the commonality of the speaker and the hearer), or use a negative politeness strategy (i.e., show deference to the hearer by respecting his or her right to be free of imposition).

7. Although the main categories of requests can be found in different languages, there are cross-linguistic differences relating to the preferred form of a request in the same situation (cf. Blum-Kulka et al., 1989b). Cross-linguistic differences are also evident in other linguistic features of requests (e.g., use of modification devices).

It is clear from this summary of the main features of requests, that the target-like performance of this particular illocutionary act calls for considerable linguistic and sociolinguistic knowledge on the part of the learner. The learner needs to develop a range of linguistic devices and also to learn how to use these in socially appropriate ways. Furthermore, English requests may differ in a number of ways from the learner's first language (L1) requests.

There have been a number of studies that have investigated how L2 learners perform requests. Most of them have been cross-sectional. Tanaka (1988) compared the English requests produced by Japanese and Australian students in a role-play task. She analyzed the request exchanges that took place into five parts (opening the conversation, notice and small talk, the request, thanking, and closing), and found a number of differences between the native and nonnative speakers in each part. For example, in the request part she found that the Japanese learners did not give very concrete reasons for their requests, did not show the same degree of uncertainty regarding whether the conditions for a request were met, and were less indirect and tentative. Thus, whereas the Australians were likely to say "Do you think I could have . . . ?" when requesting a book from a lecturer, the Japanese used "Can I . . . ?"

The CCSARP provides a wealth of information about how L2 learners with different language backgrounds perform requests. Blum-Kulka et al. (1989b) summarized the main findings of a number of separate studies that have investigated elicited requests produced primarily by advanced L2 learners. The studies showed that these learners' requests display a number of nontargetlike features. For example, their requests are verbose in comparison to those of native speakers as a result of more supportive moves such as lengthy explanations and justifications. House and Kasper (1987) reported that Danish and German learners of English opt for higher levels of directness in their requests than native speakers and use fewer mitigating devices such as syntactic downgraders. Faerch and Kasper (1989) reported that Danish learners of L2 English tend to use lexical rather than syntactic mitigating devices. Their requests display more double markings than native speakers (e.g., *Could* you *possibly* present your paper this week?), which Faerch and Kasper suggested is the result of a "playing it safe" strategy. In general, external modification of the request is preferred to internal modification. However, the learners in these studies did tend to avoid the transfer of language-specific structures. These studies need to be treated circumspectly, as the results may reflect in part the way in which the data were collected. In addition, they do not provide any information about how learners at different stages of interlanguage development perform requests.

Unfortunately, there have been few longitudinal studies. In an interesting study of a Japanese painter, Wes, Schmidt (1983) found evidence of substantial development in Wes's ability to perform requests and other directives over a 3-year period. Initially, Wes relied on a small set of formulas (e.g., "Can I have a . . . ?"). He used V-ing in place of the imperative form and tended to rely heavily on lexical clues such as "please." He also made substantial use of hints in ways that could not always be interpreted by native speakers. However, "by the end of the period, gross errors in the performance of directives had largely been eliminated" (p. 154). Wes could use request formulas productively, no longer used V-ing, increased the range of request patterns (e.g., "Let's . . ." and "Shall we . . .?") at his disposal, and, in general, showed more elaboration in his requesting behavior. However, Wes was still limited in his ability to vary the use of directive type in accordance with the situation and also sometimes extended a particular pattern (e.g., "Can I . . . ?") in inappropriate ways.

Little is known about how L2 learners perform requests in a classroom. Cathcart (1986), in the cross-sectional study already referred to, reported on the use of control acts (i.e., calls for attention, requests for objects, and requests for actions) performed by her learners. She found that two factors influenced the length and complexity of their requests: task and interlocutors. Requests directed at adults tended to be longer and more complex than those directed at other children. Requests to other pupils also increased in length and complexity in tasks with a joint goal.

The choice of requests as a subject for study appears justified on a number of fronts. First, requests call for considerable linguistic expertise. Second, they are highly sensitive to situational and cultural factors. Third, even advanced learners experience some difficulty in performing requests. Fourth, there is some evidence to suggest that the acquisition of requests follows a developmental path.

The Study

Subjects

The subjects were two boys, aged 10 and 11 years. Both were almost complete beginners in English. "J" had arrived in London a few months before the study started and could understand a few simple context-embedded instructions but was unable to speak (except for "yes" and "no") when the study started. "R" had been in London only a few days and could neither understand nor speak English.

J was literate in his mother tongue (Portuguese) and was familiar with the "rules of speaking" of the classroom. He was a lively, adventurous boy, a confident learner who enjoyed games but who was also capable of serious, independent work. He used English most of the time as, except for one short period, there was no other Portuguese speaker in his class.

R was not literate in his first language (Punjabi) or Urdu, having had very little formal schooling in Pakistan. Initially, he was withdrawn and very dependent on his older sister, who had arrived in England at the same time and who sat next to him in class. He used his first language extensively in the classroom. As R became familiar with classroom tasks, he grew more confident and independent although he continued to struggle to carry out even simple tasks.

The School and Classroom Settings

Both learners were placed in a Language Unit designed to provide initial instruction in English as a preparation for transfer to local secondary schools. J stayed full-time for three school terms (i.e., a full school year—from September to July) and part-time for a fourth term. R arrived in November, halfway through the school term, and remained at the unit on a full-time basis for the duration of the study (i.e., six school terms). The two learners joined different classes of recent arrivals, all of whom were relative beginners in English. Except for the staff of the unit, there were no native speakers of English in the school setting. The other learners, including those in J's and R's classes, were culturally and linguistically very varied, including children from Asia, Africa, Europe, and South America.

The language aims of the unit were to develop basic interpersonal communication skills in English and then the proficiency to use English for studying school subjects. The instructions did not follow a prepared syllabus—teachers were free to decide on their own approach and to choose their own teaching-learning activities. Teachers did not usually stay with a class for more than a term. J and R, therefore, experienced both a variety of teachers and a variety of teaching styles. Some of the lessons consisted of formal language instruction directed at specific linguistic points (grammar and vocabulary), although no attempt was made to teach specific language functions such as requests. Many of the lessons were informal in nature, and there were various out-of-class activities—sports, visits to places of interest, and assemblies—all conducted in English. The school and classroom environments, then, were varied—the children interacted as much among themselves as they did with the teacher. The learners were engaged in activities along the full range of the analytic-experiential continuum (Stern, 1990). Moreover, English served not only as the pedagogic target but also as the means for conducting the day-by-day business of the classroom—giving and checking instructions, making arrangements, dealing with breaches of discipline, socializing, and so forth.

The Data Base

The data for this study were obtained as part of the longitudinal study of the sequence of acquisition followed by classroom learners (cf. Ellis, 1982). The learners' classrooms were visited regularly—for four school terms in the case of J and for six in the Case of R—approximately once every 2 weeks to begin with and more frequently later.

The role of the researcher changed during the course of the study. Initially he functioned as a nonparticipant observer but subsequently he became a participant in many of the classroom activities. It is not clear to what extent the researcher's presence changed the behavior of the learners, but judging from reports from their various teachers, it had little effect.

Data were collected primarily by means of a paper-and-pencil record of the utterances that the learners produced. The researcher sat close to each learner and wrote down everything that he said, numbering each turn and adding as much contextual information as possible. This method proved the only way to obtain an accurate record of the learners' speech in a classroom that was often very noisy. Many lessons were audiorecorded, and the recordings were used to check the accuracy of the paper-and-pencil records and also to fill out the discourse context of each utterance. The data collection methods may have had a contaminating effect, but given the regularity of the visits and the rapidity with which the learners appeared to adjust to the researcher, this seems unlikely.

For the purposes of this study, all turns that included a request produced by each learner were identified. A *turn* consisted of a continuous stretch of speech bounded on either side (and sometimes overlapping with) turns produced by other speakers. A *request* consisted of a speech act whose illocutionary purpose was to ask another person to perform some nonverbal action. Usually a turn contained a single request:

> show me *ruler* on the board (R was asking the researcher to show him the word *ruler* on the chalk board).

In some cases, however, several sequentially connected requests occurred within the same turn:

> put it back inside, sir can you put it here please and take little one (R wanted the researcher to replace a piece of a jigsaw puzzle in the box and choose another, smaller piece).

There were also a few occasions when a turn was more or less continuous and overlapping with other pupils' or the teacher's turns and a whole string of requests could occur.

Analysis

The total number of request turns containing one or more request(s) produced by each learner in each term was computed. The following analyses, based on the request turn as a discourse unit, were then carried out.

A. FORMAL COMPLEXITY

    1. Propositional completeness

        a. – verb:

> sir sir sir pencil (the teacher had walked off with R's pencil and he wanted it back).

b. + verb:

give me my paper (R wanted the teacher to give him back his piece of paper).

2. Modification: The CCSARP (cf. Blum-Kulka et al., 1989b) identified a number of ways in which the *head act* of a request can be modified. The following categories represent a simplification of their scheme:

a. Internal (i.e., part of the head act)

i. Downgrade (i.e., attempts to mitigate the force of the request by means of either a syntactic or lexical modifier such as *please*)

ii. Upgrade (i.e., attempts to increase the force of the request, e.g., by repetition)

b. External (i.e., move before or after the head act)

i. Downgrade (e.g., by supplying a reason for the request)

ii. Upgrade (e.g., by adding an insult)

B. LEVEL OF DIRECTNESS: The CCSARP identifies the following types of requests, according to their level of directness:

1. Direct

a. Mood derivable (i.e., the grammatical mood of the verb signals the illocutionary force):

You shut up (R addressing another pupil).

b. Performative (i.e., the illocutionary force is explicitly named):

I am telling you to shut up.

c. Hedged performative (i.e., the naming of the illocutionary force is modified by hedging expressions):

I would like to ask you to shut up.

d. Locution derivable (i.e., the illocutionary force is derivable directly from the semantic content of the request):

I want it (R wanted the teacher to give him the big piece of paper she had).

2. Conventionally indirect

a. Suggestory formulas (i.e., a suggestion to do the action):

Come, let's play a game (J wanted the teacher to play a game).

b. Query preparatory (i.e., reference to preparatory conditions such as ability or willingness):

Can you draw it? (R wanted the teacher to draw a car for him).

   3.   Nonconventionally indirect

      a.   Strong hint (i.e., partial reference to the object or element needed for implementation of the act):

This paper is not very good to color blue (The teacher issued a different color).

      b.   Mild hint (i.e., no reference to the request proper)

C. PERSPECTIVE: Blum-Kulka et al. (1989b) distinguished requests according to whether they emphasize the role of:

   1.   speaker (e.g., can I have my ruler back please?),

   2.   hearer (e.g., miss can you write?),

   3.   both (i.e., inclusive, e.g., come let's play a game), and

   4.   neither (e.g., it would be nice to play a game).

D. CONTEXT

   1.   Addressee

      a.   adult (i.e., teacher or researcher)

      b.   another pupil

   2.   Interactive goal (cf. Ellis, 1984, p. 101)

      a.   core (i.e., the request turn occurred as part of the pedagogic discourse)

      b.   framework (i.e., the request turn occurred as part of that discourse directed at the management of classroom behavior)

      c.   social (i.e., the request turn occurred within discourse concerned with the social relations)

E. MOOD: A request turn can be:

   1.   Positive (i.e., the speaker requires the hearer to perform an action)

   2.   Negative (i.e., the speaker requires the hearer to desist from performing an action by using either a formal negative device [e.g., *don't*] or a lexical verb [e.g., *stop*])

F. PURPOSE: The learners' request turns had a variety of purposes, reflecting the different *objects* of their requests.

   1.   Goods:

Can I have one yellow book please (J wanted a new book from the teacher).

   2.   Services:

Sharpening please (J gave the teacher his pencil which he wanted sharpened).

3. Attention:

   Sir sir excuse me sir (J wanted the teacher to attend to him).

4. Pedagogic activity:

   Come let's play a game (J wanted the teacher to play a preposition game that they had played yesterday).

5. Action (i.e., where the speaker requests the hearer to perform an action or desist from performing an action):

   Look and be quiet and shut up (J wanted the other pupils to behave in a manner conducive to playing word bingo).

To some extent, (5) functions as a miscellaneous category as it includes all request turns that were not coded (1) to (4). However, it can be distinguished from the other categories in that the main force of a request belonging to this category is placed on the performance of the action itself rather than on the object of the action.

Results

The data for J consist of 108 request turns covering approximately 16 months of observation. For R there are 302 request turns produced in about 21 months.[1]

Formal Complexity: Propositional Completeness

Table 1 shows the number of request utterances with and without verbs for both learners. J produced a number of verbless requests in term 1, but the majority contained a verb right from the beginning of the study. R's requests, however, were initially all verbless, consisting of only an indicator of need:

sir (R: term 1—R wanted the teacher to put a staple in his card).

Shortly afterwards, R began to encode the object of the request, but his requests remained verbless:

big circle (R: term 1—R needed a cutout of a big circle).

In the case of both learners, propositionally complete requests seemed formulaic to begin with:

leave it, leave it (J: term 1—J wanted another pupil to stop trying to take his card);

---

[1]The considerable difference in the number of requests produced by the two learners is in part the result of data collection procedures and in part a reflection of their different communication styles in the classroom. R was observed somewhat more frequently than J. However, the average number of requests per observation was also greater for R, reflecting the difficulty that he experienced in performing many classroom tasks. Many of his requests related to actions involved in getting started on and staying with a task.

TABLE I. Formal Complexity

LEARNER	TERM	Propositional Completeness		Modification			
				Internal		External	
		− VERB	+ VERB	DOWNGRADE	UPGRADE	DOWNGRADE	UPGRADE
J	1	13	38	3	3	1	0
	2	5	12	0	0	1	1
	3	4	16	2	0	0	0
	4	4	16	0	0	0	0
	Totals	26	82	5	3	2	1
R	1	8	0	0	0	0	0
	2	24	34	13	19	0	0
	3	9	45	6	4	2	0
	4	9	94	10	8	4	1
	5	0	57	2	4	3	0
	6	2	20	2	2	1	0
	Totals	52	250	33	37	10	1

give me (R: term 2—R wanted a ruler from another pupil).

However, they soon became highly productive. By the end of the second term both learners were able to use a variety of lexical verbs in their requests and increasingly also included a lexicalized object. Verbless requests never completely disappeared from the data.

There were relatively few instances of modification in J's requests (only 10%). R used more modification (27%). Both learners relied primarily on internal rather than external modification (i.e., there were few supportive moves of the request act itself). The only internal downgrader used was the lexical item *please,* while the upgraders consisted of repetition or paraphrase of the request act. The only type of supportive move used was the *grounder* (defined by Blum-Kulka et al., 1989a, as a "reason, justification or explanation of the request"). Grounders were used sparingly, however. Modification does not appear to increase over time.

Level of Directness

Table 2 shows the different types of requests according to their level of directness. The great majority of the two learners' propositionally complete requests were direct (78% in the case of J and 58% in the case of R). Mood derivable requests accounted for nearly all the direct requests. There were, in fact, no instances of obligation and want statements. Conventionally indirect requests were also used with some frequency, particularly by R (18% for J and 20% for R), Nonconventional requests hardly occurred at all, and the few instances were all strong hints (i.e., there were no weak hints).

The order of development of the main types of requests was much the same for both learners. Mood derivable requests were used first, closely followed by query preparatory requests (as formulas) with want statements appearing some time later. Obligation statements, which did not appear in J's data, were not used by R until term 4. J first used a suggestory formula in term 2.

Perspective

Table 3 provides information about the perspective of the learners' requests. Most requests (84% for J and 74% for R) emphasized the role of the hearer, reflecting the preponderance of mood derivable utterances in the corpus. As learners acquire other types of requests (i.e., query preparatory and want statements), the speaker perspective is more strongly evident in the data, although the hearer perspective continues to dominate. Very few utterances encode a joint or impersonal perspective.

Context

Table 4 provides information relating to the context of the two learners' request turns. Both learners addressed far more requests at adults (the teacher

TABLE 2. Level of Directness

LEARNER	TERM	Direct			Conventionally Indirect		Non-conventionally Indirect
		MOOD DERIVABLE	OBLIGATION STATEMENTS	WANT STATEMENTS	SUGGESTORY FORMULAS	QUERY PREPARATORY	STRONG HINTS
J	1	37	0	0	0	1	0
	2	10	0	0	1	1	0
	3	8	0	1	1	6	0
	4	9	0	1	0	5	1
	Totals	64	0	2	2	13	1
R	1	0	0	0	0	0	0
	2	22	0	1	0	9	2
	3	35	0	3	0	4	3
	4	57	2	5	0	30	0
	5	18	8	3	0	25	3
	6	14	0	0	0	5	1
	Totals	146	10	12	0	73	9

TABLE 3.   Perspective

LEARNER	TERM	SPEAKER	HEARER	BOTH	NEITHER
J	1	1	37	0	0
	2	1	10	1	0
	3	4	12	0	0
	4	6	13	0	1
	Totals	12	72	1	1
R	1	0	0	0	0
	2	10	22	0	2
	3	7	37	1	0
	4	20	73	0	1
	5	19	37	1	0
	6	5	20	0	0
	Totals	61	189	2	3

Note: Only propositionally complex utterances have been coded for perspective.

TABLE 4.   The Context of Requests

LEARNER	TERM	Addressee		Interactive Goal		
		ADULT	PUPIL	CORE	FRAMEWORK	SOCIAL
J	1	28	23	6	43	2
	2	12	5	1	12	4
	3	10	10	0	20	20
	4	13	7	1	17	2
R	1	8	0	0	8	0
	2	37	21	1	43	14
	3	37	17	0	46	9
	4	77	26	4	77	22
	5	38	19	2	39	16
	6	18	4	0	19	3

and the researcher) than they did at other pupils. The vast majority of their requests occurred in interactions centering on framework goals, primarily the organization and management of classroom activities. Both learners also used requests in social interactions in the classroom (e.g., in order to protect their rights and possessions in the face of threats to these from other pupils). Interestingly, very few requests were uttered in core interactions, where the predominant class of speech act was the *representative,* which was generally used in response to a teacher question.

Native speaker requests have been shown to be sensitive to addressee factors (cf., Blum-Kulka & House, 1989; Ervin-Tripp, 1976). To test whether the requests produced by the two children varied according to whether they were speaking to an adult (i.e., the teacher or the researcher) or another pupil, the requests were classified as either (a) simple (i.e., a request without a verb or one with a verb but without any mitigating device such as *please,*) or (b) elaborated (i.e., a request containing a verb and a mitigating device or an indirect request). The results are shown in Table 5. Initially only simple requests occur; these are used with both adult and pupil addressees. When elaborate requests appear they are used more or less indiscriminately, and although they gradually come to be used more frequently with adult than pupil addressees, neither learner displays much sensitivity to his addressee.

TABLE 5.   Distribution of Requests According to Addressee

LEARNER	TERM	Adult		Pupil	
		SIMPLE	ELABORATE	SIMPLE	ELABORATE
J	1	26	2	22	1
	2	10	2	4	1
	3	6	4	6	4
	4	7	6	6	1
	Totals	49	14	38	7
R	1	8	0	0	0
	2	22	15	18	3
	3	33	14	13	4
	4	53	24	18	8
	5	17	21	10	9
	6	10	8	3	1
	Totals	143	82	62	25

Mood

Table 6 shows the mood of the learners' requests. The majority were positive, but there were also a substantial number of negative requests. Early negative requests made use of lexical rather than grammatical markers of negativity:

Be quiet (term 1—J wanted the other pupils to keep quiet so that the teacher could start the game).

Negative requests with *no + verb* or *don't + verb* appeared later:

Don't touch (term 3—R was telling another pupil to leave the stapler alone);

TABLE 6.   The Mood of the Requests

LEARNER	TERM	POSITIVE	NEGATIVE
J	1	39	12
	2	14	3
	3	17	3
	4	18	2
	Total	88	20
R	1	8	0
	2	48	10
	3	51	3
	4	87	16
	5	50	7
	6	19	3
	Total	263	39

Sir don't sit in that one chair (term 2—J was warning the teacher not to sit in a chair that was dirty).

As the above examples illustrate, negative requests were generally addressed to other pupils rather than an adult. Table 7 shows the overall distribution of negative requests according to addressee. To begin with, both learners directed

TABLE 7.   The Distribution of Negative Requests According to Addressee

LEARNER	TERM	Addressee	
		ADULT	PUPIL
J	1	0	12
	2	1	2
	3	0	3
	4	1	1
	Totals	2	18
R	1	0	0
	2	0	11
	3	1	2
	4	5	12
	5	3	5
	6	1	2
	Totals	7	32

all their negative requests at pupils. Later, however, they addressed some negative requests to adults but continued to direct the majority at other pupils.

Purpose

Table 8 shows the use of requests for different purposes. J used them throughout all four terms primarily to request various actions to do with such objects as paper, pencils, pens, and books, and to attract the teacher's attention.

TABLE 8.   The Purpose of the Requests

LEARNER	TERM	Purpose				
		GOODS	SERVICES	ACTIONS	ATTENTION	ACTIVITY
J	1	10	1	27	12	1
	2	0	0	12	3	2
	3	6	0	10	3	1
	4	3	1	11	4	1
	Totals	19	2	60	22	5
R	1	7	0	1	0	0
	2	29	0	20	6	3
	3	19	1	20	9	6
	4	29	16	51	3	4
	5	22	12	22	1	0
	6	9	3	7	3	0
	Totals	115	32	121	22	12

All of R's early requests were aimed at obtaining goods, and this purpose continued to account for a large proportion of R's total requests right up to the end of term 6. Increasingly, however, R used requests for other purposes, in particular for general actions and, to a lesser extent, to obtain services and to gain the teacher's attention.

To provide an indication of what kind of development takes place in relation to purpose, an analysis of requests for goods was undertaken. Initially, the requests are verbless (see examples under Formal Complexity). As the learners' linguistic ability develops, they produce requests for goods with verbs, first using imperatives:

Give me a paper (J: term 1—the teacher was giving out pieces of paper);

Give me (R: term 1—wanted another pupil to give him his ruler);

and shortly afterward with the "Can I have . . . ?" formula. This formula is very frequent in the data, accounting for the great majority of query preparatory requests. Alternative ways of requesting goods do not appear until much later.

J begins to use the colloquial "You got a...?" formula with other pupils in term 3:

> You got a rubber?

and in term 4 he employs a strong hint to obtain goods from the teacher:

> This paper is not very good to color blue.

but is otherwise restricted to imperatives and "Can I have . . . ?" R proves more versatile in his linguistic choice, and want statements appear in term 3:

> Miss I want (i.e., the stapler).

and from that point on are used fairly productively. In term 4 "Have you got . . . ?" appears:

> Tasleem, have you got glue?

while from term 5 onwards, query preparatory requests for goods with *can* employ a range of lexical verbs:

> Can I take book with me?
>
> Can you pass me my pencil?

suggesting that the "Can I have . . . ?" formula has been finally analyzed. Neither learner uses the more polite forms for requesting goods (e.g., "Could I have . . . ?" or "Would you mind . . . ?"), although R does use *could* on a few occasions to request services from term 5 onwards.

Discussion

The discussion of the two learners' requests will consider the three general research questions that motivated the study (see Research Questions). There is clear evidence to suggest that the particular classroom setting in which the two learners received instruction in English provided ample opportunity for the use of requests. Both learners performed substantial numbers of them. In fact, requests constituted one of the first productive illocutionary acts performed by both learners.

Most of the requests occurred in interactions based on framework goals and very few in interactions based on core goals. In other words, it would seem that requests were acquired largely as a result of the communicative needs that arose in the course of setting up and staying on tasks of various kinds rather than as a result of direct instruction. The learners were strongly motivated to obtain the materials they needed, gain the teacher's attention, have the teacher check their work, demand to answer a teacher's question, request a favorite classroom activity, obtain assistance from the teacher in completing a task, and so on. These kinds of communicative opportunities occurred with great regularity in the classroom because English served as the language as well as the target of instruction.

However, although the classroom setting provided plenty of occasions for the use of requests, it appeared to restrict the kind of request typically produced. First, the purposes of the learners' requests were restricted to asking for a fairly small set of classroom goods (books, pencils, colors, etc.) and to the performance of a predictable set of actions (sitting, standing, moving, showing, removing things, starting, stopping, keeping quiet, helping, etc.). In such cases, the rights of the speaker were well established and generally recognized by the interactants. Thus, there was little opportunity to perform requests that placed a heavy imposition on the addressee. Second, most of the requests were addressed to a familiar, friendly adult (the teacher or researcher). There was no opportunity to address a nonintimate or socially distant hearer. Wolfson (1988) has pointed out that the performance of illocutionary acts such as compliments, invitations, partings, refusals, and expressions of disapproval appears to be strongly influenced by whether there is an established framework of social contact. In general, greater negotiation, as evident in longer utterances and more frequent use of preparatory acts, is required with nonintimates. There is every reason to believe that the same holds true for requests. The classroom context investigated in this study did not afford opportunities for the kind of elaborated request that is needed when the speakers' relationships are not so fixed. The sheer routineness of classroom business may have provided a context for the acquisition of *basic* request forms but may not have encouraged the acquisition of more *elaborate* forms. It should be noted that even when learners have opportunities to work together in groups there is little pressure to develop sociolinguistic competence (cf. Porter, 1986).

The second research question concerned the nature of the linguistic devices that the learners use to perform requests and how these change over time. The results show that the majority of the two learners' requests were propositionally complete (i.e., contained a verb). There does not appear to be any obvious need for the use of complete requests in the classroom setting. Both "Pencil, please" and "Can I have a pencil please?" will serve the speaker equally well. Indeed, both learners were able to successfully convey their requests through propositionally reduced directives from the beginning of the study. Clearly, then, something other than communicative necessity motivated the use of complete requests.

Both learners learned to use a variety of formal devices to perform requests. Both J and R used mood derivable requests, want statements, query preparatory requests, and strong hints. In addition, J used the occasional suggestory formula and R, a few obligation statements. There is also evidence that the learners succeeded in acquiring a range of linguistic devices to perform the different types of requests. Thus, query preparatory requests were realized by the formulas, "Can I have . . . ?" "Can I + verb . . . ?" "Can you + verb . . . ?" and "Could you . . . ?" Also, both learners performed negative as well as positive requests. The vast majority of the two learners' requests were well formed, although this may reflect the formulaic nature of many of them.

There is clear evidence of development progression in the two learners:

1. Both learners produced fewer instances of verbless requests as time passed.

2. Both learners systematically extended the range of request types.

3. Whereas nearly all early requests were encoded according to the hearer's perspective, a significant proportion of later requests were encoded according to the speaker's perspective.

4. Both learners systematically extended the range of exponents of specific request types (e.g., query preparatory requests).

By the end of the study, both learners had achieved considerable competence in the use of requests.

It is important to ask, though, whether the learners succeeded in acquiring the full range of request types and forms—the third research question. The results suggest that the learners' ability to use requests is still limited in a number of ways:

1. Direct requests predominate throughout. The learners rely extensively on mood derivable requests (specifically those with imperative verbs) throughout the period of study. This contrasts with the results reported by the CCSARP, which showed that both native speakers of English and advanced L2 learners show a preference for indirect request forms (query preparatory) in a variety of situations (Blum-Kulka et al., 1989b).

2. There are very few examples of nonconventional requests. Hints, when they are used, are of the strong rather than weak kind, but this may also be a feature of requests in naturalistic settings (cf. Weizman, 1989).

3. Certain types of requests (performatives and hedged performatives) do not occur in the data at all, but again these may also be rare in naturalistic settings.

4. The range of formal devices used by the two learners is rather limited, and many of their requests are formulaic. Query preparatory requests are realized primarily by means of "Can I have . . . ?" Mood derivable requests make use of a fairly restricted set of lexical verbs.

5. The great majority of the directives (even at the end of the study) are simple—there is little attempt at either internal or external modification. In addition, the modifying devices used are restricted (e.g., *please,* the use of repetition, and a few grounders). Again this

contrasts with the results reported in the CCSARP (cf. Faerch & Kasper, 1989), which showed that the requests elicited from advanced adult L2 learners displayed considerable modification.

6.   The learners do not appear to systematically vary their use of request types or forms according to addressee (with the exception of negative directives, which are addressed primarily to pupils). There is very little evidence to suggest that the two learners have mastered the encoding of the various politeness strategies described by Brown and Levinson (1978). In general, the two learners fail to demonstrate that they have developed a targetlike sociolinguistic competence.

There are two possible explanations for these developmental limitations. One is that the features listed above are late-acquired and that the two learners did not reach the stage of development where they emerge. Such an explanation may account in part for the relative simplicity of the learners' requests, but it is not entirely convincing. Late acquisition cannot offer an adequate explanation for the continued predominance of direct request types throughout the study, as both learners developed the means for realizing indirect types early on. The more likely explanation rests in the nature of the communicative setting. The classroom constitutes an environment where the interactants achieve great familiarity with each other, removing the need for the kind of careful face-work that results in the use of indirect request types and extensive modification. Moreover, because many of the requests relate to routine events, the level of imposition on the addressee is minimized. In other words, there simply was no need to go much further than the two learners went. Several studies (Faerch & Kasper, 1989; Rintell & Mitchell, 1989) have noted that L2 learners' requests are typically verbose—Faerch and Kasper go so far as to suggest that learners follow a "the more the better" principle when they make requests. The requests produced by R and J are, however, typically lean and very much to the point, a reflection, perhaps, of the importance of getting a speech act over and done with in a setting in which there were often many speakers bidding for the floor at any one time.

Conclusion

The classroom context in which J and R learned English afforded ample opportunities for natural language use. It enabled J and R to develop a basic ability to perform requests using target language forms. In addition, it proved sufficient to motivate the acquisition of a variety of linguistic exponents for encoding requests, thus affording the learners some degree of choice in the realization of their requests. Most of the learners' requests occurred as part of the organizational language associated with framework goals, suggesting the importance of using the target language as the medium of communication in the classroom. In organizational activity, the learners have an opportunity to perform a range of speech acts associated with negotiating the transfer of goods and services (e.g., requests, offers, promises, giving advice, apologies), whereas in pedagogic activity they are generally restricted to referential acts (e.g., stating facts, giving opinions, explaining). The opportunity to communicate a varied set of illocutionary acts may be important for successful L2 acquisition. If so, the use of the L2 for classroom management may be of crucial importance for creating an "acquisition-rich" environment.

However, the study also found that J and R failed to acquire a full range of request types and forms. It also showed that they developed only a limited ability to vary their choice of request strategy in accordance with situational factors. One explanation for this is that the developmental process was not complete. However, it may be that even with more time the classroom environment is insufficient to guarantee the development of full target language norms, possibly because the kind of "communicative need" that the learners experienced was insufficient to ensure development of the full range of request types and strategies. Three types of communicative need can be distinguished:

1. *Interpersonal need* (i.e., the learner has a felt need to perform a speech act in order to give or obtain information or goods/services),

2. *Expressive need* (i.e., the learner has a personal need to realize a speech act using different formal means—this need reflects a general desire for variety for its own sake, analogous, perhaps, with the desire to have a selection of clothes to choose from), and

3. *Sociolinguistic need* (i.e., the learner has the need to vary the use of the formal means at his or her disposal in accordance with situational factors in order to realize social meanings associated with such concepts as politeness).

J and R had a clear interpersonal need to learn how to perform requests, and they also appeared to experience an expressive need to vary the way in which they performed them. It is less certain, however, that in the classroom situation they found themselves in they recognized any definite sociolinguistic need. It may be necessary to create such a need artificially and perhaps, also, to draw learners' conscious attention to the way in which language is used to encode social meaning.

This conclusion needs to be treated with caution, however. This study has examined only two learners in one classroom setting. It has provided no data to show how the two learners might have performed in a naturalistic setting; we do not know whether the two learners had the capacity to use a fuller range of request strategies if called on to do so. The study has also provided no baseline data from native speaking children in a similar classroom context. It is difficult, therefore, to judge to what extent these two learners have or have not achieved the target levels associated with this particular context. Moreover, no information regarding the kinds of requests to which the learners were exposed in the teacher's and other pupils' input has been given. The study does suggest that the detailed study of how specific illocutionary acts are performed over time in pedagogic settings is a promising line of inquiry for investigating the relationship between classroom communication and acquisition.

References

Allen, P., Swain, M., Harley, B., & Cummins, J. (1990). Aspects of classroom treatment: Toward a more comprehensive view of second language education. In B. Harley, P. Allen, J. Cummins, & M. Swain (Eds.), *The development of bilingual proficiency* (pp. 57–81). Cambridge: Cambridge University Press.

Allwright, R. (1984). The importance of interaction in classroom language learning. *Applied Linguistics, 5,* 156–171.

Blum-Kulka, S., & House, J. (1989). Cross-cultural and situational requesting behavior. In S. Blum-Kulka, J. House, & G. Kasper (Eds.), *Cross-cultural pragmatics: Requests and apologies* (pp. 123–154). Norwood, NJ: Ablex.

Blum-Kulka, S., House, J., & Kasper, G. (Eds.). (1989a). *Cross-cultural pragmatics: Requests and apologies.* Norwood, NJ: Ablex.

Blum-Kulka, S., House, J., & Kasper, G. (1989b). Investigating cross-cultural pragmatics: An introductory overview. In S. Blum-Kulka, J. House, & G. Kasper (Eds.), *Cross-cultural pragmatics: Requests and apologies* (pp. 1–34). Norwood, NJ: Ablex.

Blum-Kulka, S., & Olshtain, E. (1986). Too many words: Length of utterance and pragmatic failure. *Studies in Second Language Acquisition, 8,* 47–61.

Brown, P., & Levinson, S. (1978). Universals of language usage: Politeness phenomena. In E. Goody (Ed.), *Questions and politeness* (pp. 56–289). Cambridge: Cambridge University Press.

Cathcart, R. (1986). Situational differences and the sampling of young children's school language. In R. Day (Ed.), *Talking to learn: Conversation in a second language* (pp. 118–140). Rowley, Mass.: Newbury House.

Day, R. (1984). Student participation in the ESL classroom. *Language Learning, 34,* 69–98.

De Beaugrande, R., & Dressler, W. (1981). *Introduction to text linguistics.* Oxford: Oxford University Press.

Ellis, R. (1982). *Discourse processes in the second language classroom.* Unpublished doctoral dissertation, University of London.

Ellis, R. (1984). *Classroom second language development.* Oxford: Pergamon.

Ervin-Tripp, S. (1976). "Is Sybil there?" The structure of American English directives. *Language in Society, 5,* 25–66.

Faerch, C., & Kasper, G. (1989). Internal and external modification in interlanguage request realization. In S. Blum-Kulka, J. House, & G. Kasper (Eds.), *Cross-cultural pragmatics: Requests and apologies* (pp. 221–247). Norwood, NJ: Ablex.

Flowerdew, J. (1990). Problems of speech act theory from an applied perspective. *Language Learning, 40,* 79–105.

Hatch, E. (1978). Discourse analysis and second language acquisition. In E. Hatch (Ed.), *Second language acquisition* (pp. 401–435). Rowley, Mass.: Newbury House.

House, J., & Kasper, G. (1987). Interlanguage pragmatics: Requesting in a foreign language. In W. Lorscher & R. Schulze (Eds.), *Perspectives on language and performance. Festschrift for Werner Hüllen* (pp. 1250–1288). Tübingen: Gunter Narr.

Kasper, G., & Dahl, M. (1991). Research methods in interlanguage pragmatics. *Studies in Second Language Acquisition, 13,* 215–247.

Levinson, S. (1981). The essential inadequacies of speech act models of dialogue. In H. Parret, M. Sbisa, & J. Vershueren (Eds.), *Possibilities and limitations of pragmatics: Proceedings of the conference in pragmatics at Urbino, July 8–14, 1979* (pp. 473–492). Amsterdam: Benjamins.

Long, M. (1983). Native speaker/nonnative speaker conversation in the second language classroom. In M. Clarke & J. Handscombe (Eds.), *On TESOL '82: Pacific perspectives on language learning and teaching* (pp. 339–354). Washington, DC: TESOL.

McNamara, J. (1973). Nurseries, streets and classrooms: Some comparisons and deductions. *Modern Language Journal, 57,* 250–254.

Pica, T. (1987). Second language acquisition, social interaction and the classroom. *Applied Linguistics, 8,* 3–21.

Porter, P. (1986). How learners talk to each other: Input and interaction in task-centered discussion. In R. Day (Ed.), *Talking to learn: Conversation in a second language* (pp. 200–222). Rowley, Mass.: Newbury House.

Rintell, E., & Mitchell, C. (1989). Studying requests and apologies: An inquiry into method. In S. Blum-Kulka, J. House, & G. Kasper (Eds.), *Cross-cultural pragmatics: Requests and apologies* (pp. 221–247). Norwood, NJ: Ablex.

Schmidt, R. (1983). Interaction, acculturation and the acquisition of communicative competence. In N. Wolfson & E. Judd (Eds.), *Sociolinguistics and second language acquisition* (pp. 137–174). Rowley, Mass.: Newbury House.

Searle, J. (1976). Indirect speech acts. In P. Cole & J. Morgan (Eds.), *Syntax and semantics 3: Speech acts* (pp. 59–82). New York: Academic.

Sinclair, M., & Coulthard, M. (1975). *Towards an analysis of discourse.* Oxford: Oxford University Press.

Slimani, A. (1987). *The teaching/learning relationship: Learning opportunities and learning outcomes. An Algerian case study.* Unpublished doctoral dissertation, University of Lancaster, England.

Stern, H. (1990). Analysis and experience as variables in second language pedagogy. In S. Harley, P. Allen, J. Cummins, & M. Swain (Eds.), *The development of second language proficiency* (pp. 93–109). Cambridge: Cambridge University Press.

Swain, M. (1985). Communicative competence: Some roles of comprehensible input and comprehensible output. In S. Gass & C. Madden (Eds.), *Input in second language acquisition* (pp. 235–253). Rowley, Mass.: Newbury House.

Tanaka, N. (1988). Politeness: Some problems for Japanese speakers of English. *JALT Journal, 9,* 81–102.

Van Lier, L. (1988). *The classroom and the language learner.* London: Longman.

Weizman, E. (1989). Requestive hints. In S. Blum-Kulka, J. House, & G. Kasper (Eds.), *Cross-cultural pragmatics: Requests and apologies* (pp. 71–95). Norwood, NJ: Ablex.

Wolfson, N. (1983). An empirically based analysis of complimenting in American English. In N. Wolfson & E. Judd (Eds.), *Sociolinguistics and second language acquisition* (pp. 82–95). Rowley, Mass.: Newbury House.

Wolfson, N. (1988). The bulge: A theory of speech behavior and social distance. In J. Fine (Ed.), *Second language discourse: A textbook of current research* (pp. 17–38). Norwood, NJ: Ablex.

Wolfson, N., Marmor, T., & Jones, S. (1989). Problems in the comparison of speech acts across cultures. In S. Blum-Kulka, J. House, & G. Kasper (Eds.), *Cross-cultural pragmatics: Requests and apologies* (pp. 175–196). Norwood, NJ: Ablex.

Understanding the Article

1. How does the current study differ from previous research on (a) the performance of illocutionary acts in a second language and (b) the relationship between classroom communication and the acquisition of new linguistic features?

2. What is the author's rationale for selecting requests as the illocutionary act to focus on in this study?

3. What characteristics of the study allow it to be classified as a longitudinal case study? What was the method of data collection?

4. Based on the analysis of the results, as displayed in Tables 1 through 8, what generalizations can be made about changes in the characteristics of the requests made by the subjects over the course of the study?

5. What were the answers to the research questions? What does the researcher believe is the best explanation for the subjects' failure to acquire the full range of request types and forms?

Reflecting on Wider Issues

1. What are some of the advantages and disadvantages of the paper-and-pencil method of data collection versus using audio-tapes (supplemented by either videotapes or paper-and-pencil notes on the visual context)? What evidence does the researcher provide to suggest that his presence did not have an effect on the behavior of the subjects?

2. To what extent do the categories used by Ellis reflect an analyst's perspective or a participant's perspective? What does this tell you about the family of research (experimental or ethnographic) to which this study belongs?

3. To what extent do you believe that the researcher's conclusions are valid, given the admitted absence of comparable data from native speakers of the same age, in the same setting, as well as the absence of data from both native speakers and the subjects themselves in a natural setting?

Going Beyond the Article

If you would like to learn more about the cross-cultural pragmatics of requests, read some of the articles in *Cross-Cultural Pragmatics: Requests and Apologies,* S. Blum-Kulka, J. House, and G. Kasper (Eds.) (Norwood, N.J.: Ablex, 1989). The book includes articles such as the following: Blum-Kulka and House, "Cross-cultural and situational requesting behavior"; Faerch and Kasper, "Internal and external modification in Interlanguage request realization"; and Wolfson, Marmor, and Jones, "Problems in the comparison of speech acts across cultures."

14

SEX DIFFERENCES AND APOLOGIES: ONE ASPECT OF COMMUNICATIVE COMPETENCE

Janet Holmes
Victoria University of Wellington

Previewing the Article

Differences in the ways men and women use language—a dimension of communication that can unintentionally cause misunderstanding and breakdown—have recently interested a growing number of researchers. Awareness of gender differences in language has the potential of enabling people to communicate more clearly and effectively. In this article by Janet Holmes, an important and complex aspect of language and gender—apologizing—is studied in detail.

In preparation for reading the article, refer to whatever resources you can on language and gender issues and on theories of communicative competence (see *PLLT,* Chapter 9). You should also take note of whatever gender-based linguistic differences you may be able to observe in your own surroundings. Then answer the following questions:

1. What is the purpose of the study?
2. What are the data for the study?
3. What kinds of statistics are used?
4. Look ahead at the Conclusions section, and as you read, look for evidence of the seven findings described there.

Reprinted from *Applied Linguistics, 10*:194–213, 1989.

This paper examines sex differences in the distribution of apologies in order to illuminate the complexity of the language learner's task in acquiring communicative competence. Apologies express negative politeness. They signal the speaker's awareness of having impinged on the hearer's negative face and restricted her/his freedom of action in some way. A corpus of apologies permits an analysis of the range of strategies used by New Zealanders for expressing this aspect of negative politeness as well as the distributional patterns for women and men. The offences which elicit apologies and the strategies selected to realize them provide clues to the kind of speech acts the community regards as FTAs (face-threatening acts) and the relative seriousness of different FTAs. As with other speech acts, apologies can serve as illuminating sources of information on the sociocultural values of a speech community, including possible differences between female and male values. Learning how to produce, interpret, and respond to them appropriately requires a thorough familiarity with those values.

Introduction

Hymes's theoretical and "programatic" papers (for example, 1962, 1964, 1967, 1972, 1974) have provided the inspiration and stimulus for an enormous amount of empirical work in sociolinguistics over the last twenty-five years. Hymes defined the fundamental problem facing linguists as "to discover and explicate the competence that enables members of a community to conduct and interpret speech" (1977, p. 43). The method of attack was to be an empirical study: "The primary concern now must be with descriptive analyses from a variety of communities" (1977, p. 43). And Hymes set about providing a "heuristic schema" whose value was immediately recognized and which became an indispensable framework for descriptive sociolinguistic work. Concepts such as "speech situation," "speech event," and "speech act," introduced in Hymes's earliest writings (1962, 1964), are now regarded as the basic tools of all sociolinguistic research. The research reported in this paper describes the use and interpretation of a particular speech act, the apology, in a particular speech community.

Hymes pointed out that "facets of the cultural values and beliefs, social institutions and forms, roles and personalities, history and ecology of a community may have to be examined in their bearing on communicative events and patterns" (1977, p. 4). Correspondingly systematic observation of speech acts can yield important cultural information (for example, Coulmas, 1981; Wolfson, 1988; Wolfson & Judd, 1983). Researchers have paid attention, as Hymes enjoined (1964, p. 8), to the effects of a range of sociolinguistic factors in determining the way speech acts are realized in particular cultural contexts. Factors such as the social setting, the channel of communication, the content or topic, and features of the participants in communicative events such as ethnic group, relative status, and social distance have been studied. One aspect of interaction which has received relatively little attention, however, despite Hymes's comments on its relevance, is the influence of gender on the distribution of particular speech acts (Holmes, 1987, 1988a; Wolfson, 1984). Hymes commented in an address to the Georgetown University Round Table in 1972 that women are "communicatively second-class citizens" because of the restrictions on what they may say, and on when and where they may say it (Hymes, 1977, p. 205). Though there is now a large body of research comparing women's and men's speech (see, for example, Coates, 1986; Thorne, Kramarae, & Henley, 1983), the ways in which women's use of particular speech acts differ from men's has not yet attracted much attention. This essay focuses on sex differences in some pragmatic and sociolinguistic features of a particular speech act—the apology. In order to illuminate the complexity of the language learner's task in acquiring communicative competence, the analysis will explore both features of the distribution of apologies, and also the functions they may serve in remedial exchanges between New Zealand women and men in a variety of contexts.

There is a real risk that teaching material which ignores the influence of the sex of participants in interaction will misrepresent the sociolinguistic norms of the community concerned. There is often a tendency to assume, in the absence of explicit analyses to the contrary, that male ways of speaking represent the norm (Cameron & Coates, 1985; Spender, 1980). But many of the norms of the classroom are female ones. It is possible that in teaching learners of English when and to whom and how one should pay a compliment or make an apology, teachers unconsciously use norms specific to their own gender. In this essay I present some evidence of differences in gender norms in the use of apologies. If the patterns observed in the New Zealand corpus are generalizable, there are obvious implications for language teaching methodology, including materials development.

The Function of an Apology

Apologies, like compliments (Holmes, 1986, 1987b), are speech acts which pay attention to the "face" needs of the addressee (Goffman, 1967). I will therefore refer to them as examples of "face-supportive acts" (FSAs). While it would be possible to restrict the term "apology" to expressions such as *Sorry* and *I apologize*, it has generally been used to describe what Goffman refers to as a "remedy" (1971, p. 140), one element in a "remedial interchange." This term nicely highlights the central function of apologies—to provide a remedy for an offence and restore social equilibrium or harmony (cf. Edmondson, 1981, p. 280; Leech, 1983, p. 125). The broad definition of an apology used in this paper takes function as the crucial criterion:

> An apology is a speech act addressed to V's face-needs and intended to remedy an offence for which A takes responsibility, and thus to restore equilib-

rium between A and V (where A is the apologist, and V is the victim or person offended).

It is difficult to further specify the content of an apology in any helpful manner since this function may be achieved in an infinite number of ways depending on the offence addressed.[1] It is possible, however, to categorize the range of strategies used, as I will illustrate below.

An apology will typically address an offence performed by the speaker/apologist:

1. *Context:* A bumps into V, who is standing still.

A: Sorry.

V: That's OK.

It is sometimes the case, however, that an apology will be made on behalf of someone for whom the apologist feels responsible, such as a child, a spouse, a friend, or a member of the same group as the person apologizing.

2. *Context:* A's child spills her drink on V's carpet.

A: Oh look I'm terribly sorry. I'll clean it up. Have you got a cloth?

V: Don't worry. I'll do it. It wasn't very much.

Thus the definition given above refers to the person who takes responsibility for the offence rather than the offender herself.

Apologies, like compliments, are primarily aimed at maintaining, enhancing, anointing, or supporting the addressee's "face" (Goffman, 1967). While compliments focus on the addressee's positive face wants (Holmes, 1987, 1988a), apologies are generally aimed at face-redress associated with FTAs (face-threatening acts), in Brown and Levinson's terms (1978, p. 65), and can therefore be regarded as negative politeness strategies (Brown & Levinson, 1978, p. 192). Apologies redress negative face most obviously when the offence has ignored V's "want that his [*sic*] actions be unimpeded by others" (Brown & Levinson, 1978, p. 67). Examples 1 and 2 above illustrate apologies which are very clearly intended to remedy a threat to V's negative face.

Utterances which serve as apologies can, of course, express other functions too. They may be bivalent or plurivalent speech acts, expressing more than one illocutionary or pragmatic force (Thomas, 1985). Utterances which express regret for an offence may also serve as an admission, with the addressee learning of the offence through the utterance which serves as an apology. While the overt function is apology, the utterance simultaneously performs the indirect function of conveying bad news (cf. Brown & Levinson, 1978, p. 73; Coulmas, 1981b).

---

[1]See Holmes (1988b) for a fuller discussion of this issue.

3. *Context:* In trying to undo a bottle for V, A Breaks the cap.

A: Oh dear, I'm afraid I've broken it.

V: Never mind, at least it's open now!

Utterances like these illustrate the complexity of interaction, since they simultaneously express an indirect FTA, while administering face-redress as a politeness strategy mitigating the effect of the FTA. The discussion of apology strategies below will illustrate this point further.

The Corpus

Austin, in an article called "A plea for excuses," comments whimsically on his method of collecting examples of apologies and excuses: "I do not know how many of you keep a list of the kinds of fool you make of yourselves" (Austin, 1961, p. 186). The data collection method used in this study was a refinement of Austin's—an ethnographic approach—and was identical to that used in collecting compliments (described in Holmes, 1988b). This ethnographic method derives from anthropology and has been advocated by Hymes over many years (1962, 1964), and very successfully adopted by researchers such as Wolfson (1984, 1988) on whose work I am building.

The apologies corpus consists of 183 remedial interchanges, that is, apologies and apology responses collected over a wide range of contexts with the assistance of New Zealand students who volunteered for the task.[2] The instances collected were predominantly produced by adult pakeha[3] New Zealanders and it is therefore the apology norms of this group which are the focus of the study.

Sex of Apologizers and Recipients

Investigation of sex differences in the use of apologies is still at a preliminary stage. Olshtain and Cohen (1983, p. 31) comment on interesting sex differences between English, Japanese, and Spanish speakers' responses to complaints in role-play situations. By contrast Fraser (1981, p. 269), on the basis of examples noted ethnographically but not quantified, comments that "contrary to popular stereotype, we did not find women offering more apologies than men." There was "no apparent systematic or predictable frequency" in the occurrence or nonoccurrence of apologies from women and men in a range of contexts (Fraser, 1981, p. 269).

---

[2]The following students contributed examples to the corpus: Jane Crew, Jennifer Fouhy, Jennifer Jacob, Eletheria Lemontzi, Hedy Manders, Fiona Read, Mig Wright. Two students preferred to remain anonymous.

[3]Pakeha is the term generally used for New Zealanders of European descent.

In this corpus it is clear that there are significant sex differences in the distribution of apologies ($\chi^2 = 54.487$); in fact the pattern for apologies is remarkably similar to that for compliments. Table 1 summarizes the apology patterns and Table 2 provides the distribution of compliments for comparison.[4]

TABLE 1.   Apologies Analysed According to Sex of Participants

APOLOGIZER-VICTIM	NUMBER	%
Female–Female (F–F)	99	56.3
Female–Male (F–M)	32	18.2
Male–Female (M–F)	30	17.0
Male–Male (M–M)	15	8.5
Total 176	100	

Women gave 74.5% of all the apologies recorded and received 73.3% of them. It is always possible with ethnographic data that the environments in which the data were collected provided a higher proportion of female than male speech acts of the kind under investigation. The sampling method, which involved researchers collecting twenty consecutive apologies without interruption or editing, was an attempt to protect against such bias. Hence in this corpus at least, over a range of contexts, New Zealand women apologize more than New Zealand men do, and they are apologized to more frequently than men are. The table also illustrates the fact that apologies were most frequent between women, while apologies between males were relatively rare (only 8.5%). As Table 2 demonstrates, all these patterns are also typical of the distribution of New Zealand compliments (Holmes, 1988a).[5]

TABLE 2.   Compliments Analysed According to Sex of Participants

COMPLIMENTER-RECIPIENT	NUMBER	%
Female-Female (F–F)	248	51.2
Female-Male (F–M)	80	16.5
Male-Female (M–F)	112	23.1
Male-Male (M–M)	44	9.1
Total	484	100

[4]The total number of apologies varies slightly from table to table. This variation relates to the number of apologies which were unclassifiable for a range of reasons. Most involved unspecified speakers or unspecified or multiple addressees (for example, excusing oneself in a crowd, an apology in a notice, a broadcast public apology).

[5]In the analysis of compliment data (Holmes, 1988a) the question of the influence of the sex of the data collectors was explored. It was demonstrated that, even with equal numbers of male and female data collectors, compliments between women would be more frequent than compliments between men, though the imbalance would be less marked. There is no reason to suspect that the same is not true for the apology data.

It is superficially surprising that apologies to males are so much less frequent than apologies to females (26.7% versus 73.3%). One would expect negative politeness strategies to be used more to the powerful and to those with status. As signals of concern for offending or interfering with the addressee's freedom of action, apologies could be expected to occur most often "upwards." In female-male interaction in western culture it is generally accepted that males are perceived as the dominant and powerful group. On this analysis one would expect in particular more apologies to men from women. But the number of apologies between the sexes is remarkably evenly distributed. The resolution of this puzzle will involve exploring other social features of apology behaviour between the sexes.

Part of the answer may lie in differential perceptions by women and men of verbal politeness devices. The contexts, types of relationship, and kinds of offence which elicit apologies may differ between the sexes. Women may regard explicit apologies for offences as more important in maintaining relationships than men do. The very low frequency of apologies between males would support this hypothesis. In other words, apologies may function differently for women and men.

In order to explore the meaning and possible significance of the frequency differences identified it is necessary, then, to consider other aspects of the apologizing behaviour of women and men. Before examining features of the social interactions in which apologies occurred, I will describe the apology strategies used by women and men in the data.

Apology Strategies

A number of researchers have developed classification systems for apology strategies (Blum-Kulka & Olshtain, 1984; Fraser, 1981; Olshtain & Cohen, 1983; Owen, 1983; Trosberg, 1987). I have built on their work in developing a satisfactory categorization system for the New Zealand data. Four broad basic categories were used, with a number of subcategories where required. The categories are thoroughly discussed elsewhere (Holmes, 1988b). Here, however, they are summarized and briefly illustrated in Table 3, which compares female and male preferences in strategy selection.

Table 3 includes all the apology strategies used by women and men in the 183 remedial exchanges in the corpus. In many cases an apologist used more than one strategy as part of the overall apology; hence the total number of apology strategies in Table 3 is 295.[6]

An examination of the distribution of female and male apology strategies in the four major subcategories shown in Table 3 shows a very similar pattern overall. There is little difference in the number of explicit apology strategies

---

[6]The combinations of apology strategies in the data are described in Holmes (1988b). There are no significant differences in the combinations used by women compared to men.

TABLE 3. Analysis of Apology Strategies According to Apologizer Sex

| | Apologizer Sex | | | |
APOLOGY STRATEGY	F NUMBER	%	M NUMBER	%
A. *Explicit expression of apology*				
1. An offer of apology/IFID	8	3.7	7	8.6
e.g. *I apologize*				
2. An expression of regret	114	53.3	34	42.0
e.g. *I'm afraid, I'm sorry*				
3. A request for forgiveness	10	4.7	7	8.6
e.g. *Excuse me, Forgive me*				
Subtotal ('A's)	132	61.7	48	59.2
B. *Explanation or account*				
e.g. *I wasn't expecting it to be you*	50	23.4	17	21.0
C. *Acknowledgement of responsibility*				
1. Accepting the blame	4	1.9	5	6.2
e.g. *It is my fault*				
2. Expressing self-deficiency	5	2.3	4	4.9
e.g. *I was confused*				
3. Recognizing V as entitled to an apology e.g. *You are right*	2	0.9	—	—
4. Expressing lack of intent	7	3.3	—	—
e.g. *I didn't mean to*				
5. An offer of repair/redress	11	5.1	5	6.2
e.g. *We'll replace it for you*				
Subtotal ('C's)	29	13.5	14	17.3
D. *A promise of forbearance*				
e.g. *I promise that it won't happen again*	3	1.4	2	2.5
Total	214	100	81	100

used by women and men, though men appear to use more formal substrategies more often than women. This preference contributes to a statistically significant difference ($\chi^2 = 30.33$) in the male and female distribution of strategies, but the numbers involved are very small.[7] If it represented a trend which was

---

[7]This finding is supported by an examination of syntactic-semantic patterns which shows men preferring more formal structures than women (11.4% versus 6.2%) but again the numbers involved are very small (13 apologies in all).

sustained over a large number of interactions it would support the view that men treat apologies differently from women. Use of more formal formulae suggests that men may regard apologies as signals of social distance or as devices to be used only in cases of relatively serious offence. This would be consistent with Brown and Levinson's (1978, p. 75) description of negative politeness strategies as "avoidance-based" and "characterized by . . . formality and restraint" (1978, p. 75).

The overall proportion of explanations included in the apologies is almost identical for the two sexes: the differences are too small to be significant. There is little difference in the likelihood that women rather than men will acknowledge responsibility for the offence, though it is perhaps worth noting that only women use the substrategies of expressing lack of intent and recognizing the other's right to an apology. With such a small number of apologies involved this may be due to pure chance, but again it is suggestive. If the pattern were sustained, it supports an argument that women's motivation for apologies may be related to their perception of what is necessary to maintain the relationship with the person offended. These two substrategies could be described as "other-oriented." They make explicit the apologist's concern that the offence should not damage the relationship. Finally, promises of forbearance are used by both sexes with numbers too small to indicate anything more.

It appears then that in global terms both women and men make use of the same apology strategies and that they use them in the same proportions overall. The differences in preferred substrategies are small but suggest that perhaps women and men regard apologies as doing different jobs. If they do then it is likely that they use them in different circumstances and for different reasons. It therefore seems important to examine further the contexts in which women and men use apologies. It is possible that the overall lower number of apologies used by men reflects a different assessment by women and men concerning when an apology is required. In that case, even though women and men largely use the same strategies, they presumably carry different weight.

Type of Offence

One of the most obviously relevant components of the situation in describing apologies in discourse is the type of offence which appears to require remedial work. Though it may need further refinement, the categorization of offence types used here provides a useful indication of the range of offences in the data.[8] Table 4 illustrates the differences in the type of offence which women and men apologized for.

The differences between females and males in this area appear most obviously in relation to space and time offences, both of which contribute to a significant difference in the distribution of female versus male apologies

---

[8]The categorization is discussed in more detail in Holmes (1988b).

TABLE 4.   Interaction of Apologizer Sex with Offence Type

| OFFENCE TYPE | Apologizer Sex | | | |
| | F | | M | |
	NUMBER	%	NUMBER	%
1. Inconvenience	51	38.1	18	39.1
e.g. inadequate goods or services				
2. Space	26	19.4	4	8.7
e.g. bumping into V				
3. Talk	24	17.9	6	13.0
e.g. interrupting V				
4. Time	16	11.9	10	21.7
e.g. keeping V waiting				
5. Possessions	14	10.5	6	13.0
e.g. damaging V's pen				
6. Social gaffe	3	2.2	2	4.3
e.g. burping				
Total	134	100	46	100

($\chi^2 = 17.94$). Women apologized more than men for intrusions on the space of another, while men apologized more for time offences. Wolfson (1988, p. 27) comments that "The notion that [middle class Americans] consider themselves under obligation to be prompt and/or to avoid keeping another person waiting is, in fact, evidenced by the large number of apologies that refer to just this situation." Wolfson does not provide figures, so it is difficult to know how time apologies compare with other types of offence in her American data. In the New Zealand data it is clear that time offences are more frequent reasons for apologies among men than women. Hence it may be that when we think of time as a very valuable commodity, we are reflecting "male as norm" values (Spender, 1980).

Women are more likely to apologize for bumping into people or accidentally taking their place. A predominance of apologies for accidental body contact is not surprising in a group who are the main victims of sexual harassment. It is very plausible that women are more sensitive to such impositions and, as a result, readily apologize for "space" intrusions. An apology would make it crystal clear that the contact had been unintentional. Men, on the other hand, may not regard space impositions as offences at all, perhaps regarding bumping into one another as inevitable and normal interaction. In support of this it is worth noting that there are no examples in the corpus of "space" apologies between men.

Other differences are no more than tendencies, with men apologizing for possession offences more than women, and women for talk offences more than men. "Possession" apologies related to damage to, or loss of, a range of things including the other person's pen, car, books, clothes, and washing machine. Offences which cost the other person money were also included in this category. The finding here that men seem to apologize more often than women for offences involving another's possession is consistent with the finding that men also pay compliments relating to possessions more often than women do.

Women apologized more than men for interrupting, taking up too much of the available talking time, or not hearing what the other person said. The fact that women apologize more than men for such "talk" offences, if generalizable, is somewhat ironic, since there is an extensive literature demonstrating that women are clearly more often the victims of talk offences than men (Spender 1980; West & Zimmerman, 1983; Zimmerman & West, 1975).[9] Like "space" offences, however, it may be that women are for this very reason particularly sensitive to such offences.

The number of examples involving a social gaffe is too small to indicate any trend. By contrast, a large proportion of the apologies relate to actions which have inconvenienced the addressee in some way, such as where the apologizer could not provide the correct change or the required information, or had provided inadequate service. It is clear that there are no sex differences in the proportion of this type of offence compared to others. It is possible that a more detailed analysis of the examples within this category will provide further interesting information.

If the offences we consider worth an apology reflect our concerns and preoccupations, then these data suggest that, while both sexes are concerned about inconvenience to another, women are particularly concerned about intrusions relating to a person's space and talking rights, while men are more concerned by inconvenience which costs another time, and damage to another's possessions. There is certainly support here for the hypothesis that the reason for differences in women's and men's apology behaviour may relate to differences in their perceptions of the kind of situations which require an apology.

Seriousness of Offence

Further support is provided by a consideration of the relative seriousness of the offence in the relevant culture. An attempt was made to calculate the seriousness of the offence independently of the overall weighting of the FTA in Brown and Levinson's terms.[10] The weightiness of a FTA involves considering

---

[9]See especially Section V in the annotated bibliography in Thorne, Kramarae, and Henley (1983).

[10]Judgements of the relative seriousness of the offence as well as of the relative power and distance between the participants were made on the basis of the contextual information provided by the data collectors.

the ranking of the imposition (R) as well as the relationship between the participants measured in terms of relative power (P) and social distance (D) (Brown & Levinson, 1978, p. 81). In analysing the apologies an estimate was made of the weighting of the imposition independently of the relative power and social distance of the participants. But the assessment did of course take account of other relevant factors of the situation (cf. Brown & Levinson, 1978, p. 84). The relative cost of the imposition of losing someone's book, for instance, depends on factors such as how urgently they need it, as well as its rarity or monetary value. Table 5 summarizes the differences found in the

TABLE 5.   Interaction of Apologizer Sex with Offence Weight

| | Apologizer Sex | | | |
| | F | | M | |
OFFENCE WEIGHT	NUMBER	%	NUMBER	%
1. Light	72	53.7	19	41.3
e.g. bumped into someone				
2. Medium	54	40.3	22	47.8
e.g. broke someone's stapler				
3. Heavy	8	6.0	5	10.9
e.g. caused someone to miss an important engagement				
Total	134	100	46	100

number of offences of different weights which elicited apologies from women compared to men. The relevance of the relationship between the participants to the overall interpretation of the degree of offence caused, is discussed separately below.

Table 5 provides some support for the suggestion that women and men weight offences differently—that women apologize more readily than men. Men's apologies take up a greater proportion of the more heavily weighted offences than women's do while a greater proportion of women's apologies relate to the least weighty offences. Though the differences are not very significant ($\chi^2 = 8.26$), this suggests that men and women may interpret situations differently. The "same" behaviour may elicit an apology from a woman but not from a man. If this is so, then it would help to account for the disproportionate number of female versus male apologies in the corpus.

Power or Status

It is worth considering next what contribution relative power makes to the distribution of apologies between the sexes. Determining the relative power relations in an interaction is often a difficult task. One relevant factor is the relative status of the participants, but other factors such as relative experience, knowledge, or expertise will be crucial in particular contexts.[11] Three categories were used:

U—upwards, that is, apology to a person with more P

E—equal, that is, apology to a person of equal P

D—downwards, that is, apology to a person with less P.

Do women and men apologize more to the more powerful or to equals, and what are the implications of their apology patterns? Do people apologize more than would be expected to higher status women or are most apologies directed upwards to powerful men as Brown and Levinson's (1978, 1987) model would predict? Table 6 shows the patterns in this corpus.

TABLE 6.   Apologizer Sex by Relative Power of Recipient

| | Apologizer Sex | | | |
| | F | | M | |
RELATIVE POWER	NUMBER	%	NUMBER	%
U	29	21.6	11	29.4
E	90	67.2	25	55.6
D	15	11.2	9	20.0
Total	134	100	46	100

Though most apologies occur between equals, both sexes direct more apologies upwards than downwards, as one might expect. However, men apologize proportionately more to those with unequal power than women do ($\chi^2 =$ 11.73). Correspondingly, men use fewer apologies to equals than women do. This tendency is consistent with their tendency to use apologies for more heavily weighted offences. It may be that men regard apologies as more often superfluous or dispensable between equals than do women.

If the interaction between the sex of the apologizers and that of the recipients is examined, one finds some support for the view that the society in question recognizes that women attach more importance to apologies than men do. In other words, the data suggest women are widely recognized as sensitive to the importance of providing apologies.

Table 7 shows that both women and men apologize more to women regardless of relative power. It also shows the very high priority women place on apologies to female equals: these are by far the most frequent apologies in the sample, and they contribute to an overall significantly different distribu-

---

[11]The basis for assigning interactions to different categories is more fully described in Holmes (1988b).

TABLE 7. Apologizer Sex by Relative Power and Sex of Recipient

RELATIVE POWER AND SEX OF RECIPIENT	Apologizer Sex			
	F		*M*	
	NUMBER	%	NUMBER	%
U F	15	11.5	7	15.9
M	13	9.9	4	9.1
E F	74	56.5	16	36.4
M	14	10.7	9	20.5
D F	10	7.6	6	13.6
M	5	3.8	2	4.5
Total	131	100	44	100

tion of female and male apologies in this table ($\chi^2 = 22.74$). In addition, however, the table provides data which are consistent with the suggestion that men are sensitive to the importance women attach to apologies. While men apologize most frequently to women who are their equals, though the figures are very small, it appears that they are more likely to apologize to females in more—and particularly in less—powerful positions than they are to more and less powerful males. In every category, then, women are likely to be apologized to more than men. This analysis is consistent with the view that the society as a whole recognizes the high priority which women place on politeness strategies as interactive tokens.

Social Distance

Social distance was identified very early in sociolinguistic research as an important and influential factor across a range of communities (Hymes, 1977, p. 104). The corpus includes apologies between participants who differ widely in terms of how well they know each other or the degree of social distance which characterizes the relationship. Three categories were used to classify the data:

I—very close friends or intimates, for example, spouses, partners, family members

F—friends or colleagues

S—distant acquaintances or strangers.

Table 8 shows the distribution of the apologies according to how well the participants knew each other.

It is interesting to interpret this table in the light of Brown and Levinson's (1978, 1987) model. They suggest that the greater the social distance, the

TABLE 8. Sex of Apologizer by Relative Distance of Recipient

| RELATIVE DISTANCE OF RECIPIENT | Apologizer Sex | | | |
	F NUMBER	%	M NUMBER	%
S	62	46.6	24	53.3
F	62	46.6	12	26.7
I	9	6.8	9	20.0
Total	133	100	45	100

heavier the weighting of the FTA. Thus one might expect to find apologies to strangers occurring more often than to friends and intimates. Table 8 provides support for the view that men rather than women give weight to the kind of computation of P, D, and R predicted by Brown and Levinson. It shows that there are twice as many examples of men apologizing to those who are strangers or acquaintances as to friends, while women apologize as often to their friends as to strangers. (I will return to the interpretation of this point in the concluding section.) This result is also consistent, of course, with the hypothesis that men regard apologies to friends as less crucial and as more dispensable than those to strangers. Men may reflect or signal friendship by *not* apologizing for what they regard as "trivial" offences. To apologize to a mate for a minor offence may be regarded as an insult or a distancing device. This would be consistent with the finding that men do not pay compliments to their friends as often as women do. Face attention of this kind appears to be considered unnecessary between males and may even be perceived as threatening (Holmes, 1988a).

The data on apologies to intimates, with men apologizing more to intimates than women do, is intriguing. It is the major contributor to a sex difference in the distribution on apologies in this table ($\chi^2 = 35.08$). It may simply reflect the difficulties of obtaining examples in this category, since the actual numbers are small for both sexes. But it is worth looking at the sex of the recipients before speculating further on this.

Further analysis shows that the difference between female and male usage is very sensitive to the sex of the recipient. It was noted earlier that both men and women tend to apologize more to women than to men. Table 9 demonstrates that women apologized most to their women friends (41%), a proportion which contributes most to the overall statistically significant distribution of female versus male apologies in this table ($\chi^2 = 21.185$), while by far the largest proportion (39%) of male apologies are directed to female strangers or acquaintances. These figures suggest that both women and men are aware of the importance that women attach to face needs, and both sexes recognize that it is important to apologize to women one has offended. It appears that women, however, rate offences as much heavier when friends are involved,

TABLE 9.   Sex of Apologizer by Relative Distance and Sex of Recipient

RELATIVE DISTANCE AND SEX OF RECIPIENT	Apologizer Sex			
	F		*M*	
	NUMBER	%	NUMBER	%
S F	38	29.2	17	38.6
M	22	16.9	6	13.6
F F	53	40.8	5	11.4
M	8	6.2	7	15.9
I F	7	5.4	7	15.9
M	2	1.5	2	4.5
Total	130	100	44	100

while men perceive offences to unfamiliar women as most heavily weighted. It is interesting to speculate on the reasons for this. The potentially dangerous social interpretations of such offences may be relevant. The apology may thus act to ensure unintended offences are properly perceived.[12]

Both sexes appear to apologize more to females than to males with whom they have a closer relationship, though the numbers here are very small. They are, however, consistent with the argument that men are least likely to apologize to a close male mate, and that they differentiate between females and males with whom they are close, using apologies to the women more often than the men. Once men have developed close relationships with women it may be that they use the face-supportive strategies which women value in an effort to maintain the relationship.

The distribution of apologies according to the social distance between the participants thus suggests quite strongly that women evaluate D differently from men. It appears that women may regard an offence against a friend as weighing more heavily than one against a stranger, while the reverse may be true for men. Men, on the other hand, appear to weigh offences against intimates more heavily than do women. These tendencies certainly suggest the need for apologies is differently assessed in different contexts by the two sexes.

Response Strategies

Responses to apologies provide an indication to the apologizer of whether the goal of reestablishing social harmony or equilibrium has been achieved. Six categories of response strategies were developed and these have been analysed by the sex of the responder in Table 10.[13]

---

[12]This point was suggested by Allan Bell (personal communication).

[13]The basis for assigning responses to different categories as well as the identification of a number of subcategories are more fully described in Holmes (1988b).

TABLE 10.   Sex of Responder by Response Strategy

| | Responder Sex | | | |
| | F | | M | |
RESPONSE STRATEGY	NUMBER	%	NUMBER	%
A. *Accept* e.g. *That's OK*	49	38.0	13	27.7
B. *Acknowledge* e.g. *OK (but)*	14	10.9	5	10.6
C. *Reject* e.g. Marked silence	15	11.6	9	19.1
D. *Evade* e.g. *Let's make another time*	28	21.7	12	25.5
E. *No response expected/provided*	16	12.4	7	14.9
F. *Other* e.g. Another apology; a humorous rejection	7	5.4	1	2.1
Total	129	100	47	100

It is clear that the most likely response from both sexes is to accept the apology, with a remark such as *That's OK* or *No problem*. An evasive lateral comment, sometimes responding to some other aspect of the apology, is the next most frequent response. **4.** provides an example:

> **4.** **Context:** A is phoning V, a close friend, to cancel a lunch-date.
>
> A: I'm sorry—I can't make it after all. I've got an unexpected meeting. It's a real pain.
>
> V: Let's make another time.

While the distributional difference between female versus male responses just fails to reach significance for this table ($X^2 = 10.835$), the patterns nevertheless provide suggestive trends. Women appear to be more likely to accept an apology than men, while men are more likely than women to reject an apology, though it should be noted that most of the rejections (7 of the 9 in category C) involve a withholding response rather than an overt rejection.[14] Women responded to an apology with an apology more often than men (6 of the 7 in the "Other" category) but the numbers are obviously too small to be more than suggestive.

---

[14]It would be useful to know whether the sex of the interpreter affects the classification of these responses. The absence of an overt response to the apology can be interpreted as either a rejection or as an appropriate way of continuing with the discourse. Much depends on the context and the interpretation of the researcher.

Accepting an apology can be interpreted as a threat to the victim's face, since the acceptance implicitly confirms that the addressee has imposed on and offended the speaker. An acceptance is other-oriented in restoring the balance and thus preserving the offender's face. A rejection threatens the offender's and preserves the victim's face, and is thus more self-oriented. An evasion allows the speaker an "out" in these circumstances and avoids admitting the loss of face resulting from the offence. Men are less other-oriented than women in these data in that a higher proportion of their responses (44.6% compared to 33.3%) fall into the "Reject" and "Evade" categories than into the "Accept" category.

Conclusion

The ability to use and interpret remedial exchanges appropriately is a complex aspect of communicative competence. Knowing when and how to apologize is an important component of "politeness" in many western speech communities.

In the initial discussion of the function of apologies it was suggested that, like compliments, they are hearer-oriented FSAs (face-supportive acts). While compliments are generally regarded as positive politeness strategies (but see Holmes, 1988a, for further discussion), apologies are most obviously negative politeness strategies aimed at remedying the effects of an offence or FTA and restoring social harmony and equilibrium. It is also true, however, that apologies inevitably damage the apologizer's face "to some degree," as pointed out by Brown and Levinson (1978, p. 73). This may provide some insight into possible reasons why men and women perceive apologies differently. Men may perceive them as self-oriented FTAs, damaging the speaker's face and therefore to be avoided where possible. Women, by contrast, may perceive them as "other-oriented" speech acts and as ways of facilitating social harmony.

It is clear from the distribution of apologies in the corpus that women use these politeness strategies more than men. Moreover, just as with compliments, there are obviously grounds for suggesting that the reasons for the frequency difference between the sexes may be related to alternative interpretations of these speech acts. Detailed contextual analysis will be necessary to resolve many of the questions raised by the distributional evidence, but that evidence does provide some basis for exploring further the hypothesis that men and women attach different weight to the "same" offences and thus assess the need for an apology differently. The evidence can be summarized as follows:

1. Women use significantly more apologies than men; they use more to each other than to men, and they use many more to each other than men do to each other.

2. Women tend more than men to use apology strategies which recognize the claims of the victim. Men tend more than women to use more formal strategies which focus on the speaker.

3. Women's apologies more often than men's serve as remedies for "space" and "talk" offences—areas of interaction where women are particularly vulnerable and where they appear to have developed a greater sensitivity. Men, on the other hand, pay particular attention to "time" offences, suggesting that they have different priorities from women.

4. Women's apologies are predominantly directed to light offences whereas men use more for medium-weighted offences.

5. Whereas both sexes use most apologies to power equals, men use proportionately more than women to women of different status, that is, "upwards" and "downwards."

6. Women use most apologies to female friends whereas men use most to socially distant women.

7. Though the most frequent response for both sexes is to accept apologies, men reject apologies more than women do and women accept them proportionately more than men do.

All these facts are consistent with an interpretation of the data which proposes that women and men evaluate the need for apologies differently; an interpretation which suggests men avoid apologies where possible, using them only in cases where they judge they are likely to cause greater offence by the omission of an apology. Between female friends apologies appear to play an important part in the normal face-attention required of such a relationship. Between men apologies may be much more dispensable; indeed an appropriate signal of friendship may be to omit an apology. Face-saving appears to be more important and is perhaps recognized as such between men.

One way of interpreting the data described in this paper is to suggest that men's apology behaviour broadly conforms to Brown and Levinson's model of politeness: the frequency of men's apologies is sensitive to increased social distance and offence weight. Women's apology behaviour, on the other hand, appears to conform more closely to Wolfson's "bulge" theory. Wolfson outlines the model as follows:

> . . . when we examine the ways in which different speech acts are realised in actual everyday speech, and when we compare these behaviours in terms of the social relationships of the interlocutors, we find again and again that the two extremes of social distance—minimum and maximum—seem to call forth very similar behavior, while relationships which are more toward the center show marked differences. (Wolfson, 1988, p. 32)

Wolfson points to the evidence that most compliments, for instance, occur between speakers who are neither total strangers nor intimates, and so do negotiated imprecise invitations. Wolfson's theory is based on the relative certainty of the relationships involved. It is less certain relationships (i.e., between those who are neither strangers nor intimates) which need expressions of solidarity to bolster them, and invitations with escape clauses to avoid rejections. This describes very neatly the women's pattern of apologizing to friends more than to strangers or intimates. Though further analysis of the relative distance of relationships is needed, it seems possible that women apologize more to those to whom they feel a need to signal positive attitudes and concern for "face" in order to resolve possibly threatening alternative interpretations, and less to those with whom their relationships are clear-cut and unambiguous, because intimate or "transactional" (Blom & Gumperz, 1986).

These interpretations can be no more than suggestive at this stage. Closer analysis of the type of apologies which occur in different types of context could shed interesting illumination on the reasons for the differences identified in women's and men's apologizing behaviour.

Finally, this description has demonstrated, as Hymes suggested, that research on speech acts can yield interesting cultural information of considerable value for cross-cultural comparison. Wolfson, a researcher who has made an enormous contribution in following up Hymes's work, says (1988, p. 29) that "by observing what people apologise for, we learn what cultural expectations are with respect to what people owe one another" and we also learn "about the rights and obligations that members of a community have toward one another, information which is culture specific and not necessarily available to the intuitions of the native speaker" (Wolfson, 1988, p. 26). My contention is that information about differences in the pragmatic and sociolinguistic behaviour of women and men is an important aspect of communicative competence. Once identified, it can be used as the basis for developing appropriate methods of assisting language learners to acquire this competence (cf. Holmes & Brown, 1987).

This paper has illustrated the range of differences in women's and men's behaviour in relation to remedial exchanges, and has attempted to illustrate the complexity involved in unravelling a satisfactory interpretation of these differences. Sociocultural information of this sort constitutes a vital facet of communicative competence: learners need both productive communicative competence (the knowledge and ability involved in interpreting apologies appropriately) and receptive communicative competence (the knowledge and ability involved in interpreting apologies appropriately. To help them acquire this, researchers must provide adequate accounts both of the patterns they observe and their meaning. With this information teachers can provide learners with the information they need to make informed choices in using English. As Thomas (1983) has pointed out, the teacher's role is to empower the learner, in other words, to provide the information learners need about the way native speakers use and interpret speech so that they may choose how they wish to present themselves. This perhaps helps to make clear that far from suggesting that we teach female learners to apologize more than males, I am suggesting that we inform all learners of the patterns observed in the target speech community so that they may choose how they wish to appear, and so that they can interpret accurately the behaviour they encounter.

References

Austin, J. L. (1961). A plea for excuses. In J. O. Urmson & G. J. Warnock (Eds.), *Philosophical papers* (3rd ed.). Oxford: Oxford University Press.

Blom, J-P. & Gumperz, J. J. (1986). Social meaning in linguistic structures: Code-switching in Norway. In J. J. Gumperz and D. Hymes (Eds.), *Directions in Sociolinguistics.* New York: Holt Rinehart and Winston.

Blum-Kulka, S., & Olshtain, E. (1984). Requests and apologies: A cross-cultural study of speech and act realisation patterns (CCSARP). *Applied Linguistics, 5,* 196–213.

Borkin, N., & Reinhart, S. M. (1978). "Excuse me" and "I'm sorry." *TESOL Quarterly, 12,* 57–70.

Brown, P., & Levinson, S. (1978). Universals in language usage: Politeness phenomena. In E. N. Goody (Ed.), *Questions and Politeness.* Cambridge: Cambridge University Press.

Brown, P., & Levinson, S. (1987). *Politeness: Some universals in language usage.* Cambridge: Cambridge University Press.

Cameron, D., & Coates, J. (1985). Some problems in the sociolinguistic explanation of sex differences. *Language and Communication, 5,* 143–151.

Coates, J. (1986). *Women, men and language.* London: Longman.

Cohen, A., & Olshtain, E. (1981). Developing a measure of sociocultural competence: The case of apology. *Language Learning, 31,* 113–134.

Coulmas, F. (Ed.) (1981a). *Conversational Routine.* The Hague: Mouton.

Coulmas, F. (1981b). Poison to your soul. Thanks and apologies contrastively viewed. In F. Coulmas (Ed.), *Conversational routine.* The Hague: Mouton.

Edmondson, W. J. (1981). On saying you're sorry. In F. Coulmas (Ed.), *Conversational routine.* The Hague: Mouton.

Fraser, B. (1981). On apologising. In F. Coulmas (Ed.), *Conversational routine.* The Hague: Mouton.

Goffman, E. (1967). *Interaction ritual.* New York: Anchor Books.

Goffman, E. (1971). *Relations in public* New York: Basic Books.

Holmes, J. (1986). Compliments and compliment responses in New Zealand English. *Anthropological Linguistics, 28,* 485–508.

Holmes, J. (1987). Sex differences and language use in the ESL classroom. In Bikram K. Das (Ed.), *Communication and learning in the classroom community.* Anthology Series 19. Singapore: SEAMEO Regional Language Centre.

Holmes, J. (1988a). Paying compliments: A sex-preferential positive politeness strategy. *Journal of Pragmatics, 12.*

Holmes, J. (1988b). *Apologies in New Zealand English.* Mimeo.

Holmes, J., & Brown, D. (1987). Teachers and students learning about compliments. *TESOL Quarterly, 21,* 523–546.

Hymes, D. (1962). The ethnography of speaking. In T. Gladwin and W. Sturtevant (Eds.), *Anthropology and Human Behaviour.* Washington, DC: Anthropological Society of Washington.

Hymes, D. (1964). Introduction: Toward ethnographies of communication. *American Anthropologist, 66,* Part 2: 1–34.

Hymes, D. (1967). Models of the interaction of language and social setting. *Journal of Social Issues, 23,* 8–28.

Hymes, D. (1972). On communicative competence. In J. B. Pride & J. Holmes (Eds.), *Sociolinguistics.* Harmondsworth: Penguin.

Hymes, D. (1974). Ways of speaking. In R. Baumann & J. Sherzer (Eds.), *Explorations in the ethnography of speaking.* Cambridge: Cambridge University Press.

Hymes, D. (1977). *Foundations in sociolinguistics.* London: Tavistock.

Leech, G. N. (1983). *Principles of pragmatics.* London: Longman.

Olshtain, E. (1983). Sociocultural competence and language transfer: The case of apology. In S. Gass & L. Selinker (Eds.), *Language transfer in language learning.* Rowley, Mass.: Newbury House.

Olshtain, E, & Cohen, A. D. (1983). Apology: A speech act set. In N. Wolfson & E. Judd (Eds.), *Sociolinguistics and language acquisition.* Rowley, Mass.: Newbury House.

Owen, M. (1983). *Apologies and remedial interchanges: A study of language use in social interaction.* Berlin: Mouton de Gruyter.

Spender, D. (1980). *Man made language.* London: Routledge and Kegan Paul.

Thomas, J. (1983). Cross-cultural pragmatic failure. *Applied Linguistics, 4,* 91–112.

Thomas, J. (1985). Complex illocutionary acts and the analysis of discourse. *Lancaster Papers in Linguistics, 11.* Lancaster: University of Lancaster.

Thorne, B., Kramarae, C., & Henley, N. (Eds.) (1983). *Language, gender and society.* Rowley, Mass.: Newbury House.

Trosberg, A. (1987). Apology strategies in natives/nonnatives. *Journal of Pragmatics, 11,* 147–167.

West, C., & Zimmerman, D. H. (1983). Small insults: A study of interruptions in cross-sex conversations between unacquainted persons. In B. Thorne, C. Kramarae, & N. Henley (Eds.), *Language, gender and society.* Rowley, Mass.: Newbury House.

Wolfson, N. (1984). Pretty is as pretty does: A speech act view of sex roles. *Applied Linguistics, 5,* 236–244.

Wolfson, N. (1988). The bulge: A theory of speech behaviour and social distance. In J. Fine (Ed.), *Second language discourse: A textbook of current research.* Norwood, NJ: Ablex.

Wolfson, N., & Judd, E. (Eds.) (1983). *Sociolinguistics and language acquisition.* Rowley, Mass.: Newbury House.

Zimmerman, D.H., & West, C. (1975). Sex roles, interruptions and silences in conversation. In B. Thorne & N. Henley (Eds.), *Language and sex: Difference and dominance.* Rowley, Mass.: Newbury House.

Understanding the Article

1. What is covered in the Literature Review section of the paper?

2. Describe the subject and the data (the "corpus"). Where can you find more information on the method of data collection used?

3. In your own words, what does Table 1 show about the relationship between apologies and the sex of the participants? On page 369, Holmes uses a χ^2 test (chi-square) to measure whether the distribution of apologies based on gender was statistically significant. Go back to J. D. Brown's article for an explanation of what this test is used for and evaluate whether it has been appropriately used in this study.

4. How did Holmes categorize the apology strategies used by the subjects? Where could you find more information on her categorization system?

5. Why did the results of the analysis of apology strategies lead Holmes to look at other ways of categorizing apologies? What were these other categories and what were the results of her analysis (as displayed in Tables 4 through 10)?

6. Which conclusions follow directly from the results of Holmes's analysis and which seem more speculative? (Look back over the article and notice the researcher's use of language—for example, "perhaps," "suggests," "it is possible that . . .," "there is support here for . . ., "one finds some support for the view . . .," "it appears . . .").

Reflecting on Wider Issues

1. In terms of Bachman's concept of language competence (see page 427 this volume, or *PLLT,* Chapter 9), how does the example below (from Holmes) exemplify the different aspects of language competence?

   Context: A's child spills her drink on V's carpet.

   A: Oh look! I'm so sorry. I'll clean it up. Have you got a cloth?

   B. Don't worry. I'll do it. It wasn't very much.

2. Research suggests that the pragmatic conventions of a language are sometimes difficult to learn because of the disparity between

Going Beyond the Article

For a clearer understanding of Holmes's system for categorizing apologies, read her 1988 article, "Paying compliments: A sex-preferential positive politeness strategy" (*Journal of Pragmatics, 12.* For a look at problems in language transfer and aspects of sociolinguistic competence, read Olshtain (1983), "Sociolinguistic competence and language transfer: The case of apology," in *Language Transfer in Language Learning,* S. Gass and L. Selinker (Eds.) (New York: Newbury House).

UNIT VIII

LANGUAGE TESTING

15

CLOZE METHOD: WHAT DIFFERENCE DOES IT MAKE?

Carol A. Chapelle and Roberta G. Abraham
Iowa State University

Previewing the Article

As early as 1971, John Oller was advocating cloze testing as an excellent "integrative" test, a method he would later use to support his *unitary trait hypothesis.* In over two decades of subsequent research on the efficacy of cloze, questions are still being asked about what competencies might underlie the ability to fill in blanks in a reading passage. In this article, Carol Chapelle and Roberta Abraham shed some further light on how various types of cloze tests might measure different abilities.

Before digging into this study, make sure you understand what cloze passages are and review, if possible, the issues surrounding this fascinating testing method (*PLLT,* Chapter 10). Then, ascertain the following:

1. What is the purpose of the study?
2. Scan Section II and identify the four different types of cloze tests.
3. What are the research questions?
4. What kind of statistical test is used to support the research hypotheses?

Reprinted from *Language Testing,* 7:121–146, 1990.

Considerable evidence suggests that cloze techniques can create tests which measure aspects of students' second language competence. However, it remains unclear how variations in the cloze procedure affect measurement. This study compared results obtained from cloze passages constructed from the same text using four different procedures: fixed-ratio, rational, (rational) multiple choice, and C-test. The four procedures produced tests similar in reliabilities but distinct in levels of difficulty and patterns of correlations with other tests. These results are discussed in view of theoretically-based expectations for convergent and discriminate relationships of the four cloze tests with other tests.

I. Introduction

Although cloze procedures do not produce perfect tests of overall language proficiency, they do hold potential for measuring aspects of students' written grammatical competence, consisting of "knowledge of vocabulary, morphology, syntax and phonology/graphology," and textual competence, knowledge of the cohesive and rhetorical properties of text (Bachman, 1990, pp. 87–88). The specific traits measured by a particular cloze test should depend, in part, on methods of test construction and student response. Because the effects of various cloze methods are not well understood, this study hypothesized that performance on four types of cloze tests (a fixed-ratio, a rational cloze, a (rational) multiple-choice cloze, and a C-test) would vary and then evaluated empirical data to test this hypothesis. The four tests are compared on the basis of their difficulty, reliability, and convergent and discriminant correlations with five other tests.

II. Four Types of Cloze Tests

The cloze procedure is used to construct a language test by deleting from a passage some information which the test-taker must fill in. This basic procedure for writing second language tests has been realized in several different ways, presumably resulting in tests that differ in the specific language trait they measure, or their accuracy of measurement. The first type, the fixed-ratio cloze test, is constructed by deleting words according to a fixed pattern (e.g., every seventh word). This procedure is intended to sample regularly various types of words, some of which are governed by local grammatical constraints, others of which are governed by long-range textual constraints. A second cloze procedure, the rational cloze, allows the test developer control over the types of words deleted, and thus the language traits measured. A third cloze is constructed by altering the mode of expected response, having the student not construct an answer to fill in a blank but simply select the correct word from choices given. A fourth clozelike procedure, the C-test, specifies that deletions are made on the second half of every other word in a short segment of text.

Because of the shorter segment of text and the importance of clues in the immediate environment, this procedure most likely results in tests of more grammatical and less textual competence. Each of these types of tests has been used and investigated; however, it remains unknown exactly how these four different test-construction procedures compare.

Fixed-Ratio Cloze

The fixed-ratio cloze procedure for second language testing was proposed as a test of nothing less than global language proficiency (Oller, 1979). Consequently, much cloze research seeks evidence for this claim, offering little substance to the definition of specific traits that may comprise global proficiency (as indicated by cloze performance). Such studies consisted of analyses of the cloze and other language tests, which were all shown to correlate to some degree (e.g., Hanania & Shikhani, 1986; Irvine, Atai, & Oller, 1974; Oller & Conrad, 1971) or to load on one general factor (e.g., Oller, 1983). With foci on common language-test variance attributable to overall proficiency and predictive evidence for cloze validity, the theoretical relevance of different correlations between the cloze and other tests was not thoroughly explored (Oller, 1979)[1]. Along with this external component of construct validation, however, a substantial amount of research on cloze items has found evidence for some cloze items as measures of textual competence, and others as measures of grammatical competence (Chavez-Oller, Chihara, Weaver & Oller, 1985; Lado, 1986; Markham, 1987; Shanahan, Kamil, & Tobin, 1982). Overall, these and other studies have found positive evidence for the fixed-ratio cloze as a measure of language traits, more specifically, written grammatical and textual competence.

Investigating the suggestion (Carroll, Carton, & Wilds, 1959) that cloze performance may be related to cognitive abilities other than language, a few studies have uncovered evidence suggesting that cloze variance may also be related to the nonlinguistic trait, field independence (the ability to perceive analytically; McKenna, 1984), as measured by the Group Embedded Figures Test (GEFT). Hansen and Stansfield (1981) report significant disattenuated correlations between an apparently fixed-ratio cloze test (multiple-choice) and the GEFT (r = .43, and r = .22, with "scholastic aptitude" partialed out). They concluded that cloze tests may be biased toward field independent test takers. In another study, for four out of nine groups (n = 19–59), Hansen (1984) found

---

[1]In fact, some differences in the strengths of correlation were, of course, found. The one that is given most attention is the stronger correlation between the cloze and listening tests (e.g., the Listening part of the TOEFL, or dictation tests). However, rather than interpreting these correlations as indicators of specific shared variance among these tests, they are used as an argument that both types of tests must be measures of overall language proficiency. The cloze-listening correlations observed in early studies have not been found consistently (e.g., Ilyin et al., 1987).

significant correlations between a fixed-ratio cloze and the GEFT (r = .33–.48). On the basis of higher correlations between the cloze and GEFT than between the GEFT and other language measures, Hansen asserts "some support [for] the Stansfield and Hansen hypothesis of field sensitivity bias in the cloze procedure" but notes that "the wide variation in the relationship between FD/I cognitive style and cloze test performance among the nine classes tested ... speaks for a cautious interpretation" (pp. 320–321)[2]. In a third study, Chapelle (1988) found no correlation between a fixed-ratio cloze and the GEFT for ESL students but on the same test found moderate disattenuated correlations between the two measures for remedial native speakers of English (r = .42) and regular freshman native speakers (r = .63). When verbal ability as measured by the English ACT was partialed out for the two groups of native speakers, the partial correlation was significant for the latter (r = .53; n = 29). If cloze tests do in fact measure a nonlanguage trait as well as distinct language traits, inconsistent results from one cloze to another can be expected.

Such inconsistencies, even when different deletion ratios are used for the same text, have been noted by Alderson (1979, 1980, and 1983), who attributed them to uneven sampling of traits measured from one cloze to the next[3]. Other explanations of cloze inconsistencies are text and item difficulties relative to the group tested (Brown, 1983; Klein-Braley, 1983). Brown (1984) clarifies the relevance of a test's difficulty to its reliability and hence correlations with other measures, concluding that "effectiveness in terms of reliability and validity, appears to be related to how well a given cloze passage fits a given sample" (Brown, 1984, p. 118). Passage fit refers to characteristics of the text as a whole such as reading level and topic (Alderson & Urquhart, 1985a, 1985b), but it also depends on individual items, each of which contributes to overall variance. Because items are at the root of cloze performance, it has been suggested that the cloze procedure can be improved by selecting explicitly the words to be deleted, thus creating a rational cloze.

Rational Cloze

The theoretical underpinning of the rational cloze procedure, in which the test writer selects particular items, diverges somewhat from that of the fixed-ratio cloze, which relies on regular sampling of words in the text. Ratio-

---

[2]That variation is difficult to interpret, as it may be a function of the differential reliabilities of the cloze tests (and the GEFT) for the groups, which, on the basis of their anecdotal descriptions (Hansen, 1984, pp. 313–314) appear to differ in language proficiency.

[3]Cloze inconsistencies are even more apparent when summarized over a number of studies. In fact, J.D. Brown (1988) notes that reported internal consistency reliability estimates have ranged from .31 to .96 and correlations between cloze and other language tests have ranged from .43 to .91.

nal cloze research and practice rests on the assumption that different cloze items can be explicitly chosen to measure different language traits. Some evidence indicates that test writers can select words reflecting distinct aspects of the learners' grammatical and textual competence (Bachman, 1982). Despite these findings, the factors influencing item performance remain under investigation (e.g., Brown, 1988). While researchers continue to seek theoretical and statistical bases for cloze item performance, it is useful to note that, practically speaking, items selected by experienced test writers may produce tests that are more reliable and more highly correlated with other language tests, especially tests measuring traits similar to those that particular cloze items were chosen to measure.

The empirical findings related to these expectations have been mixed. The rational cloze procedure produced a test that was easier than the fixed-ratio cloze in Bachman's study (1985), while in Greene's (1965) research (using native speakers), overall test difficulty of the two were the same. Rational deletion procedures resulted in a test with higher reliability than its fixed-ratio counterpart in Greene's study (Split-half = .76 and .52, respectively), but not in Bachman's study (Split-half = .86 for both tests, for all subjects in the study). Bachman's (1985) comparison of correlations of fixed-ratio and rational cloze tests found the two to correlate comparably with six other language tests (rational, r = .62–.82.; fixed-ratio, r = .68–.81).

Despite these empirical results, on theoretical grounds the rational cloze procedure should have the advantage of allowing more consistent and controllable results to the extent that distinct item types can be understood and identified. As with the fixed-ratio cloze, a problem in characterizing the rational cloze as a test genre is the individual nature of each such test. In attempting to synthesize rational cloze research, one finds that the types of items used in various studies tend to be inequivalent; moreover, rational cloze tests differ from one study to another in their 'facet of expected response' (Bachman, 1990).

Multiple-Choice

How does the multiple-choice response method affect students' performance on the cloze? Research has demonstrated that constructing a test response is more difficult for test takers than selecting one (Shohamy, 1984)[4]; however, as Shohamy points out, finding that one method produces an easier test than another does not indicate which method is the more valid. An overall shift in difficulty alone, if not extreme, may not significantly alter the test's

---

[4]As Porter (1976) points out, the difficulty of a multiple choice cloze is also a function of the alternatives provided for items.

reliability or its convergent and discriminant correlations. Past research provides some comparative information between the two cloze methods. Cranney (1972) reports comparable reliabilities for multiple-choice and fill-in versions of a cloze test. Hale, Stansfield, Rock, Hicks, Butler, and Oller (1989) interpreted the research of Pike (1979) and Hinofotis and Snow (1978) to indicate "a similarity of processes measured by the MC cloze and the completion cloze procedures" (p. 51), attributing the lower-than-expected correlations in the latter study to possible unreliability of measures. Bensoussan and Ramraz (1984) also report a lower-than-expected correlation (r = .43) between their multiple-choice cloze and completion cloze, but lacking reliabilities estimated for that sample, it is difficult to interpret the strength of that relationship. Ilyin, Spurling and Seymour (1987) report for their fill-in and multiple-choice cloze tests almost equal difficulty levels and a .76 correlation.

Comparative questions aside, some data exist for adequate reliabilities of multiple-choice cloze tests and for reasonable correlations with other tests. The following reliabilities have been estimated for various multiple-choice cloze tests: KR-20 = .76 (Jonz, 1976); KR-20 = .82 & .84 (Bensoussan & Ramraz, 1984); KR-21 = .86 (Ilyin et al., 1987); adjusted reliabilities ranging from .88 to .94 (Hale et al., 1989). Strong correlations with reading tests have been hypothesized by Porter (1976) and Ozete (1977) who suggested that the multiple-choice cloze is similar to tests of reading comprehension, in other words, tests of written textual competence, requiring selected rather than constructed responses. Ilyin et al. (1987) found a slightly higher correlation of their multiple-choice cloze with their reading test (r = .77) than with their listening tests (r - .71 and .64), but the strongest correlation was found between the multiple choice cloze and their structure test (r = .81). When Jonz (1976) calculated correlations of the multiple-choice cloze with other language tests, the correlation with reading was not among the strongest: Composition, r = .80; Structure, r = .70; Reading, r = .61; Vocabulary, r = .54 and Aural, r = .29. Hale et al. (1989) found predictably stronger correlations between the multiple-choice cloze and the written-text portions (Structure, Written Expression, Vocabulary, and Reading Comprehension) of the TOEFL (r = .88; median across language groups) and weaker correlations between the cloze and the listening portion of the TOEFL (r = .77; median across language groups). However, they failed to find notable distinctions among correlations of the cloze with the four written text parts of the TOEFL.

These results appear to relate multiple-choice cloze performance to tests of written competence more clearly than has research on the fill-in cloze, indicating that this facet of test method may indeed affect not only test difficulty but also the language trait measured. However, because previous research has combined rational items and multiple-choice responses inconsistently, the hypothesis concerning the relationship between multiple-choice cloze and reading tests, or any other tests, requires additional support.

C-Test

The C-test, claimed, like the fixed-ratio cloze, to be a measure of global language proficiency, was proposed to solve several cloze problems (Klein-Braley, 1985). One major problem was the unpredictable results obtained by various fixed-ratio deletion procedures (e.g., Alderson, 1979). The every-other-word C-test procedure improves on the fixed-ratio cloze by producing a large number of "random samples of the word classes of the text involved" (Klein-Braley, 1985, p. 84)[5]. A second problem with the cloze, the effect of text topic and difficulty on test performance, is minimized by the C-test's use of several different short tests. A third cloze problem, the lack of criterion reference point defined by performance of educated native speakers, does not exist with the C-procedures; Klein-Braley (1985, p. 84) reports, "Adult educated native speakers achieve virtually perfect scores."

Indeed, these features of the C-test appear to improve on the psychometric properties of the cloze. However, like early research on the cloze, C-test research has failed to clarify evidence for the specific language traits that this technique may measure. This evidence must, then, be procured from descriptions of test items, analysis of the test task, and details of reported validity research. The method of C-test construction, designed to improve on cloze text and item sampling through the use of more and shorter passages, also has the effect of eliminating or at least reducing the number of cloze-type items which are governed by long-range constraints. The C-test requires students to fill in missing second halves of words. In completing a given word, the most important clue for the test taker is often in the immediate environment of the blank (Klein-Braley, 1985, p. 98), including the first half of the word itself. Error analysis of students' responses indicated that "recognition of syntactical relationships comes first" in making responses, although semantic processing is essential for perfect performance (Klein-Braley, 1985, p. 100). On the basis of item and task description, then, the C-test appears to reflect more grammatical than textual competence.

Interpretations of validity research, on the other hand, argue that the C-test is a measure of overall language proficiency. Such arguments include the observation that C-test scores increase regularly and predictably with an individual's native language ability. However, this argument for the predictable increase in C-test performance with maturational linguistic development would be equally compelling with respect to maturational development of grammatical competence alone. A second argument is Klein-Braley's report of weak to moderate correlations between C-test performance and scores on non-verbal intelligence tests. She asserts that the increase of these correlations with the subjects' age is evidence for consistency of C-test results with theoretical

---

[5]The numbers of different word classes deleted by C-tests were calculated for over 100 English and 100 German texts (Klein-Braley, 1985).

expectations. An alternative interpretation is that correlation of a language test with a nonverbal ability indicates undesirable convergent relationships between constructs for which divergent relationships are predicted by theory. Such an argument is precisely the one made from similar research which found the cloze test related to the nonverbal characteristic, field independence (Stansfield & Hansen, 1983).

On the basis of the C-test research reviewed by Klein-Braley, it is clear that this procedure can produce results which are psychometrically superior to the cloze. Examination of test items and task analysis suggest the C-test may be a measure of relatively grammatical competence, while validity research does not provide evidence for the specific traits it may measure and indicates problematic convergent relationships with a nonverbal measure. Thus, questions remain concerning exactly what the C-test measures and how it can be distinguished from comparable cloze tests.

In summary, cloze-type techniques produce tests that can measure, with some degree of accuracy, aspects of the students' written grammatical and/or textual competence. The accuracy of measurement and specific traits measured may depend on how deletions are made and the manner of students' expected response. This research sheds light on the effects of these methods by hypothesizing their theoretical impact on correlations with other tests and providing empirical evidence for the following question: How do cloze tests constructed from a single passage using the four procedures outlined above compare in difficulty, reliability, and convergent and discriminant correlation coefficients?

III. Research Design

Subjects

The subjects were 201 nonnative speakers of English (from a wide variety of language backgrounds) who were enrolled in intermediate and advanced ESL composition courses at Iowa State University in Fall 1985. All students had met the University's admission requirement of 500 on the TOEFL and were working toward degrees in a wide range of subject area across campus.

Measures

All four cloze tests (*Appendix A*) were constructed from a single text adapted from a *Scientific American* article entitled "Compartmentalization of Decay in Trees" (Shigo, 1985). The academic genre of this text is typical of the type these students are likely to encounter in their classes at Iowa State, yet it is not overly technical and dependent on previous knowledge. It is apparent that the author intended a general audience, as the technical terms used are defined within the text.

The fixed-ratio cloze was constructed by deleting every 11th word—an arbitrarily chosen rate—from the text following the first two sentences, which were left intact. An *a posteriori* analysis (using the item classifications introduced by Perkins and German, 1985) revealed that the procedure had resulted in four items relying on clues in the immediate context, 12 items relying on clues within the same clause, six items relying on clues beyond the clause but within the sentence, and 13 items relying on clues beyond the sentence.

The same contextual categories were used to explicitly choose items for the rational cloze. The number of each type of item for the rational cloze was approximately the same as the ones for the fixed-ratio cloze (3, 13, 5, 14, respectively) so comparisons could be made between deliberate and chance deletions without radically confounding item type as defined by context clues. The major difference, then, between the fixed ratio and rational cloze was that for the latter we chose each item as having clearly identifiable clues in the passage.

The multiple-choice cloze had exactly the same words deleted as the rational cloze. For each blank, four alternatives were given; in most cases the three distractors were the same part of speech as the correct answer.

The C-test was constructed based on the instructions given by Klein-Braley and Raatz (1984) and Klein-Braley (1985). For each of the five paragraphs of suitable length, a short intact introduction was provided, followed by the deletion of the second half of every second word. Fifteen such deletions were made for each of the five paragraphs and then the rest of the paragraph was presented intact. This procedure differed from the prototypical C-test which would have used paragraphs from different texts for each of the five parts. For the purpose of this study, it was necessary to keep the text constant across the four test-construction methods to make valid method comparisons.

The Iowa State University English Placement Test (EPT) has three multiple-choice parts: listening (35 items), reading (35 items), and vocabulary (30 items). The listening section, with aural questions about spoken segments of text, is considered a test of both grammatical and textual competence. Some items require students to discern the grammatical details of what they heard while others require overall comprehension of discourse. The reading test consists of short passages followed by multiple-choice questions intended to test discourse comprehension (i.e., textual competence). The vocabulary items require students to select the correct university-level vocabulary word to fit into a one-sentence defining context. The focus on specific lexical items within a limited context makes this test primarily a grammatical one, in Bachman's sense. These tests have been used successfully over the past decade for making rough distinctions among students. KR-20 reliabilities for the whole group taking the tests each semester are adequate (above .80). However, because subjects in this study consisted only of low scorers who, after taking the tests, were required to take an ESL class, the variance in this sample was reduced; consequently the sample reliabilities are relatively low. (See Appendix B for reliabilities for all tests.)

The writing test required students to compose an essay on the topic, "describe something you have learned in one of your non-English courses this semester." Each composition was rated by two ESL instructors (other than the student's own) using Jacobs, Zinkgraf, Wormuth, Hartfiel and Hughey's (1981) ESL Composition Profile, which produces a score between 34 and 100.

The Group Embedded Figures Test (GEFT) by Oltman, Raskin, and Witkin (1971) was used as a measure of field independence. The GEFT consists of a booklet containing 18 "complex figures" within which subjects are asked to find a given "simple figure". Their ability to identify the simple figure from the distracting context of the complex figure is used as a measure of their field independence. One point is given for each correctly identified simple figure, producing scores from 0 to 18. The GEFT, used extensively in second language research, is not without problems (see Brown, 1987; Chapelle, 1988); however, it was chosen because of the unanswered question of whether it, a nonverbal measure, would produce the desirable discriminant correlations with cloze tests.

Procedures

Most students took the listening, reading, and vocabulary tests at the beginning of Fall semester, 1985. Twenty-one (about 10%) had taken the same tests two and a half months earlier. All subjects wrote the composition during the eighth week of the semester. Within the next three weeks, each student was given a cloze test and the GEFT during one class period. To distribute the four types of cloze tests, the same type of cloze was assigned to every fourth student on alphabetized class lists, so approximately equal numbers of students took each type. Students were given 25 minutes to complete their assigned cloze tests; the GEFT was administered according to the procedures given in the test manual. Verification of the desired similarities among the four groups was obtained from the results of an ANOVA comparing the scores on all tests (except the cloze). None of the small observed differences among groups was statistically significant.

Analysis

SPSS-X (SPSS-X, Inc.) was used to estimate KR-20 reliabilities for the four cloze tests and the GEFT. Reliability for the composition was estimated by calculating the correlation between raters, and then applying the Spearman-Brown Prophecy correction for use of two raters (Thorndike & Hagen, 1977, p. 90–91). Reliabilities for the listening, reading, and vocabulary tests were estimated using the KR-21 formula for practical reasons: it was not possible to recover the item data for the sample. SPSS-X was used to perform an ANOVA with Sheffé follow-up tests indicating differences between cloze tests, and to perform correlations among all tests. To allow accurate comparisons of correlations, all were corrected for attenuation (Thorndike & Hagen, 1977, p. 101). Disattenuated correlations among all tests are given in Appendix C.

IV. Results

How Does the Difficulty of the Four Types of Cloze Tests Compare?

The fixed-ratio and rational tests were predicted to be the most difficult and the multiple-choice cloze the easiest. The C-test, hypothesized to measure relatively more grammatical competence, but requiring the student to construct a response, should be easier than the two cloze tests, but more difficult than the multiple-choice cloze. Of the two most difficult cloze tests, the fixed-ratio was predicted to be the more difficult because no deliberation over items took place during test construction in contrast to the rational cloze in which items with clearly identifiable clues were selected. An ANOVA with a Scheffé follow-up test comparing the tests' percentage scores found the differences among mean scores, which fell in the predicted order, to be statistically significant (fixed-ratio, $\bar{x}$ = 41.7%; rational, $\bar{x}$ = 50.9%; multiple-choice, $\bar{x}$ = 82.3%; C-test, $\bar{x}$ = 61.8%; F = 79.3; p<.001)

How Did the Reliabilities of the Four Tests Compare?

Estimation of reliability for cloze tests is theoretically problematic because of the interdependence of cloze items; however, Brown (1983) concluded that in practice this problem is negligible. Moreover, for the purpose of comparing the cloze reliabilities in this study, if there is an overestimation problem, it should affect the three word-deletion cloze tests equally. The interdependence of C-test items, however, requires reliability to be calculated in the manner described by Raatz (1985), which treats each segment of text with a series of blanks as one item (referred to as a "super item"). The C-test used in this study had 5 "super items", each scored from 0 to 15. Lower reliabilities were predicted for tests with the most extreme difficulties: the fixed-ratio and multiple-choice tests. These predictions were accurate, but the differences among reliabilities were not great: fixed-ratio, KR-20 = .76; rational, KR-20 = .80; multiple-choice, KR-20 = .76; C-test, KR-20 = .81.

How Do the Convergent and Discriminant Correlations of the Four Tests Compare?

Messick (1989) terms convergent and discriminant evidence for the validity of a test "the external component of construct validity" which "refers to the extent to which the test's relationships with other tests ... reflect the expected high, low, and interactive relations implied in the theory of the construct being assessed" (p. 45). Theory indicates that these relations are affected by two sources of variance: that attributable to the trait measured by the test and that associated with the test method. Bachman's (1990) theoretical foundations— asserting the relevance of traits and methods for test performance—suggest that such a framework "may provide language testers with an appropriate means of codifying and describing, at a very useful level of detail, the tests they are developing, using, or researching, for purposes of improved . . . communication within the field of language testing" (Bachman, 1990, p. 154). Accordingly, aspects of Bachman's overall framework are used here to predict convergent and discriminant relationships of each of the cloze tests with the listening, reading, vocabulary, writing, and GEFT tests.

The language tests are sufficiently narrow in the traits they measure to be characterized by using only one component of Bachman's definition of language competence and by distinguishing aural from written competence. Within Bachman's "organizational competence" exists what we shall consider a continuum from grammatical competence (vocabulary, morphology, etc.) to textual competence (cohesion and rhetorical organization). To clarify which of these traits each test was hypothesized to measure, each language test was placed at the appropriate position along the three-point continuum under either written or aural components (Table 1). Under written, the reading and writing tests are most textually based; vocabulary is most grammatically based. The listening test, the only one under aural trait, was placed in the middle because it addresses specific grammar points with some items, while other segments require comprehension of longer discourse. The three word-deletion cloze tests were placed at the written midpoint and the C-test at the grammatical end for reasons described above. A nonlanguage trait was distinguished from the language traits and the GEFT, a nonlanguage measure, was placed under that heading.

With this designation of the traits hypothesized to be measured by each test, it was possible to estimate the degree of similarity or difference between the cloze and the other tests. These estimations are marked under each trait in Table 1[A] using the notation "same," "same—" (same minus) and "different". Any tests which fell under the "same" category would be hypothesized to measure the same trait as the cloze; "same—" indicates that a test measures close to the same trait as the cloze. Additional minuses added to "same" indicate a greater trait difference between that test and the cloze. The three word-deletion cloze tests displayed in Table 1[A] are presumed to measure the same trait so their trait similarities and differences with other tests should be equivalent. Table 1[B] displays the similarities and differences between the other tests and the C-test. On the basis of trait similarities alone, different patterns of correlations are predicted for the C-test than for the word-deletion cloze tests. In keeping with Bachman's theory, however, method facets should also be considered.

TABLE I.   Hypothesized Sources of Trait Variance

Part A   Similarities and differences between the cloze tests (fixed-ratio, rational, and multiple-choice) and the other tests

TRAITS	Language (same) — Written (same) — → Textual (same)	Language (same) — Written (same) — Grammatical ← (same-)	Language (same) — Aural (same-) — → Textual (same--)	Nonlanguage (different)
Organizational Competence				
Grammatical ← (same-)	Reading Writing	Vocabulary CLOZE (F-R) CLOZE (RAT) CLOZE (M-C)	Listening	GEFT

Part B   Similarities and differences between the C-test and the other tests

TRAITS	Language (same) — Written (same) — → Textual (same--)	Language (same) — Written (same) — Grammatical ← (same-)	Language (same) — Aural (same-) — → Textual (same--)	Nonlanguage (different)
Organizational Competence				
Grammatical ← (same)	Reading Writing	C-TEST Vocabulary	Listening	GEFT

Two facets of test method were taken into account: input format and the format of expected response. Input format refers to how the student receives information while taking a test. Input can be received either through the use of language or nonlanguage material, the values for the parameter "form of presentation" in Table 2. Language input can be further subdivided on the basis of

TABLE 2.   Hypothesized Sources of Method Variance: Similarities and Differences of Input Format Between the Cloze/C-tests and the Other Tests

FORM OF PRESENTATION	LANGUAGE (SAME)		NONLANGUAGE (DIFFERENT)
Channel & Mode	Visual *(same)*	Aural *(same-)*	
	Vocabulary Reading Writing CLOZEs	Listening	GEFT

its channel and mode into primarily visual, and primarily aural, represented by the two descriptors under "language." In Table 2, each test is listed at its appropriate position and, using the same notation described for Table 1, similarities and differences with the cloze tests and the C-test are marked.

A second method facet, format of the expected response, can also be distinguished as "language" or "nonlanguage" as indicated in Table 3. When the form is "language," the type can be either "constructed" when the student is expected to produce some language, or "selected" when the student is expected to choose an answer. Constructed language can differ in its length, with a test such as a cloze or C-test requiring students to construct a word or less, and a writing test requiring students to construct an entire essay. Table 3 indicates where each of the tests is placed with respect to its method of expected response. Table 3[A] marks each category for its similarity to or difference from the fixed-ratio cloze, the rational cloze and the C-test; Table 3[B] does the same for the multiple-choice cloze test.

On the basis of these three sources of variance—one trait and two method facets—estimations were made of the relative degree of similarity between each cloze test and the other measures. These estimations resulted from adding, for each of the cloze tests, the "sames," "same minuses" and the "differents" for each test on each of the three dimensions. For example, relative relationships of other tests with the fixed-ratio and rational cloze tests are

TABLE 3.   Hypothesized Sources of Method Variance: Expected Response

Part A Similarities and differences between the fixed-ratio/rational/C-test and the other tests

FORM OF OUTPUT				
Type of output	**Constructed** (same)		**Selected** (same--)	**Nonlanguage** (different)
Length of output	**Word** (same)	**Text** (same-)		
	CLOZE (F-R) CLOZE (RAT) C-TEST	Writing	Vocabulary Reading Listening	GEFT

Part B Similarities and Differences between the multiple-choice cloze and the other tests

FORM OF OUTPUT				
Type of output	**Constructed** (same-)		**Selected** (same)	**Nonlanguage** (different)
Length of output	**Word** (same-)	**Text** (same-)		
		Writing	Vocabulary Reading Listening CLOZE (M-C)	GEFT

estimated as demonstrated in Table 4. On the basis of this analysis, the performance on the writing test (same—) should be most highly correlated with the fixed-ratio and rational cloze tests, vocabulary and reading (same—) should be

TABLE 4.   Estimation of Relative Similarities Between Other Tests and the Fixed-Ratio and Rational Cloze Tests

TEST		TRAIT		INPUT		RESPONSE		
listening	→	same-	+	same-	+	same--	=	same----
reading	→	same-	+	same	+	same--	=	same---
vocabulary	→	same-	+	same	+	same--	=	same---
writing	→	same-	+	same	+	same-	=	same--
GEFT	→	different	+	different	+	different	=	different

tied for second, listening (same----) should be third, and the GEFT (different) should be uncorrelated. By adding the similarities and differences of the tests for each cloze test, predictions for relative correlations were obtained, thereby allowing for a theoretically motivated interpretation of the obtained correlations.

Table 5 displays the estimated ranks of correlations and the comparison between the predicted and actual disattenuated correlations of the cloze tests with the other tests. In the column labeled "Predicted Rankings," the test named at the top of each list is the one predicted to have the strongest correlation with the cloze test indicated. Tests predicted to have the same relative correlation (e.g., vocabulary and reading with the fixed-ratio cloze) are on the same line. The actual correlations are also listed with the strongest one on the top, and clustered (i.e., without a blank line between them) when they were close to one another (i.e., less than .1 different). The typeface of the tests listed under "Actual Correlations" indicates accuracy of prediction. Regular type denotes perfect prediction of rank, while italics indicates slight differences between predicted and actual correlations (differences in the way that correlations are clustered or their order within a cluster). Bold indicates major discrepancies in the order of predicted and actual correlations. These results are discussed in terms of the agreement between predicted and actual convergent and discriminate relationships as well as the absolute strengths of correlations.

With respect to relative convergent and discriminant relationships, the fixed-ratio cloze conforms most closely to its expectations. The correlation with the writing test is the strongest, followed by vocabulary; the correlation with the reading test is slightly lower than predicted, but the listening ranks fourth and, as predicted, there is no correlation between the cloze and the GEFT. In fact, the fixed-ratio cloze is the only one for which the theoretically-predicted lack of correlation with the GEFT appears. However, despite the

TABLE 5.   Predicted and Actual Relationships of the Cloze Tests to the Other Tests

ESTIMATES	PREDICTED RANKINGS	ACTUAL CORRELATIONS	
Fixed-ratio cloze with:			
(same--)	writing	writing	.621
(same---)	vocabulary/reading	vocabulary	.490
(same----)	listening	reading	.380
		listening	.296
(different)	GEFT	GEFT	.026
Rational cloze with:			
(same--)	writing	reading	.767
		vocabulary	.695
(same---)	vocabulary/reading	writing	.659
(same----)	listening	listening	.338
(different)	GEFT	GEFT	.293
Multiple choice cloze with:			
(same-)	vocabulary/reading	reading	.862
(same--)	listening/writing	writing	.433
		listening	.366
(different)	GEFT	GEFT	.226
		vocabulary	.180
C-test with:			
(same--)	vocabulary	vocabulary	.836
(same---)	writing	writing	.639
(same----)	reading	reading	.604
(same-----)	listening	listening	.472
(different)	GEFT	GEFT	.399

consistency of the predictions with the results, the fixed-ratio cloze, overall, correlates most poorly with the language measures; its highest correlation with a language measure is r = .621, the next is r = .490, and the correlation with the reading test is only r = .380. Despite the desirable lack of correlation with the GEFT, it would be difficult to argue for the fixed-ratio cloze as a clear measure of any of these traits given the moderate to low correlations obtained with other language measures.

Even with approximately the same item types as the fixed-ratio cloze, the rational cloze contrasts in its strength of correlations with the written language tests: r = .767 to r = .659. With these language test correlations, however, also appears a higher-than-zero correlation with the GEFT. Although this correlation is greater than one would predict in absolute terms, the observed correlations fall close to their predicted order, with less discrimination among the written-text correlations than predicted. All three were moderately high rather than the writing test correlation being higher than the reading and vocabulary tests. On the basis of these results, then, the rational cloze demonstrates moderately high, fairly predictable correlations with other tests, providing evidence for the superiority of carefully selected items over items selected by their positions in the text alone.

These benefits of the rational cloze did not appear when it was modified into a multiple choice format. While the correlations with reading correspond to expectations, the multiple choice cloze has the pattern of relationships most deviant from predictions. The strangest of these correlations is the one with the vocabulary test, r = .180, a correlation which is lower than that between the multiple choice and the GEFT. One might suspect something strange about the vocabulary test for this sample; however, that suspicion is allayed somewhat by the correlation of r = .784 between the vocabulary and the reading test, one similar to that of the other groups. (See Appendix C.) This multiple choice cloze, then, is apparently a poor measure of vocabulary relative to its fill-in counterpart, which correlates with the vocabulary test at a predictable .695, despite the method differences between these two tests. The absolute strengths of correlations provide evidence for the hypothesis (Porter, 1976) that the multiple choice cloze may be a measure of reading comprehension. Empirical evidence supporting this assertion has not been obtained from previous research, in which the correlation between multiple choice cloze and reading has been about the same as that between the cloze and other measures (Hale et al., 1989) or less (Ilyin et al., 1987; Jonz, 1976). However, here the correlation obtained between the multiple-choice cloze and the reading test was the highest one obtained in the study (r = .862). The fact that the multiple choice and rational cloze tests were exactly the same except for their facet of expected response offers clear evidence for the effect of this method facet on convergent correlations.

The C-test's observed correlations were quite close to those expected, its correlation with reading being slightly higher, and with the GEFT considerably higher than predicted. While the correlation with the GEFT is relatively the lowest, in absolute terms it is not much lower than that with the listening test. The observed strong correlation between the C-test and the vocabulary test (the most grammatically-based test) provides empirical support for placing the C-test at the "grammatical" end of the "grammatical-textual" continuum, as suggested earlier. However, the C-test shares considerable variance with the other less grammatically-based tests, with none below r = .472.

Conclusion

Examining the cloze as a measure of second language traits, this study described results obtained from altering trait and method facets of the cloze procedure while holding text and student ability constant. The data substantiated predictions of the fixed-ratio as the most difficult and the multiple choice as the easiest of these methods. The fact that the rational and multiple choice were exactly the same tests except for their format of expected response pinpoints this facet as a determinant of difficulty level. Although statistically significant, these differences in difficulty were not sufficiently large to affect reliability substantially. The reliabilities were adequate, although not as high as desired. The homogeneity of this advanced-level group had the predictable effect of yielding only moderate cloze reliabilities.[6]

Differences in cloze methods had striking effects on their external relationships, suggesting directions for further investigation. The multiple-choice cloze was strongly related to the reading test, but not to the other language tests, including the vocabulary test. Why did the multiple choice cloze measure traits so similar to those measured by the reading test but so different from those measured by the vocabulary test? Facet of expected response apparently accounted for differences between the multiple choice and rational cloze tests, but why did the fixed-ratio and rational cloze produce different strengths of correlations with the other tests? Is it possible to explain these differences by comparing characteristics of explicitly selected items with those of items chosen by their position in the text or are these simply to be added to the many documented cases of cloze inconsistencies? Analysis of items by the amount of context needed to complete blanks does not account for test differences, since the number of items at each context level in the two tests was almost the same; therefore, other explanations are needed for the differences between these "parallel" tests. The C-test, correlating most strongly with the vocabulary test, produced, on average, the highest correlations with the language tests. Why did this apparently more grammatically-based test correlate so well with written text-based tests—even better than the fixed-ratio cloze? Why did the GEFT correlate more strongly than theory predicts with the three cloze tests which correlated well with language measures? Can we learn more about cloze/GEFT correlations by identifying particular types of items with which performance on the GEFT is associated? The consistent relationship of cloze performance with the nonverbal characteristic, field independence, is worthy of further investigation and interpretation.

Along with the empirical research directions suggested by these results are observations concerning the viability of systematizing theoretical assump-

---

[6]It should be noted that these moderate cloze reliabilities are consistently higher than those obtained with this group for the other language tests used in this study.

tions about language tests to make predictions of relationships among tests. The framework we devised for making hypotheses about expected correlations was our first attempt at formalizing and manipulating elements from Bachman's overall framework. As a first attempt, and as one which defines categories for some noncategorical constructs, it is crude and incomplete in some respects. Despite its shortcomings, we found it very useful to systematize our intuitions of expected correlational outcomes. This calculated development of hypotheses pinpointed effects of components of test variance, thereby helping us to isolate components we wished to consider. Generation of clear-cut hypotheses, moreover, facilitated discussion of correlational results because comparisons with predictions were possible as opposed to the familiar *ad hoc* explanations. There is much that could be added, rethought and reshuffled in this initial scheme; on the basis of our work with it, we foresee that time spent on further developments will be time well spent.

References

Alderson, J. C. (1979). The cloze procedure and proficiency in English as a foreign language. *TESOL Quarterly, 13,* 219–227.

Alderson, J. C. (1980). Native and nonnative speaker performance on cloze tests. *Language Learning, 30,* 59–76.

Alderson, J. C. (1983). The cloze procedure and proficiency in English as a foreign language. In Oller, J. (Ed.). *Issues in language testing research* (pp. 205–217). Rowley, Mass.: Newbury House.

Alderson, J. C., & Urquhart, A. H. (1985a). The effect of students' academic discipline on their performance on ESP reading tests. *Language Testing, 2,* 192–204.

Alderson, J. C., & Urquhart, A. H. (1985b). This test is unfair: I'm not an economist. In P. Hauptman, R. LeBlanc, and M. Wesche (Eds.). *Second language performance testing* (pp. 25–43). Ottawa: University of Ottawa Press.

Bachman, L. (1982). The trait structure of cloze test scores. *TESOL Quarterly, 16,* 61–70.

Bachman, L. (1985). Performance on cloze tests with fixed-ratio and rational deletions. *TESOL Quarterly, 19,* 535–556.

Bachman, L. (1990). *Fundamental Considerations in Language testing.* Oxford: Oxford University Press.

Bensoussan, M., & Ramraz, R. (1984). Testing EFL reading comprehension using a multiple-choice rational cloze. *Modern Language Journal, 68,* 230–239.

Brown, H. D. (1987). *Principles of languge learning and teaching.* 2d ed. Englewood Cliffs, NJ: Prentice-Hall.

Brown, J. D. (1983). A closer look at cloze: Validity and reliability. In J.W. Oller (Ed.). *Issues in language testing research* (pp. 237–250). Rowley, Mass.: Newbury House.

Brown, J. D., (1984). A cloze is a cloze is a cloze? In J. Handscombe, R. Orem, & B. Taylor (Eds.), *On TESOL 83* (pp. 109–119). Washington DC.: TESOL Publications.

Brown, J. D., (1988). What makes a cloze item difficult? *University of Hawai'i Working Papers in ESL, 7,* 17–39.

Chapelle, C. (1988). Field independence: A source of language test variance? *Language Testing, 5,* 62–82.

Chavez-Oller, M. A., Chihara, T., Weaver, K. A., & Oller, J. (1985). When are cloze items sensitive to constraints across sentences? *Language Learning, 35,* 63–73.

Cranney, A. G. (1972). The construction of two types of cloze reading tests for college students. *Journal of Reading Behavior, 5,* 60–64.

Greene, F. P. (1965). Modifications of the cloze procedure and changes in reading test performances. *Journal of Educational Measurement 2,* 213–217.

Hale, G., Stansfield, C., Rock, D., Hicks, M., Butler, F., & Oller, J. (1989). The relation of multiple-choice cloze items to the Test of English as a Foreign Language. *Language Testing, 6,* 49–78.

Hanania, E., & Shikhani, M. (1986). Interrelationships among three tests of language proficiency: Standardized ESL, cloze, and writing. *TESOL Quarterly, 20,* 97–109.

Hansen, J., & Stansfield, C. (1981). The relationship of field dependent-independent cognitive styles to foreign language achievement. *Language Learning, 31,* 349–367.

Hansen, L. (1984). Field dependence-independence and language testing: Evidence from six Pacific island cultures. *TESOL Quarterly, 18,* 311–324.

Hinofotis, F., & Snow, B.G. (1980). An alternative cloze testing procedure: Multiple-choice format. In J. W. Oller, & K. Perkins (Eds.), *Research in language testing.* Rowley, Mass.: Newbury House.

Ilyin, D., Spurling, S., & Seymour, S. (1987). Do learner variables affect cloze correlations? *System, 15,* 149–160.

Irvine, P., Atai, P, & Oller, J. (1974). Cloze, dictation and the test of English as a foreign language. *Language Learning, 24,* 245–252.

Jacobs, H. L., Zinkgraf, S. A., Wormuth, D. R., Hartfiel, V. F., & Hughey, J. B. (1981). *Testing ESL composition: A practical approach.* Rowley, MA: Newbury House.

Jonz, J. (1976). Improving on the basic egg: The M-C cloze. *Language Learning, 26,* 255–265.

Klein-Braley, C. (1983). A cloze is a question. In J.W. Oller (Ed.), *Issues in language testing research.* Rowley, MA: Newbury House.

Klein-Braley, C., & Raatz, U. (1984). A survey of research on the C-test. *Language Testing,* 134–146.

Klein-Braley, C. (1985). A cloze-up on the C-Test. *Language Testing, 2,* 76–104.

Lado, R. (1986). Analysis of native speaker performance on a cloze test. *Language Testing, 3,* 130–146.

Markham, P. (1987). Rational deletion cloze processing strategies: ESL and native English. *System, 15,* 303–311.

McKenna, F.P. (1984). Measures of field dependence: Cognitive style of cognitive ability. *Journal of Personality and Social Psychology, 47,* 593–603.

Messick, S. (1989). Validity. In R. Linn (Ed.), *Educational measurement.* NY: Macmillan.

Oller, J. W., & Conrad, C. A. (1971). The cloze technique and ESL proficiency. *Language Learning, 21,* 183–195.

Oller, J. W. (1979). *Language tests at school.* NY.: Longman.

Oller, J. W. (1983). Evidence for a general language proficiency: An expectancy grammar. In Oller, J. W. (Ed.), *Issues in language testing research.* Rowley, Mass.: Newbury House.

Oltman, P., Raskin, E., & Witkin, H. (1971). *Group embedded figures test.* Palo Alto, CA.: Consulting Psychologists Press.

Ozete (1977). The cloze procedure: A modification. *Foreign Language Annals, 10,* 565–568.

Pike, L. W. (1979). *An evaluation of alternative item formats for testing English as a foreign language* TOEFL Research Report No. 2). Princeton, New Jersey: Educational Testing Service.

Perkins, K., & German, P. (1985, October). *The effect of information gain on different structural category deletions in a cloze test.* Paper presented at Midwest TESOL, Milwaukee, WI.

Porter, D. (1976). Modified cloze procedure: A more valid reading comprehension test. *English Language Teaching, 30,* 151–155.

Raatz, U. (1985). Better theory for better tests? *Language Testing, 2,* 60–75.

Shigo, A. L. (1985). Compartmentalization of decay in trees: *Scientific American, 252,* 96–103.

Shohamy, E. (1984): Does the testing method make a difference? The case of reading comprehension. *Language Testing, 1,* 147–170.

Shanahan, T., Kamil, M., & Tobin, A. (1982). Cloze as a measure of intersentential comprehension. *Reading Research Quarterly, 17,* 229–255.

SPSS Inc. SPSS-X *User's Guide 3rd Edition.* Chicago: Author.

Stansfield, C., & Hansen, J. (1983). Field dependence-independence as a variable in second language cloze test performance. *TESOL Quarterly, 17,* 29–38.

Thorndike, R. L., & Hagen, E. P. (1977). *Measurement and evaluation in psychology and education* (4th ed.). NY: John Wiley & Sons.

Appendix A: Cloze Test – Compartmentalization of Decay in Trees

Trees have a spectacular survival record. Over a period of more than 400 million *years* (2)* they have evolved as the tallest, most massive, and longest-lived organisms ever to inhabit the earth. Yet [trees lack a means of defense *that* (2) almost every *animal* (1) has: trees cannot move away *from* (2) destruc-

---

*Italicized words represent blanks in one or more of the clozes. Blanks designated as (1) appear in the fixed-ratio cloze; those designated as (2) appear in the rational and rational multiple-choice cloze.

tive forces. Because they *cannot* (1) move, all types of living and nonliving]** enemies—fire, storms, *microorganisms* (1), insects, animals and man—have wounded *them* (2) throughout their history. *Trees* (1) (2) have survived *because* (2) their evolution has made them into highly *compartmentalized* (1) organisms; that is, they wall off injured and infected wood.

In (1) (2) that respect trees are radically different from animals. Fundamentally, [animals *heal* (1): they preserve their lives by making billions of repairs, installing *new* (1) cells or rejuvenated cells in the positions of old *ones* (2). *Trees* (1) cannot heal; they make] no *repairs* (2). Instead, they defend themselves *against* (1) consequences of injury and infection by walling *off* (2) the damage. *In* (1) a word, they compartmentalize. At *the* (2) same time they put *new* (1) cells in new positions; in effect, they grow a new *tree* (1) over the *old* (2) one every year. The most obvious results *of* (1) the process are growth rings, which are visible on the *cross* (1) section of a trunk, *a* (2) root or a branch.

Trees *have* (1) been guided through evolution by their need to defend against *attack* (1) while standing their ground. They always defend by *compartmentalizing* (2): they *attempt* (1) to wall off the injured or infected region.

After (2) a *tree* (1) has been injured, microorganisms can *infect* (2) the wound in several *ways* (1). Some [bacteria infect inner bark and stay *there* (2), creating diseases *known* (1) as annual cankers. *Other* (2) bacteria move into the tree's wood, *causing* (1) so-called wound rots. Still other microorganisms begin by] infecting the *inner* (1) bark *and* (2) then move in to *infect* (2) the wood as *well* (1). Finally, some microorganisms attack the wood first and *then* (2) move *to* (1) infect the inner bark *too* (2). Trees neither kill *nor* (2) arrest *the* (1) activity of these microorganisms. Nor do they respond in specific *ways* (1) (2) to specific microorganisms; the compartmentalization comes in response to the *fact* (1) of the injury.

Broadly *speaking* (2), the tree makes three responses *to* (1) injury and infection. In [the first of them, the boundaries *of* (1) compartments already in place are strengthened to resist the spread *of* (1) *infection* (2). *In* (2) the second, the *tree* (2) creates a new wall *by* (1)] anatomical and chemical means. The *third* (2) response the tree makes *is* (1) to continue growing. Trees survive injury and infection *if* (2) they *have* (1) enough time, energy and genetic capacity *to* (2) recognize and compartmentalize *injured* (1) and infected tissue while generating the new tissue that will maintain the *life* (2) of the tree.

This new understanding of trees as compartmentalizing organisms did not arise long ago. Indeed, [it came as a contradiction of earlier notions, some of *which* (2) were developed soon after the foundations of modern biology were established a century ago. It seems a] trite thing to say, but trees are fundamentally different from *animals* (2), and much of the failure to understand trees derives from unconsciously confusing the *two* (2).

**Deletions for the C-test begin with the first word in each bracketed section and continue with every second word to the end of the section.

APPENDIX B.   Descriptive Statistics and Reliability* Estimates for All Tests for the Four Groups

GROUP	Cloze	Listen	Vocabulary	Reading	Writing	GEFT
FIXED-RATIO						
n	53	53	53	53	52	53
x̄	14.6	21.2	23.0	23.4	78.2	13.0
s.d.	4.9	4.3	3.7	4.9	9.6	4.9
Reliability	.76	.56	.63	0.7	.85	.91
RATIONAL						
n	50	50	50	50	49	50
x̄	17.8	21.8	23.4	23.9	78.9	13.4
s.d.	5.6	4.4	3.8	4.9	7.8	3.9
Reliability	.80	.59	.67	.70	.76	.84
MULTIPLE CHOICE						
n	49	49	49	49	49	49
x̄	28.8	22.4	23.4	23.5	77.7	13.9
s.d.	3.9	4.4	3.0	4.5	7.3	3.5
Reliability	.76	.60	.44	.64	.68	.81
C-TEST						
n	49	49	49	49	49	49
x̄	46.6	20.7	23.4	23.6	78.4	13.8
s.d.	10.5	4.7	3.3	5.1	7.6	4.1
Reliability	.81	.64	.55	.73	.72	.87

*Reliability for writing calculated by correlations between raters corrected by the Spearman-Brown Prophecy Formula. Cloze and GEFT reliabilities calculated by KR-20. Listening, Vocabulary, and Reading reliabilities calculated by KR-21.

APPENDIX C.   Disattenuated Correlations Between All Tests for All Groups

GROUP	Cloze	Listen	Vocabulary	Reading	Writing	GEFT
FIXED-RATIO	---					
Listen	.296	---				
Vocabulary	.490	.030	---			
Reading	.380	-.013	1.000	---		
Writing	.621	.128	.765	.583	---	
GEFT	.026	-.052	.034	.293	.073	---
RATIONAL	---					
Listen	.338	---				
Vocabulary	.695	.000	---			
Reading	.767	.490	.654	---		
Writing	.659	.218	.776	.727	---	
GEFT	.293	.038	.012	-.069	-.238	---
MULTIPLE CHOICE	---					
Listen	.366	---				
Vocabulary	.180	.241	---			
Reading	.862	.386	.784	---		
Writing	.433	.759	.031	.487	---	
GEFT	.226	.000	-.089	.158	.016	---
C-TEST	---					
Listen	.472	---				
Vocabulary	.836	.320	---			
Reading	.604	.293	.685	---		
Writing	.639	.579	.263	.484	---	
GEFT	.399	-.280	.400	.122	.087	---

Understanding the Article

1. Using the text in Appendix A, rewrite the first paragraph to demonstrate each of the four cloze types that were examined in this study.

2. Who were the subjects and what tests were administered? Were all four types of cloze test administered to each student?

3. On the basis of previous research, the authors were able to predict the relationships (correlations) between the four cloze tests and the other tests. How do their predictions compare with the results of the present study (as depicted in Table 5)?

4. Did the results confirm the researchers' predictions of the comparative difficulty of the four cloze types?

5. What did the researchers conclude about the effects of the differences in cloze method on the correlations of the cloze tests with other tests?

Reflecting on Wider Issues

1. Some researchers would argue that cloze tests are biased in favor of field independent learners. What characteristics of cloze tests might lead researchers to make this claim? Do you think this argument would hold equally well for all four types of cloze test discussed in this study? Why or why not?

2. To what extent do you think cloze tests can measure the various traits of communicative competence?

Going Beyond the Article

Since the TOEFL is the test used by most U.S. colleges and universities for determining the English proficiency of nonnative speakers before admission, there is a great deal of interest in the relationship between TOEFL and other language tests. You might want to read Hale et al. (1989), "The relation of multiple-choice cloze items to the Test of English as a Foreign Language" (*Language Testing, 6,* 49–78).

As you can see from the study by Chapelle and Abraham, cloze testing is not uncontroversial. In a recent article, Jonz (1990) addresses one controversy in cloze testing—whether this procedure can measure comprehension beyond the immediate context of the deleted item ("Another turn in the conversation: What does cloze measure?" *TESOL Quarterly, 24,* 61–83).

16

WHAT DOES LANGUAGE TESTING HAVE TO OFFER?

Lyle F. Bachman
University of California, Los Angeles

Previewing the Article

One of the more rapidly advancing subfields of second language acquisition research is language testing. From its naive beginnings in the 1960s, with a handful of researchers devoting themselves specifically to testing in a second language, this subfield has grown into a highly sophisticated area of expertise that easily boggles the minds of us who are not "experts" in the area. In this article, Lyle Bachman provides an excellent summary of current issues in terms that are sometimes technical, but nevertheless written for the nonexpert.

Before you tackle this study, you should review basic testing concepts and principles such as validity, reliability, types and purposes of language testing, and the construct of communicative competence (see *PLLT,* Chapter 10 as well as the first part of Chapter 9). Then answer the following questions:

1. What is the purpose of the article (see paragraph 2)?

2. Scan to get a sense of some of the theoretical and methodological ideas Bachman spells out in Part 1.

3. Skim through Part 2 to get the gist of what is meant by an *interactional* approach to testing.

Reprinted from *TESOL Quarterly,* 25:671–704, 1991.

Advances in language testing in the past decade have occurred in three areas: (a) the development of a theoretical view that considers language ability to be multicomponential and recognizes the influence of the test method and test taker characteristics on test performance, (b) applications of more sophisticated measurement and statistical tools, and (c) the development of "communicative" language tests that incorporate principles of "communicative" language teaching. After reviewing these advances, this paper describes an interactional model of language test performance that includes two components, language ability and test method. Language ability consists of language knowledge and metacognitive strategies, whereas test method includes characteristics of the environment, rubric, input, expected response, and relationship between input and expected response. Two aspects of authenticity are derived from this model. The situational authenticity of a given test task depends on the relationship between its test method characteristics and the features of a specific language use situation, while its interactional authenticity pertains to the degree to which it invokes the test taker's language ability. The application of this definition of authenticity to test development is discussed.

Since 1989, four papers reviewing the state of the art in the field of language testing have appeared (Alderson, 1991; Bachman, 1990a; Skehan, 1988, 1989, 1991). All four have argued that language testing has come of age as a discipline in its own right within applied linguistics and have presented substantial evidence, I believe, in support of this assertion. A common theme in all these articles is that the field of language testing has much to offer in terms of theoretical, methodological, and practical accomplishments to its sister disciplines in applied linguistics. Since these papers provide excellent critical surveys and discussions of the field of language testing, I will simply summarize some of the common themes in these reviews in Part 1 of this article in order to whet the appetite of readers who may be interested in knowing what are the issues and problems of current interest to language testers. These articles are nontechnical and accessible to those who are not themselves language testing specialists. Furthermore, Skehan (1991) and Alderson (1991) appear in collections of papers from recent conferences that focus on current issues in language testing. These collections include a wide variety of topics of current interest within language testing, discussed from many perspectives, and thus constitute major contributions to the literature on language testing.

The purpose of this article is to address a question that is, I believe, implicit in all of the review articles mentioned above, What does language testing have to offer to researchers and practitioners in other areas of applied linguistics, particularly in language learning and language teaching? These reviews discuss several specific areas in which valuable contributions can be expected (e.g., program evaluation, second language acquisition, classroom learning, research methodology). Part 2 of this article focuses on two recent developments in language testing, discussing their potential contributions to language learning and language teaching. I argue first that a theoretical model of second language ability that has emerged on the basis of research in language testing can be useful for both researchers and practitioners in language learning and language teaching. Specifically, I believe it provides a basis for both conceptualizing second language abilities whose acquisition is the object of considerable research and instructional effort, and for designing language tests for use both in instructional settings and for research in language learning and language teaching. Second, I will describe an approach to characterize the authenticity of a language task which I believe can help us to better understand the nature of the tasks we set, either for students in instructional programs or for subjects in language learning research and which can thus aid in the design and development of tasks that are more useful for these purposes.

Part 1: Language Testing in the 1990s

In echoing Alderson's (1991) title, I acknowledge the commonalities among the review articles mentioned above in the themes they discuss and the issues they raise. While each review emphasizes specific areas, all approach the task with essentially the same rhetorical organization: a review of the achievements in language testing, or lack thereof, over the past decade; a discussion of areas of likely continued development; and suggestions of areas in need of increased emphasis to assure developments in the future. Both Alderson and Skehan argue that while language testing has made progress in some areas, on the whole "there has been relatively little progress in language testing until recently" (Skehan, 1991, p. 3). Skehan discusses the contextual factors—theory, practical considerations, and human considerations—that have influenced language testing in terms of whether these factors act as "forces for conservatism" or "forces for change" (p. 3). The former, he argues, "all have the consequence of retarding change, reducing openness, and generally justifying inaction in testing" (p. 3), while the latter are "pressures which are likely to bring about more beneficial outcomes" (p. 7). All of the reviews present essentially optimistic views of where language testing is going and what it has to offer other areas of applied linguistics. I will group the common themes of these reviews into the general areas of (a) theoretical issues and their implications for practical application, (b) methodological advances, and (c) language test development.

Theoretical Issues

One of the major preoccupations of language testers in the past decade has been investigating the nature of language proficiency. In 1980 the "unitary competence hypothesis" (Oller, 1979), which claimed that language proficiency consists of a single, global ability was widely accepted. By 1983 this view of language proficiency had been challenged by several empirical studies and abandoned by its chief proponent (Oller, 1983). The unitary trait view has been replaced, through both empirical research and theorizing, by the view that language proficiency is multicomponential, consisting of a number of interrelated specific abilities as well as a general ability or set of general strategies or procedures. Skehan and Alderson both suggest that the model of language test performance proposed by Bachman (1990b) represents progress in this area, since it includes both components of language ability and characteristics of test methods, thereby making it possible "to make statements about actual performance as well as underlying abilities'" (Skehan, 1991, p. 9). At the same time, Skehan correctly points out that as research progresses, this model will be modified and eventually superseded. Both Alderson and Skehan indicate that an area where further progress is needed is in the application of theoretical models of language proficiency to the design and development of language tests. Alderson, for example, states that "we need to be concerned not only with . . . the nature of language proficiency, but also with language learning and the design and researching of achievement tests; not only with testers, and the problems of our professionalism, but also with testees, with students, and their interests, perspectives and insights" (Alderson, 1991, p. 5).

A second area of research and progress is in our understanding of the effects of the method of testing on test performance. A number of empirical studies conducted in the 1980s clearly demonstrated that the kind of test tasks used can affect test performance as much as the abilities we want to measure (e.g., Bachman & Palmer, 1981, 1982, 1988; Clifford, 1981; Shohamy, 1983, 1984). Other studies demonstrated that the topical content of test tasks can affect performance (e.g., Alderson & Urquhart, 1985; Erickson & Molloy, 1983). Results of these studies have stimulated a renewed interest in the investigation of test content. And here the results have been mixed. Alderson and colleagues (Alderson, 1986, 1990; Alderson, Henning, & Lukmani, 1987; Alderson & Lukmani, 1986) have been investigating (a) the extent to which "experts" agree in their judgments about what specific skills EFL reading test items measure, and at what levels, and (b) whether these expert judgments about ability levels are related to the difficulty of items. Their results indicate first, that these experts, who included test designers assessing the content of their own tests, do not agree and, second, that there is virtually no relationship between judgments of the levels of ability tested and empirical item difficulty. Bachman and colleagues, on the other hand (Bachman, Davidson, Lynch, & Ryan, 1989; Bachman, Davidson, & Milanovic, 1991; Bachman, Davidson, Ryan, & Choi, in press) have found that by using a content-rating instrument based on a taxonomy of test method characteristics (Bachman, 1990b) and by training raters, a high degree of agreement among raters can be obtained, and such content ratings are related to item difficulty and item discrimination. In my view, these results are not inconsistent. The research of Alderson and colleagues presents,

I believe, a sobering picture of actual practice in the design and development of language tests: Test designers and experts in the field disagree about what language tests measure, and neither the designers nor the experts have a clear sense of the levels of ability measured by their tests. This research uncovers a potentially serious problem in the way language testers practice their trade. Bachman's research, on the other hand, presents what can be accomplished in a highly controlled situation, and provides one approach to solving this problem. Thus, an important area for future research in the years to come will be in the refinement of approaches to the analysis of test method characteristics, of which content is a substantial component, and the investigation of how specific characteristics of test method affect test performance. Progress will be realized in the area of language testing practice when insights from this area of research inform the design and development of language tests. The research on test content analysis that has been conducted by the University of Cambridge Local Examinations Syndicate, and the incorporation of that research into the design and development of EFL tests is illustrative of this kind of integrated approach (Bachman et al., 1991).

The 1980s saw a wealth of research into the characteristics of test takers and how these are related to test performance, generally under the rubric of investigations into potential sources of test bias; I can do little more than list these here. A number of studies have shown differences in test performance across different cultural, linguistic or ethnic groups (e.g., Alderman & Holland, 1981; Chen & Henning, 1985; Politzer & McGroarty, 1985; Swinton & Powers, 1980; Zeidner, 1986), while others have found differential performance between sexes (e.g., Farhady, 1982; Zeidner, 1987). Other studies have found relationships between field dependence and test performance (e.g., Chapelle, 1988; Chapelle & Roberts, 1986; Hansen, 1984; Hansen & Stansfield, 1981; Stansfield & Hansen, 1983). Such studies demonstrate the effects of various test taker characteristics on test performance, and suggest that such characteristics need to be considered in both the design of language tests and in the interpretation of test scores. To date, however, no clear direction has emerged to suggest how such considerations translate into testing practice. Two issues that need to be resolved in this regard are (a) whether and how we assess the specific characteristics of a given group of test takers, and (b) whether and how we can incorporate such information into the way we design language tests. Do we treat these characteristics as sources of test bias and seek ways to somehow "correct" for this in the way we write and select test items, for example? Or, if many of these characteristics are known to also influence language learning, do we reconsider our definition of language ability? The investigation of test taker characteristics and their effects on language test performance also has implications for research in second language acquisition (SLA), and represents what Bachman (1989) has called an "interface" between SLA and language testing research.

Methodological Advances

Many of the developments mentioned above—changes in the way we view language ability, the effects of test method and test taker characteristics—have been facilitated by advances in the tools that are available for test analysis. These advances have been in three areas: psychometrics, statistical analysis, and quantitative approaches to the description of test performance. The 1980s saw the application of several modern psychometric tools to language testing: item response theory (IRT), generalizability theory (G theory), criterion-referenced (CR) measurement, and the Mantel-Haenszel procedure. As these tools are fairly technical, I will simply refer readers to discussions of them: IRT (Henning, 1987), G theory (Bachman, 1990b; Bolus, Hinofotis, & Bailey, 1982), CR measurement (Bachman, 1990b; Hudson & Lynch, 1984), Mantel-Haenszel (Ryan & Bachman, in press). The application of IRT to language tests has brought with it advances in computer-adaptive language testing, which promises to make language tests more efficient and adaptable to individual test takers, and thus potentially more useful in the types of information they provide (e.g., Tung, 1986), but which also presents a challenge not to complacently continue using familiar testing techniques simply because they can be administered easily via computer (Canale, 1986). Alderson (1988a) and the papers in Stansfield (1986) provide extensive discussions of the applications of computers to language testing.

The major advance in the area of statistical analysis has been the application of structural equation modeling to language testing research. (Relatively nontechnical discussions of structural equation modeling can be found in Long, 1983a, 1983b.) The use of confirmatory factor analysis was instrumental in demonstrating the untenability of the unitary trait hypothesis, and this type of analysis, in conjunction with the multitrait/multimethod research design, continues to be a productive approach to the process of construct validation. Structural equation modeling has also facilitated the investigation of relationships between language test performance and test taker characteristics (e.g., Fouly, 1985; Purcell, 1983) and different types of language instruction (e.g., Sang, Schmitz, Vollmer, Baumert, & Roeder, 1986).

A third methodological advance has been in the use of introspection to investigate the processes or strategies that test takers employ in attempting to complete test tasks. Studies using this approach have demonstrated that test takers use a variety of strategies in solving language test tasks (e.g., Alderson, 1988c; Cohen, 1984) and that these strategies are related to test performance (e.g., Anderson, Cohen, Perkins, & Bachman, 1991; Nevo, 1989).

Perhaps the single most important theoretical development in language testing in the 1980s was the realization that a language test score represents a complexity of multiple influences. As both Alderson and Skehan point out, this advance has been spurred on, to a considerable extent, by the application of the methodological tools discussed above. But, as Alderson (1991) notes, "the use of more sophisticated techniques reveals how complex responses to test items can be and therefore how complex a test score can be" (p. 12). Thus, one legacy of the 1980s is that we now know that a language test score cannot be interpreted simplistically as an indicator of the particular language ability we want to measure; it is also affected to some extent by the characteristics and content of the test tasks, the characteristics of the test taker, and the strategies the test taker employs in attempting to complete the test task. What makes the interpretation of test scores particularly difficult is that these factors undoubtedly interact with each other. The particular strategy adopted by a given test taker, for example, is likely to be a function of both the characteristics of the test task and the test taker's personal characteristics. This realization clearly indicates that we need to consider very carefully the interpretations and uses we make of language test scores and thus should sound a note of caution to language testing practitioners. At the same time, our expanded knowledge of the complexity of language test performance, along with the methodological tools now at our disposal, provide a basis for designing and developing language tests that are potentially more suitable for specific groups of test takers and more useful for their intended purposes.

Advances in Language Test Development

For language testing, the 1980s could be characterized as the decade of "communicative" testing. Although two strains of communicative approaches to language testing can be traced, as with many innovations in language testing over the years, the major impetus has come from language teaching. One strain of communicative tests, illustrated by the *Ontario Assessment Pool* (Canale & Swain, 1980a) and the *A Vous la Parole* testing unit described by Swain (1985), traces its roots to the Canale/Swain framework of communicative competence (Canale, 1983; Canale & Swain, 1980b). The other, exemplified by the *Test of English for Educational Purposes* (Associated Examining Board, 1987; Weir, 1983), the *Ontario Test of English as a Second Language* (Wesche et al., 1987), and the *International English Language Testing Service* (e.g., Alderson, 1988b; Alderson, Foulkes, Clapham, & Ingram, 1990; Criper & Davies, 1988; Seaton, 1983) has grown out of the English for specific purposes tradition. While a number of lists of characteristics of communicative language tests has been proposed (e.g., Alderson, 1981a; Canale, 1984; Carroll, 1980; Harrison, 1983; Morrow, 1977, 1979), I will mention four characteristics that would appear to distinguish communicative language tests. First, such tests create an "information gap," requiring test takers to process complementary information through the use of multiple sources of input. Test takers, for example, might be required to perform a writing task that is based on input from both a short recorded lecture and a reading passage on the same topic. A second characteristic is that of task dependency, with tasks in one section of the test building upon the content of earlier sections, including the test taker's answers to those sections. Third, communicative tests can be characterized by their integration of test tasks and content within a given domain of discourse. Finally, communicative tests attempt to measure a much broader range of language abilities—including knowledge of cohesion, functions, and sociolinguistic appropriateness—than did earlier tests, which tended to focus on the formal aspects of language—grammar, vocabulary, and pronunciation.

A different approach to language testing that evolved during the 1980s is the adaptation of the FSI oral interview guidelines (Wilds, 1975) to the assessment of the oral language proficiency in contexts outside agencies of the U.S. government. This "AEI" (For *A*merican Council for the Teaching of Foreign Languages/*E*ducational Testing Service/*I*nteragency Language Roundtable) approach to language assessment is based on a view of language proficiency as a unitary ability (Lowe, 1988), and thus diverges from the view that has emerged in language testing research and other areas of applied linguistics. This approach to oral language assessment has been criticized by both linguists and applied linguists, including language testers and language teachers, on a number of grounds (e.g., Alderson, 1981b; Bachman, 1988; Bachman & Savignon, 1986; Candlin, 1986; Kramsch, 1986; Lantolf & Frawley, 1985, 1988; Savignon, 1985). Nevertheless, the approach and ability levels defined have been widely accepted as a standard for assessing oral proficiency in a foreign language in the U.S. and have provided the basis for the development of "simulated oral proficiency interviews" in various languages (e.g., Stansfield & Kenyon, 1988, 1989). In addition, the approach has been adapted to the assessment of EFL proficiency in other countries (e.g., Ingram, 1984).

These two approaches to language assessment—communicative and AEI—are based on differing views of the nature of language proficiency, and are thus likely to continue as separate, unrelated approaches in the years to come. Lowe (1988) has explicitly articulated such a separatist view, in stating that the "concept of Communicative Language Proficiency (CLP), renamed Communicative Language Ability (CLA), and AEI proficiency may prove incompatible" (p. 14). Communicative language testing and AEI assessment represent two different approaches to language test design, and each has developed a number of specific manifestations in language tests. As a result, language testing will be enriched in the years to come by the variety of tests and testing techniques that emerge from these approaches.

This summary has focused on common areas among four recent reviews of language testing. In addition to these common areas, each of the reviews mentions specific areas of progress or concern. Skehan (1991) and Alderson (1991) both note that until very recently other areas of applied linguistics have provided very little input into language testing. Skehan, however, is encouraged by the relevance to language testing of recent work in sociolinguistics, second language acquisition, and language teaching, and points out the need for language testing to be aware of and receptive to input from developments in other areas of applied linguistics such as the SLA-based approach to assessing language development of Pienemann, Johnston, & Brindley (1988). Skehan and Alderson both argue that language testing must continue to investigate new avenues to assessment, such as formats that measure communicative abilities more successfully (e.g., Milanovic, 1988); "series tasks," in which specified language interactions are scored in terms of how particular aspects of information are communicated; group testing; self-assessment; and computer-based language testing. Alderson discusses two additional areas to which language testing needs to turn its attention in the years to come: "washback" effects and learner-centered testing. He points out that while we generally assume that tests have an impact on instruction (washback), there is virtually no empirical research into how, if at all, instructional impact functions, under what conditions, and whether deliberate attempts to design tests with positive instructional impact are effective. Alderson also argues persuasively for the greater involvement of learners in the activity of testing, in the design and writing of tests, and in the setting of standards for success. In this regard, I would mention the work of Brindley (1989) in assessing language achievement in learner-centered instructional settings and the papers in de Jong & Stevenson (1990), which address issues in individualizing language testing. A final area of development, mentioned by Bachman (1990b), is the renewed interest in language aptitude and developments in both the definition of the theoretical construct and in approaches to its measurement (Perry & Stansfield, 1990).

As a result of the developments of the 1980s, language testing has emerged as a discipline in its own right within applied linguistics. Alderson (1991) notes that since 1980 language testing has seen the creation of an internationally respected journal, *Language Testing,* as well as several regular newsletters; five new texts on language testing as well as over a dozen volumes of collected papers have been published; and there are now at least two regular major international conferences each year devoted to language testing. The field of language testing has seen the development of both a model of language test performance that can guide empirical research, and the application of a variety of research approaches and tools to facilitate such research. In sum, language testing can now claim its own research questions and research methodology. As Bachman (1990a) states, "perhaps for the first time in the history of language testing it is possible to see a genuine symbiotic relationship between applied linguistic theory and the tools of empirical research as they are applied to both the development and the examination of a theory of performance on language tests [and to] the development and use of better language tests" (p. 220).

Also as a result of developments in the past decade, language testing is in a better position, I believe, both to make contributions to its sister disciplines in applied linguistics and to be enriched by developments in those disciplines.

The next part of this paper briefly describes what I consider two contributions that language testing has to offer to the areas of language learning and language teaching.

Part 2: An Interactional Approach to Language Test Development

Language tests are used for a variety of purposes; these can be grouped into two broad categories. First, the results of language tests may be used to make inferences about test takers' language abilities or to make predictions about their capacity for using language to perform future tasks in contexts outside the test itself. Second, decisions (e.g., selection, diagnosis, placement, progress, grading, certification, employment) may be made about test takers on the basis of what we infer from test scores about their levels of ability or their capacity for nontest language use. A major consideration in both the design and use of language tests, therefore, is the extent to which the specific test tasks we include elicit instances of language use from which we can make such inferences or predictions. What this implies is that in order to investigate and demonstrate the validity of the uses we make of test scores, we need a theoretical framework within which we can describe language test performance as a specific instance of language use. Specifically, in order to make inferences about levels or profiles of ability, or predictions about capacity for using language to perform future tasks in nontest language use contexts, we need to demonstrate two kinds of correspondences: (a) that the language abilities measured by our language tests correspond in specifiable ways to the language abilities involved in nontest language use, and (b) that the characteristics of the test tasks correspond to the features of a target language use context.

In an instructional setting, for example, in which we may want to use a test to measure learners' degrees of mastery of different components of language ability that have been covered in the curriculum, we need to demonstrate that the content of the test is representative of the content of the course. Specifically, we will want to demonstrate that the components of language ability included in the test correspond to those covered in the course and that the characteristics of the test tasks correspond to the types of classroom learning activities included in the program. Demonstrating correspondences such as these provides some justification for interpreting test scores as evidence of levels of ability in the different components tested.

Another example would be a situation in which we need to select individuals for possible employment in a job which requires a specified level of proficiency in a foreign language. In this case, we need to demonstrate that the tasks included in the test are representative of the language use tasks required by the future job. Demonstrating this correspondence provides some justification for using the test scores to predict future capacity for using the foreign language effectively in the target employment situation.

Demonstrating correspondences between test performance and language use is equally important for justifying the use of language tests in applied linguistics research. For example, if we were interested in investigating the interlanguage development of a specific component of ability in a target language, for example, sensitivity to appropriate register, and wanted to use a test as one of our research instruments, we would need to be sure that the test we used measured this aspect of language ability. Similarly, we would want to specify the characteristics of the tasks included in the test, so as to minimize any variations that may arise between performance on this test and other elicitation procedures we may want to use.

In this part of the article I will present a framework that I believe provides a basis for relating test performance to nontest language use. This framework includes a model of language ability for describing the abilities involved in language use and test performance and a framework of test method characteristics for relating the characteristics of tests and test tasks to features of the language use context. I will then suggest how this framework can be used to clarify our thinking about the notion of authenticity and for designing test tasks that are authentic.

Language Ability

The language ability of the language user is one feature of language use. When we design a language test, we hypothesize that the test taker's language ability will be engaged by the test tasks. Thus, in order to relate the abilities we believe are involved in test performance to the abilities involved in language use, we need a model of language ability. The model I will describe here is a refinement of my 1990 model that Adrian Palmer and I are developing (Bachman & Palmer, in press). We define language ability essentially in Widdowson's (1983) terms as the capacity for using the knowledge of language in conjunction with the features of the language use context to create and interpret meaning. Our model of language ability includes two types of components: (a) areas of language knowledge, which we would hypothesize to be unique to language use (as opposed to, for example, mathematical knowledge or musical knowledge), and (b) metacognitive strategies that are probably general to all mental activity.

This view of language ability is consistent with research in applied linguistics that has increasingly come to view language ability as consisting of two components: (a) language knowledge, sometimes referred to as competence, and (b) cognitive processes, or procedures, that implement that knowledge in language use (e.g., Bachman, 1990a; Bialystok, 1990; Spolsky, 1989; Widdowson, 1983). It is also consistent with information-processing, or cognitive, models of mental abilities, which also distinguish processes or heuristics from domains of knowledge (e.g., Sternberg, 1985, 1988).

Language use involves the integration of multiple components and processes, not the least of which are those that constitute language ability. It is unlikely that every language test we develop or use will be intended to measure all the components in our model. Nevertheless, even though we may be interested in focusing on only one or a few of these in a given testing context, we need to be aware of the full range of language abilities as we design and develop language tests and interpret language test scores. For example, even though we may only be interested in measuring an individual's knowledge of vocabulary, the kinds of test items, tasks or text we use need to be selected with an awareness of what other components of language ability they may evoke. We believe, therefore, that even though a given language test may focus on a narrow range of language abilities, its design must be informed by a broad view of language ability.

Language Knowledge[1]

What we refer to as language knowledge can be regarded as a domain of information that is specific to language ability and that is stored in long-term memory. For our purposes, we do not attempt to characterize how this knowledge is stored. That is, we use the term *knowledge* to refer to both conscious and tacit, analyzed and unanalyzed knowledge. While the importance of such distinctions has been recognized in other areas of applied linguistics, it remains to be seen how relevant they are to the design, development, and use of language tests.

Language knowledge includes two broad areas: organizational knowledge and pragmatic knowledge. These are constantly changing, as new elements are learned or acquired, and existing elements restructured. The learning or acquisition of areas of language knowledge is beyond the scope of my discussion here, and for purposes of describing how they pertain to language use, I will treat them as more or less stable traits or constructs. The areas of language knowledge are given in Figure 1.

Discussion of these elements of language knowledge is beyond the scope of this paper. I would simply indicate that this model of language ability has evolved from earlier models, particularly that of Canale & Swain (Canale, 1983; Canale & Swain, 1980b) as a result of both empirical research and review of relevant literature in applied linguistics. The model presented here thus includes a much wider range of elements and provides a more comprehensive view of language ability than have earlier models.

---

[1]This description of *language knowledge* is essentially the same as Bachman's (1990b) discussion of *language competence*. The change in terminology from *competence* to *knowledge* reflects the view that the former term now carries with it a great deal of unnecessary semantic baggage that makes it less useful conceptually than it once was. I would note two changes from Bachman's 1990 model: (a) "Vocabulary" has been removed from "organizational competence" and placed within a new area, "propositional knowledge," under "pragmatic knowledge," and (b) "illocutionary competence" has been renamed "functional knowledge."

Organizational knowledge

(Determines how tests—oral or written—are organized)

Grammatical knowledge
(Determines how individual utterances or sentences are organized)

Textual knowledge
(Determines how utterances or sentences are organized to form texts)

Pragmatic knowledge

(Determines how utterances/sentences, intentions, and contexts are related to form meaning)

Propositional knowledge
(Determines how utterances/sentences are related to propositional content)

Functional knowledge
(Determines how utterances/sentences are related to intentions of language users)

Sociolinguistic knowledge
(Determines how utterances/sentences are related to features of the language use context)

FIGURE 1. Areas of Language Knowledge

From *Language Testing in Practice* by L. F. Bachman and A. S. Palmer, in press, Oxford, Oxford University Press. Copyright by Oxford University Press. Reprinted by permission.

Strategic Competence

The second component of language ability is what I have called strategic competence, and have described as consisting of three sets of processes: assessment, planning, and execution (Bachman, 1990b). In applying this model to the practical design and development of language tests, Adrian Palmer and I have refined this view of strategic competence as consisting of three sets of metacognitive strategies: assessment, goal setting, and planning. These are given in Figure 2 on page 428.

Since I will be referring to these in the following discussion of interactional authenticity, I briefly discuss these metacognitive strategies here. First, however, I would point out a dilemma in describing a set of strategies that we hypothesize operate simultaneously and are thus essentially unordered. In situated language use, the metacognitive strategies and areas of language knowledge interact with each other simultaneously. Thus there is no particular

Assessment	(Taking stock of what you need, what you have to work with, and how well you've done)

1. Determining the desirability of achieving a particular goal and what is needed to achieve it in a particular context
2. Determining what knowledge components—language knowledge, schemata, and affective schemata—are available for accomplishing that goal
3. Determining the extent to which the communicative goal has been achieved by a given utterance

Goal-setting	(Deciding what you're going to do)

1. Identifying and selecting one or more communicative goals that you want to achieve
2. Deciding to attempt or not attempt achieving the communicative goal selected

Planning	(Deciding how to use what you have)

1. Selecting relevant areas of language knowledge for accomplishing the given communicative goal
2. Formulating a plan for implementing these areas in the production or interpretation of an utterance

FIGURE 2.   Metacognitive Strategies

From *Language Testing in Practice* by L. F. Bachman and A. S. Palmer, in press, Oxford, Oxford University Press. Copyright by Oxford University Press. Reprinted by permission.

ordering or sequencing in the way they operate. Furthermore, the strategies and areas of language knowledge are integrated and interactive, by which I mean that all the components of language ability, although distinct from each other, interact with each other and are fully integrated in any instance of language use. However, since the language used to describe the model is linear, only one strategy can be described at a time; I must begin with one and end with another. This dilemma applies to examples, as well, which must necessarily be described in terms of a sequence of events. However, if the reader will keep in mind that my purpose here is to provide a general conceptualization for guiding test development and use, rather than to give a detailed description of how language is processed in the mind, I believe that this dilemma in presentation will not be a problem.

    Assessment.   The strategies of assessment provide a direct link between the context in which language use takes place, the discourse that is used, and the areas of language knowledge that the language user employs in producing or interpreting utterances. Assessment strategies perform three types of functions:

1. Assessing features of the context to determine whether it is feasible to achieve a given goal and if feasible, what is needed to achieve it in a particular context

2. Assessing what areas of language knowledge are available for accomplishing that goal

3. Assessing the extent to which the communicative goal has been achieved

In performing these functions, assessment strategies draw upon and interact with the different areas of language knowledge as well as with real-world knowledge schemata and affective schemata.

Goal setting.   From the perspective of the language user, goal setting involves, essentially, deciding what you are going to do, and includes the following functions:

1. Identifying a set of possible communicative goals

2. Choosing one or more goals from this set of possible goals

3. Deciding whether or not to attempt to achieve the goal(s)

Since one of the primary advantages of a language test, as opposed to other ways of obtaining information about an individual's language ability (such as naturalistic observation), is that it is designed to elicit a specific sample of language use, the test taker's flexibility in setting goals for performance on test tasks is necessarily limited. Thus, even though test takers may have some flexibility in setting goals for test performance, this is generally not as much as language users enjoy in nontest language use. As I will argue below, however, one way to increase the degree of interactional authenticity of a language test task is to increase the test taker's involvement in goal setting.

Planning.   Strategies of planning involve the following:

1. Selecting the relevant areas of language knowledge for accomplishing the given communicative goal

2. Formulating a plan for implementing these areas in the production or interpretation of an utterance

Strategies in Language Use

Using language involves interpreting or producing utterances with propositional content, functional purpose, and contextual appropriateness. This involves all the strategies and areas of language knowledge simultaneously and interactively. As discussed above, each of the three strategies interacts with all of the areas of language knowledge. In addition, the strategies themselves function interactively. Consider goal setting and assessment: We may modify or abandon a particular goal on the basis of assessment strategies. If, for example, we wanted to invite someone over for dinner, and saw that person at a party, we might decide to speak to them. If, however, we determined that it was inappropriate to extend the invitation in the presence of another person whom we did not want to invite, we would most likely modify our communicative goal and engage in polite conversation until the opportunity to extend the dinner invitation arose.

One implication of this model is that variations in language ability can be attributed to two sources. First, the areas of language knowledge may vary over time and across different language users, so that language knowledge may contain varying combinations of elements from the native language, interlanguage, and the target language. These areas of knowledge may vary both in terms of the presence or absence of different elements and in the nature of the elements that are present. Second, the metacognitive strategies may vary over time and across different language users. Thus these strategies may be used more or less effectively by different individuals in completing a given language test task or by the same individual in completing different test tasks. Furthermore, the strategies may be used in differing proportions and in differing degrees for different language test tasks. This means that test takers' performance on a given test task reflects both their knowledge of the language elements being measured and their capacity for effectively relating this language knowledge to the characteristics of the test task so as to arrive at a successful solution to the problem posed.

Test Method Characteristics

So far I have described a model of language ability that consists of areas of language knowledge and metacognitive processes. I have argued that this model can provide a basis for demonstrating the correspondences between the abilities measured by the test and the abilities required for nontest language use.

The second correspondence we need to demonstrate in order to make inferences about abilities or to make predictions about future language use on the basis of language test scores is the correspondence between the characteristics of the test task and the features of a target language use context. It is widely recognized that the features of the language use context, such as the relationship between the language users, the topic, and the purpose, influence the way we use language. It would thus not be surprising to find that characteristics of the method of testing affect the way individuals perform on tests. Indeed, one of the major findings of language testing research over the past decade is that performance on language tests is affected not only by the ability we are trying to measure but also by the method we use to measure it (cf. references in the

Theoretical Issues section of Part 1). In a language test, the instances of language use that we elicit are shaped, as it were, by the test tasks we present. Thus, it is the discourse that is included in the test question and the nature of the test task that will determine, to a large extent, how the test taker processes the information presented and responds to the particular task.

Language teachers also realize that the selection of a testing method is important. Frequently one of the first questions asked in testing classes or at conferences is the speaker's opinion of the "best" way to test a particular component of language ability. Teachers are clearly aware that the way they test language ability affects how their students perform on language tests and hence the quality of the information obtained from their tests. These teachers also want to be sure that this test method effect works in ways that will be fair to their students and that will enable them, the teachers, to make inferences about the language abilities they want to measure.

When we consider the different test methods that are commonly used for language tests, we realize that they are not single wholes, but rather collections of characteristics. "Multiple-choice" test items, for example, vary in a number of ways, such as in their length, syntactic complexity, level of vocabulary, topical content, and type of response required, to name but a few. Similarly, the "composition" test method encompasses a wide variety of prompts that can differ in terms of characteristics such as the intended audience, purpose, and specific organizational pattern requested. It is thus clear that we cannot be very precise in our thinking about test methods if we think of them only as holistic types. In order to organize our thinking about test methods, therefore, we first need a way to characterize them. A framework for doing this is presented in Figure 3 on page 432.

Again, given space limitations, I will not discuss these here, but will simply point out that these test method characteristics have been used in several empirical studies to analyze the content of test items and to investigate the relationships between test content and the difficulty and discrimination of test items (Bachman, Kunnan, Vanniarajan, & Lynch, 1988; Bachman et al., 1989; Bachman et al., 1991; Bachman et al., in press).

Characterizing Authenticity

I have argued that in order to justify the use of language tests, we need to be able to demonstrate that performance on language tests corresponds in specified ways to nontest language use. I have described a model of language ability that I believe provides a basis for specifying the language ability of the language user as test taker. I have also presented a framework for specifying the characteristics of test tasks in a way that I believe enables us to investigate how these are related to the features of a given target language use context. In

Characteristics of the testing environment
Characteristics of the test rubric

Test organization
Time allocation
Scoring
Instructions

Characteristics of the test input

Format
Language of input
    Length
    Organizational characteristics
    Pragmatic characteristics

Characteristics of the expected response

Format
Language of expected response
    Length
    Organizational characteristics
    Pragmatic characteristics

Relationship between input and response

Reciprocal
Nonreciprocal
Adaptive

FIGURE 3.   Test Method Characteristics

From *Fundamental Considerations in Language Testing* (p. 119) by L. F. Bachman, 1990, Oxford, Oxford University Press. Copyright 1990 by Oxford University Press. Reprinted by permission.

the remainder of this paper I will attempt to describe how these models can be used to assess the "authenticity" of a given test task, and suggest some ways this notion of authenticity can be used in the practical design of test tasks.

A number of language testing specialists have discussed the features that characterize an authentic test task (e.g., Alderson, 1981b; Canale, 1984; Carroll, 1980; Harrison, 1983; Morrow, 1977, 1979). When we try to define *authenticity*, however, we notice that it is one of those words like *real* (as in "He's really real") that sounds good but leaves us wondering exactly what it means. In fact, in language testing circles, authenticity has been defined in a number of different ways. One approach, for example has been to define it as direct, in the sense of getting at the ability without going through an intermediate representation of the ability. However, it is impossible to directly observe the neurological programming in the brain that may account for language ability. Thus, all language tests are indirect; they simply permit us to observe behavior from which we can make inferences about language ability.

A second approach has been to define authenticity in terms of similarity to real life. The problem with this definition is that "real life" language use consists of an infinite set of unique and widely varied speech events. Thus, the way in which language is used in real life can vary enormously and includes language use situations as different as announcing a sporting event and keying information from a questionnaire into a computer. Because of the great variation in the language used in real life, we have no basis for knowing what kind of real life language tasks to use as our primary criteria for authenticity.

A third approach to defining authenticity is to appeal to what was once called face validity, which is really nothing more than face appeal. This is just as problematic as the previous two approaches, but in a different way. This definition refers to a purely subjective response on the part of the evaluator and offers us no criteria for use in creating appealing tests. Moreover, there is also the issue, noted by Davies (1977) some years ago, that what is appealing to experts in language testing might be different from what is appealing to teachers, students, or to parents of students.

All three of these approaches to authenticity capture some intuitively useful aspects of authenticity, but they are problematic in many ways. Furthermore, they are not clearly enough defined, I believe, to provide a basis for test development. Adrian Palmer and I (Bachman & Palmer, in press) have attempted to define authenticity in a way that we think still captures the spirit of these approaches but does so in a way that avoids the problems of these approaches and is also specific enough to guide test development. For this purpose, we define two different types of authenticity: situational authenticity and interactional authenticity.

Situational Authenticity

We define situational authenticity as the perceived relevance of the test method characteristics to the features of a specific target language use situation. Thus, for a test task to be perceived as situationally authentic, the characteristics of the test task need to be perceived as corresponding to the features of a target language use situation. For example, one set of test method characteristics relates to certain characteristics of vocabulary (e.g., infrequent, specialized) and topics (e.g., academic, technical) included in the test input. If test takers were specialists in engineering, it is likely that inclusion of technical terms and topics from engineering would tend to increase the situational authenticity of the test. While situational authenticity may appear to be essentially the same as the real-life approach described above, it is fundamentally different in a critical way. The real-life approach assumes that there is a well-defined domain of target language use tasks outside the test itself and that these tasks themselves can be sampled in order to achieve authenticity. In contrast, we define the situational authenticity of a given test task in terms of the distinctive features that characterize a set of target language use tasks. Thus, in designing a situationally authentic test, we do not attempt to sample actual tasks from a domain of nontest language use, but rather try to design tasks that have the same critical features as tasks in that domain.

This definition allows for possibly different perceptions of situational authenticity. Thus, different test takers may have different ideas about their target language use situations. And the perceptions of test takers about the relevance of the characteristics of the test task to their target language use situations may be different from those of the test developers. What this implies is that situational authenticity must be assessed from a number of perspectives and that these all must be taken into consideration in the development and use of language tests.

Language testers and teachers alike are concerned with this kind of authenticity, for we all want to do our best to make our teaching and testing relevant to our students' language use needs. For a reading test, for example, we are likely to choose a passage whose topic and genre (characteristics of the test input) match the topic and genre of material the test user is likely to read outside of the testing situation. Or, if the target language use situation requires reciprocal language use, then we will design a test task in which reciprocity is a characteristic of the relationship between test input and expected response.

Interactional Authenticity

What we call interactional authenticity is essentially Widdowson's (1978) definition of authenticity and is a function of the extent and type of involvement of test takers' language ability in accomplishing a test task. The different areas of language knowledge and the different strategies can be involved to varying degrees in the problem presented by the test task. In contrast to situational authenticity, where the focus is on the relationship between the test task and nontest language use, interactional authenticity resides in interaction between the test taker and the test task.

In order to make these definitions of authenticity useful for test development, we need to be able to specify both the characteristics of the test task and the nature of the involvement of the test taker's language ability. We propose that the situational authenticity of a given test task can be assessed largely in terms of the framework of test method characteristics and that these characteristics can also provide a basis for designing test tasks that are situationally authentic. Assessing interactional authenticity and designing tasks that are interactionally authentic, however, is more complex, since this requires us to consider both the characteristics of the test task and the components of the test taker's language ability. For this reason, I will focus the remainder of the paper on a discussion of the relevance of interactional authenticity to the design of test tasks.

But before I discuss ways of increasing the relative interactional authenticity of test tasks, I present some examples of test tasks that vary in terms of their relative situational and interactional authenticity. This will accomplish a number of objectives, I hope. It will help the reader understand how actual test tasks differ in terms of their authenticity. It will also illustrate what Bachman and Palmer (in press) believe are some fundamental facts about authenticity. First, both situational and interactional authenticity are relative, so that we speak of "low" or "high" authenticity, rather than "authentic" and "inauthentic." Second, we cannot tell how authentic a test task is just by looking at it; we must also consider the characteristics of the test takers and the specific target language use context. Third, certain test tasks may be useful for their intended purposes, even though they are low in either situational or interactional authenticity. Finally, in either designing new tests or analyzing existing tests, estimates of authenticity are only best guesses. We can do our best to design test tasks that will be authentic for a given group of test takers, but we need to realize that different test takers may process the same test task in different ways, often in ways we may not anticipate.

The first example is from an institution abroad where Adrian Palmer and I once worked, in which some of the typists in our department did not understand English very well. Nevertheless they were excellent typists and produced high quality typescripts, even from handwritten documents. These typists had developed a high level of mechanical control of English, and this was all that was required for their job. A screening test for new typists in this situation might involve simply asking job applicants to type from a handwritten document. If the applicants knew that their on-the-job use of English would be limited to exactly this kind of typing, they would probably perceive the typing test as highly relevant to the job. Clearly, however, the test meets very few of the criteria for interactional authenticity. This example illustrates a test task which would be evaluated as highly situationally authentic but low in terms of interactional authenticity. The number *1* in the upper left corner of the diagram in Figure 4 indicates where this example test falls, in terms of authenticity. How useful is this test likely to be for its intended purpose? Probably quite useful.

We can use the same testing situation to invent a second example. Suppose for a moment that these applicants were capable of carrying on a conversation in English, and that we tested them by interviewing them in English. If the topics we talked about in the interview were of interest to them, the

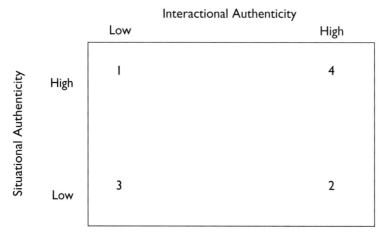

FIGURE 4.   Aspects of Authenticity

interview might actually involve the same types of interactions involved in nontest conversation. If we used the scores from this interview to select individuals whose sole use of English was to type from handwritten documents, how would this example rate with respect to authenticity? I would judge this task to be relatively low in situational authenticity and relatively high in interactional authenticity. The number *2* in the diagram indicates where this example falls. How useful is this test likely to be for predicting applicants' ability to type from handwritten documents? Probably not very useful.

For our third example, suppose we gave international students applying to U.S. universities a test of English vocabulary in which they were required to match words in one column with meanings in a second column. How does this stack up in terms of authenticity? This task, I would say, is relatively low in both situational and interactional authenticity. The number *3* in the diagram shows where this example falls. How useful is this test likely to be in predicting readiness for academic study in English? Given the generally low predictive utility of language tests for forecasting academic achievement, it is difficult to say how useful this test might be.

One final example: Suppose we used a role play in which a prospective sales person was required to attempt to sell a product. The role play might involve a face-to-face oral conversation with an interlocutor who plays the role of a potential customer. The test taker might be required to engage the hypothetical customer in a conversation, decide what kind of approach to use in the selling task, and carry out the task. How authentic is this test task? I would rate this task as relatively high in both situational and interactional authenticity. The number *4* in the diagram indicates where this test task falls. How useful is this test likely to be in selecting successful sales persons? It could be quite useful, particularly if we included some criteria about successful completion of the task in the scoring.

Increasing the Interactional Authenticity of Test Tasks

The four examples just given illustrate how test tasks can differ in their relative authenticity, and suggest how authenticity may be useful in evaluating existing tests. I now turn to considerations in designing and developing test tasks that are relatively interactionally authentic.

The two main steps in developing interactionally authentic test tasks are as follows:

1. For a given test task, assess the degree to which the strategies of language ability are involved in successfully completing the test task.

2. Explore ways of increasing the interaction of each strategy.

Assessing Levels of Interactional Authenticity

The involvement of the components of language ability in a given test task can be assessed in a number of ways. We could, for example, imagine ourselves to be typical test takers and then speculate about the levels of involvement of the strategies and areas of language knowledge. What specific areas of language knowledge will be engaged by the test task? Grammatical knowledge? Sociolinguistic knowledge? What strategies will be evoked—assessment, planning—and to what extent? Another way of assessing interactional authenticity is through observing test takers and asking them to self-report on the strategies they used in attempting a given test task. This method of introspection is being used increasingly by language testing researchers to investigate the strategies used by test takers and how these strategies are related to test performance (e.g., Anderson et al., 1991; Cohen, 1984; Nevo, 1989).

Increasing Interactional Authenticity

Interactional authenticity can be increased, I believe, by increasing the level of involvement of the test taker's language ability. Bachman and Palmer (in press) suggest that this can be done by designing the test method characteristics of the test tasks to provide for the following: (a) requirement, (b) opportunity, (c) feasibility, and (d) interest. In order to assure that the strategies or given areas of language knowledge must be involved for successful completion of the test, one might set up tasks that cannot be done without their involvement. Opportunity for involvement may be provided by allocating adequate time or providing necessary information, tools, references, and so forth. Feasibility of involvement might be increased by adjusting the difficulty of the test task so that the involvement of the strategies and areas of language knowledge will be within the test takers' ability range. Finally, involvement of language ability may be increased by making test tasks interesting to test takers. In this regard, interest may be increased through increased situational authenticity.

Let me offer an example of how one might evaluate interactional authenticity and try to increase it for a specific writing test task. Suppose we want to develop a writing test as a final examination for a composition course. And suppose one procedure that comes to mind involves simply giving the candidates one hour to write a 250-word composition on a prescribed topic. Our initial task specification, or prompt, might simply be: "Write a 250 word composition describing your most frightening experience. You will not be graded on what you say. You will be graded on how well you express your ideas."

Assessment strategies.   In this task candidates might assess their experiences with frightening situations and their ability to write about them. This could affect their choice of topics (goal-setting). As they write their essays, they might take some time to assess the correctness of their grammar and spelling. After finishing a draft of their essays, they might spend some time in revision and editing, which involve reassessment of the language produced. Since the instructions indicate that the essay will not be graded on content, however, the candidates might not reassess the information in the essay.

In this task the involvement of assessment is likely to be rather limited. Since the main focus of the task seems to be on how well the candidates express ideas, assessment is likely to be limited primarily to this domain. Moreover, since no detailed grading criteria are provided, the candidates are not prompted to assess what they have written in any particular areas. They might construe "how well you express your ideas" in the prompt to mean correct grammar and spelling. Of course, they may have a much richer set of internal criteria for assessment, both of content and of language, but nothing in the prompt specifically evokes this.

We could increase the involvement of assessment strategies in this task by providing more specific information in the prompt about the criteria for grading. We could also encourage test takers to go back and revise their writing, and provide adequate time for this.

Goal setting   In this example, test takers are assigned a topic, and the involvement of goal setting might be limited to picking a particular frightening experience to describe. They are given no purpose for writing the essay other than to produce something to be graded. And they are given no indication that what they say is of any importance. Their thinking is likely to be limited to "What can I write the best essay about?" Their emotions might be involved in this decision since the topic of the essay is about an emotional experience. On the other hand, the instructions state that the content of what is written will not influence the grade, and this might tend to cause test takers to minimize the importance of what they write, and hence their emotional involvement with it. Also, since the task does not require them to come up with anything new, it might not evoke feelings of interest, concern or excitement.

To increase the involvement of goal setting we might consider allowing the test taker a choice of topics to talk about, the choice to be made on the basis of what the test taker finds interesting. So we might provide the test taker with a list of topics including political, social, educational, and religious issues. We might also give the test taker a choice of purpose or intended audience.

Planning.   In our example writing task, no instructions are given to how to organize the essay or the role that organization plays in the grade the essay will receive. In addition, the task is such that a simple chronological organization would suffice, so the test taker might feel little need to do much planning. Because the task is one that requires little planning, the test taker needs to do very little formal organization of ideas. Thus, the way the task is specified (particularly the lack of indication that the essay needs to be well planned) is likely to result in little involvement of planning.

One way to increase the involvement of planning would be to explicitly state in the prompt that planning is part of the task, and then allowing test takers some time to organize and prepare their thoughts on the topic selected. We might even go so far as to require an outline as part of the test taker's response.

These examples suggest the following principles for increasing interactional authenticity of test tasks:

1. Tasks should consist of multiple, sequential subtasks.

2. Goal setting and planning should be required at the beginning of the task.

3. Request for and provision of feedback should be given at the end of each subtask.

4. Feedback should be used in subsequent subtasks.

5. There should be provision for changing goals and for additional planning.

Clearly, these principles are related to some of the features that have been included in the design of communicative language tests, as discussed earlier in Part 1. An information gap can be created by including complementary types of information in different tasks. Information presented aurally via a videotape recording, for example, could be complemented by different information on the same topic presented visually in a reading passage. Another feature of communicative tests is that of task dependency. This can be built into language tests by sequencing tasks so that information generated in completing one task is used to complete subsequent tasks. Answers to listening and reading comprehension questions, for example, could provide the content for a writing task. These principles are consistent with much practice in the development of communicative language tests, and thus cannot be claimed to be original. Nevertheless, it is comforting to find that principles for the design and development of language tests that are derived from theoretical models of language ability and test method characteristics are in keeping with practice that is derived from language teaching.

Conclusion

I believe the framework for language testing presented here makes two contributions to the field. First, it grounds practical considerations in test design, development, and use firmly on a theoretical framework of the nature of language ability and test tasks, and thus provides a principled basis for making practical test development decisions. Second, and equally important, this framework enables us to specify and assess the relationship between language test performance and nontest language use, and thus provides a principles basis for addressing issues of validity and authenticity.

Acknowledgments

I would like to thank Adrian Palmer for his useful comments and suggestions in preparing this essay. In particular, the material in Part 2 is largely the result of our collaborative effort to apply a theory of language test performance to the practical design and development of language tests. I also thank Charles Alderson and Peter Skehan for making available their recent reviews of language testing. I am grateful to Kari Sajavaara and Eduardo Cascallar for their valuable comments and suggestions with regard to metacognitive strategies. An earlier version of the second part of this essay was presented at the PennTESOL-East 1991 Spring Conference in Philadelphia, March 1991.

References

Alderman, D. L., & Holland, P. W. (1981). *Item performance across native language groups on the Test of English as a Foreign Language* (TOEFL Research Report No. 9). Princeton, NJ: Educational Testing Service.

Alderson, J. C. (1981a). Reaction to Morrow paper (3). In J. C. Alderson & A. Hughes (Eds.), *Issues in language testing* (ELT Documents No. 111, pp. 45–54). London: The British Council.

Alderson, J. C. (1981b). Report of the discussion on communicative language testing. In J. C. Alderson & A. Hughes (Eds.), *Issues in language testing* (ELT Documents No. 111, pp. 55–65). London: The British Council.

Alderson, J. C. (1986, January). *Levels of reading comprehension: Do they exist?* Paper delivered at Salford University, England.

Alderson, J. C. (1988a). *Innovation in language testing: Can the microcomputer help?* (Language Testing Update Special Report No. 1). Lancaster, England: Lancaster University, Institute for English Language Education.

Alderson, J. C. (1988b). New procedures for validating proficiency tests of ESP? Theory and practice. *Language Testing, 5,* 220–232.

Alderson, J. C. (1988c, March). Testing reading comprehension skills. In P. L. Carrell, J. Devine, & W. Grabe (Organizers), *Research in reading in a second language.* Colloquium conducted at the 22nd Annual TESOL Convention, Chicago, IL.

Alderson, J. C. (1990, March). *Judgments in language testing.* Paper presented at the 12th Annual Language Testing Research Colloquium, San Francisco, CA.

Alderson, J. C. (1991). Language testing in the 1990s: How far have we come? How much further have we to go? In S. Anivan (Ed.), *Current developments in language testing* (pp. 1–26). Singapore: SEAMEO Regional Language Centre.

Alderson, J. C., Foulkes, J., Clapham, C., & Ingram, D. (1990, March). *International English language testing service (IELTS).* Panel presented at the 12th Annual Language Testing Research Colloquium, San Francisco, CA.

Alderson, J. C., Henning, G., & Lukmani, Y. (1987, April). *Levels of understanding in reading comprehension tests.* Paper presented at the 9th Annual Language Testing Research Colloquium, Miami, FL.

Alderson, J. C., & Lukmani, Y. (1986, March). Reading in a second language. In D. E. Eskey, J. Devine, & P. L. Carrell (Organizers), *Research on reading in a second language.* Colloquium conducted at the 20th Annual TESOL Convention, Anaheim, CA.

Alderson, J. C., & Urquhart, A. H. (1985). The effect of students' academic discipline on their performance on ESP reading tests. *Language Testing, 2,* 192–204.

Anderson, N., Cohen, A., Perkins, K., & Bachman, L. (1991). An investigation of the relationships among test-taking strategies, item content, and item difficulty in an EFL reading test. *Language Testing, 8,* 41–66.

The Associated Examining Board. (1987). *Test in English for Educational Purposes (TEEP).* Aldershot, England: Author.

Bachman, L. F. (1988). Problems in examining the validity of the ACTFL oral proficiency interview. *Studies in Second Language Acquisition, 10,* 149–164.

Bachman, L. F. (1989). Language testing-SLA interfaces. In R. B. Kaplan (Ed.), *Annual Review of Applied Linguistics 1988* (pp. 193–209). New York: Cambridge University Press.

Bachman, L. F. (1990a). Assessment and evaluation. In R. B. Kaplan (Ed.), *Annual Review of Applied Linguistics 1989* (pp. 210–226). New York: Cambridge University Press.

Bachman, L. F. (1990b). *Fundamental considerations in language testing.* Oxford: Oxford University Press.

Bachman, L. F., Davidson, F., Lynch, B., & Ryan, K. (1989, March). *Content analysis and statistical modeling of EFL proficiency tests.* Paper presented at the 11th Annual Language Testing Research Colloquium, San Antonio, TX.

Bachman, L. F., Davidson, F., & Milanovic, M. (1991, March). *The use of test method characteristics in the content analysis and design of EFL proficiency tests.* Paper presented at the 13th Annual Language Testing Research Colloquium, Princeton, NJ.

Bachman, L. F., Davidson, F., Ryan, K., & Choi, I-C. (in press). *An investigation into the comparability of two tests of English as a foreign language: The Cambridge-TOEFL comparability study.* Cambridge: University of Cambridge Local Examinations Syndicate.

Bachman, L. F., Kunnan, A., Vanniarajan, S., & Lynch, B. (1988). Task and ability analysis as a basis for examining content and construct comparability in two EFL proficiency test batteries. *Language Testing, 5,* 128–159.

Bachman, L. F., & Palmer, A. S. (1981). The construct validation of the FSI oral interview. *Language Learning, 31,* 67–86.

Bachman, L. F., & Palmer, A. S. (1982). The construct validation of some components of communicative proficiency. *TESOL Quarterly, 16,* 449–465.

Bachman, L. F., & Palmer, A. S. (in press). *Language testing in practice.* Oxford: Oxford University Press.

Bachman, L. F., & Savignon, S. (1986). The evaluation of communicative language proficiency: A critique of the ACTFL oral interview. *Modern Language Journal, 70,* 380–390.

Bialystok, E. (1990). *Communication strategies: A psychological analysis of second-language use.* Oxford: Basil Blackwell.

Bolus, R. E., Hinofotis, F. B., & Bailey, K. M. (1982). An introduction to generalizability theory in second language research. *Language Learning, 32,* 245–258.

Brindley, G. (1989). *Assessing achievement in the learner-centered curriculum.* Sydney, Australia: National Centre for English Language Teaching and Research.

Canale, M. (1983). On some dimensions of language proficiency. In J. W. Oller (Ed.), *Issues in language testing research* (pp. 333–342). Rowley, Mass.: Newbury House.

Canale, M. (1984). Testing in a communicative approach. In G. A. Jarvis (Ed.), *The challenge for excellence in foreign language education* (pp. 79–92). Middlebury, VT: The Northeast Conference Organization.

Canale, M. (1986). The promise and threat of computerized adaptive assessment of reading comprehension. In C. W. Standfield (Ed.), *Technology and language testing* (pp. 29–45). Washington, DC: TESOL.

Canale, M., & Swain, M. (1980a). A domain description for core FSL: Communication skills. In *The Ontario assessment instrument pool: French as a second language, junior and intermediate divisions* (pp. 27–39). Toronto, Canada: Ontario Ministry of Education.

Canale, M., & Swain, M. (1980b). Theoretical bases of communicative approaches to second language teaching and testing. *Applied Linguistics, 1,* 1–47.

Candlin, C. (1986). Explaining communicative competence limits of testability? In C. W. Standfield (Ed.), *Toward communicative competence testing: Proceedings of the second TOEFL invitational conference* (pp. 38–57). Princeton, NJ: Educational Testing Service.

Carroll, B. J. (1980). *Testing communicative performance.* London: Pergamon Institute of English.

Chapelle, C. (1988). Field independence: A source of language test variance? *Language Testing, 5,* 62–82.

Chapelle, C., & Roberts, C. (1986). Ambiguity tolerance and field dependence as predictors of proficiency in English as a second language. *Language Learning, 36,* 27–45.

Chen, Z., & Henning, G. (1985). Linguistic and cultural bias in language proficiency tests. *Language Testing, 2,* 155–163.

Clifford, R. T. (1981). Convergent and discriminant validation of integrated and unitary language skills: The need for a research model. In A. S. Palmer, P. J. M. Groot, & G. A. Trosper (Eds.), *The construct validation of tests of communicative competence* (pp. 62–70). Washington, DC: TESOL.

Cohen, A. D. (1984). On taking tests: What the students report. *Language Testing, 1,* 70–81.

Criper, C., & Davies, A. (1988). *ELTS validation project report.* London: The British Council and the University of Cambridge Local Examinations Syndicate.

Davies, A. (1977). The construction of language tests. In J. P. B. Allen & A. Davies (Eds.), *The Edinburgh course in applied linguistics: Vol. 4. Testing and experimental methods* (pp. 38–194). London: Oxford University Press.

de Jong, J. H. A. L., & Stevenson, D. K. (1990). *Individualizing the assessment of language abilities.* Clevedon, England: Multilingual Matters.

Erickson, M., & Molloy, J. (1983). ESP test development for engineering students. In J. W. Oller, Jr. (Ed.), *Issues in language testing research* (pp. 280–288). Rowley, Mass.: Newbury House.

Farhady, H. (1982). Measures of language proficiency from the learner's perspective. *TESOL Quarterly, 16,* 43–59.

Fouly, K. A. (1985). *A confirmatory multivariate study of the nature of second language proficiency and its relationship to learner variables.* Unpublished doctoral dissertation. University of Illinois at Urbana-Champaign.

Hansen, L. (1984). Field dependence-independence and language testing: Evidence from six Pacific Island cultures. *TESOL Quarterly, 18,* 311–324.

Hansen, J., & Standfield, C. (1981). The relationship between field dependent-independent cognitive styles and foreign language achievement. *Language Learning, 31,* 349–367.

Harrison, A. (1983). Communicative testing: Jam tomorrow? In A. Hughes & D. Porter (Eds.), *Current developments in language testing* (pp. 77–85). London: Academic Press.

Henning, G. (1987). *A guide to language testing.* Cambridge, Mass.: Newbury House.

Hudson, T., & Lynch, B. (1984). A criterion-referenced measurement approach to ESL. *Language Testing, 1,* 171–201.

Ingram, D. E. (1984). *Australian second language proficiency ratings.* Canberra: Department of Immigration and Ethnic Affairs.

Kramsch, C. (1986). From language proficiency to interactional competence. *The Modern Language Journal, 70,* 366–372.

Lantolf, J. P., & Frawley, W. (1985). Oral proficiency testing: A critical analysis. *The Modern Language Journal, 69,* 337–345.

Lantolf, J. P., & Frawley, W. (1988). Proficiency: Understanding the construct. *Studies in Second Language Acquisition, 10,* 181–195.

Long, J. S. (1983a). *Confirmatory factor analysis.* Beverly Hills, CA: Sage.

Long, J. S. (1983b). *Covariance structure models: An introduction to LISREL.* Beverly Hills, CA: Sage.

Lowe, P., Jr. (1988). The unassimilated history. In P. Lowe, Jr., & C. W. Stansfield (Eds.), *Second language proficiency assessment: Current issue.* Englewood Cliffs, NJ: Prentice Hall.

Milanovic, M. (1988). *The construction and validation of a performance-based battery of English language progress tests.* Unpublished doctoral dissertation, London University, Institute of Education.

Morrow, K. (1977). *Techniques of evaluation for a notional syllabus.* London: Royal Society of Arts.

Morrow, K. (1979). Communicative language testing: Revolution or evolution? In C. J. Brumfit & K. Johnson (Eds.), *The communicative approach to language teaching* (pp. 143–157). Oxford: Oxford University Press.

Nevo, N. (1989). Test-taking strategies on a multiple-choice test of reading comprehension. *Language Testing, 6,* 199–215.

Oller, J. W., Jr. (1979). *Language tests at school: A pragmatic approach.* London: Longman.

Oller, J. W., Jr. (1983). A consensus for the eighties? In J. W. Oller, Jr. (Ed.), *Issues in language testing research* (pp. 351–356). Rowley, Mass.: Newbury House.

Perry, T., & Stansfield, C. W. (Eds.). (1990). *Language aptitude revisited.* Englewood Cliffs, NJ: Prentice Hall.

Pienemann, M., Johnston, M., & Brindley, G. (1988). Constructing an acquisition-based procedure for second language assessment. In A. Valdman (Ed.), *The assessment of foreign language proficiency* [Theme issue]. *Studies in Second Language Acquisition, 10,* 121–243.

Politzer, R. L., & McGroarty, M. (1985). An exploratory study of learning behaviors and their relationship to gains in linguistic and communicative competence. *TESOL Quarterly, 19,* 103–123.

Purcell, E. T. (1983). Models of pronunciation accuracy. In J. W. Oller, Jr. (Ed.), *Issues in language testing research* (pp. 133–151). Rowley, Mass.: Newbury House.

Ryan, K., & Bachman, L. F. (in press). Differential item functioning on two tests of EFL proficiency. *Language Testing.*

Sang, F., Schmitz, B., Vollmer, H. J., Baumert, J., & Roeder, P. M. (1986). Models of second language competence: A structural equation approach. *Language Testing, 3,* 54–79.

Savignon, S. J. (1985). Evaluation of communicative competence: The ACTFL provisional proficiency guidelines. *The Modern Language Journal, 69,* 129–134.

Seaton, I. (1983). The English Language Testing Service (ELTS): Two issues in the design of the new "nonacademic module." In A. Hughes & D. Porter (Eds.), *Current developments in language testing* (pp. 129–139). London: Academic Press.

Shohamy, E. (1983). The stability of oral proficiency assessment on the oral interview testing procedures. *Language Learning, 33,* 527–540.

Shohamy, E. (1984). Does the testing method make a difference? The case of reading comprehension. *Language Testing, 1,* 147–170.

Skehan, P. (1988). State of the art article: Language testing I. *Language Teaching, 21,* 211–221.

Skehan, P. (1989). State of the art article: Language Testing II. *Language Teaching, 22,* 1–13.

Skehan, P. (1991). Progress in language testing: The 1990s. In J. C. Alderson & B. North (Eds.), *Language testing in the 1990s: The communicative legacy* (pp. 3–21). London: Modern English Publications and The British Council.

Spolsky, B. (1989). *Conditions for second language learning.* Oxford: Oxford University Press.

Stansfield, C. W. (Ed.). (1986). *Technology and language testing.* Washington, DC: TESOL.

Stansfield, C. W., & Hansen, J. (1983). Field dependence-independence as a variable in second language cloze test performance. *TESOL Quarterly, 17,* 29–38.

Stansfield, C. W., & Kenyon, D. M. (1988). *Development of the Portuguese speaking test.* Washington, DC: Center for Applied Linguistics.

Stansfield, C. W., & Kenyon, D. M. (1989). *Development of the Hausa, Hebrew, and Indonesian speaking tests.* Washington, DC: Center for Applied Linguistics.

Sternberg, R. J. (1985). *Beyond IQ: A triarchic theory of human intelligence.* New York: Cambridge University Press.

Sternberg, R. J. (1988). *The triarchic mind.* New York: Viking.

Swain, M. (1985). Large-scale communicative language testing: A case study. In Y. P. Lee, A. C. Y. Y. Fok, R. Lord, & G. Low (Eds.), *New directions in language testing* (pp. 35–46). Oxford: Pergamon Press.

Swinton, S., & Powers, D. E. (1980). *Factor analysis of the Test of English as a Foreign Language for several language groups* (TOEFL Research Rep. No. 6). Princeton, NJ: Educational Testing Service.

Tung, P. (1986). Computerized adaptive testing: Implications for language test developers. In C. W. Stansfield (Ed.), *Technology and language testing* (pp. 13–28). Washington, DC: TESOL.

Weir, C. J. (1983). The Associated Examining Board's Test of English for academic purposes: An exercise in content validation events. In A. Hughes & D. Porter (Eds.), *Current developments in language testing* (pp. 147–153). London: Academic Press.

Wesche, M., Canale, M., Cray, E., Jones, S., Mendelsohn, D., Tumpane, M., & Tyacke, M. (1987). *The Ontario Test of English as a Second Language (OTESL): A report on the research.* Ottawa, Canada: Ontario Ministry of Colleges and Universities.

Widdowson, H. G. (1978). *Teaching language as communication.* Oxford: Oxford University Press.

Widdowson, H. G. (1983). *Learning purpose and language use.* London: Oxford University Press.

Wilds, C. P. (1975). The oral interview test. In R. L. Jones & B. Spolsky (Eds.), *Testing language proficiency* (pp. 29–38). Washington, DC: Center for Applied Linguistics.

Zeidner, M. (1986). Are English language aptitude tests biased towards culturally different minority groups? Some Israeli findings. *Language Testing, 3,* 80–95.

Zeidner, M. (1987). A comparison of ethnic, sex and age biases in the predictive validity of English language aptitude tests: Some Israeli data. *Language Testing, 4,* 55–71.

Understanding the Article

1. How has our view of language proficiency changed since 1980?

2. Explain the differences between *communicative* language testing and the AEI approach. How does Bachman explain the existence of these two distinct approaches to language assessment?

3. In your own words, explain the two broad purposes that language tests serve, and provide examples of each.

4. How is test authenticity related to language ability (language knowledge and strategic competence)?

5. According to Bachman, you cannot judge the authenticity (both situational and interactional) unless you know the purpose of the test. Explain why this is true.

6. How can test writers increase interactional authenticity?

Reflecting on Wider Issues

1. How are the metacognitive strategies that make up Bachman's *strategic competence* similar to or different from learning strategies discussed in the article by O'Malley et al.?

2. Bachman argues that to justify the use of language tests, we have to show that the performance on the tests corresponds in specified ways to language use in a nontest situation. Can you think of examples of language tests you have taken in which the task on the test seemed to you quite different from a real-life or "authentic" language use situation? What characteristics of the test do you think were "unauthentic"? What could be done to improve on the test's authenticity?

3. One way to assess interactional authenticity, Bachman suggests, would be to ask test-takers to self-report on the strategies they used in attempting various test tasks. What might some of the advantages and disadvantages of this approach be?

Going Beyond the Article

For an excellent review of the state of the art in language testing, read Skehan (1988, 1989), "Language testing: Part I" (*Language Teaching, 21,* 211–221), and "Language Testing: Part II" (*Language Teaching, 22,* 1–13).

UNIT IX

THEORIES OF SECOND LANGUAGE ACQUISITION

17

UNIVERSAL GRAMMAR: IS IT JUST A NEW NAME FOR OLD PROBLEMS?

Lydia White
McGill University

Previewing the Article

In the 1960s, Noam Chomsky's assertion of an innate Language Acquisition Device (LAD) in every human being inspired a new paradigm of research on language acquisition. In the early 1980s, again inspired by Chomsky's writing, this widely accepted paradigm shifted to a focus on the universal grammatical properties of the hypothetical LAD, or universal grammar (UG). In the present article, Lydia White outlines how UG can offer new insights into the phenomena associated with language transfer.

Before you read the article, review some of the arguments that were advanced in the earlier LAD hypothesis (see *PLLT*, Chapter 2); then try to familiarize yourself with the thrust of UG research (*PLLT*, Chapters 8 and 11). You should also review the approach to language transfer taken by earlier SLA theories (see *PLLT*, Chapter 8). Then scan the article to answer the following questions:

Reprinted from Gass and Selinker (Eds.), *Language Transfer in Language Learning.* Philadelphia: J. Benjamins, pp. 217–232, 1992.

1. What is the general purpose of the article?
2. Are there specific research questions to be addressed? If so, what are they?
3. What four issues does the author use to describe differences between traditional accounts of transfer and those inspired by UG? In general, what kinds of data are cited as evidence for UG?

Introduction

Within generative grammar, certain aspects of language structure are assumed to be innately present in the first language (L1) learner, helping to account for the fact that the child acquires all the complexities and subtleties of language although these are underdetermined by the input data. This innate structure is referred to as *Universal Grammar* (UG); it consists of principles which underlie native speaker knowledge of language. Current Government and Binding (GB) Theory (Chomsky, 1981, 1986) constitutes one attempt to characterize the principles of UG. In addition to fixed principles, UG is assumed to contain parameters, with a limited number of values, known as parameter settings. Input data from the L1 "trigger" the appropriate setting for the language being learned (see Lightfoot, 1989 for discussion). In other words, the input determines the choice between the built-in settings.

GB theory has attracted considerable attention as a potential theory of second language (L2) learner competence, with the focus of much recent GB-based L2 research being on whether or not UG is still available to L2 learners. Arguments in favor of a role for UG in L2 acquisition center on the "projection problem"; native speakers end up with a highly complex unconscious mental representation of their language, even though many properties of language are not explicit in the input, suggesting that universal principles must mediate L1 acquisition and shape knowledge of language. It seems most unlikely that L2 input will contain explicit information about these kinds of properties in the L2; thus, if L2 learners attain unconscious knowledge of the L2 which goes beyond the input in similar ways, it suggests that UG must still be involved (see White, 1989a, for more detailed discussion). Arguments against UG in L2 acquisition emphasize difficulties faced by L2 learners, and differences between L1 and L2 acquisition; it is claimed that these can best be explained on the assumption that UG is no longer available to adult L2 learners, that there is a "fundamental difference" between L1 and L2 acquisition (Bley-Vroman, 1989, 1990; Clahsen, 1988a, 1988b; Clahsen and Muysken, 1986, 1989; Schachter, 1988).

In this chapter, I will concentrate on research which has pursued the implications of parameter theory for L2 acquisition. Two opposing trends are apparent in this research: on the one hand, researchers use parameters of UG to offer an explanation of language transfer: if UG is available to L2 learners, parameters can explain and predict cases of language transfer, on the assumption that learners apply their L1 parameter settings to the L2 (e.g., White, 1985, 1988) or are otherwise affected by L1 settings (Flynn, 1987). Conversely, some researchers use transfer to question the full operation of UG in L2 acquisition; if L2 learners can only adopt principles or parameter values found in the L1, this indicates that access to UG is essentially "incomplete," and helps to account for differences between L1 and L2 acquisition (e.g., Schachter, 1991).

The theory of UG is currently being applied to two areas which have long been of concern in L2 acquisition research, namely the role of transfer and the question of L1/L2 acquisition differences. These two areas are interconnected. I will suggest in this chapter that UG provides new insights in these domains, and a different perspective on old problems.

Parameters and Transfer

When considering the potential operation of UG in L2 acquisition, the fact that L2 learners already know a language raises the issue of language transfer. It might seem that universal principles should be unaffected by transfer. However, parameterized principles are of obvious potential relevance whenever the L1 and L2 differ as to the value they adopt for some parameter.[1]

An example is the parameter of head-position, which determines the ordering of heads (nouns, prepositions, etc.) and their complements (e.g., relative or appositive clauses, and the objects of verbs and prepositions) (Chomsky, 1986; Travis, 1984). Head-initial languages have heads before complements; head-final languages have complements before heads. The Head-position Parameter applies across categories within a language.[2] In a head-initial language, the complements of the verb will occur after the verb, the complements of the noun after the noun, the complements of prepositions and adjectives after the preposition or adjective; in head final languages, complements will all precede their heads. English, for example is a head-initial language, where direct objects follow verbs and relative clauses follow their head nouns, whereas Japanese is head-final, with direct objects preceding verbs, and relative

---

[1]In addition, languages can differ as to the fixed principles that they instantiate, in that certain properties of a language may render a principle inoperative. Situations where the L1 and L2 differ with respect to the operation of a principle can lead to L1 influence. See, for example, Johnson (1988), Schachter (1989, 1991) for relevant work on the Subjacency Principle.

[2]There are languages (e.g., Chinese) which, on the surface at least, do not show consistent head-complement orders. The Head-position Parameter is a claim about D-structure orders; certain derived orders show up at S-structure which are not the same as the underlying order.

clauses preceding nouns. In L2 acquisition, Japanese learners of English or English learners of Japanese will have to acquire a different setting for the Head-position Parameter if their L2 acquisition is to be successful.

A considerable amount of recent research has addressed itself to the influence of the L1 parameter setting on the L2 learner's hypotheses about the L2. Before looking in more detail at UG-based transfer research, let us consider some general possibilities as far as parameters are concerned. If the L1 and the L2 share a parameter setting, this might be expected to offer an advantage to the language learner, and lead to some kind of "positive transfer." For instance, if the L1 and L2 share the same value of the Head-position Parameter, the L2 learner might be at an advantage in learning L2 word order. On the other hand, if the L1 and L2 settings differ, some form of "negative transfer" might be expected; an L2 learner whose L1 had a different value for head-position would be expected to have problems resetting the parameter and might produce word order errors reflecting the L1 order. (However, when combined with certain learnability considerations, the GB perspective does not necessarily predict difficulties for all cases of parametric differences between the L1 and the L2. See *Learnability* section for further discussion.)

Most researchers who argue for a UG perspective on transfer make some such general assumption but they differ as to the precise form of influence that is attributed to the L1. One possibility is that the L1 parameter setting actually constitutes the learner's interim theory about the L2 data, until subsequent resetting to the L2 value (or some other value) takes place. In other words, L1 parameter settings are part of the interlanguage grammar, either briefly or for a longer period of time, and as such they influence the way the L2 learner attempts to comprehend and produce the L2 (e.g., Phinney, 1987; Schwartz, 1987; White, 1985, 1986, 1988).

In contrast, Flynn (e.g., 1987), looking specifically at the Head-position parameter and its effects on pronominal anaphora interpretation, argues that while the L1 setting has an effect, it is never actually adopted in the interlanguage grammar. Where the L1 and L2 differ as to the settings they require, the L1 setting causes difficulty and delay in acquiring the L2 setting but the difficulty does not manifest itself in the form of an inappropriate parameter setting. It is not clear on this account what the nature of the interlanguage grammar is before the learner acquires the appropriate L2 setting, that is, what guides the hypotheses if the L2 setting has not been acquired but the L1 setting is not being used either.

UG and Transfer: A New Name for Old Problems?

It might be objected that all that is achieved by claiming that transfer reflects the influence of the L1 parameter setting is to give a more fancy name to a well-known phenomenon, leaving us with nothing more than an updated version of the Contrastive Analysis Hypothesis (CAH) in the guise of parameters of UG. If approaching L2 acquisition from the perspective of GB theory yields nothing more than a redescription of existing phenomena, this is not, of course, particularly interesting. Furthermore, one of the reasons why the CAH failed was that it predicted transfer where none was in fact found; GB theory might fall into the same trap. If learners adopt L1 parameter settings, why doesn't the interlanguage grammar just resemble the L1 using L2 vocabulary?

In fact, there are certain insights that GB theory offers, which were not available under the CAH, and which offer a genuinely different perspective on transfer, and a different range of predictions. Some of the differences between UG-based theories of transfer and earlier theories are general, others are quite specific.

The general ones stem from the underlying motivation of generative grammar, the assumption that linguistic theory is a theory of the mental representation of the native speaker's unconscious knowledge of language. This means that claims that L1 parameter settings affect L2 acquisition are not claims about strategies used by L2 learners, or conscious comparisons between the L1 and the L2, or falling back on the L1 only due to temporary lack of knowledge of the L2, or the dominance of L1 habits, or whatever. Rather the claim is that certain parameter settings may be represented in the interlanguage grammar of the L2 learner, just as they are part of the internalized grammar of a native speaker. In some cases, then, the interlanguage grammar will instantiate an L1 parameter setting, rather than that appropriate for the L2.

In addition, as a theory of the principles and parameters which account for the L1 learner's ultimate attainment, and possibly for the course of language development (Hyams, 1986), UG helps to account for those aspects of L1 acquisition that have been referred to as "creative" or "developmental" in the L2 literature (Dulay and Burt, 1974). In applying parameter theory to the L2 acquisition domain, one is not claiming that this side of UG is lost. Parameters crucially interact with L2 input, so that appropriate L2 parameter settings can be attained. As frequently pointed out by Flynn (e.g., 1988) and by White (e.g., 1988), the UG perspective has the potential to bring together transfer and non-transfer aspects of L2 acquisition within one theoretical framework.

More specific ways in which the UG approach to transfer differs from earlier approaches are as follows:

i. levels—generative grammar crucially assumes that representations involve a number of different syntactic levels; transfer may affect some or all of these, with direct or indirect consequences. The CAH, in contrast, concentrated on "visible" surface similarities and differences between languages.

ii. clustering—parameters link clusters of properties, which superficially might seem to be unconnected. Thus the claim that the L1 value of a parameter will be adopted, or will color the L2 learner's perception of the L2 input, is a claim about a whole range of structures in the interlanguage.

iii. interacting parameters—since UG contains many parameters, it is likely that a number of these will have to be reset in L2 acquisition. This leads to the possibility that they will not all be reset at the same time. In that case, interlanguages will result that are neither exactly like the L1 nor the L2. Similar effects will be achieved if learners adopt parameter settings which are present in neither the L1 nor the L2.

iv. learnability—certain parameter settings may be unmarked or marked, their status determined by learnability considerations, in particular by the assumption that L1 acquisition proceeds largely on the basis of positive evidence. When applied to L2 acquisition, this perspective gives a different twist to transfer issues from traditional claims about markedness and transfer.

In the following sections, these four issues are examined in turn, using examples from the literature to show how work on parameters in L2 acquisition has been able to offer a different perspective on transfer.

Levels of Representation

One difference between traditional accounts of transfer and those inspired by generative grammar concerns the levels at which the L1 might have effects. The CAH, for example, made claims about surface differences between languages, differences that would be "obvious" to a researcher or teacher. However, this is by no means the only level at which parametric differences are to be expected. In GB theory (and earlier versions of generative grammar) there are various levels of structure. Grammatical and thematic relationships are represented at D-structure. The rule *move α* moves syntactic categories out of their D-structure positions; S-structure is the level that represents the effects of *move α*. PF (phonetic form) is the level closest to the actual form of a sentence as uttered. LF (logical form) is a level of representation for those aspects of meaning that relate to sentence structure.

It is quite possible for languages to have superficially similar sentence types, which in fact stem from very different D- or S-structures. According to the traditional CAH, these superficial similarities would be predicted not to cause problems, whereas on a GB account which proposes structural differences in their analysis, transfer effects might be expected. Haegeman (1985, 1988) offers an illustration of such a case. The following sentences in Dutch and English appear to be identical in form:

1. a. Jan kocht een boek voor zijn moeder
   b. John bought a book for his mother

However, (1a) and (1b) have very different D-structures and S-structures. The Dutch sentence is derived from a D-structure with the verb in final position, since Dutch is a head-final language (at least with respect to VP), with SOV word order. The Germanic "verb-second" rule moves the verb into second position and the subject is preposed into a topic position (technical details omitted). The English sentence, on the other hand, reflects the underlying SVO order of English. The two languages differ as to their settings for the Head-position Parameter, and with respect to the position of INFL, and also as to the possibility of verb-movement, and yet they have a range of sentences with a common word order. This means that one cannot simply look for surface similarities or differences between languages to determine the potential influence of the L1. (See Haegeman [1985, 1988] for discussion of a range of subtle effects on the interlanguage which stem from these parametric differences between Dutch and English.)

Conversely, different surface forms can result from the same D-structure. For example, in languages like Italian, two surface orders are found with unaccusatives verbs like arrive. (Unaccusatives, also called ergatives, are verbs whose sole argument is a theme.) The order can be subject verb, as in (2a) or verb subject, as in (2b). Burzio (1986) argues that unaccusative verbs should be represented at D-structure with an empty subject position and the theme in object position, as in (2c). In the case of sentences like (2a), the theme moves into subject position at S-structure, leaving a coindexed trace, as in (2d). This analysis accounts for a range of interesting properties exhibited by such verbs.

2. a. *Giovanni arriva*
    John arrived

    b. *Arriva Giovanni*
    arrived John
    "John arrived"

    c. [e [VP V NP]]

    d. [NP$_i$ [VP V t$_i$]]

Although all languages have unaccusative verbs, they do not necessarily allow the same surface orders. In English, for example, unaccusatives are found in sentences of the form of (2a) but not (2b). Nevertheless, it is assumed that they too have a D-structure like (2c).

Zobl (1989) explores the implications of the claim that unaccusatives arise from common D-structures which are realized differently in different languages. He suggests that certain errors found in the speech of L2 learners can be directly attributed to difficulties in working out how unaccusatives are realized in English. Zobl is not in fact arguing for transfer; he points out that transfer of surface patterns allowed with unaccusatives in the L1 cannot account for the L2 learner data, but nor does their language necessarily exhibit a direct reflection of D-structure. Here we have an interesting example where surface differences between languages do not lead to transfer errors (as the CAH would have predicted), although they do lead to errors.

By making predictions based on a theory which assumes the importance of a number of levels of representation, researchers have been able to look beyond surface similarities and differences, to try and establish more precisely where and when the L1 will have an influence, and what that influence will be.

Clustering

Parameter settings usually account for clusters of properties, which superficially might seem to be unrelated. One of the first parameters to be proposed in linguistic theory was the Prodrop or Null Subject Parameter (Chomsky, 1981); this parameter was also one of the first to be investigated in the L2 acquisition context, particularly from the point of view of the claim that UG can account for language transfer (e.g., Hilles, 1986; Liceras, 1988, 1989; Phinney, 1987; White, 1985, 1986). The Null Subject Parameter has a cluster of properties associated with each of its values, and all the L2 research on this parameter has looked at the clustering issue.

There are certain languages, such as Italian and Spanish, which allow the omission of subject pronouns. These languages exhibit the [+ null subject] value of the parameter. Other languages, such as English, require lexical subjects, in accordance with the [− null subject] value. In other words, the subject position in an English sentence cannot be empty, whereas it may in Spanish, as shown in (3):

3. *Leemos muchos libros*
    Read many books
    "We read many books"

In addition, other properties cluster with the presence or absence of null subjects. The following have been proposed as clustering with the [+ null subject] value: rich agreement systems, the possibility of postponing the subject, the possibility of extracting the subject of an embedded clause over a complementizer (the so-called *that-trace effect*), the absence of a distinct category of modal auxiliaries.

There have been a number of studies on the acquisition of English, a [− null subject] language, by native speakers of Spanish, a [+ null subject] language (e.g., Hilles, 1986; Phinney, 1987; White, 1985, 1986) and of the acquisition of Spanish by native speakers of English or French (also a [− null subject] language) (Liceras, 1988, 1989; Phinney, 1987). The detailed results of these studies will not be discussed here. However, there are trends common to all of them. With the exception of the study by Hilles, which looks at longitudinal production data from only one native speaker of Spanish learning English, all the experimental studies have found that the associated properties do not in fact consistently cluster together in the interlanguage. That is, while Spanish-speaking learners of English show evidence of transferring the possibility of null subjects from Spanish to English (as all of the studies have found), they do not transfer other aspects of the parameter, such as subject postposing. When English- or French-speaking learners of Spanish make correct use of null subjects in the L2, they do not necessarily show evidence of having acquired other aspects of the [+ null subject] value of the parameter, such as the possibility of that-trace sequences.

In other words, studies so far conducted on the Null Subject Parameter suggest that L2 learners fail to show the full cluster of properties associated with that parameter, either in terms of what they transfer from the L1, or in terms of what properties of the L2 they successfully acquire. There are a number of possible explanations for this failure. These range from the possibility that parameters of UG no longer operate in L2 acquisition, hence the breakup of the cluster of properties, to methodological problems with the ways in which the cluster was tested. In addition, there is considerable disagreement among linguists as to precisely what the cluster consists of. The important point is not which of these explanations ultimately proves to be correct, but rather that research conducted within this perspective has led people to look for potential relationships between different structures in the interlanguage, and has led to the assumption that transfer might have quite a different range of effects from what has traditionally been assumed. Even where the full cluster does not seem to have been operative in the interlanguage grammar, nevertheless some properties of the parameter (i.e., a subset of the full cluster) do appear to be linked, suggesting that exploring connections between structures linked by parameters is a fruitful way of gaining insight into the effects of the L1 on the interlanguage grammar.

Multivalued and Interacting Parameters

Many parameters of UG are assumed to be binary, having only two values. If L2 learners are guided by UG, there would seem to be only two possibilities for such parameters in the interlanguage grammar, namely that learners adopt either the L1 value or the L2.[3] However, there are proposals for multivalued parameters as well as binary ones. In such cases, L2 learners might adopt a parameter setting which is found neither in the L1 nor in the L2. Finer and Broselow (1986), Finer (1991) look at a parameter which has five values rather than two, namely the Governing Category Parameter (Wexler and Manzini, 1987), taking L1 Japanese or Korean and English as the L2. They argue that L2

---

[3]In some cases, however, parameters might be left unset. For example, if a learner is learning a language without wh-movement, the question of parameterized bounding nodes for Subjacency will not arise, because Subjacency will not operate, since it is a constraint on movement.

learners adopt a value for this parameter which is that of neither the L1 nor the L2, but is found in other languages.

Furthermore, since parameters do not operate in isolation, some parameters may be set by the learner at the L1 value and others at the L2, leading to an interlanguage which does not look like the L1 grammar, even though some L1 parameter settings are involved. UG is an intricate system of principles and parameters. In the studies discussed above, researchers have isolated one parameter and then looked for evidence of its effects on the interlanguage grammar. Many properties of the L2 will in fact derive from the interactions of a number of parameters. L2 researchers have just begun to look at this issue, particularly in the context of Germanic word order. Clahsen and Muysken (1986), Clahsen (1988b) have argued that adult L2 learners do not have access to UG (not even L1 parameter settings), and that adult stages of acquisition of German word order are best explained on the assumption that they are driven by more general learning and processing strategies. They back up their claim with comparative data from child L1 and adult L2 learners of German, pointing out that there are systematic differences in the way these groups acquire German word order, and in their error patterns.

Responding to these claims, du Plessis et al. (1987), Schwartz, and Tomaselli (1990) have argued that German word order is explained by a number of different parameters, including the Head-position Parameter. They propose that adult learners of German initially adopt the L1 values of the parameters in question, and that they do not set all these parameters to their appropriate L2 value at the same time, the Head-position Parameter being reset before the others. The gradual resetting of the various parameters in fact can account for the stages of development that Clahsen and Muysken describe. Where multiple parameters are concerned, the interlanguage grammar does not necessarily conform to either the mother tongue or the L2 settings, but may show a combination of values characteristic of some other language. (See also Hulk [1991] for work assuming similar patterns of parameter resetting in the acquisition of French by native speakers of Dutch.) L1 parameter settings, then, are not adopted exclusively.

The above authors do not, on the whole, discuss why some parameters should retain their L1 setting longer than others in the interlanguage grammar, but this may well relate to the issue to be discussed in the next section, namely the nature of the evidence available to motivate a resetting.

Learnability

Another way in which the UG perspective on transfer differs from more traditional perspectives is in the attention it pays to arguments from language learnability, and particularly the role played by positive evidence in the acquisition of language. It is standardly assumed that L1 acquisition proceeds on the basis of positive evidence, since children do not get relevant and consistent negative evidence (for a recent statement of this position, see Pinker, 1989). In addition, it is assumed that children are somehow constrained to start with the most conservative hypothesis compatible with the input. This has recently been formulated in terms of the Subset Principle, whose purpose is to ensure that children do not pick a parameter setting which is incorrect for the language being acquired and which would require negative evidence for disconfirmation (Berwick, 1985; Wexler and Manzini, 1987).

For example, Wexler and Manzini (1987) propose a Proper Antecedent Parameter, a modified version of which is given in (4):

4. A proper antecedent for a reflexive is

    a. a subject

    or

    b. any NP

This parameter determines what kind of NP can serve as the antecedent for a reflexive. Languages like Korean or Japanese only allow subjects as the antecedents or reflexives, whereas languages like English allow subjects and nonsubjects. Sentences like (5) are ambiguous in English, but the equivalent sentences are not ambiguous in Korean or Japanese. In English, Susan or Nancy can serve as the antecedent of the reflexive; in the Korean equivalent, only the subject, i.e., Susan, can:

5. Susan showed Nancy a picture of herself

Korean, then, allows a subset of the sentences allowed by English with respect to this property. In other words, English allows the sentence types allowed by Korean, and additional ones as well.

The learnability problem is as follows. Suppose that the Korean or Japanese L1 acquirer, on hearing any sentence involving a reflexive, makes the incorrect generalization that reflexives can be bound to any NP. It is not clear what positive input will indicate that the interpretation of (5) is excluded, where *Nancy* is the antecedent of *herself.*

The Subset Principle solves this problem by stipulating that where an L1 learner is faced with input which could be accommodated by either of two parameter settings, the parameter setting which generates the subset language (the unmarked value) should be adopted, unless there is positive evidence to the contrary, in which case the value generating the superset language will be adopted (the marked value). In other words, Korean children, on being exposed to Korean sentences containing reflexives, will adopt value (a) of the Proper Antecedent Parameter, and will never encounter evidence causes them to change this analysis. The English child, on the other hand, will at some point hear sentences like (6), where the antecedent of the reflexive is clearly not the subject, and will set the parameter to value (b).

6.   Bill showed Nancy a picture of herself

How do these claims about the Subset Principle and L1 acquisition relate to transfer in the L2 acquisition context? There will be differences depending on whether L1 or the L2 has the subset (unmarked) value of a parameter. Consider an English learner of Korean or Japanese. If the learner adopts the marked English value of the Proper Antecedent Parameter, it is not clear what positive L2 input will motivate a retreat to the unmarked setting actually required by these languages. What input will indicate to the learner that *Nancy* is excluded as the antecedent of *herself* in the Japanese equivalent of (5)? Presumably context will indicate on particular occasions that *Susan* is the antecedent, but finding out that the object happens not to be the antecedent on a particular occasion is not the same thing as finding out that it may *never* be the antecedent. In such cases, then, the effects of transfer are expected to be serious because there is no positive L2 evidence to lead to parameter resetting, and fossilization of the L1 setting is more likely to occur. (Such situations also motivate the possibility that negative evidence might play a role in L2 acquisition [cf. White, 1990a, 1991]). Thomas (1990, 1991) found that English learners of Japanese do indeed incorrectly assume that nonsubjects can be antecedents of the Japanese reflexive *zibun*. A number of recent papers have looked at other situations where the L1 has a parameter value which generates a superset of the sentences allowed by the L2. In these cases, transfer of the L1 setting has been reported (Hirakawa, 1990; White, 1989b; Zobl, 1988).

In contrast, the Korean learner of English has the unmarked value of the parameter instantiated in the L1, and is learning an L2 which requires the marked value. There will be positive evidence in the L2, in the form of sentences like (6) or sentences like (5) with a disambiguating context, which indicate that the antecedents of reflexives are not restricted to subjects, and which motivate the marked value of the parameter. Here, then, L2 acquisition can proceed on the basis of positive evidence, and transfer of the L1 setting, even if it occurs, is not expected to be permanent. Several recent studies are relevant for this issue (Finer, 1991; Hirakawa, 1990; Thomas, 1991). In these studies, Korean and Japanese learners of English were found to behave very similarly to native speakers of English with respect to choice of antecedents for reflexives. That is, they showed a preference for subjects as antecedents, but objects were also permitted, suggesting that the L2 value for the Proper Antecedent Parameter had been successfully acquired.

In principle, in cases where the positive L2 evidence motivates a different setting from that instantiated in the L1, resetting could be (almost) immediate, predicting little or no transfer, especially if the relevant positive evidence is readily available in the input. This is true both for cases similar to the one just described, where the L2 parameter setting generates a wider language than the L1, and also where the L1 and L2 differ without markedness being at issue, as is the case for head-position, where the head-initial and head-final values of the parameter do not yield languages in a subset/superset relationship but nevertheless there is ample positive evidence (from various aspects of word order) as to the difference in the settings. The Japanese learner of English or the English learner of Japanese should early on encounter evidence that indicates the word order differences between the two languages. In these cases, then, the Head-position Parameter should be reset without difficulty, predicting little transfer.[4]

Using markedness predictions to make claims about transfer is, of course, not new in L2 acquisition research (e.g., Eckman, 1977; Hyltenstam, 1984; Kellerman, 1978). These researchers have argued, from a variety of perspectives, that unmarked properties of language are in some sense privileged and will be more likely to transfer, whereas marked properties will not be liable to transfer, and will be harder to acquire in the L2. The studies that take learnability into consideration differ from these approaches in focusing on the nature of the evidence required to arrive at correct properties of the L2. Learnability theory claims that acquisition can proceed when positive evidence is available but that it is problematic where the learner makes certain kinds of overgeneralizations requiring negative evidence. Applying L1 parameter settings to the L2 in certain cases leads to such overgeneralizations. Markedness claims deriving from learnability theory, then, are (a) that marked parameter settings may be transferred from the L1, and (b) that marked L2 settings can be acquired, given appropriate positive L2 input. Thus, unmarked properties of language are not particularly privileged in the L2 acquisition context. (I should point out that the above claim is not accepted by all researchers working on markedness and transfer within a GB perspective; Liceras [1989], and Phinney [1987] adopt an approach which is closer to the more traditional one, namely the assumption that unmarked properties of the L2 will be readily accessible even when the L1 instantiates the marked value of a parameter.)

Transfer and Access to UG in Adult L2 Acquisition

Implicit or explicit in most studies so far mentioned is the assumption that UG plays an active role in adult L2 acquisition, even though L1 parameter settings are adopted, or exert other forms of influence. Thus, properties of UG, in particular parameters, contribute to an explanation of language transfer. The considerations discussed above suggest that working on language transfer within the framework of generative grammar offers rather more than new names for old problems. Different predictions are made about L2 acquisition

---

[4]This contrasts with the acquisition of German word order, where internal inconsistencies in surface word orders allowed by German make it hard for the L2 learner to establish immediately that German is SOV, as discussed in the section *Multivalued and Interacting Parameters.*

and explanations are proposed which are different from those found under previous views of transfer.

In contrast, there are researchers who draw a very different conclusion from data which suggest the adoption of the L1 parameter setting. These researchers argue that UG is essentially inactive in adult L2 acquisition and that adults' **only** access to UG is via whatever is instantiated in the L1 (Bley-Vroman, 1989, 1990; Clahsen and Muysken, 1989; Schachter, 1988). On this view, then, UG does not offer an explanation of transfer since UG is no longer available. Instead, data that reflect transfer suggest that UG is inactive.

Both the view that UG is available and the view that it is not assume that L1 parameter settings will be applied to the L2; however, there is a crucial difference between them, concerning the question of resetting a parameter to the appropriate L2 value. If UG is still available, the learner is not assumed to be "stuck" with L1 parameter settings; parameter resetting to the L2 value is possible, on the basis of input from the L2 interacting with a still active UG (White, 1989a, 1990b). On the second view, on the other hand, only L1 parameter settings (as well as fixed principles exemplified in the L1) will be accessible to the L2 learner (Clahsen and Muysken, 1989). Parameters cannot be reset; if the L1 and the L2 differ as to the values they have for some parameter, the L1 value will be adopted, and the L2 value will not be attainable, nor should there be "mixed" settings like those described above where some parameters are set at their L1 value, others at their L2, others at values found in different natural languages. Thus, transfer data are compatible with two radically different theories about the mechanisms involved in L2 acquisition; any data that demonstrate only the operation of the L1 value of a parameter in L2 acquisition cannot be used to determine whether UG is active or inactive, but research which demonstrates evidence of the attainment of any non–L1 value, or any combination of L1 and L2 values, favors the hypothesis that UG is still active in L2 acquisition.

Conclusion

An advantage of conducting research on language transfer from within the framework of GB theory is that this theory offers very specific and testable claims about the nature of native speaker linguistic competence. UG is a theory of knowledge in a particular domain, a theory of abstract principles and parameters, which both constrain child language acquisition and form part of adult native speaker knowledge of language. By looking at the operation of parameters in L2 acquisition, a greater understanding of the precise influence of the mother tongue can be achieved, as well as insight into the overall accessibility of UG in nonprimary acquisition.

I should, however, like to emphasize that since second language acquisition is not a unitary phenomenon, it is unrealistic to expect there to be one paradigm that will be able to embrace the whole field. Generative grammar certainly cannot provide an explanation of everything that L2 learners do or fail to do. Its relevance is strictly limited to providing a potential explanation of the acquisition of rather formal aspects of language structure. It is highly likely that language transfer will also be involved in domains that fall outside the scope of UG. But, sticking within these circumscribed limits, it appears that generative grammar provides a suitable paradigm from which to address issues of importance within second language acquisition, including the issue of transfer, and that adopting this framework is not simply a matter of renaming old problems; instead, it offers new insights and suggests new lines of research.

Acknowledgments

This research was conducted with the assistance of the following research grants: Social Sciences and Humanities Research Council Canada Research Fellowship #455-87-0201, Social Sciences and Humanities Research Council of Canada research grant #410-87-1071 (to Lisa Travis and Lydia White), Government of Québec FCAR research grant #88 EQ 3630 (to Lisa Travis and Lydia White).

References

Berwick, R. (1985). *The acquisition of syntactic knowledge.* Cambridge, Mass.: MIT Press.

Bley-Vroman, R. (1989). What is the logical problem of foreign language learning? In S. Gass and J. Schachter (Eds.), *Linguistic perspectives on second language acquisition.* Cambridge: Cambridge University Press.

Bley-Vroman, R. (1990). The logical problem of foreign language learning. *Linguistic Analysis, 20,* 3–49.

Burzio, L. (1986). *Italian syntax: A government-binding approach.* Dordrecht: Reidel.

Chomsky, N. (1981). *Lectures on government and binding.* Dordrecht: Foris.

Chomsky, N. (1986). *Knowledge of language: Its nature, origin, and use.* New York: Praeger.

Clahsen, H. (1988a). Critical phases of grammar development: A study of the acquisition of negation in children and adults. In P. Jordens & J. Lalleman (Eds.), *Language development.* Dordrecht: Foris.

Clahsen, H. (1988b). Parameterized grammatical theory and language acquisition: A study of the acquisition of verb placement and inflection by children and adults. In S. Flynn & W. O'Neil (Eds.), *Linguistic theory in second language acquisition.* Dordrecht: Kluwer Academic Publishers.

Clahsen, H., & Muysken, P. (1986). The availability of universal grammar to adult and child learners: A study of the acquisition of German word order. *Second Language Research, 2,* 93–119.

Clahsen, H. & Muysken, P. (1989). The UG paradox in L2 acquisition. *Second Language Research, 5,* 1–29.

Dulay, H., & Burt, M. (1974). A new perspective on the creative construction processes in child second language acquisition. *Language Learning, 24,* 253–258.

du Plessis, J., Solin, D., Travis, L. & White, L. (1987). UG or not UG, that is the question: A reply to Clahsen and Muysken. *Second Language Research, 3,* 56–75.

Eckman, F. (1977). Markedness and the contrastive analysis hypothesis. *Language Learning, 27,* 315–330.

Finer, D. (1991). Binding parameters in second language acquisition. In L. Eubank (Ed.), *Point counterpoint: Universal grammar in the second language.* Amsterdam: John Benjamins.

Finer, D., & Broselow, E. (1986). Second language acquisition of reflexive-binding. *Proceedings of NELS 16.* University of Massachusetts at Amherst: Graduate Linguistics Students Association.

Flynn, S. (1987). *A parameter setting model of L2 acquisition.* Dordrecht: Reidel.

Flynn, S. (1988). Second language acquisition and grammatical theory. In F. Newmeyer (Ed.), *Linguistics: The Cambridge survey, Vol. II.* Cambridge: Cambridge University Press.

Haegeman, L. (1985). Scope phenomena in English and Dutch and L2 acquisition: A case study. *Second Language Research, 1,* 118–150.

Haegeman, L. (1988). The categorial status of modals and L2 acquisition. In S. Flynn & W. O'Neil (Eds.), *Linguistic theory in second language acquisition.* Cambridge, Mass.: MIT Press.

Hilles, S. (1986). Interlanguage and the pro-drop parameter. *Second Language Research, 2,* 33–52.

Hirakawa, M. (1990). L2 acquisition of English reflexives by speakers of Japanese. *Second Language Research, 6,* 60–85.

Hulk, A. (1991). Parameter setting and the acquisition of word order in L2 French. *Second Language Research, 7,* 1–34.

Hyams, N. (1986). *Language acquisition and the theory of parameters.* Dordrecht: Reidel.

Hyltenstam, K. (1984). The use of typological markedness conditions as predictors in second language acquisition: The case of pronominal copies in relative clauses. In R. Andersen (Ed.), *Second languages: a cross-linguistic perspective.* Rowley, Mass.: Newbury House.

Johnson, J. (1988). *Critical period effects on universal properties of language: The status of subjacency in the acquisition of a second language.* Unpublished doctoral dissertation, University of Illinois at Urbana-Champaign.

Kellerman, E. (1978). Transfer and nontransfer: Where are we now? *Studies in Second Language Acquisition, 2,* 37–57.

Liceras, J. (1988). Syntax and stylistics: More on the prodrop parameter. In J. Pankhurst, M. Sharwood Smith, & P. Van Buren, (Eds.), *Learnability and second languages: A book of readings.* Dordrecht: Foris.

Liceras, J. (1989). On some properties of the "prodrop" parameter: Looking for missing subjects in nonnative Spanish. In S. Gass & J. Schachter (Eds.), *Linguistic perspectives on second language acquisition.* Cambridge: Cambridge University Press.

Lightfoot, D. (1989). The child's trigger experience: Degree-0 learnability. *Behavioral and Brain Sciences, 12,* 321–375.

Phinney, M. (1987). The prodrop parameter in second language acquisition. In T. Roeper & E. Williams, (Eds.), *Parameter setting.* Dordrecht: Reidel.

Pinker, S. (1989). *Learnability and cognition.* Cambridge, Mass.: MIT Press.

Schachter, J. (1988). Second language acquisition and its relationship to Universal Grammar. *Applied Linguistics, 9,* 219–235.

Schachter, J. (1989). Testing a proposed universal. In S. Gass & J. Schachter, (Eds.), *Linguistic perspectives on second language acquisition.* Cambridge: Cambridge University Press.

Schachter, J. (1991). On the issue of completeness in second language acquisition. *Second Language Research, 6,* 93–124.

Schwartz, B. (1987). *The modular basis of second language acquisition.* Unpublished doctoral dissertation, University of Southern California.

Schwartz, B., & Tomaselli, A. (1990). Some implications from an analysis of German word order. In W. Abraham, W. Kosmeijer, & E. Reuland (Eds.), *Issues in Germanic syntax.* The Hague: Mouton.

Thomas, M. (1990). Acquisition of the Japanese reflexive *zibun* by unilingual and multilingual learners. *Proceedings of SLRF 1990.* Eugene, OR: University of Oregon.

Thomas, M. (1991). Universal Grammar and the interpretation of reflexives in a second language. *Language, 67,* 211–239.

Travis, L. (1984). *Parameters and effects of word order variation.* Unpublished doctoral dissertation, MIT.

Wexler, K., & Manzini, R. (1987). Parameters and learnability in binding theory. In T. Roeper & E. Williams (Eds.), *Parameter Setting.* Dordrecht: Reidel.

White, L. (1985). The prodrop parameter in adult second language acquisition. *Language Learning, 35,* 47–62.

White, L. (1986). Implications of parametric variation for adult second language acquisition: An investigation of the "prodrop" parameter. In V. Cook (Ed.), *Experimental approaches to second language acquisition.* Oxford: Pergamon Press.

White, L. (1988). Universal grammar and language transfer. In J. Pankhurst, M. Sharwood Smith, & P. Van Buren (Eds.), *Learnability and second languages: A book of readings.* Dordrecht: Foris.

White, L. (1989a). *Universal grammar and second language acquisition.* Amsterdam: John Benjamins.

White, L. (1989b). The principle of adjacency in second language acquisition: Do L2 learners observe the subset principle? In S. Gass & J. Schachter (Eds.), *Linguistic perspectives on second language acquisition.* Cambridge: Cambridge University Press.

White, L. (1990a). Implications of learnability theories for second language learning and teaching. In M.A.K. Halliday, J. Gibbons, & H. Nicholas (Eds.), *Learning, keeping and using language.* Amsterdam: John Benjamins.

White, L. (1990b). Another look at the logical problem of foreign language learning: A reply to Bley-Vroman. *Linguistic Analysis, 20,* 50–63.

White, L. (1991). Adverb placement in second language acquisition: Some effects of positive and negative evidence in the classroom. *Second Language Research, 7,* 133–161.

Zobl, H. (1988). Configurationality and the subset principle: The acquisition of V¢ by Japanese learners of English. In J. Pankhurst, M. Sharwood Smith, & P. Van Buren (Eds.), *Learnability and second languages: A book of readings.* Dordrecht: Foris.

Zobl, H. (1989). Canonical typological structures and ergativity in English L2 acquisition. In S. Gass, & J. Schachter (Eds.), *Linguistic perspectives on second language acquisition.* Cambridge: Cambridge University Press.

Understanding the Article

1. Describe the role of input within a theory of SLA based on Universal Grammar.

2. In your own words, explain what UG *parameters* are and describe how they can be used to explain *transfer.*

3. White claims that adopting a UG framework allows for very different explanations about the role of the native language in L2 acquisition that were not possible in previous models such as CAH. Explain how her discussion of levels of representation and clustering supports this claim.

4. Explain the concepts of *negative* and *positive* evidence. How are these concepts related to *learnability?*

5. How does White use the following data to illustrate the Proper Antecedent Parameter and the Subset Principle?

   a. i. Tom$_1$ gave Bob a picture of himself$_1$. (English)

      ii. Tom gave Bob$_1$ a picture of himself$_1$. (English)

   b. i. Tom$_1$ gave Bob a picture of himself$_1$. (Japanese)

      ii. *Tom gave Bob$_1$ a picture of himself$_1$. (Japanese)

   How can the operation of UG explain why speakers of English learning Japanese have difficulty learning that (b) (ii) is ungrammatical in Japanese, whereas speakers of Japanese are able to learn with relative ease that (a) (ii) is grammatical in English?

6. Briefly outline White's conclusion about the question of whether Universal Grammar is just a new name for old problems.

Reflecting on Wider Issues

1. Some researchers claim that UG does not have a role in adult SLA, arguing that the "fundamental difference" between L1 and L2 acquisition can best be explained by assuming that UG is no longer available to adult foreign/second language learners. Describe the characteristics of adult SLA that might lend support to this position.

2. How would you go about testing whether adults have access to the universal principles and parameters of Universal Grammar (UG) when they are learning a second language? What kind of experiment could you design to test the hypothesis that UG is available to adult foreign language learners?

Going Beyond the Article

Researchers who support the Chomskyan position that humans are innately endowed with both knowledge of what a human language can be and procedures for acquiring the grammar of a specific language frequently cite what is referred to as the "logical problem of language acquisition." To see how this logical problem is applied to foreign/second language learning, read Bley-Vroman's "The logical problem of foreign language learning," *Linguistic Analysis, 20,* 3–49, 1990, in which he concludes that UG is unavailable to the L2 learner. Then read Lydia White's response, "Another look at the logical problem of foreign language acquisition," (pages 50–63 in the same journal) in which she reaches a different conclusion.

For a lucid review of the issues involved and of some of the more important research on the role of UG in SLA, read Eubank's "Introduction: Universal grammar in the second language" (*Point Counterpoint: Universal Grammar in the Second Language,* L. Eubank (Ed.), Philadelphia: J. Benjamins, 1991.) You might also want to follow up by reading some of the other chapters in the book.

If you want to know more about recent views of the role of language transfer in SLA, look at other chapters in the book from which Lydia White's chapter was taken (e.g., *Language Transfer in Language Learning,* S. Gass & L. Selinker, (Eds.) Philadelphia: J. Benjamins, 1992).

18

THE LEAST A SECOND LANGUAGE ACQUISITION THEORY NEEDS TO EXPLAIN

Michael H. Long
University of Hawaii at Manoa

Previewing the Article

Second language acquisition, as a professional discipline, is still relatively young. Part of that youth is manifested in some theoretical vacillations as the pendulum of trends and beliefs has swung back and forth. However, as we approach the twenty-first century, theoretical positions in second language acquisition seem to be stabilizing; we seem to be more capable of identifying just what we do indeed know about the process. In Michael Long's thought-provoking article, he sets forth major foundation stones for the construction of a sound, pervasive theory of second language acquisition.

Before you read the article, ask yourself what we mean by the term *theory* (see *PLLT*, Chapter 1), and review some of the more popular theories that prevail today (see *PLLT*, Chapter 11). Then answer the following:

Reprinted from *TESOL Quarterly, 24*:649–666, 1990.

1. What is the purpose of this article?

2. How is it organized to achieve that purpose?

3. Before a careful reading, jot down what you think are some of the major "accepted findings" about second language acquisition—some of the major principles that are widely accepted throughout the language teaching profession. Then, as you read, see if some of your principles are also included in the article.

Theories of second language acquisition (SLA) are attempts to explain well-attested empirical findings about relationships between process and product in interlanguage development and universals, and variance in learners and learning environments. An important component of such theories will be one or more mechanisms to account for interlanguage change. While theories differ in scope and so often relate only to partial descriptions, they must account for major accepted findings within their domains if they are to be credible. Identification of "accepted findings," therefore, is an important part of theory construction and evaluation. Such findings will be the least an SLA theory needs to explain. Sample accepted findings on learners, environments, and interlanguages are proposed along with some implications for current SLA theories.

Second Language Acquisition: Some Structural Characteristics

Second language acquisition (SLA) is a relatively new, interdisciplinary field of inquiry. While several important studies appeared much earlier (see Hatch, 1978a, for review), most empirical research has been conducted since 1960 by researchers drawing heavily (although some would say not heavily enough) upon theory, research findings, and research methods in a variety of fields, including education, psychology, linguistics, anthropology, foreign languages, ESL, and applied linguistics. Data-based SLA research is presented at a variety of conferences, most of which were originally designed with focuses other than reporting SLA research results,[1] and is published in a wide range of journals, only three of which (*Language Learning, Studies in Second Language Acquisition* and *Second Language Research*) are primarily devoted to it.

---

[1]Examples include TESOL, the International Association of Applied Linguistics (AILA), and the American Educational Research Association (AERA). The Second Language Research Forum (SLRF) is the only regular international conference (first held in 1977) devoted exclusively to SLA research findings although two new organizations, the European Second Language Association (EUROSLA) and Second Language Research Forum for the Pacific (PacSLRF), will begin holding regular annual SLA conferences in 1991 and 1992, respectively.

Important results often go unnoticed because they appear in obscure regional publications or remain buried between the covers of master's and doctoral theses. There is very little funding available, and virtually none at all in the U.S., where many SLA researchers work.

SLA's brief history means that few issues have yet been investigated exhaustively. The dearth of funding causes what tends to be labor-intensive work to be conducted cross-sectionally (that is, using data collected on different subjects at one point in time only, instead of on the same subjects over time, or longitudinally) and on small samples. The diversity of disciplines represented in the field often results in skepticism about findings when research methods from other traditions are used—from controlled laboratory experiments, through work using interview data, grammaticality judgments and other kinds of introspection, to case studies and ethnographies. Also, SLA research with origins in one source discipline, for example, theoretical linguistics, often seems irrelevant to that inspired by developments in another, for example, social psychology. To illustrate, it is difficult to relate research findings on access to Universal Grammar in adult SLA motivated by Chomsky's ideas to the results of studies of nonnative speech accommodation to an interlocutor motivated by Giles' Accommodation Theory. Finally, the shortage of specialist SLA conferences and the fragmented publication of research findings makes it difficult to review the literature to assess what is known about a given topic. What *is* "the literature" on SLA?

Description and Explanation in Theory Construction

It is often difficult to determine just what is known, or thought to be known about second language acquisition. It becomes very dangerous to claim that X is an established *fact* or that Y has attained the status of a *generalization* or perhaps even of a *law* when there is disagreement over what constitutes legitimate data and when researchers and textbook writers are not reading or respecting the same literature. Yet the identification of at least some uncontroversial results is a prerequisite for developing and evaluating theories in any field. A synthesis of well-attested empirical findings about process and product in interlanguage development related to universals and variance in learners and learning environments is essential for a valid *description* of SLA. The description delineates the scope of the problem to be solved; it becomes part of the data for which a theory needs to account and against which it may be testable. The description specifies what is acquired; the theory explains how.

Several qualifications are in order, however. First, not all forms of theory attempt to explain how. Axiomatic and causal-process forms, for example, do. The set-of-laws form does not. It consists of a compilation of repeatedly observed patterns, but does not necessarily seek to explain them (Reynolds, 1971; Long, 1985).

Second, what counts as an explanation varies from one discipline and scientific subcommunity to another, and over time (Bunge, 1985; Cummins, 1983; Trusted, 1979). For some, such as behaviorists in several fields, biochemists, and many psychologists, explanation means the empirically verified ability to predict future events (either that they will occur or when they will occur); for others, such as some ethnographers and anthropologists, it can mean post hoc understanding of a single past event. For some, a purported explanation must be empirically testable; for others, it need not, and for still others, for example, theorists in some branches of contemporary physics, a theory cannot be tested due to the current unavailability of technology required to conduct such a test.

Finally, the work undertaken to produce a description really does more than provide a mere collation of the data to be explained. A description has the beginning of explanation embedded within it; explaining and theorizing are not separate activities, as is often thought (Pronko, 1988). Description and explanation are better viewed as two overlapping circles or as two points on a continuum (Figure 1). What researchers select for observation is seldom arbitrary, but a reflection of their own or others' biases about what is likely to be

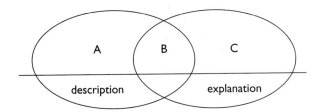

FIGURE 1.   Description and Explanation in Theory Construction

important, or "worth studying." That is, the choice is already an implicit theoretical claim. In addition, with the possible exception of certain kinds of constitutive ethnography (e.g., Mehan, 1978), what is incorporated into the resulting description is both far less and far more than what was observed.

What emerges from a study is far *less* than what was observed because researchers eliminate what they consider to be irrelevant detail and draw attention to recurrent patterns. Thus, in the following examples, it is safe to assume that subjects exhibited some deviation from the norms, that is, that there was variation in the data, but this information has not been retained.

1. The frequency of *no V* constructions declined as that of *don't V* constructions increased.

2. Subjects' suppliance of plural *s* was more target-like on the picture description task than in the narrative.

3. Whether or not learners exhibited adverb-fronting on the pretest predicted their control of particle separation after instruction.

Descriptive statements like 1–3 (those in area A of Figure 1) are ostensibly observations. They record *that* learning or some kind of interlanguage change occurred or failed to occur and are neutral as to *how* or *why*. Their very inclusion in a final report, however, inevitably reflects the investigator's initial assessment of their potential significance for explanation. To the extent that messy detail has been eliminated, they are already low-level generalizations about the data collected from particular samples although not yet generalizations about behavior across studies or to populations.

On the other hand, what emerges from a study is far *more* than what was observed because many descriptive statements about patterns do take the form of generalizations and/or link two or more variables in a way that implies a potential causal relationship. To a greater or lesser degree, that is, they are abstractions from the data, and abstraction is an essential step in constructing theories of every kind. In the following examples, patterns are being claimed to exist across samples (or across performance by the same subjects on different task types) and/or across studies and in populations.

4. Accuracy was greater on tasks performed after planning than on tasks performed with no planning.

5. After equivalent periods of exposure, child starters score higher on proficiency tests than learners who begin as adults.

6. Constructions (such as topicalization) which involve movement of an element from final to initial position are learned before constructions (such as particle separation) which require both disruption of a string and movement of an internal element to a salient (initial or final) position.

Consciously or not, descriptive statements like 4-6 (those in area B of Figure 1) already suggest at least low-level potential explanations for the findings they record.

While descriptions are the basis for theory construction, theories need not account for all the facts in every description to be viable. Theories rarely purport to address every kind of aspect of SLA; they vary greatly in scope. A particular theory may deal with naturalistic, instructed, or mixed learning, with children or adults, with specific language skills and modalities (oral or written, comprehension or production), with a specific cognitive capacity or resource (such as memory, attention, or aptitude), a specific psycholinguistic process (such as transfer, restructuring, or stabilization), a specific linguistic system (such as phonology, syntax, or pragmatics), a specific subsystem (such as syllable structure, tense-aspect-modality, relative clauses, or politeness), and so on. The variance in scope makes it legitimate for theories to relate to different partial descriptions, or to selected findings in the field.

7. SLA is just one aspect of acculturation and the degree to which a learner acculturates to the TL [target language] group will control the degree to which he [*sic*] acquires the second language. (Schumann, 1978, p. 34)

8. There are two independent ways of developing ability in a second language. "Acquisition" is a subconscious process identical in all important ways to the process children utilize in acquiring their first language, while "learning" is a conscious process that results in "knowing about" language. (Krashen, 1985, p. 1)

9. Second language learning, like any other complex cognitive skill, involves the gradual integration of subskills as controlled processes initially predominate and then become automatic. (McLaughlin, 1987, p. 139)

In fact, as these statements (area C of Figure 1) show, in addition to ignoring vast bodies of SLA research findings, theoretical claims of greater or lesser scope, that is, explanations, may not refer explicitly to SLA research findings at all.

Mechanisms

A theory that referred to every accepted finding about SLA would still not necessarily provide an explanation of the SLA process, even in the unlikely event that all the findings were correct. For explanatory power, a theorist needs to propose one or more *mechanisms* to account for change. In the present context, mechanisms are devices that specify how cognitive functions operate on input to move a grammar at Time 1 to its new representation at Time 2. The output of these mechanisms is observable in learner data, in this case, an interlanguage sample.

Mechanisms in theories of first language acquisition are discussed, among others, by Atkinson (1982), McShane (1987), MacWhinney (1987), and Jensen and Kiel (1988). Behaviorist theories, they note, have relied upon data-driven mechanisms of association, differentiation, and generalization. Innatist theories typically employ some form of hypothesis testing constrained by innate knowledge, for example, Chomsky's language acquisition device. Flavell (1972) provides a taxonomy of mechanisms governing possible relationships between stages in a developmental sequence, including addition, substitution, modification (either by differentiation or generalization), inclusion, and mediation.

Mechanisms in the SLA literature to date are rather vaguely defined and poorly supported. A partial list includes some borrowings from first language research, plus restrictive and elaborative simplification (Meisel, 1983; Meisel,

Clahsen, & Pienemann, 1981), confirmative simplification (Stauble, 1984), regularization (Long, 1982), nativization and denativization (Anderson, 1983), and hypothesis testing constrained by innate knowledge of language universals, either syntactic (Flynn & O'Neil, 1989; White, 1985) or semantic (Adamson, 1988; Bickerton, 1984).

In addition to specifying mechanisms driving development from one stage to the next, Atkinson (1982) suggests that an adequate explanation will also identify why the stages in a developmental sequence have to occur in exactly the order they do, and cannot occur in some other order (see also Johnston, 1985). Few proposals of this type have yet been made in SLA theory, but one interesting example is Rutherford's attempt to explain various morphological and syntactic accuracy and acquisition orders in terms of markedness (Rutherford, 1982).

Another such SL example is that originally proposed by Meisel, Clahsen, and Pienemann (1981) and Clahsen (1987) to account for German as a second language word order, and later extended to a variety of morphological and syntactic constructions in ESL (Pienemann & Johnston, 1987). Meisel et al. and Clahsen claim that the surface structures observed at each of five stages in the development of German as a second language word order reflect the cumulative shedding of three underlying processing strategies: (a) *the canonical order strategy,* (b) *the initialization-finalization strategy,* and (c) *the subordinate clause strategy.*

The strategy combinations are hierarchically related such that each new one entails and adds to the sophistication of the previous one, thereby gradually allowing psycholinguistically more complex structures to be processed. At stage $X + 1$ (initialization-finalization), for example, the learner can move elements from one salient position to another (string-initial to string-final position or vice versa), but only if this does not disturb the canonical word order. Thus, an ESL learner can produce utterances like *In Vietnam, I am teacher* (adverb-fronting). At stage $X + 2$ (disruption and movement into a salient position), the learner is no longer constrained by the canonical order strategy, and can move string-internal elements to salient (initial or final) position, too, producing utterances like *Have you job?* (yes/no inversion) and *You take your coat off* (particle separation). Whatever the merits of this particular analysis, it is an attempt to move beyond presentation of observed *series* of structures as developmental *sequences* with no attempt to explain why they occur in the order they do (for a critique of the model, see White, 1989a).

Some Accepted SLA Findings

Whether or not they refer to empirical findings or specify explanatory mechanisms, theories have to account for well-attested facts in their domain if they are to be taken seriously. A proposed explanation for something that either ignored or could not account for one or more of its most salient characteristics and/or for some other well-established facts would lack credibility. For example, a theory that birds can fly because they eat flying insects would immediately be rejected because many flying birds do not eat insects, many animals that eat flying insects cannot fly, and because such an explanation would ignore a salient characteristic of all flying birds, that is, wings. Theorists need to survey such known facts when evaluating theories in a field and when constructing their own theories. (See Spolsky, 1989, for a recent attempt at SLA theory construction in this vein.)

There is an underlying assumption here that should be made explicit, namely, that SLA research is at least partly a *rational* endeavor. It is this quality that makes well-attested findings important, not merely the fact that they are well attested.

It should be noted, however, that the rational nature of science in general is not universally acknowledged. Proponents of an extreme relativist, "anything goes" view of the growth of knowledge (e.g., Feyerabend, 1975) argue that voodoo, magic, or religious beliefs are held no less certainly than are scientific beliefs, and that scientific beliefs are different, not superior. As Gould (1981) and others have shown, it is sometimes the case that the apparent superiority of science over other belief systems arises simply from scientists as a community deciding to value their work higher than others'. Then, either they are in a position of power or represent elite interests with sufficient power to impose their views on others.

The strength with which a belief is held and the value systems underlying it are not the only relevant criteria for judging an epistemology. As Newton-Smith (1982) has argued, scientists are different precisely because they recognize the threat to the validity of their work potentially posed by a lack of objectivity, unreliability of observation and measurement, and the inevitable contribution of the social construction of truth by closed communities. They, uniquely, attempt to deal with the threat. They do this through efforts to *disengage* researchers from their findings by establishing minimum criteria that they must meet when making a claim. There must be evidence for the claim, the evidence must have been obtained using certain procedures, must be replicable by third parties, and so on. The experiment is a key illustration of work carried out within this approach, as is the importance of replication and prediction. While scientists may never be able to know if they have found the truth, increasing accuracy in their predictions is one indication that they are getting closer to it.

Generalizations are only possible when empirical observations are repeatedly supported. Generalizations are crucial to, and must be accounted for by, credible theories. It is not just the existence of consensus that makes generalizations important for theory construction, but the *rationality* of the scientific process that underlies them. (For insightful discussion of these and related issues, see Beretta, 1991.)

Unfortunately, certain structural characteristics of SLA research make known facts rather easier to determine with respect to how birds fly than why some people can learn a second language and others do not. Notwithstanding these difficulties, the following are a few examples (by no means intended as a comprehensive list) of what I would claim are well-established findings about learners, environments, and interlanguages, along with some of the challenges they pose to current SLA theories. Space limitations preclude surveys of supporting literature. For each generalization, references are provided to recent reviews and/or to key studies of the phenomenon concerned. (The very existence of reviews, of course, attests to the familiarity of many of the results.)

Learners

Wide variation in learners' abilities (e.g., intelligence), states (e.g., motivation), and traits (e.g., extroversion) has relatively little effect on most aspects of (first or second) language acquisition by young children. Child language development is strikingly regular in both course, rate, and ultimate attainment, and success is the norm (Slobin, 1982). On the other hand, individual differences do affect adult first (e.g., American Sign Language) or second language acquisition. SLA processes and sequences are again fairly regular, but learning rate and ultimate SL attainment are highly variable and failure is common (Ellis, 1985; Newport, 1984).

Differences in learners' starting age (Krashen, Long, & Scarcella, 1979; Scovel, 1988), aptitude, attitude, and motivation (Skehan, 1989; Spolsky, 1989), for example, are systematically related to variance in rate of progress and ultimate attainment. The role of affective factors appears to be indirect and subordinate to more powerful developmental and maturational factors, perhaps influencing such matters as the amount of contact with the L2, or time on task (Schumann, 1986). The most positive attitudes to target language speakers and the strongest motivation, for example, cannot overcome psycholinguistic constraints on learnability at a particular stage of development (Clahsen, 1987; Meisel, Clahsen, & Pienemann, 1981; Pienemann & Johnson, 1987; Schmidt, in press) or maturational constraints on what older starters can achieve (Long, 1990). Both L1 and L2 development appear to depend on the same universal cognitive abilities (e.g., the capacity for implicit and inductive learning) and to be subject to the same cognitive constraints (e.g., limited human memory, attentional resources, and information-processing capacity) (McLaughlin, 1987; Schmidt, 1990; Schmidt, in press).

Environments

Variation in the linguistic environment has surprisingly little effect on first language acquisition by children, where a high degree of success is achieved even under conditions of quite severe linguistic deprivation (Gleitman, 1986).

The effect on adult language learning of differences in the amount and kind of input available is much greater and varies among different groups of learners, in part as a function of L1/L2 relationships (Larsen-Freeman & Long, 1991). Both children and adults need the language they encounter to be comprehensible for it to become potential intake (Krashen, 1985). Comprehensibility is not dependent on linguistic "simplification" from the source (speaker/writer), which is often absent, but may result from interactional or elaborative modifications, which are frequently the product of negotiation for meaning between the source and the learners themselves (Hatch, 1978b; Long, 1983; Parker & Chaudron, 1987). Exposure to comprehensible input is necessary but not sufficient (White, 1987). Both children and adults can learn from positive evidence alone, as evidenced by successful untutored development in the absence of negative input, such as overt error correction (Bley-Vroman, 1986), but a focus on form (which overt error correction can sometimes induce in the learner), along with any other behaviors or tasks that make certain L2 features salient, improves rate and ultimate SL attainment (Doughty, in press; Long, 1988). Attention to form is necessary for mastery of certain types of L1/L2 contrasts, for example, where the way the L2 encodes a grammatical relationship is more marked than the equivalent L1 structure (Eckman, 1981; Schachter, 1989), and where the L1 allows two options (such as placement of frequency adverbs before or after the direct object), only one of which is grammatical in the L2, but both of which are communicatively successful. This situation preempts negative input on the ungrammatical item via repair sequences (White, 1989b). Noticing, brought about by feedback, task structure, or other means, is necessary for input to become intake, and negative evidence must be recognized as such for it to be effective (Schmidt, in press). Much of a language is not learned unconsciously.

Interlanguages

Interlanguages, the psycholinguistic SL equivalent of idiolects, exhibit systematicity and variability at any time in their development (Huebner, 1985; Selinker, 1969). The systematicity manifests itself in many ways, including the regular suppliance and nonsuppliance of both targetlike and nontargetlike features in certain linguistic contexts and in the persistence of the same errors for often quite lengthy periods (Sato, 1990; Schmidt, 1981). Interlanguages, that is, are, or at least appear to be, rule-governed. Much of the variability they also reveal turns out to be systematically related to such factors as task, task requirements (e.g., attention to form and planning), interlocutor, and linguistic context (Crookes, 1989; Hulstijn, 1989; Kasper, 1988; Preston, 1989; Tarone, 1988). However, some of it does appear to be random, or free, as when a learner produces *no put* and *don't put* or *I born* and *I was born* within moments of one another under seemingly identical conditions (Ellis, 1985). Change over time also follows predictable paths. With some differences for first language background—L1 transfer being constrained by such factors as L1/L2 markedness relationships and perceived transferability (Eckman, 1985; Kellerman, 1984; Odlin, 1989; Zobl, 1982)—learners of different ages, with and without instruction, in foreign and second language settings (Lightbown, 1983; Pica, 1983), follow similar developmental sequences for such items as English negation (Schumann, 1979), English and Swedish relative clauses (Hyltenstam, 1984; Pavesi, 1986), German word order (Meisel, Clahsen, & Pienemann, 1981), and a variety of other morphological and syntactic constructions (Johnston, 1985). Progress is not linear; backsliding is common, giving rise to so-called U-shaped behavior observed in first and second language acquisition (Huebner, 1983; Kellerman, 1985). Development is for the most part gradual and incremental, but some sudden changes in performance suggest occasional fundamental restructuring of the underlying grammar (McLaughlin, 1990).

Sample Implications for Current SLA Theories

If the above can be considered a sample of "accepted findings" in the sense indicated earlier, and so some of the facts in need of explanation and/or constituting part of that explanation, a number of implications follow for any theories that purport to be comprehensive accounts of SLA. The following eight are offered by way of illustration:

1. Common patterns in development in different kinds of learners under diverse conditions of exposure means that a theory that says nothing about universals in language and cognition is incomplete or, if considered complete, inadequate.

2. Systematic differences in the problems posed learners of different L1 backgrounds by certain kinds of L1/L2 configurations and by other qualitative features of the input, such as the salience of certain linguistic features or lack thereof, means that a theory that says nothing about environmental factors is incomplete or, if considered complete, inadequate.

3. Differences in rate of acquisition and the level of proficiency achievable by children and adults under comparable conditions of exposure requires that viable theories specify either different mechanisms driving development in learners of different starting ages or differential access to the same mechanisms.

4. The subordination of affective factors to linguistic and cognitive factors means that a theory that purports to explain development solely in terms of affective factors can, at most, be an account of facilitating conditions, not an explanatory theory of acquisition itself.

5. The need for awareness of and/or attention to language form for the learning of some aspects of a SL means that a theory that holds all

language learning to be unconscious is inadequate.

6. The impossibility of learning some L2 items from positive evidence alone means that a theory that holds that nativelike mastery of a SL can result simply from exposure to comprehensible samples of that language is inadequate.

7. Interlanguage systematicity, including adherence to regular developmental sequences and systematic production of nontargetlike forms never modeled in the input indicates a strong cognitive contribution on the learner's part and means that environmentalist theories of SLA are inadequate.

8. The gradualist, often U-shaped course of much interlanguage development renders inadequate a theory that assumes sudden, categorical acquisition of grammatical knowledge triggered by recognition of linguistic features of the input. A theory that assumes that change is a product of the steady accumulation of generalizations based upon the learner's perception of the frequencies of forms in the input is also incomplete.

Conclusion

It is perfectly reasonable for particular theories to discount or ignore certain supposed empirical findings in the field because they lie outside a theorist's domain of interest or because a theorist's assumptions preclude the findings being correct and/or from holding explanatory relevance. Nevertheless, a theory must account for at least some of the major accepted findings within its scope if it is to be useful. The same descriptions of findings to which a theory is accountable may often simultaneously serve as the beginning of an explanation for them, but an adequate SLA theory also needs to specify one or more mechanisms to explain interlanguage change.

Accepted research findings show that SLA is a multidimensional phenomenon, with many (although by no means all potential) learner and environmental variables determining variation in developmental processes and product. Consequently, theories that attempt to explain acquisition by recourse to a single factor (for example, motivation, comprehensible input, or the workings of an innate language acquisition device) or to a single type of factor (for example, affect variables) lack face validity.

An explanatory theory of SLA that hopes to be viable will have to be interactionist. That is to say, it will need to do two things. First, it will need to recognize the role of both learner variables and environmental variables in language development: Which aspects of SLA are universal (presumably as a result of all learners possessing common cognitive abilities and constraints), and which aspects vary systematically as a function, for example, of age, aptitude, and attention, or of the kind of input different learners encounter? Second, it will need to specify which of those learner and environmental variables exert a constant influence and which ones interact, when and how. Which variables' effect on development is mediated by which others, and when? For example, is increasing age of first exposure to the L2 always negatively related to ultimate attainment, or only up to a particular age after which it makes no difference? Are affective factors important in second language settings, where, for example, positive attitudes may lead learners to seek out and obtain more input or different kinds of input, but only relevant for L2 literacy skills in foreign language settings, where increased contact with native speakers may be unavailable even when attitudes are positive? Is increased attention to form useful only for adults or only for certain classes of linguistic items? Does the structure of a learner's L1 facilitate acquisition of some features in a particular L2, impede acquisition of certain others, and have no effect on still others?

As can be seen from the above examples, interactionist theories are more powerful than unidimensional or single factor solutions in their ability to account for the same set of data because they invoke two or more (often many more) variables, types of variables, and relationships among variables. This is always undesirable from a theory construction perspective, where parsimony is valued. However, the increase in power is clearly justified by the intriguing combination of universals and variability in adult language learning, which is the least an SLA theory needs to explain.

Acknowledgements

This is a revised version of a paper presented at the 24th Annual TESOL Convention in San Francisco, March 1990. I thank Graham Crookes, Alan Beretta, and *TESOL Quarterly* editor Sandra Silberstein for helpful comments on earlier versions.

References

Adamson, H. (1988). *Variation theory and second language acquisition.* Washington, DC: Georgetown University Press.

Andersen, R. W. (1983). Introduction: A language acquisition interpretation of pidginization and creolization. In R. W. Andersen (Ed.), *Pidginization and creolization as language acquisition* (pp. 1–56). Rowley, Mass.: Newbury House.

Atkinson, M. (1982). *Explanations in the study of child language development.* Cambridge: Cambridge University Press.

Beretta, A. (1991). Theory construction in SLA: Complementarity or opposition? *Studies in Second Language Acquisition, 13,* 493–511.

Bickerton, D. (1984). The language bioprogram hypothesis and second language acquisition. In W. E. Rutherford (Ed.), *Language universals and second language acquisition* (pp. 141–161). Amsterdam: John Benjamins.

Bley-Vroman, R. (1986). Hypothesis testing in second language acquisition. *Language Learning, 36,* 353–376.

Bunge, M. (1985). Types of psychological explanation. In J. McGaugh (Ed.), *Contemporary psychology: Biological processes and theoretical issues* (pp. 489–501). Amsterdam: Elsevier Science Publishers.

Clahsen, H. (1987). Connecting theories of language processing and (second) language acquisition. In C. Pfaff (Ed.), *First and second language acquisition processes* (pp. 103–116). Cambridge, Mass.: Newbury House.

Crookes, G. (1989). Planning and interlanguage variation. *Studies in Second Language Acquisition, 11*(4), 367–387.

Cummins, R. (1983). *Psychological explanation. Cambridge, Mass.: MIT Press.*

Doughty, C. (1991). Second language instruction does make a difference: Evidence from an empirical study of SL relativization. *Studies in Second Language Acquisition, 3,* 431–469.

Eckman, F. (1981). On the naturalness of interlanguage phonological rules. *Language Learning, 31,* 195–216.

Eckman, F. (1985). The markedness differential hypothesis: Theory and applications. In B. Wheatley, A. Hastings, F. Eckman, L. Bell, G. Krukar, & R. Rutkowski (Eds.), *Current approaches to second language acquisition: Proceedings of the 1984 University of Wisconsin-Milwaukee Linguistics Symposium* (pp. 3–21). Bloomington, IN: Indiana University Linguistics Club.

Ellis, R. (1985). *Understanding second language acquisition.* Oxford: Oxford University Press.

Feyerabend, P. (1975). *Against method.* London: Verso.

Flavell, J. (1972). An analysis of cognitive-developmental sequences. *Genetic Psychology Monographs, 86,* 279–350.

Flynn, S., & O'Neil, W. (Eds.). (1989). *Linguistic theory in second language acquisition.* Dordrecht, The Netherlands: Reidel.

Gleitman, L. R. (1986). Biological programming for language learning. In S. L. Friedman, K. A. Klivington, & R. W. Peterson (Eds.), *The brain, cognition, and education* (pp. 119–149). New York: Academic Press.

Gould, S. J. (1981). *The mismeasure of man.* New York: Norton.

Hatch, E. M. (1978a). Introduction. In E. M. Hatch (Ed.), *Second language acquisition: A book of readings* (pp. 1–18). Rowley, Mass.: Newbury House.

Hatch, E. M. (1978b). Discourse analysis and second language acquisition. In E. M. Hatch (Ed.), *Second language acquisition: A book of readings* (pp. 402–435). Rowley, Mass.: Newbury House.

Huebner, T. (1983). Linguistic system and linguistic change in an interlanguage. *Studies in Second Language Acquisition, 6,* 33–53.

Huebner, T. (1985). System and variability in interlanguage syntax. *Language Learning 35,* 141–163.

Hulstijn, J. H. (1989). A cognitive view on interlanguage variability. In M. Eisenstein (Ed.), *The dynamic interlanguage* (pp. 17–31). New York: Plenum Press.

Hyltenstam, K. (1984). The use of typological markedness conditions as predictors in second language acquisition: The case of pronominal copies in relative clauses. In R. W. Andersen (Ed.), *Second language: A cross-linguistic perspective* (pp. 39–58). Rowley, Mass.: Newbury House.

Jensen, K. A., & Kiel, E. (1988). Innateness and language acquisition: Two perspectives. *Pluridicta, 10.* Odense University, Denmark.

Johnston, M. (1985). *Syntactic and morphological progressions in learner English* (Research report). Canberra, Australia: Department of Immigration and Ethnic Affairs.

Kasper, G. (1988). Variation in interlanguage speech act realization. *University of Hawai'i Working Papers in ESL, 7,* 117–142.

Kellerman, E. (1984). The empirical evidence for the influence of the L1 in interlanguage. In A. Davies, C. Criper, & A. P. R. Howatt (Eds.), *Interlanguage* (pp. 98–122). Edinburgh: Edinburgh University Press.

Kellerman, E. (1985). If at first you do succeed . . . . In S. Gass & C. Madden (Eds.), *Input in second language acquisition* (pp. 345–353). Rowley, Mass.: Newbury House.

Krashen, S. D. (1985). *The input hypothesis: Issues and implications.* New York: Longman.

Krashen, S. D., Long, M. H., & Scarcella, R. (1979). Age, rate, and eventual attainment in second language acquisition. *TESOL Quarterly, 13,* 573–582.

Larsen-Freeman, D., & Long, M. H. (1991). *An introduction to second language acquisition research.* London: Longman.

Lightbown, P. M. (1983). Exploring relationships between developmental and instructional sequences in L2 acquisition. In H. W. Seliger & M. H. Long (Eds.), *Classroom oriented research in second language acquisition* (pp. 217–243). Rowley, Mass.: Newbury House.

Long, M. H. (1982, August). *Foreigner talk and early interlanguage: A cross-linguistic study.* Paper presented at the 2nd European-North American Workshop on Cross-Linguistic Second Language Acquisition Research, Gorde, West Germany.

Long, M. H. (1983). Linguistic and conversational adjustments to nonnative speakers. *Studies in Second Language Acquisition, 5,* 177–193.

Long, M. H. (1985). Input and second language acquisition theory. In S. Gass & C. Madden (Eds.), *Input and second language acquisition* (pp. 377–393). Rowley, Mass.: Newbury House.

Long, M. H. (1988). Instructed interlanguage development. In L. M. Beebe (Ed.), *Second language acquisition: Multiple perspectives* (pp. 115–141). Cambridge, Mass.: Newbury House.

Long, M. H. (1990). Maturational constraints on language development. *Studies in Second Language Acquisition, 12,* 251–285.

McLaughlin, B. (1987). *Theories of second language learning.* London: Edward Arnold.

McLaughlin, B. (1990). Restructuring. *Applied Linguistics, 11,* 1–16.

McShane, J. (1987). Do we need a metatheory of language development? *Language and Communication 7,* 111–121.

MacWhinney, B. (Ed.) (1987). *Mechanisms of language acquisition.* Hillsdale, NJ: Lawrence Erlbaum.

Mehan, H. (1978). Structuring school structure. *Harvard Educational Review, 48,* 32–64.

Meisel, J. (1983). Strategies of second language acquisition: More than one kind of simplification. In R. W. Andersen (Ed.), *Pidginization and creolization as language acquisition* (pp. 120–157). Rowley, Mass.: Newbury House.

Meisel, J., Clahsen, H., & Pienemann, M. (1981). On determining developmental stages in natural second language acquisition. *Studies in Second Language Acquisition, 3,* 109–135.

Newport, E. (1984). Constraints on learning: Studies in the acquisition of American Sign Language. *Papers and Reports on Child Language Development, 23,* 1–22.

Newton-Smith, W. (1982). Relativism and the possibility of interpretation. In M. Hollis & S. Lukes (Eds.), *Rationality and relativism* (pp. 106–122). Oxford: Basil Blackwell.

Odlin, T. (1989). *Language transfer. Cross-linguistic influence in language learning.* Cambridge: Cambridge University Press.

Parker, K., & Chaudron, C. (1987). The effects of linguistic simplifications and elaborative modifications on L2 comprehension. *University of Hawai'i Working Papers in ESL, 6,* 107–133.

Paesi, M. (1986). Markedness, discoursal modes, and relative clause formation in a formal and an informal context. *Studies in Second Language Acquisition, 8,* 38–55.

Pica, T. (1983). Adult acquisition of English as a second language under different conditions of exposure. *Language Learning, 33,* 465–497.

Pienemann, M. (1984). Psychological constraints on the teachability of languages. *Studies in Second Language Acquisition, 6,* 186–214.

Pienemann, M., & Johnston, M. (1987). Factors influencing the development of language proficiency. In D. Nunan (Ed.), *Applying second language acquisition research* (pp. 45–141). Adelaide, Australia: National Curriculum Resource Centre.

Preston, D. (1989). Sociolinguistics and the learning and teaching of foreign and second languages. In D. Preston, *Sociolinguistics and second language acquisition* (pp. 239–272). Oxford: Basil Blackwell.

Pronko, N. H. (1988). Explanation or description? In N. H. Pronko, *From A1 to zeitgeist* (pp. 55–6). New York: Greenwood Press.

Reynolds, P. (1971). *A primer in theory construction.* Indianapolis: Bobbs-Merrill.

Rutherford, W. E. (1982). Markedness in second language acquisition. *Language Learning, 32,* 85–108.

Sato, C. J. (1990). *The syntax of conversation in interlanguage development.* Tübingen, Germany: Gunter Narr.

Schachter, J. (1989). *On the issue of completeness in second language acquisition.* Unpublished manuscript. University of Southern California, Department of Linguistics, Los Angeles.

Schmidt, R. W. (1981). Interaction, acculturation and the acquisition of communicative competence. *University of Hawai'i Working Papers in Linguistics, 13,* 29–77.

Schmidt, R. W. (1990). The role of consciousness in second language learning. *Applied Linguistics, 11,* 17–46.

Schmidt, R. W. (in press). Consciousness, learning, and interlanguage pragmatics. In G. Kasper and S. Blum-Kalka (Eds.), *Research in second language pragmatics.* Oxford: Oxford University Press.

Schumann, J. H. (1978). The acculturation model for second language acquisition. In R. Gingras (Ed.), *Second language acquisition and foreign language teaching* (pp. 27–50). Arlington, VA: Center for Applied Linguistics.

Schumann, J. H. (1979). The acquisition of English negation by speakers of Spanish: A review of the literature. In R. W. Andersen (Ed.), *The acquisition and use of Spanish and English as first and second languages* (pp. 3–32). Washington, DC: TESOL.

Schumann, J. H. (1986). Research on the acculturation model for second language acquisition. *Journal of Multilingual and Multicultural Development, 7,* 379–392.

Scovel, T. (1988). *A time to speak. A psycholinguistic inquiry into the critical period for human speech.* Cambridge, Mass.: Newbury House.

Selinker, L. (1969). Language transfer. *General Linguistics, 9,* 67–92.

Skehan, P. (1989). *Individual differences in second language learning.* London: Edward Arnold.

Slobin, D. I. (1982). Universal and particular in the acquisition of language. In E. Wanner & L. Gleitman (Eds.), *Language acquisition: State of the art* (pp. 128–170). Cambridge: Cambridge University Press.

Spolsky, B. (1989). *Conditions for second language learning.* Oxford: Oxford University Press.

Stauble, A-M. (1984). A comparison of the Spanish-English and Japanese-English interlanguage continuum. In R. W. Andersen (Ed.), *Second languages: A cross-linguistic perspective* (pp. 323–353). Rowley, Mass.: Newbury House.

Tarone, E. (1988). *Variation in interlanguage.* London: Edward Arnold.

Trusted, J. (1979). *The logic of scientific inference.* London: Macmillan.

White, L. (1985). Universal grammar as a source of explanation in second language acquisition. In B. Wheatley, A. Hastings, F. Eckman, L. Bell, G. Krukar, & R. Rutkowsky (Eds.), *Current approaches to second language acquisition.* Bloomington: Indiana University Press.

White, L. (1987). Against comprehensible input: The input hypothesis and the development of L2 competence. *Applied Linguistics, 8,* 95–110.

White, L. (1989a, February). *Processing strategies: Are they sufficient to explain adult second language acquisition?* Paper presented at the Ninth Second Language Research Forum, University of California, Los Angeles.

White, L. (1989b, October). *The principle of adjacency in second language acquisition: Do L2 learners observe the subset principle?* Paper presented at the Boston Conference on Child Language Development, Boston.

Zoble, H. (1982). A direction for contrastive analysis: The comparative study of developmental sequences. *TESOL Quarterly, 16,* 169–183.

Understanding the Article

1. Long claims that second language acquisition (SLA) is an interdisciplinary field. What are the disciplines on which SLA draws? What does this tell you about where you might look for research on SLA in scholarly books and journals?

2. According to Long, the diversity of disciplines from which SLA research comes leads to a diversity in research methods (and "skepticism about the findings when research methods from other traditions are used.") Can you find examples from the essays in this book of the following kinds of research methods?

    a. case studies

    b. ethnographies

    c. grammaticality judgments

    d. interview data

    e. controlled experiments

3. Suppose that you are studying learner language in the classroom, using audiotapes and videotapes of the classes. How could your description of what you heard and saw be described as "both far less and far more than what was observed"?

4. Long says that before you can develop a theory of SLA, you must have at least some uncontroversial results that serve as the description of SLA. In your own words, list at least five of Long's accepted findings about SLA.

Reflecting on Wider Issues

1. Although Long says that theories do not have to account for all the facts in every description to be viable, his position is clearly

that certain facts about SLA must be taken into account if a theory of SLA is to be comprehensive. Do you believe that all of Long's *facts* about SLA are as uncontroversial as he suggests? If not, what are some of the issues related to his *facts* that still need to be resolved?

2. List some *facts* about SLA that you might add to Long's list, and explain why you think they should be added.

3. Long says that it is reasonable for a particular theory to ignore certain *facts* about SLA because they lie outside the theorist's domain of interest. For each of the theories listed below, list at least one important fact about SLA that the theory ignores, and tell why you think its omission from the theory is or is not justifiable.

    a. Universal Grammar
    b. Krashen's Input Hypothesis
    c. Schumann's Pidginization/Acculturation Model

Going Beyond the Article

For an excellent review of second language acquisition research—where it has been, where it is now, and where it is going—read Larsen-Freeman (1991), "Second language acquisition research: Staking out the territory" (*TESOL Quarterly, 25,* 315–350). The essay also provides an extensive bibliography that should enable you to follow up on issues in the essay that you would like to learn more about.

Editors' Appendix

I. Some Major Journals in Second and Foreign Language Learning

Applied Linguistics: Oxford, England: Oxford University Press. Published quarterly.

Canadian Modern Language Review. Toronto, Ontario: Canadian Modern Language Association. Published quarterly.

ELT Journal. Oxford: Oxford University Press. Published quarterly.

Issues in Applied Linguistics. Los Angeles: University of California at Los Angeles. Published twice yearly.

Language in Society. Cambridge: Cambridge University Press. Published quarterly.

Language Learning. Ann Arbor, MI: University of Michigan. Published quarterly.

Language Teaching: The International Abstracting Journal for Language Teachers and Applied Linguists. Cambridge: Cambridge University Press. Published quarterly.

Language Testing. London: Edward Arnold. Published three times a year.

The Modern Language Journal. Madison, WI: University of Wisconsin Press. Published quarterly.

Second Language Research. London: Edward Arnold. Published twice yearly.

Studies in Second Language Acquisition. Cambridge, England: Cambridge University Press. Published quarterly.

TESOL Quarterly. Alexandria, VA: Teachers of English to Speakers of Other Languages. Published quarterly.

World Englishes. Oxford: Basil Blackwell. Published three times a year.

II. Suggested Supplementary Texts on Research

Allwright, D., & Bailey, K. M. (1991). *Focus on the language classroom: An introduction to classroom research for language teachers.* Cambridge, England: Cambridge University Press.

Brown, J. D. (1988). *Understanding research in second language learning: A teacher's guide to statistics and research design.* Cambridge, England: Cambridge University Press.

Hatch, E., & Farhady, H. (1982). *Research design and statistics for applied linguistics.* Cambridge: Newbury House.

Hatch, E., & Lazaraton, A. (1991). *The research manual: Design and statistics for applied linguistics.* New York: HarperCollins–Newbury House.

Johnson, D. M. (1992). *Approaches to research in second language learning.* New York: Longman.

Nunan, D. (1992). *Research methods in language learning.* Cambridge, England: Cambridge University Press.